Handbook of
Cross-Cultural Psychology

Handbook of Cross-Cultural Psychology
Second Edition

Edited by John W. Berry, Ype H. Poortinga, Janak Pandey,
Pierre R. Dasen, T. S. Saraswathi, Marshall H. Segall,
and Cigdem Kagitçibasi

VOLUME 1
Theory and Method

VOLUME 2
Basic Processes and Human Development

VOLUME 3
Social Behavior and Applications

性相近　習相遠

**Basic human nature is similar at birth;
Different habits make us seem remote.**

From the *San Zi Jing*

Second Edition

Handbook of
Cross-Cultural Psychology

VOLUME 3
SOCIAL BEHAVIOR
AND APPLICATIONS

Edited by

John W. Berry
Queen's University, Canada

Marshall H. Segall
Syracuse University, U.S.A.

Cigdem Kagitçibasi
Koç University, Turkey

Allyn and Bacon
Boston • London • Toronto • Sydney • Tokyo • Singapore

This volume is dedicated to
the memory of Donald T. Campbell
1917–1996

Copyright © 1997, 1980 by Allyn & Bacon
A Viacom Company
Needham Heights, MA 02194

First edition published under the titles *Handbook of Cross-Cultural Psychology*,
Volume 5, *Social Psychology*, edited by Harry C. Triandis and Richard W. Brislin,
and *Handbook of Cross-Cultural Psychology*, Volume 6, *Psychopathology*, edited by
Harry C. Triandis and Juris G. Draguns, copyright © 1980 by Allyn & Bacon.

Library of Congress Cataloging-in-Publication Data

Handbook of cross-cultural psychology. -- 2nd ed.
    p.   cm.
   Includes bibliographical references and index.
   Contents: v. 1. Theory and method / edited by John W. Berry, Ype
H. Poortinga, Janak Pandey.
    ISBN 0-205-16074-3 (v. 1)
    1. Ethnopsychology.   I. Berry, John W.
GN502.H36   1996
155.82—dc20
                                           96-16261
                                              CIP

Printed in the United States of America
10 9 8 7 6 5 4 3 2   01 00 99 98

CONTENTS

VOLUME 3: SOCIAL BEHAVIOR AND APPLICATIONS
Edited by J. W. Berry, M. H. Segall, & C. Kagitçibasi

VOLUME 2: BASIC PROCESSES AND HUMAN DEVELOPMENT
Edited by J. W. Berry, P. R. Dasen & T. S. Saraswathi

FOREWORD

Humans have been interested in how culture influences "naive psychology" (beliefs, customs, ways of life) from the time when they had the leisure to do so, and they have been recording their impressions since Herodotus. The scientific study of the link between culture and psychology started in the 19th century, perhaps with Comte's *Cours de philosophie positive* (6 volumes, 1830 to 1842). Much of the knowledge that had accumulated between the 19th century and the mid-1970s was presented in the first edition of the *Handbook of Cross-Cultural Psychology* (6 volumes, 1980 to 1981).

But science provides an ever-changing panorama. Between 1975 and today some of the ideas about what culture and psychology are have changed. Culture has become a less static, more dynamic, and "constructed" conception. Psychology has finally realized that culture has a major role to play in the way psychology is shaped.

That is so because we humans are all ethnocentric. This is a fundamental reality, reflecting that we all grow up in a specific culture (even when it is cosmopolitan and a mixture of other cultures) and learn to believe that the standards, principles, perspectives, and expectations that we acquire from our culture are *the* way to look at the world. Unexamined assumptions are one of the central aspects of culture. When we construct psychological theories, the more the subject matter deviates from biological and physiological phenomena, the more our culture intrudes in the shaping of the theories that we construct. In social and clinical psychology, for instance, much of what we present as "the truth" reflects our culture. The only way to correct the "false consensus" we perceive as "the truth" is to compare our ideas with the ideas that have been generated in other contexts. This can be done by emphasizing general issues of how culture influences psychological processes, as is done in "cultural psychology." It can also be revealed very sharply when we study different "indigenous psychologies." Much can be learned, in addition, by comparing data from several cultures, as is done in "cross-cultural psychology," and by examining how cultures interact with each other, as is done in "intercultural psychology."

John Berry has wisely included many of these perspectives in the *Second Edition*. He has done this by including more editors and authors from different cultures, traditions, and theoretical perspectives, and by broadening the definition of what is to be included in this edition. Thus, the second edition is broader, with authors who are more diverse in age, culture, and theoretical perspectives, than the first edition.

In this edition there are chapters on indigenous and evolutionary psychologies that were not included in the first edition. The research methods covered in chapters of the *First Edition* have not changed much, so these chapters are "archived" in the *Second Edition;* but two new methodological chapters have been added. Relatively new research areas—the examination of the developmental niche, the construction of identity, individualism and collectivism, intergroup relations, sex and gender issues, aggression, crime, and warfare, cross-cultural training, and health—now have separate chapters.

Some of these topics had a minor presence in 1972, when the first edition was formulated. For instance, the individualism and collectivism theme was not yet a focus of cross-cultural research, but became quite important after the first edition was published. I should have included a chapter on cross-cultural training in the first edition, but I was so concerned that the *Handbook* might include too much material reflecting my own interests that I went too far in holding back such material. It is gratifying that the *Second Edition* corrects this mistake.

The constellation of editors and authors of the *Second Edition* consists of about one-fifth old and four-fifths new writers, of diverse ages and cultures. I am delighted to see that the new generation of cross-cultural psychologists is moving the field forward.

Summer of 1995

Harry C. Triandis
Champaign, Illinois

Harry Triandis is Professor of Psychology at the University of Illinois. His recent books include *Culture and Social Behavior* (1994, New York: McGraw-Hill) and *Individualism and Collectivism* (1995, Boulder, CO: Westview Press). He edited (with W. W. Lambert, J. W. Berry, W. J. Lonner, R. Brislin, A. Heron, & J. Draguns) the first edition of the *Handbook of Cross-Cultural Psychology* (1980–81), and the international volume of the *Second Edition of the Handbook of Industrial and Organizational Psychology* (M. D. Dunnette and L. M. Hough 1990–1994, Palo Alto, CA: Consulting Psychologists). In 1994 he received the Otto Klineberg Award for his work on cultural syndromes, and the American Psychological Association's Award for Distinguished Contributions to the International Advancement of Psychology.

PREFACE

Cross-cultural psychology is the systematic study of relationships between the cultural context of human development and the behaviors that become established in the repertoire of individuals growing up in a particular culture. The field is diverse: some psychologists work intensively within one culture, some work comparatively across cultures, and some work with ethnic groups within culturally plural societies; all are seeking to provide an understanding of these culture-behavior relationships. This inclusive view about the diversity of the field has guided the editing of this second edition of the *Handbook of Cross-Cultural Psychology.*

The field of cross-cultural psychology has greatly evolved and expanded since the publication of the first edition of the *Handbook* in 1980. Under the general editorship of Harry Triandis, the six volumes of the first edition established the field as a wide-ranging but focused and coherent approach to understanding human experience and behavior in cultural context. The fifty-one chapters covered a vast territory, exploring virtually every corner of the discipline of psychology. The focus was consistently on how cultural factors influence psychological development and guide behavioral expression, and the integration was achieved through editorial coordination and collegial exchanges among authors.

Usually, second editions must exhibit both continuity and change. In this edition of the *Handbook,* continuity is represented by similar organization and coverage of materials to those in the first edition. More specifically: the present Volume 1 (Theory and Method) is a sequel to first edition Volumes 1 and 2 (Perspectives, and Methodology); the present Volume 2 (Basic Processes and Human Development) stems from Volumes 3 and 4 (Basic Processes, and Developmental); and the present Volume 3 (Social Behavior and Applications) follows mostly from Volumes 5 and 6 (Social, and Psychopathology). However, in this edition there has been no attempt to replicate the original compendium. Instead, the current editors decided to "archive" many of the earlier chapters, letting them stand as important and comprehensive statements of contemporary knowledge; where appropriate, present chapters refer readers to these earlier treatments. Chapters in the first edition that are considered as "archived" should be consulted by readers who want to have a comprehensive view of the field. These include: in Volume 1, a consideration of psychological universals and of the politics and ethics of cross-cultural research; in Volume 2, presentations of various methods (ethnographic, observational, surveying and interviewing, psychometric assessment, projective testing, experiments, unobtrusive measures, translation and content analysis, and holocultural methods); in Volume 3, surveys of research on motivation; in Volume 4, overviews of Piagetian theory, personality development and games and sports; in Volume 5, examinations of exchange theory, and small group behavior; and in Volume 6, reviews of alienation and depression. The topics of all other chapters in the first edition have, in one way or another, been updated and incorporated in the various chapters in this second edition.

This *Handbook,* in fewer chapters (34), focuses on topics for which there have been important theoretical and empirical advances since the late 1970s. Some chapters are true sequels to earlier ones; authors who are continuing earlier topics were asked to assume that readers have (or can) read the original chapter, and to start their review where the other chapter left off (usually around 1978). Other chapters attend to new topics that were barely evident in 1980; authors of these were asked to develop their material from earlier and more basic sources. The overall results, we hope, is a *Handbook* that can be used alone, or in sequence with the first edition.

The field of cross-cultural psychology has changed considerably over the past two decades. Four changes in particular have been important. One substantial change is in diversification in the concept of *culture* and how it may be related to psychology. Some of this change has followed a move in cultural anthropology away from a view of culture as objectively knowable and describable, providing a relatively stable context for individual human development, to a more interactive and creative relationship between individuals and their sociocultural surroundings. This move in anthropology has led to a parallel shift in cross-cultural psychology, stimulating the emergence of a subfield known as "cultural psychology." This aspect of diversification is represented particularly in Volume 1 by pairs of chapters on Theory and on Method that portray these contrasting perspectives on the concept of culture. A final chapter in Volume 1 attempts to provide an integrative framework within which this recent diversification can be viewed.

There can be no doubt that for many years cross-cultural psychology was done mostly by those in Western, economically and politically powerful nations; the objects of their attention were usually "others." When these others lived elsewhere, they were "tribes," and when they were closer at hand they were "subcultures" or "minorities." Recognizing the ethnocentrism in this arrangement, two other changes have occurred that represent moves away from this position. In the first emergent subfield, cross-cultural psychology has been increasingly carried out with cultural groups that co-reside in culturally plural societies, influencing each other, and being influenced in common by the many institutions that are widely shared in the larger society (e.g., public education, mass media, justice). This new subfield itself has a number of variants, and many terms have been used to describe them: "acculturation psychology," "ethnic psychology," and, in the French language tradition, "psychologie interculturelle." Much of this work has been accomplished by psychologists whose ethnic heritage is within the groups being studied.

In the second emergent subfield there has been increasing interest among the "others" in understanding themselves in their own terms, drawing upon their own culturally-rooted concepts and intellectual traditions. This move has brought about new approaches, known variously as "indigenous psychology," or "ethnopsychology." In these, a single cultural tradition is the locus of interest, and leadership is being provided by psychologists whose cultural backgrounds are also from within the cultural groups being studied, and which cumulatively span an ever-widening range. This search for indigenous origins and outcomes has been advocated both as a valuable activity in its own right, and as an important step towards achieving a more inclusive, panhuman psychology: it is argued that only when the universe of indigenous psychologies has been sampled can a universal psychology be achieved.

A last change has involved a shift away from the search for, and cataloging of, differences in psychological phenomena toward an interest in also identifying similarities. This interest in similarities has been present for many decades but recent developments in human ethology have begun to influence psychology, and are providing a base for this increasing interest in similarities. At the same time, the field has been increasingly clear in its conceptualization of the difference–similarity contrast as a dimension ranging from *relativism* at one pole to *universalism* at the other. All positions on this dimension are represented in this *Handbook.*

Given this diversification, it is no longer possible to give a single definition of key concepts (such as *culture*), to characterize the typical method used (such as the comparative method), or even to provide one definition of the field of cross-cultural psychology that the editors (never mind all the authors) would find to their liking. However, it is possible to identify what does hold the field, and this *Handbook,* together: the field rejects the long-standing exclusion of *culture* by the discipline of psychology; in contrast, it seeks to incorporate cultural aspects of human life as a major factor in behavior. The various ways in which cultural factors are conceptualized and linked to behavior constitutes the diversity of the field. In a sense, this combination of an underlying communality, but with variation in expression, corresponds to the perspective of *universalism,* which makes the assumption that basic psychological processes are shared panhuman characteristics of the species, but that culture provides an opportunity to develop and express these processes in highly variable ways.

In many respects, these changes in the field correspond to the sequence of three methodological orientations to the field outlined in 1969 and later elaborated as three goals of cross-cultural psychology in 1974. As outlined in Chapter 2 in Volume 1, the first goal was to *transport* current hypotheses and conclusions to other cultural contexts in order to *test* their validity. This goal was associated with the *imposed etic* methodological approach, and it has now resulted in a massive amount of data on psychological differences across cultures. For some critics of the field it has also become identified (somewhat erroneously) as the whole of cross-cultural psychology. The second goal was to *explore* new cultural systems to *discover* psychological phenomena not available in the first culture. This goal was associated with the *emic* methodological approach and it can be identified with the moves toward "cultural," "indigenous," and "ethnic" psychologies that we have witnessed over the past decade. The third was to *integrate* psychological knowledge gained from these first two activities, and to *generate* a more panhuman psychology that would be valid for all people. This goal was associated with the *derived etic* methodological approach, and it can be identified with the increased contemporary interest in psychological similarities and the search for a universal psychology. Cross-cultural psychology thus appears to be evolving in a sensible and understandable way.

Cross-cultural psychology is fundamentally concerned with understanding human diversity. As we have just noted, a basic proposition of the field is that cultural factors affect human behavior; it thus follows that cultural factors must also affect the psychology that we do, including the way we conceive of behavior, study it, interpret it, and apply it. In recognition of this cultural impact on psychology, one goal of this second edition of the *Handbook* is to incorporate as much cultural diversity as possible, both by the selection of editors and authors, and by the coverage of the literature. In this endeavor, we have succeeded to some extent: the editors have different cultures of origin, representing Asia, Europe, and North America; their teaching and research experience also include Africa and Oceania (but not South America). Chapter authors include those whose cultural origins are in all continents, representing over twenty mother tongues and with access to psychological literature in all major languages. However, there are evident failures to represent all cultural diversity: research rooted in Western Academic Scientific Psychology (W.A.S.P.), and written in English, overwhelms this *Handbook* as it does any other contemporary psychological work, although hopefully not as much. Moreover, within chapters, there are obvious cultural perspectives taken, and selections made, that result in coverage that falls well short of a pan-cultural treatment. Despite these shortcomings, this *Handbook* represents a serious and honest attempt to engage human diversity where it exists in the psychological literature.

Cross-cultural psychology, while still dominated by Western views and psychologists, is no longer their exclusive preserve. What started as a Western-based attempt to understand the "others" is now a field well-populated by these "others." In part, this has come about by many developing world psychologists having experienced Western psychology (as graduate students, as research collaborators, or as "consumers"), and being both attracted to, and wary of it. The attraction has brought them to the field, while the wariness has brought critical and culturally-rooted alternative perspectives. This process of enrichment by cultural diversification has had a major impact on the field, and continues at an accelerating pace.

The institutions of cross-cultural psychology reflect this growth and diversification. Almost thirty years ago, a meeting of social psychologists concerned with cultural influences took place in Nigeria, and led to the initiation of the *Cross-Cultural Social Psychology Newsletter* (edited by Harry Triandis). A year later (1968) the first of a series of a *Directory of Cross-Cultural Psychological Research* (edited by John Berry) was published in the *International Journal of Psychology* (which was founded in 1966 in part to promote the cross-cultural point of view). Walt Lonner established the *Journal of Cross-Cultural Psychology* in 1970, and John Dawson pulled these various activities and people together in 1972 to found the International Association for Cross-Cultural Psychology (IACCP). This Association has met every two years in a different country since its inaugural meeting in Hong Kong. In 1984, the French-language Association pour la Recherche Interculturelle (ARIC) was founded, primarily through the efforts of Pierre Dasen. These two associations held a joint meeting in Liège in 1992 in an effort to establish closer ties. Conference proceedings of both associations are a core resource in the field.

Other publications in the field have appeared with increasing frequency. For example, in 1974 Walt Lonner and John Berry initiated the Sage Series on Cross-Cultural Research and Methodology, publishing eighteen volumes on a wide variety of topics in psychology and cognate disciplines; this series has been reconstituted (in 1996) as the Sage Series on Cross-Cultural Psychology. Another series, *Cross-Cultural Psychology Monographs* was established by the IACCP in 1991, under the editorship of Fons van de Vijver and Ype Poortinga. Chapters in the *Annual Review of Psychology* focusing on cross-cultural research have appeared at regular intervals since 1973. In addition to these publications, there has been a virtual explosion of textbooks in the field, some covering all domains in which cross-cultural psychologists are active, and some focusing on specific domains, such as social or developmental psychology.

The three volumes of this *Handbook* attempt to extend these publications in two ways. First, the most recent ideas and information in an area have been incorporated in the chapters; the treatment should thus be the most up-to-date available. Second, the writing has been pitched at a level suitable for graduate students and professionals who have a substantial background in psychology, but not necessarily in cross-cultural psychology. All authors were asked to provide basic definitions and descriptions of their area, and then move on to the main tasks of evaluating and integrating the area.

In Volume 1, theoretical and methodological issues are presented as an initial orientation to the broad features of cross-cultural psychology. In Volumes 2 and 3 the field is reviewed and evaluated in the more or less conventional categories used by general psychology. Readers may prefer to use the *Handbook* by beginning with the chapter that comes closest to their own substantive area, move to cognate areas of interest, and then delve into the broader issues addressed in Volume 1. Whatever your approach to the materials in these volumes, we hope that your understanding of the myriad ways in which culture and behavior can be intertwined will be enriched, and that you will be more convinced than ever about the importance of culture as a factor in the production and display of human diversity.

The process of developing an outline for this *Handbook,* and suggesting appropriate chapter authors, was primarily the responsibility of the team of co-editors. However, we were assisted by an editorial advisory group made up of the Editors of the First Edition of this *Handbook,* including Harry Triandis, Bill Lambert, Walt Lonner, Alastair Heron, Rich Brislin, and Juris Draguns. The task of reviewing drafts of chapters, recommending revisions, and keeping authors on track and on schedule largely fell to my volume co-editors. And, of course, the main work of any writing project has fallen to the chapter authors themselves. Najum Rashid has managed the chapter texts and their numerous revisions with accuracy and diligence. I thank all of them for their efforts, and for their contribution to this *Handbook.*

J. W. Berry
Department of Psychology
Queen's University
Kingston, Ontario
Canada

ABOUT THE EDITORS

John W. Berry

John Berry is a Professor of Psychology at Queen's University, Kingston. He received his B.A. from Sir George Williams University (Montreal) in 1963, and his Ph.D. from the University of Edinburgh in 1966. He has been a lecturer at the University of Sydney for three years, a Fellow of Netherlands Institute for Advanced Study and a visiting Professor at the Université de Nice and the Université de Genève. He is a past Secretary-General, past President and Honorary Fellow of the International Association for Cross-Cultural Psychology, and has been an Associate Editor of the *Journal of Cross-Cultural Psychology* and co-editor of the first edition of this *Handbook*. He is the author or editor of over twenty books in the areas of cross-cultural, social, and cognitive psychology, and is particularly interested in the application of cross-cultural psychology to public policy and programs in the areas of acculturation, multiculturalism, immigration, health, and education.

Cigdem Kagitçibasi

Cigdem Kagitçibasi, a Turkish citizen, is a social and cross-cultural psychologist with a special interest in human development and the self in cultural context. She has a B.A. from Wellesley College in Wellesley, Massachusetts, U.S.A., and a Ph.D. from the University of California in Berkeley, California, U.S.A.

She is an executive board member of the International Union of Psychological Science and a past president of the International Association for Cross-Cultural Psychology and the Turkish Psychological Association. She is one of the ten founding members of the Turkish Academy of Sciences and is a member of the Council of the Academy. She holds several awards and honors, including the APA 1993 Distinguished Contributions to the International Advancement of Psychology Award; Fellow of the Netherlands Institute for Advanced Study; Fulbright Scholar at Harvard University; Fellow of the Bunting Institute, Radcliffe College; Alumna Phi Beta Kappa of Wellesley College; honorary fellow of the Population Council; and a number of research awards.

Kagitçibasi was involved in a nine-country study on the value of children and motivations for childbearing, and more recently directed a ten-year longitudinal intervention project on early childhood enrichment. The latter has produced a mother–child education program which is in wide scale use with low-income families in Turkey. Her publications in English and Turkish include 17 books (authored and edited) and more than 100 journal articles and chapters. She is deeply concerned with and actively involved in promoting the relevance of psychology in contributing to the solution of global "human development issues."

Marshall H. Segall

Marshall H. Segall is Professor Emeritus of Social and Political Psychology in the Department of Political Science in the Maxwell School at Syracuse University, where he has been since 1966. He did psychological fieldwork in collaboration with anthropologist colleagues in Uganda in 1959. His cross-cultural research earlier focused on visual perception (with Donald Campbell and Melville Herskovits) and later on adolescence, aggression, and intergroup relations. President of the International Association for Cross-Cultural Psychology (IACCP) from 1996 through 1998, he earlier served as President of the Society for Cross-Cultural Research. During the decade of the 1990s, he has collaborated with Pierre Dasen, John Berry, and Ype Poortinga in textbooks in cross-cultural psychology, and he notes with pleasure their translation into Italian, Greek, and Japanese. His most recent writing project was done in Geneva, with support from the Johann Jacobs Foundation.

ABOUT THE CONTRIBUTORS

Irwin Altman   Irwin Altman is Distinguished Professor of Psychology at the University of Utah, U.S.A. His work focuses on cross-cultural and environmental aspects of interpersonal relationships. Recent publications include the *Handbook of Environment Psychology* (1987) co-edited with Dan Stokols, and edited volumes on *Place Attachment* (1992) co-edited with Setha Low, and *Women and Environment* (1994) co-edited with Arza Churchman. He is also co-author with Joseph Ginat of *Polygamous Families in Contemporary Society* (1996).

Lisa Marie Beardsley   Lisa Marie Beardsley is Assistant Dean for medical education and evaluation and an Associate Professor in the department of medicine at the University of Illinois College of Medicine at Peoria. In addition to a Ph.D. in educational psychology, she has a Master of Public Health and has worked in health education in Hawaii, Finland, and the Philippines. Current research interests include culture and health behavior, acculturation training for physicians who are international medical graduates, and clinical performance assessment methods.

Deborah L. Best and **John E. Williams**   Deborah Best and John Williams are Professors of Psychology at Wake Forest University in Winston-Salem, North Carolina. Best, a native of North Carolina, is a developmental psychologist while Williams, a native of West Virginia, is a personality–social psychologist. Their common interests in cross-cultural psychology have resulted in their 32-country study of gender stereotypes, their 14-country study of self-concepts, and their 19-country study of age stereotypes. A current 20-country project involves similarities and differences in the importance attached to different psychological traits. Both have been active in organizational affairs, with Best currently completing her seventh year of service as treasurer of the International Association for Cross-Cultural Psychology and Williams completing his fifth year as editor of the *Journal of Cross-Cultural Psychology.*

Michael Harris Bond   Michael Harris Bond was born in Toronto, Canada, where he received a transplanted public school education from teachers with British accents. His cultural confusion was reinforced by trips to Quebec, where he heard a euphonic language and saw people drinking wine at lunch. His fate was sealed when he was enchanted by another foreigner, Edwin Hollander, whose television programs on social psychology were beamed across the border from Buffalo. Subsequent travels took him to exotic cultures, such as California, where he received a Ph.D. from Stanford in 1970. His appetite for the extraordinary thus whetted, he continued going west as a young man until he arrived in the Far East, where he has now reached middle age, teaching psychology at the Chinese University of Hong Kong (Department of Psychology, Chinese University of Hong Kong, Shatin, N.T., Hong Kong). His most recent act of cultural hubris was editing the *Handbook of Chinese Psychology*.

Richard W. Brislin   Richard W. Brislin is a professor in the College of Business Administration at the University of Hawaii. He directs yearly programs for university professors planning to introduce cross-cultural studies into their courses, and for community leaders asked to prepare various types of cross-cultural training programs (e.g., *Intercultural Interactions: A Practical Guide*, 2nd ed. (1996)) and is author of a text in cross-cultural psychology, *Understanding Culture's Influence on Behavior* (1993). One of his books, *The Art of Getting Things Done: A Practical Guide to the Use of Power*, was a Book-of-the-Month Club Selection in 1992. He is frequently asked to give workshops for American and Asian managers working on international assignments.

Barbara Brown   Barbara Brown is an Associate Professor in the Environment and Behavior Area of the Family and Consumer Studies Department at the University of Utah. Her primary research interests include the processes of human territoriality, privacy regulation, and place attachment, with applications to the problems of university retention, environmental disruptions, residential burglary, and neighborhood revitalization.

Juris G. Draguns   Juris Draguns was born in Latvia in 1932 where he completed his primary schooling. He graduated from high school in Augsburg, Germany. In the United States, he obtained his bachelor's degree from Utica College of Syracuse University in 1954 and was awarded a Ph.D. in clinical psychology from the University of Rochester in 1962. After employment as a clinical and research psychologist at the Rochester, New York State Hospital and Worcester, Massachusetts State Hospital, he accepted a faculty appointment at The Pennsylvania State University in 1967 where he is Professor of Psychology. He also taught part-time at Clark University, Leicester Junior College, University of Rochester, and Florida Institute of Technology. He held visiting faculty appointments at the Johannes Gutenberg University in Mainz, Germany, East-West Center in Honolulu, Flinders University in Bedford, South Australia, and National Taiwan University in Taipei. Dr. Draguns' cross-cultural research interests have been focused upon psychological disturbance. They have expanded to include personality characteristics, complex social behavior, and therapeutic and counseling relationships. At this time, he is especially interested in the role of cultural factors in mediating economic, political, and social change in Eastern and Central Europe. He is a member of the Advisory Board of the Multicultural Research Center in Daugavpils, Latvia. Dr. Draguns has published over 100 articles, chapters, and monographs in psychological, psychiatric, and interdisciplinary publications, many of which deal with cultural topics.

Carol R. Ember and **Melvin Ember**   Carol Ember is Director of Operations at the Human Relations Area Files (HRAF), a research agency of Yale University. She did anthropological fieldwork on sex differences among the Luo of western Kenya and, before joining the HRAF, was Professor of Anthropology at Hunter College in New York City. Her cross-cultural comparative research has focused on social organization, warfare, and sex roles. She has served as President of the Society for Cross-Cultural Research and has been the principal investigator on NSF-sponsored cross-cultural tests of competing explanations of aggression and warfare.

Melvin Ember is President of HRAF. He did anthropological fieldwork on cultural change in American Samoa and before joining HRAF was chairman of the Department of Anthropology at Hunter College. His comparative research has focused on human social organization. He has served as President of the Society for Cross-Cultural Research, is the editor of its official organ *Cross-Cultural Research: The Journal of Comparative Social Science,* and was the co-principal investigator on the NSF-sponsored project mentioned above.

Together, Carol and Melvin Ember have co-authored eight editions of a general anthropology textbook and the same number of editions of a cultural anthropology textbook. They have also collaborated with Burton Pasternak on the forthcoming volume entitled *Social Structure: Sex, Gender, and Kinship in Cross-Cultural Perspective.*

William S. Gudykunst   William Gudykunst was born in Manning, Iowa, U.S.A., and raised in Glendale, Arizona, U.S.A. His first extended intercultural experience came after he completed his M.A. when he served as an intercultural relations specialist in Yokosuka, Japan, conducting training designed to help naval personnel and their families adjust to living and working in Japan. After being discharged from the Navy, he went to Minnesota to pursue his interest in intercultural communication, completing his Ph.D. in 1977. His work focuses on developing a theory of interpersonal and intergroup communication. He has written and edited several books including *Bridging Differences, Bridging Japanese/North American Differences* (with Tsukasa Nishida), and *Communicating with Strangers* (with Young Yun Kim). He currently teaches in the Department of Speech Communication at California State University, Fullerton, California, U.S.A.

Ann-Marie Horvath   Ann-Marie Horvath has an M.A. in psychology and currently is a student in the clinical studies Ph.D. program in psychology at the University of Hawaii. She is an East-West Center degree fellow with the Program on Education and Training. Her special emphasis is in cross-cultural and intercultural mental health. Current research projects center on the measurement of ethnocultural identity in multicultural populations. She is author of a training module on ethnocultural identity published in *Improving Intercultural Interactions: Modules for Cross-Cultural Training Programs, 2nd edition* (1997).

C. Harry Hui   C. Harry Hui is a Hong Kong native. He has published on topics such as the effects of second language proficiency on person perception, methods to determine cross-cultural equivalence of psychological instruments, individualism-collectivism, and work psychology of the Chinese. Some of his publications were on topics related to the psychology of the Hispanics, whom he first came to know when he was a graduate student and research assistant at the University of llinois at Urbana-Champaign, U.S.A. He has also been developing indigenous psychological instruments for use among the Chinese. Harry's academic pursuit has greatly enriched and informed his work as a consultant to Hong Kong, Chinese, and multinational organizations. Working with these organizations also brings new insights to his study of cross-cultural industrial/organizational psychology. Harry is now at the University of Hong Kong, his Alma Mater, and where he has been teaching since he received his doctorate in 1984.

Chung Leung Luk   Chung Leung Luk is currently a Ph.D. candidate at the University of Hong Kong. He is a Hong Kong Chinese, born, raised, and educated in Hong Kong. The academic training that he received was a blend of psychology and anthropology. The cultures particularly attractive and interesting to him were those of traditional societies in Indo-China. Recently he is working on models of managerial decision-making, the role of cultural factors in these models, and their implications to economic development.

Paul Pedersen   Paul Pedersen is a professor in the department of human studies at the University of Alabama, Birmingham. He is a leader in the field of cross-cultural counseling and has authored 28 books. He is a fellow in Division 17, 9, and 45 in the American Psychological Association. He was PI for the NIMH Grant, *Developing Interculturally Skilled Counselors* (University of Hawaii) and was Senior Fellow at the East-West Center from 1978–81. He has taught at the university level and conducted research in Indonesia, Taiwan, and the University of Malaya in Malaysia.

David Sam   David Sam is a Norwegian researcher of Ghanaian origin, who has rapidly established his position as an expert in cross-cultural psychology in Norway. He has a B.Sc. degree from the University of Ghana, and a doctorate degree in psychology from the University of Bergen, Norway. His research interests lie in the domain of adaptation in a foreign society, a subject with which he is familiar also through personal experience. Sam has published quite extensively in international scientific journals during the past few years. He has also been active in initiating and conducting international research projects within and outside Europe.

Shalom H. Schwartz   Shalom Schwartz was born and educated in the United States, receiving his Ph.D. in social psychology from the University of Michigan. He taught in the sociology department of the University of Wisconsin-Madison for 12 years, researching moral decision making, altruism, and helping behavior. In 1979, he moved to Israel. A desire to test whether his theory of the contents and structure of individual values captures basic psychological processes kindled his interest in cross-cultural psychology. To test the cross-cultural generalizability of the theory, he sought co-workers in ten countries. Gradually this network expanded to over 55 countries. The availability of data from so many countries encouraged him to develop a new theory of the dimensions of values on which cultures can be compared. Currently he is studying origins and consequences of both individual differences and national differences in value priorities.

Gün R. Semin   Gün Semin received his Ph.D. from the University of London, England. His teaching and research has been at the Universities of Essex, Sussex, in England; Mannheim, Germany; and the Maison des Sciences des Hommes in Paris, France. Currently he is Professor and Chair of the Department of Social Psychology at the Free University of Amsterdam, the Netherlands.

Peter B. Smith   Peter Smith was born in England and has lived there for most of his life. He obtained his Ph.D. in social psychology from the University of Cambridge in 1962. For some years thereafter he studied leadership and group influence. He has taught at the University of Sussex since 1966, where he is now Professor of Social Psychology. He became interested in cross-cultural psychology during the mid-eighties, when he made a series of studies comparing leadership in Japanese and Western organizations. More recently he has attempted to develop an understanding of leadership processes with applicability to a broad range of cultural contexts, collaborating with others in a 30-nation survey. He has also analyzed the 43-nation values databank assembled by Fons Trompenaars. With Michael Bond, he is author of *Social Psychology Across Cultures* (1993). He is currently editor of the *Journal of Cross-Cultural Psychology*.

Junko Tanaka-Matsumi   Junko Tanaka-Matsumi was born in Osaka, Japan, and educated in Japan, Australia, and the United States. She received her Ph.D. in clinical psychology from the University of Hawaii and was an East-West Center student from Japan. She is an Associate Professor of Psychology at Hofstra University, Hempstead, New York, and teaches graduate courses on psychopathology and cross-cultural psychology, and an undergraduate course on behavior modification. She serves on the editorial boards of *Journal of Cross-Cultural Psychology, Psychological Assessment,* and *the Behavior Therapist.* Her research interests include analyses of dyadic interactions of depressed people, culture and psychopathology, communication of emotions, and functional analytic approaches to cross-cultural therapy. She lives in Rockville Centre, Long Island, New York.

Carol Werner   Carol Werner is a professor in the psychology department at the University of Utah. Her current research examines the social and psychological underpinnings of such conservation behaviors as recycling and adherence to wilderness signs. Her writings with Drs. Altman and Brown have explored implications of transactional/dialectical approaches to interpersonal relationships, such as how rituals provide opportunities for managing tensions between individual and social identities.

Sandra M. Zwier   Sandra Zwier is one of Professor Semin's graduate students. Following programs at the Universities of Amsterdam, the Netherlands, and Exeter, England, she finished a first degree in social psychology in 1992. Her current research focuses on the interactions between culture, social cognition, and communication.

INTRODUCTION TO VOLUME 3

Social and Applied Psychology, Then and Now

This volume merges Volume 5 (Social Psychology) and Volume 6 (Psychopathology) from the first edition of the *Handbook of Cross-Cultural Psychology*, including them here under the overarching title "Social Behavior and Applications." In many respects, this volume covers several of the same topics and engages the talents of some of the same scholars. Authors whose contributions enriched Volume 5 of the first edition and who are represented in this volume are Richard Brislin, John Berry, and Irwin Altman, all of whom are co-authors of new chapters. In addition, Juris Draguns, who served as co-editor of Volume 6 (Psychopathology) in the first edition, and who authored a chapter in that volume, is a co-author of a chapter in this volume.

That all these veteran contributors are co-authors, rather than solo authors, is no mere coincidence. In nearly every instance in this volume, chapters have been co-authored, because the editors tried to cast a wide net when searching for authors, seeking to include both younger scholars and persons with more than one foot planted in societies other than the North American and Western European societies in which our discipline was first nourished. This discipline is, after all, an international enterprise and it is evolving and growing, attracting new adherents from diverse generations and home settings. So, the authorship of this volume reflects those facts about cross-cultural psychology—facts that are more true now than they were in 1980.

Our topic range (rather like a frequent characteristic of findings in cross-cultural psychology studies) is both similar to and different from the range of topics in the first edition. A cursory comparison is instructive regarding ways in which the field may have changed during the intervening 15 years.

Similarities and Differences

In both editions, coverage includes attitudes, beliefs, and values, but whereas in the first edition (henceforth referred to as "then") one chapter covered "attitudes and beliefs" while another was entitled "values," in this edition (henceforth "now") the two (roughly) corresponding chapters are called "social cognition" and "values." The word "attitude" does not appear in the title of any of our present chapters. But, as readers will surely discover, attitudes are in fact being studied under various rubrics, and findings related to various kinds of attitudes (toward self, toward others, intergroup, etc.) fill the pages of many of the chapters in this edition, especially in this volume. As a domain title, "attitude" has apparently lost favor, but the processes formerly studied under that heading are often found under "social cognition" and remain a major concern of cross-cultural social psychologists. For evidence supporting this assertion, see, especially, Chapters 1 through 8.

"Social and cultural change," a chapter then, is also a chapter now, this time called "acculturation and adaptation." Obviously, there has been no decline in interest in the processes of cultural change. However, there have been shifts in what is studied and how it is discussed. Theoretical perspectives once popularly applied to overall societal change, such as the modernization paradigm and the achievement motivation notion, are currently out of favor. On the increase are studies of cultural changes reflecting contact among members of various ethnic or cultural groups in increasingly multicultural settings. In fact, interest and research activity have burgeoned in the interim between editions. The ever-increasing international migration of workers and refugees, among others, and the arguably temporary resurgence of "ethnic" identities have stimulated research in this domain, the results of which are reflected in three chapters (4, 8, and 9) of this volume.

Similarly, the domain "environment–behavior relationships," with a focus on behavioral implications of culturally variable spatial arrangements, merited a chapter then, and has one now. What was called "organizational psychology" then is now found in a chapter on "industrial–organizational psychology." And, psychopathology, to which a whole volume was devoted then, is covered in a chapter now, one that covers psychotherapy as well. Related issues pertaining to physical and psychological well-being, which were covered then in Volume 6, are treated now in a chapter which includes in its broad sweep many issues relating to health and counseling.

Featured then, but hidden now, are "behavior exchange," and "small groups" and the many issues covered by these rubrics. Where have all these topics gone? No longer highlighted as chapter headings, the phenomena to which these terms once provided a categorical home, can, we believe, still be found in many of the present chapters.

Occupying center stage now, but still waiting in the wings then, are sex and gender, and aggression, crime, and warfare. While the world in which we all live may not have gotten any sexier or any more violent (both questionable propositions), how people in all cultures relate to each other across gender and ethnic boundaries (and within them) has certainly become a more salient set of concerns, both to lay persons and to cross-cultural psychologists. So, all to the better, this volume has chapters newly devoted to these domains.

Other topics of both historical and contemporary interest, such as the self, social identity, leadership, social influence, and conformity, while they do not appear in chapter titles, are discussed in various chapters in this volume; for example, the self is a focus of Chapter 1, social influence and conformity in Chapter

4, leadership appears in Chapter 10, and social identity is treated from a developmental perspective in Volume 2 of this *Handbook.*

Compared with the first edition, here there is a greater emphasis on applied issues, reflecting, perhaps, a wider acceptance by cross-cultural psychologists of the propriety, if not sometimes the necessity, of taking a problem-oriented, policy-relevant stance with respect to real-world problems.

Finally, the era we are here calling "then," which was circa 1980, was just beginning to hear about "individualism/collectivism." These ideas, while deeply rooted in intellectual history, were then new enough in their latest guise that they hardly made it into the first edition of this *Handbook.* Now, the concept has earned pride of place as the subject of the first chapter in this volume, and it appears with great frequency in many of the other eleven chapters. In case anyone failed to notice, this volume makes very clear that individualism/collectivism is currently the favorite heuristic of many cross-cultural social psychologists. Since 1980, increasing legions of them have been tempted to hang their facts on this concept, organizing principle, or paradigm, as some have been tempted to call it. Readers will find it frequently in this volume, despite the efforts of the editors to winnow away the striking overlap that was present in first drafts of chapters, as authors, independently of each other, felt compelled to cover "individualism/collectivism" in great detail, whatever the topic of their particular chapters. So, this volume is, in some measure, a testimony to the popularity of this concept. It is also, as we noted earlier, evidence of both continuity and change in the field of cross-cultural social psychology from circa 1980 to circa 1995.

Before we conclude our discussion of where the cross-cultural study of social behavior and of applications now stands, as well as the difficulties it confronts and the promise it foresees, let us indicate in some detail what each chapter in this volume sets out to accomplish.

Brief Chapter Descriptions

Individualism/Collectivism

As was just noted, ideas relating to these concepts have, in the views of many, attained the status of a paradigm in cross-cultural psychology. Whether true or not, they require focused attention, clear presentation, and fair but penetrating analysis and critique. The editors decided to precede all other topics in this volume with a chapter on individualism/collectivism and assigned the task of preparing the opening to one of us, Cigdem Kagitçibasi, based in the Koç University in Turkey, herself a long-time contributor to the development of the domain and a sometimes strict, but always friendly, critic. What she produced, to a considerable degree, takes the place of a chapter that would try to bring together the diverse threads of cross-cultural social psychology, since the I/C concept purports to (and in the views of many, actually does) provide some unity to the field.

Social Cognition

The authors of this chapter, both at the Free University of Amsterdam, provide an overview of research on attribution processes (whereby persons perceive the causes of various acts), the one domain in social cognition which has long attracted attention from a cultural perspective. What Semin and Zwier find to be new about this attention is that the very process of attribution, and not merely its content, is culturally shaped. This evolution is described more generally in the chapter as an "infusion" of culture into social cognition, which includes the "recognition" that the self itself is fundamentally culturally situated. While the individualism/collectivism dimension is cited in this chapter as well, the authors conclude with a plea for a multiple or convergent construct approach to the many phenomena of social cognition.

Values

This chapter reminds us that most of the currently popular models of variation among cultures rest upon analyses of their values. Smith and Schwartz (the former at the University of Sussex in England, the latter at Hebrew University in Israel) acknowledge the importance of eco-cultural theories in cross-cultural social psychology (which tend to explain cultural adaptations by reference to ecological and socio-political contexts) but the authors of this chapter find "values" appealing as mediating variables, which seem to be more closely related to psychology than either ecological or sociopolitical variables. (See a related discussion of mediating variables in the chapter by Lonner and Adamopoulos in Volume 1 of this *Handbook*.) Certainly, Smith and Schwartz opine, the value priorities which prevail in a society are perhaps the most central element in its culture. Individualism/collectivism, which Kagitcibasi in Chapter 1 refers to as a paradigm, is featured in the Smith and Schwartz chapter as a value. This one, like other values, can be treated as either a characteristic of individuals or a characteristic of societies. The distinction between individual-level and cultural-level value dimensions is treated as crucial in this chapter, and it is shown, especially in the case of individualism/collectivism, how failure to take this distinction seriously has led to some errors of interpretation in the cross-cultural literature.

Accordingly, here there are separate sections dealing with individual-level values and with cultural-level ones. In the former, the Rokeach legacy is reviewed and serves as a springboard to the more recent Schwartz project which revolves around a theory of dynamic relations among "motivationally distinct" value types. Attempts to derive individual-level measures of individualism/collectivism are also reviewed in this section. In the latter, where cultural-level values are considered, most of the attention is given to individualism/collectivism from before Hofstede up to Schwartz. The chapter concludes with a review of some studies that explain national differences in the light of value priorities, accompanied by some methodological and theoretical pointers for future research.

Intergroup Relations

Although relegated to one of several sections of this chapter by Gudykunst of the California State University and Bond of the Chinese University of Hong Kong, social cognition appears again, this time as applied to intergroup relations. And, once more, individualism/collectivism is introduced early in the chapter, this time in a section on measuring variations across cultures in intergroup behavior. The chapter ranges more widely, however, over several topics, including social and ethnolinguistic identity, intergroup expectations (e.g., stereotypes and intergroup attitudes), intergroup communication and intergroup conflict. Theories brought to bear on intergroup relations include social identity theory, ethnocentrism theory, and uncertainty avoidance theory, among other intriguing ideas. The authors advocate attention to diverse theoretical frameworks, noting that the recent focus on "collectivism and its associated constructs" may be excessively narrow, a narrowness arising, they say, "because of the Americocentrism characterizing social science, with Americans and its social scientists occupying the extreme end of the individualism dimension." So they would have us widen our theoretical net as well as our sampling of cultural groups. They leave us wondering how we would understand intergroup relations if we had more data on groups in South America and Africa, for example, instead of mostly from one or two Asian societies (almost always compared with the United States).

Sex, Gender, and Culture

Best and Williams, both at Wake Forest University in the United States, describe the intent of their chapter as providing a review of studies in developmental psychology, personality, and social psychology that deal with the ways in which males and females view themselves and one another and the way in which they interact with each other. Because all of these are heavily influenced by culture, while at the same time reflecting biological influences, the authors can demonstrate in this chapter both similarities and differences across cultures in gender roles and in inter-gender relations. Both biology and socialization are shown to play roles in shaping these phenomena and, hence, both biology and socialization are featured in various theories of gender role development. However, these authors find most striking their central finding that pan-cultural similarities outweigh cultural differences in respect to many issues of sex and gender. Among the particular issues discussed in this chapter are the bases for mate selection, concepts of romantic love and intimacy, and, contrastingly, harassment and rape.

Various kinds of research methods are shown to have been applied to the study of the sexes, including hologeistic research (comparing ethnographic accounts of many societies described and indexed in the Human Relations Area Files), a research strategy also featured in the following chapter. It is notable that in their conclusion, Best and Williams include a plea for anthropologists and psychologists to bridge their disciplines, to learn more from each other in their efforts to understand the impact of culture on behavior.

Aggression, Crime, and Warfare

An anthropology/psychology team, including the psychologist Segall at Syracuse University in the United States and the two anthropologists, C. Ember and M. Ember, from the Human Relations Area Files in New Haven, United States, co-authored this chapter and, as Best and Williams would have expected, did indeed learn from each other. Ember and Ember brought to bear on the construction of this chapter HRAF research on sex differences in aggression and on the perplexing question of what causes warfare. And, despite the fact that HRAF studies are fundamentally correlational, their findings can be applied in theory-building efforts, as they are in this chapter. Segall brought to bear mostly psychological research and theory to such issues as the socialization of aggression, the role of the absent father in the development of male aggression (and hence, of sex differences in aggression, an issue also treated by the HRAF research), and effects of the mass media in the United States and other societies. Attention is paid in this chapter to societal reactions to aggressive behavior, because these constitute some of the mechanisms whereby culture shapes aggressive behavior, although the biological bases of aggressive behaviors are by no means ignored in this chapter.

Near the end of their chapter, Segall, Ember, and Ember sadly note that, although aggression is surely a "real-world concern," cross-cultural psychologists have thus far contributed very little of practical significance to a search for a less aggressive, less violent, less warfare-prone world. But they find a few hopeful signs, including some recent examples of attempts to address policy concerns from the perspective of what is known, cross-culturally, about this most costly mode of action.

Environmental Psychology

This chapter, by Werner, Brown, and Altman, based in the University of Utah in the United States, reflects a view of the physical environment as an essential backdrop to all human activity and the source of essential resources, which are differentially used in ways that reflect individual and cultural aspects of identity. Ongoing social and economic change in various parts of the world, which include increased urbanization, and increased population size and density in many nations, when added to pre-existing cultural variations in the use of physical environments, serve to underscore the fundamental significance of the physical and human-made environment. The authors employ a "transactional/dialectical" perspective which presumes that human behavior is inseparable from sociophysical contexts and that opposition and change are integral to human events. They also discuss culturally variant conceptions of the human being/natural environment relationship (subservient, dominant, in harmony) and recent changes in these conceptions in some parts of the world as concern about the health of ecosystems has grown. Readers will also find in this chapter some rich descriptions of reactions to changing population pressures, changes in gender roles and in other political, economic, and technological environments, revealing some complex interactions. One of the clearest ideas to emerge from this chapter is that environments are not merely "out there" nor unchanging. An ecocultural view of human behavior is one that must be dynamic, for all aspects of such a view are themselves in flux.

Acculturation and Adaptation

An ecocultural view is certainly clear in the chapter by Berry, of Queen's University in Canada, and Sam, of the University of Bergen in Norway. So, of course, is change. Indeed, this is a chapter all about changing cultural contexts due to contacts with other cultures. The cultural changes themselves are described as acculturation and their consequent psychological changes are termed adaptation. Diverse theoretical and conceptual issues are raised by Berry and Sam, who then review empirical studies pertaining to various groups of people experiencing cultural contacts—immigrants, sojourners, refugees, asylum seekers, indigenous peoples, and other ethnocultural groups resident in plural societies. An updated version of a conceptual framework for acculturation research is included in this chapter and its fit with advancing knowledge is assessed.

Cross-Cultural Training and Multicultural Education

Opportunities for intercultural contacts are accelerating, especially for sojourners pursuing educational opportunities in cultural settings other than their own, and persons engaged in the global economy, within which national boundaries count hardly at all in the domains of commerce and industry. Hence, training persons to function effectively in such situations is a growing enterprise. Clearly an application of cross-cultural psychology, it nonetheless has its own research literature and some of its own theoretical frameworks. These are reviewed by a team of co-authors based in the East-West Center in Hawaii, where cross-cultural training has a long history. Brislin and Horvath present detailed descriptions of different approaches to cross-cultural training, and they consider various ways to assess their effectiveness. The chapter also attends to the related issues of cross-cultural, multi-ethnic, and international education. More general than training, education for all who live in a shrinking world, whose lives both in and out of school, both as children and later as adults in whatever communities they will live, will increasingly require the ability to interact, work and live with diverse "others," is beginning to attract widespread attention from psychologists and educators. But, the chapter makes clear, research in this domain, at least in North America, and to some extent elsewhere, is only a beginning. Much more is badly needed.

Industrial–Organizational Psychology

Industrial/organizational psychology is a field that is clearly an application of social psychology. When treated from a cross-cultural perspective, as it is in this chapter by co-authors in the University of Hong Kong, it becomes also an application of cross-cultural psychology. However, as so often is the case with "applications," its own research findings and related theoretical developments come to inform, in meaningful ways, their more "basic" relatives. Thus, to no one's sur-prise, we find that Hui and Luk launch their chapter with an account of research on work-related values, findings from which are interpreted, as they have been since 1980, in the light of the Individualism/Collectivism concept. Clearly this concept, although rooted in I/O psychology, has come to play a central role in many aspects of cross-cultural social psychology. This chapter covers other issues as well, however, including problems relating to intra-organizational communica-tion, managerial techniques, organizational development and business activities, for all of which cultural variables are shown to be significant. The global economy, referred to briefly earlier in our comments on cross-cultural training, is salient in this chapter as well. The authors review research on work values, management, and commerce in the light of the growth of this economy. Because so many of the earlier principles of management were derived from research which originated in North America and Europe, but with the economy now very global indeed, a cul-turally-based second look at those principles is, according to this chapter, clearly in order.

Health and Culture-Centered Intervention

In another chapter that exemplifies this volume's concern for applications of cross-cultural psychology to real-world problems, Beardsley of the University of Illinois and Pedersen of the University of Alabama, both in the United States, show that when culture is made central to health interventions, behavior can be measured more accurately, personal identity becomes clearer, and the consequences of prob-lems relating to health and illness are better understood. Noting that "All illness has a psychological component that is influenced by culture and that interacts with biological processes of disease," they try in their chapter to integrate biologi-cal factors with cultural ones and to inform health providers and public health policy makers of insight gained into questions of health and illness from studies of psychological, social, and cultural factors. Among the chapter's emphases are culturally-sensitive definitions of health, illness, and disease, the role of cultural factors in differences in health morbidity and mortality, and variations in diagno-sis and treatments across cultures. The chapter also includes recommendations for the training of culture-centered counselors and health care providers. An in-triguing feature of the chapter is a section containing some success stories (e.g., a dramatic decline in river blindness in West Africa through environmental inter-vention and a similar drop in Guinea worm disease through health education and other efforts coordinated by the World Health Organization). In contrast, the ac-count found here of the spread of AIDS in many cultures has little to offer by way of achieved success, but reveals how a culturally sensitive research program holds promise of better understanding of behavioral interventions (e.g., "safe sex" edu-cation, encouragement of clean needles by intravenous drug users) that might contribute to enhanced control of the world-wide epidemic. Acculturation as a factor in health and disease is clearly revealed in this chapter (e.g., the account of changes in behavior and health status of Japanese migrants in Hawaii and California and studies of other immigrant populations), which argues for reading it alongside the Berry and Sam chapter on acculturation and adaptation in this volume. Another inter-chapter linkage is with the Tanaka -Matsumi and Draguns chapter, which follows immediately upon the Beardsley and Pedersen chapter.

Psychopathology

In the first edition of this *Handbook* (1980), Draguns stated that "no disorder has been found to be immune to cultural shaping." He and his co-author, Tanaka-Matsumi, reaffirm this here, but go on to ask whether a "universalist" or "culturally relativist" position provides the better orientation for interpreting the interplay of abnormal behavior and culture. These two orientations lead to somewhat different research projects and yield findings which serve in some instances to support a universalist orientation and in others the culturally relativist one. Tanaka-Matsumi and Draguns, based respectively in Hofstra University and Pennsylvania State University, both in the United States, organize the largest portion of their chapter under the universalist approach, revealing many pan-cultural commonalties with respect to affective disorders, suicide, schizophrenia, alcoholism, anxiety disorders, and other, while certain cultural idioms of distress and certain culture-bound syndromes are classified under the cultural-relativist orientation. In both categories, the empirical research reveals the role of cultural factors. This is true not only for psychopathology, but for psychotherapy as well.

As in other chapters in this volume (notably the Training chapter and the Acculturation chapter), multiculturalism, migration, and acculturation issues are treated as of increasing importance in efforts to understand psychopathology. Again as in other chapters, Individualism/Collectivism finds favor as a concept.

Some Common Threads and Some Nagging Questions

Individualism/Collectivism, as we have stated, is mentioned in most chapters in this volume. An ecocultural framework is at least implicit in many chapters. These popular conceptualizations do not compete with each other, nor is the relationship between the two very clear, although Berry (1994)[1] proposes a linkage between them. In any case, most cross-cultural social psychologists, circa late 1990s, tend to conceptualize relations between environments (both physical and social) and behaviors (both overt and inferred internal psychological states) as a complex of interacting variables. And, most of these same social psychologists seem primed to describe, if not explain, cross-cultural differences as reflecting differences in individualism/ collectivism. (Significantly, perhaps, most contributors to this *Handbook*'s Volume 2, on Developmental Psychology, were not similarly disposed.)

Are Individualism/Collectivism and the ecocultural framework both paradigms? If so, will either or both go the way of many other paradigms, some of which were once as popular but are now forgotten?

In every chapter, culture, not usually well-defined, is given a heavy burden of explanation to carry. Is this notion up to the task? Elsewhere in this *Handbook* (especially in Volume 1), we learn that the concept is undergoing a wrenching investigation from many quarters, post-modernist and social constructionist among them. Yet, in this volume, it seems to have weathered the storm.

Nevertheless, as social psychologists, we should remain alert to the possibility that when we compare samples, both within and across nations, they may be not only samples representing different "cultures" but samples of different social and economic class. Thus, what we take to be a cross-cultural difference might well be a social class difference.

Of course, this last point could be applied to any particular interpretation of a "cross-cultural" difference, such as an attribution of a behavioral difference between, say, (to choose that almost-going-steady couple) a sample from China with a sample from the United States, to a reflection of the two samples' positions on the individualism/collectivism dimension (individualist in the case of the Americans, collectivistic in the case of the Chinese). Although it is seldom mentioned in the cross-cultural psychological research literature, China and the United States are vastly different from each other in terms of several socioeconomic variables, including and especially, level and distribution of wealth. Thus, it was recently reported by the American news service, Associated Press, that in the United States, a country in which three out of four households have at least two cars, and where are found more than one-third of all the world's cars, there is approximately one privately owned automobile per 1.7 people (men, women, and children). In stark contrast, in China, there is one car per 18,000 people! One *could* argue, of course, that it is the American individualism implied by "privately owned" that matters, but one has to wonder if the wealth differences that are reflected in the dramatic differences in persons/cars ratios in China and the United States (about 11,000-to-1) are not responsible for the many behavioral differences between their two populations! But then again, wealth is a cultural variable, so maybe, after all, as the chapters in this volume collectively argue, we can't understand social behavior without searching for the cultural variables (whether individualism/collectivism or other things much more concrete) which influence it.

In any event, the editors of this volume commend it to its readers. We ask you to note the diversity of research methods employed in contemporary social psychology when it is done cross-culturally, and enjoy the many fruits of this diversity. We hope that you also note the emergence of cross-cultural research and theory from some parts of the world other than North America and Western Europe, while remaining cautious about our ability to generalize to human social behavior, because vast populations from many areas continue to be under-researched.

Recalling the ways in which the domain has both stayed the same and changed in the decade and a half since the first edition of this *Handbook*, we expect you, our present and future colleagues, to build on, add to, and depart from, in a culturally evolutionary manner, what is offered in this volume as the state of the art, circa the end of the twentieth and beginning of the twenty-first century, in cross-cultural social psychology and related applications.

A final note: We, the editors, enjoyed eliciting, cajoling, arguing, and praising, in various orders and to varying degrees, the cross-cultural social psychologists who contributed much solid effort to this project. Thanks to them, our task as editors was never less than tolerable, often entertaining, and always enlightening.

M. H. Segall
C. Kagitçibasi

Endnote

1. Berry, J. W. (1994) Ecology of individualism and collectivism. In U. Kim, H. C. Triandis, C. Kagitçibasi, S. Choi, & G. Yoon (Eds.), *Individual-ism and collectivism: Theory, method and applications* (pp. 77–84). Thousand Oaks, CA: Sage.

1

INDIVIDUALISM AND COLLECTIVISM

CIGDEM KAGITÇIBASI
Koç University
Istanbul, Turkey

Contents

Introduction

The Individualism/Collectivism concept has been popular since the publication of Hofstede's *Culture's Consequences* (1980). In this chapter I will discuss its place in cross-cultural psychology and will consider why it enjoys such popularity. I will review the various models and conceptualizations of individualism and collectivism, followed by a selective presentation of research and a critical appraisal of the constructs, with a discussion of the problems of conceptualization. I will then propose a scheme for refinement in conceptualization.

Recent publications show the salience of Individualism/Collectivism. It constitutes a special section of the most recent *Annual Review of Psychology* article on cross-cultural psychology under "New Directions" (Kagitçibasi & Berry, 1989). It is one of the six main topics (entitled "Individualism and Collectivism: A Universal Dimension?") of an International Association for Cross-Cultural Psychology (IACCP) international conference proceedings volume (Kagitçibasi, 1987). It also constitutes a chapter of a recent volume of the Nebraska Symposium on Motivation on *Cross-Cultural Perspectives* (Triandis, 1990).

One recent book comprises selected papers from the international conference held in Korea July 9–13, 1990, on "Individualism and Collectivism: Psychocultural Perspectives from East and West " (Kim, Triandis, Kagitçibasi, Choi, & Yoon, 1994). The other, by Triandis (1995), provides comprehensive coverage. Individualism/Collectivism also constitutes a general theoretical background for a recently published cross-cultural social psychology textbook (Smith & Bond, 1993) and a cross-cultural (minority) child development book (Greenfield & Cocking, 1994). Finally, many research reports and conceptual studies using this framework continue to be published in international journals. About one third of recently published studies cited this construct as at least a partial explanation of observed cross-cultural differences (Hui & Yee, 1994).

The Background: How Did We Get Here?

Individualism and collectivism are not confined to psychology. In all the fields of the social and behavioral sciences and humanities, ranging from literary criticism to religion, from political philosophy to sociology, these concepts figure importantly. Since the 1970s, there has been a growing concern in American psychology and social sciences with unbridled individualism in Western (American) society. This has increased the salience of the Individualism/Collectivism concept.

The History of Individualism/Collectivism

The roots of individualism in the Western world have been traced in the history of ideas (e.g., Lukes, 1973), in political and economic history (e.g., Macfarlane, 1978) in religious history (e.g., Capps & Fenn, 1992), and in psychosocial history (e.g., Westen, 1985). Individualism/Collectivism is dealt with by the ancient Greeks, with collectivistic themes being apparent in Plato's *Republic* and individualistic values in Sophists' teaching. Individualism has been attributed to the earliest Christian renouncers or has been linked to the emergence of private property in England, around 1200 (MacFarlane, 1978). Closer to cross-cultural psychologists' understanding of the historical precursors of Individualism/Collectivism, however, are Tönnies's (1887/1957) *Gesellschaft* and *Gemeinschaft*, often translated as society and community, respectively.

Individualism is notable in Britain. Starting with Hobbes in the 17th century, for whom the self-interested individual, *homo economicus*, is primary, economic individualism is rooted in the ideas of Adam Smith (*The Wealth of Nations*, 1776) and Jeremy Bentham's "Utilitarianism," claiming that a free expression of individuals' wills and interests would provide natural harmony and maximal efficiency. Epistemological individualism can be traced to British Empiricism (Bishop Berkeley, David Hume, and John Locke), which rejected *a priori* truths and considered individual experience as the only source of knowledge (see also Jahoda & Krewer chapter in Vol. 1).

Predating British empiricists, Descartes had endorsed epistemological individualism from a rationalist perspective. He pointed to the individual mind as the source of knowledge in his *Cogito ergo sum* (I think therefore I am). These strong philosophical trends in Western Europe contributed to an individualistic human model that was further reinforced in the 19th century by Spencer's Social Darwinism. Social Darwinism legitimized the *laissez-faire* doctrine, upholding the individual, and became especially popular in the United States. In Europe individualism possibly reached its apex in phenomenology and existential philosophy (Kierkegaard, Husserl, Heidegger, and Sartre).

Collectivist themes are also found in continental European philosophy and social thought. For example, in Jean-Jacques Rousseau's *Du Contrat Social* (1762), voluntary submission to the "general will" is proposed. In the early 19th century the German philosopher Hegel considered the nation state as the highest embodiment of social morality, and Karl Marx later put forth his influential collectivist treatise. After the Second World War "ethical socialism," espoused by social democratic movements in Germany, France, and the Netherlands, for example, attempted to integrate individualism with socialist collectivism. It paved the way for the rise of social welfare states in Western Europe.

Nevertheless, individualism has been the hallmark of European social history especially since the early modern period (the beginning of the 16th century). Historical demographic records and court rolls point to individualistic themes in family interactions, marriages, residence patterns, and inheritance in Western Europe, particularly in England. Some historians (Bennett, 1984; Hanawalt, 1986; MacFarlane, 1987) trace these back to the Medieval period.

Certainly, individualistic family systems were prevalent by the early modern period (Lesthaeghe, 1983; Razi, 1993; Thadani, 1978; Thornton, 1984). There are similar reports of individualism from preindustrial North America (Aries, 1980; Thornton & Fricke, 1987). It is important to keep in mind this historical background of an individualistic ethos in the Western world.

In contrast, the teachings of Confucius in the East in the 5th century B.C. emphasized "virtue," including loyalty to one's true nature, reciprocity in human relations, righteousness, and filial piety. Such social morality, underpinning a collectivist worldview, is also seen in other eastern religions and philosophies, such as Taoism, Buddhism, Hinduism, and Shintoism. The monotheistic religions arising in the Middle East (Judaism, Christianity, Islam) also stressed collective loyalties, though the European reformation in Christianity later emphasized individual responsibility. Thus, Westen (1985) sees the rise of the great religions contributing to greater collectivism in sedentary agrarian populations, compared with the animistic nomadic groups or hunters–gatherers.

Today, the majority of humankind share at least some aspects of collectivism. The West, where individualism is more widespread, constitutes less than 30 percent of humanity and even there ethnic minorities and lower socioeconomic status groups tend to be more collectivistic (Singelis, Triandis, Bhawuk, & Gelfand, 1995).

It appears that all societies must deal with tensions between collectivism and individualism and that there is some of both everywhere. Nevertheless, differences in emphasis appear to be real. Thus individualism is to a large extent a characteristic of Western society, and this may engender a bias in psychological theory which is predominantly Western.

More Recent Developments

Individualism/Collectivism finds expression in sociological and anthropological thinking, in addition to psychological approaches. For example, Parsons proposed the pattern variable of "self-orientation/collectivity-orientation." The former reflected the "pursuit of private interests" and the latter the "pursuit of the common interests of the collectivity" (Parsons, 1951, p. 60). Kluckhohn and Strodtbeck (1961) posited "lineal," "collateral," and "individualistic" human relations in all cultures. The former two refer to biologically and culturally determined human ties through time, whereas the latter refers to autonomous and independent individual goals.

Bellah et al. (1985) wrote a seminal treatise on individualism in the United States, taking their clue from Alexis de Tocqueville, who in the 1830s visited the United States and was impressed by American individualism. They pointed to widely shared values, epitomized by individualism. Several other conceptualizations of individualism and collectivism have been proposed, reflecting a wide scope of coverage. A sample is presented in Table 1–1 to show the comprehensive nature of the constructs under consideration. As seen in the table, a number of characteristics purported to be components of individualism and collectivism appear rather to be traditions or customs (e.g., filial piety, sacrifice of women, involvement in community life) or not necessarily implicated by Individualism/Collectivism (e.g., large military spending, equality of individuals). The tendency to identify general cultural differences with Individualism/Collectivism is a serious problem which is one of the main issues discussed in this chapter.

TABLE 1–1   Features and Component Ideas of Individualism/Collectivism

	Individualism	Collectivism
Janzx (1991)	Human beings as the fundamental "building block" of society; "dignity," of the individual; individual as the primary source of value (ethical individualism); collective goals subsumed under personal ones; individual having firm boundaries (Homo Clausus); "equality" of individuals (at least in principle); and "liberty" from interference of others.	Emphasis on the group or community; the group as the source of value; the interests of the group taking precedence over those of the individual, with "commitment" as the moral aspect of ideology; individual not separate from others, but inextricably linked with them or embedded in group; individual freedom "restricted" by the group.
Hsu (1983)	Self reliance, competitiveness; aggressive creativity; conformity; insecurity; large military spending; prejudice toward different racial and religious groups; unrealistic interpersonal (and international relations—policeman of the world).	Low emotionality; seeking group protection; not interested in competition; low in creativity.
Triandis (1990) (after Gould & Kolb, 1964)	Individual is an end in himself, and as such ought to realize his "self" and cultivate his own judgment, notwithstanding social pressures toward conformity.	Emphasis on (a) the views, needs, and goals of the (in)group; (b) social norms and duty defined by the group rather than pleasure seeking; (c) beliefs shared with the group rather than beliefs that separate self from group; and (d) readiness to cooperate with the group.
Ho & Chiu (1994)	Value of the individual; autonomy; individual responsibility (consequences of action affect the individual); individual achievement; self-reliance (individual interests; security in individual's strength).	Value of the group; conformity; collective responsibility (consequences of action affect the whole group); group achievement; interdependence (group interests; security in group solidarity).
Cha (1994)	—	Korean collectivism: dependence; hierarchy; courtesy; heartfulness/fraternity; family line; filial piety; and sacrifice of women.

TABLE 1–1 *(Continued)*

	Individualism	Collectivism
Bellah et al. (1985)	American individualism: self-reliance, independence and separation from family, religion, and community; hedonism, utilitarianism, and emphasis on exchange; competition; equity and fairness in the distribution of rewards; trust in others; emphasis on competence; involvement in community life (getting something in return); equality of people and the rejection of arbitrary authority; the self as the only source of reality.	—
Yamaguchi (1994)	—	Japanese collectivism: expectation of rewards and punishments from the ingroup lead to "collectivistic tendencies"; low need for uniqueness, high self-monitoring, and external locus of control.

Beginning in the 1970s, there have been many (somewhat moralistic) critiques of individualism in the United States. The self-indulgence of the "me-generation," in search of self-satisfaction and a lack of social commitment have been called "social ills" engendered by excessive individualism. This has been a double criticism, focusing on both the society and the social sciences, in particular psychology (Batson, 1990; Baumeister, 1991; Bellah et al., 1985; Capps & Fenn, 1992; Cushman, 1990; Donohue, 1990; Etzioni, 1993; Gergen, 1991; Hogan, 1975; Jansz, 1991; Lasch, 1978; Sampson, 1987, 1988, 1989; Schwartz, 1986; M. B. Smith, 1978, 1994; Spence, 1985; Taylor, 1989; Wallach & Wallach, 1983, 1990).

A viewpoint shared by most of the critics is that too much is expected of the individual self as a source of life purpose and goals, overburdening it to replace other (fading) moral social values. There is a questioning of the vulnerability of "lives organized around self-actualization and the pursuit of gratification" and a conviction that "human lives seem most meaningful and satisfying when they are devoted to projects and guided by values that transcend the self" (M. B. Smith, 1994, p. 407). There is a search for a merger of social commitment with individual autonomy—a bringing together of the benefits of individualism and collectivism, as, for example, proposed in "communitarianism" (Etzioni, 1993; Taylor, 1985) and in Kanfer's (1979) work, which deals with the balancing of individualistic and collectivistic tendencies, as desirable for good mental health. It is claimed that social science shares a responsibility in reinforcing and legitimizing excessive individualism in society. This is particularly notable in Wallach and Wallach's (1983, 1990) critique of psychology as sanctioning "selfishness," in Batson's questioning of the "assumed egoisms of humans" in psychology, and in B. Schwartz's (1986) argument that economics, evolutionary biology, and the behavioral sciences (behavior theory) are based on *cultural* individualistic assumptions which are presented as "human nature." Spence (1985) called upon psychology to be a part of the solution, *not* of the problem (of social ills in society).

Why Individualism/Collectivism?

Given this above background, it is obvious that Individualism/Collectivism has long been of significance in social thought about human nature and the relationships among human beings. The basic question confronted by social philosophers and social scientists, "How is social order possible?" has been answered by stressing either the individualistic or the collectivistic elements in the human–society interface.

The recent upsurge of interest in Individualism/Collectivism in cross-cultural psychology still needs explanation. It may be seen as an example of a general "trend toward universals" (Kagitçibasi & Berry, 1989). The promise of Individualism/Collectivism as "perhaps the most important dimension of cultural difference in social behavior across the diverse cultures of the world (Triandis, 1988, p. 60) renders it an attractive construct for explaining cross-cultural variation.

A related reason for the widespread interest in Individualism/Collectivism may have to do with its perceived potential to explain variations in economic development. In this respect, it resembles the once popular construct of achievement motivation that was seen as a key to understanding and even producing societal economic achievement (McClelland, 1961, 1969). Though "N Ach" did not fulfill its promise, some of the intriguing issues raised by the theory and research on achievement motivation continue to draw interest. Specifically, the relationship between the psychological characteristics of a people and their economic development, that is, the non-economic factors underlying economic development, is of great current interest.

Indeed, Hofstede (1980) showed a correlation of .82 between individualism (at the cultural level) and the level of national economic development. Even though such a correlation does not provide information about causation, the common tendency to see individualism as a cause of economic achievement is reinforced by it. This is in line with views about the "deficiency" or incompatibility of collectivistic orientations with economic development (as discussed by Marsella & Choi, 1994; and by Sinha, 1988). As such views are challenged today by the rapid economic growth of the collectivist countries in the Pacific Rim, new conceptualizations are called for. This challenge has triggered further interest in Individualism/ Collectivism.

There are doubtless other reasons for the research interest in Individualism/ Collectivism arising from within cross-cultural psychology, such as the seminal work of Hofstede (1980), followed by the research program of Triandis and his students. Nevertheless, academic reasons, by themselves, could probably not have triggered so much research without a favorable "zeitgeist." After all, Individualism/Collectivism constitutes only *one* of the four dimensions articulated by Hofstede, and even then it is not a new discovery. As shown above, it has been with us for a long time, and with quite some salience at least since Tönnies's (1887/ 1957) *Gesellschaft* and *Gemeinschaft*.

Another possible reason for the popularity of Individualism/Collectivism is its apparent simplicity as *one* dimension. The law of parsimony dictates that the more we can explain by assuming less (or using less explanatory factors), the better it is. There is an inherent attraction to single key explanations. Neverthless, single key explanations are highly problematic, particularly in the social sciences, as demonstrated historically. There is a danger that Individualism/Collectivism is too readily used as an explanation for every behavioral variation between the so-called individualistic and collectivistic cultures—an all-purpose construct. If Individualism/Collectivism is used to explain everything, it may explain nothing.

Recently the validity of Individualism/Collectivism as "a high level psychological concept" has been questioned (Fijneman, Willemsen, & Poortinga, 1995). In a comparative study involving students from five countries (Hong Kong, Greece, Turkey, Netherlands, and the United States), these researchers found very similar patterns in all the countries in the tendency to give, and the expectation to receive, resources from others of varying degrees of emotional closeness. They showed that there was not a greater readiness to give (and receive) resources among collectivists compared with individualists, the main explanatory factor being emotional closeness. Thus, "sharing resources," a presumed characteristic of collectivists (Hui & Triandis, 1986; J. B. P. Sinha & Verma, 1987), does not appear to be greater in collectivistic than in individualistic contexts.

Notwithstanding the challenge posited by Fijneman et al., there is accumulated evidence pointing to Individualism/Collectivism as a factor explaining several kinds of variance. First, there are systematic variations among societies on Individualism/Collectivism at the cultural level (e.g., Chinese Culture Connection, 1987; Hofstede, 1980; Schwartz, 1992a, 1994). Second, individuals from individualistic cultures tend to have individualistic values and manifest individualistic behaviors, and the reverse appears to be the case for those from collectivistic societies. Thus predictions can be made for a wide variety of behaviors (e.g., Triandis, 1989 , 1994a, 1995). Finally, in addition to cultural difference, Individualism/Collectivism also shows within-culture variability and can be used in explaining individual/group differences in a society (Triandis et al., 1985).

Nevertheless, it behooves the researchers to demonstrate whether the observed differences are actually due to variations in Individualism/Collectivism or to some other cultural/group characteristics that may overlap with it at least partially.

There is good reason for addressing Individualism/Collectivism in cross-cultural research. There is also a need to view it critically and to develop it further through more refined conceptualization and operationalization.

Models of Individualism/Collectivism: The Value Orientation

Some of the main conceptualizations and research programs in this field overlap in time and are interrelated; nevertheless, they will be reviewed here separately. Their interfaces will be examined also. Much of this research shares a focus on individualism and collectivism as values. This is in line with the ideological traditions apparent in the backgrounds of these concepts, described earlier, rendering them akin to world views. Individualism and collectivism are construed as broad tendencies or preferences spanning varied realms of human activity (see also Smith & Schwartz chapter, in this volume).

Hofstede

Hofstede's *Culture's Consequences* (1980) revived the concepts of individualism and collectivism. He administered questionnaires in 1968 and 1972 to 117,000 IBM employees. Answers to 14 work goal items were factor analyzed. The 40-country sample was subsequently expanded to a total of 50 national cultures and three regions (Hofstede, 1980, 1983). It is still the most comprehensive comparative study in terms of both the range of countries and the number of respondents involved.

Hofstede conceptualized culture in terms of meanings; he therefore studied it by assessing the values of people. Culture-level, rather than individual-level, factor analyses (using country mean scores) produced four factors; "individualism," "power distance," "masculinity," and "uncertainty avoidance." In subsequent research Individualism/Collectivism far exceeded the other factors in popularity. Because Power Distance and Individualism/Collectivism were differentiated from a single factor in an original 3-factor solution, they are highly correlated (.67) (Hofstede, 1980).

Hofstede notes (1991, p.160) that his definitions of individualism and collectivism, as well as of the other value dimensions, derive from his Western "mental programming." "Individualism stands for a society in which the ties between individuals are loose; everyone is expected to look after himself or herself and his or her immediate family only," and "collectivism stands for a society in which people from birth onwards are integrated into strong, cohesive ingroups, which throughout people's lifetime continue to protect them in exchange for unquestioning loyalty" (pp. 260–261). These characterizations involve both interpersonal and normative aspects (or dimensions) of individualism and collectivism. This is a conceptual issue which will be discussed later.

These general definitions appear to have little to do with their operationalization in Hoftede's research. The three work goal items associated with individualism stressed having a job that gives one sufficient time for personal or family life, having freedom to adapt one's own approach to the job, and having challenging work to do (providing a personal sense of accomplishment). Those associated with collectivism stressed having training opportunities, having good physical working conditions, and having the possibility of fully using skills and abilities on the job (Hofstede, 1991, pp. 51–52).

It is not clear how these six items, both in terms of number and in terms of content, assess individualism and collectivism as broadly defined. These items, particularly those measuring collectivism, do not appear to be conceptually similar to the definitions of these constructs, which exceed the items in scope. Hofstede (1991, p. 52) points to this problem also, and explains that these items make sense within an organizational context and represent issues in the IBM research. He nevertheless claims that the relative emphasis on individual freedom versus dependence on the organization provides some clues regarding Individualism/Collectivism.

It is also true that the IBM individualism country scores correlate with other measures in predictive ways, thus providing intriguing empirical comparison and convergent validity. We will next turn to these studies that have produced different measures and conceptualizations but use Hofstede's work as a point of reference (see also Smith & Schwartz chapter, this volume).

Bond and the Chinese Culture Connection

In 1982, a study of values was published (Ng et al., 1982), using a modified version of the Rokeach Value Survey (RVS) with university students in nine Asian and Pacific countries. Later Bond, from the research team, reanalyzed the data using Hofstede's approach. This reanalysis produced five factors, four of which corresponded to the four Hofstede dimensions across the six countries where both studies had been conducted (Hofstede & Bond, 1984).

The similarity of factors may be questioned. For example, Schwartz (1994, p. 119) notes that only two values ("exciting life" and "world of beauty") loaded on the factor considered to replicate Individualism/Collectivism. These values do not appear to reflect Individualism/Collectivism. Nevertheless, the researchers claim that given the different samples and instruments, any correspondences obtained may still be considered as "an example of synergy between two cross-cultural studies" (Hofstede & Bond, 1984, p. 432).

Both Hofstede and Ng et al. were using instruments developed in the West, which might have had something to do with some of the obtained correspondance. Bond proceeded to develop a non-Western instrument, a Chinese emic, to deal with this problem. Chinese social scientists from Hong Kong and Taiwan worked on basic Chinese values, and a resultant 40-item "Chinese Value Survey" (CVS) was constructed (Chinese Culture Connection, 1987).

The CVS was administered to university students in twenty-two countries. Following Hofstede's (1980) approach, an "ecological" factor analysis was conducted, using culture means. Again four factors were obtained, and country scores on these were correlated with those of Hofstede, obtained from the twenty countries common to the two studies. Three of the factors from the CVS correlated with three of Hofstede's: Social Integration corresponded positively with Individualism and negatively with Power Distance; Human-Heartedness corresponded with Masculinity (Femininity); and Moral Discipline corresponded with High Power Distance. The fourth CVS factor, Confucian Work Dynamism, and Hofstede's Uncertainty Avoidance did not relate to any of the others.

This work provided partial validation of some of the Hofstede dimensions, including Individualism/Collectivism. It also pointed to a new conceptual dimension, Confucian Work Dynamism, which was found to correlate highly (.70) with *economic growth*. Individualism, on the other hand, did not correlate with economic growth even though it was correlated with GNP.

Bond (1988) reanalyzed the CVS data at the individual level and contrasted Social Integration with Cultural Inwardness as a basic value dimension. Here values of openness, noncompetitiveness, and tolerance of others (subsumed under the former) are contrasted with values exhalting the ingroup, such as respect for tradition and a sense of cultural superiority. The parallels between Social Integration, Openness to Change (Schwartz, 1992a), and Individualism (Hofstede, 1980) are noted (see Gudykunst & Bond and Smith & Schwartz chapters in this volume). These studies of values contributed to conceptual development in the field, followed by further studies of values by Schwartz, to be examined later. In the meantime, a separate but related program of research and model building was being carried out by Triandis and his co-workers.

Triandis

Triandis has popularized Individualism/Collectivism in cross-cultural psychology with a research program that started in the early 1980s and currently continues. He first attempted to define the construct cross-culturally, based on a review of previous research (Triandis et al., 1984). Hui and Triandis (1986) conceptualized collectivism as "concern" (for others) and asked a total of 81 psychologists and anthropologists in many parts of the world to indicate how an individualist and a collectivist would respond to seven questions tapping aspects of this concern. The responses converged, showing some consensus in the construal of collectivism as subordination of individual goals to the goals of the collective, in line with the conceptualization of the authors (e.g., "Consider behaviors [e.g., fishing, singing] that the person enjoys doing very much. Would the person be likely to give up such activities to save time or money for the other, when the other has indicated that he or she needs such sacrifices?").

Triandis et al. (1986) replicated some of Hofstede's results with 15 samples from different parts of the world. They obtained four factors: Family Integrity (e.g., "Children should live with their parents until they get married."); Interdependence (e.g., "I like to live close to my good friends."), representing collectivism; Self-Reliance (e.g., "It is best to work alone than in a group."), and Separation from Ingroups (e.g., "If a family member is honored, this honor is not shared by other family members."), representing individualism. However, different results were obtained at cultural and individual levels of analyses. Family Integrity and Distance from Ingroups explained more of the variance across cultures, and Interdependence, Sociability, and Self-Reliance (with hedonism or with competition) at the individual level.

The terms "allocentrism" and "idiocentrism" were used to replace collectivism and individualism, respectively, at the individual level (Triandis et al., 1985). However, this distinction between levels of analysis, though important in methodological terms, is often not attended to, and commonly the terms individualism and collectivism are used at both levels. This usage is also open to a problem of "circularity" (Berry, 1992), that is, the lack of independent measurement at the two levels combined with the use of correlations between them.

A great deal of effort has been expended to devise methods for the measurement of individualism and collectivism and to conduct convergent and discriminant analyses (e.g., Hui, 1984, 1988; Hui & Yee, 1994; Triandis et al., 1985; Triandis, et al., 1986). Several factor analyses confirmed the cross-cultural versus the within culture (mainly U.S.) distinction. The Family Integrity factor discriminated the most among national samples and was the only one to correlate with Hofstede's collectivism (rho .73, p < .05). Triandis (1990, p.113) concludes from this research and others that the defining attributes of individualism are distance from ingroups, emotional detachment, and competition, while the defining attributes of collectivism are family integrity and solidarity.

However, there are many other characteristics that emerge from factor analyses used with different measures. For example, allocentric students in the United States are found to be low on anomie, alienation, and loneliness; they report that they receive greater social support of better quality, and value most cooperation, equality, and honesty. Idiocentric students show the opposite pattern and value a comfortable life, competition, pleasure, and social recognition (Triandis et al., 1985). A higher order factor analysis in another study (Triandis, et al. 1988) finds Subordination of Ingroup Goals to Personal Goals to be the most important aspect of U.S. individualism. It is also found that concepts such as self-reliance, achievement, and competition have different meanings in different societies, and that the type of in-group, context, and behavior determine responses to questions tapping individualism and collectivism.

Going beyond these, several other indicators (antecedents/correlates) of individualism and collectivism are proposed by Triandis (1988, 1990, 1994b, 1995; Triandis et al., 1988; Triandis, McCusker, & Hui, 1990). Among these are ecology (sedentary agriculturalists being more collectivistic than hunters/gatherers) and societal complexity (the higher the complexity, the higher the individualism, after the establishment of sedentary lifestyles). Both of these "indicators" have been challenged and will be taken up later in the Problems of Conceptualization section.

As correlates of collectivism, Triandis proposes societal tightness; sharp ingroup–outgroup distinctions; small number of ingroups; ingroups being ascribed rather than achieved; hierarchy; corrupt governments; ingroup harmony; low creativity; low stress and stress-related disease and mental illness rates; greater and better social support; low criminality and social pathology (suicide, divorce, child abuse); low economic development; and low modernity (traditionalism).

Some of these "correlates" are obtained on the basis of empirical evidence; others appear to be rather stereotypic attributions not implicated by Individualism/Collectivism in any logical sense, but based on personal observations (e.g., corrupt governments, low creativity, low economic development). Nevertheless, personal observations can provide hypotheses. For example, Triandis (personal communication) is currently testing the hypothesis that corruption that favors the ingroup is more likely in collectivistic cultures. Such studies are needed on many of the attributes of Individualism/Collectivism that have been proposed in the literature and as yet have received little empirical support. In different writings, different characterizations are proposed (Triandis et al., 1990).

Following Campbell (1986), multimethod approaches are recommended and pursued (Triandis, McCusker, & Hui, 1990). Thus, in addition to the more common attitudinal and value measures, self perceptions, judgments of the homogeneity of ingroups and outgroups, social perception (social distance judgments), naturalistic observations of the frequency of collective behaviors, and so forth, are used as indicators of Individualism/Collectivism (Triandis, 1990, 1995; Triandis, McCusker, & Hui, 1990).

There is an attempt at preliminary model building, based on extensive research (Hui & Triandis, 1986; Triandis, 1989, 1990; Triandis et al., 1985, 1986, 1988; Triandis, McCusker, & Hui, 1990). The model is given in Table 1–2. It contains a rather informal listing of attributes, together with antecedents and consequents of Individualism/Collectivism. The attributes are based on factor analyses of scores obtained with several measures. The antecedents derive from research and writings in cross-cultural psychology, anthropology, and other social sciences. In some cases they are "logically" rather than empirically derived and may be considered speculative. Some of the consequents have to do with research findings regarding behavioral concomitants of Individualism/Collectivism; others are again "logical" derivations.

What is presented in Table 1–2 is more a heuristic device than a theory, because it does not identify exclusively the conditions that lead to individualism and collectivism and in turn their exclusive consequents in terms of any "necessary" causal relations. It is also apparent that many of the characterizations mentioned previously are not given in this model. Nevertheless, there is an attempt to link background (ecological, social structural, economic) factors to individualism and collectivism, treated as mediating variables, which are in turn linked to behavioral outcomes. Some aspects of the model will be discussed later on. It is presented here to give a general portrait of the topics attended to by Triandis and his coworkers.

Schwartz

Schwartz initiated an extensive study of values, based on a theory being revised and elaborated through ongoing work by a team of researchers (Schwartz, 1990,

TABLE 1–2   Attributes defining Individualism and Collectivism and their antecedents and consequents

Antecedents	Attributes	Consequents
Individualism		
Affluence	Emotional detachment from	Socialization for self-reliance
Cultural complexity	ingroup	and independence
Hunting/food gathering	Personal goals have primacy	Good skills when entering new
	over ingroup goals	group
Upper social class	Behavior regulated by attitudes	Loneliness
Migration	and cost-benefit analyses	
Urbanism	Confrontation is okay	
Collectivism		
Unit of survival is food	Family integrity	Socialization for obedience and
Ingroup		duty
Agriculture	Self defined in ingroup terms	Sacrifice for ingroup
Large families	Behavior regulated by ingroup	Cognition: Focus on common
	norms	elements with ingroup
	Hierarchy and harmony within	members
	ingroup	
	Ingroup is seen as homogeneous	Behavior: intimate, saving face,
	Strong ingroup/outgroup	reflects hierarchy, social sup-
	distinctions	port, interdependence

Source: Triandis, McCusker, and Hui, 1990

1992a, b, 1994; Schwartz & Bilsky, 1987, 1990) (see Smith & Schwartz chapter, this volume). Ten types of values were derived theoretically, in terms of underlying motivations reflected in needs (organism), social motives (interaction), and social institutional demands: Universalism, Benevolence, Tradition, Conformity, Security, Power, Achievement, Hedonism, Stimulation, and Self-Direction. Many of the specific values within these were derived from the Rokeach Value Survey (1973); others were added. Numerous applications have been carried out with the number of values reaching 56, and the number of samples of students and teachers reaching 87 from 41 cultural groups in 38 nations (Schwartz, 1994). Ten individual-level and seven culture level value types have been established through applications and revisions of the model (see also P. B. Smith & Schwartz chapter, this volume).

Individualism/Collectivism figured importantly in this endeavor from the start. Collectivism and individualism (affective and intellectual) were differentiated by "smallest space analysis" at the culture level (Schwartz, 1992b). Hedonism, Achievement, Self-Direction, Social Power, and Stimulation were considered to be individualistic types of values, while Pro-Social, Restrictive Conformity, Security, and Tradition were collectivistic types of values (Schwartz, 1990).

Nevertheless, in reformulating his theory, Schwartz has replaced Individualism/Collectivism with two higher order dimensions at the individual level. One of these is Openness to Change (Self Direction and Stimulation) vs. Conservation (Conformity, Tradition and Security) at the individual level; their counterparts at the culture level being Autonomy versus Conservation (Schwartz, 1994). Openness to Change versus Conservation dimension is similar to Bond's Social Integration versus Cultural Inwardness and Hofstede's Individualism versus Collectivism. They all refer to the normative (value) aspects of Individualism/Collectivism where collectivism implies a traditional, conservative worldview.

The other dimension is Self-Transcendence (Universalism and Benevolence) versus Self-Enhancement (Achievement and Power) at the individual level; culture level counterparts being Hierarchy and Mastery (Schwartz, 1994). In terms of individual–group relations, Self-Transcendence would appear to be akin to Collectivism, and Self-Enhancement to individualism.

These terms better reflect the specific values involved and do not carry the additional meanings that Individualism/Collectivism connote. Indeed, the component values Conformity, Tradition, and Security connote conservatism more than collectivism; and Self-Direction and Stimulation imply openness to change, more than individualism, as previously suggested by the present author (Kagitçibasi, 1992).

Schwartz (1994) notes that Self-Transcendence versus Self-Enhancement parallels a common characterization of Individualism/Collectivism with regard to the priority of group versus individual interests (respectively). His Openness to Change versus Conservation dimension parallels the other characterization of Individualism/Collectivism in terms of autonomy–embeddedness (respectively). He considers the latter to be the more fundamental theme because if persons are truly embedded in their groups, conflict of interests do not arise with regard to the priority of the individual or the group.

It is not clear why conservation implies embeddedness; it is also not clear exactly what kind of a conceptual contrast inheres in the Autonomy–Conservation dimension at the culture level. The two terms do not connote opposing tendencies/values. Autonomy sounds more like an individual characteristic, which indeed Schwartz also contrasts with embeddedness. The latter dimension (autonomy–embeddedness) makes more heuristic sense with regard to interpersonal relations at the individual level. Similarly, while self-enhancement versus self-transcendence make sense at the individual level, their cultural counterparts, mastery versus hierarchy, hardly convey the same meaning. As is also true with other value orientations, mentioned before, the discrepancies between culture level and individual level constructs do not make immediate psychological sense and are confusing.

Finally, Schwartz (1990, 1994) points out that the Individualism/Collectivism dichotomy is insufficient because it leaves out some universal goals and values tapped by his model that do not serve the ingroup, such as equality for all, social justice, a world at peace, and preserving the natural environment. Similarly, some values, such as maturity, may serve both individual and group goals.

Further Studies on Values and Individualism/Collectivism

Triandis (1994a) has differentiated between horizontal and vertical Individualism/Collectivism. The distinction refers mainly to equalitarian versus hierarchical interpersonal relations, respectively, and is akin to Hofstede's power distance dimension. This conceptualization is in line with Fiske's (1990, 1992) "Four elementary forms of sociality," involving Communal Sharing (where group resources are shared according to need), Authority Ranking (resources are shared according to rank), Equality Matching (equal sharing), and Market Pricing (equity in resource sharing, based on merit). The framework regarding horizontal–vertical individualism and collectivism promises to contribute to theoretical advancement in the field, particularly in dismantling the broad construct of Individualism/Collectivism.

There is a recognition here of the independence of hierarchy–equality dimension from a merging–separation dimension. There can be separated or connected self–other relations in both hierarchical and equalitarian value contexts. Separating the normative (value) and the interpersonal (relational) dimensions will be discussed further later in the chapter.

Further links are proposed between these categorizations and Rokeach values regarding equality and freedom and political systems (Singelis et al., 1995), as shown in Table 1–3. This is an attempt to form a more encompassing conceptual pattern. Similarities between Fiske's categories, Hofstede's (1980) concepts and Schwartz's values have also been recognized (P. B. Smith & Bond, 1993), as presented in Table 1–4. Tables 1–3 and 1–4 show how Individualism/Collectivism is thought to relate to other value orientations within overall value structures.

It is to be noted that while both Singelis et al. (1995) and P. B. Smith and Bond (1993) relate communal sharing to collectivism, the latter see authority ranking (verticality) as similar to power distance and hierarchy, and equality matching (horizontality) as akin to femininity and harmony; market pricing is associated with masculinity and mastery, rather than with individualism. Thus there is not a one-to-one correspondence among the different patterns of categories used by the different scholars. Some varying conceptualizations are seen with different value structures, and interrelations are proposed. If these conceptual categories are carefully examined, they may be found to be more appropriate than Individualism/Collectivism to explain certain behaviors; this would help provide fine-tuning and prevent the overuse of the latter constructs.

An example is the recent work of P. B. Smith, Dugan, and Trompenaars (1995) in analyzing the values of 8,841 managers and organization employees from 43 countries (see Smith & Schwartz chapter in this volume). The countries covered in the survey parallelled those studied by Hofstede (1980), but also included many East European ones. Measures based on "pattern variables" (Parsons, 1951) of Universalism–Particularism, Achievement–Ascription and Individualism–Collectivism were used. Out of the three dimensions obtained, the two main ones represent Conservatism versus Egalitarian Commitment (terms taken from Schwartz, 1994), reflecting value orientations toward the obligations of social relationship, and Utilitarian Involvement versus Loyal Involvement, reflecting value orienta-

TABLE 1–3   Characteristics of vertical and horizontal individualism and collectivism

	Vertical		Horizontal	
	Collectivism	Individualism	Collectivism	Individualism
	Interdependent Different from others	Independent Different from others	Interdependent Same as others	Independent-self Same as others
Fiske	Communal sharing	Market pricing	Communal sharing	Market pricing
Orientation	Authority ranking	Authority ranking	Equality matching	Equality matching
Values	Low freedom	High freedom	Low freedom	High freedom
Political	Communalism	Market democracy	Communal living	Democratic Socialism
System	(e.g., rural village in India)	(e.g., U.S.A., France)	(e.g., Israeli Kibbutz)	(e.g., Sweden, British Labour Party)

Source: Singelis, Triandis, Bhawuk, and Gelfand, 1995.

TABLE 1–4   Possible relations between the concepts of Hofstede, Fiske, and Schwartz

Hofstede	Fiske	Schwartz
Individualism	Low communal sharing	Affective individualism
Collectivism	High communal sharing	Collectivism
High power distance	High authority ranking	Hierarchy
Low power distance	Low authority ranking	Social concern
Low uncertainty avoidance	—	Intellectual individualism
Masculinity	Market pricing	Mastery
Femininity	Equality matching	Harmony

Source: Smith and Bond, 1993.

Note: The Schwartz concepts in this table are those derived from his country-level analyses.

tions toward continuity of group membership. These are found to define better Hofstede's Individualism/Collectivism and Power Distance dimensions.

P. B. Smith et al. (1995) claim, similar to Schwartz (1994), that Egalitarian Commitment and its polar opposite, Conservatism, are not the same as Individualism/Collectivism, but the countries located at the positive pole of this dimension are found to be those labeled as individualistic by Hofstede (1980). Nevertheless,

Hofstede's ordering of nations in terms of Individualism/Collectivism is found to follow *both* dimensions here (r = .70 with Conservatism versus Egalitarian Commitment, and −.74 with Utilitarian Involvement versus Loyal Involvement), pointing to the confounding of these two different constructs within Individualism/ Collectivism, as it has often been used.

The advantage of distinguishing these two dimensions is apparent also in their similarity to "vertical" and "horizontal" Individualism/Collectivism (Triandis, 1995) mentioned previously. P. B. Smith et al. (1995) provide some evidence of the utility of these concepts at the cultural level, and Singelis et al. (1995) present evidence of their validity at the individual level.

In a recent book, Triandis (1995) uses a "polythetic" definition of Individualism/Collectivism in terms of four attributes and 60 others to define its many kinds. The four defining attributes relate to others' work; they are: (a) the self is interdependent with one or more ingroups or independent of ingroups (Markus & Kitayama, 1991), (b) personal goals have lower priority or are often given more priority than ingroup goals (Yamaguchi, 1994), (c) norms are more important than attitudes or vice versa (Bontempo & Rivero, 1992), (d) social behavior is communal (based on the needs of the other) more often than it is based on social exchanges or vice versa (Mills & Clark, 1982). Among the attributes that define different kinds of individualism and collectivism are the vertical and the horizontal dimensions and others such as the importance of ingroup harmony. Triandis stresses the situational factors that "pull" individualistic or collectivistic tendencies; situations, in turn, are affected by ecological and social factors. Both intra- and intercultural variance in individualism and collectivism are noted and their advantages and disadvantages are evaluated.

The Self Orientation

In the last two decades, there has been a renewed interest in the "self" in social psychology and in cultural and cross-cultural psychology. A number of volumes published in the 1980s included this basic theme, from mainly an anthropological "culture and self" perspective (e.g., Heelas & Locke, 1981; Marsella, DeVos, & Hsu, 1985; Marsella & White, 1984; Roland, 1988; Shweder & LeVine, 1984; White & Kirkpatrick, 1985). The basic distinction drawn is that between a self-contained, individuated, separated, independent self defined by clear boundaries from others, and a relational, interdependent self with fluid boundaries. Obviously, this is more a variability than a duality; nevertheless sharp contrasts are commonly made to stress the point.

In American scholarship on the self, especially among psychologists who are critical of the continuing mainstream conventions, cross-cultural and contextual evidence is used, pointing to the above diversity in self construals (e.g., Pepitone, 1987; Sampson, 1988, 1989; M. B. Smith, 1994). Historical evidence is also searched (e.g., Cushman, 1990; Gergen, 1991; Sampson, 1987, 1989; Taylor, 1989). Feminist theory, too, stresses the "relational–separated" self distinction in the study of gender (Chodorow, 1989; Gilligan, 1982; Lykes, 1985). Cross-cultural comparisons of person perception (Shweder & Bourne, 1984), self-perception (Bond & Cheung, 1983; Cousins, 1989), and attribution (Miller, 1984) provide further evidence for variability in self construals; and reviews of cross-cultural research (Markus & Kitayama, 1991; Triandis, 1989) attempt systematic analysis.

The relevance of self theory to Individualism/Collectivism is that the former provides a micro (individual–interpersonal) level framework for the latter. The independent, separated self with clearly defined boundaries reflects individualism, and the interdependent, embedded self reflects collectivism at the psychological (individual) level.

In a functional–contextual model of self development and family change, Kagitçibasi (1990, 1996) studied the antecedents of self development in different cultural and socioeconomic contexts, mediated by the family. She differentiated between the Relational and the Separated Self. The Relational Self develops especially in "the family model of total (emotional and material) interdependence," typical in subsistence economies and agrarian lifestyles, with collectivistic cultures, requiring intergenerational interdependence for family livelihood. This is often reflected in the "economic and old-age security value of children" for parents (Kagitçibasi, 1982, 1990). The Separated Self typically develops in "the family model of independence," seen in the western urban contexts, with individualistic cultures, where inter-generational interdependence is not required for family livelihood.

Kagitçibasi proposed a third category of self that combines a relational orientation with autonomy, in a dialectical synthesis of the above two types of self. It develops in "the family model of emotional interdependence," seen particularly in the developed urban areas of societies with collectivistic cultures, where material intergenerational interdependencies weaken but emotional interdependencies continue. This allows for the introduction of an autonomy orientation in childrearing, as complete intergenerational interdependence is no longer required, rendering dysfunctional total obedience and dependence of the growing child. With continuing emotional interdependencies, however, a related self is still the outcome (Kagitçibasi, 1990, 1996). The "autonomous-related self" emerging in the family model of emotional interdependence combines within itself both collectivistic (relational) and individualistic (autonomous) elements, at the individual level. It is a dialectical or coexistence (D. Sinha & Tripathi, 1994) model, which is also recognized in other self theories, to be discussed.

Thus, whether an individualistic (separated) or collectivistic (relational) self development or a third category (autonomous-related) self is seen depends on the environmental requirements rendering one of these more functional than the others. With socioeconomic change, therefore, changes in family patterns and self configurations can be expected. Kagitçibasi (1990, 1996) proposes the main shift in the world to be toward the combined (coexistence) model, as this model better satisfies the two basic human needs for agency (autonomy) and relatedness.

Markus and Kitayama (1991) proposed a very similar distinction between the "independent" and the "interdependent" construal of the self. This is in line with the diverse literature on the topic, referred to previously. While Kagitçibasi exam-

ined the antecedents of the self, Markus and Kitayama elaborated upon its consequents, particularly its implications for cognition, emotion, and motivation. They
presented the independent versus the interdependent construal of the self as a
key psychological phenomenon in understanding psychological processes that
show variations across cultures. Reviewing a great deal of relevant research, they
pointed to the key differences between the two conceptual representations of the
self.

They differentiated between "ego-focused" emotions, which foster independence, and "other focused" emotions, which foster and create interdependence.
Similar distinctions in cognitive and motivational processes were proposed, based
on whether the self or the other is more focal. A great deal of research evidence is
provided to support these distinctions in self construals (Markus & Kitayama, 1991).
This research will be presented later in the section on Behavioral Differences Across
Societies.

The connections with Individualism/Collectivism are clear. The interdependent self reflects collectivistic self–other relational patterns, and the independent
self reflects individualistic patterns. However, in this approach analysis remains
at the individual level, and normative or ideological aspects are not dealt with.

Further attempts at studying the self from a perspective of Individualism/
Collectivism have been made by Triandis and Singelis (Singelis, 1994; Singelis &
Brown, 1995; Singelis et al., 1995; Triandis, 1989, 1995). They build upon Markus
and Kitayama conceptualization of independent and interdependent selves, as
appropriate intermediate level constructs between culture level Individualism/
Collectivism and the specific behavioral outcomes such as Self-Reliance with
Competition.

Triandis (1989, 1995) has elaborated upon his theoretical conceptualizations to
include "the self." Three aspects of the self (private, public, and the collective) are
linked to Individualism/Collectivism, societal tightness/looseness, and cultural
complexity. Different conceptualizations of self also figure in horizontally and vertically arranged human relations, following Fiske (1990). As discussed before, vertical collectivism involves the self merged with a hierarchical ingroup; horizontal
collectivism implies the same interdependent self as a member of an equalitarian
ingroup. Vertical individualism refers to an autonomous self in a group of unequal individuals, whereas horizontal individualism involves the independent self
in an equalitarian ingroup.

Independent and interdependent self construals have also been integrated with
communication styles (Singelis, 1994; Singelis & Brown, 1995; Singelis et al., 1995).
Within a social cognitive perspective, incorporating Hall's (1976) "high and low
context communication" framework, culture is linked to individual behavior
through self and communication.

Finally, Kim (1994) has proposed two sets of contrasting facets of Individual-
ism/Collectivism. The three different facets of individualism are called the aggregate, distributive, and static modes. The three different facets of collectivism are
labeled the undifferentiated, relational, and coexistence modes. Empirical evidence
is provided from the literature in support of these modes, which are based on the
individual–group level distinctions regarding firm or fluid self boundaries (after

Markus & Kitayama, 1991), characteristics of interrelationships among individuals and internal structures, and characteristics of groups. Kim (1994) also relates the contrasting facets of Individualism/Collectivism to similar conceptualizations proposed by other researchers, providing some conceptual convergence.

The numerous conceptualizations of Individualism/Collectivism presented in this section point to the diversity of meaning in the connotations of Individualism/Collectivism. Further increasing the complexity are the additional behavioral, cognitive, emotional, and motivational correlates of Individualism/Collectivism.

Behavioral Differences Across Societies Considered Individualistic or Collectivistic

The research on Individualism/Collectivism is extensive, spanning the full spectrum of behavioral, cognitive, emotional, and motivational domains. Some relevant research has already been mentioned regarding conceptualizations; here the emphasis will shift to more specific empirical evidence. A selective and brief review will be presented, to give an idea of how far Individualism/Collectivism is claimed to explain variations in human behavior. Other reviews are available (Kim et al., 1994; Markus & Kitayama, 1991; Triandis, 1990, 1995). In most cases, the levels of individualism or collectivism of the subjects are not directly measured but are assumed on the basis of their national/ethnic status. This is a general weakness pervading research in this area that should be kept in mind in considering the following studies. Given this caveat, we will take the researchers' grouping of the subjects at face value, for the sake of simplicity.

Social Perception and Cognition

Bond and Forgas (1984; Forgas & Bond, 1985) showed variations in social perception between Chinese and Australian subjects. The Chinese attended to certain "prosocial" personality traits such as agreeableness and perceived social episodes as reflecting more social solidarity and acceptance of authority, while the Australians emphasized individual competitiveness, self confidence and freedom. Several other studies looking into social perception from a social–cognition and attribution framework have come up with significant cross-cultural differences paralleling Individualism/Collectivism (see also Semin & Zwier chapter in this volume).

In a much quoted study, Shweder and Bourne (1984) found person perception among adults in India to be more concrete and "relational" than in the United States. While American subjects used more individual, "egocentric" constructs (46% of Americans' descriptions were of this type, compared with only 20% of the Indians'), Indians used more contextual, "sociocentric" ones (p. 110) in describing persons they know. Thus, while Americans tended to use more trait descriptions ("she is friendly"), Indians contextualized ("she brings cakes to my family on festive occasions"). This distinction seems to reflect a more "independent" view of the self as comprising traits that have generality over time and situations, as opposed to a more situational understanding of the self. The American subjects had middle-class standing and were college educated. The Indian sample showed a greater range in social class (as well as caste) and education; nevertheless, the differences obtained were stable across the entire sample (p. 112).

Similar results are also found for self-perception. Cousins (1989) used the Twenty Statements Test (TST) (Kuhn & McPartland, 1954), which repeatedly asks "Who am I?," with American and Japanese students. The Americans used more trait or attribute descriptions of themselves, whereas the Japanese were more situational and role specific. The reverse result was obtained, however, when a modified version of the test was used, specifying situations (in relation to others). Because this was more "natural" for the Japanese, they could give enduring trait descriptions, whereas the Americans tended to qualify their self-descriptions to make sure that their self-images could be independent of the situational constraints. Other work using the TST also found Americans to use more trait descriptions in self-perception than subjects from more collectivistic cultures, such as the Japanese and the Chinese (Bond & Cheung, 1983; Triandis et al., 1990).

Self–other similarity perceptions also show variations. Kitayama et al. (1991) found students from Eastern cultural backgrounds to perceive greater self-to-other similarity than other-to-self similarity. The reverse finding was obtained for American students, in line with earlier studies (Srull & Gaelick, 1983). Their preferred explanation for this finding was that in the individualistic context, there is a more elaborated representation of the self than of the other, which is reversed in the collectivistic context.

Emotions

Emotions are found by Markus and Kitayama (1991) to vary in individualistic and collectivistic contexts. "Ego focused" emotions (such as anger, frustration, and pride) with the individual's internal attributes as the primary referent are found to be more marked among independent selves (individualists). "Other focused" emotions (such as sympathy, shame, and feelings of interpersonal communion) that have the other person as the primary referent, are more marked among interdependent selves (collectivists). Markus and Kitayama (1991) point to other research evidence also substantiating this differentiation in emotions. For example, Matsumoto (1989) studied emotions in 15 countries and found them to be more subdued in hierarchical societies. However, this appears to relate more to power distance (Hofstede), hierarchy (Schwartz), or vertical collectivism (Triandis, Singelis) rather than to interdependent–independent self construals or horizontal (relational) individualism–collectivism. More extensive coverage is provided in Markus and Kitayama (1994).

Attribution and Moral Reasoning

In studying attributions for others' deviant and prosocial behaviors, Miller (1984) found a preponderance of dispositional (person) attributions among Americans, in line with the so-called Fundamental Attribution Error (Ross, 1977). Among the

Indians, however, situational attributions were more marked (36% of the Americans made dispositional and 17% situational attributions; the corresponding figures were 15% and 32% for the Indians). This finding questions the universality of the "fundamental attribution error" and points to more contextual–relational thinking among the Indians where the person is situated in the interpersonal context and is seen to be affected by it.

Such thinking also has implications for moral reasoning. Miller, Bersoff, and Harwood (1990) found that Indians consider social responsibilities as moral issues while Americans do not; the latter consider them to be matters of personal decision. While beneficience is for Indians a key concept in morality, it is not so for Americans; in fact, it may be seen as an imposition conflicting with individual freedom of choice. There are implications of this finding for the issue of egoism–altruism, salient in the criticism of American psychology, mentioned earlier.

Social Interaction

A strong "social orientation" is reflected in social interaction in collectivistic contexts. Comparing Hong Kong Chinese and American students Wheeler, Reis, and Bond (1989) found Hong Kong students to have longer but fewer interactions, a higher percentage of group and task interactions, and greater self-and-other disclosure. The habit of hard work among the more select Hong Kong students may explain their lower level of socializing, compared with the American students. However, Chinese students' longer interactions, more group interactions, and greater self disclosure reflect their "social orientation" as different from the stronger "individual orientation" of the American students.

Self-Serving Bias and Self-Focusing

Self-serving bias is found to be more common among Americans than among the Japanese (Chandler et al., 1981; Kashima & Triandis, 1986; Shikanai, 1978, cited by Markus & Kitayama, 1991). The high value put on modesty in "Eastern" societies may be a factor here. Thus, Bond, Leung, and Wan (1982) found Chinese students to give humble or self-effacing attributions for their success, and those students who were humble were better liked by their peers. A developmental study by Yoshido et al. (cited in Markus & Kitayama, 1991) with second, third, and fifth grade students showed that self promotion is also perceived negatively in Japan, even among children. A self-enhancing hypothetical peer was perceived negatively and was also evaluated as less competent than a modest peer. Research conducted with Americans, on the other hand, finds self enhancement to be a common tendency, also expressed in "false uniqueness" (seeing oneself better than the average), as reviewed by Markus and Kitayama (1991).

Another factor accounting for little self-serving bias may be a low degree of "self focusing," which the self-serving bias reflects (Ross & Fletcher, 1985). Stipek,

Weiner, and Li (1989) found that when asked to recall situations that made them angry, American subjects remembered events that had happened to them personally, whereas Chinese subjects remembered more events that had happened to other people. The Chinese subjects were also less likely to express pride in success. In a different cultural context, Boski (1983) studied two groups in Nigeria and found that the more traditional Hausa, compared with the Igbos, attributed their successes more to contextual factors. Similarly, comparing Canadian and Asian Indian Canadian children, Fry and Ghosh (1980) found the self-serving attributional pattern among the former but not among the latter. Such findings have implications for self-esteem, also. The so-called collective self (Triandis, 1989) or the interdependent self (Markus & Kitayama, 1991) might have a "collective self-esteem" rather than an individual self-esteem (Crocker & Luhtanen, 1990).

This may be the reason for the typically lower scores obtained, by the Japanese for example, on self esteem scales. Those scales, devised by Western researchers, focus on individual self esteem. Some of the above findings regarding modesty may be related to this less self-focused orientation, as well. This would also implicate an ingroup enhancing bias rather than an (individual) self-serving bias, as substantiated in research by Crocker and Luhtanen (1990).

Achievement Motivation

Achievement, too, may expand beyond the individual self, as a "socially-oriented achievement motivation," proposed to be prevalent in collectivistic contexts (Agarwal & Misra, 1986; DeVos, 1968; Ho & Chiu, 1994; Phalet & Claeys, 1993; Yang, 1988; Yu, 1995; Yu & Yang, 1994). Similar to self-esteem, when assessed with traditional achievement motivation measures, with an individualistic construal of achievement, people in collectivistic societies typically emerge as low in achievement motivation (Bradburn, 1963; Rosen, 1962). Yet, some of the greatest feats of economic achievement at societal levels are seen in the collectivistic societies of the Pacific rim, and Japanese and Chinese students excel in academic achievement, as demonstrated in international competitive tests of science and mathematics, for example .

A socially-oriented achievement motivation would exalt both the self and a collectivity (usually the family) encompassing the self. It is not, as often assumed, debasing the self or sacrificing self-interest for the group, but rather merging the self with the group (related self), so that achievement elevates *both*. For example, Phalet and Claeys (1993) found *combined* preferences among Turkish youth for both "loyalty" to the family and society and "self-realization," contrasted with "self-realization," alone, among Belgian youth. J. B. P. Sinha (1993) also states that the need for achievement in India is often combined with the need for extension, the latter reflecting care and concern for others (see also Hui & Luk chapter in this volume). Finally, Nevis (1983) proposed the concept of "collectivist self-actualization" in China, which is embodied in serving one's community and nation.

Distributive Justice

In the realm of interpersonal and group behavior, ingroup values in collectivistic societies favor an equality orientation rather than an equity orientation in distributive justice (Bond, Leung, & Wan, 1982; Hui, Triandis, & Yee, 1991; Leung & Bond, 1982). This is particularly the case where the goal is group harmony; when productivity is the goal, equity orientation is adopted by collectivists, also. Thus, goals affect preferences regarding distributive justice (Leung & Park, 1986). When the goal is not spelled out, collectivistic groups tend to use an equality orientation because of the greater salience of group harmony.

Equality orientation, conflict avoidance, and nonadversarial conflict resolution, which is believed to be most likely to reduce animosity, all point to group orientedness in collectivistic cultures (Leung, 1987). Triandis et al. (1985) found the same difference in reward allocation between allocentrics and idiocentrics in the United States, and Mann and others obtained parallel findings with Australian and Japanese children (Mann, 1986).

Need norm in distributive justice is also found to be more common in collectivistic contexts than in individualistic contexts. Studies comparing Indian and American subjects found the former to allocate resources more in line with the needs of the individuals concerned (Berman, Murphy-Berman, & Singh, 1985). Whether this is due to collectivism of the Indian subjects or some other characteristic will be taken up later.

Cooperation–Competition

There is long-standing evidence for competition to be more prevalent in individualistic than in collectivistic societies and in middle-class groups than in lower SES or rural groups within the same country (Domino, 1992; Eliram & Schwarzwald, 1987; Ho & Chiu, 1994; Madsen, 1971). For example, Domino (1992), in a game-like choice task with Chinese and American children found the former to give equality responses most often, followed by group enhancement responses, whereas the latter gave individualistic and competitive responses more frequently. From a different perspective, Ho & Chiu (1994) found in a content analysis of Chinese popular sayings that achievement through cooperative group effort is affirmed, but achievement through individual effort is negated (p. 152), in line with a socially oriented achievement orientation, discussed previously. Self interest is rejected while a self-reliant but cooperative orientation is valued. The latter pattern is of interest as an "exemplary synthesis of individualistic and collectivist values" (p. 154); it will be discussed again later. Social loafing is found less in collectivistic societies (Gabrenya, Wang, & Lataner, 1985) owing to "group orientedness" and cooperative tendencies, as would be expected from the above. The tendency to perceive consensus in group ("false consensus effect"; Ross et al., 1977) is also found to relate to collectivism (Yamaguchi, 1994).

Communication

As mentioned before, research on communication finds distinctive communication styles and communication-linked phenomena in collectivist and individualist contexts (Gudykunst, Ting-Toomey & Chua, 1988; Singelis, 1994; Singelis & Brown, 1995) (see chapter by Gudykunst and Bond in this volume). Building on Markus and Kitayama's (1991) independent–interdependent self construal on the one hand and on Hall's (1976) "high context-low context" communication on the other, this research shows that it is the interdependent nature of the self that orients the person toward greater sensitivity to context and more meaning to be drawn from context. This results in high-context communication and contextual attributions, and leads to emotional contagion. Cultural collectivism is proposed to be linked to high-context communication and resultant cognitive and emotional states through the mediation of the interdependent self (see also Gudykunst & Bond chapter in this volume).

Problems of Conceptualization

Some of the conceptualizations of Individualism/Collectivism reviewed in this chapter reflect rather impressionistic, stereotypic and global (general) characterizations of what individualists and collectivists are like. Studies too often merely compare national groups assumed to be high or low on these attributes, but do not measure Individualism/Collectivism.

When measurement is attempted, factor analyses conducted on scales formed by stereotypic characterizations are often limited by the items making up these scales. They show what goes with what, but they cannot guarantee construct validity. Obviously, this is a general issue, not confined only to Individualism/Collectivism. Nevertheless, it would appear to be especially serious here, given that these terms have a long ideological history and have been used in different disciplines with somewhat different connotations.

A basic question can be asked regarding these conceptualizations or characterizations of Individualism/Collectivism: Are they the features/correlates of Individualism/Collectivism, as such, or could they be caused by or associated with other (background) factors?

Have the Individualism/Collectivism Proponents Overreached?

Individualism and collectivism tend to get associated with a great number of societal, group, and individual characteristics. For example, individualism is associated with such diverse characteristics as cultural complexity, economic development, modernity, crime and social pathology, stress and stress related illness, (capacity for) social organization, mobility, low primary group orientation, small family size, using universalistic rather than particularistic exchanges in ingroups, equity orientation, having many ingroups, creativity, and cognitive complexity (e.g., Hofstede, 1980; Triandis, 1987, 1988; Triandis et al., 1988). Collectivism is associated with their opposites, together with corrupt governments and such traditional values/customs as filial piety (and ancestor worship), subordination of women, obedience to authority, and deference to parents (Cha, 1994; Triandis, 1987, 1988; Triandis et al., 1988).

Such overextension is highly problematic, because some of it is not based on empirical evidence. Even when there is empirical evidence of relationships, it is not clear if Individualism/Collectivism is causally associated (either as cause or effect) or whether some other factor might be involved. Research designs are needed that control for the effects of confounding variables.

Much research is needed to determine the limits of the constructs of individualism and collectivism. For example, multi-method measurements of each of these need to be interrelated to determine if they converge. Thus far the alphas of scales that measure the constructs have been no greater than .7 and often as low as .5. Convergence findings have been in the .2 to .5 range, which is expected when low reliabilities are present. Some current studies explore the issue of how narrow or broad the constructs of Individualism/Collectivism should be, and whether they should be measured with many narrow constructs with high reliabilities or few broad ones of low reliability (Triandis et al., 1995).

There is a need, also, for studies that will link the measures of Individualism/Collectivism with outside variables. Background factors such as socioeconomic development, in particular education, income, urban–rural standing, type of employment, all defining conditions under which people live, can account for some of the characteristics assumed to be correlates of Individualism/ Collectivism. For example, the use of an equality orientation or need norm in the allocation of rewards by Indian subjects, compared with American subjects (Berman, Murphy-Berman, & Singh, 1985) may reflect the greater sensitivity of Indians to poverty and scarce resources (Leung, 1988; Greenberg, 1981), rather than to their greater collectivism.

Indeed, Hui, Triandis, and Yee (1991) have shown that scarcity of resources has a different impact on Chinese and American subjects. It tends to intensify the generosity motive (using an allocation rule that is to the partner's advantage) of the Chinese but not the Americans. Furthermore, generosity cannot be accounted for by collectivism, because when measured collectivism was statistically controlled, Chinese subjects' tendency toward generosity was not affected but their tendency toward equality was reduced. Thus collectivism appears to account for equality in resource allocation but not for generosity. Whether the need norm is related more to generosity or to collectivism needs to be examined. Such unraveling of causal variables is required for sound analysis and theory construction. Collectivism may indeed play a role, but this needs to be demonstrated rather than assumed.

Similarly, (capacity for) social organization and public interest may be prevented more by poverty and lack of education than by collectivism, because it takes affluence to be altruistic and education to develop public awareness. Corrupt governments may be associated more with power orientation, power distance, greed, individual interests of rulers, and international political and financial interests (e.g., war industry) together with low levels of education and suppression and poverty in society, which prevent public action. These factors appear as more likely causes than the collectivism of people in general.

There is an assumption that loyalty to the family or ingroup (a facet of collectivism) is a source of corruption, because it interferes with more extensive concerns and therefore public good. However, both early research (Gillespie & Allport, 1955; Kagitçibasi, 1970, 1973) and more recent work (Nevis, 1983; Phalet & Claeys, 1993) have shown that loyalties in collectivist societies often extend far beyond the family and other kin all the way to national loyalties. In contrast, in the individualist society personal interests are most important, which can threaten social harmony and public good (e.g., Sampson, 1987, 1989; M. B. Smith, 1994).

Nevertheless, universalistic values (world at peace, protecting the environment, social justice, equality, etc., at the individual level) of Schwartz (1992a, b, 1994) were found to be stressed more in the so-called individualistic societies. Again whether it is individualism *per se* that is the key here or some other characteristics of these societies is an open question. The latter may include higher levels of education and secularism (Schwartz, 1990, 1992; Triandis, 1990). Some additional determining factors may be greater access to mass media, more global involvement (domination) and integration, and therefore a more globally informed public opinion.

These are important considerations in the sense that an attributional error may be involved in our thinking with regard to Individualism/Collectivism. Some of its alleged effects (observed behaviors) may be determined, rather, by other (societal) antecedent conditions. These antecedent conditions may be also causing Individualism/Collectivism, while the latter may not have a causal relationship with the observed behaviors in question. Thus, codetermination by a third factor may be overlooked when assuming causation between two correlated outcomes.

One reason for this attributional error is the tendency of psychologists toward psychological reductionism. They look for psychological explanations for behavioral regularities that may in fact have socioeconomic bases. Given the self-contained nature of psychology, much sociological evidence is simply overlooked.

The Social Evolutionary Stance

A specific instance of ignoring current sociological thinking may be seen in the social evolutionistic approach to Individualism/Collectivism, which treats individualism as modernity (see also Kagitçibasi, 1994). Given the assumption that individualism is more compatible with economic development, social organization, and social–cultural complexity (Hofstede, 1980; Triandis, 1984, 1988), it is expected to predominate with societal development and modernization, through some kind of social evolutionary progression. As Hofstede claims, "Modernization corresponds to individualization" (1991, p. 74).

Indeed, an examination of the "individual modernity" syndrome shows that most of its characteristics reflect individualism (Yang, 1988), thus a revival of the 1960s modernization paradigm is seen in the 1980s conceptualization of individualism. It is to be noted, however, that the Individual Modernity paradigm made sense in understanding orientations adaptive to urbanization and shifts from tribal to national identities in many developing countries going through socioeconomic transformations in the 1950s and 1960s. It included such attitudinal characteristics as preference for urban life, exposure to mass media, openness to innovation, belief in science rather than religiosity, freedom from primordial ties and parental authority, interest in participation in national activities, participation in secondary groups, high educational and occupational aspirations, and activism (Dawson, 1967; Doob, 1960; Inkeles, 1969; Inkeles & Smith, 1974; Kahl, 1968; Kagitçibasi, 1973; D. H. Smith & Inkeles, 1966; see also Berry chapter in the first edition of the Handbook, Volume 5, 1980).

Many of these characteristics are now commonplace, because they are required to some extent by urban life styles. However, some aspects of human behavior that are not incompatible with the demands of urban life styles endure, even though they may be different from Western patterns. For example, close-knit human bonds may be just such a characteristic. There appear to be functional shifts and adjustments in psychological orientations rather than a general progression to a higher level of social development (Bendix, 1967; Gusfield, 1967).

Modernization has been equated with Westernization, and the path of modernization has been drawn as a unidirectional converging toward the Western pattern. Any different human/societal characteristics have been deemed deficient in the sense of being incompatible with economic/societal development (e.g., Hoselitz, 1965; Kapp, 1963). Though these views are rejected by many (e.g., Bendix, 1967; Gusfield, 1967; Kagitçibasi, 1994; Mazrui, 1968; D. Sinha, 1988), the "convergence hypothesis" is still commonly accepted. It also continues to color some of the thinking in Individualism/Collectivism.

Recently Marsella and Choi (1993) have further questioned the modernization theory assumptions and have claimed "Easternization" to reflect the current "modernization" in East Asia. This refers to a process of societal/economic development involving alternative cultural and psychosocial aspects to those characterizing Western societies. Thus there may be alternative pathways to societal development.

The same applies to Individualism/Collectivism. Some aspects of individualism are adaptive to urban living conditions and can be expected to spread with social change in the world. However, those aspects of collectivism that do not conflict with urban lifestyles need not change, or new styles of individualism or collectivism may emerge and may coexist (D. Sinha & Tripathi, 1994). Because individualism and collectivism are manifested in different situations, it is important to study how modernization affects some situations and leaves others unchanged. Thus Individualism/Collectivism needs to be unconfounded from modernity (Kagitçibasi, 1994).

Some examples of the above conceptual confounding have been already mentioned. Such values/customs as filial piety and ancestor worship, subordination of women, orthodox Islamic belief, and so forth (Cha, 1994; Weinreich & Kelley, 1990) may reflect traditional lifestyles more than psychological collectivism. Conservatism, rather than collectivism (Kagitçibasi, 1992; Schwartz, 1994), may be the more appropriate antecedent of characteristics prevalent in premodern (rural–traditional) living contexts. "Sharing of material resources," one of the attributes of collectivism as conceived by Hui and Triandis (1986), may have more to do with rural–traditional life styles and poverty than with collectivism. It reflects "material interdependencies" that are functional in certain socioeconomic contexts (Kagitçibasi, 1990).

The correspondance between economic development and individualism may be less than assumed. Indeed the high correlation (.82) obtained by Hofstede (1980) with the 1970 GNP per capita figures is found to be much less (.40) by Schwartz, using the 1988 GNP figures. Schwartz used the Autonomy–Conservatism dimension (replacing Individualism/Collectivism). Beyond the differences in the specific items used, however, this great reduction is probably due more to the recent economic boom in East Asia. In other words, it is no longer only the so-called individualistic countries that are rich.

Similarly, the contention that social/cultural complexity is associated with individualism and simplicity with collectivism (Triandis, 1988, 1989, 1995; Triandis et al., 1988) makes sense only within isolated tribal conditions or when comparing preindustrial lifestyles. It is questionable beyond the point of shift from isolated, rural/tribal agrarian existence patterns into mostly urban nations, even if "developing" (Kagitçibasi, 1994). Contemporary societies are all highly complex but vary in Individualism/Collectivism (see also Berry, 1994).

It is important to distinguish Individualism/Collectivism from modernization, cultural complexity, and socioeconomic development (Kagitçibasi, 1994). Indeed, Bond (1994, p. 75) points out that if individualism is just another name for modernization, then this implies that cross-cultural differences in behavior would disappear with time and together with it cross- cultural psychology! In fact, equating individualism with modernization amounts to "psychologizing" a sociological phenomenon. Sociologists are no longer assuming that modernity will replace tradition. Today "modernism" is not being contrasted with tradition but rather with "postmodernism," where new "traditions" emerge, and no progression from a less to a more "developed" societal state is assumed.

Dimensionality, Generality, and Levels of Measurement

There is a pervasive tendency to treat individualism and collectivism as polar opposites. Their semantics and historical–philosophical treatments may be seen as contributing to this dichotomous conceptualization. In research there is often an imposed dichotomy in forced choice measures. However, recent theorizing and empirical evidence suggests that these constructs do not necessarily form opposite poles and may coexist in individuals or groups at the same time in different situations or with different target groups or toward different interactional goals (Berry, 1994; Ho & Chiu, 1994; Kagitçibasi, 1987; Kim, 1994; Mishra, 1994; Schwartz, 1990; Sinha & Tripathi, 1994; Triandis, 1990; Triandis et al., 1986, 1988; Triandis, McCusker, & Hui, 1990; Yang, 1988; Yu & Yang, 1994) (see also Gudykunst & Bond in this volume).

For example, using the Schwartz Values Survey with Turkish and Bulgarian (ethnic Turkish) teachers, Kusdil (1991) found Bulgarian teachers to have higher collectivistic values than Turkish teachers, but the two groups were not different from each other in individualistic values. Furthermore, emotional giving, emotional receiving, embeddedness, and family extendedness all correlated with collectivism but not with individualism.

Yamaguchi, Kuhlman, and Sugimori (1992), working with two American and one Korean sample, found a two-factor model to fit best their individualist and collectivist items. The two scales of individualism and collectivism did not correlate in the U.S. sample and correlated only moderately negatively in the Korean sample. Affiliative tendency and need for uniqueness showed correlations with one but not with the other.

If Individualism/Collectivism were a single dimension, its two poles would be equally and inversely related to other variables. As shown by the previously mentioned research and others, this is not found to be the case. Singelis and Brown (1995) also note that such equal inverse relationships do not hold with communication outcomes; they point to the growing evidence for the coexistence of independent and interdependent selves.

Ho and Chiu (1994) distinguish between dimensionality and polarity, stating that individualism and collectivism can be multidimensional but polar opposites on each dimension. They nevertheless claim that highly individualist and collectivist attributes can be displayed on *a given* dimension (p. 156), as they found within their two major components of Self Reliance/Interdependence and Responsibility. This finding contradicts their contention of polarity and provides evidence for the coexistence of individualist and collectivist attributes.

Hofstede (1980) derived "individualism" empirically as a unidimensional construct at the cultural level. He finds a single bipolar dimension useful at the culture level, recognizing, however, that a multidimensional structure may be more valid at the individual level. Other work has suggested a better fit for multidimensional conceptualization even at the cultural level (Chinese Culture Connection, 1987; Schwartz, 1994; Triandis, 1990; Triandis et al., 1986) (see also Gudykunst & Bond chapter in this volume).

A related question is whether Individualism/Collectivism is situation and target specific or has trait-like generality over situations and targets (Kagitçibasi, 1987). The general inclination is to attribute a trait-like characteristic to individualism and collectivism and to see them as determined by culture or personality. Possible situational determination is overlooked. Yet a great deal of research points to variation in dispositions with different targets and changing situational demands. Who the other is and the very definition of the "ingroup" make a difference in the response emitted.

For example, Leung and Bond (1984) showed that the equality orientation in collectivistic societies is the case in dealing with ingroups; with outgroups they found Chinese subjects to abide with the "equity" norm even more closely than American subjects. Other research also finds differences between ingroup and outgroup behaviors (Gudykunst, Yoon, & Nishida, 1987). Thus, behaviors change according to situations. This is recognized in several assessment instruments where target-specific questions are used (e.g., Hui, 1988; Hui & Yee, 1994). It may be wise to construe Individualism/Collectivism in probabilistic terms, as the likelihood of a person or a group of people behaving in individualist or collectivist ways in various situations (Kagitçibasi, 1994; Triandis, 1989, 1994b, 1995).

These considerations point to the need to conceptualize and operationalize Individualism/Collectivism at the individual level of analysis. As mentioned before, discrepancies between the conceptualizations at the cultural level and the individual level do not make much psychological sense. This is the case even though statistically it is clear that a country-level analysis uses country scores and an individual-level analysis uses individual scores. Because the so-called country scores are themselves derived from averaging the responses of a sample of individuals, they are expected to have parallel psychological meaning (Berry, 1992). Yet the results of the two analytical procedures are not identical (Leung, 1988) and, especially with different labels, it is difficult to make much sense of the different country-level dimensions.

Without a theoretical explanation of the meaning of the discrepancies between the individual and the cultural levels, the picture is confused. Thus it is not always clear whether the different factor structures at the cultural and the individual levels imply different construals of Individualism/Collectivism, or whether we are talking about a statistical (arti)fact. For example, there are differences between the culture-level and individual-level characterization of Individualism/Collectivism in Triandis' model. Collectivism is best described by Family Integrity at the culture level but by Interdependence and Sociability at the individual level; the corresponding factors for individualism are Emotional Detachment and Self Reliance. Why these differences are obtained is not clear. Similar distinctions are seen in Schwartz's values.

There have been attempts to devise statistical procedures to compute individual-level scores in ways not overlaid by differences between country means (Bond, 1988; Leung & Bond, 1989). More work needs to be done along these lines, given the lack of correspondence between the individual- and the culture-level measures. For example, Hofstede (1980, 1991) warns against the "ecological fallacy" of applying culture-level characteristics to individuals. Hui (1988) reports that when he applied Hofstede's Individualism scale, developed on the basis of an "ecological" factor analysis using the country mean scores, to undergraduate students, he found inter-item correlations and Cronbach alphas to be virtually zero. Hofstede and Spangenberg (1987) also acknowledge that the instrument has limited use at the individual level of measurement.

Before concluding the discussion of the problems of conceptualization, we need to point to a pervasive artifactual problem. Most of the recent research, and theorizing emerging from it, have focused on East Asia, contrasted mainly with North American behavioral patterns. The result is a distinctly East Asian variant of Collectivism (see also Gudykunst & Bond in this volume). For example, the so-called modesty bias, low levels each of self-focused emotions, self-serving bias, self-esteem, and self-focusing in general found in research with Chinese and Japanese subjects may reflect some other values and conventions in these cultures and may not replicate with Latin American or Mediterranean "collectivists," for example. Research covering a greater variety of societies is badly needed.

Refinement in Conceptualization

Previously we asked whether some of the features or correlates of Individualism/Collectivism could be due to other background factors. That questioning led us to consider some problems of conceptualization, such as overextension. At this point we need to ask two more interrelated questions regarding those features that *are* found to be associated with Individualism/Collectivism: Which aspects of Individualism/Collectivism do these features represent? Is it possible to dismantle the unwieldy characterization of Individualism/Collectivism by detecting some basic dimensions?

Research and conceptualization reviewed in this chapter reveal two different ways in which Individualism/Collectivism has been construed. One of these is the normative or value orientation that has stressed ideology and how people think individual–group relations should be organized. The other construal is in terms of human relatedness and considers Individualism/Collectivism as a dimension of self–other relations. Though interrelated, these two construals of Individualism/Collectivism are distinctly different, both theoretically and in terms of research and applications. While the value orientation deals more with the normative aspects of the relationship between the individual and the group (or society), the self orientation deals with the definition of the self (its boundaries and relationship to others).

Normative Individualism/Collectivism

Normative collectivism is based on the premise that individual interests are to be subordinated to group interests. This has direct implications for individual–group interaction at all levels ranging from the family to the state. The family, kin, neighborhood, society, or whatever the relevant "ingroup" under consideration, is expected to protect and support the individual in return for unquestioning loyalty (Hofstede, 1980, 1991). Normative individualism, in turn, upholds individual rights, freedom, and integrity *against* group domination. The rise of Western individualism can be seen as a struggle against oppressive collectivities such as the feudal state and the church.

Normative Individualism/Collectivism has permeated research and theorizing in cross-cultural psychology, as we have seen. From 1980 on, with the influential research of Hofstede and Triandis on attitudes and values, such a normative conceptualization of individualism and collectivism has been in the forefront. It has been further reinforced by work on values conducted by Schwartz, Bond, and others. This can be seen as a natural outgrowth of Western ideological tradition, pitting the individual against the group (Kagitçibasi, 1987). For example, in the construction of the first scales, questions were based on giving up (or not giving up) personal interest for group interest (or for others), reinforced by responses from many psychologists and anthropologists (Hui & Triandis, 1986). More recently, also, Yamaguchi (1994) has developed a scale that explicitly deals with individual and group goals.

Normative Individualism/Collectivism is more relevant at the cultural than at the individual level, because it has more to do with societal values and conventions than individual tendencies. For example, Triandis found that Family Integrity discriminated the most among national samples and was the only factor to correlate with Hofstede's collectivism. Family Integrity (e.g., the idea that children should live with their parents until they get married) reflects traditional family ideology.

It is normative Individualism/Collectivism that gets confounded with modernization/tradition. Since normative orientations, customs and practices change in response to socioeconomic development, normative collectivism weakens with changing lifestyles and is replaced by normative individualism, as predicted by modernization theory. For example, with increased affluence, old people become more self-sufficient financially and *material* interdependencies between generations decrease (Kagitçibasi, 1990). Together with this change, filial piety may weaken because it includes financial support of parents together with respect for them (Chinese Culture Connection, 1987). As filial piety is a collectivistic value, this is an instance of normative collectivism decreasing with changing lifestyles. However, the close *emotional* bonds between generations may continue, even though material interdependencies weaken (Kagitçibasi, 1990, 1996). This latter has to do with the other construal of collectivism, at the interpersonal psychological level, rather than at the normative level.

Normative aspects of collectivism reflect tradition and conservative ideology. Thus, as mentioned before, Schwartz (1994) has replaced his earlier label of Collectivism dimension with Conservation (Conformity, Tradition, and Security). Conservatism regarding sex roles, for example, is closely associated with tradition rather than modernity, and this latter dimension overlaps with Hofstede's individualism–collectivism (Buss et al., 1990; see also Best & Williams chapter in this volume).

Together with tradition and conservatism go power distance and hierarchy in human organization. Some converging is apparent between the different conceptualizations or dimensions used by the different researchers. Thus normative collectivism relates to combined collectivism and power distance (Hofstede), authority ranking (Fiske), hierarchy (Schwartz), cultural inwardness (Bond), and vertical collectivism (Triandis).

The strong emphasis on normative Individualism/Collectivism has implied an attitudinal and value orientation in conceptualization and operationalization. Even though multiple methods for assessment are recommended (Triandis et al., 1990), most measures utilize values and attitudes. The degree of correspondence between values/attitudes and behavior is a perennial problem in social psychology. In collectivistic contexts this would appear to be an even more serious issue, given the greater sensitivity to situational demands (others' expectations, etc.).

Thus Ho and Chiu (1994) with Chinese subjects showed that an individualist or collectivist orientation may be role specific and not predictable from a person's "global attitudes toward traditional values" (p. 154). Similarly, Kashima et al. (1992) found a stronger belief in the consistency between attitudes and behavior in Australia than in Japan. In individualistic contexts there are less situational constraints on behavior, which therefore better reflects personal attitudes or values; in collectivistic contexts the greater embeddedness of persons in groups weakens this connection. This is substantiated by much cross-cultural research on attributions, which we have reviewed.

There is also the related problem of the degree of correspondence between attitudinal/value measures and other types of assessment. For example Chan (1994), in a comparison of different measures of individualism and collectivism, found that a collectivist values index (Schwartz's Security, Conformity, Tradition items) did not relate (r = .08) to a measure of social content of the self (percent S on the Kuhn & McPartland, 1954, "Who am I?").

Relational Individualism/Collectivism

These considerations bring us to the other (relational) construal of Individualism/Collectivism. Conceptualizations that emphasize the hierarchical status positions versus equality have addressed mainly normative Individualism/ Collectivism, whereas those that focus on interpersonal distance versus embeddedness have dealt with relational Individualism/Collectivism. There is a need to differentiate these dimensions of hierarchy–equality and interpersonal distance. Closely-knit relatedness or separateness can exist within both hierarchical and equalitarian groups, as also expressed by the distinction between vertical and horizontal Individualism/Collectivism.

Even though the normative construal of Individualism/Collectivism has been pervasive, particularly in the sense of whether the individual is or is not subservient to the group, a number of researchers have recognized that relational individualism/collectivism is the more basic construal (Bond, 1994; Hui & Villareal, 1989; Kagitçibasi, 1994; Schwartz, 1994). This construal has found expression particularly in the "self" orientation, as previously discussed.

The main distinction drawn is that between a relatively self-contained, individuated, separated, independent self defined by clear boundaries from others and a relational , interdependent self with fluid boundaries (Kagitçibasi, 1990; Markus & Kitayama, 1991). This distinction holds in both self-perception and in social perception (perception of others). A great deal of research evidence has already been reviewed regarding self and other descriptions, attributions, perceptions of similarity, emotions, cognitions, communication, and so forth, which reflect this basic distinction.

Some line is drawn between self and non-self at an existential level, which is probably universal. Beyond this, however, there is variability as to *where* that line is drawn (Heelas & Lock, 1981) and how sharply and clearly it is drawn. American (and Western) psychology, both reflecting and reinforcing the individualistic cultural ethos, has drawn the line narrowly and sharply, constituting a clear boundary between self and non-self. Other cultural conceptions differ in varying degrees.

A relational construal of Individualism/Collectivism can be seen at different levels of analysis. For example, the present author originally proposed the constructs "culture of separateness–culture of relatedness," to refer to general closeness-distance in human relations at the cultural level (Kagitçibasi, 1985). Later, focusing more on self–other relations, "psychology of relatedness" (Kagitçibasi, 1994) was construed at the individual level. Most theorizing in relational Individualism/Collectivism is at the individual level of analysis.

The "Relational" and the "Separated" self distinction can also be construed along a dimension of "(Inter)dependence–Independence" (Kagitçibasi, 1990, 1996). This dimension provides the link in family socialization between the background (cultural, social structural) variables and the self. As mentioned before, intergenerational familial interdependence engenders the development of the interdependent self. Where family culture entails independence (between generations), the separated self develops. In interpersonal relations, in general also, the (inter)dependence–independence dimension defines relational Individualism/Collectivism.

The relational–separated self or the (inter)dependence–independence distinction has to do with basic human merging and separation. In personality psychology it finds its first expression in the "conflict theories" of personality (Angyal, 1951; Bakan, 1966), which propose two basic human needs for merging with and separation from "the other." From a psychoanalytic perspective, reinterpreted by object relations theory, it derives from the "resolution" of the "individuation–separation" problem (e.g., Chodorow, 1989; Mahler, Pine, & Bergman, 1975) and is considered a natural early developmental process leading to autonomy from the environment.

Similar views are shared by ego psychologists (Hartman, 1939/1958) and by family systems theorists (Minuchin, 1974), where there is an emphasis on clear boundaries separating the selves (in the family). Though "conflict theories" recognize the importance of both merging and separation, the other personality theories have stressed the latter, reflecting the Western individualistic ethos. As mentioned before, this emphasis has been challenged generally in recent criticism and particularly in feminist theory that has stressed the relational self (e.g., Chodorow, 1989; Gilligan, 1982; Lykes, 1985).

Brewer's "optimal distinctiveness" theory (1991) recognizes two contrasting needs for being similar to and different from the ingroup, called the need for "assimilation" and the need for "differentiation," respectively. Extrapolating from this theory, it may be proposed that individualists have a sharp gradient for differentiation and a flat gradient for assimilation, and the opposite is the case for collectivists (Triandis, 1995). As mentioned before, Triandis (1995) has also included relational aspects to the conceptualization of Individualism/Collectivism, following Markus and Kitayama's self orientation.

A great deal of the research evidence presented in this chapter has to do with relational Individualism/Collectivism. The relevance of the relational conceptualization is made explicit particularly in communication research from a self theory perspective (Singelis, 1994; Singelis & Brown, 1995, Singelis et al., 1995). An independent or an interdependent self construal (Markus & Kitayama, 1991) is seen as mediating between cultural collectivism and the resultant communication outcomes. In many other areas of psychological functioning, also, relational Individualism/Collectivism appears more relevant than normative Individualism/Collectivism. For example, situational or dispositional attribution, "sociocentric" or "egocentric" person perception and self perception, self to other or other to self similarity perception, ego- or other-focused emotions, individual- or social-achievement, and self esteem can all be explained in terms of relational–separated self other relations.

The very definition of independence may be culturally bound. For example, Osterweil and Nagano (1991) and Fujinaga (1991) found that Japanese mothers, like American and Israeli mothers, value independence, but for the Japanese mother this means that children are capable of interacting with other children or engaging in relationships. Thus, independence connotes interdependence in the development of the Japanese self, where the self is defined "in terms of the relationship one has with others" (Befu, 1986, p. 22). Similarly, "control" may be situated interpersonally rather than within the individual. Weisz, Rothbaum, and Blackburn (1984) showed that while in the United States "primary control" (influencing existing realities) is valued, in Japan "secondary control" (accommodating to existing realities) assumes greater importance. The same point was made earlier by Diaz-Guerrero (1979) in Mexico.

The implications of relational Individualism/Collectivism for psychological functioning are significant. Its antecedents are to be found in familial (intergenerational) interdependencies that are reflected in family socialization. For example, Choi (1992) showed the prevalence of a "communicative pattern relationally-attuned to one another in a fused state" in mother-child interaction among Koreans, where "mothers merged themselves with the children." In contrast the Canadian mothers were found to "detach themselves from the children . . . withdrawing themselves from the children's reality, so that the children's reality can remain autonomous" (pp. 119–120). Similar "enmeshment" in child rearing is found among Puerto Rican (Coll, 1990) and Japanese families (Azuma, 1994), where mothers view their infants as "extensions of themselves."

Thus, three different types of conceptualizations appear to be of importance. One of these would show that there are different types of selves (separated–relational, varying in degrees), and that they differ in several psychological processes, ranging from self-perceptions to emotions. A second one would throw light on the kinds of family socialization engendering these different selves. A third one would reveal why a certain kind of socialization occurs in a particular socio-economic–cultural context (in terms of a functional analysis) and when a change in this process of self development may be expected. A relational construal of Individualism/Collectivism would be greatly enriched by these complementary conceptualizations.

A relational construal of Individualism/Collectivism does not mean mutually exclusive polar opposites. The merging and the separating tendencies coexist in individuals as basic human needs. This is also reflected in family socialization stressing both autonomy and control in contexts where emotional interdependencies (close-knit family ties) continue while material interdependencies weaken (Cha, 1994; Kagitçibasi, 1990, 1996; Lin & Fu, 1990). Coexistence in different degrees of idiocentrism and allocentrism, of public and private self, of autonomy and relatedness, and of self reliance and interdependence is proposed by many (Ho & Chiu, 1994; Kagitçibasi, 1990, 1996; Kim, 1994; Singelis, 1994; Sinha & Tripathi, 1994; Triandis, 1994a; Yu & Yang, 1994).

It is possible to introduce an even finer tuning of this conceptualization by differentiating further between an autonomy versus heteronomy dimension (agency) and a relatedness versus separation dimension (interpersonal distance). Distinguishing agency from interpersonal distance provides a conceptual basis for the coexistence of autonomy and relatedness, as proposed to emerge in the family model of emotional interdependence and evidenced in research (Kagitçibasi, 1990, 1996). This view allows for the existence of autonomy within both relational individualism and collectivism and renders the previously mentioned dualities nonconflictual.

Future Prospects

Judging from the research activity in Individualism/Collectivism up to now, we can expect this field to be active in the near future also. Conceptual and methodological refinements are called for, however, for research to contribute to a better understanding of the phenomena under consideration. These are particularly needed before causal inferences may be drawn. Methodologically, issues of the level of analysis and dimensionality need to be addressed. Overextension and broad coverage present measurement problems, such as low reliabilities. Very general (overinclusive) constructs and very specific ones (e.g., sociability) do not provide optimal levels of measurement (Singelis et al., 1995), thus intermediate level constructs are needed. Attempts such as integrating the independent/interdependent self with the equality/inequality dimension in the context of horizontal/vertical individualism and collectivism are promising developments (Singelis et al., 1995).

Conceptually, also, smaller-range models and theories focusing on delimited areas would be more effective than all-encompassing theoretical schemes. Of particular importance would be the distinction between normative and relational construals of Individualism/Collectivism. Researchers should be sensitive to the choices they make with regard to which type of a conceptualization (and operationalization) they undertake, in terms of cultural norms, values, individual attitudes, cognitions, behaviors, and so forth. When these are intermixed, conceptual and methodological confounding may result.

Research and conceptualization at the level of basic psychological processes and behavioral correlates of Individualism/Collectivism are needed. The psychology of relatedness, including interpersonal relations along (inter)dependence–independence dimension and relational-separated self variations emerges as a promising area for the cross-cultural study of relational Individualism/Collectivism. This may be an area that comes closest to being *core* Individualism/Collectivism. This is because the extent to which the self is perceived as separate from or overlapping with others is conceptually more basic than any other aspects of Individualism/Collectivism. Whether there are significant differences in these basic self-concepts across cultures has implications for all other behavioral outcomes. Furthermore, how these differences come about and whether they are decreasing (converging) or not are important research questions. Going beyond basic psychological processes, situational determinants of Individualism/Collectivism also require research attention, because evidence points to their importance, as mentioned before.

Future research may point to alternative outcomes regarding commonality and diversity in Individualism/Collectivism across cultures. If research focuses on the most fundamental level, such as the two basic needs for merging and separation, commonality may ensue. Nevertheless, even at this level of the self and relational patterns, there would be differences in the relative emphasis put on the two basic needs, with resulting variations in the prevalence of the relational and the separated selves.

If research focuses on normative Individualism/Collectivism, a convergence toward the Western pattern may ensue, given the changing lifestyles toward urban patterns and the Western dominated mass media engendering cultural diffusion, even though acculturation need not be unidirectional (see Berry & Sam chapter). The convergence would be limited, however, with relational Individualism/Collectivism continuing to show diversity. This is because relational patterns may be more or less independent of socioeconomic development, which needs to be researched.

Thus, both commonality and diversity would be expected to prevail in Individualism/Collectivism, depending on how it is construed and operationalized. New combinations would be expected to emerge with changes in normative–, but continuities in relational–Individualism/Collectivism. An example would be the relational-autonomous self construal (Kagitçibasi, 1990, 1996) developing in a family context of emotional interdependencies but decreased material interdependencies entailing both autonomy and control in childrearing. Coexistence of seemingly opposing orientations and new syntheses would need to be considered within dialectic outlooks, fine tuning, and new perspectives going beyond what has been commonly used in psychology. Recognition of the existing complexities would help enrich our understanding. Cross-cultural thinking has benefited from the Individualism/Collectivism paradigm. More refined conceptualization and sophisticated second-generation research, building upon the valuable first-generation research of the 1980s and early 1990s, may be expected to contribute to further advancement within this paradigm.

References

Agarwal, R. & Misra, G. (1986). A factor analytic study of achievement goals and means: An Indian view. *International Journal of Psychology, 21*, 717–731.

Angyal, A. (1951). A theoretical model for personality studies. *Journal of Personality, 20*, 131–142.

Aries, P. (1980). Two successive motivations for the declining birth rate in the West. *Population and Development Review, 6*, 645–650.

Azuma, H. (1994). Two modes of cognitive socialization in Japan and the United States. In P. M. Greenfield & R. R. Cocking, *Cross-cultural roots of minority child development* (pp. 275–284). Hillsdale, NJ: Lawrence Erlbaum.

Bakan, D. (1966). *The duality of human existence.* Chicago: Rand McNally.

Batson, C. D. (1990). How social an animal? *American Psychologist, 45*, 336–346.

Baumeister, R. F. (1991). *Meanings of life.* New York and London: Guilford.

Befu, H. (1986). The social and cultural background of child development in Japan and the United States. In H. Stevenson, H. Azuma, & K. Hakuta (Eds.), *Child development and education in Japan* (pp. 13–25). New York: Freeman.

Bellah, R.N., Madsen, R., Sullivan, W., Swidler, A. & Tipton, S. M. (1985). *Habits of the heart: Individualism and commitment in American life.* Berkeley: University of California Press.

Bendix, R. (1967). Tradition and modernity reconsidered. *Comparative Studies in Society and History, 9*, 292–346.

Bennett, J. (1984). The tie that binds: Peasant marriage and families in late Medieval England. *Journal of Interdisciplinary History, 15*, 111–129.

Berman, J. J., Murphy-Berman, V. M., & Singh, P. (1985). Cross-cultural similarities and differences in perception of fairness. *Journal of Cross-Cultural Psychology, 16*, 55–67.

Berry, J. W. (1980). Social and cultural change. In H. C. Triandis & R. W. Brislin (Eds.), *Handbook of cross-cultural psychology* (Vol. 5, pp. 211–280). Boston: Allyn and Bacon.

Berry, J. W. (1992). The cross-cultural study of values: The Jack Horner strategy and alternative approaches. Paper presented at the Symposium "Antecedents and Consequences of Value Priorities: Cross-Cultural Perspectives," 25th International Congress of Psychology, Brussels, July 19–24, 1992.

Berry, J. W. (1994). Ecology of individualism and collectivism. In U. Kim, H. C. Triandis, C. Kagitçibasi, S-C. Choi, & G. Yoon (Eds.), *Individualism and collectivism: Theory, method and applications* (pp. 77–84). Thousand Oaks, CA: Sage.

Berry, J. W., Poortinga, Y. H., Segall, M. H., & Dasen, P. R. (1992). *Cross-cultural psychology: Research and applications.* New York: Cambridge University Press.

Bhawuk, D. P. S. & Brislin, R. W. (1992). The measurement of intercultural sensitivity using the concepts of individualism and collectivism. *International Journal of Intercultural Relations, 16*, 413–436.

Billings, D. K. & Majors, F. (1989). Individualism and group orientation: Contrasting personalities in Melanesian cultures. In D. Keats & L. Mann (Eds.), *Heterogeneity in cross-cultural psychology* (pp. 92–103). Lisse, Netherlands: Swets and Zeitlinger.

Bond, M. H. (Ed.). (1988). *The cross-cultural challenge to social psychology.* Newbury Park, CA: Sage.

Bond, M. H. (1994). Into the heart of collectivism: A personal and scientific journey. In U. Kim, H. C. Triandis, C. Kagitçibasi, S-C. Choi, & G.

Yoon (Eds.), *Individualism and collectivism: Theory, method and applications* (pp. 66–76). Thousand Oaks, CA: Sage.

Bond, M. H. & Cheung, T. S. (1983). The spontaneous self-concept of college students in Hong Kong, Japan and the United States. *Journal of Cross-Cultural Psychology, 14,* 153–171.

Bond, M. H. & Forgas, J. P. (1984). Linking person perception to behavior intention across cultures: The role of cultural collectivism. *Journal of Cross-Cultural Psychology, 15*(3), 337–352.

Bond, M. H., Leung, K., & Wan, K. C. (1982). How does cultural collectivism operate? The impact of task and maintenance contributions on reward distribution. *Journal of Cross-Cultural Psychology, 13,* 186–200.

Bontempo, R. & Rivero, J. C. (1992). Cultural variation in cognition: The role of self concept in the attitude–behavior link. Paper presented at the meetings of the American Academy of Management, Las Vegas, Nevada, August, 1992.

Boski, P. (1983). A study of person perception in Nigeria: Ethnicity and self versus other attributions for achievement-related outcomes. *Journal of Cross-Cultural Psychology, 14,* 85–108.

Bradburn, N. M. (1963). N achievement and father dominance in Turkey. *Journal of Abnormal and Social Psychology, 67,* 464–468.

Brewer, M. B. (1991). The social self: On being the same and different at the same time. *Personality and Social Psychology Bulletin 17,* 475–482.

Buss, D. M. and 49 co-authors. (1990). International preferences in selecting mates: A study of 37 cultures. *Journal of Cross-Cultural Psychology, 21,* 5–47.

Campbell, D. T. (1986). Science's social system of validity enhancing collective belief change and the problems of social sciences. In D. W. Fiske & R. A. Shweder (Eds.), *Metatheory in social science.* Chicago: University of Chicago Press.

Capps, D. & Fenn, R. (1992). *Individualism reconsidered: Bearing on the endangered self in modern society.* Center for Religion, Self, and Society, Princeton Theological Seminary Monograph Series, #1. Princeton, NJ: A & A Printing.

Cha, J-H. (1994). Aspects of individualism and collectivism in Korea. In U. Kim, H. C. Triandis, C. Kagitçibasi, S-C. Choi, & G. Yoon (Eds.), *Individualism and collectivism: Theory, method and applications* (pp. 157–174). Thousand Oaks, CA: Sage.

Chan, D. Y-F. (1994). COLINDEX: A refinement of three collectivism measures. In U. Kim, H. C. Triandis, C. Kagitçibasi, S-C. Choi, & G. Yoon (Eds.), *Individualism and collectivism: Theory, method and applications* (pp. 200–210). Thousand Oaks, CA: Sage.

Chandler, T. A., Shama, D. D., Wolf, F. M., & Planchard, S. K. (1981). Multiattributional causality: A five cross-national samples study. *Journal of Cross-Cultural Psychology, 12,* 207–221.

The Chinese Culture Connection. (1987). Chinese values and the search for culture-free dimensions of culture. *Journal of Cross-Cultural Psychology, 18,* 143–164.

Chodorow, N. (1989). *Feminism and psychoanalytic theory.* New Haven: Yale University Press.

Cousins, S. (1989). Culture and selfhood in Japan and the U.S. *Journal of Personality and Social Psychology, 56,* 124–131.

Choi, S. H. (1992). Communicative socialization processes: Korea and Canada. In S. Iwawaki, Y. Kashima, & K. Leung (Eds.), *Innovations in cross-cultural psychology* (pp. 103–121). Lisse: Swets & Zeitlinger.

Coll, C. T. G. (1990). Developmental outcome of minority infants: A process-oriented look into our beginnings. *Child Development, 61,* 270–289.

Crocker, J. & Luhanen, R. (1990). Collective self-esteem and ingroup bias. *Journal of Personality and Social Psychology, 58,* 60–67.

Cushman, P. (1990). Why the self is empty: Toward a historically situated psychology. *American Psychologist, 45,* 599–611.

Dawson, J. L. M. (1967). Traditional versus Western attitudes in west Africa: The construction, validation and application of a measuring device. *British Journal of Social and Clinical Psychology, 6,* 81–96.

De Vos, G. (1968). Achievement and innovation in culture and personality. In E. Norbeck, D. Price-Williams, & E. W. McCord (Eds.), *The study of personality* (pp. 348–370). New York: Holt, Rinehart & Winston.

Diaz-Guerrero, R. (1979). The development of coping style. *Human Development, 22,* 320–331.

Domino, G. (1992). Cooperation and competition in Chinese and American children. *Journal of Cross-Cultural Psychology, 23,* 456–467.

Donohue, W. A. (1990). *The new freedom: Individualism and collectivism in the social lives of Americans.* New Brunswick, NJ: Transaction.

Doob, L. W. (1960). *Becoming more civilized.* New Haven: Yale University Press.

Eliriam, T. & Schwartzwald, J. (1987). Social orientation among Israeli youth. *Journal of Cross-Cultural Psychology, 18,* 31–44.

Etzioni, A. (1993). *Spirit of community: Rights, responsibilities and the communitarian agenda.* New York: Crown.

Fijneman, Y. A., Willemsen, M. E., & Poortinga, Y. H., in cooperation with Erelcin, F.G., Georgas, J., Hui, H. C., Leung, K., & Malpass, R. S. (1995). Individualism–collectivism: An empirical study of a conceptual issue. *Journal of Cross-Cultural Psychology, 27,* 381–402..

Fiske, A. P. (1990). *Structures of social life.* New York: Free Press.

Fiske, A. P. (1992). The four elementary forms of sociality: Framework for a unified theory of social relations. *Psychological Review, 99,* 689–723.

Forgas, J. P. & Bond, M. H. (1985). Cultural influences on the perception of interaction episodes. *Personality and Social Psychology Bulletin, 11,* 75–88.

Fry, P. S. & Ghosh, R. (1980). Attribution of success and failure: Comparisons of cross-cultural differences between Asian and Caucasion children. *Journal of Cross-Cultural Psychology, 11,* 343–363.

Fujinaga, T. (1991). *Development of personality and among Japanese children.* Paper presented at the International Society for the Study of Behavioural Development, Workshop on Asian Perspectives of Psychology, Ann Arbor, MI.

Gabrenya, W. K., Jr., Wang, Y. E., & Lataner, B. (1985). Social loafing on an optimizing task: Cross-cultural differences among Chinese and Americans. *Journal of Cross-Cultural Psychology, 16*(2), 223–242.

Gergen, K. J. (1991). *The saturated self: Dilemmas of identity in contemporary life.* New York: Basic.

Gillespie, J. M. & Allport, G. W. (1955). *Youth's outlook on the future: A cross national study.* Garden City, NY: Doubleday.

Gilligan, C. (1982). *In a different voice.* Cambridge, MA: Harvard University Press.

Greenberg, J. (1981). The justice of distributing scarce and abundant resources. In M. J. Lerner & S. C. Lerner (Eds.), *The justice motive.* New York: Plenum.

Greenfield, P. M. & Cocking, R. R. (Eds.). (1994). *Cross-cultural roots of minority child development.* Hillsdale, NJ: Lawrence Erlbaum.

Gudykunst, W. B., Yoon, Y., & Nishida, T. (1987). The influence of individualism–collectivism on perceptions of communication in ingroup and outgroup relationships. *Communication Monographs, 54,* 295–306.

Gudykunst, W. B., Ting-Toomey, S., & Chua, E. (1988). *Culture and interpersonal communication.* Newbury Park, CA: Sage.

Gusfield, J. R. (1967). Tradition and modernity: Misplaced polarities in the study of social change. *American Journal of Sociology, 73,* 351–362.

Hall, E. T. (1976). *Beyond culture.* New York: Doubleday.

Hanawalt, A. A. (1986). *The ties that bound: Peasant families in Medieval England.* New York: Oxford University Press.

Hartman, H. (1939/1958). *Ego psychology and the problem of adaptation* (D. Rapaport, Trans). New York: International Universities Press. (Original work published, 1939).

Heelas, P. & Lock, A. (Eds.). (1981). *Indigenous psychologies: The anthropology of the self.* London: Academic.

Ho, D. Y-F. & Chiu, C-Y. (1994). Component ideas of individualism, collectivism and social organisation: An application in the study of Chinese culture. In U. Kim, H. C. Triandis, C. Kagitçibasi, S-C. Choi, & G. Yoon (Eds.), *Individualism and collectivism: Theory, method and applications* (pp. 137–156). Thousand Oaks, CA: Sage.

Hofstede, G. (1980). *Culture's consequences: International differences in work-related values.* Beverly Hills: Sage.

Hofstede, G. (1983). Dimensions of national cultures in fifty countries and three regions. In J. B. Deregowski, S. Driurawiec, & R. C. Annis (Eds.), *Expiscations in cross-cultural psychology* (pp. 335–355). Lisse, Netherlands: Swets and Zeitlinger.

Hofstede, G. (1991). *Cultures and organizations: Software of the mind.* London: McGraw-Hill.

Hofstede, G. & Bond, M. H. (1984). Hofstede's culture dimensions: An independent validation using Rokeach's value survey. *Journal of Cross-Cultural Psychology, 15,* 417–433.

Hofstede, G. & Spangenberg, J. (1987). Measuring individualism and collectivism at occupational and organizational levels. In C. Kagitçibasi (Ed.), *Growth and progress in cross-cultural psychology* (pp. 113–129). Lisse, Netherlands: Swets and Zeitlinger.

Hogan, R. (1975). Theoretical egocentrism and the problem of compliance. *American Psychologist, 30,* 533–540.

Hoselitz, B. (1965). *Economics and the idea of mankind.* New York: Columbia University Press.

Hsu, F. L. K. (1983). *Rugged individualism reconsidered.* Knoxville: University of Tennessee Press.

Hui, C. H. (1984). *Individualism–collectivism: Theory, measurement and its relationship to reward allocation.* Unpublished doctoral dissertation, Department of Psychology, University of Illinois at Champaign-Urbana.

Hui, C. H. (1988). Measurement of individualism and collectivism. *Journal for Research in Personality, 22,* 17–36.

Hui, C. H. & Triandis, H. C. (1986). Individualism-Collectivism: A study of cross-cultural researchers. *Journal of Cross-Cultural Psychology, 17,* 225–248.

Hui, C. H., Triandis, H. C., & Yee, C. (1991). Cultural differences in reward allocation: Is collectivism an explanation? *British Journal of Social Psychology, 30,* 145–157.

Hui, C. H. & Villareal, M. (1989). Individualism–collectivism and psychological needs: Their relationship in two cultures. *Journal of Cross-Cultural Psychology, 20,* 310–323.

Hui, C. H. & Yee, C. (1994). The shortened individualism–collectivism scale: Its relationship to demographic and work-related variables. *Journal of Research in Personality, 28,* 409–424.

Inkeles, A. (1969). Making men modern: On the causes and consequences of individual change in six developing countries. *American Journal of Sociology, 75,* 208–225.

Inkeles, A. & Smith, D. H. (1974). *Becoming modern: Individual changes in six developing countries.* Cambridge, MA: Harvard University Press.

Jansz, J. (1991). *Person, self and moral demands.* Leiden, The Netherlands: DSWO Press.

Kagitçibasi, C. (1970). Social norms and authoritarianism: A Turkish-American comparison. *Journal of Personality and Social Psychology, 16,* 444–451.

Kagitçibasi, C. (1973). Psychological aspects of modernization in Turkey. *Journal of Cross-Cultural Psychology, 4,* 157–174.

Kagitçibasi, C. (1982). Old-age security value of children: Cross-national socio-economic evidence. *Journal of Cross-Cultural Psychology, 13,* 29–42.

Kagitçibasi, C. (1985). Culture of separateness-culture of relatedness. In C. Klopp (Ed.), *1984 Vision and Reality. Papers in Comparative Studies* (Vol. 4, pp. 91–99). Columbus, OH: Ohio State University.

Kagitçibasi, C. (1987). Individual and group loyalties: Are they compatible? In C. Kagitçibasi (Ed.), *Growth and progress in cross-cultural psychology* (pp. 94–104). Lisse, Netherlands: Swets and Zeitlinger.

Kagitçibasi, C. (1990). Family and socialization in cross-cultural perspective: A model of change. In J. Berman (Ed.) *Cross-cultural perspectives: Nebraska Symposium on motivation, 1989* (pp. 135–200). Lincoln: University of Nebraska Press.

Kagitçibasi, C. (1992). Value priorities in Muslim-influenced countries: A cross-cultural perspective. Paper presented at the 25th International Congress of Psychology, Brussels, July 19–24, 1992.

Kagitçibasi, C. (1994). A critical appraisal of individualism and collectivism: Toward a new formulation. In U. Kim, H. C. Triandis, C. Kagitçibasi, S-C. Choi, & G. Yoon (Eds.), *Individualism and collectivism: Theory, method and applications* (pp. 52–65). Thousand Oaks, CA: Sage.

Kagitçibasi, C. (1996). *Family and human development across cultures: A view from the other side.* Hillsdale, NJ: Lawrence Erlbaum.

Kagitçibasi, C. & Berry, J. W. (1989). Cross-cultural psychology: Current research and trends. *Annual Review of Psychology, 40,* 493–531.

Kahl, J. A. (1968). *The measurement of modernism: Study of values in Brazil and Mexico.* Austin: University of Texas Press.

Kanfer, F. (1979). Personal control, social control and altruism: Can society survive the age of egocentrism? *American Psychologist, 34,* 231–239.

Kapp, W. K. (1963). *Hindu culture, economic development and economic planning in India.* Bombay: Asia Publishing House.

Kashima, Y. & Triandis, H. C. (1986). The self-serving bias in attributions as a coping strategy: A cross-cultural study. *Journal of Cross-Cultural Psychology, 17,* 83–97.

Kashima, Y., Siegal, M., Tanaka, K., & Kashima, E. S. (1992). Do people believe behaviours are consistent with attitudes? Towards a cultural psychology of attribution processes. *British Journal of Social Psychology, 31,* 111–24.

Kim, U. (1994). Individualism and collectivism: Conceptual clarification and elaboration. In U. Kim, H. C. Triandis, C. Kagitçibasi, S-C. Choi, & G. Yoon (Eds.), *Individualism and collectivism: Theory, method and applications* (pp. 19–41). Thousand Oaks, CA: Sage.

Kim, U., Triandis, H. C., Kagitçibasi, C., Choi, S-C., & Yoon, G. (Eds.). (1994). *Individualism and collectivism: Theory, method and applications.* Newbury Park, CA: Sage.

Kitayama, S., Markus, H. R., Kurokawa, M., Tummala P., Kato, K. (1991). Self–Other similarity judgements depend on culture. *University of Oregon, Institute of Cognitive Decision Sciences, Technical Report,* No. 91–17.

Kluckhohn, F. & Strodtbeck, F. (1961). *Variations in value orientations.* Evanston, IL: Row Peterson.

Kuhn, M. H. & McPartland, T. (1954). An emprirical investigation of self attitudes. *American Sociological Review, 19,* 68–76.

Kusdil, E. (1991). *Core characteristics of collectivism: A comparison between Bulgarian-Turkish and Turkish teachers.* Unpublished Masters thesis, Psychology Department, Bogaziçi University, Istanbul.

Lasch, C. (1978). *The culture of narcissism: American life in an age of diminishing expectations.* New York: Norton.

Lebra, T. S. (1994). Mother and child in Japanese socialization: A Japan–U.S. comparison. In P. M. Greenfield & R. R. Cocking, *Cross-cultural roots of minority child development.* Hillsdale, NJ: Lawrence Erlbaum.

Lesthaeghe, R. (1983). A century of demographic and cultural change in Western Europe: An exploration of underlying dimensions. *Population and Development Review, 9,* 411–437.

Leung, K. (1987). Some determinants of reactions to procedural models for conflict resolution: A cross-national study. *Journal of Personality and Social Psychology, 53,* 898–908.

Leung, K. (1988). Theoretical advances in justice behavior: Some cross-cultural inputs. In M. H. Bond (Ed.), *The cross-cultural challenge to social psychology* (pp. 218–229). Newbury Park, CA: Sage.

Leung, K. & Bond, M. H. (1982). How Chinese and Americans reward task-related contributions: A preliminary study. *Psychologia, 25,* 32–39.

Leung, K. & Bond, M. H. (1984). The impact of cultural collectivism on reward allocation. *Journal of Personality and Social Psychology, 47,* 793–804.

Leung, K. & Bond, M. H. (1989). On the empirical identification of dimensions for cross-cultural comparisons. *Journal of Cross-Cultural Psychology, 20,* 133–151.

Leung, K. and Park, H. J. (1986). Effects of interactional goal on choice of allocation rules: A cross-national study. *Organizational Behaviour and Human Decision Processes, 37,* 111–20.

Lin, C-Y. C. & Fu, V. R. (1990). A comparison of child-rearing practices among Chinese, immigrant Chinese, and Caucasian-American parents. *Child Development, 61,* 429–433.

Lukes, S. (1973). *Individualism*. Oxford: Basil Blackwell.

Lykes, M. B. (1985). Gender and individualistic vs. collectivistic bases for notions about the self. *Journal of Personality, 53,* 356–383.

MacFarlane, A. (1987). *The origins of English individualism: The family, property and social transition.* New York: Cambridge University Press.

Madsen,M. C. (1971). Developmental and cross-cultural differences in the cooperative and competitive behavior of young children. *Journal of Cross-Cultural Psychology, 2,* 365–371.

Mahler, M., Pine, F., & Bergman,A. (1975). *The psychological birth of the human infant.* New York: Basic Books.

Mann, L. (1986). Cross-cultural studies of rules for determining majority and minority decision rights. *Australian Journal of Psychology, 38,* 319–328.

Markus, H. R. & Kitayama, S. (1991). Culture and the self: Implications for cognition, emotion and motivation. *Psychological Review, 98*(2), 224–253.

Markus, H. R. & Kitayama, S. (Eds.). (1994) *Emotion and culture: Empirical studies of mutual influence.* Washington, DC: American Psychological Associaton.

Marsella, A. J. & Choi, S-C. (1994). Psychosocial aspects of modernization and economic development in East Asian Nations. *Psychologia, 36,* 201–213.

Marsella, A. J., DeVos, G., & Hsu, F. L. K. (Eds). (1985). *Culture and self: Asian and Western perspectives.* New York: Tavistock.

Marsella, A. J. & White, G. M. (Eds). (1984). *Cultural conceptions of mental health and therapy.* Boston: D. Reidel.

Matsumoto, D. (1989). Cultural influences on the perception of emotion. *Journal of Cross-Cultural Psychology, 20,* 92–105.

Mazrui, A. (1968). From social Darwinism to current theories of modernization. *World Politics, 21,* 69–83.

McClelland, D.C. (1961). *The achieving society.* Princeton: Van Nostrand.

McClelland, D. C., & Winters, D. G. (1969). *Motivating economic achievement.* New York: Free Press.

Miller, J. G. (1984). Culture and the development of everyday social explanation. *Journal of Personality and Social Psychology, 46,* 961–978.

Miller, J. G., Bersoff, D. M., & Harwood, R. L. (1990). Perceptions of social responsibilities in India and the United States: Moral imperatives or personal decisions? *Journal of Personality and Social Psychology, 58,* 33–47.

Mills, J. & Clark, M. S. (1982). Exchange and communal relationships. In L. Wheeler (Ed.), *Review of personality and social psychology* (Vol. 3, pp. 121–144). Beverly Hills: Sage.

Minuchin, S. (1974). *Families and family therapy.* Cambridge, MA: Harvard University Press.

Mishra, R. C. (1994). Individualism and collectivism orientations across generations. In U. Kim, H. C. Triandis, C. Kagitçibasi, S-C. Choi, & G. Yoon (Eds.), *Individualism and collectivism: Theory, method and applications* (pp. 225–238). Thousand Oaks, CA: Sage.

Nevis, E. C. (1983). Using an American perspective in understanding another culture: Toward a hierarchy of needs for the People's Republic of China. *The Journal of Applied Behavioral Science, 19*(3), 249–264.

Ng, S. H., Akhatar-Hossain, A. B. M., Ball, P., Bond, M. H., Hayashi, K., Lim, S. P., O'Driscoll, M. P., Sinha, D., & Yang, K. S. (1982). Human values in nine countries. In R. Rath, H. S. Asthara, D. Sinha, & J. B. H. Sinha (Eds.), *Diversity and unity in cross-cultural psychology: Selected papers from the 5th International Conference of the International Association for Cross-Cultural Psychology* (pp. 196–205). Lisse, Netherlands: Swets and Zeitlinger.

Osterweil, Z. & Nagano, K. N. (1991). Maternal views on autonomy: Japan and Israel. *Journal of Cross-Cultural Psychology, 22,* 363–375.

Parsons, T. (1951). *The social system.* Glencoe, IL: Free Press.

Pepitone, A. (1987). The role of culture in theories of social psychology. In Kagitçibasi, C. (Ed.), *Growth and progress in cross-cultural psychology* (pp. 12–22). Lisse, Netherlands: Swets and Zeitlinger.

Phalet, K. & Claeys, W. (1993). A comparative study of Turkish and Belgian youth. *Journal of Cross-Cultural Psychology, 24,* 319–343.

Razi, Z. (1993). The myth of the immutable English family. *Past and Present: A Journal of Historical Studies, 140,* 3–44.

Rokeach, M. (1973). *The nature of human values.* New York: Free Press.

Roland, A. (1988). *In search of self in India and Japan.* Princeton: Princeton University Press.

Rosen, B. C. (1962). Socialization and achievement motivation in Brazil. *American Sociological Review, 27,* 612–624.

Ross, L. (1977). The intuitive psychologist and his shortcomings: In L. Berkowitz (Ed.), *Advances in experimental social psychology* (Vol. 10), New York: Academic Press.

Ross, M. & Fletcher, G. J. O. (1985). Attribution and social perception. In G. Lindzey & E. Aronson (Eds.), *The handbook of social psychology* (3rd ed., Vol. 2, pp. 73–122). New York: Random House.

Sampson, E. E. (1987). Individuation and domination: Undermining the social bond. In C. Kagitçibasi (Ed.), *Growth and progress in cross-cultural psychology* (pp. 84–93). Lisse, Netherlands: Swets and Zeitlinger.

Sampson, E. E.(1988). The debate on individualism: Indigenous psychologies of the individual and their role in personal and societal functioning. *American Psychologist, 43,* 15–22.

Sampson, E. E. (1989). The challenge of social change for psychology: Globalization and psychology's theory of the person. *American Psychologist, 44,* 914–921.

Schwartz, B. (1986). *The battle of human nature: Science, morality, and modern life.* New York: Norton.

Schwartz, S. H. (1990). Individualism–collectivism: Critique and proposed refinements. *Journal of Cross-Cultural Psychology, 21,* 139–157.

Schwartz, S. H. (1992a). Universals in the content and structure of values: Theoretical advances and empirical tests in 20 countries. In M. Zanna (Ed.), *Advances in experimental social psychology, 25* (pp. 1–65). Orlando, FL: Academic.

Schwartz, S. H. (1992b). Cultural dimensions of values: Toward an understanding of national differences. Paper presented at the 25th International Congress of Psychology, Brussels, July 19–24, 1992.

Schwartz, S. H. (1994). Beyond individualism/collectivism: New cultural dimensions of values. In U. Kim, H. C. Triandis, C. Kagitçibasi, S-C. Choi, & G. Yoon (Eds.), *Individualism and collectivism: Theory, method and applications* (pp. 85–122). Thousand Oaks, CA: Sage.

Schwartz, S. H. & Bilsky, W. (1987). Toward a psychological structure of human values. *Journal of Personality and Social Psychology, 53,* 550–562.

Schwartz, S. H. & Bilsky, W. (1990). Toward a theory of the universal content and structure of values: Extentions and cross-cultural replications. *Journal of Personality and Social Psychology, 58,* 878–891.

Shweder, R. A. & Bourne, E. J. (1984). Does the concept of the person vary cross-culturally? In R. A. Shweder & R. A. LeVine (Eds.), *Culture theory: Essays on mind, self and emotion* (pp. 158–199). Cambridge: Cambridge University Press.

Shweder, R. A. & LeVine, R. A. (Eds.). (1984). *Culture theory.* New York: Cambridge University Press.

Singelis, T. M. (1994). The measurement of independent and interdependent self-construals. *Personality and Social Psychology Bulletin, 20,* 580–591.

Singelis, T. M. & Brown, W. P. (1995). Culture, self and collectivist communication: Linking culture to individual behavior. *Human Communication Research, 21,* 354–389.

Singelis, T. M., Triandis, H. C., Bhawuk, D. S., & Gelfand, M. (1995). Horizontal and vertical dimensions of individualism and collectivism: A theoretical and measurement refinement. *Cross-Cultural Research, 29,* 240–275.

Sinha, D. (1988). The family scenario in a developing country and its implications for mental health: The case of India. In P. R. Dasen, J. W. Berry, & N. Sartorius (Eds.), *Health and cross-cultural psychology: Toward applications* (pp. 48–70). Newbury Park, CA: Sage.

Sinha, D. & Tripathi, R. C. (1994). Individualism in a collectivist culture: A case of coexistence of opposites. In U. Kim, H. C. Triandis, C. Kagitçibasi, S-C. Choi, & G. Yoon (Eds.), *Individualism and collectivism: Theory, method and applications* (pp. 123–136). Thousand Oaks, CA: Sage.

Sinha, J. B. P. (1993). The bulk and the front of psychology in India. *Psychology and Developing Societies, 5,* 135–150.

Sinha, J. B. P. & Verma, J. (1987). Structure of collectivism. In C. Kagitçibasi (Ed.), *Growth and progress in cross-cultural psychology* (pp. 123–129). Lisse, Netherlands: Swets and Zeitlinger.

Smith, D. H. & Inkeles, A. (1966). The OM scale: A comparative social-psychological measure of individual modernity. *Sociometry, 29,* 353–377.

Smith, M. B. (1978). Perspectives on selfhood. *American Psychologist, 33,* 1053–1064.

Smith, M. B. (1994). Selfhood at risk: Post-modern perils and the perils of post-modernism. *American Psychologist, 49,* 405–411.

Smith, P. B. & Bond, M. H. (1993). *Social psychology across cultures.* Hartfordshire, England: Harvester/Wheatsheaf.

Smith, P. B., Dugan S., & Trompenaars, F. (1996). National culture and the values of organizational employees: A dimensional analysis across 43 nations. *Journal of Cross-Cultural Psychology, 27,* 231–264.

Spence, J.(1985). Achievement American style: The rewards and costs of individualism. *American Psychologist, 40,* 1285–1295.

Srull, T. K. & Gaelick, L. (1983). General principles and individual differences in the self as a habitual reference point: An examination of self–other judgements of similarity. *Social Cognition, 2,* 108–121.

Stipek, D., Weiner, B., & Li, K. (1989). Testing some attributio-emotion relations in the People's Republic of China. *Journal of Personality and Social Psychology, 56,* 109–116.

Taylor, C. (1985). *Philosophy and the human sciences: Philosophical papers, Vol. II.* Cambridge: Cambridge University Press.

Taylor, C. (1989). *Sources of the self: The making of the modern identity.* Cambridge, MA: Harvard University Press.

Thadani, V. N. (1978). The logic of sentiment: The family and social change. *Population and Development Review, 4*(3), 457–499.

Thornton, A. (1984). Modernization and family change. In *Social Change and Family Policies: Proceedings of the 20th International CFR Seminar.* Melbourne: Australian Institute of Family Studies.

Thornton, A. & Fricke, T. E. (1987). Social change and the family: Comparative perspectives from the West, China and South Asia. *Sociological Forum, 2,* 746–779.

Tönnies, F. (1887/1957). *Community and society.* (C. P. Loomis, trans.) East Lansing: Michigan State Press.

Triandis, H. C. (1984). Toward a psychological theory of economic growth. *International Journal of Psychology, 19,* 79–95.

Triandis, H. C. (1987). Individualism and social psychological theory. In C. Kagitçibasi (Ed.), *Growth and progress in cross-cultural psychology* (pp. 78–83). Lisse, Netherlands: Swets and Zeitlinger.

Triandis, H. C. (1988). Collectivism and individualism: A reconceptualization of a basic concept in cross-cultural psychology. In G. K. Verma & C. Bagley (Eds.), *Personality, attitudes and cognitions* (pp. 60–95). London: MacMillan.

Triandis, H. C. (1989). The self and social behavior in differing cultural contexts. *Psychological Review, 96*(3), 506–520.

Triandis, H. C. (1990). Cross-cultural studies of individualism and collectivism. In J. Berman (Ed.), *Cross-cultural perspectives: Nebraska Symposium on Motivation, 1989* (pp. 41–133). Lincoln: University of Nebraska Press.

Triandis, H. C. (1994a). *Culture and social behavior.* New York: McGraw-Hill.

Triandis, H. C. (1994b). Theoretical and methodological approaches to the study of collectivism and individualism. In U. Kim, H. C. Triandis, C. Kagitçibasi, S-C. Choi, & G. Yoon (Eds.), *Individualism and collectivism: Theory, method and applications* (pp. 41–51). Thousand Oaks, CA: Sage.

Triandis, H. C. (1995). *Individualism and collectivism.* Boulder, CO: Westview.

Triandis, H. C., Bontempo, R., Betancourt, H., Bond, M., Leung, K., Brenes, A., Georgas, J., Hui, C. H., Marin, G., Setiadi, B., Sinha, J. B. P., Verma, J., Spangenberg, J., Touzard, H., & de Montmollin, G. (1986). The measurement of etic aspects of individualism and collectivism across cultures. *Australian Journal of Psychology, 38,* 257–267.

Triandis, H. C., Bontempo, R., Villareal, M. J., Asai, M., & Lucca, N. (1988). Individualism and collectivism: Cross-cultural perspectives on self-ingroup relationships. *Journal of Personality and Social Psychology, 54,* 323–338.

Triandis, H.C., Chan, D. K.-S., Bhawuk, D. P. S., Iwao, S. & Sinha, J.B.P. (1995) Multimethod probes of allocentrism and idio-centrism. *International Journal of Psychology, 30,* 461–480.

Triandis, H. C., Hui, C. H., Albert, R. D., Leung, K., & Lisansky, J. (1984). Individual models of social behavior. *Journal of Personality and Social Psychology, 46,* 1389–1404.

Triandis, H. C., Leung, K., Villareal, M. V., & Clark, F. L. (1985). Allocentric versus idiocentric tendencies: Convergent and discriminant validation. *Journal of Research in Personality, 19,* 395–415.

Triandis, H. C., Marin, G., Lisansky, J., & Betancourt, H. (1984). *Simpatia* as a cultural script of Hispanics. *Journal of Personality and Social Psychology, 47,* 1363–1374.

Triandis, H. C., McCusker, C. & Hui, C. H. (1990). Multi-method probes of individualism and collectivism. *Journal of Personality and Social Psychology, 59,* 1006–1020.

Wallach, M. A. & Wallach, L. (1983). *Psychology's sanction for selfishness: The error of egoism in theory and therapy.* New York: Freeman.

Wallach, M. A. & Wallach, L. (1990). *Rethinking goodness.* Albany: State University of New York Press.

Weinreich, P. & Kelly, A. (1990). Collectivism and individualism in identity development: Muslim British and Anglo-Saxon British identities. Paper presented at the Individualism/Collectivism Workshop, Seoul, Korea, July, 1990.

Weisz, J. R., Rothbaum, F. M., & Blackburn, T. C. (1984). Standing out and standing in. *American Psychologist, 39,* 955–969.

Westen, D. (1985). *Self and society.* Cambridge: Cambridge University Press..

Wheeler, L., Reis, H. T., & Bond, M. H. (1989). Collectivism–individualism in everyday social life: The Middle Kingdom and the melting pot. *Journal of Personality and Social Psychology, 57,* 79–86.

White, G. & Kirkpatrick, J. (Eds.). (1985). *Person, self and experience: Exploring Pacific ethnopsychologies.* Berkeley: University of California Press.

Yamaguchi, S. (1994). Collectivism among the Japanese: A perspective from the self. In U. Kim, H. C. Triandis, C. Kagitçibasi, S-C. Choi, & G. Yoon (Eds.), *Individualism and collectivism: Theory, method and applications* (pp. 175–188). Thousand Oaks, CA: Sage.

Yamaguchi, S., Kuhlman, D. M., & Sugimori, S. (1992). *Universality of personality correlates and dimensionality of person's collectivistic tendencies.* Paper presented at the center for Korean Studies Colloquium, University of Hawaii, Honolulu, May, 1992.

Yang, C. F. (1988). Familism and development: An examination of the role of family in contemporary China Mainland, Hong Kong, and Taiwan. In D. Sinha & H. S. R. Kao (Eds.), *Social values and development: Asian perspectives* (pp. 93–123). London: Sage.

Yang, K-S. (1988). Will societal modernization eventually eliminate cross-cultural psychological differences? In M. H. Bond (Ed.), *The cross-cultural challenge to social psychology* (pp. 67–85). London: Sage.

Yu, A-B. & Yang, K-S. (1994). The nature of achievement motivation in collectivistic societies. In U. Kim, H. C. Triandis, C. Kagitçibasi, S-C. Choi, & G. Yoon (Eds.), *Individualism and collectivism: Theory, method, and applications* (pp. 239–250). Thousand Oaks, CA: Sage.

2

SOCIAL COGNITION

GÜN R. SEMIN[1]
Free University Amsterdam
The Netherlands

SANDRA M. ZWIER
Free University Amsterdam
The Netherlands

Contents

Introduction

The interface between social cognition and culture has a long history. It is an age-old concern and a central theme in the intellectual history of several disciplines including anthropology, and it is at the root of numerous issues that have long occupied philosophers of science.

As a theme, the culture–cognition interface enters the beginnings of systematic psychology through Wilhelm von Humboldt's (1767–1835) work on the relationship between language and thinking from a cultural perspective. His approach attempted, on the one hand, to combine variations in culture and mentality as they impact thinking and, on the other, it was concerned with a search for the "governing principle of human universality" (von Humboldt, 1836/1988). This work had a strong influence on the Völkerpsychologie that was to emerge with Lazarus and Steinhal (1860), which, among other things, was also concerned with examining the interplay between culture and cognition (cf. Jahoda, 1992; chapter by Jahoda & Krewer, volume 1, this *Handbook*).

In social psychology, the culture–cognition interface has not been a prominent domain for a long time, aside from sporadic excursions or theoretical debates on the status of social psychological knowledge (cf. Semin & Manstead, 1983). Analytic examinations of the cultural formation of the person have a long-standing tradition in the social sciences though (e.g., Mauss, 1938/1985). It is only with the growing awareness of the psychological relevance of systematic variations in how the person is culturally formed that a tradition of work on social cognition in culture has emerged (cf. Markus & Kitayama, 1991; Shweder, 1991; Shweder & Sullivan, 1990; Triandis, 1989, 1990; see also chapters by Miller, Volume 1, and Kagitçibasi, this volume). This tradition is in the process of developing a systematic framework of how the cultural formation of a person influences cognitive processes. In its extension, this approach has begun to systematically examine cultural variations in social cognitive processes, emotionality, and morality.

The domain in social cognition that has consistently attracted attention from a cultural perspective has been attribution processes. This is not surprising considering that attribution theory has been one of the most prolific research domains in social cognition since the late 1960s. Consequently, research conducted within an attribution theoretical framework will occupy a substantial part of this chapter. Indeed, the distinctive characteristic of this research is that whereas earlier cross-cultural attribution research was conducted with the vision of uncovering pan-cultural attribution processes, the more recent work has entailed the acknowledgement of cultural variations in attributional processes. In other words, the more recent developments consider *process* as being shaped by culture. Indeed, the gradual recognition of the culturally situated nature of cognition has led to a radical reversal in conceptions of social cognition. From a view that has considered the examination of *process* as fundamental and has deemed social psychology and cognitive social psychology as "nearly synonymous" (Markus & Zajonc, 1985, p. 137), the move has been toward regarding *content as process* (Markus &

Kitayama, 1991; Moscovici, 1984) and therefore argues that process must be culturally shaped. Thus, the earlier search for generality, namely the search for universally valid features or processes of social cognition, has increasingly had to come to terms with a more complex conceptual problem. This has been the exploration of the general within-cultural variation. In order to be able to achieve this, one of the distinctive developments has been the incorporation of cultural models into the conceptualization of social cognition—such that one could more profitably be speaking of *sociocultural cognition*. The distinctive character of this more recent theorizing and research is primarily that, in contrast to earlier research, there has been an increasing acknowledgment of the impact of culturally specific theories upon cognitive processes (e.g., Miller & Bersoff, 1992; Morris & Peng, 1994; Semin, Nandram, Goossens & Taris, 1995; Shweder & Bourne, 1982). The most widely utilized framework in this context has to do with the conceptualization of the person as a carrier of culture, that is, with the "cultural formation of the person" (Geertz, 1974; Shweder & Miller, 1991; Semin, 1995a). It is precisely the cultural context within which and by which the person is formed that has contributed to a more contextualized and systematic examination of cognitive processes. This development has proceeded in a manner in which it has influenced both attributional research, as we shall review in the following sections, and current mainstream social cognition that has to do with memory processes and spontaneous trait inferences (e.g., Newman, 1993; Uleman, in press; see also Shoda & Mischel, 1993). The pattern of work on attributional processes displays this pattern of change from a pan-cultural view of attribution processes to a culture-bound perspective of how people come to causal explanations for their own and others' behaviors.

The interest in social cognitive processes as a function of cultural variations has evolved alongside the older tradition of the language and cognition interface, which enjoys the status of being one of the older quests in Western intellectual history. The second central domain that is reviewed here is the recent work that has emerged on the interface between language and social cognition. Despite the centrality of this issue, the amount of systematic research from a cultural perspective on this subject is highly limited. This is in our view largely because social psychology has not been able to develop a clear handle on language that would make it amenable to systematic analysis (cf. Semin & Fiedler, 1991). The reason for this is that most work on language has not advanced a systematic framework that operationalizes the properties of linguistic devices in a way that allows researchers to generalize beyond highly specific phenomena.

In this chapter, we shall first provide an overview of research on attribution processes from a cultural perspective. We shall then turn to research on social cognition that has entailed an analysis of the influence of linguistic factors from a cultural perspective. We shall conclude with a series of observations about the directions in which social cognition work can profitably proceed and the advances that could be made by the introduction of conceptual and methodological discipline.

Culture and Attribution: The Cultural Context of Causal Explanations

Broadly speaking, attribution refers to the process by which social perceivers arrive at causal explanations for their own, as well as others', behaviors. It is not surprising that attributional processes have been the subject of substantial research from a cultural perspective given the long-standing influence of attribution theories within social and developmental psychology. In the following discussion, we shall provide an overview of the research that has evolved from the early seventies. As we suggested, the distinctive character of this research is that earlier research focused primarily upon attributional processes as "process." The conceptual separation of content from process, which was a hallmark of social cognition in general and attribution in particular, has however, turned out not to be a viable conceptual avenue in the examination of social cognition.

Individual Differences in Attributional Style

Given that attribution theory's main concern is the explanation of the perceived causes of behavior, an individual difference measure that allows one to distinguish between a preferentially internal or external attribution is of considerable interest. This becomes particularly relevant in a cross-cultural context where differences in attributional style across cultures are of central concern. It is within such a context that the "locus of control" concept (Rotter, Seeman, & Liverant, 1962; Rotter, 1966) has attracted considerable attention in cross-cultural psychology from the late 1960s onward.

Locus of control, as formulated by Rotter and colleagues, is a cognitive construct that uses the concept of reinforcement. *Internal* locus of control is a belief that reinforcement depends primarily upon one's own actions or, in other words, that one is in control of the events in one's life. *External* locus of control is the reverse belief, namely that reinforcement is primarily outside of one's control; consequently, the assumption is that one is not in control of the events in one's life. The introduction of the locus of control concept in 1966 resulted in an immediate and broadly shared interest in its cross-cultural variability. The most prominent question in this research is whether or not people from different cultural communities vary in the degree to which they display an external or internal locus of control. The most common prediction is that non-Western people display a stronger external locus of control than Western people because they may have, for example, less access to power, material recourses, social mobility, and so forth (cf. DuCette, Wolk, & Friedman, 1972; Hui, 1982; see also Tobacyk, 1992). Differences between rural and urban people (e.g., Kagan, 1976), high and low socioeconomic status (e.g., Scott & Phelan, 1969), minorities and majorities within a country (e.g., Alvarez & Padar, 1978), or women and men (e.g., Lee & Dengerink, 1992) have also been predicted, where the expectation was that urban, high SES, majority, and male participants will have higher internal locus of control than participants who are rural, low SES minority women.

Hui reviewed no less than ninety studies in 1982. These studies address questions much like the ones previously mentioned. His review covers a wide range of cultural communities from Puerto Rico (e.g., Pehazur & Wheeler, 1971), to Israel (e.g., Horowitz, 1979), to Ghana (e.g., Jahoda, 1970) and Thailand (Reitz & Groff, 1974). This comprehensive overview shows that there is scarcely any systematic pattern that would allow one to come to some general conclusions about variability in locus of control across cultures. For instance, when compared with Anglo-Americans, Hispanic populations within the United States have been found to be more external (e.g., Pehazur & Wheeler, 1971), equally external (e.g., Alvarez & Padar, 1978) as well as more internal (e.g., Cole & Cole, 1977) in locus of control and this is just one of the inconsistencies that has emerged in this research.

More recent research reports that Swedish women and Polish students have a more external locus of control than Americans (Lee & Dengerink, 1992; Tobacyk & Tobacyk, 1992), and that Fijian-Indians have a more internal control than Fijians (Kishor, 1983). Other recent studies have looked at some psychological consequences of locus of control. Ward and Kennedy (1993), for example, find that internal locus of control promotes psychological adjustment to novel environments and Kelley (1986) reports that in the United States, India, and Hong Kong external locus of control relates to self-destructiveness (e.g., heavy drinking, dangerous driving), but not in Venezuela.

The research to date suggests an inconsistent pattern and this appears to be due in large part to the absence of a theory relating culture to the conception of locus of control. The conception and application of the locus of control idea is founded on a tacit assumption of constituting a pan-cultural measure of systematic differences in attributional tendencies. Given that there is no provision for cultural variation in this individual differences measure and no attempt has been made to link it to any culture theory, the research to date inevitably remains an accumulation of noncumulative correlational evidence as a number of assessments of this research suggest. Indeed, the overall picture is rather inconsistent (cf. Fletcher & Ward, 1988) mainly for its lack of a culturally informed basis. For instance, Hui (1982) states that "while we can defend the construct's unidimensionality at least partially for a single culture, extending it to other cultures reflects insensitivity to cultural differences" (p. 315). Other authors have raised the question of the validity of a global measure. The critical question has been whether a global measure of generalized expectation for internal versus external control of reinforcement can capture the subtle differences across cultures. Trimble and Richardson (1982), for instance, maintain that in some cultural communities a distinction between personal control and ideological or societal control is of critical relevance. Munro (1986) maintains that for his Zimbabwean samples the questionnaire is not emically valid.

As a consequence of the diverse conceptual and methodological problems a number of authors have advanced alternative conceptions of control that may be expected to vary across cultures. Collins (1974) identifies four separate factors of the locus of control construct—difficult versus easy, predictable versus unpredictable, just versus unjust, and politically responsive versus unresponsive worlds.

Fletcher and Ward (1988) and Hui and Triandis (1983) suggest on the basis of their own research that the first two or three of these may be universally valid. More systematic research on this issue is lacking to date, however; it remains to be seen whether these approaches can be anchored with an informed and psychologically informative culture theory.

Attribution of Success and Failure

Achievement has been a focus of cultural research for a considerable amount of time. Earlier research focused on cultural variations in achievement motivation, which was concerned with the "need" to do things well and to the highest standards possible (McClelland, 1961). The more recent work has addressed achievement attribution theory (Weiner, 1986, 1992; Weiner et al., 1972), which is concerned with the thought processes underlying the perceived reasons as to why one succeeded or failed. The theory postulates that three dimensions are important in the causal analysis of success and failure situations. These are *stability* (stable versus unstable), *locus* (internal versus external) and a third dimension, namely *controllability* (Is the cause of failure or success controllable?). People react upon their assessment of whether they have succeeded or failed in an emotional way and then search for the cause of the outcome based upon the three postulated dimensions. This search is regarded as leading to a number of causes, which vary on the three dimensions, such as aptitude, effort, task difficulty, luck, and so forth.

In most general terms, the achievement attribution theory has found substantial support from a number of cross-cultural studies[2] (e.g., Bar-Tal, Goldberg, & Knaani, 1984; Louw & Louw-Potgieter, 1986; Schuster, Försterling, & Weiner, 1989; Stipek, Weiner, & Li, 1989; Watkins & Astilla, 1984; inter alia). Nevertheless, studies report differences between Western and non-Western samples (e.g., Crittenden, 1991; Dalal, Sharma, & Bisht, 1983; Gupta & Singh, 1981; Holloway, Kashiwagi, Hess, & Azuma, 1986; L'Armand, Pepitone, & Shanmugan, 1981; Mizokawa & Ryckman, 1990; Yan & Gaier, 1994; inter alia). However, to make sense of the many different results it is useful to distinguish between two separate questions, namely: (a) Are the dimensions of stability, locus, and controllability universally valid? and (b) Do people pan-culturally attribute success and failure to the same factors?

As we saw in the previous section on locus of control, the practice of offering people pre-selected response categories is highly problematic because such categories may not be emically valid everywhere (cf. Duda & Allison, 1989). This issue has been addressed by a number of authors who have used free- instead of prestructured response categories (e.g., Hortacsu & Karanci, 1987; Kashima & Triandis, 1986; L'Armand, Pepitone, & Shanmugam, 1981; Misra & Agarwal, 1985; Watkins & Astilla, 1984; inter alia). This research suggests that the factors of ability, effort, and task difficulty are commonly mentioned factors of achievement attribution across cultures (cf. Fletcher & Ward, 1988). The second question, which would appear to be answered affirmatively by the previously mentioned research is, however, not so straitforward. It invites consideration of a more basic issue.

This issue lies at the very heart of the curriculum of current social psychology. It is an inquiry into whether achievement attributions in particular, and attributional activities in general, are such a central or salient part of people's mental lives across cultures as it is generally (pre-)supposed (cf. Fiske & Taylor, 1991). No doubt, people across the world engage in attributional activity if asked, but this does not mean that this is a central feature of discourse in everyday life. In fact, the research reviewed in the following section puts the achievement attribution findings precisely into a culturally relative framework. It suggests that the biases in success and failure attribution are relative to cultural dimensions of self-conceptions (cf. Markus & Kitayama, 1991) that have to be taken into consideration in explaining the cultural differences in attribution patterns.

Self-Serving and Group-Serving Biases

The self-serving, or *egocentric* bias is defined as a tendency for actors to take credit for success and to disclaim responsibility for failure, and is a relatively well-established phenomenon (cf. Zuckerman, 1979; Nisbett & Ross, 1980). A study by Chandler, Shama, Wolf and Planchard (1981) that employed Indian, Japanese, South African, American, as well as Yugoslavian samples found an egocentric bias in all the cultures examined, with the exception of the Japanese sample where no such bias was found. In contrast, Watkins and Regmi (1990) did not find such a self-serving bias in Nepal, nor did Fry and Ghosh (1980), who report that Indian Asian children actually show a reversal of the self-serving bias; they chiefly attribute their own successes to luck and their failures to personal (in)abilities. This reversal of the self-serving bias, also referred to as a *modesty bias* (Markus & Kitayama, 1991), has now been documented by several authors, including Markus and Kitayama who review a number of studies employing samples mainly from Asian cultures. Kashima and Triandis (1986), who employed a sample of Japanese graduate students, also find evidence for a modesty bias (see also Boski, 1983; Hannover, 1995; Mizokawa & Ryckman, 1990; Nurmi, 1992 respectively, for Nigerian, East German, more Asian, and Finnish samples. See also Meijer & Semin, 1996). Finally, Yamaguchi (1988) also finds evidence for a modesty bias among Japanese students. In contrast, his data show that when explaining *others'* success and failure, these participants are more likely to attribute success to internal factors and failure to external factors. The latter is in essence a reversal of the so-called *group-serving bias* (cf. Hewstone & Jaspars, 1988). The group-serving bias refers to a tendency of making internal attributions for the in-group's success and the out-group's failure. The reverse tendency is found for in-group failure and out-group success, namely a tendency to make external attributions for the in-group's failure and the out-group's success. Thus, this is essentially an egocentric bias for explanations of the in-group's achievements, and a reverse tendency regarding achievements of the out-group. As the research reviewed in the previous section suggests, evidence for the existence of an egocentric bias in cross-cultural perspective is not unequivocal, nor is evidence for the existence of a group-serving bias in this perspective (e.g., Taylor & Jaggi, 1974, versus Boski, 1983). Recent evidence, however, suggests that the self-serving as well as the group-serving bias may be moderated by a number of factors (cf. Smith & Bond, 1993; Fletcher & Ward, 1988). Bond, Hewstone, Wan, and Chui (1985) show, for example, that for Chinese subjects anonymity can play a central role in the emergence or non- emergence of a group-serving bias. Chinese participants showed a group-serving bias in explaining gender characteristics. However, this was only evident in the absence of an audience. In the presence of an audience the Chinese showed a reversal of the group-serving bias. Consistent with earlier American evidence, Bond et al.'s American participants displayed a group-serving bias under both the presence and absence of an audience. Wan and Bond (1982) replicated these results with respect to the egocentric/modesty bias. They found evidence for an egocentric bias for the Chinese under conditions of anonymity. However, this egocentric bias disappeared under non-anonymity conditions.

In considering the group-serving bias, additional sociocultural factors such as group rivalry have been noted to play a mediating role. Hewstone and Ward (1985), for example, report that the minority group of Chinese students in Malaysia show a reversal of the group-serving bias. In contrast, the majority group of Malay students show a group-serving bias. The same study further showed that Chinese students in Singapore, where Chinese people are not negatively stereotyped, do not show a reversal of the group-serving bias. A study by Hunter, Stringer, and Coleman (1993) on a difference between Protestant and Catholic adolescents in Northern Ireland also shows the role of similar mediating factors. The results of these studies suggest that social–political dominance of the in-group to which one belongs, group rivalry, and conditions under which responses are given can be of crucial importance with respect to the existence of group-serving or modesty biases. Indeed, such factors have also been shown to be of critical importance in research examining these issues from a noncomparative perspective (cf. Tajfel & Turner, 1979; Maass & Arcuri, 1996).

The Infusion of Culture into Social Cognition

The most important feature of the work reviewed in the previous section is that the theories (e.g., Kelley, 1967; Rotter, Seeman, & Liverant, 1962; Weiner et al., 1972) that have driven comparative work across cultures have not considered how cultural factors might affect the properties or processes that they postulate. The implicit assumption was that the processes or properties postulated by the theory are pan-cultural. This tacit assumption was largely predicated by a Western cultural perspective that regards the individual as a fundamental analytic unit. Thus, the individual is regarded as a self-contained whole, whose cognitive, motivational, and behavioral processes constitute the core of any psychological analysis. This view has met with an increasingly critical reception in the social sciences.

One source of challenge has come from a group of interrelated and influential meta-theoretical orientations such as social constructionism and ethnogenetics. The other challenge, which predates these meta-theoretical orientations, comes from cross-cultural sociology, anthropology, social history, and literary and art history. These disciplines have questioned the treatment of the individual as an independent unit of analysis, both scientifically and socially. In particular, they have advanced converging evidence for the fundamental cultural formation of the person. It is within this framework that psychologists have become increasingly aware of the impact of culture and have imported the construct of individualism–collectivism (cf. Hofstede, 1980) and developed a number of aligned terms (e.g., independence versus interdependence, Markus & Kitayama, 1991; ego-centered versus socio-centered, Shweder & Bourne, 1982; inter alia) to mark the psychological translation of this cultural difference in the formation of the person (see chapter by Kagitçibasi, this volume, for detail). The introduction of these constructs has had critical implications for conceptions of social cognition. Markus and Kitayama (1991), in this context, suggest the following: "How a given object is culturally construed and represented in memory should importantly influence and even determine how one thinks about the object" (p. 231). In earlier social cognition research the introduction of the cultural dimension constituted an interesting, but essentially unnecessary, luxury. The growing trend in social cognition research is, however, a move toward the increasing inevitability of investigating cultural dimensions as integral constituents to not only understand and explain social cognition but also to construct any theory that proposes any claim to generality (cf. Semin, 1995a). The recent influential work by Markus and Kitayama (1991), Shweder and Sullivan (1990, 1993), or Triandis (1989, 1990) has introduced precisely such an intellectual innovation within social cognition research. This development marks an important departure from earlier work that was driven by a concern of examining variations between cultures on "culture-free" psychological variables or processes.

The basic idea that increasingly impacts on social cognition research[3] is that the self is fundamentally culturally situated. "The self or the identity is critical because it is the psychological locus of cultural effects. It functions as a mediating, orienting, and interpretative framework that will systematically bias how members of a given sociocultural group will think, feel, and act." (Markus & Kitayama, 1991, p. 6). For Markus and Kitayama, a viable starting point is the assumption of an essential difference between independent and interdependent self-construals which have to do with the extent to which the self and others are seen as fundamentally connected to each other. Likewise, Shweder and Bourne (1982) stress the cultural situatedness of social thought as a function of the way the person is culturally constituted by distinguishing between socio-centered and ego-centered conceptions of the person. Essentially, these distinctions refer to the different reference points by which identities are regulated in different cultures (cf. Trafimow, Triandis, & Goto, 1991; Triandis, 1989). Whereas collectivist, interdependent, or socio-centered conceptions of the person are to be found in cultural communities in which the group is more important, identity definition is largely reliant upon the interdependencies that persons have, and norms, obligations and duties regulate social relationships; the contrasting analytic distinction is made for cultures that engage in practices emphasizing an individualistic, independent, or ego-centered conception of the person. Autonomy, rules, and independence from others characterize the person here (see chapter by Kagitçibasi, this volume, for detail). The major implication of this analytic distinction for social cognition has been that all cognitive processes that implicate identities will systematically vary as a function of the manner in which identity is culturally constituted (cf. Markus & Kitayama, 1991). This has led to the beginning of an interesting change in the way in which researchers are beginning to approach social cognition.

Cultural Variations in Social Cognition

Research on cultural social cognition has consistently found variations in the types of social representations that exist in a number of cultural communities. One such variation is a systematic difference between concrete and abstracted social representations (e.g., Cousins, 1989; Gudykunst, Ting-Toomey, & Chua, 1988; Miller, 1984; Semin, Nandram, & Goossens, 1996; Shweder & Miller, 1991). By social representations, we refer here to the types of explanatory frameworks subjects espouse in investigations into, for instance, attributional processes. Within attributional approaches this has been expressed by a reference to dispositional, trait-like explanations manifested by individualistically oriented people versus situationally oriented explanations of social events as a function of a more collectivistic self-construal. Newman (1993), for instance, was able to demonstrate that American participants who were strongly individualistic were more likely to spontaneously interpret behavior in dispositional or trait terms than participants who were less strongly individualistic. That is, he was able to demonstrate in a reaction-time study that spontaneous trait inferences, which are assumed to mediate recall process for social events, are moderated by cultural factors. A cued recall paradigm provided partial support for this outcome (cf. Uleman, in press).

Miller (1984) examined different patterns of explanation used by American and Indian Hindu children. The question she addressed was whether Indian Hindu children will show a growing trend toward explaining the causes of social behavior (deviant and pro-social) in dispositional terms with age. Such a growing trend has been reported for American children (cf. Eisert & Kahle, 1986). However, because Indian Hindu children live in societies where socio-centered rather than ego-centered conceptions of the person are prevalent, Miller predicted that Indian Hindu children will not show this same trend toward a dispositional explanatory mode. Indeed, on average she finds that whereas American children display an increasing preferential dispositional explanation for the causes of social behavior with age, such an increase is absent in the case of Hindu Indian children. Thus, Indian Hindu children do not display the fundamental attribution error (cf. Nisbett & Ross, 1980), namely a tendency to underestimate the impact of the social–situational factors and overestimate the role of dispositional factors in controlling behavior. American subjects, however, display precisely this tendency. Miller's work

(1984) shows that dispositional attribution is a cultural (i.e., individualistic) model of explanation that abstracts properties that are centered upon the person from contextual factors.

The ecological validity of Miller's study was tested by Morris and Peng (1994, study 2). They selected two sets of articles from English and Chinese newspapers, both involving comparable crimes utilizing the same content analytic framework as the one employed by Miller (1984), namely, segmenting articles into clauses and coding each unit according to whether it constituted a disposition-based causal explanation for the event or a contextual–situational explanation. Their research shows that whereas American reporters used more personal dispositions to explain the crime, Chinese reporters used more situational attributions. Thus, while American reporters displayed the "fundamental attribution error," Chinese reporters did not. In their third study, Morris and Peng (1994) show that the weightings of dispositional and situational causes for recent murders varied as a function of the cultural background of respondents.

Both Miller (1984) and Morris and Peng (1994) regard their studies as bolstering the view that variable concepts of the person translate into differences in the way social events are referred to and explained. They have not attempted so far, however, to empirically clarify the contribution of such a dimension as a mediating variable. An explanation of cultural differences in attributional patterns in terms of interdependent versus independent concepts of the person was, however, bolstered in a recent study by Meijer and Semin (1996). They found that participants from a more individualistic background (Dutch) showed more of a self-serving tendency in their attribution of life-events than did a comparable Japanese sample with a more collectivistic background. In this study, it was subsequently shown, however, that the very cultural dimension that differentiated the two samples from one another also co-varied with the observed attributional tendencies, thereby bolstering the view that concepts of the person indeed can explain a critical amount of variance in attributional tendencies.

Further explorations of the influence of cultural models of the person on attribution can be found in Kashima, Siegal, Tanaka, and Kashima (1992). These authors show that the cultural models for the explanation of behaviors in everyday life are also driven by different references, namely a dispositional explanation by individualists and a situational one by collectivists. When subjects are presented with an essay expressing extreme political views, the Australian participants regard this as expressing the author's own attitude on the subject. In contrast, Japanese respondents are found not to make the same strong inferences regarding the author's attitudes. This research suggests that the attitude–behavior link may also be driven by cultural models. Overall, the diverse research studies (Cousins, 1989; Kashima et al., 1992; Miller, 1984; Morris & Peng, 1994; Shweder & Bourne, 1982; Shweder & Miller, 1991) that explore the relationship between cultural formation of the person and attributional preferences in the explanation of the causes of social behavior show that a theory incorporating assumptions about the cultural formation of the person leads to predictions that cannot be derived from a culture-free theory of attribution and furnish a better understanding of how sociocultural cognition functions.

The interesting question that arises in the context of causal explanations is whether cultural models of explanation make different provisions for social events versus nonsocial events. This is, indeed, one specific approach to the question of universal versus those cognitive processes that are more specifically influenced by cultural frames. Morris and Peng (1994) address this question with an ingenious experiment in which they are able to show that whereas Chinese and American students do not differ in their causal perceptions of physical events, they are shown to differ in their causal perceptions of social behavior. Whereas the American students rely on internal causes, Chinese students are shown to rely on external causes.

The collectivistic tendency for a more situational or social explanation of the causes of behavior versus the individualistic tendency for a more abstracted dispositional explanation is the common pattern displayed across these studies. This is the more general principle of concrete versus abstracted explanatory modes that seems to co-vary with the different cultural formations of the person.

The next section shows that this attributional tendency can be seen also in the case of how people across different cultural communities that vary in individualism and collectivism attribute morality.

Cultural Bases of the Attribution of Morality

The reconceptualization of culture with regard to how it shapes the psychological field of the person has similarly given research on morality and attributions of morality a renewed impetus (e.g., Haidt, Koller, & Dias, 1993; Miller, 1994). The formulation of culture and the cultural constitution of the person in a thus operationally tangible manner dovetailed with the emerging critique of the prominent Kohlbergian conception of morality (e.g., Kohlberg, 1981) by Gilligan (1977, 1982). The earlier Kohlbergian work was shaped by a conceptual paradigm that regarded morality as based on principles of justice and regarded the stages of moral development as universal (cf. chapter by Eckensberger & Zimba, Volume 2, this *Handbook*). Gilligan's critique emphasized the justice-based model's neglect of a contextually sensitive morality that is based on benevolence and care. Her view is that Kohlbergian morality typically ignores gender differences in the constitution of morality. Similarly, Miller and her colleagues (e.g., Miller & Bersoff, 1992, 1994; Miller, Bersoff, & Harwood, 1990) argue that conceptions of morality vary across cultures: A justice-based notion of morality that emphasizes the autonomy of the individual and individual rights is a cultural framework for morality that is found predominantly in individualistic cultural contexts. This type of morality entails the application of rules that are impartial, and relies upon standards and principles that are equally applicable to everybody. In contrast, in cultural communities where a collectivistic or interdependent orientation is predominant, as in the case of Hindu Indians, Miller argues (1994) that morality constitutes a social practice that should be understood in terms of a duty-based interpersonal code. She further argues that a caring or benevolence framework as suggested by Gilligan (e.g., 1977) is also integrally an individually oriented moral code. Miller's research (Bersoff & Miller, 1993; Miller & Bersoff, 1992; Miller & Luthar, 1989) suggests that conceptions of morality vary cross-culturally. For instance, whereas helping friends and strangers in a variety of situations is perceived to be a personal choice in the United States, in India subjects perceive such situations to entail a moral obligation. Further, these researchers demonstrated that in situations where Americans attribute a right to choose one's own actions, Hindu Indians endorse social regulation, interference, or punishment. Overall, this research strand demonstrates that attributions of morality are strongly embedded in cultural frames. The analytic construct of contrasting the cultural formation of the person between individualistic and collectivistic orientations provides a useful perspective in explaining not only cultural variations in the attribution of morality, but such an analysis also puts scientific conceptions of morality into a relative perspective.

More recently, Haidt, Koller, and Dias (1993) have extended the cultural approach to morality (cf. Shweder, 1991) by showing that culturally shaped emotions have a strong impact on morality and ascription of morality. In particular, they showed that in a collectivistic community affective reactions were better predictors of moral judgments with reference to actions that were disgusting or disrespectful than in more individualistic communities. In such collectivistic communities these actions were also judged with a moralizing stance, whereas North American students judged such acts as having to do with social conventions or personal preferences.

Haidt et al.'s (1993) research points to a direction in which the research on attributions of morality can fruitfully progress, that is, a direction in which careful consideration of affect and emotion and their role in moral judgments are made. This is a sorely neglected area, in large part because this domain has always been considered a prerogative of cognition rather than emotion. In fact, this orientation in itself can be regarded as conditioned by a Western individualistic conception of morality—namely, to consider attribution of morality as the domain of cold cognition. No doubt, even in individualistic cultural contexts issues entailing morality are highly emotive and entail emotion-arousing dilemmas. In our view, it is this direction that future research on the cultural examination of attributions of morality could follow.

The Language–Cognition Interface

Despite the age of the linguistic relativism hypothesis (Berry, Poortinga, Segall, & Dasen, 1992; Brown, 1986; Whorf, 1956) and its precursors, the literature on social cognition merely displays a sporadic and certainly nonsystematic interest in the role that language plays in social cognition. Language research has not contributed to the study of social cognition until recently for at least two reasons. The first one is similar to the reluctance of addressing cultural variations in cognition, namely the distinction between content and process and the *implicit* view that anything to do with language is largely content. The second one is due to the difficulty in developing a handle on language that allows one to examine it in a clearly objective and systematic manner within the context of the types of questions that arise in social cognition. It is therefore not surprising that a variety of the recent studies displaying differences in the causal explanations of social behavior, or the explanation of morality, rely on "intuitive" analyses of often open-ended verbal material. Indeed, most of the innovative recent work relies on content analytic investigations of verbal material produced by respondents (e.g., Miller, 1984; Morris & Peng, 1994) with regard to the types of causal explanations people employ. These types of investigations can also be conducted with a careful analysis of the predicates that are employed in the narratives supplied by participants, if one has a grounded theory of the implicational properties of interpersonal predicates (e.g., Semin & Fiedler, 1991). It is therefore quite important for cultural research in social cognition to develop a clearer understanding of linguistic tools and their properties, if the aim is to understand how linguistic tools in their culturally located use reflect specific theories about, for instance, differing explanations of the causes of social behavior. The original and long-standing intellectual interest in the interface between language and thought referred to at the beginning of this chapter was motivated precisely by a concern to understand the impact of culture on thought via language. We now turn to those aspects of this issue that are relevant to social cognition. For the reasons noted earlier, the amount of systematic research on this subject is relatively limited. Furthermore, interest in more general research on linguistic relativity has been waning over the years (cf. Brown, 1986). We now focus on the work on language and social cognition that derives from the Sapir-Whorfian heritage.[4]

The Whorfian Hypothesis and Social Cognition

The literature addressing the issue of the language–cognition interface has begun to depart from the original formulations of this conceptual problem toward treating language as a tool (cf. Semin, 1995b) and investigating how the availability of different linguistic tools in alternative cultural communities introduces differential cognitive "burdens" (Hunt & Banaji, 1988). Consequently, the availability of specific linguistic devices or tools in a particular language can diminish, for instance, the load on working memory. An experiment by Hoffman, Lau, and Johnson (1986) supports this view. These authors hypothesized that the differential availability of certain trait terms (adjectives) in English and Chinese will influence memory-related schematic functions. For example, in English it is possible to combine a number of diverse behaviors under the adjectives *artistic* or *liberal*. These devices do not exist in Chinese. That is, the potential behaviors that characterize the two types described by these adjectives are also available in Chinese, but not embedded in one overarching adjective. In contrast, there are no overarching adjectives available in English for the two Chinese adjectives *shì gù* (greater than average experience of the world, strong family orientation, and well-developed social and interpersonal skills) and *shēn cáng bú lòu* (very knowledgeable and skilled, reluctant to display this knowledge and skill, and inconspicuous). When Chinese–English bilinguals, who were randomly assigned to the Chinese or English-speaking conditions, are given the character descriptions to read and subsequently asked to make a number of behavioral inferences an interesting pattern of inferences emerged. Subjects made stronger schema-congruent inferences as a function of the language condition; that is, the availability of the linguistic schema (adjective) is seen to facilitate within-language condition inferences. Thus, if, for example, a specific behavioral description of the artistic type was read in English, then subjects were more likely to infer from such a behavioral description that this person "drinks heavily at times and likes to try out hallucinogenic drugs" than if it was read in Chinese. The idea is that the behavior description activates a higher order concept (adjective) which then mediates further inferences that would have been less likely if the adjective was not available in language. Note then, that since Hoffman et al. used Chinese bilinguals randomly assigned to either the English- or the Chinese speaking conditions, it seems relatively unlikely that any such effect could be attributed to cultural differences between the two groups.[5] These findings are in line with Hunt and Banaji's (1988) concept label availability notion that different linguistic devices or tools have different facilitating effects on schematic cognitive processing. An extension of this framework is to consider the function of linguistic tools in communication. Hunt and Agnoli (1991) suggest that "different languages lend themselves to the transmission of different types of messages. People consider the costs of computation when they reason about a topic. The language that they use will partly determine those costs. In this sense, language does influence cognition" (p. 379).

The main tenor of this work is to emphasize the differential burdens that languages may place on different cognitive processes (e.g., those involved in memory processes as well as those in the transmission of messages). The view that this approach suggests is that certain thought processes are more likely to occur or be communicated in one language than in another. These ideas, which have potential relevance to social cognition, are still in need of more systematic empirical investigation however.

The question as to whether there are systematic differences between Western and non-Western language and thinking was raised by Bloom's work (1981). The general question can be phrased in terms of the degree to which abstract versus concrete forms of reasoning characterize the respective cultural communities. Bloom (1981) introduced this discussion after an investigation of political thinking in Hong Kong. When he asked his respondents the question, *"If the Chinese government had . . . how would you have reacted?,"* Bloom was startled by the fact that the majority of his respondents answered *"It hasn't."* Bloom then made a study of the Chinese language and concluded that English has a particular constellation of linguistic patterns that encourages a mode of abstract thinking among speakers of English that cannot be found in Chinese. To test his argument, he focused, among others, on counterfactual thinking.[6] Bloom claims that although the Chinese language has a grammatical construction for counterfactual statements such as "If the government had . . . how would you" this is in fact rarely used in daily life. As a result, the Chinese may be less inclined to think counterfactually than, for instance, the English. Bloom supported his hypotheses with some experiments but was severely criticized by Au (1983) who argued that Bloom's findings were chiefly due to un-idiomatic translations rather than anything else. She showed that using her own translations of Bloom's tasks, Chinese were perfectly able to engage in counterfactual reasoning (cf. Au, 1984; Bloom, 1984).

The crux of this debate concerned the question of whether the Chinese were in fact less capable of counterfactual, or rather abstract thinking, than the Americans. This does not seem to be the case (see also Liu, 1985; Takano, 1989; Vorster & Schuring, 1989). What this debate missed out on is, however, an emphasis on the general *use* of language or performance rather than the competence notion. That is, are forms such as counterfactuals more likely to occur within an American everyday conversation rather than a Chinese one? Bloom's observations may be seen as concurring with the earlier arguments we presented. These suggest that collectivistically oriented communities may have a more concrete style of social thought than individualistic communities (e.g., Shweder & Bourne, 1982; Miller, 1984). As argued above, and as, for example, shown by Miller (1984), such differences are not due to general cognitive deficits but rather are due to different cultural orientations. Unfortunately, these typically social cognition studies have not assessed the types of linguistic devices upon which their findings are based. What is thus required is a systematic examination of which linguistic tools or devices are available across different cultural communities (cf. Dixon, 1977) and how they are used. This type of systematic investigation is one direction that could contribute to a clearer understanding of the relationship between language and social cognition in terms of both what the linguistic toolbox of a cultural community contains in terms of devices or tools, and which of these devices are used, when, and for which purposes. The focus of such an approach to the shaping of linguistic practices on conceptions of reality dates back to Hoijer (1954) and Hymes (1964) who argued that the active use of lexical and grammatical categories has a bearing on the everyday analysis of experience and not the mere presence or absence of these categories. In our view, this is the direction that a convergence between a cultural social cognition approach and language could fruitfully take. One tentative study showing whether the tools available across different linguistic communities have comparable properties is supplied by Brown (1986). He provides evidence that a particular inferential property of interpersonal verbs (that is, verbs that are used to describe social events and relations between people) is shared by distinctly different linguistic communities. The inferential property in question is what has originally been termed 'implicit causality' (Brown & Fish, 1983). This can be best illustrated with the following examples. In the following two sentences:

1. John trusts David because of the type of person *he is.*
2. John helps David because of the type of person *he* is.

The personal pronoun in the subsidiary clauses of 1 and 2 are ambiguous. When asked, participants predominantly disambiguate the first "he" to David and the "he" in the second sentence to John. This disambiguation is assumed to be mediated by an inference process that has been referred to as the "causality implicit in interpersonal verbs." The general assumption and finding is that in a "Subject–verb–Object" sentences *verbs of state* (e.g., trust, like, hate) mediate an inference to the grammatical sentence object as the (cause) *initiator of an event*. In contrast, in similar sentences constructed with *verbs of action* (e.g., help, cheat, push) the inference is to the grammatical sentence subject as the (cause) *initiator of the event*. Such interpersonal verbs thus mediate inferences that have to do with causal inferences in an attributional sense (cf. Semin & Fiedler, 1991). Brown's (1986) research suggests that these inferences are comparable across different linguistic communities (i.e., Chinese, English, and Japanese). This work on the properties of interpersonal language and the research we reviewed on culturally informed social cognition (e.g., Miller, 1984; Morris & Peng, 1994) has as yet not converged but could be one potential avenue to illuminate differences and similarities in tool *use*, which would complement differences and similarities in tool *availability*.

Conclusions and Future Directions

The distinctive feature of what has been happening over the recent years in social cognition is the transition from an acultural, process-oriented modus to one that has increasingly become more aware of the contribution of cultural factors to social cognitive processes. This impetus is primarily attributable to the fruitful translation of an analytic framework that has emerged in the social sciences about the cultural formation of the person. The psychological translation of this analytic framework, particularly in the hands of authors such as Triandis (1989), Markus and Kitayama (1991), or Shweder and Sullivan (1990, 1993), has led to innovative and pacesetting studies that may change the face of social cognition work. Yet, there is still a substantial degree of theoretical and methodological sophistication that is possible and that could contribute to further inroads into the informed explanation of variations and generalities in social cognition, or better sociocultural cognition.

There are two major inroads that the more immediate research in this field can easily make. On a theoretical front, the major change, in our view, is a move from a single construct examination of phenomena to a multiple or convergent construct examination. We already noted an instance of this approach in the context of research on the attribution of moral responsibility. As we mentioned, affect and emotion play an integral role in situations where moral judgements are made. Haidt, Koller, and Dias's (1993) research has begun to show that there is a clear link between affective and cognitive processes in moral judgment, but this is only one facet of what we intend when referring to convergent construct investigations that are theoretically linked. If we pursue the moral judgement example, aside from the emotional features of such situations that require more systematic examination, there are also a number of other interrelated judgments such as those of attributions of responsibility, the influence that others have upon the decisions made in such situations, and so on. In our view, a cultural approach to social cognition invites considering a multiple construct approach (cf. Semin, Nandram, Goossens, & Taris, 1995) which investigates interrelationships between diverse cognitive, emotive, and interpersonal facets of social phenomena in a systematic dependence from cultural factors. One of the advantages of such a "syndromic" approach to the examination of social cognition is that while it increases the complexity of the phenomena under examination it also reduces the possible variations that are afforded by alternative explanations. That is, the more the constructs postulated to vary in interdependence and as a function of culture are interrelated, the more grounded an explanation one can afford. The number of interdependent constructs that are postulated in such an explanatory framework effectively increases the strength of explanation, assuming that the empirical evidence is convergent. In fact, part of the reasoning that is behind a convergent construct approach leads to the type of methodological concern that has to be addressed more systematically in future research.

The distinctive feature of the more recent social cognition work from a cultural perspective is, as we have repeatedly noted, its attendance to incorporating a psychological translation of particular cultural dimensions that are significant for psychological functioning, such as the cultural formation of the person. And, yet, with no exception, the work on cultural social cognition does not empirically demonstrate the contribution of this factor (however operationalized) to the systematic differences observed in social cognitive processing. That is, there are at least two substantial shortcomings of the research that can be avoided. The first one is a clear indication that the samples being compared and being postulated to be coming from distinct cultural communities are also clearly different on the cultural dimension that they are assumed to be varying. Assuming that there are no differences on a number of variables other than those that are postulated to account for the variation in cognitive processes is useful but not sufficient. What is required is: (a) a clear indication that the two (or more) samples assumed to be different on the postulated cultural dimension also *do* vary on this dimension. And, more importantly, it should be a methodological requirement that (b) the cultural dimension that is postulated to contribute to the variation in social cognition is also shown to co-vary with or mediate the process that is under investigation. The absence of such an indication or measure has, as a consequence, the inevitable uncertainty that the differences that are obtained co-vary with other variables that are not measured but nevertheless differ between the two samples that have provided the data. The absence of such measures is somewhat surprising considering that there are numerous suggestions of how to measure differences in cultural orientations with respect to how the person is culturally formed (e.g., Hui, 1988; Kim, Triandis, Kagitçibasi, Choi, & Yoon, 1994; Triandis, McCusker, & Hui, 1990; inter alia). The manner in which it should be possible to achieve the detection of patterns of generality within variation in social cognition is, in our view, by expanding the theoretical net that is cast by a convergent construct approach and making sure that the conceptual fish are ecologically viable by ascertaining that they fit the dimensions that are relevant for their intellectual consumption.

Endnotes

1. The writing of this chapter was in part facilitated by a grant from the Netherlands Organization for Scientific Research (NWO), grantnr. PGS 56-381, to the first author.

2. Kelley's (1967) attribution theory did not get nearly as much attention. For an exception, see a study by Cha and Nam (1985) which shows that Korean subjects essentially use consensus, distinctiveness, and consistency information in the way Kelley's theory suggests.

3. It should be noted that the impact of this work is not only on social cognition, but also on emotion processes, inter alia (cf. Markus & Kitayama, 1994).

4. Recent work that does not fall within the immediate domain of psychology will thus not be discussed, but see for example Lucy (1992), Friedriech (1990), or Silverstein, (1987).

5. In fact, there was a third condition consisting of English monolinguals only. The difference between both English speaking conditions was non-significant, which bolsters the hypothesis that this effect was due to language rather than culture. Subsequently, it must be noted that not all hypotheses in this experiment regarding the effects of concept labels on schematic thinking were supported.

6. Counterfactuals are after-the-fact thoughts, such as "If James Dean would still be alive, people would have forgotten about him."

References

Alvarez, C. M. & Padar, O. F. (1978). Locus of control among Anglo-Americans and Cuban-Americans. *The Journal of Social Psychology, 105,* 195–198.

Au, T. K-F. (1983). Chinese and English counterfactuals: The Sapir–Whorf hypothesis revisited. *Cognition, 15,* 155–187.

Au, T. K-F. (1984). Counterfactuals: In reply to Bloom. *Cognition, 17,* 289–302.

Bar-Tal, D., Goldberg, M., & Knaani, A. (1984). Causes of success and failure and their dimensions as a function of SES and gender: A phenomenological analysis. *British Journal of Educational Psychology, 54,* 51–61.

Berry, J. W., Poortinga, Y. H., Segall, M. H., & Dasen, P. R. (1992). *Cross-cultural psychology: Research and applications.* Cambridge: Cambridge University Press.

Bersoff, D. M. & Miller, J. G. (1993). Culture, context and the development of moral accountability judgments. *Developmental Psychology, 29,* 664–676.

Bloom, A. H. (1981). *The linguistic shaping of thought: A study of the impact of language on thinking in China and the West.* Hillsdale, NJ: Lawrence Erlbaum.

Bloom, A. H. (1984). Caution—the words you use may affect what you say: A response to Au. *Cognition, 17,* 275–87.

Bond, M. H., Hewstone, M., Wan, K. C., & Chui, C. K. (1985). Group-serving attributions across intergroup contexts: Cultural differences in the explanation of sex-typed behaviors. *European Journal of Social Psychology, 15,* 435–451.

Boski, P. (1983). A study of person perception in Nigeria: Ethnicity and self vs. other attributions for achievement-related outcomes. *Journal of Cross-Cultural Psychology, 14,* 85–108.

Brown, R. (1986). Linguistic relativity. In S. H. Hulse & B. F. Green (Eds.), *One hundred years of psychological research in America: G. Stanley Hall and the Johns Hopkins tradition* (pp. 241–276). Baltimore: Johns Hopkins University Press.

Brown, R. & Fish, D. (1983). The psychological causality implicit in language. *Cognition, 14,* 237–273.

Cha, J. H. & Nam, K. D. (1985). A test of Kelley's cube theory of attribution: A cross-cultural replication of McArthur's study. *Korean Social Science Journal, 12,* 151–180.

Chandler, T. A., Shama, D. D., Wolf, F. M., & Planchard, S. K. (1981). Multiattributional causality: A five cross-national samples study. *Journal of Cross-Cultural Psychology, 12*, 207–221.

Cole, D. & Cole, S. (1977). Counternormative behavior and locus of control. *Personality and Social Psychology Bulletin, 1*, 351–353.

Collins, B. E. (1974). Four components of the Rotter internal–external scale: Belief in a difficult world, a just world, a predictable world, a politically responsive world. *Journal of Personality and Social Psychology, 29*, 381–391.

Cousins, S. D. (1989). Culture and self-perception in Japan and the United States. *Journal of Personality and Social Psychology, 56*, 124–131.

Crittenden, K. S. (1991). Asian self-effacement or feminine modesty? Attributional patterns of women university students in Taiwan. *Gender and Society, 5*, 98–117.

Dalal, A. K., Sharma, R., & Bisht, S. (1983). Causal attributions of ex-criminal tribal and urban children in India. *The Journal of Social Psychology, 119*, 163–171.

Dixon, R. M. W. (1977). Where have all the adjectives gone? *Studies in Language I, 1*, 19–80.

Duda, J. L. & Allison, M. T. (1989). The attributional theory of achievement motivation: Cross-cultural considerations. *International Journal of Intercultural Relations, 13*, 37–55.

Du Cette, J., Wolk, S., & Friedman, S. (1972). Locus of control and creativity in black and white children. *The Journal of Social Psychology, 88*, 297–298.

Eisert, D. C. & Kahle, L. R. (1986). The development of social attributions: An integration of probability and logic. *Human Development, 29*, 61–81.

Fiske, S. T. & Taylor, S. E. (1991). *Social cognition.* New York: McGraw-Hill.

Fletcher, G. J. O. & Ward, C. (1988). Attribution theory and processes: A cross-cultural perspective. In M. H. Bond (Ed.), *The cross-cultural challenge to social psychology* (pp. 230–244). Beverly Hills: Sage.

Friedriech, P. (1990). Language, ideology, and political economy. *American Anthropologist, 91*, 295–312.

Fry, P. S. & Ghosh, R. (1980). Attributions of success and failure: Comparisons of cultural differences between Asian and Caucasian children. *Journal of Cross-Cultural Psychology, 11*, 343–363.

Geertz, C. (1974). From the native's point of view: On the nature of anthropological understanding. In K. Basso & H. Selby (Eds.), *Meaning in anthropology* (pp. 221–237). Albuquerque: University of New Mexico Press.

Gilligan, C. (1977). In a different voice: Women's conception of the self and of morality. *Harvard Educational Review, 47*, 481–517.

Gilligan, C. (1982). *In a different voice: Psychological theory and women's development.* Cambridge, MA: Harvard University Press.

Gudykunst, W. B., Ting-Toomey, S., & Chua, E. (1988). *Culture and interpersonal communication.* Newbury Park, CA: Sage.

Gupta, M. & Singh, R. (1981). An integration-theoretical analysis of cultural and development differences in attribution of performance. *Developmental Psychology, 17*, 816–825.

Haidt, J., Koller, S. H., & Dias, M. G. (1993). Affect, culture, and morality, or is it wrong to eat your dog? *Journal of Personality and Social Psychology, 65*, 613–628.

Hannover, B. (1995). Self-serving biases and self-satisfaction in East versus West German subjects. *Journal of Cross-Cultural Psychology, 26*, 176–188.

Hewstone, M. & Jaspars, J. M. F. (1988). Intergroup relations and attribution processes. In H. Tajfel (Ed.), *Social identity and intergroup relations* (pp. 121–141). Cambridge: Cambridge University Press.

Hewstone, M. & Ward, C. (1985). Ethnocentrism and causal attribution in Southeast Asia. *Journal of Personality and Social Psychology, 48*, 614–623.

Hoffman, C., Lau, I., & Johnson, D. R. (1986). The linguistic relativity of person cognition: An English–Chinese comparison. *Journal of Personality and Social Psychology, 51*, 1097–1105.

Hofstede, G. (1980). *Culture's consequences: International differences in work-related values.* Beverly Hills: Sage.

Hoijer, H. (1954). The Sapir–Whorf hypothesis. In

H. Hoijer (Ed.), *Language in Culture* (pp. 92–105). Chicago: University of Chicago Press.

Holloway, S. D., Kashiwagi, K., Hess, R. D., & Azuma, H. (1986). Causal attributions by Japanese and American mothers and children about performance in mathematics. *International Journal of Psychology, 21,* 269–286.

Horowitz, R. T. (1979). Jewish immigrants to Israel: Self-reported powerlessness and alienation among immigrants from the Soviet Union and North America. *Journal of Cross-Cultural Psychology, 10,* 366–374.

Hortacsu, N. & Karanci, A. N. (1987). Premarital break-ups in a Turkish sample: Perceived reasons, attributional dimensions and affective reactions. *International Journal of Psychology, 22,* 57–74.

Hui, C. H. (1982). Locus of control: A review of cross-cultural research. *International Journal of Intercultural Relations, 6,* 301–323.

Hui, C. H. (1988). Measurement of individualism–collectivism. *Journal of Research in Personality, 22,* 17–36.

Hui, C. H. & Triandis, H. C. (1983). Multistrategy approach to cross-cultural research: The case of locus of control. *Journal of Cross-Cultural Psychology, 14,* 65–83.

Humboldt, W., von. (1836/1988). *On language.* Cambridge: Cambridge University Press.

Hunt, E. & Agnoli, F. (1991). The Whorfian hypothesis: A cognitive psychology perspective. *Psychological Review, 98,* 377–389.

Hunt, E. & Banaji, M. R. (1988). The Whorfian hypothesis revisited: A cognitive science view of linguistic and cultural effects on thought. In J. W. Berry, S. H. Irvine, & E. B. Hunt (Eds.), *Indigenous cognition: Functioning in cultural context* (pp. 57–84). Dordrecht, Netherlands: Nijhoff.

Hunter, J. A., Stringer, M., & Coleman, J. T. (1993). Social explanations and self-esteem in Northern Ireland. *The Journal of Social Psychology, 133,* 643–650.

Hymes, D. (1964). Two types of linguistic relativity (with examples from Amerindian ethnography). In W. Bright (Ed.), *Sociolinguistics: Proceedings of the UCLA Sociolinguistics Conference* (pp. 114–167). The Hague: Morton de Gruyter.

Jahoda, G. (1970). Supernatural beliefs and changing cognitive structures among Ghanaian university students. *Journal of Cross-Cultural Psychology, 1,* 115–130.

Jahoda, G. (1992). *Crossroads between culture and mind.* Hemel Hempstead, England: Harvester/Wheatsheaf.

Kagan, S. (1976). Preference for control in rural Mexican and urban Anglo-American children. *Revista Interamericana de Psicologia, 10,* 51–59.

Kashima, Y., Siegal, M., Tanaka, K., & Kashima, E. S. (1992). Do people believe behaviors are consistent with attitudes? Towards a cultural psychology of attribution processes. *British Journal of Social Psychology, 31,* 111–124.

Kashima, Y. & Triandis, H. C. (1986). The self-serving bias in attributions as a coping strategy: A cross-cultural study. *Journal of Cross-Cultural Psychology, 17,* 83–97.

Kelley, H. H. (1967). Attribution theory in social psychology. In D. Levine (Ed.), *Nebraska Symposium on Motivation* (pp. 192–241). Lincoln: University of Nebraska Press.

Kelley, K. (1986). Chronic self-destructiveness and locus of control in cross-cultural perspective. *The Journal of Social Psychology, 126,* 573–577.

Kim, U., Triandis, H. C., Kagitçibasi, C., Choi, S-C., & Yoon, G. (1994). *Individualism and collectivism: Theory, method, and applications.* Thousand Oaks, CA: Sage.

Kishor, N. (1983). Locus of control and academic achievement: Ethnic discrepancies among Fijians. *Journal of Cross-Cultural Psychology, 14,* 297–308.

Kohlberg, L. (1981). *The philosophy of moral development: Moral stages and the idea of justice: Vol. 1. Essays on moral development.* New York: Harper and Row.

L'Armand, K., Pepitone, A., & Shanmugan, T. E. (1981). Attitudes toward rape: A comparison of the role of chastity in India and the United States. *Journal of Cross-Cultural Psychology, 12,* 284–303.

Lazarus, M. & Steinthal, H. (1860). Einleitende Gedanken über die Völkerpsychologie, als Einladung zu einer Zeitschrift für Völkerpsychologie und Sprachwissenschaft. *Zeitschrift für Völkerpsychologie und Sprachwissenschaft, 1,* 1–73.

Lee, V. K. & Dengerink, H. A. (1992). Locus of control in relation to sex and nationality. *Journal of Cross-Cultural Psychology, 23,* 488–497.

Liu, L. (1985). Reasoning counterfactually in Chinese: Are there any obstacles? *Cognition, 21,* 239–270.

Louw, J. & Louw-Potgieter, J. L. (1986). Achievement-related causal attributions: A South African cross-cultural study. *Journal of Cross-Cultural Psychology, 17,* 269–282.

Lucy, J. A. (1992). *Language diversity and thought: A reformulation of the linguistic relativity hypothesis.* Cambridge: Cambridge University Press.

Maass, A. & Arcuri, L. (1996). Language and stereotyping. In N. Macrae, M. Hewstone & C. Stangor (Eds.), *The foundations of stereotypes and stereotyping* (pp. 17–28). New York: Guilford Press.

Markus, H. & Zajonc, R. B. (1985). The cognitive perspective in social psychology. In G. Lindzey & E. Aronson (Eds.), *The handbook of social psychology,* 3d ed. (Vol. 1, pp. 127–230). New York: Random House.

Markus, H. R. & Kitayama, S. (1991). Culture and the self: Implications for cognition, emotion and motivation. *Psychological Review, 98,* 224–253.

Markus, H. R. & Kitayama, S. (Eds.). (1994). *Emotion and culture: Empirical studies of mutual influence.* Washington, DC: American Psychological Associations.

Mauss, M. (1938/1985). A category of the human mind: The notion of self. In M. Carrithers, S. Collins, & S. Lukes (Eds.), *The category of the person* (pp. 1–25). Cambridge: Cambridge University Press.

McClelland, D. C. (1961). *The achieving society.* New York: Free Press.

Meijer, Z. Y. & Semin, G. R. (1996). When the self-serving bias does not serve the self: Attributions of success and failure in cultural perspective. Unpublished ms. under editorial consideration.

Miller, J. G. (1984). Culture and the development of everyday social explanation. *Journal of Personality and Social Psychology, 46,* 961–978.

Miller, J. G. (1994). Cultural diversity in the morality of caring: Individually oriented versus duty based interpersonal moral codes. *Cross-Cultural Research, 28,* 3–39.

Miller, J. G. & Bersoff, D. M. (1992). Culture and moral judgment: How are conflicts between justice and interpersonal responsibilities resolved? *Journal of Personality and Social Psychology, 62,* 541–554.

Miller, J. G. & Bersoff, D. M. (1994). Cultural influences on the moral status of reciprocity and the discounting of endogenous motivation. *Personality and Social Psychology Bulletin, 97,* 592–602.

Miller, J. G., Bersoff, D. M., & Harwood, R. L. (1990). Perceptions of social responsibilities in India and the United States: Moral imperatives or personal decisions? *Journal of Personality and Social Psychology, 58,* 33–47.

Miller, J. G. & Luthar, S. (1989). Issues of interpersonal responsibility and accountability: A comparison of Indians' and Americans' moral judgments. *Social Cognition, 7,* 237–261.

Misra, G. & Agarwal, R. (1985). The meaning of achievement: Implications for cross-cultural theory of achievement motivation. In I. R. Lagunes & Y. H. Poortinga (Eds.), *From a different perspective: Studies of behavior across cultures* (pp. 250–266). Lisse, Netherlands: Swets and Zeitlinger.

Mizokowa, D. T. & Ryckman, D. B. (1990). Attributions of academic success and failure: A comparison of six Asian-American ethnic groups. *Journal of Cross-Cultural Psychology, 21,* 434–451.

Morris, M. W. & Peng, K. (1994). Culture and cause: American and Chinese attributions for social and physical events. *Journal of Personality and Social Psychology, 67,* 949–971.

Moscovici, S. (1984). The phenomenon of social representation. In R. Farr & S. Moscovici (Eds.), *Social representations* (pp. 5–71). Cambridge: Cambridge University Press.

Munro, D. (1986). Work motivation and values: Problems and possibilities in and out of Africa. *Australian Journal of Psychology, 38,* 285–296.

Newman, L. S. (1993). How individualists interpret behavior: Idiocentrism and spontaneous trait inference. *Social Cognition, 11,* 243–269.

Nisbett, R. & Ross, L. (1980). *Human inference: Strat-*

egies and shortcoming of social judgment. Englewood Cliffs, NJ: Prentice Hall.

Nurmi, J. E. (1992). Cross-cultural differences in self-serving bias: Responses to the attributional style questionnaire by American and Finnish students. *The Journal of Social Psychology, 132,* 217–222.

Pehazur, L. & Wheeler, L. (1971). Locus of perceived control and need achievement. *Perceptual and Motor Skills, 33,* 1281–1282.

Reitz, H. J. & Groff, G. K. (1974). Comparisons of locus of control categories among American, Mexican and Thai workers. *Proceedings of the Annual Convention of the APA, 7,* 263–264.

Rotter, J. (1966). Generalized expectancies for internal versus external control of reinforcement. *Psychological Monograph, 80*(1), 1–28.

Rotter, J., Seeman, M., & Liverant, S. (1962). Internal versus external locus of control of reinforcement: A major variable in behavior theory. In F. Washburne (Ed.), *Decisions, values and groups.* Elmsford, NY: Pergamon.

Schuster, B., Försterling, F., & Weiner, B. (1989). Perceiving the causes of success and failure: A cross-cultural examination of attributional concepts. *Journal of Cross-Cultural Psychology, 20,*191–213.

Scott, J. D. & Phelan, J. G. (1969). Expectancies of unemployable males regarding source of control reinforcement. *Psychological Reports, 25,* 911–913.

Semin, G. R. (1995a). Individualism–collectivism. In A. S. R. Manstead & M. Hewstone (Eds.), *An encyclopaedic dictionary of social psychology* (pp. 320–324). Oxford: Blackwell.

Semin, G. R. (1995b). Interfacing language and social cognition. *Journal of Language and Social Psychology, 14,* 182-194.

Semin, G. R. & Fiedler, K. (1991). The linguistic category model, its basis, applications, and range. In W. Stroebe & M. Hewstone (Eds.), *European review of social psychology* (Vol. 2, pp. 1–31). Chichester, England: Wiley.

Semin, G. R. & Manstead, A. S. R. (1983). The epistemological foundations of accountability of conduct. In G. R. Semin & A. S. R. Manstead, *The accountability of conduct: A social psychological analysis* (pp. 156–177). London: Academic.

Semin, G. R., Nandram, S., Goossens, A., & Taris, T. (1996). The cultural configuration of emotion: A convergent construct approach. Under editorial consideration.

Shoda, Y. & Mischel, W. (1993). Cognitive social approach to dispositional inferences: What if the perceiver is a cognitive social theorist? *Personality and Social Psychology Bulletin, 19,* 574–585.

Shweder, R. A. (1991). Cultural psychology: What is it? In R. A. Shweder, *Thinking through cultures* (pp. 73–110). Cambridge, MA: Harvard University Press.

Shweder, R. A. & Bourne, E. J. (1982). Does the concept of the person vary cross-culturally? In A. J. Marsella & G. White (Eds.), *Cultural conceptions of mental health and therapy.* Boston: D. Reidel.

Shweder, R. A. & Miller, J. G. (1991). The social construction of the person: How is it possible? In R. A. Shweder, *Thinking through cultures* (pp. 156–185). Cambridge, MA: Harvard University Press.

Shweder, R. A. & Sullivan, M. A. (1990). The semiotic subject of cultural psychology. In L. A. Pervin (Ed.), *Handbook of personality: Theory and research* (pp. 399–415). New York: Guilford.

Shweder, R. A. & Sullivan, M. A. (1993). Cultural psychology: Who needs it? *Annual Review of Psychology, 44,* 497–523.

Silverstein, M. (1987). Cognitive implications of a referential hierarchy. In M. Hickmann (Ed.), *Social and functional approaches to language and thought* (pp. 17–38). Cambridge: Cambridge University Press.

Smith, P. B. & Bond, M. H. (1993). *Social psychology across cultures: Analysis and perspectives.* Hemel Hempstead, England: Harvester/ Wheatsheaf.

Stipek, D., Weiner, B., & Li, K. (1989). Testing some attribution–emotion relations in the People's Republic of China. *Journal of Personality and Social Psychology, 56,* 109–116.

Tajfel, H. & Turner, J. C. (1979). An integrative theory of intergroup conflict. In S. Worchel & W.G. Austin (Eds.), *The social psychology of intergroup relations* (pp. 33–47). Monterey, CA: Brooks/Cole.

Takano, Y. (1989). Methodological problems in cross-cultural studies of linguistic relativity. *Cognition, 31*, 141–162.

Taylor, D. M. & Jaggi, V. (1974). Ethnocentrism and causal attribution in a South India context. *Journal of Cross-Cultural Psychology, 5*, 162–171.

Tobacyk, J. J. (1992). Changes in locus of control beliefs in Polish university students before and after democratization. *The Journal of Social Psychology, 132*, 217–222.

Tobacyk, J. J. & Tobacyk, Z. S. (1992). Comparisons of belief-based personality constructs in Polish and American university students: Paranormal beliefs, locus of control, irrational beliefs, and social interests. *Journal of Cross-Cultural Psychology, 23*, 311-325.

Trafimow, D., Triandis, H.C. & Goto, S.G. (1991). Some tests of the distinction between the private self and the collective self. *Journal of Personality and Social Psychology, 60*, 649–655.

Triandis, H. C. (1989). The self and social behavior in differing cultural contexts. *Psychological Review, 96*, 506–520.

Triandis, H. C. (1990). Cross-cultural studies of individualism and collectivism. In J. Berman (Ed.), *Nebraska Symposium on Motivation* (pp. 41–133). Lincoln: University of Nebraska Press.

Triandis, H. C., McCusker, C., & Hui, C. H. (1990). Multimethod probes of individualism and collectivism. *Journal of Personality and Social Psychology, 59*, 1006–1020.

Trimble, J. E. & Richardson, S. S. (1982). Locus of control measures among American Indians: Cluster structure, analytic characteristics. *Journal of Cross-Cultural Psychology, 13*, 228–238.

Uleman, J. S. (In press). Toward a view of personality traits as experience-near, theory-based, language- and culture-bound concepts. In G. R. Semin & K. Fiedler (Eds.), *Culture, language and social cognition.*

Vorster, J. & Schuring, G. (1989). Language and thought: Developmental perspectives on counterfactual conditionals. *South African Journal of Psychology, 19*, 34–41.

Wan, K. C. & Bond, M. H. (1982). Chinese attributions for success and failure under public and anonymous conditions of rating. *Acta Psychologica Taiwanica, 24*, 23–31.

Ward, C. & Kennedy, A. (1993). Psychological and socio-cultural adjustment of foreign students in Singapore and New Zealand. *Journal of Cross-Cultural Psychology, 24*, 146–158.

Watkins, D. & Astilla, E. (1984). The dimensionality, antecedents, and study methods correlates of the causal attribution in Filipino children. *The Journal of Social Psychology, 124*, 191– 199.

Watkins, D. & Regmi, M. (1990). Self-serving bias: A Nepalese investigation. *The Journal of Social Psychology, 130*, 555–556.

Weiner, B. (1986). *An attributional theory of motivation and emotion.* New York: Springer-Verlag.

Weiner, B. (1992). *Human motivation: Metaphors, theories and research.* Newbury Park, CA: Sage.

Weiner, B., Frieze, I., Kukla, A., Reed, L., Rest, S., & Rosenbaum, R. M. (1972). Perceiving the causes of success and failure. In E. E. Jones, D. E. Kanouse, H. H. Kelley, R. E. Nisbett, S. Valines & B. Weiner (Eds.), *Attribution: Perceiving the causes of behavior.* Morristown, NJ: General Learning Press.

Whorf, B. L. (1956). *Language, thought and reality: Selected writings of Benjamin Lee Whorf.* New York: Wiley.

Yamaguchi, H. (1988). Effects of actor's and observer's roles on causal atttribution by Japanese subjects for success and failure in competative situations. *Psychological Reports, 63*, 619–626.

Yan, W. & Gaier, E. L. (1994). Causal attributions for college success and failure. *Journal of Cross-Cultural Psychology, 25*, 146–158.

Zuckerman, M. (1979). Attribution of success and failure revisited, or the motivational bias is alive and well in attribution theory. *Journal of Personality, 47*, 245–287.

3

VALUES[1]

PETER B. SMITH
University of Sussex
England

SHALOM H. SCHWARTZ
The Hebrew University
Israel

Contents

Introduction

In her chapter on values in the first edition of this *Handbook,* Zavalloni (1980) concluded that values were likely to reappear as a major focus of psychological research. At least in the delimited area of cross-cultural psychology, this expectation has been substantially fulfilled (Bond & Smith, 1996). Most of the currently popular models of cultural variation rest upon analyses of value differences. Indeed, the Individualism/Collectivism model has become so influential as to merit a separate chapter in this *Handbook* (Kagitçibasi, this volume). The present chapter places this development within a broader framework and should be read in conjunction with Kagitçibasi's chapter. We will locate values studies in the wider context of cross-cultural psychology and clarify the distinction between individual-level and culture-level value dimensions. We will then examine the nature of these two sets of dimensions and how they have been used to describe and explain individual and cultural differences. This is an exciting and very active field of investigation; but because it is still young, there are many methodological problems and theoretical confusions to which attention must be drawn.

Why Study Values as a Way of Understanding Culture?

The early phase in the development of cross-cultural psychology was largely preoccupied with comparisons of different cultural groups on various attributes. As both differences and similarities were detected, an increasing need was felt for a theoretical framework to guide enquiries. Researchers recognized the decreasing benefits attained from simple comparisons of two or three cultural groups, selected on grounds of convenience, and the potential gains from sample selection guided by a theory that could suggest where to seek the data and how to explain observed differences in attributes.

Ecocultural theories have been one important advance (Berry, 1979; Berry, 1994; Georgas & Berry, 1995). They seek to clarify how the ecological (physical environment, climate, resources, etc.) and sociopolitical contexts may lead to cultural adaptations that, in turn, influence individual behavior and characteristics. Sample selection that represents different contexts can therefore aid in developing explanations for differences in cultural practices and psychological variables. However, ecological and sociopolitical contexts are distant from the cultural and psychological variables that cross-cultural psychologists usually wish to understand. Spelling out and testing possible explanatory links would be facilitated by working with mediating variables more closely related to culture and to psychology. The appeal of values is that they can play this role.

On the one hand, as we shall elaborate, the value priorities prevalent in a society are a key element, perhaps the most central, in its culture, and the value priorities of individuals represent central goals that relate to all aspects of behavior. On the other hand, values are directly influenced by everyday experiences in changing ecological and sociopolitical contexts. Values are therefore well-suited for examining the ongoing processes of cultural and individual change in response to historical and social changes. They can also be used to differentiate among the cultural and subcultural groups that have emerged as human communities have evolved in different directions in response to their unique experiences.

A summary of the many definitions of values suggests the main features on which most theorists agree (Schwartz & Bilsky, 1987):

1. Values are beliefs. But they are not objective, cold ideas. Rather, when values are activated, they become infused with feeling.
2. Values refer to desirable goals (e.g., equality) and to the modes of conduct that promote these goals (e.g., fairness, helpfulness).
3. Values transcend specific actions and situations. Obedience, for example, is relevant at work or in school, in sports or in business, with family, friends or strangers
4. Values serve as standards to guide the selection or evaluation of behavior, people, and events.
5. Values are ordered by importance relative to one another. The ordered set of values forms a system of value priorities. Cultures and individuals can be characterized by their systems of value priorities.

A major virtue of the concept of values for cross-cultural research is its relative abstraction and generality. Attitudes and behaviors have specific situational referents and studies of them are therefore often less well-suited to the formulation of cross-cultural generalizations. The observation that people's behavior is often inconsistent with their declared values has caused skepticism regarding the utility of building a psychology based on values. There is growing evidence, however, that analyses of the multiple, competing value priorities relevant in a situation can reveal consistent relations of individual's values to their attitudes (Feather, 1995) and behavior (Schwartz, 1996). Moreover, as we will discuss, the prevailing value priorities in societies also show meaningful and consistent relations to other societal attributes.

Measuring Values: Methods and Special Cross-Cultural Problems

Individual persons and cultural spokespersons may not have conscious access to abstractly defined systems of values (Zavalloni, 1980). Accepting this point, some cross-cultural researchers prefer to infer values indirectly from nonverbal behaviors, from responses to questions on specific topics that may express underlying values, or from cultural products like movies or literature. But indirect inferences are also problematic: researchers' own interpretations color all inferences, and they may easily misconstrue the effects of situational or behavior-specific factors as evidence of underlying values. Most researchers ask about basic values directly. This follows the tradition, initiated by Rokeach (1973), that focuses on the values that people consciously use to guide and justify decisions.

While many early studies measured values by means of interviews, essays, or open-ended questions, almost all contemporary cross-cultural studies of values use structured questionnaires. Most exceptions are found within studies of indigenous psychologies (Kim & Berry, 1993). The most widely used method is to ask respondents about their endorsement of particular values presented as single words, short phrases, or paragraphs describing a general goal orientation. Typically, the response format enables the respondent to differentiate the strength of endorsement along a rating scale. Van de Vijver & Leung (see chapter in Volume 1, this *Handbook*) explore the full range of methodological hazards inherent in this and other types of cross-cultural measurement. We discuss here only two issues that are absolutely central to the validity of cross-cultural studies of values and are often ignored.

Response Bias

Respondents from different cultures vary in the way they typically respond to rating scale formats, some using more extreme responses, for example, while others use more moderate responses. The researcher's dilemma is that there is no certain way to determine whether such variations are best understood as an artifact induced by the measurement instrument or as "true" differences in the attributes of samples from different cultures. Treating response bias as artifact and employing procedures that eliminate it may actually remove substantively important cross-cultural variance. Leaving bias untreated may cause misattribution of artifactual differences to culture. Theoretically grounded hypotheses about how value priorities relate to other variables can help in distinguishing whether differences in use of response scales reflect substantive differences or measurement bias (Schwartz, Verkasalo, Antonovsky, & Sagiv, in press). Bias probably accounts for response scale differences more than substance, if hypotheses are confirmed more strongly after correcting for scale use.

Several procedures for correcting response bias, both at the level of culture means and of individual differences, have been proposed (Leung, 1989; Leung & Bond, 1989; see van de Vijver & Leung, Volume 1, this *Handbook*, for a full review). Most commonly used is standardizing data within subjects (e.g., Hofstede, 1980). An alternative approach is to ask respondents to rank values in terms of relative importance (e.g., Rokeach, 1973), thereby avoiding rating scales entirely.

Meaning Equivalence

The second problem is to establish whether the values studied have the same meaning in different cultures. Even with the best translations, we cannot be confident that value expressions have equivalent meanings in different languages and cultures. On the other hand, working with the local value expressions in each language and culture provides no obvious way to determine whether these value expressions are distinctive or overlap with those found elsewhere. The predominant emphasis of the discipline of psychology has been upon identifying universals, whether of cognition, affect, or behavior. This emphasis has led, in cross-cultural psychology, to the predominance of measures termed "imposed-etics" by

Berry (1969). That is, instruments formulated within one culture (most frequently the United States) are imposed on other cultures, with the untested assumption that their meaning is relatively unchanged. There is obviously good reason to question this assumption.

Values researchers sometimes cope with the problem of meaning equivalence by asking whether the structure of relations among the values they study is similar within each culture (Bond, 1988; Schwartz, 1992; Triandis et al., 1993). The meaning of a value is understood as its associations—positive, negative, and neutral—with other concepts. If values have similar meanings across cultures, the intercorrelations among these values should be similar too. If the meanings of values differ from one culture to another, the intercorrelations among the values should differ as well. Researchers usually assess the degree of similarity in the patterns of intercorrelations by performing factor analyses or multidimensional scaling analyses on the whole set of values, separately within each culture. They then compare the factors, dimensions or regional configurations of values that emerge in each culture. Values are taken to have reasonably equivalent meanings in the different cultures if they are located on similar factors or dimensions, or in similar spatial regions. If similar factors, dimensions or regions do not emerge in each culture, or if values have quite different locations, meaning equivalence must be rejected.

Pan-cultural factor analysis (Leung & Bond, 1989) is another method used to identify basic individual value dimensions across cultures (e.g., Bond, 1988; Triandis et al., 1993). In this method, individuals from all the cultural groups are included in a single factor analysis, usually following within-subject and within-group standardizations of individual responses. Although this method extracts individual-level dimensions, it does not address the question of meaning equivalence. If the meanings of the items are equivalent across the set of cultures studied, the pan-cultural factors will be meaningful. There is no assurance, however, that the dimensions extracted represent the structure of values within any of the separate cultures. Only if the pan-cultural dimensions also emerge in the within-culture analyses can they be used confidently in cross-cultural work.

Progress in clarifying the basic dimensions of values depends upon more rigorous application of existing criteria for assessing the equivalence of factors and dimensions against chance levels of similarity or upon developing and applying new criteria. Many of the claims for equivalence in the literature do not fulfill existing criteria.

Levels of Analysis: Individual and Cultural

Cross-cultural research on values takes place at two distinct levels of analysis, individual and cultural. For individual persons, values represent the motivational goals that serve as guiding principles in their lives (Rokeach, 1973; Schwartz & Bilsky, 1987, 1990). Relations among different values reflect the psychological dynamics of conflict and compatibility that individuals experience when pursuing values in everyday life. Individuals cannot easily seek authority for themselves and try to be humble at the same time, for example, but they can simultaneously pursue authority and wealth. The intercorrelations among the value ratings made by individual persons reflect the underlying dimensions that organize individual values.

Less well-understood is the distinctive cultural level. When values are used to characterize cultures, what is sought are the socially shared, abstract ideas about what is good, right, and desirable in a society or other bounded cultural group (Williams, 1968). The societal institutions in which people pass their lives express cultural value priorities by their goals and modes of operation (Schwartz, in press). For example, in societies where individual ambition and success are highly valued, the economic and legal systems are likely to be competitive (e.g., capitalist markets and adversarial legal proceedings). In contrast, a cultural emphasis on group well-being is likely to be expressed in more cooperative systems (e.g., socialism and mediation).

When people carry out their roles in social institutions, they draw upon cultural values to decide what behavior is appropriate and to justify their choices to others. Cultural value priorities also affect the way social resources are invested. For example, the relative importance attributed to values such as wealth, justice, and beauty in a society partly determines whether the money, land, and human capital that are available are invested more in industrialization, social welfare, or preserving the environment. As standards, cultural value priorities also influence how organizational performance is evaluated—for instance, in terms of productivity, social responsibility, innovativeness, or support for the existing power structure.

Relations among different values at the cultural level reflect the social dynamics of conflict and compatibility that emerge as social institutions pursue their goals. These relations are not necessarily the same as those at the individual level. For instance, although a simultaneous emphasis on authority and humility is incompatible at the individual level, as noted above, it is compatible at the cultural level. The social system will run more smoothly if people accept authority as a desirable basis for organizing human relations and humility as the appropriate response toward those with greater authority. Because relations among value priorities at the two levels may differ, the underlying dimensions that organize values may differ too. Culture-level dimensions must be derived from the correlations among value priorities that characterize cultural groups, that is, by taking the group (e.g., nation) as the unit of analysis and computing correlations across many cultural groups.

The relations of prevailing cultural values to other attributes of cultures may also differ from the relations of parallel individual level values to parallel attributes of individuals. For instance, Hui, Yee, and Eastman (1995) found that scores on Hofstede's culture-level individualism variable correlated positively across 45 nations with mean scores for job satisfaction. In contrast, their individual-level analysis in Hong Kong revealed a negative correlation between high job satisfaction and individualist attitudes. To assume that a finding obtained at one level of analysis will hold true at the other is to commit the ecological fallacy (Hofstede,

1980). Cross-cultural research on values has been insufficiently vigilant against this error.

Preliminary Conclusion

For the most part, cross-cultural research on values has been driven by the results of influential studies (especially that of Hofstede, 1980) whose conclusions rest upon data derived from imposed-etic measures. Such studies have given substantial impetus to the study of cross-cultural psychology in general. Now that this momentum has been achieved, it is time to attend more closely to improving our data. In particular, it is critical to establish that our instruments have reasonably equivalent meanings across the cultures studied. We will note those studies that have at least tried to do this. The most defensible approach is to start with parallel, emic studies within many different cultures, seeking convergence in the structures of values chosen for study. This accords with Berry's (1989) recommendations for finding "derived-etics."

The structure of this chapter reflects the importance we attribute to the distinction between individual- and culture-level studies of values. Two aspects of the distinction should be noted. First, the dimensions that underlie value priorities at the two levels may not be the same. Second, the choice of appropriate level depends upon the type of question asked: If it is about relations of individual differences in value priorities to variation on other individual attributes, individual-level value dimensions should be used, even when individuals from different cultural groups are studied. If the question is about relations of cultural differences in prevailing values to variation across cultures on other variables, culture-level value dimensions should be used, even if these other variables are frequencies of individual behavior. Below we address studies at these two levels in separate sections.[2]

Individual-Level Dimensions of Values

Contemporary individual-level studies of values fall rather clearly into two groups, those whose approach builds upon the work of Rokeach and those who were influenced by the conceptions advanced by Hofstede and Triandis.

The Rokeach Legacy

Rokeach (1973) stimulated renewed interest in values among psychologists by providing a clear definition of the concept and developing an easily administered instrument that operationalized his view of values as guiding principles in life. The specific values included in the Rokeach Value Survey (RVS) were intended to be comprehensive while avoiding redundancy. Respondents ranked two lists of 18 values each according to their personal importance. Cross-cultural applications compared the rank orders of values in different cultural groups. Rokeach reported differences within the United States, for example, between groups defined by race, age, and education, as well as cross-national comparisons to be discussed later. He also reported how values and value change relate to many types of attitudes and behaviors (political, racial, gender, and personal habits; see also Ball-Rokeach, Rokeach, & Grube, 1984). Feather (1975, 1986) summarized numerous studies using the Rokeach Value Survey for comparisons both within and between nations.

The ranking procedure of the RVS has been widely criticized, for reasons discussed below (Feather, 1975; Zavalloni, 1980; Schwartz & Bilsky, 1987). Many subsequent researchers have standardized the ranks or used ratings of each value instead. To understand the dimensionality of values and to determine whether this dimensionality is cross-culturally stable, researchers have investigated the structure of the RVS. Rokeach himself proposed two dimensions, personal (e.g., comfortable life) versus social (equality) values and moral (honest) versus competence (logical) values. His factor analyses of U.S. data did not support this structure, however. Feather and Peay (1975) used multidimensional scaling of standardized ranks to reexamine the structure of the U.S. data and compare it with Australian data. They found between five and seven dimensions in both countries, but the structures were somewhat different and did not parallel Rokeach's proposal.

Ng, Akhtar-Hossain, Ball, Bond, and Hayashi et al. (1982) obtained ratings of the RVS values from students in nine countries. Bond (1988) reanalyzed these data in a pan-cultural factor analysis, after standardizing to remove cultural response biases. He identified four dimensions that overlap somewhat with Rokeach's ideas: Competence vs. Security, Personal Morality versus Success, Social Reliability versus Beauty, and Political Harmony versus Personal Sociability. Bond (1988) also reported a pan-cultural factor analysis of responses to values presumably central to Chinese culture, collected by the Chinese Culture Connection (1987) from students in 23 countries. This analysis yielded two quite different factors.[3]

These studies suggest only minimal similarity in the structure of individual-level value systems within different cultural settings, using the RVS and other imposed etic instruments. Greater similarity emerged, however, when Schwartz and Bilsky (1987, 1990) reanalyzed RVS data from six countries. Applying both a different theory of the content and structure of value systems and a different analytic approach (see below), they were able to discern the same seven types of values in analyses in each country. These value types gave some support to Rokeach's competence/morality and personal/social distinctions. From this starting point, Schwartz (1992) developed a new theory and methodology for studying values.

The Schwartz Project

Schwartz postulated that the crucial content aspect that distinguishes among values is the type of motivational goal they express. He therefore grouped single values into value types according to their common goals. He reasoned that the basic human values likely to be found in all cultures are those that represent universal requirements of human existence (biological needs, requisites of coordinated social interaction, and demands of group functioning) as conscious goals. Drawing on the values identified by previous researchers and found in religious and philosophical writings about values from many cultures, he grouped them into ten motivationally distinct types that he thought might be comprehensive of the basic types. The following are capsule definitions of the value types in terms of their central goal:

- Power—social status, dominance over people and resources
- Achievement—personal success according to social standards
- Hedonism—pleasure or sensuous gratification
- Stimulation—excitement and novelty
- Self-Direction—independence of thought and action
- Universalism—understanding, tolerance and protection for the welfare of *all* people and nature
- Benevolence—preserving and enhancing the welfare of people to whom one is close
- Tradition—respect and commitment to cultural or religious customs and ideas
- Conformity—restraint of actions and impulses that may harm others and violate social expectations
- Security—safety and stability of society, relationships and self

In order to understand the conceptual organization of value systems, Schwartz developed a theory of the dynamic relations among these value types. He postulated that actions taken in pursuit of each type of values have psychological, practical, and social consequences that may conflict or may be compatible with the pursuit of other types. For example, pursuing achievement values may conflict with pursuing benevolence values: seeking personal success may obstruct actions aimed at enhancing the welfare of others. The total pattern of conflict and compatibility among value types yielded the theoretical structure of value systems portrayed in Figure 3–1. Competing value types emanate in opposing directions from the center; complementary types are in close proximity around the circle.

Findings of later research (Schwartz, 1992, 1994b) confirmed this structure, revealing that the ten value types are organized in the two bipolar dimensions shown in Figure 3–1: Openness to Change (including self-direction and stimulation values) versus Conservation (security, conformity and tradition) and Self-Enhancement (power and achievement) versus Self-Transcendence (universalism and benevolence). Hedonism includes elements of both Openness to Change and Self-Enhancement. Because value types form an integrated motivational structure, Schwartz further postulated that the value types relate as a total system to other variables of interest (attitudes, behaviors, group membership, etc.). Specifically, any variable tends to have similar associations with value types that are adjacent in the value structure, and these associations will decrease as one moves around

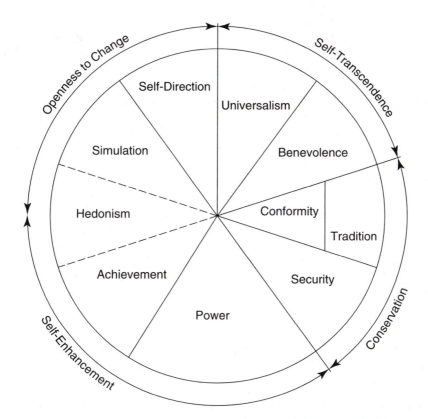

FIGURE 3–1   Structural relations among ten motivational types of values

the circular structure in both directions from the most positively to the least positively associated value type.

Based on this theory, Schwartz (1992) developed a survey consisting of 56 values selected to represent each of the value types. To avoid a Western imposed-etic, values were drawn from all the world's major religions and from surveys developed in Asia and Africa as well as in the West. Collaborators in many countries added values. To avoid dependence on one language of origin, Hebrew, Finnish, and English versions were developed together. Thus far, collaborators in 54 countries have gathered data from about 44,000 respondents, usually including a sample of urban school teachers and one of college students. Teachers were the focal occupational group because they play a key role in value socialization. Respondents rate the importance of values as guiding principles in their lives. The response scale permits a negative rating because values important in one culture may be rejected in another.

The correspondence between the actual and theorized content and structure of value types was assessed by comparing two-dimensional spatial representations of the intercorrelations among the 56 single values to the theoretical spatial arrangement in Figure 3–1. Separate multidimensional scaling analyses have been reported for 97 samples (Schwartz, 1992, 1994b). These analyses provided substantial support for the near universality of the ten value types and of their structural relations. The two bipolar dimensions were found in almost every sample. Each of the ten value types formed a distinct region or a joint region with its postulated neighbors in over 90 percent of samples. All the single values emerged most frequently in the region of their a priori value type.

Schwartz concluded that 45 values demonstrate sufficient equivalence of motivational meaning across cultures to justify their use to form indexes of the importance of the value types in different cultures. To correct the main response bias in value rating—the tendency to rate all values more or less important regardless of content—individuals' average rating of all values is partialled out of their scores. Ways of identifying culture-specific meanings of values against the background of measurement error have also been proposed (Schwartz & Sagiv, 1995). This project provides a cross-culturally validated instrument for measuring values, a comprehensive, near-universal set of value types for studying individual differences, and a basis for relating value systems as integrated wholes to other variables of interest.

Dimensions Derived from Individualism/Collectivism

Individualism/Collectivism, as formulated by Hofstede (1980), is a culture-level concept and not an attribute of individuals. Many researchers have, however, transposed this concept into an individual difference or personality variable—the degree to which individuals endorse values, norms, and attitudes associated with cultural individualism or collectivism. Rather than seeking to identify all basic dimensions of individual values, these researchers have sought one general dimension that distinguishes individualists from collectivists. The central features of this dimension are a tendency to give priority to personal interests or to ingroup interests and a tendency to value independence, emotional detachment, personal achievement, and competition versus interdependence, emotional closeness, group achievement, and cooperation (Triandis, 1995). Another major theme (Markus & Kitayama, 1991) concerns thinking about or construing the self as an independent entity motivated by personal standards or as an interdependent part of social groups motivated by social expectations.

Triandis, Leung, Villareal and Clack (1985) proposed the terms "idiocentrism" and "allocentrism" to describe individualism/collectivism as an individual-level variable. But these terms have not been adopted widely, with most studies using the labels "individualists" and "collectivists" instead. Confusion regarding levels of analysis is rife in these studies. From a methodological point of view, the problem is that the labels are used, sometimes interchangeably, to refer both to persons within a society who differ on the personality variable (individual-level) and to all members of a society or other cultural group who are treated as reflecting the presumed level of individualism or collectivism in their group (culture-level). From a conceptual point of view, the problem is that many researchers assume it is appropriate to use the same dimensions to describe individuals and cultures. Thus, they adopt either a reductionist, personological view of culture or a reductionist, cultural view of persons. This section describes only clearly individual-level research and follows the authors' choice of labels.

Several instruments have been devised to measure this individual-level variable. Triandis and colleagues developed a 21-item attitude scale that they administered to students in nine countries (Triandis et al., 1986) and later in ten partly overlapping countries (Triandis et al., 1993). In the second study, separate factor analyses were performed in each country. These analyses yielded several factors in each country, suggesting that idiocentrism/allocentrism is a multidimensional concept rather than a unitary, bipolar dimension. Empirical support for the view that neither idiocentrism or allocentrism is a coherent unitary construct whose necessary criterial attributes are clearly defined comes from analyses of indigenous scales developed to measure it in China (Ho & Chiu, 1994), India (Sinha & Tripathi, 1994), and Korea (Cha, 1994). All of these analyses yielded multiple factors rather than a single biploar factor. A second finding of the Triandis et al. (1993) within-country analyses was that different factors were extracted in different countries. This suggests that the meanings of the items in this scale varied across cultures and that both idiocentrism and allocentrism have culturally different meanings. If this is so, then indigenous scales are indeed necessary to measure them in different cultures.

The INDCOL scale (Hui, 1988) addresses one aspect of the complexity of this purported individual-level personality construct—the possibility that people exhibit varying degrees of individualism/collectivism in relations with different others (e.g., spouse, kin, coworkers). Research confirms that this is indeed the case. Research with the INDCOL scale also reveals that this construct may have a different structure and hence different meanings in different cultures. For instance, people in one cultural group may respond as individualists to both friends and coworkers but as collectivists to kin, whereas those in another cultural group may respond as individualists to coworkers but as collectivists to both friends and kin.

Other scales have been designed to measure more narrowly defined aspects of the personality construct derived from culture-level individualism/collectivism. Yamaguchi (1994) devised a collectivism scale whose ten items measure exclusively the tendency to weigh group goals more heavily than personal goals when the two are in conflict. Factor analyses of this scale, after appropriate standardization of items, yielded a single robust factor in samples from Japan, Korea, and the United States. This indicates both conceptual unity and cross-cultural comparability (Yamaguchi, Kuhlman, & Sugimori, 1995). Scales intended primarily to measure the self-construal aspect of the personality construct (but not the values aspect) have been developed by Singelis (1994) and by Gudykunst, Matsumoto, Ting-Toomey, Nishida, Kim, and Heyman (1994). These scales also show coherence in analyses of student samples in a number of countries. Of course, narrow scales do not capture the richness of the purported individualism/collectivism personality construct. But findings of many studies indicate that this construct has probably been defined in an overly inclusive global manner that is not justified conceptually.

A number of studies have examined relations between the self-construal aspect of the personality construct and individuals' value priorities. Gudykunst et al. (1994) related individuals' independent and interdependent self-construals to their endorsement of clusters of values chosen to represent priorities for independence and interdependence. Correlations in separate samples from the United States, Japan, Korea, and Australia confirmed the expected links. Three other studies (Chan, 1994; Ip & Bond, 1995; Roccas, unpublished data) related people's values to their tendency to refer to social categories (such as family or religion) when describing themselves—a presumed index of interdependent self-concepts. Students in Hong Kong, the United States, and Israel were sampled, as were Israeli adults. References to social categories correlated positively with values from Schwartz's conservation value types and negatively with values from his openness types, as expected. Correlations were often weak, however, and not all were significant. The weakness of these findings reinforces the view that the individualism/collectivism personality construct might better be understood as encompassing loosely connected elements rather than as a coherent unitary concept.

Triandis (1995) has also recently proposed subdividing the concept of allocentrism/idiocentrism into "horizontal" and "vertical" types of what he reverts to calling collectivism and individualism. Both types of collectivists perceive the self as an interdependent part of a collective, but horizontal collectivists stress equality because all members of the collective are seen as equal, whereas vertical collectivists accept inequalities within the collective. Both types of individualists view the self as autonomous, but horizontal individualists emphasize equality whereas vertical individualists accept inequality. Singelis, Triandis, Bhawuk, and Gelfand (1995) report preliminary studies of methods intended to measure these concepts with ethnically diverse American students. Items include attitudes, norms, behavioral intentions, behaviors, and self-construals, but not values. Scores on the dimensions are treated as equally appropriate for comparing individual persons and comparing cultures, with no empirical test of this assumption, thereby adding to the conceptual confusion in the literature.

As our review suggests, much work has yet to be done to establish the optimal conceptualization and measurement of individual difference variable(s) derived from culture-level individualism/collectivism. Empirical research shows that the aspects of this syndrome are related in different ways across some cultures and rarely form a unitary dimension. One might ask: How useful and how methodologically defensible is it, especially given the need for equivalence of meaning across cultures, to squeeze these aspects under one conceptual roof? The Schwartz studies provide a theoretically-grounded alternative, encompassing a broader range of values. The critique provided by Kagitçibasi (this volume) suggests a different line of development. She proposes that certain values related to individualism/ collectivism are more salient within the interpersonal domain, while others are more salient when persons consider societal issues. This may well prove to be the case, but it should be noted that her proposal relates exclusively to the individual-level of analysis as defined within this chapter. Even when values pertain to how societal issues should be handled, if the analysis concerns individual differences in these values, it remains an individual-level analysis. Only when value scores are aggregated across whole cultures would we consider a study to be a culture-level study.

We have considered the main approaches currently available for formulating and measuring individual differences in value priorities within cultures. We turn next to the results of studies that examine the relations of individual values to other individual attributes.

Cross-Culturally Consistent Correlates of Individual-Level Values

The following review is limited to patterns of correlation that have emerged consistently in at least three or more countries or ethnic groups. First we examine the background variables (age, education, occupational status, urban/rural residence, and gender) that shape experiences of individuals and are therefore likely to affect their values. We then consider a number of attitudes and behaviors that may be influenced largely or in part by individual differences in value priorities.

Social Background

Young people attribute greater importance to openness (stimulation and hedonism) values than their elders do, and less importance to conservation (tradition, conformity, and security) values, in a wide variety of nations (Schwartz, 1992). Similarly, young people express more individualist and less collectivist values and preferences in studies in Japan (Yamaguchi, 1994) and India (Mishra, 1994). More educated people, as compared to less, show the same value patterns and preferences as younger people in numerous countries (Cha, 1994—Korea; Mishra, 1994—India; Reykowski, 1994—Poland; Schwartz, 1994c—Estonia, Finland, Israel, Japan, West Germany). Using instruments quite different from those described previously, Kohn (1969) and his colleagues (Kohn, Schonbach, Schooler, & Slomczynski, 1990) found that education relates positively to self-direction values and negatively to conformity values in Italy, Japan, Poland, and the United States. Occupational status showed the same pattern as education in the Kohn studies and also related positively to individualist and negatively to collectivist orientations in Reykowski's (1994) Polish study. Finally, residents of urban as compared to rural areas typically show more individualist and less collectivist orientations and attribute more importance to openness to change and universalism values and less to conservation values (Cha, 1994; Georgas, 1993; Mishra, 1994; Schwartz, unpublished data).

It seems logical that the different social experiences associated with gender would also lead to value differences between men and women. Yet the studies by Cha (1994), Yamaguchi (1994), and Reykowski (1994) revealed no gender differences in individualist versus collectivist orientations. Kashima, Yamaguchi, Kim, Choi, Gelfand and Yuki (1995) propose that gender is unrelated to some components of these orientations but may influence endorsement of relatedness. They found gender differences in relatedness but not in collectivism in samples of students in Japan, Korea, Australia, Hawaii, and mainland United States.

When values have been studied directly, gender differences predictable from sex-typed socialization and role experiences have been found. A meta-analysis of differences on the Schwartz value types, in samples from 47 countries, revealed that women attribute greater importance to security and benevolence values and men to self-direction, stimulation, hedonism, achievement, and power values (Prince-Gibson & Schwartz, 1994). Differences were strongest for the benevolence and power value types. The sizes of the differences varied greatly across cultures, however, a finding parallel to Bond's (1988) report of numerous culture by gender interactions in his 23-nation study with the Chinese value survey. Moreover, the largest mean gender difference was much weaker than differences typically found for age, education, status, and cultural group. Rokeach (1973) and Feather (1987), using the Rokeach values scale, reported similar gender differences in large U.S. and Australian samples. In sum, there are cross-culturally consistent gender differences in values, but they may be missed in small samples. These differences vary in size across cultures.

Attitudes and Behavior

A number of single-country studies have established that individuals' values relate systematically to their attitudes and behavior (reviews in Ball-Rokeach, Rokeach, & Grube, 1984; Mayton et al., 1994, and Seligman et al., 1996). The causal processes that explain these relations are a matter of continuing debate, however. Very few studies have asked whether the same relations hold consistently across cultures. Our concern here is only with evidence that may bear on this question. If these relations reflect basic psychological processes, cross-cultural consistency might be expected. To the extent that they are context-dependent, however, inconsistency might be the rule. Culture may constitute a powerful context, giving more or less legitimacy, for example, to acting on one's personal values regardless of social expectations (R. A. Bond & Smith, 1996). Such cultural variation might enhance the value-behavior link or attenuate it.

Religion

A series of studies has examined relations of the ten Schwartz value types with individual commitment to religion among Catholics, Muslims, Jews, Orthodox and several denominations of Protestants in 13 countries (Huismans, 1994; Roccas & Schwartz, 1995; Schwartz & Huismans, 1995). The same pattern of correlations emerged, with only minor variations, in all groups: Religiosity correlated most positively with tradition values, and correlations for the other value types decreased progressively going around the value structure (see Figure 3–1) in both directions toward hedonism and stimulation values, which correlated most negatively. In one interesting variation, universalism values correlated quite negatively with religiosity in the Orthodox and Muslim samples. The magnitudes of correlation were also affected by whether the relations between church and state were cordial (e.g., in Western Europe) or oppositional (e.g., in communist states). The researchers conclude that relations of values to religiosity reflect the opportunities for attaining valued goals through religious involvement. They interpret the observed variations as evidence that the social position of religious groups influences the extent to which religious commitment can express particular values (e.g., exclusivity vis-à-vis out-groups blocks the expression of universalism values).

Politics
Rokeach (1973) postulated that freedom and equality are orthogonal values whose relative importance largely determines political ideology and behavior across cultures. He found support for this view in political treatises from various countries and in American voting patterns. However, many subsequent studies in Australia, Britain, and the United States (summarized in Braithwaite, 1994) indicated that, while endorsement or rejection of equality divided protagonists of the political left and right, position on freedom had few clear political implications.

Braithwaite (1994) derived two other value orientations, "International harmony and equality" and "National strength and order," from factor analyses of the social values in the Rokeach survey, plus some added social values (e.g., the rule of law, international cooperation). She postulated that these value orientations underlie individual political attitudes and behavior. Multi-item indexes of each were administered to Australian (Braithwaite, 1994; Heaven, 1991) and to South African (black and white) students (Heaven, Stones, Nel, Huysamen, & Louw, 1994). The two orientations showed the expected, opposite correlations with support for foreign policy goals, positions on election issues, political radicalism–conservatism, willingness to engage in political protest, and voting.

Conceptually, and in terms of how they are measured, the Braithwaite international harmony and equality orientation parallels Schwartz's universalism values, and national strength and order parallels security values. Universalism and security values are opposed in the Schwartz value structure (Figure 3–1), and they showed opposing correlations with voting for liberal versus conservative political parties in Israel (Barnea & Schwartz, 1996). Discriminant function analyses of data from Hungary, Israel, the Netherlands, and Spain indicated that, in general, the values in opposing positions in the value structure predict support for opposing political parties (Barnea & Schwartz, 1994).

Mayton and Furnham (1994) investigated relations of individual values to antinuclear political activism in England, Japan, New Zealand, and the United States. The researchers used responses to the Rokeach survey to construct indexes for nine of the Schwartz value types. In all countries, universalism values correlated positively with activism and power values correlated negatively. Correlations for self-direction were mostly positive and those for security and conformity mostly negative. This pattern of findings reinforces the importance of the universalism/ self-direction versus power/security/conformity axis of values for political attitudes and behavior. Interestingly, correlations were consistently weak in the Japanese sample. This might reflect the unique experience of Japanese with nuclear war or a cultural tendency to attend more to social expectations than to inner standards (Markus & Kitayama, 1991).

Social Relations

Singelis and Sharkey (1995) studied self-rated embarrassability among samples of Anglo-, Japanese-, Korean-, Chinese-, and Filipino-American students in Hawaii. In each cultural group, individuals with more interdependent and less independent self-concepts reported greater embarrassment on a cross-situational measure of embarrassability. Using the same self-concept measures, Smith and Hooker (1995) studied self-reported assertiveness of students from the United Kingdom and Turkey in five types of situations. In the British sample, having an independent self-concept related to assertiveness across situations. In the Turkish sample, however, the relations of independent versus interdependent self-concepts to assertiveness varied more across situations. Thus, this study provides suggestive evidence that internal constructs like the self-concept may relate less consistently to social behavior in some cultures than in others. Cultural characteristics that may account for this variation are discussed in the section on culture-level dimensions.

Sagiv and Schwartz (1995) studied the readiness of schoolteachers from three Israeli ethnic groups for contact with groups other than their own. For Jews, an hypothesis that referred to the value system as a whole was confirmed: Universalism values correlated most positively with readiness for contact and tradition values correlated most negatively, while the relative size of correlations for the other value types reflected their order in the circular value structure (see Figure 3–1). For Christian and Muslim Arabs, different predictions that took account of group variation in motivation to integrate into the dominant society or to preserve ethnic uniqueness were largely confirmed. Thus this study provides evidence that group location in the social structure can elicit predictably different value-behavior linkages.

Because values represent desirable goals, one might ask how they relate to the seeking of social approval. For example, those who seek social approval might attribute especially great importance to the values viewed as most important in their society and little importance to the values viewed as least important in their society. Schwartz, Verkasalo, Antonovsky, and Sagiv (in press) addressed this question with Finnish social work students and Israeli adults, measuring approval seeking with the Marlowe-Crowne scale. There was no tendency for people high in social approval to endorse values in accord with the societal importance of these values. However, as predicted, those who scored high on approval were the individuals whose values emphasized social harmony and rejected any challenge to social conventions, in both countries. Correlations followed the order of the circular value structure from most positive for conformity values to most negative for hedonism and stimulation. Replication of the same pattern of correlations in two countries, despite substantial country differences in the importance of different value types, suggests that these associations reflect basic psychological processes.

Culture-Level Dimensions of Values

We turn now to studies that treat cultures rather than individuals as the unit of analysis. Investigations of the dimensions on which cultures vary and comparisons of different cultural groups encounter special methodological problems that researchers often overlook. We will therefore describe some of the more significant problems and attempts to cope with them in our discussion of this literature. After presenting the different approaches to culture-level dimensions, we offer a first attempt to integrate them conceptually and empirically.

The shared cultural value emphases in a society help to shape the reward contingencies to which people must adapt in the institutions in which they spend most of their time—families, schools, factories, businesses, and so forth. As a result, the members of each cultural group share many value-relevant social experiences and they come to accept similar values. The *average* value priorities of societal members reflect the central thrust of their shared enculturation, independent of individual differences due to unique experiences or heredity. These average societal priorities point to the underlying common cultural values. Hence researchers have used the average of individual value priorities to measure the prevailing culture.

There are hundreds, perhaps thousands, of values on which societies and other cultural groups could be compared. Some values are relevant in all societies, others are known only in particular societies. Hence, a way must be found to organize the profusion of cultural values into a limited number of dimensions on which to compare societies effectively. For identifying critical cultural value dimensions, an approach that starts with societies is needed.

Theorists who address this issue make the assumption that cultural dimensions of values reflect the basic issues or problems that societies must confront in order to regulate human activity (Hofstede, 1980; Kluckhohn & Strodtbeck, 1961; Schwartz, 1994a). Societal members, especially decision-makers, recognize these problems, plan responses to them, and motivate one another to cope with them. Values are the vocabulary of socially approved goals that they use to motivate action and to express and justify the solutions (Schwartz, in press).

The vast majority of cross-cultural studies of values have compared nations. Often, national boundaries do not encompass homogeneous societies with a shared culture. But there are strong forces towards integration in nations that have existed for some time (Hofstede, 1991, p. 12). There is usually a single dominant language, educational system, army, and political system, and shared mass media, markets, services, and national symbols (e.g., flag, sports teams). These can produce substantial sharing of basic values among residents of a nation. This is less the case, of course, in nations with sharp cleavages among ethnic groups.

Early Studies

Of the early studies that compared the values of cultural groups, only Kluckhohn and Strodtbeck (1961) were sensitive to the need to use dimensions of comparison appropriate to the culture level. They specified five dimensions that refer to basic philosophical issues: human nature as good or evil; past, present, or future time perspective; linearity–collaterality–individualism; being–becoming–doing; relation of humankind to nature. For each issue, the researchers formulated several detailed positions that might be preferred in a culture. In interviews, respondents ranked these positions, thereby expressing their preferences (= values) on each issue. In this way, predictions about the prevailing value orientations of five cultural groups in the American Southwest were tested. There was no empirical examination, however, of whether these were appropriate dimensions for comparing the cultures and whether the specific items were understood in equivalent ways in the different cultural groups.

Rokeach (1973) compared the rankings of instrumental and terminal values in his survey (described earlier) by students in the United States, Australia, Canada, and Israel, while Feather (1986) compared rankings by students in Australia, Papua New Guinea, and China. Ranking is not vulnerable to the same response biases as rating, but differences in ranking are hard to interpret. Is a value ranked fourth in one culture necessarily less important than a value ranked third in another? The large number of values compared in these studies, and the absence of a theory that organized values into dimensions on which cultures were known to differ, made it difficult to draw general conclusions about cultural differences from their findings. Revisiting these results, guided by the approaches presented below, might reveal a more integrated picture.

The Hofstede Project

Hofstede's (1980, 1991) study of IBM employees in 50 nations and three regions has defined the agenda for cross-cultural researchers into values for the past 15 years. Hofstede suggested that four basic societal problems underlie cultural value dimensions:

1. Social inequality, including the relationship with authority
2. The relationship between individual and group
3. Concepts of masculinity and femininity—the social implications of gender
4. Dealing with uncertainty, including the control of aggression and the expression of emotions

Hofstede defined four cultural dimensions that reflect the way members of a society typically cope with each of these problems, respectively:

1. *Power Distance:* Accepting an unequal distribution of power in institutions as legitimate versus illegitimate (from the viewpoint of less powerful persons)
2. *Individualism/Collectivism:* Valuing loosely knit social relations in which individuals are expected to care only for themselves and their immediate families versus tightly knit relations in which they can expect their wider in-group (e.g., extended family, clan) to look after them in exchange for unquestioning loyalty
3. *Masculinity/Femininity:* Valuing achievement, heroism, assertiveness, and material success versus relationships, modesty, caring for the weak, and interpersonal harmony
4. *Uncertainty Avoidance:* Feeling uncomfortable or comfortable with uncertainty and ambiguity and therefore valuing or devaluing beliefs and institutions that provide certainty and conformity

Hofstede used data derived from questionnaires originally designed for audits of company morale. The sheer size of his sample of 117,000 respondents enabled him to achieve several methodological advances on any previous study. For instance, he discarded data from respondents who were not matched with respondents in other countries. Consequently, he selected the type of IBM employees who were most widely dispersed around the world, namely those engaged in marketing and servicing. Using these matched samples, he computed an average score on each questionnaire item for each national group, taking the sample as his unit of analysis. He then factor analyzed these average national scores to uncover the dimensions that underlie them and found four factors.

Hofstede computed nation scores on each dimension by combining the questions that loaded on the relevant factor. Because the questionnaire was not designed to test the theory, it is perhaps not surprising that the factor-based indexes fit the conceptual definitions of the dimensions only loosely. High scores on Power Distance indicated, for instance, that respondents reportedly fear to express disagreement with their manager, perceive the boss as autocratic or paternalistic and do not want a boss who is consultative. High scores on Individualism versus Collectivism were defined by emphases on work goals of freedom to work in one's own way, sufficient time for personal life and challenging work versus work goals of good working conditions, opportunities for training and full use of skills and abilities. High scores on Uncertainty Avoidance reflected high reported job stress, beliefs that company rules should not be broken, and expectations of continuing to work for IBM for a long time. High scores on Masculinity versus Femininity reflected emphases on earnings, recognition, advancement, and challenge in one's work versus good relations with the boss and others, living in a desirable area, and having high job security. Hofstede assumed that the *order* of nations on each of the four dimensions, based on the IBM samples, is close to the "true" order traceable to cultural differences. He reasoned that, because the samples were well-matched on a large variety of variables other than their nationality, national culture itself is the most likely explanation for consistent differences between the national groups.

Hofstede's findings have posed a variety of challenges to subsequent researchers. For example: Did the dimensions that emerged depend upon the particular items that the questionnaire happened to include? Did the type of respondents studied affect the results? Did the countries where IBM was located adequately sample global variations in values (e.g., no Soviet bloc nations)? Have the national value priorities measured from 1967 to 1972 remained stable over subsequent decades? The simplest way to begin addressing these questions is to consider studies using Hofstede's own measures.

In 1984, Hoppe (1990) gave the Hofstede survey to 1,544 very senior administrators from business, government, academia, and nonprofit organizations, drawn from 17 West European nations, Turkey, and the United States, who attended seminars in Austria. Using the Hofstede indexes, Hoppe computed nation scores on each dimension and correlated these with the nation scores Hofstede had obtained. Correlations ranged from .56 (Masculinity, after dropping Sweden, which diverged greatly) to .69 (Individualism). This suggests that Hofstede's ordering of nations was not determined by his use of IBM samples and that this ordering remained fairly stable over more than a decade. Hoppe also performed a culture-level factor analysis across his 19 nations in an attempt to replicate the four factors representing Hofstede's dimensions. Three factors emerged, none of which replicated any of the Hofstede factors (with congruence coefficients all below .77). Although this independent test failed to replicate the Hofstede dimensions, even with the same items, it is hardly definitive. Hoppe included almost exclusively in his analyses economically developed Western democracies, which may well have influenced the emergent dimensions. Although many other studies have employed Hofstede's instrument (Shackleton & Ali, 1990; Sondergaard, 1994), these studies shed little light on the previously raised questions.

The Chinese Value Survey

Bond (Chinese Culture Connection, 1987) extended the Hofstede research and addressed questions it raised by adopting a novel strategy. He constructed an instrument intentionally based on Eastern rather than on Western culture. After asking Chinese scholars to nominate values "of fundamental importance in Chinese culture," he developed an emic Chinese value survey (CVS). He proposed no theory of value dimensions, asking instead whether the factors extracted from responses of students from 23 countries to the CVS matched Hofstede's factors. A country-level factor analysis yielded four orthogonal factors. Bond computed nation scores for each of these factors and correlated them with the nation scores Hofstede reported for his dimensions in 20 overlapping countries. Scores on three of the CVS factors correlated substantially with scores on a Hofstede dimension.

Scores on one CVS factor correlated negatively with scores on Power Distance and positively with Individualism, while scores on a second CVS factor correlated positively with Power Distance and negatively with Individualism. This pattern of correlation, based on factors obtained by different methods, supports the universality of Power Distance and Individualism, but it reinforces doubts about the distinctiveness of these two dimensions from one another. Scores on the third CVS factor correlated positively with scores on Masculinity. Although Hofstede (1991) viewed this finding as supportive, the items defining the CVS factor (patience, courtesy, kindness, forgiveness, compassion versus patriotism and a sense of righteousness) seem to contradict his definition of Masculinity, coming closer to his definition of Femininity. No CVS factor correlated with Uncertainty Avoidance, raising doubts about its universality. Bond named the fourth, unique CVS factor "Confucian Work Dynamism," and Hofstede (1991) adopted it as an added value dimension of cultural variation missing from his theory. Hofstede interpreted it as opposing a dynamic orientation towards the future to a more static orientation towards the past and present, and therefore renamed it "Long-Term Orientation."

The Schwartz Culture-Level Approach

The Schwartz (1994a; Schwartz & Ros, 1995) culture-level approach to values is conceptually independent of his individual-level work just described. He argues that the content of cultural value dimensions reflects the alternative solutions that emerge as groups cope with basic societal problems. Schwartz began with three basic societal issues:

1. Relations between individual and group: to what extent are persons autonomous versus embedded in groups?
2. Assuring responsible social behavior: how to motivate people to consider others' welfare and coordinate with them?
3. The role of humankind in the natural and social world: is it more to submit, to fit in, or to exploit?

The cultural adaptations that evolve to resolve each of these issues are arrayed along bipolar cultural dimensions. Each adaptation is expressed, maintained, and justified by a particular interrelated set of values, called a value type.

Dimension 1: Conservatism versus Autonomy
In cultures at the Conservatism pole of this dimension, the person is viewed as embedded in a collectivity, finding meaning in life largely through social relationships, through identifying with the group and participating in its shared way of life. This value type emphasizes maintenance of the status quo, propriety, and restraint of actions that might disrupt the solidary group or the traditional order. Exemplary specific values are social order, respect for tradition, family security, and self-discipline. In cultures at the Autonomy pole of this dimension, the person is viewed as an autonomous, bounded entity who finds meaning in his or her own uniqueness, who seeks to express his or her own internal attributes (preferences, traits, feelings, motives) and is encouraged to do so. Schwartz distinguishes two related types of Autonomy: *Intellectual* autonomy emphasizes the independent ideas and rights of the individual to pursue his/her own intellectual directions

(exemplary values include curiosity, broadmindedness, creativity). *Affective* autonomy emphasizes the individual's independent pursuit of affectively positive experience (pleasure, exciting life, varied life).

Dimension 2: Hierarchy versus Egalitarianism

In high Hierarchy cultures, a hierarchical system of ascribed roles assures socially responsible behavior. People are socialized to comply with the obligations and rules attached to their roles and sanctioned if they do not. This value type emphasizes the legitimacy of an unequal distribution of power, roles, and resources (social power, authority, humility, wealth). High Egalitarianism cultures portray individuals as moral equals who share basic interests as human beings. People are socialized to internalize a commitment to voluntary cooperation with others and to feel concern for everyone's welfare. This value type emphasizes transcendence of selfish interests (equality, social justice, freedom, responsibility, honesty). Egalitarianism values are a focus of socialization in cultures where the person is viewed as autonomous rather than interdependent, because autonomous persons have no natural commitment to others.

Dimension 3: Mastery versus Harmony

In high Mastery cultures, people actively seek to master and change the natural and social world, to assert control and exploit it in order to further personal or group interests. This value type emphasizes getting ahead through active self-assertion (ambition, success, daring, competence). High Harmony cultures accept the world as it is, trying to preserve rather than to change or exploit it. This value type emphasizes fitting harmoniously into the environment (unity with nature, protecting the environment, world of beauty). In contemporary national cultures, the potential adaptation of submitting to the environment is uncommon.

Responses to the 56-item value survey described earlier—from teachers, students and adults in 54 countries, including ten from the former Soviet bloc—were also used for the culture-level analyses. For the culture-level analysis, however, the mean scores on the values for each entire sample were used , as done by Hofstede. Because of this procedure, there is no statistical dependence between the empirical study of culture- and of individual-level value dimension.[4] Only those 45 values demonstrated to have relatively stable cross-cultural meanings in studies within each nation (Schwartz, 1994b) were included. Scores for 121 samples were entered into a multidimensional scaling analysis to test the validity of the theoretical specification of seven value types, organized into three bipolar dimensions. Partitioning of the observed value space into regions confirmed the structure of value types and dimensions. In order to check whether the results depended on the particular sample types and set of nations analyzed, separate analyses were repeated with subsets of samples split in two other ways: (1) samples of urban school teachers from 47 nations and of college students from 48 nations (12 non-overlapping nations), and (2) samples from richer and poorer nations (above and below the median on gross national product per capita). All of these analyses also supported the content and dimensional structure of the seven culture-level value types.

Nation scores were computed for each value type by combining the mean ratings on the values designated a priori as representing that type and confirmed in the preceding analyses. Schwartz (1994b) reported scores for 32 national groups, based on teacher samples. The assumption that different kinds of matched samples from the same nations yield a similar *order* of nations on the three cultural value dimensions was also assessed. Nation scores were computed for each dimension (one polar type minus the other), and the scores from teacher samples were correlated with those from student samples across 40 nations. Correlations of between .83 and .70, for the three dimensions, provided support for this assumption.

Scores on the Schwartz culture-level value types and dimensions provide an alternative to the Hofstede dimensions for sampling nations with particular value cultures, for explaining national differences on other variables, and for characterizing national cultures when studying culture as a moderator variable. Next we examine some applications of this approach.

The Trompenaars Value Survey

Unrelated to the above approaches, Trompenaars (1985) drew upon sociological literature to derive dimensions of cultural difference that might affect behavior in business organizations. He developed a questionnaire intended to measure preferred ways of handling five basic elements of social relationships specified by Parsons and Shils (1951) as well as preferred ways of managing in organizations. Although the questionnaire was meant to tap the values of organizational employees, the format of many items differed from usual ways of measuring values. Some items presented vignettes of situations and asked how the protagonist in the situation should act. Others asked respondents to choose the one statement in a pair that best represented their view. During the past decade, about 15,000 organization employees in over 50 countries, including nine former Soviet bloc nations, have completed the questionnaire.

Trompenaars (1993) cited country means for responses to some questionnaire items and suggested several cultural dimensions, but he undertook no empirical analyses to assess the validity of these dimensions. Smith, Dugan, and Trompenaars (1996) selected items from the questionnaire that were suitable for the empirical analysis of dimensions. These items measured preferences for using universalistic versus particularistic standards in relationships, for granting status on the basis of ascribed versus achieved qualities, for orientation to the interests of the self versus the collective, and for different styles of organizational management. After appropriate standardization of individual responses, item means for 43 nations were entered into a multidimensional scaling analysis. Three dimensions emerged. The first, labeled "Conservatism/Egalitarian Commitment," contrasted preferences for particularistic relations and status based on ascription with preferences for univeralistic relations and status based on achievement. The second, labeled "Loyal

Involvement/Utilitarian Involvement," contrasted preferences for family loyalty and sharing responsibility for mistakes with individual responsibility. The third dimension was not clearly interpretable.

In contrast to Hofstede and Schwartz, Trompenaars did not match the demographic profiles of his samples. Respondents were mostly managers and other employees who attended training programs. It was crucial therefore to determine whether the dimensions found in his data were influenced by sample differences on demographic variables. For this purpose, Smith, Dugan, and Trompenaars (1996) reran their analyses with controls for age, gender, and status. They concluded that demographic variability did not materially affect the results of the MDS solutions. There is, however, no evidence regarding the equivalence of meaning of the items within the various cultural groups.

Relations among Different Dimensional Approaches

We have reviewed four studies that each sampled at least 23 nations. The availability of these different analyses of the structure of values at the culture level makes it possible to seek some theoretical and empirical integration. As noted, the studies varied in methodological strength. Hofstede and Schwartz have the most extensive and globally representative samples. Only Schwartz derived the value contents from diverse Western and non-Western sources, empirically controlled for meaning equivalence, and demonstrated replicability of dimensions with different types of samples. Nonetheless, consistencies across the different studies may point to the most central and reliable dimensions of cultural values.

With this purpose, Bond (1996) conducted a second-order factor analysis of country means for the 12 nations whose scores were available from the studies of Hofstede (1991), Chinese Culture Connection (1987), and Schwartz (1994a). His analysis yielded four factors. The first opposed Egalitarianism (S),[5] Individualism (H), and the related CVS factor to Conservatism (S) and Hierarchy (S). The second, a unipolar factor, included Uncertainty Avoidance (H), Intellectual Autonomy (S), and Harmony (S). The third opposed Confucian Work Dynamism (C) and a CVS factor called Moral Discipline (C) to Affective Autonomy (S) and Mastery (S). The fourth, also unipolar, included Masculinity (H) and its correlated CVS factor (C).

The first factor makes good conceptual sense: It opposes a view that social relations should be governed by voluntary and negotiated coordination among independent individuals who are moral equals to a view that social relations should be governed by compliance to traditional, hierarchically ordered role obligations. The second factor does not seem conceptually coherent, though it might suggest a preference for finding harmony and certainty through application of intellect. The third factor also makes good sense: It opposes a preference for disciplined, persistent work within an accepted social framework to a preference for emotionally expressive and assertive action likely to threaten conventional constraints. The fourth factor is puzzling, combining conceptually opposed dimensions, as noted earlier.

Although Bond's second-order factor analysis has the virtue of combining data from three studies, it suffered from the small number of nations included—fewer than the number of separate dimensions. Moreover, exploratory factor analysis in general, and orthogonal rotation in particular, may be ill-suited to the task at hand. The basic cultural dimensions probably form a complex, circular structure of interrelated concepts (Schwartz, 1994a), a structure that is not easily represented with factor analytic methods (Shye, 1988).

An alternative approach correlates the country means on each dimension in one study with those on each dimension in another study, looking for dimensions that are highly correlated. Smith, Dugan, and Trompenaars (1996, supplemented by later data) computed correlations of the country means on the dimensions emerging from the Trompenaars data with those on the dimensions from the other studies (Hofstede, 33 nations; Schwartz, 26 nations; Chinese Culture Connection, 17 nations). Scores on the first Trompenaars dimension (Conservatism vs. Egalitarian Commitment) correlated positively with Conservatism (S) and Power Distance (H) and negatively with Egalitarianism (S), Individualism (H), and Integration (C). This clearly reinforces the first factor in the Bond analyses. Thus, this dimension emerges most consistently and strongly from all the country-level surveys. The second dimension from the Trompenaars data (Loyal Involvement vs. Utilitarian Involvement) correlates positively with Power Distance (H) and Hierarchy (S) and negatively with Intellectual Autonomy (S).

Correlations between the Schwartz (1994a, supplemented by later data) means and those of Hofstede revealed several meaningful findings. Correlations were based on 33 nations. Parallel to the first factor identified above by Bond, Egalitarianism (S) correlated positively with Individualism (I) and both Conservatism (S) and Hierarchy (S) correlated negatively with Individualism (H). There were no correlations corresponding to Bond's conceptually questionable second factor. Replicating Bond's third factor (with data from only 17 nations), Affective Autonomy (S) correlated negatively with Long-Term Orientation (Confucian Work Dynamism) (C, H).

These analyses reinforce the view of cultural dimensions as non-orthogonal. Intellectual Autonomy (S), Affective Autonomy (S), and Egalitarianism (S) all correlated negatively with Power Distance (H) and positively with Individualism (H), whereas Conservatism (S) and Hierarchy (S) exhibited the opposite patterns of correlation. This set of correlations points to a close positive association between two basic dimensions identified in different ways by different authors:

1. The preferred cultural view of individual-group relations (autonomous versus embedded
2. The preferred cultural mode of motivating responsible social behavior and allocating resources (negotiation among equals versus acceptance of unequal, hierarchical roles*)*

These dimensions are virtually identical to the first two culture-level dimensions identified by Schwartz (1994a, in press). The first is also very similar to what

Kagitçibasi (this volume) refers to as "relational Individualism/Collectivism" (calling it an *individual-level* dimension in her approach to levels of analysis); the second is similar to her culture-level "normative Individualism/Collectivism." Moreover, Triandis's (1995) new horizontal dimension of Individualism/Collectivism is an adaptation of the first dimension, and his new vertical dimension is an adaptation of the second dimension. In contrast to other theorists and to the data examined here, however, Triandis appears to think of these as orthogonal dimensions.

Culture-Level Differences in Values: Findings, Implications, and Explanations

Mapping the Nations of the World

Each of the major studies of culture-level dimensions has yielded mappings of national cultures relative to one another. Two key questions may be asked: (1) Do the world's national cultures form meaningful clusters? That is, do the clusters of countries that emerge in an empirical analysis of their value profiles have common or similar histories and/or socio-demographic characteristics that might account for why they have evolved similar cultures? (2) What value profiles characterize these clusters? A third question, what are the origins of these value profiles, is addressed in the section following this one.

Hofstede (1980) reported a hierarchical cluster analysis of 40 nations based on their scores on the four cultural dimensions he identified. This analysis yielded 11 clusters which he regrouped into seven meaningful "culture areas": Nordic, Anglo, Germanic, Near Eastern, less developed Asian, less developed Latin, and more developed Latin. Japan stood alone as a more developed Asian nation. Hofstede provided a detailed description of the value profiles of each culture area. The Nordic and Anglo areas, for example, were both relatively low in Power Distance, high in Individualism, and low to medium in Uncertainty Avoidance, but the Nordic cluster was low in Masculinity whereas the Anglo cluster was high. Thus, it is mainly in their emphases on caring for the weak and interpersonal harmony versus assertiveness and material success, respectively, that these cultural areas differed.

The Near Eastern and less developed Asian areas were both high in Power Distance, low in Individualism, and medium in Masculinity, but the Near Eastern cluster was high in Uncertainty Avoidance whereas the less developed Asian cluster was low to medium. Thus, these cultural areas differed mainly in whether they valued or devalued beliefs and institutions that provide certainty and conformity. The comparison between the Nordic and Anglo culture areas, on the one hand, and the Near Eastern and less developed Asian culture areas, on the other, contrasts opposing sets of scores on Power Distance and Individualism. In light of these scores, the former pair of culture areas has often been seen as prototypically Individualist, while the latter has been seen as prototypically Collectivist.

Schwartz (1994a, in press; Schwartz & Ros, 1995) conducted multidimensional scaling analyses using nation scores on the seven culture-level value types he identified. He replicated these analyses with data from both teachers (44 nations) and students (40 nations). The same six culture areas were clearly distinguishable in both analyses: West European, Anglo, East European, Islamic, East Asian, and Latin American. Again, Japan was distinctive. The similarity between the Hofstede and Schwartz culture areas is remarkable. Some of the differences doubtless reflect the different sampling of nations, for example, no East European nations in Hofstede. Other differences may reflect cultural change over two decades, such as increasing cultural homogeneity in Western Europe.

Some examples of the value profiles that Schwartz reported for culture areas may also be noted. East Asian nations were especially high on Hierarchy and Conservatism and low on Autonomy and Egalitarianism. Thus, this cultural area emphasized compliance with ascribed, unequal, role obligations and maintenance of the traditional order in contrast to developing individual independence and uniqueness and voluntary commitment to the welfare of others who are seen as equals. West European nations showed exactly the opposite pattern of priorities, reflecting opposing cultural emphases.

The value profiles of the East Asian and West European clusters again appear to suggest a simple East-West cultural dichotomy resembling Collectivism versus Individualism. However, the profile of the Anglo cluster reveals that this would be a misreading of world culture. The Anglo profile was unusual in the high importance attributed to Mastery, Affective Autonomy, and Hierarchy values at the expense of Harmony and Conservatism values. This culture area, including the United States, fell between the West European and East Asian. This cultural area combined an emphasis on active self-assertion and emotional expression, rather than acceptance and preservation of the world as it is, with a legitimation of the unequal distribution of power and resources.

Smith, Dugan, and Trompenaars (1996) present a plot of 43 nations on their two meaningful dimensions. Two clear culture areas emerged, one for Eastern Europe and the other for Northern Europe. Somewhat less clear Far Eastern, Latin, and Anglo areas were also discernible. The overlap of these results with those reported by Hofstede and Schwartz is substantial. The North European cluster was high on Egalitarian Commitment and on Utilitarian Involvement. According to the items that formed these dimensions, this profile signifies a cultural emphasis on achievement of status through personal merit, equality of individual rights, and rejection of paternalism, together with an emphasis on utilitarian rather than loyalty considerations in interpersonal relations. This profile is virtually the same as the one found by Schwartz for Western Europe.

The East European cluster, like the North European, was high on Utilitarian Involvement, but it was also high on Conservatism. Thus it differed in emphasizing acceptance of hierarchical, paternalistic system of ascribed roles rather than an emphasis on individual rights and responsibilities. This profile is very similar to the one Schwartz found for the East European culture area, one that emphasized Conservatism and Hierarchy at the expense of Autonomy, Egalitarianism, and Mastery values.

Explaining National Differences in Value Priorities

In an effort to explain the origins of the meaningful national differences in cultural values, researchers have studied their correlates. A key issue in these studies is the direction of causality. Consider, for example, the substantial positive correlations of national level of economic development with cultural emphases on Individualism ($r = .82$, Hofstede, 1980) and Autonomy ($r = .58$, Schwartz, 1993). This correlation might arise because wealthier economies provide individuals with more varied opportunities and can afford to permit greater freedom of choice. On the other hand, these value emphases might promote economic development by motivating individual members of society to work harder and be more productive. In this instance, the causal path from development to values is probably stronger than the path from values to development, as suggested by the fact that Individualism and Autonomy are related to level of development but not to rate of economic growth. Detailed theorizing about the causal links of national value priorities with social structural and demographic variables and careful testing of alternative explanations with appropriate statistical models are much needed.

Hofstede (1980) provided the correlations of national scores on his four cultural value dimensions with national wealth, economic growth, latitude, population size, growth, and density. Gross national product per capita was the strongest "predictor" of Power Distance (negative) Individualism (positive), and Uncertainty Avoidance (negative), across 40 countries. Neither population density nor economic growth correlated with any of the culture dimensions across the countries, but the remaining variables had substantial correlations with at least two culture dimensions. Hofstede also noted that different patterns of correlation are sometimes found among richer and among poorer countries. He offered tentative explanations for many of these correlations. For example, he attributed the strong positive correlation of distance from the equator with Individualism to the need for individual initiative in order to survive in colder climates. Hofstede also speculated about historical influences on culture-level values. For example, he traced high Power Distance to a heritage shaped by life in centralized empires such as the Roman and Chinese empires.

The Confucian Work Dynamism dimension is the only value dimension to correlate reliably with economic growth (Hofstede & Bond, 1988). A correlation of .70 was observed with high growth in GNP per capita in 23 nations during the 1965–87 period. The Far Eastern countries that underwent the most rapid growth were doubtless high on Confucian Work Dynamism before this period. Hence the cultural values may be implicated in the causation of economic growth, rather than an effect of it. Of course, numerous economic, technological, and political factors may be implicated in why economic growth occurred in these countries at this particular point in history as well.

Schwartz (1993) also examined social structural and demographic correlates of national scores on his cultural value dimensions. National wealth and other indicators of economic development correlated strongly negatively with Conservatism versus Autonomy and with Hierarchy versus Egalitarianism. However, the strongest predictor was household size, which correlated positively with these two dimensions as well as with Mastery versus Harmony. Schwartz reasoned that the smooth functioning of family units with large numbers of people living together, including many young children, requires a hierarchically organized social system in which people identify with the collectivity, comply with role obligations, and exploit the material environment to satisfy group needs. He also explained how this type of family unit, in turn, might influence value priorities. Other important "predictors" of cultural values included political democratization, ethnic heterogeneity, and percentage of Christians.

Because the many correlates of national differences in culture are naturally intertwined, neither the examination of single variables nor the use of hierarchical regression analyses to identify the best "predictors" is likely to fully clarify the causal picture. The most successful approaches will probably have to consider the interplay of historical, intellectual, economic, technological, political, religious and other forces in forming cultural values. Statistical analyses of the sort described above should be integrated into these approaches, however, in order to insure that their reasoning is compatible with the empirical data. Two recent studies adopted this strategy to explain the distinctive value profiles of the West European (Schwartz & Ros, 1995) and East European (Schwartz & Bardi, in press) culture areas. The latter study, for example, explained the East European pattern as an adaptation to the life circumstances imposed by communist regimes—pervasive demands for conformity, close surveillance, unpredictable application of rules, suppression of initiative, and rewards not contingent on effort and performance. It then employed statistical analyses to test this explanation against alternative historical, economic, and religious explanations. This work makes clear the interdisciplinary nature of cross-cultural research on values.

Implications of Differences in National Value Priorities

In this section, we explore possible influences of national culture, as measured by culture-level value means, on the characteristics of nations and the behavior of their residents. As noted, correlational studies of this type cannot form a strong basis for inferences about causal relationships. However, when complemented by careful reasoning and empirical comparison of possible alternative causal links, they can suggest how societal value priorities influence social policy and affect the lives of citizens.

Social Indicators

Hofstede (1980) initiated this line of analysis. We cite a few of more than 20 findings he reports across at least 20 countries. Countries scoring high in Power Distance had more domestic political violence and sectoral inequality, less press freedom, and a lower proportion of women in professions. Individualism had the inverse pattern of correlations with these variables. Countries high on Uncertainty Avoidance had more domestic political violence and less press freedom and segregation in higher education. Countries low on Masculinity donated a higher proportion of their budget to overseas aid, a finding that remained true with later data (Hofstede, 1991). The interrelatedness of the different value dimensions must be considered in order to clarify the causal processes that may explain these associations. Even more important, researchers must consider the effects of the social structural variables associated with value priorities as alternative or supplementary explanations. National wealth, for example, affects a country's ability to allocate resources in a way that reflects its value priorities. Researchers can partial out the effects of structural variables before testing other relationships, but this should be guided by theory and not done automatically.

Bond (1991) employed the partialling strategy in a study of relations between national values and health indices in 23 countries. Assuming that national health rates reflect material conditions, he partialled out GNP per capita before computing correlations of health indices with country scores on the two dimensions from the Chinese Value Survey. After partialling, he found, for example, that countries scoring higher on the CVS factor related to Hofstede's Individualism and Schwartz's Autonomy and Egalitarianism had lower rates of early childhood mortality and higher rates of tumors and ulcers. In the realm of social well-being, these countries provided greater protection of human rights and higher status for women. About one-third of the partial correlations were significant.

Social Psychological Processes

The studies in this next section did not collect data from the respondents they studied to provide culture-level value means. Rather, they assumed that the means provided by existing large cross-national surveys could be used as reasonable estimates in their studies too. This assumption may not be justified unless the populations sampled were similar and value change was low. Nonetheless, many of these studies obtained results that supported their predictions concerning the relation of culture-level value means and other indices of social psychological processes. Gudykunst & Bond (this volume) discuss studies of national differences in intergroup relations, emotions, and expectations from interaction, and relate them to national differences on the Hofstede dimensions. Many studies based on the Individualism/Collectivism dimension are covered by Kagitçibasi (this volume). We include only those studies that refer to other dimensions as well.

Only one study considered all the value dimensions from Hofstede, Schwartz, and Trompenaars. Bond and Smith (1996) reported a meta-analysis of 134 Asch-type conformity studies from many nations. After controlling for variations in experimental design, they found that the level of conforming responses was higher in countries that score high on the related Collectivism (H) and Conservatism (S; Trompenaars as in Smith, Dugan, & Trompenaars, 1996) dimensions and that score low on Intellectual and Affective Autonomy (S). This fitted their predictions. However, the authors caution, the same behaviors that signify conformity in cultures high on Individualism and Autonomy may signify sensitivity to others in cultures high on Collectivism and Conservatism. Thus, cultural effects on the connotations of conformity may moderate the responses of individuals to social influence.

National differences in culture-level values have also been linked to work-related variables. Peterson et al. (1995) compared the incidence of role overload and role ambiguity among middle managers in 21 nations. Role overload was greatest in nations high on Power Distance, whereas role ambiguity was greatest in nations low on Power Distance. The Meaning of Working International Team (MOW, 1987) studied the centrality of work in people's lives in nine nations. Work was most central in Japan, an effect which may relate to Confucian Work Dynamism/Long-Term Orientation. Using MOW data, Schwartz (in press) found that work is more central to people's lives in cultures high on Hierarchy and Mastery. He also found that the tendency to view work as an obligation one owes to society rather than as an individual right (England & Quintanilla, 1994) is greater in cultures high on Conservatism versus Autonomy and on Hierarchy versus Egalitarianism.

Barnea and Schwartz (1994b) hypothesized that culture moderates relations between individuals' value priorities and their voting behavior, in their four-country study cited earlier. In support of this hypothesis, the values-voting association was stronger in nations high on Autonomy values and low on Conservatism values. This finding is compatible with Schwartz's view of autonomous cultures as encouraging people to express their internal attributes while conservative cultures expect people to follow social norms.

The remaining studies drew upon Hofstede's Power Distance and Masculinity dimensions. We present them according to the primary dimension they utilized.

Power Distance

Smith, Peterson, and Leung (1995) studied how managers handled disagreements with out-groups in 23 nations. They found a preference for applying formal rules and procedures in high Power Distance nations, but a preference for relying on colleagues, subordinates, and their own experience and training in low Power Distance nations. Best and Williams (1994) studied self-concepts of male and female students in 14 countries. The affective meaning (favorability, strength, and activity) of male and female self-concepts varied across nations. This variability was related to national culture: male and female self-concepts were more divergent the greater the cultural Power Distance.

Masculinity–Femininity

Leung and his colleagues investigated whether the preferred procedures for resolving conflicts in a cultural group depend upon the importance of Masculinity vs. Femininity in the culture. In one study (Leung, Bond, Carment, Krishnan, & Liebrand, 1990), they compared preferred procedures in student samples from Holland (highly feminine) and Canada (moderately masculine). Both countries scored high on Individualism and were similar on the other Hofstede dimensions. Dutch students preferred mediation more while Canadian students yielded more to the other party's demands and ignored differences less than the Dutch. The same experimental design was repeated in the second study (Leung, Au, Fernandez-Dols, & Iwawaki, 1992) of students from Spain (moderately feminine) and Japan (highly masculine). Both these countries scored moderately high on collectivism and were similar on the other dimensions. This time, those from the highly masculine country (Japan) favored mediation more strongly. Leung et al. (1992) concluded that preferences for conflict resolution are unrelated to masculinity–femininity.

Williams and Best (1982) studied variability in the gender stereotypes held by students in 30 countries. This variability was moderated by national culture: the stereotypes of males and females overlapped more in nations high on Hofstede's Masculinity dimension and were more differentiated in nations high on Femininity. Best and Williams (1994) reported a similar finding in their 14 country study: gender self-concepts were also more differentiated in Feminine than in Masculine cultures. No convincing explanation of these apparently counterintuitive results has yet been proposed. Perhaps the results appear counterintuitive only because of surplus expectations created by Hofstede's label for this dimension. The items defining Masculinity imply a unidimensional work-centered view of life. Those defining Femininity are more diverse and might be associated with a more cognitively complex understanding of oneself and others.

Conclusions

We conclude by considering how well current studies encompass the temporal and global diversity of values, how ways of studying values might be extended, and how far the field of values studies has come in the 16 years since Zavalloni's (1980) review.

Temporal and Global Diversity of Value Studies

For the most part, this chapter has reported upon values, value types, and value dimensions as though they were a fixed element within the cultures of the world. At best, this is a necessary simplification, but there are substantial reasons to believe that global change in values over the past decades has been both continuous and important. The impact of modernization upon traditional cultures has included substantial changes in all those social institutions that define and implement cultural value emphases (Yang, 1988). Such changes are not restricted to the impact of industrialization. Social scientists from different disciplines have noted continuing changes in values and attitudes in Western societies over the past 25 years (e.g., Inglehart, 1977, 1990; Ester, Halman, & de Moor, 1994). However, the crucial question for firmly basing the cross-cultural study of values is not whether changes in the endorsement of particular values have occurred but whether more profound change in the structure of relations among values is also underway. We return to this issue next.

The convergence regarding two culture-level dimensions in all the studies that covered numerous countries could be taken as an indication that the major dimensions of culture-level variation in values have now been identified. This conclusion must be treated with caution, however. The dimensions that emerge from such studies are affected by the locations that are sampled. No study has sampled many more than 50 of the nearly 200 current national entities. Europe, North America, and the Pacific Rim are well represented, but African and Arab countries are badly underrepresented in all studies. The dimensions identified may represent well variation in values across industrialized nations but not across nations in earlier stages of socioeconomic development. Moreover, the dimensions that emerge are affected by the values included in the survey questionnaires. Dimensions identified in some studies but not replicated in others may provide clues as to what has been missed. The field is too young to foreclose on the possibility that further theorizing and consideration of values found in indigenous studies will yet point to additional major dimensions.

Future Directions

We consider next two ways in which the focus of value studies could usefully be broadened.

Perceived Value Priorities

Most studies of values ask respondents to report their own values. This procedure has conceptual and face validity for the study of individual-level values and has been justified conceptually for studying culture-level values. But it is problematic if respondents have little ability or desire to communicate their values in this way, for example, in cultures where indirect modes of communication are favored. Asking about the values perceived to prevail in society is a potentially fruitful alternative. This directly measures the "cultural press" to which people feel they are exposed. As such, it is appropriate for studying culture-level but not individual-level values. For instance, Sinha and Verma (1994) asked Indian respondents to rate the behavior of "people in general," and some Trompenaars (1993) items requested estimates of the response "most people in your country" would choose. Use of such procedures could help to clarify the adequacy of current methods for representing the value priorities in some nations.

Value Consensus

As noted, nations are not necessarily an appropriate unit of comparison for cross-cultural studies. If the level of value consensus in a nation is low, separate reporting of the values of different cultural or subcultural groups would be preferable. Many people believe that there are major regional and/or ethnic differences in values within their country. Multiple samples from single countries are needed to test the validity of these beliefs. When assessing intergroup differences within a nation, however, it is important to view their magnitude against the background of cross-national differences in order to keep them in perspective. For example, statistically significant differences on some value dimensions among samples from three regions in China, three in Japan, and five in the United States were dwarfed by the much larger differences between nations (Schwartz & Ros, 1995).

Cross-cultural research on values has focused almost exclusively on value importance. The study of value consensus as a variable in its own right would take research on values in a new direction. According to Durkheim (1947), Parsons (1968), and other sociologists, value consensus provides the underpinnings for social order by increasing cooperation and facilitating accommodation rather than violence in resolving conflicting interests. In a first study of consensus, Sagie and Schwartz (1996) drew on data from the Schwartz project to examine differences in value consensus across national groups. The findings are compatible with their causal hypotheses that socioeconomic development increases value consensus but political democratization decreases consensus. Development and democratization are both widely pursued goals in the contemporary world, yet their effects on the underpinnings of social order are apparently contradictory. Research on these and other antecedents of societal value consensus, and on its social and psychological consequences, can increase the contribution of cross-cultural psychology to the understanding of social change.

Structural Approaches as the Key to Integrating Different Conceptualizations

There is widespread agreement that the methodological problems inherent in any form of psychological research are intensified if one takes on the challenge of addressing global cultural diversity. In this chapter we have proposed two crucial guidelines that can assist values researchers in contributing effectively to this promising research area. First, it is essential to make and to maintain a sharp distinction between individual- and culture-level analyses. Only by doing so can we avoid erroneous inferences about the relations of values to other aspects of social processes. These two levels differ in the questions for which they are appropriate, in the psychological and social dynamics that give rise to value systems and in the dimensions of values that they provide for comparison.

Second, clarity can be promoted by focusing upon the dimensional structure of value systems rather than on specific single values. A sufficiently wide range of studies is now available to discern at least two of the key culture-level dimensions of values. Because these studies used data obtained in different ways and from different types of samples, it is apparent that they are relatively robust. There is also evidence that they are relatively stable over time. They emerged both from Hofstede's data collected nearly 30 years ago and from much more recent studies. Moreover, the Schwartz (1994b) analysis yielded similar structures of values among samples of rich and of poor nations. This would not be expected if the massive changes that accompany socioeconomic development also cause change in the structure of values. Our confidence in the utility of the culture-level dimensions that have so far proved replicable is increased by the fact that the culture-level analyses that yielded the Schwartz dimensions were preceded by within-country analyses that clarified the degree to which particular values had equivalent meanings in different cultures. Identification of additional dimensions must also be based upon evidence of meaning equivalence.

The period of 16 years since the first edition of this *Handbook* has proved a fruitful one for cross-cultural values researchers. At that time, research into values was considered by most one among many possible directions that might become central to cross-cultural psychology. Conceptual and methodological advances have now reached the point where values research can claim one of the more central positions. The dimensions of values and the locations of cultural groups on them provide a framework that can be used to derive predictions and to integrate our understanding of cross-cultural variations in many aspects of social processes.

Endnotes

1. Work on this chapter was supported by grant R 000 22 1552 from the Economic and Social Research Council, U.K. to the first author; and by grant 94-00063 from the United States-Israel Binational Science Foundation (BSF), Jerusalem, Israel to the second author, whose work was also faciliated by the Leon and Clara Sznajderman Chair Professorship in Psychology.

2. Kagitçibasi (this volume) uses the idea of individual and culture levels of analysis in a way quite different from ours. She distinguishes two construals of individualism–collectivism, relational and normative, that she locates at the individual and culture levels, respectively. As we define levels, this distinction refers not to the level of analysis of the construals but to their content. Indeed, Kagitçibasi uses both construals to describe both individual differences within cultures and cultural differences across nations. The criteria for distinguishing levels of analysis proposed and applied in this chapter can clear up such confusions.

3. Because separate analyses were not reported within each country in these studies, it is not known whether either set of pan-cultural factors constitutes dimensions useful for cross-cultural comparison.

4. Because this point sometimes seems counterintuitive, we elaborate further. Individual-level dimensions are derived from individual differences in value priorities within samples or cultures, that is, from intra-cultural variance. This intra-cultural variance is omitted from culture-level analyses: sample/culture means are entered into these analyses, not the value scores of individual persons. Hence, the culture-level dimensions are derived exclusively from variance across cultures and are in no way affected by individual difference variation within cultures.

Pairs of values that are strongly correlated in individual-level analyses, because they are psychologically consistent for individuals, can be negatively correlated in the culture-level analysis, because their emphases reflect polar responses to the same societal problem. Thus wisdom and broadmindedness are closely related as universalism values at the individual level, but they are opposed as Conservatism versus Intellectual Autonomy at the culture level. Moreover, pairs of values that are uncorrelated at the individual level because they are psychologically unrelated (e.g., authority and humility) can be positively correlated at the culture level, because they express the same response to a societal problem (e.g., legitimating a hierarchical, unequal distribution of power and resources). For a detailed discussion of the empirical relations among levels of analysis, see Leung and Bond (1989).

5. To facilitate identification, the sources of the types of values that were related in the integrative analyses are labelled as follows: C = Chinese Culture Connection, H = Hofstede, S = Schwartz, T = Trompenaars.

References

Ball-Rokeach, S. J., Rokeach, M., & Grube, J. (1984). *The great American values test.* New York: Free Press.

Barnea, M. & Schwartz, S. H. (1994). *Value dimensions of political conflict: A cross-national perspective.* Paper presented at the Twelfth Congress of the International Association of Cross-Cultural Psychology, Pamplona, Spain, July, 1994.

Barnea, M. & Schwartz, S. H. (1996). *Values and voting.* Submitted manuscript, The Hebrew University of Jerusalem, Israel.

Berry, J. W. (1969). On cross-cultural comparability. *International Journal of Psychology, 4,* 119–128.

Berry, J. W. (1979). A cultural ecology of social behavior. In L. Berkowitz (Ed.), *Advances in experimental social psychology* (Vol. 12, pp.177–206). New York: Academic.

Berry, J. W. (1989). Imposed etics—emics—derived etics: The operationalization of a compelling idea. *International Journal of Psychology, 24,* 721–734.

Berry, J. W. (1994). Ecology of individualism and collectivism. In U. Kim, H. C. Triandis, C. Kagitçibasi, S-C. Choi, & G.Yoon (Eds.), *Individualism and collectivism: Theory, method and applications* (pp. 77–84). Thousand Oaks, CA: Sage.

Best, D. L. & Williams, J. E. (1994). Masculinity/ femininity in the self- and ideal-self descriptions of students in 14 countries. In A-M. Bouvy, F. van de Vijver, P. Boski, & P. Schmitz (Eds.), *Journeys into cross-cultural psychology* (pp. 297–306). Lisse, Netherlands: Swets and Zeitlinger.

Bond, M. H. (1988). Finding universal dimensions of individual variation in multi-cultural studies of values: The Rokeach and Chinese value surveys. *Journal of Personality and Social Psychology, 55,* 1009–1115.

Bond, M. H. (1991). Chinese values and health: A cultural-level examination. *Psychology and Health, 5,* 137–152.

Bond, M. H. (1996). Chinese values. In M. H. Bond (Ed.), *Handbook of Chinese psychology* (pp. 208–226). Hong Kong: Oxford University Press.

Bond, M. H., & Smith, P. B. (1996). Cross-cultural social and organizational psychology. *Annual Review of Psychology, 47,* 205–235.

Bond, R. A. & Smith, P. B. (1996). Culture and conformity: A meta-analysis of studies using the Asch line judgment task. *Psychological Bulletin, 119,* 111–137.

Braithwaite, V. (1994). Beyond Rokeach's equality–freedom model: Two-dimensional values in a one-dimensional world. *Journal of Social Issues, 50,* 67–94.

Cha, J. H. (1994). Aspects of individualism and collectivism in Korea. In U. Kim, H. C. Triandis, C. Kagitçibasi, S-C. Choi, & G.Yoon (Eds.), *Individualism and collectivism: Theory, method and applications* (pp. 157–174). Thousand Oaks, CA: Sage.

Chan, S. N. C. (1994). COLINDEX: A refinement of three collectivism measures. In U. Kim, H. C. Triandis, C. Kagitçibasi, S-C. Choi, & G.Yoon (Eds.), *Individualism and collectivism: Theory, method and applications* (pp. 200–210). Thousand Oaks, CA: Sage.

Chen, C. C., Meindl, J. R., & Hunt, R. G. (in press). Testing effects of horizontal and vertical collectivism: A study of rewards allocation preferences in China. *Journal of Cross-Cultural Psychology.*

Chinese Culture Connection. (1987). Chinese values and the search for culture-free dimensions of culture. *Journal of Cross-Cultural Psychology, 18,* 143–164.

Durkheim, E. (1947). *The division of labor in society.* Glencoe, IL: Free Press.

England, G. W. & Quintanilla, S. A. R. (1994). *Work*

meanings: Their structure and stability. WORC Paper 94.11.046/6. Tilburg University, Netherlands.

Ester, P., Halman, L., & de Moor, R. (Eds.). (1994). *The individualizing society: Value change in Europe and North America.* Tilburg, Netherlands: Tilburg University Press.

Feather, N. T. (1975). *Values in education and society.* New York: Free Press.

Feather, N. T. (1986). Cross-cultural studies with the Rokeach Value Survey: The Flinders program of research on values. *Australian Journal of Psychology, 38,* 269–283.

Feather, N. T. (1987). Gender differences in values: Implications of the expectancy value model. In F. Halish & J. Kuhl (Eds.), *Motivation, intention and volition* (pp. 31–45). New York: Springer-Verlag.

Feather, N. T. (1995). Values, valences, and choice: The influence of values on the perceived attractiveness and choice of alternatives. *Journal of Personality and Social Psychology, 8,* 1135–1151.

Feather, N. T. & Peay, E. R. (1975). The structure of terminal and instrumental values: Dimensions and clusters. *Australian Journal of Psychology, 27,* 151–164.

Georgas, J. (1993). Ecological–social model of Greek psychology. In U. Kim, H. C. Triandis, C. Kagitçibasi, S-C. Choi, & G.Yoon (Eds.), *Individualism and collectivism: Theory, method and applications* (pp. 56–78). Thousand Oaks, CA: Sage.

Georgas, J. & Berry, J. W. (1995). An eco-cultural taxonomy for cross-cultural psychology. *Cross-Cultural Research, 29,* 121–157.

Gudykunst, W. B., Matsumoto, Y., Ting-Toomey, S., Nishida, T., Kim, K. S., & Heyman, S. (1994). *Measuring self-construals across cultures.* Paper presented at the International Communication Association Convention, Sydney, Australia, July, 1994.

Heaven, P. C. L. (1991). Voting intention and the two-value model: A further investigation. *Australian Journal of Psychology, 43,* 75–77.

Heaven, P. C. L., Stones, C., Nel, E., Huysamen, G., & Louw, J. (1994). Human values and voting in South Africa. *British Journal of Social Psychology, 33,* 223–232.

Ho, D. Y-F. & Chiu, C-Y. (1994). Component ideas of individualism, collectivism and social organization: An application in the study of Chinese culture. In U. Kim, H. C. Triandis, C. Kagitcibasi, S-C. Choi, & G.Yoon (Eds.), *Individualism and collectivism: Theory, method and applications* (pp. 137–156). Thousand Oaks, CA: Sage.

Hofstede, G. (1980). *Culture's consequences: International differences in work-related values.* Beverly Hills: Sage.

Hofstede, G. (1991). *Cultures and organizations: Software of the mind.* London: McGraw Hill.

Hofstede, G. & Bond, M. H. (1988). The Confucius connection: From cultural roots to economic growth. *Organizational Dynamics, 16,* 4–21.

Hoppe, M. H. (1990). *A comparative study of country elites: International differences in work- related values and learning and their implications for management training and development.* Unpublished Ph.D. thesis, Department of Education, University of North Carolina at Chapel Hill.

Hui, C. H. (1988) Measurement of individualism–collectivism. *Journal of Research on Personality, 22,* 17–36.

Hui, C. H., Yee, C., & Eastman, K. L. (1995). The relationship between individualism–collectivism and job satisfaction. *Applied Psychology: An International Review, 44,* 276–282.

Huismans, S. (1994). The impact of differences in religion on the relation between religiosity and values. In A-M. Bouvy, F. van de Vijver, P. Boski, & P. Schmitz (Eds.), *Journeys into cross- cultural psychology* (pp. 255–267). Lisse, Netherlands: Swets and Zeitlinger.

Inglehart, R. (1977). *The silent revolution: Changing values and political styles among Western publics.* Princeton: Princeton University Press.

Inglehart, R. (1990). *Culture shift in advanced industrial society.* Princeton: Princeton University Press.

Ip, G. W. H. & Bond, M. H. (1995). Culture, values and the spontaneous self-concept. *Asian Journal of Psychology, 1,* 29–35.

Kashima, Y., Yamaguchi, S., Kim, U., Choi, S-C., Gelfand, M. & Yuki, M. (1995). Culture, gender and self: A perspective from individualism–collectivism research. *Journal of Personality and Social Psychology, 59,* 925–937.

Kim, U. & Berry, J. W. (Eds.). (1993). *Indigenous psychologies: Research and experience in cultural context.* Newbury Park, CA: Sage.

Kluckhohn, C. & Strodtbeck, F. L. (1961). *Variations in value orientations.* Evanston, IL: Row Peterson.

Kohn, M. L. (1969). *Class and conformity: A study in values.* Homewood, IL: Dorsey.

Kohn, M. L., Schoenbach, C., Schooler, C., & Slomczynski, K. M. (1990). Position in the class structure and psychological functioning in the United States, Japan and Poland. *American Journal of Sociology, 95,* 964–1008.

Leung, K. (1989). Cross-cultural differences: Individual-level and culture-level analysis. *International Journal of Psychology, 24,* 703–719.

Leung, K., Au, Y. F., Fernandez-Dols, J. M., & Iwawaki, S. (1992). Preference for methods of conflict processing in two collectivist cultures. *International Journal of Psychology, 27,* 195–202.

Leung, K. & Bond, M. H. (1989). On the empirical identification of dimensions for cross-cultural comparison. *Journal of Cross-Cultural Psychology, 20,* 133–151.

Leung, K., Bond, M. H., Carment, D. W., Krishnan, L., & Liebrand, W. B. G. (1990). Effects of cultural femininity on preference for methods of conflict processing: A cross-cultural study. *Journal of Experimental Social Psychology, 26,* 373–388. Correction published: (1991), *27,* 201–202.

Markus, H. R. & Kitayama, S. (1991). Culture and the self : Implications for cognition, emotion, and motivation. *Psychological Review, 98,* 224–253.

Mayton, D. M. & Furnham, A. (1994). Value underpinnings of antinuclear political activism: A cross-national study. *Journal of Social Issues, 50,* 117–128.

Mayton, D. M., Loges, W. E., Ball-Rokeach, S. J., & Grube, J. W. (Eds.). (1994). Human values and social issues. *Journal of Social Issues, 50,* whole issue.

Meaning of Work International Team. (1987). *The meaning of work: An international view.* New York: Academic.

Mishra, R. C. (1994). Individualist and collectivist orientations across generations. In U. Kim, H. C. Triandis, C. Kagitçibasi, S-C. Choi, & G. Yoon (Eds.), *Individualism and collectivism: Theory, method and applications* (pp. 225–238). Thousand Oaks, CA: Sage.

Ng, S. H. et al. (1982). Values in nine countries. In R. Rath, J. B. P. Sinha, & H. S. Asthana (Eds.). *Diversity and unity in cross-cultural psychology* (pp. 196–205). Lisse, Netherlands: Swets & Zeittinger.

Parsons, T. (1968). *The structure of social action.* New York: Free Press.

Parsons, T. & Shils, E. A. (1951). *Toward a general theory of action.* Cambridge, MA: Harvard University Press.

Peterson, M. F., Smith, P. B., Akande, A., Ayestaran, S., Bochner, S., et al. (1995). Role conflict, ambiguity and overload: A 21-nation study. *Academy of Management Journal, 38,* 429–452.

Prince-Gibson, E. & Schwartz, S. H. (1994). *Cross-cultural gender differences in value priorities: A meta-analysis.* Paper presented at the Twelfth Congress of the International Association for Cross-Cultural Psychology, Pamplona, Spain, July, 1994.

Redding, S. G. (1990). *The spirit of Chinese capitalism.* Berlin: Mouton, de Gruyter.

Reykowski, J. (1994). Individualism and collectivism as dimensions of social change. In U. Kim, H. C. Triandis, C. Kagitçibasi, S-C. Choi, & G. Yoon (Eds.), *Individualism and collectivism: Theory, method and applications* (pp. 276–292). Thousand Oaks, CA: Sage.

Roccas, S. & Schwartz, S. H. (1995). *Church–state relations and the association of religiosity with values: A study of Catholics in six countries.* Submitted paper, Hebrew University of Jerusalem, Israel.

Rokeach, M. (1973). *The nature of human values.* New York: Free Press.

Sagie, G. & Schwartz, S. H. (1996). National differences in value consensus. In H. Grad, A. Blanco, & J. Georgas (Eds.), *Key issues in cross-cultural psychology* (pp. 217–226). Lisse, Netherlands: Swets and Zeitlinger.

Sagiv, L. & Schwartz, S. H. (1995). Value priorities and readiness for outgroup contact. *Journal of Personality and Social Psychology, 69,* 437–448.

Schwartz, S. H. (1992). Universals in the structure and content of values: Theoretical advances and empirical tests in 20 countries. In M. P.

Zanna (Ed.), *Advances in experimental social psychology* (Vol.25, pp. 1–65). Orlando, FL: Academic.

Schwartz, S. H. (1993). Comparing value priorities across nations. Invited address at XXIV Congress of the Interamerican Society of Psychology, Santiago, Chile, July.

Schwartz, S. H. (1994a). Beyond individualism/collectivism : New cultural dimensions of values. In U. Kim, H. C. Triandis, C. Kagitçibasi, S-C. Choi, & G.Yoon (Eds.), *Individualism and collectivism: Theory, method and applications* (pp. 85–119). Thousand Oaks, CA: Sage.

Schwartz, S. H. (1994b). Are there universal aspects in the structure and contents of human values? *Journal of Social Issues, 50,* 19–45.

Schwartz, S. H. (1994c). *Education and value priorities.* Paper presented at the II Congreso Internacional Familia y Sociedad, Tenerife, Islas Canarias, Spain, December, 1994.

Schwartz, S. H. (In press). Cultural value differences: Some implications for work. *Applied Psychology: An International Review.*

Schwartz, S. H. (1996). Value priorities and behavior: Applying a theory of integrated value systems. In C. Seligman, J. M. Olson, & M. P. Zanna (Eds.), *Values: The Ontario Symposium* (Vol. 8) (pp. 1–24). Hillsdale, NJ: Lawrence Erlbaum.

Schwartz, S. H. (in press). Values and culture. In D. Munro, S. Carr, & J. Schumaker (Eds.), *Motivation and culture.* New York: Routledge.

Schwartz, S. H. & Bardi, A. (In press). Influences of adaptation to communist rule on value priorities in Eastern Europe. *Political Psychology,*

Schwartz, S. H. & Bilsky, W. (1987). Towards a psychological structure of human values. *Journal of Personality and Social Psychology, 53,* 550–562.

Schwartz, S. H. & Bilsky, W. (1990). Toward a theory of the universal structure and content of values: Extensions and cross-cultural replications. *Journal of Personality and Social Psychology, 58,* 878–891.

Schwartz, S. H. & Huismans, S. (1995). Value priorities and religiosity in four Western religions. *Social Psychology Quarterly, 58,* 88–107.

Schwartz, S. H. & Ros, M. (1995). Values in the West: A theoretical and empirical challenge to the individualism–collectivism cultural dimension. *World Psychology, 1,* 91–122.

Schwartz, S. H. & Sagiv, L. (1995). Identifying culture specifics in the content and structure of values. *Journal of Cross-Cultural Psychology, 26,* 92–116.

Schwartz, S. H., Verkasalo, M., Antonovsky, A., & Sagiv, L. (in press). Value priorities and social desirability: Much substance, some style. *British Journal of Social Psychology,*

Seligman, C., Olson, J. M., & Zanna, M. P. (1996). (Eds.). *Values: The Ontario symposium.* Hillsdale, NJ: Erlbaum.

Shackleton, V. J. & Ali, A. H. (1990). Work-related values of managers : A test of the Hofstede model. *Journal of Cross-Cultural Psychology, 21,* 109–118.

Shye, S. (1988). Multidimensional scaling versus factor analysis: A methodological note [Appendix to Shye, 1982]. *Journal of Applied Psychology, 73,* 308–311.

Singelis, T. M. (1994). The measurement of independent and interdependent self-construals. *Personality and Social Psychology Bulletin, 20,* 580–591.

Singelis, T. M. & Sharkey, W. F. (1995). Culture, self-construal and embarrassability. *Journal of Cross-Cultural Psychology, 26,* 622–644.

Singelis, T. M., Triandis, H. C., Bhawuk, D. S., & Gelfand, M. (1995). Horizontal and vertical dimensions of individualism and collectivism: A theoretical and measurement refinement. *Cross-Cultural Research, 29,* 240–275.

Sinha, D. & Tripathi, R. C. (1994). Individualism in a collectivist culture: A case of coexistence of opposites. In U. Kim, H. C. Triandis, C. Kagitçibasi, S-C. Choi, & G. Yoon (Eds.), *Individualism and collectivism: Theory, method and applications* (pp. 123–136). Thousand Oaks, CA: Sage.

Sinha, J. B. P. & Verma, J. (1994). Social support as a moderator of the relationship between allocentrism and psychological well-being. In U. Kim, H. C. Triandis, C. Kagitçibasi, S-C. Choi, & G.Yoon (Eds.), *Individualism and collectivism: Theory, method and applications* (pp. 267–275). Thousand Oaks, CA: Sage.

Smith, P. B., Dugan, S., & Trompenaars, F. (1996).

National culture and the values of organizational employees: A dimensional analysis across 43 nations. *Journal of Cross-Cultural Psychology, 27*, 231–264.

Smith, P. B. & Hooker, H. (1995). *Self and situation as determinants of assertiveness in the United Kingdom and Turkey.* Paper presented at Fourth European Congress of Psychology, Athens, Greece, July, 1995.

Smith, P. B., Peterson, M. F., & Leung, K. (1995). *Individualism–collectivism and the handling of disagreement: A 23-country study.* Submitted manuscript, University of Sussex, England.

Sondergaard, M. (1994). Hofstede's consequences: A study of reviews, citations and replications. *Organization Studies, 15*, 447–456.

Triandis, H. C. (1995). *Individualism and collectivism.* Boulder, CO: Westview.

Triandis, H. C., Bontempo, R., Betancourt, H., Bond, M., Leung, K., et al. (1986). The measurement of etic aspects of individualism and collectivism across cultures. *Australian Journal of Psychology, 38*, 257–267.

Triandis, H. C., Leung, K., Villareal, M., & Clack, F. L. (1985). Allocentric versus idiocentric tendencies: Convergent and discriminant validation. *Journal of Research in Personality, 19*, 395–415.

Triandis, H.C., McCusker, C., Betancourt, H., Iwao, S., Leung, K., et al. (1993). An emic–etic analysis of individualism and collectivism. *Journal of Cross-Cultural Psychology, 24*, 366–383.

Trompenaars, F. (1985). *The organization of meaning and the meaning of organization: A compara-tive study of the conceptions of organizational structure in different cultures.* Unpublished doctoral dissertation, Wharton School of Management, University of Pennsylvania, Philadelphia.

Trompenaars, F. (1993). *Riding the waves of culture.* London: Brealey.

Williams, J. E. & Best, D. L. (1982). *Measuring sex stereotypes: A thirty nation study.* Beverly Hills: Sage.

Williams, R. M., Jr. (1968). Values. In E. Sills (Ed.), *International encyclopaedia of the social sciences* (pp. 283–287). New York: MacMillan.

Yamaguchi, S. (1994). Collectivism among the Japanese: A perspective from the self. In U. Kim, H. C. Triandis, C. Kagitçibasi, S-C. Choi, & G. Yoon (Eds.), *Individualism and collectivism: Theory, method and applications* (pp. 175–178). Thousand Oaks, CA: Sage.

Yamaguchi, S., Kuhlman, D., & Sugimori, S. (1995). Personality correlates of allocentric tendencies in individualist and collectivist cultures. *Journal of Cross-Cultural Psychology, 26*, 658–672.

Yang, K. S. (1988). Will societal modernisation eventually eliminate cross-cultural psychological differences? In M. H. Bond (Ed.), *The cross-cultural challenge to social psychology* (pp. 67–85). Newbury Park, CA: Sage.

Zavalloni, M. (1980). Values. In H. C. Triandis & R. W. Brislin (Eds.), *Handbook of cross-cultural psychology* (Vol. 5, pp.73–120). Boston: Allyn and Bacon.

4

INTERGROUP RELATIONS ACROSS CULTURES

WILLIAM B. GUDYKUNST
California State University, Fullerton
United States

MICHAEL HARRIS BOND
Chinese University of Hong Kong
Hong Kong

Contents

Introduction

The behavior of individuals is based partly on their personal characteristics and partly on their group memberships. Lewin (1948) points out that during most of one's life the adult acts not purely as an individual but as a member of a social group. However, the different groups to which a person belong are not all equally important at a given moment; sometimes belonging to one group is dominant. Generally, in every situation a person seems to know to what group or groups he or she does or does not belong. An individual knows, more or less, where he or she stands, and this position largely determines behavior (p. 46). In short, to understand an individual's behavior, group memberships must be taken into consideration.

Sherif (1966) contends that "whenever individuals belonging to one group interact collectively or individually, with another group or its members *in terms of their group identifications,* we have an instance of intergroup behavior" (p. 12). Intergroup behavior can occur at many levels—when representatives of nations interact, when representatives of different social groups within a nation interact, and when individuals interact with other individuals based on their group identities. Although different levels of interaction are mentioned throughout this chapter, focus throughout is on individuals' behavior when it is based on their group identities.

Interpersonal and intergroup factors are not easily separated. Both influence individuals' behavior in any situation. Stephenson (1981) argues that it is difficult to think of any social situation that may not have both intergroup and interpersonal significance. In any interaction with another, our apparent membership of different social groups—be it male, female, young, English, black, or European—is at least a potential allegiance to be exploited by the other, such that we act in some sense as *representatives* of fellow members of those groups. When nationality, sex, or occupation becomes salient in the interaction, it does not necessarily obliterate the interpersonal significance; indeed, it may enhance it (p. 195). Throughout this chapter, interpersonal factors that are enhanced by intergroup factors, therefore, are addressed.

Our purpose in this chapter is to examine intergroup behavior across cultures. We divide the chapter into seven sections, beginning with issues in the measurement of cultural variability in intergroup behavior. Then, in the second section, we examine social and ethnolinguistic identitites, the primary characteristics that define behavior as intergroup. Next, we summarize research on intergroup expectations, such as stereotypes, intergroup affect, and intergroup attitudes. Following this, we examine intergroup social cognitions and intergroup communication. We complete our examination of intergroup behavior across cultures by discussing intergroup conflict, concluding with suggestions for future theorizing and research.

Measuring Cross-Cultural Variation in Intergroup Behavior

Hofstede's (1980) *Culture's Consequences* and other multi-cultural studies of values (e.g., Chinese Culture Connection, 1987; Hofstede & Bond, 1984; Triandis et al.,

1986; Schwartz, 1992) have stimulated theory development (e.g., Smith, Dugan, & Trompenaars, 1996) and hypothesis-testing (e.g., Leung, Bond, Carment, Krishnan, & Liebrand, 1990) concerning culture and behavior. These studies allow researchers to link previous anthropological insights to measured dimensions of cultural variability[1] (e.g., context-dependency to collectivism by Gudykunst & Ting-Toomey, 1988, p. 44), to break down monolithic stereotypes about "Westerners" and identify the uniqueness of American culture (e.g., Hofstede, 1980), and to discriminate ways in which superficially similar cultures are in fact distinct (e.g., Bond's analysis of Chinese values in Singapore, Taiwan, Hong Kong, and China, in press).

In this chapter, we examine cross-cultural work on intergroup behavior from an eclectic group of scholars. Most researchers link the cultural variability dimension of collectivism–individualism (COL–IND) to intergroup behavior. We, therefore, emphasize this dimension throughout the chapter.

Collectivism–Individualism

COL–IND and related variants enjoy a distinguished lineage in social science (see Kagitçibasi, this volume). Its pre-eminence has been fuelled by the emergence of the Five Dragons as economic powers and hence as viable, interesting research sites; much current cross-cultural research contrasts one of the Western cultures, which are high in IND, with one of these Asian cultures, which are high in COL. So, the database has grown along with theoretical elaborations, driven by research opportunities. The danger, of course, is that these findings may be elaborating a distinctively Asian variant of COL (Singelis, 1994a).

Definitions of COL-IND abound. Gudykunst and Ting-Toomey's (1988) definition is representative:

> In individualistic cultures, "people are supposed to look after themselves and their immediate family only," while in collectivistic cultures, "people belong to ingroups or collectivities which are supposed to look after them in exchange for loyalty" (Hofstede & Bond, 1984, p. 419). The "I" identity has precedence in individualistic cultures over the "we" identity, which takes precedence in collectivistic cultures. The emphasis in individualistic societies is on individuals' initiative and achievement, while emphasis is placed on belonging to groups in collectivistic societies. (pp. 40–41)

This definition suggests some important linkages between COL–IND and behavior: the sharper distinction between ingroup and outgroup implies that people in COL cultures would interact more frequently, more widely, more deeply and more positively with ingroup members than would members of IND cultures (see e.g., Wheeler, Reis, & Bond, 1989); the processes of mutual influence, harmony enhancement, and ingroup favoritism should also be stronger in COL cultures than in IND cultures.

Hofstede (1980) provides country scores for a large number of nations on COL-

IND. Although he replicated his findings at two time periods, 1969 and 1973, they were challenged as being population-dependent (IBM employees) and instrument-dependent (an in-house, work-values survey). Subsequent work has, however, confirmed the robustness of the COL dimension, using different populations and instruments (Chinese Culture Connection, 1987; Hofstede & Bond, 1984; Schwartz, 1994; Triandis et al., 1986). Subsequently, a second-order factor analysis of the results from Hofstede (1980), the Chinese Culture Connection (1987), and Schwartz (1994) identified a multifaceted construct of COL from dimensions that group together across all three studies (Bond, 1996).[2]

Cultures can be characterized by their degree of COL–IND. Persons within any culture, however, vary in the degree to which they mirror an IND or COL orientation. Because individuals, not cultures, behave, we must clearly move toward measuring COL–IND at the level of persons (see also Singelis & Brown, 1995).

COL–IND can be assessed at the level of the individual via personality traits, values, and self construals. Triandis, Leung, Villareal, and Clack (1985), for example, propose idiocentrism-allocentrism as the personality equivalents of IND–COL, respectively. They found that allocentrism is correlated positively with social support, and negatively with alienation and anomie in the United States. Idiocentrism, in contrast, is correlated positively with an emphasis on achievement and perceived loneliness in the United States. Idiocentric individuals in IND cultures see it as natural to "do their own thing" and disregard needs of their ingroups, while allocentric individuals in IND cultures are concerned about their ingroups (Triandis et al., 1988). Allocentric individuals in COL cultures "feel positive about accepting ingroup norms and do not even raise the question of whether or not to accept them," while idiocentric individuals in COL cultures "feel ambivalent and even bitter about acceptance of ingroup norms" (Triandis et al., 1988, p. 325). Several researchers have used idiocentrism-allocentrism in the study of behavior within and across cultures (e.g., Earley, 1989, 1993; Oyserman, 1993; Triandis et al., 1985, 1986, 1988, 1993), while others have studied personality issues using different labels (e.g., Yamaguchi, 1994, uses the term COL instead of allocentrism).

Schwartz and Bilsky (1990) present a theory of the universal psychological content and structure of human values, and of value groupings called domains. Schwartz and Bilsky argue that the interests served by value domains can be IND, COL, or mixed. The value domains of enjoyment, achievement, and self-direction serve individual interests; the value domains of prosocial, restrictive conformity, and security serve collective interests; and the value domain of maturity serves mixed interests. Bond (1988) also isolates a value factor that taps COL at the individual level that includes 11 values: tolerance of others (–), patience (-), harmony with others (–), noncompetiveness (–), trustworthiness (–), persistence (–), filial piety, respect for tradition, chastity in women, a sense of cultural superiority, and observation of rites and social rituals.

Markus and Kitayama's (1991) conceptualization of self-construals has led to measures of individualism–collectivism at the individual level. They distinguished two types of self-construal, an "independent notion of the self as an entity containing significant dispositional attributes, and as detached from context" from a self characterized as "interdependent with the surrounding context [such that] it is the 'other' or 'the self-in-relation-to-other' that is focal in individual experience (p. 225). Singelis (1994b) discovered that independent and interdependent self-construals are not negatively related, but orthogonal (see also Bhawuk & Brislin, 1992; Cross & Markus, 1991; Gudykunst et al., 1994). People from COL cultures, such as Asian Americans, are likely then to be higher in interdependence but lower in independence than are people from IND cultures, like European Americans (Singelis & Sharkey, 1995).

Any dependent variable of interest can be linked to one of the ways of assessing COL–IND.[3] The use of apologies (Barnlund & Yoshioka, 1990), for example, could be associated with the degree of one's interdependence or independence both within each of the cultural groups sampled *as well as* across the cultural groups. Should the same linkage be discovered within *and* across cultures, a universal relationship would be strongly suggested (Leung & Bond, 1989). A measurable, theoretical variable would then be available to explain individual apologizing behavior that distinguishes people within as well as across cultures. The *post hoc*, speculative quality plaguing most cross-cultural work (Leung & Bond, 1989) would be replaced by integrative theory-building (Smith & Bond, 1993, ch. 11).

Other Dimensions of Culture

Other dimensions of cultural variability can predict and explain cultural variability in behavior. Not all dimensions, however, appear to be linked directly to intergroup behavior. Hofstede's (1980) power distance (PD) may be related to intergroup behavior, especially when there are power differences between the groups involved. Similarly, Hofstede's masculinity–femininity (MF) is related to intergroup behavior, especially when gender groups are involved. Hofstede's uncertainty avoidance (UA) dimension, in contrast, is related to broader issues of intergroup behavior. In comparison to members of cultures low in UA, members of cultures high in UA have a lower tolerance "for uncertainty and ambiguity, which expresses itself in higher levels of anxiety and energy release, greater need for formal rules and absolute truth, and less tolerance for people or groups with deviant ideas or behavior" (Hofstede, 1979, p. 395). There is a strong desire for consensus in high UA cultures, therefore, deviant behavior is not acceptable. People in high UA cultures tend to display emotions more than people in low UA cultures. People in low UA cultures have lower stress levels, weaker superegos, but accept dissent and risk-taking more than people in high UA cultures.

In the most recent version of Anxiety/Uncertainty Management (AUM) theory, Gudykunst (1995) argues that interaction with strangers [members of outgroups] in high UA cultures may be highly ritualistic and/or very polite. These rituals provide clear scripts for interaction and allow individuals to attune their behavior with strangers. If people from high UA cultures interact with strangers in a situation where there are not clear rules, they may ignore the strangers, treating them as though they do not exist. AUM theory also makes other predictions based on UA that are presented later in this chapter.

Cultural differences with respect to uncertainty avoidance are important because Asian cultures, while similar on COL-IND, vary widely on UA. This allows for strong tests of UA-based hypotheses across countries sharing Asian history and philosophy (e.g., Singapore or Hong Kong versus Japan or South Korea).

To summarize, social scientists can identify universally meaningful *and* measurable dimensions of psychological variation (e.g., Bond, 1988; Schwartz, 1992; Triandis et al., 1993), some of which (e.g., Bond's Social Integration versus Cultural Inwardness or Schwartz's Universalism) are conceptually like dimensions isolated at the cultural level (e.g., COL–IND). But new types of measures need to be developed. Up to now, we have relied too heavily on broad measures of value that are less closely tied to behaviors than are other constructs (Leung, Bond, & Schwartz, 1994). Expectancies (Bond, Leung, & Schwartz, 1992), self-definitions (Triandis, 1978), relationship rules (Argyle, Henderson, Bond, Iizuka, & Contarello, 1986), and social axioms (Leung & Bond, 1993) are some of the constructs with cross-cultural potential in this respect.

Given this overview of issues regarding cultural variability, we turn our attention to cultural variability in intergroup behavior, beginning with social and ethnolinguistic identities.

Social and Ethnolinguistic Identity

Tajfel (1978) argues that when individuals engage in interpersonal behavior, their behavior is driven by their personal identities, and when individuals engage in intergroup behavior, their behavior is driven by their social identities.

An intergroup interaction occurs when one of the two parties becomes aware that the other is a member of a different group. The other may or may not likewise perceive the opposite number as an outgroup member. Such mutual identification may be straightforward and salient. Gender and race may well be "primitive," universal categories in this regard (Brewer, 1988); one's physical distinctiveness in the social field may cue the awareness of different group membership (McGuire, McGuire, Child, & Fujioka, 1978); variations of language style, indeed of the language used itself, are likewise potent reminders of difference. Clothing, nonverbal behaviors, and physiognomic prototypicality all combine to further signal difference (Smith & Bond, 1993, ch. 9).

Social Identity

Social identity theory (SIT) is concerned with predicting individuals' motivations to maintain or change their group memberships and the relations among their groups and other groups (see Abrams & Hogg, 1990, for a summary). SIT's underlying assumption is that individuals want to have a positive self-concept, which includes belonging to groups that have high status. Tajfel (1978) argues that individuals engage in social categorizations by grouping people in ways that make sense to them, and compare their own groups to others' groups on dimensions that they value. One outcome of this comparison process is the development of social identities that involve individuals' knowledge of belonging to social groups and the value or emotional significance attached to that membership. Individuals develop positive social identities when they perceive their groups as higher on the valued dimensions; they develop negative social identities when they perceive their groups as lower on the valued dimensions than others' groups.

Individuals are dissatisfied when they have negative social identities. When they perceive that the intergroup situation in which their groups are emersed is unjust or changeable, individuals may take individual or collective action to change the intergroup situation as a way to develop positive identities (i.e., a social change strategy). Alternatively, individuals may try to change their group memberships and identify with groups that have high status (i.e., a social mobility strategy).

Specific categorizations activated in specific situations influence perceptions and behavior. Individuals categorize themselves, and the people with whom they interact categorize them as well. Through the process of categorization individuals select from among the available identities that could influence their behavior in the situation (e.g., they categorize themselves and others in terms of ethnicity instead of nationality). Sometimes individuals accept the categories others impose on them and act on the basis of the identities activated. At other times individuals are not constrained to accept the identities ascribed to them by others (Bond & Venus, 1991; Weinrich, 1983). The specific identity individuals use to guide their behavior in a particular situation is based on a negotiation process between themselves and the people with whom they are interacting (see Ting-Toomey, 1993, for a summary of this argument). One identity, however, tends to predominate and guide behavior in any particular interaction.

One consequence of individuals' categorizing themselves and others is an ingroup bias; that is, positive traits and rewards tend to be assigned to the ingroup (Doise & Sinclair, 1973). Ingroup bias tends to involve negative interpersonal attraction toward outgroup members (Turner, Shaver, & Hogg, 1983). Ingroup bias can occur when category membership is arbitrary, and even when a close friend is a member of the outgroup being discriminated against (Vaughan, Tajfel, & Williams, 1981). Ingroup bias is reduced when membership in social groups is "crossed"; that is, in situations in which people are members of an outgroup on one criterion (e.g., ethnicity), but members of an ingroup on another criterion (e.g., religion; Deschamps & Doise, 1978). Gaertner et al. (1994) also suggest that ingroup bias is decreased when members of different groups activate a common ingroup identity. To illustrate, the ingroup bias is reduced when individuals change their cognitions from "us" and "them" to an inclusive "we" (e.g., from individuals thinking about themselves as European American and African American to thinking about themselves as Americans). Another way to reduce ingroup bias is the use of nonevaluative niche differentiation whereby groups enact equally valued, but separate roles (Thalhofer, 1993).

While SIT was developed in IND cultures, it appears to be generalizable to COL cultures. In fact, Hinkle and Brown (1990) argue that SIT is more applicable in COL cultures than in IND cultures. Majeed and Ghosh (1982), for example, examined social identity in three ethnic groups in India. As predicted by SIT, they observed differential evaluations of self, ingroup, and outgroups in High Caste, Muslims, and Scheduled Caste members. Ghosh and Huq (1985) found similar results for Hindu and Muslim evaluations of self and ingroup in India and Bangladesh.

Brewer and Campbell's (1976) research on ingroup and outgroup evaluations in Africa and Peabody's (1985) research in Europe also are consistent with SIT. Brewer and Campbell's study further suggests that the more group identities based on different categories (e.g., race, religion, economic conditions) coincide, the more similar members of the ingroup are assumed to be.

Wetherell (1982) found that both Europeans and Polynesians in New Zealand display bias in intergroup situations, but Polynesians moderate their discrimination toward the outgroup more than Europeans. Gudykunst and Ting-Toomey (1988) argue that this study suggests that members of COL cultures moderate their outgroup discrimination more than members of IND cultures. This argument is consistent with research indicating that members of COL cultures use the equity norm with outgroup members more than members of IND cultures (e.g., Leung, 1988a). Moderation of outgroup discrimination and the use of the equity norm with outgroups in COL cultures, however, probably are limited to situations where there are not hostile relations between the groups.

Research in Hong Kong (e.g., Bond & Hewstone, 1988; Hewstone, Bond, & Wan, 1983) is compatible with Wetherell's (1982) findings. To illustrate, Bond and Hewstone found that British high school students in Hong Kong perceive social identity and intergroup differentiation to be more important than do Chinese high school students. The British students also perceived group membership to be more important and held more positive images of the ingroup than did the Chinese students. The results for the Chinese do not necessarily contradict SIT. Rather, they suggest that social differentiation in Hong Kong is "relatively muted" due to Chinese conflict avoidance (Bond & Hewstone, 1988).

Wetherell's (1982) findings also appear to be consistent with Feldman's (1968) field study in Paris, Boston, and Athens. Feldman found that outgroup members are treated better in Athens than in Boston or Paris. Feldman's results, however, may be unique to Greece where foreigners and guests are perceived as potential members of the ingroup. Foreigners in other collectivistic cultures generally are not viewed as potential ingroup members (Triandis, 1988).

Social identities are more important in COL cultures than in IND cultures, and one social identity may consistently predominate in COL cultures where there is only one major ingroup. Gabrenya and Wang (1983), for example, found that Chinese utilize more group-based self descriptions than people in the United States. This conclusion appears to be consistent with studies of the spontaneous self-concept across cultures (e.g., Bochner, 1994; Cousins, 1989; Driver & Driver, 1983; Ip & Bond, 1995). To illustrate, Bochner found that collectivists in Malaysia produce more group and fewer individual self-descriptions than individualists in Australia and Britain. Bond and Cheung (1983), however, suggest that a simple COL–IND distinction does not adequately explain all variations. They found that Hong Kong Chinese and North Americans mentioned family roles more than Japanese, while Japanese mentioned sex and age more than the other two. These differences are compatible with Hofstede's (1980) MF dimension of cultural variability (Gudykunst & Ting-Toomey, 1988).

Members of COL cultures draw a sharper distinction between members of ingroups and outgroups than members of IND cultures (Triandis, 1988). Triandis (1995) argues that individualists value ingroup heterogeneity, while collectivists value ingroup homogeneity. Gudykunst (1995) contends that the emphasis on group memberships and the relatively few ingroups in COL cultures leads to collectivists being better able than individualists to categorize members of outgroups in the same categories (groups) in which they place themselves.[4]

Ethnolinguistic Identity

Giles and Johnson (1981, 1987) isolate five components of ethnolinguistic identity: strength of identification with the ingroup, ethnolinguistic vitality (i.e., the range and functions of an ethnic group's language), interethnic comparisons, softness of group boundaries, and multiple group memberships. They argue that individuals are likely to define encounters as intergroup in nature when they identify with the ingroup, perceive the ingroup to have vitality, make insecure intergroup comparisons, perceive group boundaries to be hard, and do not have multiple group memberships (e.g., no crossed memberships with outgroup members).

Strength of ethnic identity influences attitudes toward outgroups and their languages. Kraemer and Birenbaum (1993) found that the saliency of ethnic group membership influences Arabs' and Jews' attitudes toward Arabic and Hebrew. Similarly, Gao, Schmidt, and Gudykunst (1994) observed that the strength of ethnic identity influences Mexican Americans' perceptions of the vitality of English and Spanish.

Ethnolinguistic identity is associated with outgroup language competence in intergroup settings. Giles and Johnson (1987), for example, found that strength of ingroup identification, negative interethnic comparisons, and perceived hard boundaries are related negatively to outgroup language competence in bilingual Welsh adolescents. Similar findings emerge in Hall and Gudykunst's (1986) study of international students' competence in English in the United States.

Gudykunst (1989) compared ethnolinguistic identity across cultures (using international students) and linked the variations to Hofstede's (1980) dimensions of cultural variability. He found that members of COL cultures identify with groups other than the ingroup more than members of IND cultures; members of high UA cultures make less secure intergroup comparisons than members of low UA cultures; members of COL, feminine cultures identify with the ingroup more than members of IND, masculine cultures; and members of feminine cultures perceive softer boundaries between the ingroup and outgroups than members of masculine cultures.

Concluding Issues

Identity cues for difference may not always work in concert; the Chinese-looking person may address the Hong Kong merchant in English, the petite lady may pound her fist on the table when making a point, the 50-year-old may still play basketball with skill and vigor. Personal and social factors may focus interactants on difference *or* on similarity in categorization. A history of intergroup conflict and its legacy of revenge (Kim & Smith, 1993) may push toward perceiving difference (Giles & Johnson, 1987), as may any encounter in a competitive social setting (Wish, Deutsch, & Kaplan, 1976). Likewise, the personality characteristics of ethnocentrism, aggressiveness, and insecurity may exacerbate pressures for group differentiation (Scott, 1965). Conversely, an explicit ideology of multiculturalism and group harmony as one finds in Canada and Singapore, for example, or the sharing of cooperative, superordinate goals (Sherif, 1966) push toward focusing on shared identifications. Similarly, the basic personality disposition of openmindedness (Riemann, Grubich, Hempel, Mergl, & Richter, 1993) and attitudes of internationalism (Hett, 1991) will probably counteract the salience of differences in cues, perhaps by inhibiting the automaticity of stereotype activation (Devine, 1989). The net result of these considerations is that identities are always negotiated and there is no guarantee that the result will be an outgroup categorization (Wu, 1979).

Intergroup Expectations

Intergroup expectations emerge whenever others are categorized as group members. Once individuals are categorized, stereotypes may be activated, and the affect and attitudes individuals have toward the members of other groups become salient. We begin with stereotypes.

Stereotypes

Stereotypes are packages of beliefs about typical members of groups, including our own (see Hamilton, Sherman, & Ruvolo, 1990, for a summary of research on how stereotypes create expectations). As Smith and Bond (1993) point out,

> *stereotypes vary in many aspects: they may be widely shared by others, even by the stereotyped persons themselves, or they may be idiosyncratic to the individual holding them; they may involve beliefs about the traits, values, behaviours, opinions or, indeed, beliefs of typical persons from that other group; they may be simple or differentiated, positive or negative, confidently or unsurely held . . .*

> *The early work on stereotypes was dominated by an interest in groups that typically shared a history of conflict, abuse or atrocity . . . Against such a background, stereotypes about the out-group were extreme, simple, negative and symmetrical, with members of each group rating their own group members positively while denigrating members of the out-group . . . The elimination of stereotypes was widely believed to be a prerequisite for intergroup harmony (p. 169).*

Contemporary research, however, suggests that eliminating stereotypes is not possible (e.g., Devine, 1989).

Recent researchers have assessed stereotypes of interacting groups not in a state of open hostility (e.g., Linssen & Hagendoorn, 1994). Beliefs about the traits of outgroup members are differentiated (Brewer & Campbell, 1976, p. 144). A key "goodness" or beneficence dimension (Giles & Ryan, 1982) always emerges. Some degree of ingroup enhancement on this dimension may be a necessary ideological component of any viable social group even when there is no open hostility (Mihalyi, 1984–5; Smith, 1992, p. 83). An independent "competence" dimension, however, also often is found and group ratings here usually correspond to independent assessments of the relative status enjoyed by the interacting groups (Giles & Ryan, 1982). Other dimensions of difference, such as emotional expressiveness and openness to change, can be elicited when a full range of traits is assessed (e.g., Bond, 1986).

Members of interacting groups often show consensus on the relative ranking of groups on the various characteristics in question (see Lee & Ottati, 1993). Stereotypes in this sense, then, may contain a "kernel of truth" (Allport, 1954). This consensus arises from cues associated with identifiable social/geographical factors (Linssen & Hagendoorn, 1994) and may be useful in guiding specific types of interpersonal behaviors across group lines (Bond, 1986). Additionally, the differentiation of these shared trait stereotypes allows individuals to derive a sense of esteem from their group memberships while still giving credit to members of outgroups (e.g, Berry, Kalin, & Taylor, 1977). Taylor's (1981) thesis is that such differentiated, mutual appreciation is a feature of harmonious intergroup relations.

Stereotypes generally do not lead to accurate predictions of intergroup behavior. To illustrate, a person's ethnic identification is a complex construct (Keefe, 1992; Weinreich, 1991), including strength of ethnic identification, the evaluation of that ethnic membership, perceptions of ethnic practices, and the importance attached to those practices. These components of identity are variable across the members of a given ethnic group and are only moderately inter-correlated (Rosenthal & Feldman, 1992). It is thus not possible as an outsider to ascribe a group membership to individuals and then use that ascription to accurately predict their responses to their own groups. Indeed, individuals draw a distinction between themselves and typical ingroup members (Bond, 1993), often perceiving themselves as being more similar to members of certain outgroups than to their ascribed ingroup (Weinreich, Luk, & Bond, 1994). It is these *patterns* of self, ingroup and outgroup identification that may prove decisive in predicting intergroup attitudes and behaviors, not outgroup ratings alone.

Also, a given outgroup member can be categorized in a number of ways—by age, gender, race, ethnicity, education, profession and so forth. Such potential multiplicity in applicable stereotypes makes it difficult to predict what characteristics will eventually guide that other person's behavior (see work on cross-categorization; e.g., Dorai, 1993; Hewstone, Islam, & Judd, 1993). Further complicating the process is the probability that there are cultural differences in the salience of these social categories (Triandis & Triandis, 1960), just as there are cultural differences in their content (e.g., Best & Williams, 1993, on gender stereotypes).

Certain types of stereotypes may be more critical in predicting intergroup attitudes and behaviors than others. Most work to date has examined beliefs about the *character* of outgroup members. Beliefs about the *values* of group members are also important (Bond, 1993; Schwartz & Struch, 1989; Staub, 1990). Esses, Haddock, and Zanna (1993) use the term "symbolic beliefs" to refer to "all thoughts about the relation between social groups and basic values and norms, whether the relation is negative or positive" (p. 147). Some groups are perceived to promote, others to undermine, our cherished social traditions. These symbolic beliefs are not highly correlated with beliefs about character, and, more importantly, are relatively more powerful than beliefs about character in predicting negative attitudes towards a given group and its members (Esses, Haddock, & Zanna, 1993; Haddock, Zanna, & Esses, 1993). These negative symbolic beliefs then lead to discriminatory behavior, at least for those high in authoritarianism (Haddock, Zanna, & Esses, 1993)

One neglected component of stereotypes concerns beliefs about how the outgroup deals with group diversity. Is the outgroup believed to honor and accommodate other groups, or to revile and suppress them? Is it believed to hold "ideologies of antagonism," defined by Staub (1988) as "systems of beliefs that designate others as antagonists or enemies, requiring self-defense and superior power for the sake of one's security" (p. 83)? What procedures is it believed to use in resolving group conflict and what intergroup outcomes are believed to result from its dealings with other groups? These expectations at the group level parallel those for interactional, procedural, and distributive justice at the individual level (see, e.g., Leung, 1988b). Beliefs about the outgroup's intergroup ideology may be decisive in predicting whether and how group members interact across group lines.

Intergroup Affect

Allport (1954) saw prejudice as driven by projected guilt, and Dollard, Doob, Miller, Mowrer, and Sears (1939) hypothesized that it was driven by displaced hostility. Recently, positive intergroup emotions have been shown to make distinctive contributions in predicting outgroup attitudes (Dijker, 1987; Stangor, Sullivan, & Ford, 1991). Emotions appear particularly important in determining responses to groups perceived in a relatively favorable light (Esses, Haddock, & Zanna, 1993).

Emotions, such as panic, tenor, and distrust, assume great import in historically hostile intergroup environments. Stephan and Stephan (1985) argue that intergroup anxiety arises from the expectation of negative consequences for one's group during contact. Their research with ethnic groups in the United States demonstrated that anxiety is a result of lower levels of outgroup contact, larger status differences defining that contact, and a high ratio of out- to ingroup members. Recently, Islam and Hewstone's (1993) research in Bangladesh confirmed that minority group members have higher levels of intergroup anxiety even though their outgroup contact is more frequent, demonstrating the greater impact of qualitative over quantitative aspects of the contact (see also Dijker, 1987; Haddock, Zanna & Esses, 1994). Intergroup anxiety predicted both perceptions of lower variability of outgroup member characteristics and also negative attitudes towards the outgroup.

Stereotypes about the character of outgroup members are not as effective as intergroup emotions in predicting outgroup attitudes. Esses, Haddock, and Zanna (1993) argue that "stereotypes (about character) in part determine our emotional reactions to members of other groups which then more directly influence our attitudes towards the groups" (pp. 152–3). Previous work linking stereotypes of outgroup characteristics to outgroup attitudes may have shown effects which derived from the unmeasured agency of intergroup affect. Clearly, future work on intergroup attitudes should be multivariate and include intergroup emotions as predictors.

Intergroup Attitudes

Two attitude domains are particularly important to understanding intergroup behavior: ethnocentrism and multicultural attitudes. We begin with ethnocentrism.

Sumner (1906) defines ethnocentrism as "the view of things in which one's own group is the center of everything, and all others are scaled and rated with reference to it" (p. 13). Summarizing the research of Campbell and his associates (Brewer & Campbell, 1976; Campbell & LeVine, 1968), Triandis (1994) identifies four generalizations about this universal tendency:

1. What goes on in our culture is seen as "natural" and "correct," and what goes on in other cultures is perceived as "unnatural" and "incorrect."
2. We perceive our own ingroup customs as universally valid.
3. We unquestionably think that ingroup norms, roles, and values are correct.
4. We believe that it is natural to help and cooperate with members of our ingroup, to favor our ingroup, to feel proud of our ingroup, and to be distrustful of and even hostile toward outgroups. (pp. 251–2)

Our ingroup defines the standard which guides our assessment of other groups and our willingness to associate with them (Lambert, Mermigis, & Taylor, 1986). The more similar we believe outgroups are to our standard, the less hostile we are towards them (Brewer & Campbell, 1976).

The study of ethnocentrism as an individual trait began after the Second World War with the development of the F (Facism) personality scale by Adorno et al. (1950). Using a psychoanalytic perspective, they developed a scale measuring a syndrome involving conservativism, deference towards authority figures and hostility towards outgroup members. This "authoritarian personality" was linked to antecedent conditions of parental socialization, social class, and so forth. Other measures of attitudes towards outgroups also have been developed, like Rokeach's (1960) Dogmatism measuring outgroup rejection, and Sampson and Smith's (1957) World-mindedness measuring openness to outgroups. A recent addition is Altemeyer's (1988) Right-Wing Authoritarianism scale (RWA). People high on this personality dimension are more negative in their attitudes towards various outgroups (Esses, Haddock, & Zanna, 1993). These negative attitudes are predicted by symbolic beliefs for those high in RWA, whereas negative attitudes held by those low in RWA are predicted by stereotypes of (outgroup) character and affects towards those groups. So, the processes leading to outgroup rejection by those high and low in RWA appear to differ (see also Haddock, Zanna, & Esses, 1993).

Research (e.g., Berry & Kalin, 1979; Kalin & Berry, in press) suggests that there is a reciprocity in interethnic attitudes in Canada. Members of ethnic groups have attitudes toward other ethnic groups that are similar to the attitudes that members of those ethnic groups hold toward them. Ethnocentric attitudes, however, still exist in that individual's attitudes toward their own groups and positive reference groups are more positive than attitudes toward outgroups.

Most measures of authoritarianism were developed in the United States or Canada. The personality dynamics leading to prejudice or openness in any unique culture may not operate in different cultural settings. In consequence, a given measure, like Fascism (Kagitçibasi, 1970) or World-mindedness (Der-Karabetian, 1992), does not always form a coherent constellation when exported to other countries. Cross-cultural comparisons therefore become problematic. Bond (1988) reported the results of a 22-country study of values in university students that first established the composition of two, culture-general dimensions of value. The first, Social Integration versus Cultural Inwardness, contrasted values of broad openness, such as tolerance of others and non-competitiveness, with values exhalting the ingroup, such as respect for tradition and a sense of cultural superiority. The similarity of this value dimension to (negative) Authoritarianism is striking. Persons from countries like the Netherlands or (then) West Germany were high on this value dimension; persons from India and Pakistan, low.

Social Integration versus Cultural Inwardness has much in common with Schwartz's (1992) Openness to Change versus Conservativism and Hofstede's (1980) Individualism versus Collectivism (Leung & Bond, 1989). One end endorses an acceptance of difference; the other, a rejection. The possible implications for intergroup relations for persons holding such opposing values are obvious. Staub (1990), for example, identifies the belief in cultural superiority as a condition promoting outgroup scapegoating and violence. We would therefore predict that violent suppression of minority groups would be greater in societies higher in Cultural Inwardness; institutions protecting human rights, lower (see Bond, 1991, for a discussion of human rights observances in these countries).

Smith (1992) treats ethnocentrism as meeting a need for group inclusion and the existential need for self-transcendence. National and cultural identifications anchor people in a meaning system that confers order and pathways to dignity (see also Solomon, Greenberg, & Pyszezynski, 1991, on terror management). He points out, however, that "people can be devoted to collectivities that bring transcendent meaning to their lives without buying into the full pernicious package of ethnocentrism" (p. 87). Smith supports this distinction between positive and negative ethnocentrism by citing Feshback's (1987) factor analytic separation of patriotism (concern and pride in one's country) from nationalism (striving for dominance, beliefs in superiority). Previous measures of ethnocentrism have emphasized the "pernicious," chauvinistic component of ethnocentrism, neglecting its sustaining, integrative aspect. Thus, people can value their own heritage without disparaging that of others. Kalin and Berry's (1996) research in Canada further illustrates that desiring unity (integration) and accepting diversity are not necessarily in conflict.

Berry et al. (1989) proposed a variety of acculturation attitudes for multicultural societies, isolating two orientations:

> *One pertains to the maintenance and development of one's ethnic distinctiveness in society, deciding whether or not one's cultural identity and customs are of value and to be retained. The other issue involves the desirability of inter-ethnic contact, deciding whether relations with other groups in the larger society are of value and to be sought. (Those familiar with multiculturalism policy will recognize two of the key elements in the policy: heritage maintenance, and social participation and sharing) (Berry, 1990, p. 14).*

Dichotomizing each of the orientations results in a fourfold classification of attitude constellations available to individuals or groups: integration, assimilation, separation, and marginalization. These attitude constellations have predictable relations to stress experienced by immigrants with those endorsing integration showing less, those endorsing separation and marginalization showing more (Krishnan & Berry, 1992).

Particularly important in plural societies is the acculturation profile characterizing the dominant group. This profile provides a context, and in some cases, national policies, within which acculturating groups must develop a *modus vivendi* for achieving their group goals. We need cross- national studies linking attitudes of these dominant groups to indices characterizing the intergroup relationships in these nations.[5] One way these profiles could be developed is through the use of Berry and Kalin's (1995) multicultural ideology scale.

At the psychological level, policies of "active multiculturalism" make two assumptions: (1) that ethnic group members are motivated to retain their cultural heritages, and (2) that they feel secure in the intergroup mosaic (Moghaddam, 1993). Not surprisingly, however, it is the higher status groups within a given society that feel more secure and positively oriented toward heritage culture retention by all groups; visible minorities are more ambivalent about such retention and less secure in the social hierarchy (Moghaddam & Taylor, 1987). Obviously, if the higher status groups define the criteria for status ranking, then it is more difficult for members of lower status groups to value their heritage or to feel secure. So, a tension continues to surround the intercultural issue even in societies with policies of active multiculturalism.

Security within the ethnic mosaic is not the only factor predisposing toward outgroup tolerance. Kalin and Berry (1980) controlled for ethnicity and socio-economic status, two correlates of perceived security, and found that higher geographic mobility, intranational or international, also was associated with higher ethnic tolerance. Similarly, higher degrees of ethnic mixing in a given area were related to more favorable outgroup attitudes (Kalin & Berry, 1982). Both studies were conducted in Canada, a country characterized by active, public multiculturalism. Such a superordinate, national goal undoubtedly reduces intergroup bias and hostility (Gaertner et al., 1994) These findings, therefore, may not replicate in countries where government policies and interventions fail to provide minority groups with economic access, due process and physical protection (Berry, 1991). Intergroup studies in such cultures are rare, however, perhaps because the results can be so politically sensitive.

Intergroup Social Cognition

Intergroup social cognitions deal with how members of one group think about members of other groups. We begin with intergroup contexts.

Intergroup Contexts

Interpersonal interaction across cultural lines occurs within social contexts that characterize the relations between the cultural groups and the persons involved. Bochner (1982) provided a list of variables to consider in intergroup contact, including time span of the interaction, frequency of contact, degree of intimacy, relative status, numerical balance, among others. Gallois and Callan (1991) examined the impact of situational norms involving degree of formality and threat on interethnic accommodation and speech patterns.

Sagiv and Schwartz (1995) discuss social dominance as a contextual factor, arguing that for minority group members, their social identity as group members is more salient than for dominant group members. Hence, minority group members view contact with dominant group members more in terms of group differences and characteristics. Their readiness for outgroup contact is more strongly influenced by the norms, attitudes, and stereotypes toward the outgroup prevalent in their own group. In contrast, members of dominant groups, for whom group membership is less salient, view contact with minority group members in more individual terms. They are therefore more influenced by their personal experiences and characteristics such as their values (see also Haddock, Zanna, & Esses, 1993 on determinants of outgroup attitudes).

Such approaches to understanding intergroup behavior are predicated upon interactants sharing the same "culture of contexts." Indeed, some contexts probably have the same meanings to persons from any culture. When this similarity of understanding exists, then one can proceed to analyze the intergroup and interpersonal dynamics without reference to culture (Smith & Bond, 1993). Cross-cultural research on episode representation suggests that such similarity cannot always be presumed, however (Gallimore, Goldenberg, & Weisner, 1993).

Episode Perception

Intergroup contact occurs during social episodes like arriving late to class, making a joke during a conference, bargaining with a salesclerk. Within a given culture these exchanges will be similarly construed (e.g., Forgas, 1979) and coordination of behavior relatively easy (Furnham, 1982). Problems arise interculturally if these same episodes are construed differently. If so, the interactants are participating in psychologically different events and the consequent behavior exchanges are likely to be unexpected, puzzling, and difficult to integrate for both participants.

Evidence suggests that common social episodes are very differently construed (Forgas & Bond, 1985; Oatey, 1992). Not only may different dimensions be used for episode representation, but even when the same dimension is used, a given event may be located in different positions by members of the cultural groups involved. Cross-cultural training (see Brislin & Horvath, this volume) could involve helping newcomers to master the meaning of recurring situations. Such an approach would require a set of etic dimensions for episode cognition, a resource that will require more research on this important, but curiously neglected, topic. Meanwhile, researchers cannot naively presume that the "same" episodes are similarly understood by differently cultured persons.

Perceiving the Character of Others

There is considerable evidence that people from a variety of linguistic/cultural traditions use at least five broad dimensions to characterize themselves and other persons (Bond, 1994b; McCrae & John, 1992). These dimensions within the tradition of the Five Factor Model of personality (Digman, 1990) are extroversion, agreeableness, conscientiousness, neuroticism, and openness to experience or culture. They are used to structure social perceptions in all cultures so far studied and have important functional consequences for social interaction (Bond, 1983a).

Culture enters this process of social perception in two ways. First, it is probable that the same phenotypic behavior (e.g., not responding to an insult, complimenting an employee publicly, making negative remarks about oneself, etc.) are construed as examples of different trait dimensions by persons from different cultural traditions. Self-effacing comments, for example, probably connote agreeableness in COL cultures, but neuroticism in IND cultures (Markus & Kitayama, 1991), although little systematic knowledge is available (e.g., Young, 1980). If the same behaviors are differently linked in this way, the potential for miscommunication is enhanced.

Second, people from different cultures may differentially emphasize certain of the five dimensions in their intergroup exchanges (Korten, 1974; Williams et al., 1994). Hong Kong Chinese students, for example, rely on conscientiousness judgments more strongly than Australian students in guiding their decisions to trust another. The Australians for their part placed a greater weight upon judgments of the other's emotional stability (Bond & Forgas, 1984).

Language Effects on Person Perception

In intergroup interactions, often one or more parties speak in a language that is not their native language. The language spoken affects the self-concept of the speakers (Pierson & Bond, 1982; Yang & Bond, 1980). These emergent self-concepts reflect stereotypes about the language groups involved (Bond, 1983b) and the relations between the groups (Pierson & Bond, 1982). The self-concepts that emerge appear to be true language effects, as they occur independent of the ethnicity of one's interlocutor (Grujic & Libby, 1978; Pierson & Bond, 1982). The language of interaction also affects the perceptions of one's interlocutor (Pierson & Bond, 1982) and the process by which this perception occurs. Hoffman, Lau, and Johnson (1986), for example, demonstrated that language-specific personality schemas affected both impressions and memories of individuals described in their first or second languages.

Language may also affect the perception of others indirectly by eliciting different nonverbal behaviors during speech. Pierson and Bond (1982), for example, found that Cantonese bilinguals spoke slower, gazed less at a speaking interlocutor, and used more filled pauses when conversing in English regardless of their interlocutor's ethnicity. These differences were independent of the speaker's fluency in English and could well lead to different impressions being formed about them by observers (see e.g., Gifford, 1994).

Judging the Causes of Others' Behavior

Islam and Hewstone (1993) define intergroup attribution as "the ways members of different social groups explain the behavior (as well as the outcomes and consequences of behavior) of members of their own and other social groups" (p. 936). This process is affected by the relations between the social groups, but may be further complicated if ingroup and outgroup members come from different cultures with distinctive rules for assigning behaviors with meanings (Fletcher & Ward, 1988).

Pettigrew (1979) defines the "ultimate attribution error" as the "systematic patterning of intergroup misattributions shaped in part by prejudice" (p. 464). Pettigrew (1979) advanced five hypotheses relating to the ultimate attribution error.

Hewstone (1990) concludes that there is some support for each of Pettigrew's propositions:

1. There is a tendency to attribute negative outgroup behaviour to personal causes within the actor. When found, this tendency takes the form of a categorization effect (there is more internal attribution for a negative act by an outgroup than an ingroup member), rather than an outcome effect for outgroup actors. Contrary to Taylor and Jaggi's hypothesis, there is generally *not* more internal attribution for negative than positive acts by an outgroup member. There is also a tendency for outgroup failure to be attributed more to lack of ability than is ingroup failure.

2. For positive acts, Pettigrew's predictions cannot be tested precisely, because none of the available studies has included attributions to "the exceptional case." For the remaining three causes, there is some support. Studies on attributions for positive outcomes have sometimes reported less internal attribution for a positive act by an outgroup than an ingroup member. There is also evidence that outgroup success is sometimes explained away in terms of good luck, high effort or an easy task.

3. There is evidence of group-serving attributions for subjects in many studies, but while effects can be stronger for prejudiced individuals . . . this effect has not always been found. . . .

4. The prediction that group-serving attributions are more likely when perceivers are aware of their own and the actor's group memberships is supported by the weakness or absence of effects when experimental manipulations are weak or unconvincing . . . and by stronger effects when minority groups become aware of intergroup disparities. . . .

5. Group-serving attributions do vary across intergroup situations . . . and may be stronger when the groups have histories of intense conflict and possess negative stereotypes and when group differences covary with national and socioeconomic differences. . . . The bias can, however, be extinguished, even reversed, for members of subordinate or low status groups. (pp. 327–328)

Subsequent work by Islam and Hewstone (1993) has shown a link between causal attributions and self-esteem, suggesting that intergroup attributions may be used to enhance one's social identity. Further, crossed categorizations can attenuate intergroup attributional bias (see also Brown & Turner, 1979), although certain categories, like religion for the Muslims, may be especially tenacious.

Certain cultural groups are socialized to be more biased in favor of their ingroup. Bond's (1988) findings of cultural differences on the dimension of Social Integration versus Cultural Inwardness and the general logic of COL suggests that such differential favoritism is the case, especially when there are hostile relations between the groups. Indeed, Al-Zahrani and Kaplowitz (1993) found that the more allocentric Saudis showed more intergroup bias and outgroup derogation in their attributions than the more idiocentric Americans.

Culture's effects on attribution are, however, much more basic to the process itself than its outcomes. Perhaps the most widely documented difference is the tendency for most COL cultural groups to give greater weight to external or contextual factors in explaining behavior, at least in comparison to Americans (Al-Zahrani & Kaplowitz, 1993; Crittendon, 1991; Fry & Ghosh, 1980; Lee & Seligman, 1993; Miller, 1984; Miller, Bersoff, & Harwood, 1990; Morris, Nisbett, & Peng, in press; Singelis & Brown, 1995). This emphasis on situational factors may help moderate overt responses arising from the attributions. Americans may be extreme in their assignment of personal agency, thereby rendering the fundamental attribution error (Ross, 1977) a culturally variable phenomenon. Recent multicultural work on the dimensionality of internal-external locus of control (Smith, Trompenaars, & Dugan, 1994) may help us generate predictions about how "fundamental" this error is in global terms.

In addition, researchers are beginning to search for culture-general, personality-level mediators for externality effects. Although locus of control is an obvious candidate (Bond, 1983c), the focus in previous work has been category width (Detwelier, 1978), idiocentrism (Al-Zahrani & Kaplowitz, 1993), and interdependence of self construals (Singelis & Brown, 1995). In some cases regression equations indicate that cultural differences in attribution style are mediated by the personality variable; in other cases, not.

Within the internal or external domains, cultural agendas may result in relatively greater emphases on one category of explanation or another. In Chinese culture, effort is regarded as more important than ability in explaining academic outcomes than in the United States (e.g., Chen & Uttal, 1988). For external explanations, Chinese place great stock in *yuan fun* (interpersonal fatedness) and in geographical–ecological forces called *fung shui* (Leung, 1996). Such emic emphases tend to be culturally specific, but are likely to find counterparts in other cultural belief systems when comparisons are made at levels of sufficient generality.

Part of what one learns in effective cross-cultural adaptation is to make isomorphic attributions (i.e., those likely to be made by persons from the host cultural group, not by persons from one's cultural group of origin). Cultural norms for behaviors, including public explanations, are often different, so that one's expectations for appropriate behavior are frequently violated in cross-cultural exchanges. When the outsider explains the violation using his or her own cultural logic, a misattribution occurs. This misattribution may set in motion a chain of events that generates further misunderstandings (Smith & Bond, 1993, pp. 177-187) which may result in social withdrawal or hostility.

Intergroup Communication

Triandis (1988) argues that members of collectivistic cultures draw sharper distinctions between ingroups and outgroups than members of individualistic cultures. The differences in the nature of the distinctions drawn affect the communication that occurs with ingroup and outgroup members.

Perceptions of Intergroup Communication

Gudykunst and Nishida's (1986b) research indicates that collectivists in Japan perceive that ingroup communication is more intimate than outgroup communication, but there is no significant difference for individualists in the United States.

Two studies replicating Asch's (1956) classic studies of conformity in Japan also support Triandis's (1988) position. Frager (1970) found that levels of conformity are low in Japan (in fact, the conformity was lower than in Asch's study in the United States) when the confederates in the study are strangers (i.e., not members of an ingroup). Williams and Sogon (1984), in contrast, discovered than when confederates are members of the Japanese respondents' ingroup, conformity is much higher than in Asch's original study.

Gudykunst, Nishida, and Morisaki's (1992) research in Japan and the United States supports Hoyle, Pinkley, and Insko's (1989) findings (i.e., interpersonal encounters are perceived to be more agreeable and less abrasive than intergroup encounters). In addition, Gudykunst et al. found that respondents in the United States expect encounters to be more abrasive than respondents in Japan. This finding is consistent with the United States being a low UA culture and Japan being a high UA culture. Since members of high UA cultures have clear rules for social interaction in different contexts, they would not necessarily expect intergroup encounters to be abrasive. Gudykunst et al.'s study also indicated that the strength of social identity influences expected agreeableness and abrasiveness of encounters, but personal identity does not.

Self-Disclosure and Social Penetration

Self-disclosure involves individuals telling information about themselves to others that the other people do not know (Altman & Taylor, 1973). Closely related to self-disclosure is Altman and Taylor's notion of social penetration. They argue that as relationships become more intimate, there is an increase in social penetration; that is, participants engage in self-disclosure on a larger variety of topics and with more intimacy.

Generally, self-disclosure is associated with direct communication styles that predominate in IND cultures, rather than the indirect communication styles which predominate in COL cultures (Gudykunst & Ting-Toomey, 1988). Intuitively, it might seem that individualists would engage in more self-disclosure than collectivists. Wheeler et al. (1989), however, discovered that Chinese in Hong Kong report engaging in more self-disclosure in everyday communication than Americans. On the surface, this finding appears inconsistent with the claim that self-disclosure is associated with direct communication, but this is not necessarily the case. Wheeler, Reis, and Bond point out that most of the Chinese respondents' contacts were with members of their ingroup and communication in ingroups in COL cultures tends to be intimate (e.g., involves high levels of self-disclosure). Most of the American respondents' contacts, in contrast, were with superficial acquaintances where high levels of self-disclosure are not expected.

Gudykunst et al. (1992) studied ingroup and outgroup self-disclosure in five cultures: Australia, Hong Kong, Japan, Taiwan, and the United States. They found more self-disclosure with ingroup members than with outgroup members in the two Chinese samples, both high in COL. There was, however, no difference in ingroup and outgroup self-disclosure in the Australian and United States samples, both high in IND. The Japan data, in contrast, did not fit the expected pattern. Wheeler et al. (1989) argue that this reversal of expectation may be due to other dimensions of self-disclosure mediating the process of self-disclosure. To illustrate, the expected findings might not be observed in COL cultures, like Japan, that are high in MF and/or UA. Alternatively, Wheeler et al. point out that the findings for Japan may be due to the homogeneity of the Japanese culture. Barnlund (1975) contends that "the greater the cultural homogeneity, the greater the meaning conveyed in a single word, the more that can be implied rather than stated" (p. 162). This implies that explicit self-disclosure is not needed to convey intimate information.

Gudykunst and Nishida's (1986b) data on social penetration are consistent with Triandis' description of the focus on ingroup relationships in COL cultures. The Japanese respondents in this study reported greater differences in personalization (e.g., knowing personal information), synchronization (e.g., coordination), and difficulty of communication between ingroup (classmate) and outgroup (stranger) relationships than the American respondents.

Gudykunst, Yoon, and Nishida (1987) also examined the influence of individualism on social penetration in ingroup and outgroup relationships in Japan, Korea, and the United States. They found that the greater the degree of COL present in a culture, the greater the differences between ingroup (i.e., classmate) and outgroup (i.e., stranger) communication in terms of amount of personalization (e.g., intimacy of communication) and synchronization (e.g., coordination of communication) and difficulty in communication.

Anxiety/Uncertainty Management

Anxiety/uncertainty management (AUM) theory (Gudykunst, 1988b, 1993, 1995) suggests that effective interpersonal and intergroup communication is a function of the amount of anxiety and uncertainty individuals experience when communicating with others. Uncertainty involves individuals' ability to predict and/or explain others' feelings, attitudes, and behavior (Berger & Calabrese, 1975). Managing uncertainty is a cognitive process. Anxiety is the affective equivalent of uncertainty. It stems from feeling uneasy, tense, worried, or apprehensive about what might happen and is based on a fear of potential negative consequences (Stephan & Stephan, 1985).

Consistent with the conclusions from the social penetration studies, Gudykunst and Nishida (1986a) found that Japanese students have more attributional confidence (the inverse of uncertainty) regarding classmates (members of an ingroup in Japan) than students in the United States, while the reverse pattern exists for strangers (potential members of an outgroup in Japan).

Gudykunst, Nishida, and Schmidt (1989) found differences in uncertainty reduction processes between ingroup and outgroup relationships in the Japan sample, but not in the United States sample. Gudykunst, Gao, Nishida, Bond, Leung, Wang, and Barraclough's (1992) study of uncertainty reduction processes in ingroup and outgroup relationships in Australia, Japan, Hong Kong, and the United States suppport the earlier findings. There was a main effect for group membership (ingroup vs. outgroup) in the Japan and Hong Kong samples, but not in the United States and Australia samples. As expected, uncertainty was lower for communication with members of ingroups than for communication with members of outgroups in Japan and Hong Kong, but there was no difference in Australia and the United States.

The ways that individuals gather information to reduce uncertainty differs in IND and COL cultures. Members of IND cultures seek out person-based information to reduce uncertainty about strangers, and members of COL cultures seek out group-based information to reduce uncertainty (Gudykunst & Nishida, 1986a). The focus on person-based information leads members of IND cultures to search for personal similarities when communication with outgroup members more than members of COL cultures (Gudykunst, 1995). The focus on group-based information, in contrast, leads members of COL cultures to search for group similarities when communicating with outgroup members more than members of IND cultures.

There also are differences in how members of IND and COL cultures explain others' behavior. Members of COL cultures emphasize the importance of context in explaining others' behavior more than members of IND cultures (e.g., Kashima, Siegel, Tanaka, & Kashima, 1992; Miller, 1984). The emphasis on context in COL cultures affects other aspects of their communication as well. To illustrate, adapting and accommodating to the context in which they are communicating is an important part of the high-context communication patterns used in COL cultures (Hall, 1976).

Gudykunst and Shapiro (1996) found that there is greater uncertainty in intergroup encounters (interethnic and intercultural) than in intragroup encounters. They also discovered that uncertainty is associated negatively with positive expectations, communication satisfaction, and quality of communication. Uncertainty is associated positively with the degree to which social identities are activated in the interaction, and with the amount of anxiety experienced. Hubbert, Guerrero, and Gudykunst (1995) observed uncertainty to decrease over time in intergroup encounters, but the decrease does not fit a linear pattern. This pattern holds for both respondents from IND (e.g., European Americans) and COL (e.g., Latino Americans, Asian Americans) groups. Gudykunst, Nishida, and Chua (1986) further observed uncertainty to decrease as the intimacy of intercultural relationships increase.

Actual or anticipated interaction with members of other ethnic groups can lead to anxiety. Stephan and Stephan (1985) argue that individuals fear four types of negative consequences: negative psychological consequences (e.g., frustration), negative behavioral consequences (e.g., exploitation), negative evaluations by members of outgroups (e.g., negative stereotyping), and negative evaluations by members of their ingroups (e.g., disapproval).

One behavioral consequence of anxiety is avoidance (Stephan & Stephan, 1985). When individuals are experiencing anxiety and cannot avoid outgroup members, they often terminate the interaction as soon as they can (see, e.g., Spence-Brown, 1993). Cognitively, anxiety leads to biases in how individuals process information. The more anxious individuals are, the more likely they will focus on the behaviors they expect to see, such as those based on their stereotypes, and the more likely they are to confirm these expectations and not recognize behavior that is inconsistent with their expectations (Stephan & Stephan, 1985).

Stephan and Stephan (1989) found that the amount of anxiety Hispanic Americans and Asian Americans experience interacting with European Americans is associated negatively with the quality of their prior contact. Stephan and Stephan (1992) discovered that the anxiety Americans experience interacting with Moroccans is associated negatively with the amount of nonthreatening contact and is associated positively with the amount of threatening contact experienced. Islam and Hewstone (1993) obtained similar results for Hindu–Muslim contact in Bangladesh. They found that favorable contact is associated negatively with anxiety and that having intergroup (as opposed to interpersonal) contact is associated positively with the amount of anxiety. They also discovered that the greater the anxiety individuals experience, the less variability they perceive in the outgroup, and the more negative their attitudes toward the outgroup.

Gudykunst and Shapiro (1996) found that greater anxiety is experienced in intergroup encounters (interethnic and intercultural) than in intragroup encounters, and anxiety is negatively associated with positive expectations, communication satisfaction, and quality of communication. Anxiety is associated positively with the degree to which social identities are activated in the interaction, and the amount of uncertainty experienced. Hubbert, Guerrero, and Gudykunst (1995) discovered that anxiety decreases over time, but that the decrease does not fit a straight linear pattern for members of IND and COL groups.

There should be cultural differences in the anxiety individuals experience communicating with outgroup members. Members of high uncertainty avoidance cultures experience greater stress interacting with strangers than members of low uncertainty avoidance cultures (Hofstede, 1980), so it is expected they should also experience more anxiety interacting with outgroup members (Gudykunst, 1995).

Communication Rules

Rules for intergroup communication differ across cultures. Noesjirwan (1978), for example, found that the rule for behavior with respect to the ingroup in Indonesia is that members of the ingroup should adapt to the group, so that the group can present a united front. In Australia, in contrast, the rule is that members of the ingroup are expected to act as individuals, even if it means going against the ingroup. Argyle, Henderson, Bond, Iizuke, and Contarello (1986) also found that rules regarding ingroups (e.g., maintaining harmony) are endorsed more highly in COL cultures, like Japan and Hong Kong, than in IND cultures, like Britain and Italy.

Mann, Mitsui, Beswick, and Harmoni (1994) examined respect rules for interaction with father, mother, teacher, best friend, adult neighbor, and same-age neighbor used by Japanese and Australian children. They found that Australian children endorsed rules for greeting targets respectfully, did what the target told them, and stuck up for the target more than Japanese children. The Japanese children differentiated their endorsement of rules with respect to parents and teachers compared with friends and neighbors. Mann et al. argue that Japanese rules are person- and situation-specific and that lapses of politeness are tolerated in the family because of the strong ingroup bond.

If people from high UA cultures interact with members of outgroups in a situation where there are not clear rules, they may ignore the outgroup members, treating them as though they do not exist (Hofstede, 1991). Since outgroup members may deviate from expectations, members of high UA cultures tend to have less positive expectations for interacting with outgroup members than members of low UA cultures (Gudykunst, 1995). People in high UA cultures try to avoid ambiguity and, therefore, develop rules and rituals for virtually every possible situation in which they might find themselves, including interacting with outgroup members. Interaction with outgroup members in high UA cultures tends to be highly ritualistic and/or very polite. Interaction with outgroup members may be avoided in informal situations where there are not clear norms to guide behavior in high UA cultures. The rituals that are developed in high uncertainty avoidance cultures provide clear scripts for interaction and allow individuals to attune their behavior with outgroup members. The scripts for interacting with outgroup members, however, are much more complex in high UA cultures than in low UA cultures (Gudykunst, 1995).

The degree to which cultural rules require cooperation with outgroup members appears to be a function of power differences (PD). Power differences are expected in high PD cultures. People with less power are expected to do what people with more power tell them to do. This interaction logic leads to low levels of egalitarian cooperation between people with different amounts of power. Because outgroup members are outsiders, they generally have less power than insiders. Gudykunst (1995), therefore, suggests that cultural rules require less cooperation with outgroup members in high PD cultures than in low PD cultures.

Expression of Emotions

Affective reactions are one of the major by-products of intergroup interaction (Pettigrew, 1986). Bobad and Wallbott's (1986) cross-cultural research in eight cultures reveals that there is greater fear associated with interactions with people who are unfamiliar (outgroup members) than with people who are familiar (ingroup members), and that there is less verbalization of and less control over expressing anger with people who are unfamiliar across cultures. Gudykunst and

Ting-Toomey (1988) argue that differences across the eight cultures are linked to UA. Members of low UA cultures appear to engage in more vocalization of anger toward outgroup members and control their anger toward outgroup members less than members of high UA cultures.

> *Matsumoto (1989) examined the perception of emotions in 15 cultures. He concluded that cultures high in power distance and low in individualism stress hierarchy and group cohesion ("collectivity"), while individuality is minimized. In these cultures, the communication of negative emotions threatens group solidarity and interpersonal social structure. On the other hand, cultures low in power distance and high in individualism may sanction the communication of these emotions more, as they relate to individual freedom to express and perceive negative emotions. As such, they do not threaten social structures and groups to the same extent found in high power distance, low individualism cultures. (p. 101)*

Matsumoto (1991) argues that because subjugating individuals' goals to group goals is more important in COL cultures than IND cultures, members of COL cultures will emphasize emotional displays that facilitate group cooperation, harmony, and cohesion more than members of IND cultures. He also points out that members of IND cultures display a wider variety of emotional behaviors than members of COL cultures. COL cultures are "not as tolerant of wide ranges of individual variations, and thus frown upon such variation" (p. 132).

The specific emotions displayed depends on the context and target of the emotion. In a public context in a COL culture, it would be inappropriate to display a negative emotion because it would reflect negatively on the ingroup. If the emotion is a reaction to an ingroup member and is experienced in private with the ingroup member, expressing the emotion would disturb the harmony of the group. If the emotion is a reaction to an outgroup member, however, it would be acceptable to express it because this would foster cohesion in the ingroup (see also Bond & Venus, 1991).

Matsumoto (1991) goes on to argue that people in IND cultures are more likely to express positive and not to express negative emotions with members of the outgroup than are members of COL cultures. Gudykunst and Kim (1992) agree with the conclusion regarding the "positive" emotions. Members of collective cultures avoid establishing intimacy with members of outgroups and, therefore, they would not display positive emotions in their presence.

Gudykunst and Kim (1992) disagree with Matsumoto regarding negative emotions, because members of COL cultures avoid negative behaviors with the ingroup, but not with the outgroup. Friesen's (1972) study illustrates how negative emotions are avoided with members of the ingroup. He found that students in Japan and the United States experienced similar affect when viewing a stressful film alone. When viewing the film with a member of the ingroup, however, the students in the United States displayed more negative affect than the students from Japan. Triandis et al. (1988) provide an explanation for the display of negative affect toward members of the outgroup in COL cultures. They point out that in COL cultures a "do whatever you can get away with" orientation applies toward members of outgroups. Members of outgroups in COL cultures often are treated as "nonpersons." Cole (1990) reported that members of COL cultures are more dominating with members of outgroups when trying to resolve conflict than are members of IND cultures. Given this line of reasoning, Gudykunst and Kim (1992) believe that members of COL cultures are more likely to express negative emotions with members of outgroups than are members of IND cultures.

Intergroup Conflict

Intergroup conflict is occurring at alarming rates throughout the world today (see Boucher, Landis, & Clark, 1987; Horowitz, 1985, for discussions of some of these specific conflicts). Understanding why intergroup conflict occurs and the ways that members of different groups manage conflict is necessary if these conflicts are to be handled constructively. To begin, we look at the characteristics of intergroup conflict.

Characteristics of Intergroup Conflict

Intergroup conflict is similar in kind to interpersonal conflict in some ways, but there are important differences. Condor and Brown (1988) point out that intergroup conflict is, by definition, a collective phenomenon, and requires a suitably collective "model of man." The psychological factors associated with intergroup hostility are best sought in *collective* social cognition and motivation. It is an important task . . . to examine the relationship between individual drives and cognition and those associated with the groups to which they belong (p. 19). Condor and Brown, therefore, take the position that intergroup conflict is different from interpersonal conflict.

Landis and Boucher (1987) outline several characteristics of interethnic conflict that appear to apply to other forms of intergroup conflicts as well. First, intergroup conflict involves perceived (not necessarily real) group differences that lead to the activation of social identities and stereotypes. Second, intergroup conflicts often involve claims to a given territory. Third, intergroup conflicts tend to be based on group differences in power and resources. Fourth, intergroup conflicts may involve disagreements over language usage or language policies. Fifth, intergroup conflicts are exacerbated by group differences in endorsement of the process preferred for resolving conflicts (e.g., members of one culture may prefer to resolve conflicts through a third party, while members of another culture do not use third parties and prefer direct confrontation). Sixth, intergroup conflicts often are exacerbated by religious differences. Conflicts are intensified, for example, when religious differences are compounded with other group differences (e.g., in Sri Lanka the Tamil-Sinhalese conflict is intensified because Tamils are Hindu and Sinhalese are Buddhists).

Lilli and Rehm (1988) point out that social categorization leads individuals to make evaluative judgments about members of the ingroups and outgroups, and that when conflict occurs, social categorizations are particularly important and this heightens the ingroup bias. Social categorizations lead to emphasizing social identities over personal identities. When social identities are enhanced by intergroup comparisons, the devaluation of the outgroup can lead to conflicts. The persistence of "being negatively categorized (labeled) may cause conflicts" (p. 35). Social categorizations also lead to deindividuation. Deindividuation can initiate conflicts or escalate conflicts that already exist. Social categorization also influences the way information about outgroups is processed; it is simplified (e.g., outgroups are seen as homogeneous and only stereotypical information about outgroups is obtained). Simplified information processing can lead to arguments that maintain and justify conflicts.

Contact and Conflict

Intergroup contact often is promoted as a way to manage intergroup conflicts. The contact hypothesis suggests that when contact takes place under favorable conditions (e.g., equal status, intimate contact, rewarding contact, see Stephan, 1987, for a summary), it leads to a decrease in prejudice and discrimination. Tzeng and Jackson's (1994) research further indicates that contact under favorable conditions reduces intergroup hostilities across ethnic groups in the United States.

Related work on norm violations and intergroup hostility (DeRidder & Tripathi, 1992) also suggests that perceptions that their norms have been violated lead members of an ingroup to make negative attributions about outgroups. The negative attributions that ingroup members make lead outgroup members to make negative inferences about ingroup members. Norm violations, therefore, can lead to cycles of escalating conflict. Escalations are most likely when individuals strongly identify with their group, when negative intergroup attitudes exist, when one group has feelings of relative deprivation, and when the group violating the norms has power over the group whose norms are violated.

Harmonious interpersonal contact can take place between members of different groups, even when there is a history of intergroup conflict (e.g., Trew's study in Ireland, 1986; Taylor, Dubé, & Bellerose's work in Quebec, 1986). This does not always occur, however, as Foster and Finchilescu's (1986) research in South Africa indicates. Pettigrew (1986) points out that "the use of intergroup contact as a means of alleviating conflict is largely dependent on the social structure that patterns relations between the groups" (p. 191).

To explain cross-cultural variability in this process, it is necessary to isolate the dimensions of cultural variability that apply to structural relations. Structural tightness is "the degree of hierarchical structure among sociocultural elements in a society" (Witkin & Berry, 1975, p. 15). Boldt and Roberts (1979) argue that role relatedness (e.g., the degree to which roles are interrelated) defines a culture as loose or tight. Gudykunst (1988a) contends that Ireland and Canada have a high degree of role relatedness with respect to the roles members of different groups fill, while South Africa did not have a high degree of role relatedness between blacks and whites when Foster and Finchilescu's (1986) research was conducted. He suggests that contact has a greater influence on reducing intergroup conflict in tight than in loose cultures.

Conflict Styles

Ting-Toomey's (1988) face-negotiation theory is designed to explain how people in IND and COL cultures manage conflict. She argues that members of IND cultures like the United States use dominating, integrating, and compromising styles more than members of COL cultures like Japan. Members of COL cultures, in contrast, use avoiding and obliging conflict resolution styles more than members of IND cultures in order to maintain harmony in the ingroup.

Cole (1990) found that European American students in the United States tend to use integrating and obliging styles more with members of ingroups than with members of outgroups. He also discovered that Japanese students studying in the United States tend to use an obliging style more with members of ingroups than with members of outgroups, and they tend to use a dominating style more with members of outgroups than with members of ingroups. Cole's (1990) findings are compatible with earlier work on the influence of COL–IND on ingroup and outgroup conflicts. Leung (1988a), for example, found that Chinese are more likely than North Americans to pursue conflicts with strangers (outgroup) than with friends (ingroup).

To fully understand how conflict operates with respect to ingroups in collectivistic cultures, it is necessary to take other dimensions of cultural variability into consideration. Bond, Wan, Leung, and Giacalone (1985) argue that the level of power distance in a culture mediates how collectivists respond to someone who insults members of the ingroup. They found that Chinese are less critical than Americans of people insulting ingroup members when they have higher status than the ingroup member compared to when the status is lower than the ingroup members'. Bond et al. also discovered that Americans make less of a distinction as a function of insulter's status or group membership.

Suggestions for Future Research

In this chapter, we have closely examined the current empirical and theoretical literature on intergroup relations. Combining this focus with the panorama of emerging concerns in the sociology of knowledge production leads to a number of recommendations.

First, we must culturally re-center the research enterprise (Easton, 1991). Featherman (1993) points out that "at least two-thirds of published research originates in the West. In the social sciences and humanities, as well as the natural sciences, America, especially, has exported the major theoretical frameworks, methods of research design and analysis, and with them, our disciplinary form of codifying and organizing scientific knowledge systems" (p. 41). This American dominance becomes problematic because the cultural background of its social scientists imposes distorting conceptual blinders on their productions. The linchpin concept of the "self" has, in particular, been challenged as a distinctively Western and hence unexportable concept (e.g., Kondo, 1990; Lutz, 1988).

A variety of responses have addressed this fundamental challenge. Wierzbicka (1993), for example, has championed the development of a language for social science consisting of lexical universals. These core constructs can then be used to develop culture-general instruments which transcend the peculiarities inherent in their creator's language/culture of origin. Cross-cultural comparisons thereby become meaningful rather than possible exercises in Procrustean, intellectual imperialism.

Many have called for the creation of multicultural research teams that are managed democratically to enhance intellectual synergy (e.g., Triandis, 1976). Such international collaboration requires from us the same skills in cross-cultural communication that we frequently encourage in others (e.g., Bond, 1992; Brislin & Yoshida, 1994; Gudykunst & Nishida, 1994; Gudykunst, Ting-Toomey, Sudweeks, & Stewart, 1995). Graduate programs in social science will need to be broadened in order to train such abilities (Featherman, 1993). Promotion committees will need to recognize the skill, effort, persistence, and teamspersonship required to effect such collaborations (Gabrenya, 1988).

Other resources may help us decenter culturally: Bond (1994a) has written about the daily inspirations provided by living in a foreign culture; Scollon (1993) about the suggestive richness of local metaphors concerning the communication process. These and other possibilities will expand our receptiveness in "the context of discovery."

Second, we must include other cultural groups in our research designs to explore whether they respond similarly to our manipulations. When we do so (e.g., Tzeng & Jackson, 1994), we often discover differences. These in turn promote the development of more comprehensive theorizing. These theories necessarily broaden to include social, economic, even ecological factors (e.g., Giles, Coupland, Williams, & Leets, 1992). At present too little research is tested with other cultural groups to generate such development (or to reassure us about its generalizability; see e.g., Stephan, Ageyev, Coates-Shrider, Stephen, & Abolakina, 1994).

Third, we are too focused on collectivism and its associated constructs in our theorizing about the effects of culture. In part this narrowness arises because of the Americocentrism characterizing social science, with Americans and its social scientists occupying the extreme end of the individualism dimension (e.g., Hofstede, 1980). Also, the continued use of bi-cultural contrasts involving (very individualistic) Americans as one group blinds us to the possible impact from other dimensions of cultural variation.

In both cases the solution is to widen the net of cultural groups included in our studies. Multicultural studies allow us to detect additional dimensions of cultural difference, to refine our conflated understanding of collectivism, and to locate cultural groups on these emerging dimensions (e.g., Smith, Dugan, & Trompennars, 1996). It will be especially revealing to learn what dimensions of cultural variation become apparent when South American and African countries are included in our samples. Their current exclusion impoverishes our theorizing.

Finally, we believe that it is now time to examine the *process* of communicating across cultural lines more closely. Work on process has been conducted (e.g, Giles & Johnson, 1986; Hubbert, Guerrero, & Gudykunst, 1995; Pierson & Bond, 1982), but more is needed, especially on cases of conflict-free, intercultural interactions in egalitarian contexts. We need to know more about how such successes occur (e.g., Smith & Bond, 1993, Ch. 10), as we move into our next millenium on this embattled planet.

> *The people of this world have been brought together technologically, but have not yet begun to understand what that means in a spiritual sense. We have to learn to live as brothers [and sisters] or we will perish as fools.*
>
> *Martin Luther King*

Endnotes

1. Hofstede's (1980) dimensions of cultural variation are derived from country scores themselves derived from responses of a sample from each country. This results in each country receiving scores on factors arising from country-level grouping of items. Culture scores can also be produced at the individual level of analysis. Here, the input is individual responses from a number of people from a number of countries. This much larger data set must then be carefully processed (Leung & Bond, 1989) to elicit dimensions of variation at the individual level. A culture score is then the average score of individuals in a given culture or country on any one of the resulting dimensions (e.g., Bond, 1988). So, a country-level analysis uses country scores as the initial input; an individual-level analysis uses individual scores as the initial input.

We make this distinction because the results of the two analytic procedures are not identical (Leung, 1989). More practically, it is often difficult to make sense of country-level dimensions of variation and "translate" them into psychologically sensible constructs. Some scholars (e.g., Schwartz, 1994) are addressing this linking task;

others are focusing attention on measuring psychological processes at the individual level multiculturally (Bond, 1988; Gudykunst et al., 1994; Schwartz, 1992; Triandis et al., 1993). See Kagitçibasi (this volume) for a related discussion.

2. So, we must assess the broad sweep of individualism-collectivism as a fundamental cultural variable. A country's score on some operationalization of the dimension will vary from study to study. The United States, for example, was the most individualistic country on Hofstede's (1980) survey, but it was in the middle on the survey done by the Chinese Culture Connection (1987). Smith, Dugan, and Trompenaars (1996), for example, examined value endorsement in 43 countries, including many from the former communist bloc. The first two dimensions of a country cluster analysis arrayed countries in ways which differentiate collectivism. The "First dimension has to do with the nature of one's obligations to groups and organizations" (p. 39). The second dimension "may best be defined in terms of the continuity and intensity of group membership: (p. 39). These dimensions were regarded by Hofstede (1980, ch. 5) as aspects of individualism, but now appear

separable (see also Singelis, Triandis, Bhawuk, & Gelfand, 1994). The two Smith et al. dimensions have important and different implications for behavior.

3. Because operationalizations at one level of analysis tend not to translate down to a lower level of measurement (e.g., Hofstede, Bond, & Luk, 1993; Leung, 1989) searches for individual-level measures of cultural level constructs continue (Bond, 1988; Gudykunst et al., 1994; Schwartz, 1992; Triandis et al., 1993). It is becoming evident that collectivism–individualism at the individual level is a multifaceted construct (e.g., Singelis et al., 1994). Links between these facets and communication variables will have to be carefully developed in cross-cultural studies (e.g., Singelis, Bond, Lai, & Sharkey, 1994).

4. Gudykunst (1995) argues that because members of collectivistic cultures focus on group-based information, it is easier for them to isolate simi-larities and differences between their groups and outgroups than for members of individualistic cultures. Members of individualistic cultures, in contrast, can more easily recognize personal similarities and differences between themselves and strangers than members of collectivistic cultures because they focus on person-based information. The focus on group-based information leads members of collectivistic cultures to attribute strangers' behavior to their group memberships more than members of individualistic cultures.

5. Of course, dominance may be defined in various ways—numerical, political, economic, historical, and so forth—and these criteria may be inconsistent. The Chinese in Singapore are dominant in all respects; the Blacks in South Africa, in some respects. These patterns of consistency will also have implications for intergroup relations that we must come to understand.

References

Abrams, D. & Hogg, M. (Eds.). (1990). *Social identity theory: Constructive and critical advances.* New York: Springer-Verlag.

Adorno, T. W., Frenkel-Brunswik, E., Levinson, D. J., & Sanford, R. M. (1950). *The authoritarian personality.* New York : Harper.

Allport, G. E. (1954). *The nature of prejudice.* New York: Doubleday.

Altemeyer, B. (1988). *Enemies of freedom: Understanding right-wing authoritarianism.* San Francisco: Jossey-Bass.

Altman, I. & Taylor, D. (1973). *Social penetration.* New York: Holt, Rinehart, and Winston.

Al-Zahrani, S. S. A. & Kaplowitz, S. A. (1993). Attributional biases in individualistic and collectivistic cultures. *Social Psychology Quarterly, 56,* 223–233.

Argyle, M., Henderson, M., Bond, M. H., Iizuka, Y., & Contarello, A. (1986). Cross-cultural variations in relationship rules. *International Journal of Psychology, 21,* 287–315.

Asch, S. E. (1956). Studies of independence and conformity. *Psychological Monographs, 70,* (9)(whole no. 416).

Barnlund, D. (1975). *Public and private self in Japan and the United States.* Tokyo: Simul.

Barnlund, D. & Yoshioka, M. (1990). Apologies: Japanese and American styles. *International Journal of Intercultural Relations, 14,* 193–206.

Berger, C. & Calabrese, R. (1975). Some explorations in initial interactions and beyond. *Human Communication Research, 1,* 99–112.

Berry, J. W. (1990). The role of psychology in ethnic studies. *Canadian Ethnic Studies, 12,* 8–21.

Berry, J. W. (1991). Understanding and managing multiculturalism: Some possible implications of research in Canada. *Psychology and Developing Societies, 3,* 17–49.

Berry, J. W. & Kalin, R. (1979). Reciprocity of inter-ethnic attitudes in a multicultural society. *International Journal of Intercultural Relations, 3,* 99–112.

Berry, J. W. & Kalin, R. (1995). Multicultural and ethnic attitudes in Canada: An overview of the 1991 national survey. *Canadian Journal of Behavioural Science, 27,* 301–320.

Berry, J. W., Kalin, R., & Taylor, D. M. (1977). *Multiculturalism and ethnic attitudes in Canada.* Ottawa: Ministry of Supplies and Services.

Berry, J. W., Kim, U., Power, S., Young, M., & Bujaki, M. (1989). Acculturation attitudes in plural societies. *Applied Psychology, 38,* 185–206.

Best, D. L. & Williams, J. E. (1993). A cross-cultural viewpoint. In A. E. Beall & R. J. Sternberg (Eds.), *The psychology of gender* (pp. 215–248). New York: Guilford.

Bhawuk, D. P. S. & Brislin, R. W. (1992). The measurement of intercultural sensitivity using the concepts of individualism and collectivism. *International Journal of Intercultural Relations, 16,* 413–436.

Bobad, E. Y. & Wallbott, H. (1986). The effects of social factors on emotional reactions. In K. Sherer, H. Wallbott, & A. Summerfield (Eds.), *Experiencing emotions: A cross-cultural study* (pp. 154–172). Cambridge: Cambridge University Press.

Bochner, S. (1982). The social psychology of cross-cultural relations. In S. Bochner (Ed.), *Cultures in contact: Studies in cross-cultural interaction* (pp. 5–44). Oxford: Pergamon.

Bochner, S. (1994). Cross-cultural differences in self-concept. *Journal of Cross-Cultural Psychology, 25,* 273–283.

Boldt, E. & Roberts, L. (1979). Structural tightness and social conformity. *Journal of Cross-Cultural Psychology, 10,* 221–230.

Bond, M. H. (1983a). Linking person perception dimensions to behavioral intention dimensions: The Chinese connection. *Journal of Cross-Cultural Psychology, 14,* 41–63.

Bond, M. H. (1983b). How language variation affects intercultural differentiation of values by Hong Kong bilinguals. *Journal of Language and Social Psychology, 2,* 57–66.

Bond, M. H. (1983c). A proposal for cross-cultural studies of attribution processes. In M. Hewstone (Ed.), *Attribution theory: Social and applied extensions* (pp. 144–157). Oxford: Blackwell.

Bond, M. H. (1986). Mutual stereotypes and the facilitation of interaction across cultural lines. *International Journal of Intercultural Relations, 10,* 259–276.

Bond, M. H. (1988). Finding universal dimensions of individual variation in multi-cultural studies of values: The Rokeach and Chinese value surveys. *Journal of Personality and Social Psychology, 55,* 1009–1015.

Bond, M. H. (1991). Chinese values and health: A cross-cultural examination. *Psychology and Health, 5,* 137–152.

Bond, M. H. (1992). The process of enhancing cross-cultural competence in Hong Kong organizations. *International Journal of Intercultural Relations, 16,* 395–412.

Bond, M. H. (1993). Between the Yin and the Yang: The identity of the Hong Kong Chinese. Professorial inaugural lecture, Chinese University of Hong Kong, May, 1993.

Bond, M. H. (1994a). Continuing encounters with Hong Kong. In W. J. Lonner & R. Malpass (Eds.), *Psychology and culture* (pp. 41–46). Boston: Allyn and Bacon.

Bond, M. H. (1994b). Trait theory and cross-cultural studies of person perception. *Psychological Inquiry, 5,* 114–117.

Bond, M. H. (1996). Chinese values. In M. H. Bond (Ed.), *The handbook of Chinese psychology* (pp. 208–226). Hong Kong: Oxford.

Bond, M. H. & Cheung, T. (1983). College students' spontaneous self-concept: The effect of culture among respondents in Hong Kong, Japan, and the United States. *Journal of Cross-Cultural Psychology, 14,* 153–171.

Bond, M. H. & Forgas, J. P. (1984). Linking person perception to behavioral intention across cultures. *Journal of Cross-Cultural Psychology, 15,* 337–352.

Bond, M. H. & Hewstone, M. (1988). Social identity theory and the perception of intergroup relations in Hong Kong. *International Journal of Intercultural Relations, 12,* 153–170.

Bond, M. H., Leung, K., & Schwartz, S. (1992). Explaining choices in procedural and distributive justice across cultures. *International Journal of Psychology, 27,* 211–225.

Bond, M. H. & Venus, C. K. (1991). Resistance to group or personal insults in an ingroup or outgroup context. *International Journal of Psychology, 23,* 83–94.

Bond, M. H., Wan, K., Leung, K., & Giacalone, R. (1985). How are responses to verbal insults related to cultural collectivism and power distance. *Journal of Cross-Cultural Psychology, 16,* 111–127.

Boucher, J., Landis, D., & Clark, K. (Eds.). (1987). *Ethnic conflict: International perspectives.* Beverly Hills: Sage.

Brewer, M. (1988). A dual process model of impression formation. In R. Wyer & T. Scrull (Eds.), *Advances in social cognition* (Vol. 1, pp. 1–36). Hillsdale, NJ: Erlbaum.

Brewer, M. & Campbell, D. T. (1976). *Ethnocentrism and intergroup attitudes:* East African evidence. New York: Sage/Halsted/Wiley.

Brislin, R. & Yoshida, T. (1994). *Intercultural communication training: An introduction.* Thousand Oaks, CA: Sage.

Brown, R. J. & Turner, J. C. (1979). The crisis–cross categorization effect in intergroup discrimination. *British Journal of Social and Clinical Psychology, 18,* 371–383.

Campbell, D. T. & LeVine, R. (1968). Ethnocentrism and intergroup relations. In R. P. Abelson, E. Aronson, W. McGuire, T. Newcomb, M. Rosenberg, & P. Tannenbaum (Eds.), *Theories of cognitive cognitive consistency: A sourcebook* (pp. 551–564). Chicago: Rand McNally.

Chen, C. S. & Uttal, D. H. (1988). Cultural values, parents' beliefs, and children's achievement in the United States and China. *Human Development, 31,* 351–358.

Chinese Culture Connection. (1987). Chinese values and the search for culture-free dimensions of culture. *Journal of Cross-Cultural Psychology, 18,* 143–164.

Cole, M. (1990). *Relational distance and personality influence on conflict communication styles.* Paper presented at the Speech Communication Association Convention, Chicago, November, 1990.

Condor, S. & Brown, R. (1988). Psychological processes in intergroup conflict. In W. Stroebe, A. Kruglanski, D. Bar-Tal, & M. Hewstone (Eds.), *The social psychology of intergroup conflict* (pp. 3–26). New York: Springer-Verlag.

Cousins, S. D. (1989). Culture and self-perception in Japan and the United States. *Journal of Personality and Social Psychology, 56,* 124–131.

Crittendon, K. (1991). Asian self-effacement or feminine modesty? Attributional patterns of women university students in Taiwan. *Gender and Society, 5,* 98–117.

Cross, S. E. & Markus, H. M. (1991). *Cultural adaptation and the self: Self-construal, coping, and stress.* Paper presented at the 99th annual convention of the American Psychological Association, San Francisco, July, 1991.

DeRidder, R. & Tripathi, R. (Eds.). (1992). *Norm violation and intergroup relations.* Oxford: Clarendon.

Der-Karabetian, A. (1992). World-mindedness and the nuclear threat: A multinational study. *Journal of Social Behavior and Personality, 7,* 293–308.

Deschamps, J. C. & Doise, W. (1978). Crossed category membership in intergroup relations. In H. Tajfel (Ed.), *Differentiation between social groups* (pp. 141–158). London: Academic.

Detweiler, R. A. (1978). Culture, category width, and attributions: A model-building approach to the reasons for cultural effects. *Journal of Cross-Cultural Psychology, 9,* 259–284.

Devine, P. G. (1989). Stereotypes and prejudice: Their automatic and controlled components. *Journal of Personality and Social Psychology, 56,* 5–18.

Digman, J. M. (1990). Personality structure: Emergence of the five factor model. *Annual Review of Psychology, 41,* 417–440.

Dijker, A. J. (1987). Emotional reactions to ethnic minorities. *European Journal of Social Psychology, 17,* 305–325.

Doise, W. & Sinclair, A. (1973). The categorization process in intergroup relations. *European Journal of Social Psychology, 3,* 145–157.

Dollard, J., Doob, L. W., Miller, N. E., Mowrer, O. H., & Sears, R. R. (1939). *Frustration and aggression.* New Haven: Yale University Press.

Dorai, M. (1993). Effets de la catégorisation simple et de la catégorisation croisée sur les stereotypes [Effects of simple and crossed categorization on stereotypes]. *International Journal of Psychology, 28,* 3–18.

Driver, E. & Driver, A. (1983). Gender, society, and self-conceptions. *International Journal of Comparative Sociology, 24,* 200–217.

Earley, P. C. (1989). Social loafing and collectivism. *Administrative Science Quarterly, 34,* 565–581.

Earley, P. C. (1993). East meets west: Further explorations of collectivistic and individualistic groups. *Academy of Management Journal, 36*, 319–348.

Easton, D. (1991). The division, integration, and transfer of knowledge. In D. Easton & C. S. Schelling (Eds.), *Divided knowledge* (pp. 7–36). Newbury Park, CA: Sage.

Esses, V. M., Haddock, G., & Zanna, M. P. (1993). Values, stereotypes, and emotions as determinants of intergroup attitudes. In D. M. Mackie & D. L. Hamilton (Eds.), *Affect, cognition and stereotyping: Interactive processes in group perception* (pp. 137–166). New York: Academic.

Featherman, D. L. (1993). What does society need from higher education? *Items, 47*(2/3), 38–43.

Feldman, R. (1968). Responses to compatriot and foreigner who seek assistance. *Journal of Personality and Social Psychology, 10*, 202–214.

Feshback, S. (1987). Individual aggression, national attachment, and the search for peace: Psychological perspectives. *Aggressive Behavior, 13*, 315–325.

Fletcher, G. J. O. & Ward, C. (1988). Attribution theory and processes: A cross-cultural perspective. In M.H. Bond (Ed.), *The cross-cultural challenge to social psychology* (pp. 230–244). Newbury Park, CA: Sage.

Forgas, J. P. (1979). *Social episodes: The study of interaction routines.* London: Academic.

Forgas, J. P. & Bond, M. H. (1985). Cultural influences on the perception of interaction episodes. *Personality and Social Psychology Bulletin, 11*, 75–88.

Foster, D. & Finchilescu, G. (1986). Contact in a "non-contact" society: The case of South Africa. In M. Hewstone & R. Brown (Eds.), *Contact and conflict in intergroup encounters* (pp. 119–136). Oxford: Blackwell.

Frager, R. (1970). Conformity and anti-conformity in Japan. *Journal of Personality and Social Psychology, 15*, 203–210.

Friesen, W. (1972). *Cultural differences in facial expression in a social situation.* Unpublished Ph.D. dissertation, Department of Psychology, University of California at San Francisco.

Fry, P. S., & Ghosh, R. (1980). Attribution of success and failure: Comparisons of cross-cultural differences between Asian and Caucasian children. *Journal of Cross-Cultural Psychology, 11*, 343–363.

Furnham, A. (1982). The message, the context and the medium. *Language and Communication, 2* 33–47.

Gabrenya, W. K., Jr. (1988). Social science and social psychology: The cross-cultural link. In M. H. Bond (Ed.), *The cross-cultural challenge to social psychology* (pp. 48–66). Newbury Park, CA: Sage.

Gabrenya, W. K. & Wang, Y. (1983). *Cultural differences in self schemata.* Paper presented at the Southeast Psychological Association Convention, Atlanta, March, 1983.

Gaertner, S. L., Rust, M.C., Dovidio, J. F., Bachman, B. A., & Anastasio, P. A. (1994). The contact hypothesis: The role of a common ingroup identity on reducing intergroup bias. *Small Group Research, 25*, 224–249.

Gallimore, R., Goldenberg, C. N., & Weisner, T. S. (1993). The social construction and subjective reality of activity settings: Implications for community psychology. *American Journal of Community Psychology, 21*, 537–559.

Gallois, C. & Callan, V. J. (1991). Interethnic accommodation: The role of norms. In H. Giles, J. Coupland, & N. Coupland (Eds.), *Contexts of accommodation: Developments in applied linguistics* (pp. 245–269). Cambridge: Cambridge University Press.

Gao, G., Schmidt, K., & Gudykunst, W. B. (1994). Strength of ethnic identity and perceptions of ethnolinguistic vitality. *Hispanic Journal of Behavioral Sciencces, 16*, 332–341.

Ghosh, E. & Huq, M. (1985). A study of social identity in two ethnic groups in India and Bangladesh. *Journal of Multilingual and Muticultural Development, 6*, 239–251.

Gifford, R. (1994). A lens-mapping framework for understanding the encoding and decoding of interpersonal dispositions in nonverbal behavior. *Journal of Personality and Social Psychology, 66*, 398–412.

Giles, H., Coupland, N., Williams, A., & Leets, L. (1992). Integrating theory in the study of minority languages. In R. L. Cooper & B. Spolsky (Eds.), *The influence of language on culture and thought* (pp. 113–136). The Hague: Mouton de Gruyter.

Giles, H. & Johnson, P. (1981). The role of language in ethnic group relations. In J. Turner & H. Giles (Eds.), *Intergroup behavior* (pp. 199–242). Chicago: University of Chicago Press.

Giles, H. & Johnson, P. (1986). Perceived threat, ethnic commitment, and interethnic language behaviour. In Y. Y. Kim (Ed.), *Interethnic communication: Current research* (pp. 91–116). Newbury Park, CA: Sage.

Giles, H. & Johnson, P. (1987). Ethnolinguistic identity theory: A social–psychological approach to language maintenance. *International Journal of the Sociology of Language, 68,* 69–99.

Giles, H. & Ryan, E. B. (1982). Prolegomena for developing a social psychological theory of language attitudes. In E. B. Ryan & H. Giles (Eds.), *Attitudes toward language variation* (pp. 208–223). London: Edward Arnold.

Grujic, Z. & Libby, W. L., Jr. (1978). *Nonverbal aspects of verbal behaviour in French Canadian French-English bilinguals.* Paper presented at the American Psychological Association Convention, Toronto, August, 1978.

Gudykunst, W. B. (1988a). Culture and intergroup processes. In M. H. Bond (Ed.), *The cross-cultural challenge to social psychology* (pp. 165–181). Newbury Park, CA: Sage.

Gudykunst, W. B. (1988b). Uncertainty and anxiety. In Y. Kim & W. B. Gudykunst (Eds.), *Theories in intercultural communication* (pp. 123–156). Newbury Park, CA: Sage.

Gudykunst, W. B. (1989). Cross-cultural variability in ethnolinguistic identity. In S. Ting-Toomey & F. Korzenny (Eds.), *Language, communication, and culture* (pp. 222–242). Newbury Park, CA: Sage.

Gudykunst, W. B. (1993). Toward a theory of effective interpersonal and intergroup communication: An anxiety/uncertainty management (AUM) perspective. In R. Wiseman & J. Koester (Eds.), *Intercultural communication competencce* (pp. 33–71). Newbury Park, CA: Sage.

Gudykunst, W. B. (1995). Anxiety/Uncertainty Management (AUM) theory: Current status. In R. L. Wiseman (Ed.), *Intercultural communi-nication theory* (pp. 8–57). Thousand Oaks, CA: Sage.

Gudykunst, W. B., Gao, G., Schmidt, K., Nishida, T., Bond, M. H., Leung. K., Wang, G., & Barraclough, R. (1992). The influence of individualism–collectivism on communication in ingroup and outgroup relationships. *Journal of Cross-Cultural Psychology, 23,* 196–213.

Gudykunst, W. B. & Kim, Y. Y. (1992). *Communicating with strangers,* 2d ed. New York: McGraw-Hill.

Gudykunst, W. B., Matsumoto, Y., Ting-Toomey, S., Nishida, T., Kim, K. S., & Heyman, S. (1994, July). *Measuring self-construals across cultures.* Paper presented at the International Communication Association Convention, Sydney, Australia, July, 1994.

Gudykunst, W. B. & Nishida, T. (1986a). Attributional confidence in low- and high-context cultures. *Human Communication Research 12,* 525–549.

Gudykunst, W. B. & Nishida, T. (1986b). The influence of cultural variability on perceptions of communication associated with relationship terms. *Human Communication Research, 13,* 147–166.

Gudykunst, W. B. & Nishida, T. (1994). *Bridging Japanese/North American differences.* Thousand Oaks, CA: Sage.

Gudykunst, W. B., Nishida, T., & Chua, E. (1986). Uncertainty reduction in Japanese–North American dyads. *Communication Research Reports, 3,* 39–46.

Gudykunst, W. B., Nishida, T., & Morisaki, S. (1992). *The influence of personal and social identity on expectations for interpersonal and intergroup encounters.* Paper presented at the International Communication Association Convention, Miami, May, 1992.

Gudykunst, W. B., Nishida, T., & Schmidt, K. (1989). Cultural, relational, and personality influences on uncertainty reduction processes. *Western Journal of Speech Communication, 53,* 13–29.

Gudykunst, W. B. & Shapiro, R. B. (1996). Communication in everyday interpersonal and intergroup encounters. *International Journal of Intercultural Relations, 20,* 19–45.

Gudykunst, W. B. & Ting-Toomey, S. (1988). *Culture and interpersonal communication*. Beverly Hills, CA: Sage.

Gudykunst, W. B., Ting-Toomey, S., Sudweeks, S., & Stewart, L. (1995). *Building bridges: Interpersonal skills for a changing world*. Boston: Houghton Mifflin.

Gudykunst, W. B., Yoon, Y., & Nishida, T. (1987). The influence of individualism–collectivism on perceptionss of communication in ingroup and outgroup relationships. *Communication Monographs, 54*, 295–306.

Haddock, G., Zanna, M. P., & Esses, V. M. (1993). Assessing the structure of prejudicial attitudes: The case of attitudes towards homosexuals. *Journal of Personality and Social Psychology, 65*, 1105–1118.

Haddock, G., Zanna, M. P., & Esses, V. M. (1994). The (limited) role of trait-laden stereotypes in predicting attitudes towards Native peoples. *British Journal of Social Psychology, 33*, 83–106.

Hall, E. T. (1976). *Beyond culture*. New York: Doubleday.

Hamilton, D., Sherman, S., & Ruvolo, C. (1990). Stereotyped-based expectancies. *Journal of Social Issues, 46*(2), 35–60.

Hett, J. E. (1991). The development of an instrument to measure global-mindedness. *Dissertation Abstracts International, 52*, 2099A. (University Microfilm No. 91-23-938).

Hewstone, M. (1990). The ultimate attribution error? A review of the literature on intergroup causal attribution. *European Journal of Social Psychology, 20*, 311–335.

Hewstone, M., Bond, M. H., & Wan, K. (1983). Social facts and social attributions: The exploration of intergroup differences in Hong Kong. *Social Cognition, 2*, 142–157.

Hewstone, M., Islam, M. R., & Judd, C. M. (1993). Models of crossed categorization and intergroup relations. *Journal of Personality and Social Psychology, 64*, 779–793.

Hinkle, S. & Brown, R. (1990). Intergroup comparisons and social identity. In D. Abrams & M. Hogg (Eds.), *Social identity theory: Constructive and critical advances* (pp. 48–70). London: Springer-Verlag.

Hoffman, C., Lau, I., & Johnson, D. R. (1986). The linguistic relativity of person cognition: An English–Chinese comparison. *Journal of Personality and Social Psychology, 51*, 1097–1105.

Hofstede, G. (1979). Value systems in forty countries. In J. Deregowski, S. Dzuirawiec, & R. Annis (Eds.), *Explications in cross-cultural psychology* (pp. 389–407). Lisse, Netherlands: Swets and Zeitlinger.

Hofstede, G. (1980). *Culture's consequences: International differences in work-related values*. Beverly Hills: Sage.

Hofstede, G. (1991). *Cultures and organizations: Software of the mind*. London: McGraw-Hill.

Hofstede, G. & Bond, M. H. (1984). Hofstede's culture dimensions: An independent validation using Rokeach's value survey. *Journal of Cross-Cultural Psychology, 15*, 417–433.

Hofstede, G., Bond, M. H., & Luk, C. L. (1993). Individual perceptions of organizational cultures: A methodological treatise on levels of analysis. *Organization Studies, 14*, 483–583.

Horowitz, D. (1985). *Ethnic groups in conflict*. Berkeley: University of California Press.

Hoyle, R., Pinkley, R., & Insko, C. (1989). Perceptions of social behavior: Evidence of differing expectations for interpersonal and intergroup behavior. *Personality and Social Psychology Bulletin, 15*, 365–376.

Hubbert, K., Guerrero, S., & Gudykunst, W. B. (1995). *Intergroup communication over time*. Paper presented at the International Communication Association Convention, Albuquerque, May, 1995.

Ip, G. W. & Bond, M. H. (1995). Culture, values, and the spontaneous self-concept. *Asian Journal of Psychology, 1*, 29–35.

Islam, M. R. & Hewstone, M. (1993). Dimensions of contact as predictors of intergroup anxiety, perceived outgroup variability, and outgroup attitude. *Personality and Social Psychology Bulletin, 19*, 700–710.

Kagitçibasi, C. (1970). Social norms and authoritarianism: A Turkish–American comparison. *Journal of Cross-Cultural Psychology, 4*, 157–174.

Kalin, R. & Berry, J. W. (1980). Geographic mobility and ethnic tolerance. *Journal of Social Issues, 112*, 129–134.

Kalin, R. & Berry, J. W. (1982). The social ecology

of ethnic attitudes in Canada. *Canadian Journal of Behavioural Science, 14,* 97–109.

Kalin, R. & Berry, J. W. (in press). Interethnic attitudes in Canada: Ethnocentrism, consensual hierarchy, and reciprocity. *Canadian Journal of Behavioral Science.*

Kalin, R. & Berry, J. W. (1996). Ethnic, national and provincial self-identity in Canada: Analysis of 1974 and 1991 national surveys. *Canadian Ethnic Studies.*

Kashima, Y., Siegel, M., Tanaka, K., & Kashima, E. (1992). Do people believe behaviors are consistent with attitudes? *British Journal of Social Psychology, 31,* 111–124.

Keefe, S. E. (1992). Ethnic identity: The domain of perceptions of and attachment to ethnic groups and cultures. *Human Organization, 51,* 35–43.

Kim, S. H. & Smith, R. H. (1993). Revenge and conflict escalation. *Negotiation Journal, 9,* 37–43.

Kim, U., Triandis, H. C., Kagitçibasi, C., Choi, S-C., & Yoon, G. (Eds.). (1994). *Individualism and collectivism: Theory, method, and applications.* Thousand Oaks, CA: Sage.

Kondo, D. K. (1990). *Crafting selves: Power, gender, and discourses of identity in a Japanese workplace.* Chicago: University of Chicago Press.

Korten, F. F. (1974). The influence of culture and sex on the perception of persons. *International Journal of Psychology, 9,* 31–44.

Kosterman, R. & Feshbach, S. (1989). Toward a measure of patriotic and nationalistic attitudes. *Political Psychology, 10,* 257–274.

Kraemer, R. & Birenbaum, M. (1993). Language attitudes and social group memberships. *International Journal of Intercultural Relations, 17,* 437–449.

Krishnan, A. & Berry, J. W. (1992). Acculturative stress and acculturation attitudes among Indian immigrants to the United States. *Psychology and Developing Societies, 4,* 187–212.

Lambert, W.E ., Mermigis, L., & Taylor, D. M. (1986). Greek Canadians' attitudes towards own group and other Canadian ethnic groups. *Canadian Journal of Behavioural Sciences, 18,* 35–51.

Landis, D. & Boucher, J. (1987). Themes and models of conflict. In J. Boucher, D. Landis, & K. Clark (Eds.), *Ethnic conflicts: International perspectives* (pp. 18–31). Beverly Hills, CA: Sage.

Lee, Y. T. & Ottati, V. (1993). Psychologists have biases towards stereotypes: Neglecting the kernel of truth. Manuscript submitted for publication.

Lee, Y. T., & Seligman, M. E. P. (1993). Are Americans more optimistic than Mainland Chinese? Unpublished manuscript.

Leung, K. (1988a). Some determinants of conflict avoidance. *Journal of Cross-Cultural Psychology, 19,* 125–136.

Leung, K. (1988b). Theoretical advances in justice behavior: Some cross-cultural inputs. In M. H. Bond (Ed.), *The cross-cultural challenge to social psychology* (pp. 218–229). Newbury Park, CA: Sage.

Leung, K. (1989). Cross-cultural differences: Individual-level vs cultural-level analysis. *International Journal of Psychology, 24,* 703–719.

Leung, K. (1996). Beliefs in Chinese culture. In M. H. Bond (Ed.), *The handbook of Chinese psychology* (pp. 247–262). Hong Kong: Oxford.

Leung, K. & Bond, M. H. (1989). On the empirical identification of dimensions for cross-cultural comparisons. *Journal of Cross-Cultural Psychology, 20,* 133–151.

Leung, K. & Bond, M. H. (1993). Invitation to participate in a multi-cultural study of social axioms. Unpublished manuscript, Chinese University of Hong Kong.

Leung, K., Bond, M. H., Carment, D. W., Krishnan, L., & Liebrand W. B. C. (1990). Effects of cultural femininity on preference for methods of conflict resolution: A cross-cultural study. *Journal of Experimental Social Psychology, 26,* 373–388.

Leung, K., Bond, M. H., & Schwartz, S. H. (1994). Explanatory mechanisms for cross-cultural differences: Values, valences, and expectancies. Manuscript submitted for publication.

Lewin, K. (1948). *Resolving social conflicts.* New York: Harper and Row.

Lilli, W. & Rehm, J. (1988). Judgmental processes as bases of intergroup conflict. In W. Strobe, A. Kruglanski, D. Bar-Tal, & M. Hewstone (Eds.), *The social psychology of intergroup conflict* (pp. 29–46). New York: Springer-Verlag.

Linssen, H. & Hagendoorn, L. (1994). Social and

geographical factors in the explanation of the content of European nationality stereotypes. *British Journal of Social Psychology, 33,* 165–182.

Lutz, C. (1988). *Unnatural emotions: Everyday sentiments on a Micronesian atoll and their challenge to Western theory.* Chicago: University of Chicago Press.

Majeed, A. & Ghosh, E. S. K. (1982). A study of social identity in three ethnic groups in India. *International Journal of Psychology, 17,* 455–463.

Mann, L., Mitsui, H., Beswick, G., & Harmoni, R. (1994). A study of Japanese and Australian children's respect for others. *Journal of Cross-Cultural Psychology, 25,* 133–145.

Markus, H. & Kitayama, S. (1991). Culture and the self: Implications for cognition, motivation, and emotion. *Psychological Review, 98,* 224–253.

Matsumoto, D. (1989). Cultural influences on the perceptions of emotion. *Journal of Cross-Cultural Psychology, 20,* 92–104.

Matsumoto, D. (1991). Cultural influences on facial expression of emotion. *Southern Communication Journal, 56,* 128–137.

McCrae, R. R. & John, O. P. (1992). An introduction to the five factor model and its applications. *Journal of Personality, 60,* 175–215.

McGuire, W. J., McGuire, C. V., Child, P., & Fujioka, T. (1978). Salience of ethnicity in the spontaneous self-concept as a function of one's ethnic distinctiveness in the social environment. *Journal of Personality and Social Psychology, 36,* 511–520.

Mihalyi, L. J. (1984–1985). Ethnocentrism vs. nationalism: Origin and fundamental aspects of a major problem for the future. *Journal of Social Relations, 12,* 95–113.

Miller, J. G. (1984). Culture and the development of everyday social explanation. *Journal of Personality and Social Psychology, 46,* 961–978.

Miller, J. G., Bersoff, D. M., & Harwood, R. L. (1990). Perceptions of social responsibilities in India and the United States: Moral imperatives or personal decisions? *Journal of Personality and Social Psychology, 58,* 33–47.

Moghaddam, F. (1993). Managing cultural diversity: North American experiences and suggestions for the German unification process. *International Journal of Intercultural Relations, 28,* 727–741.

Moghaddam, F. & Taylor, D. M. (1987). The meaning of multiculturalism for visible minority immigrant women. *Canadian Journal of Behavioural Science, 19,* 121–136.

Morisaki, S. & Gudykunst, W. B. Face in Japan and the United States. In S. Ting-Toomey (Ed.), *The challenge of facework* (pp. 47–93). Albany: State University of New York Press.

Morris, M. W., Nisbett, R. E., & Peng, K. (In press). Causal attribution across domains and cultures. In G. Lewis, D. Premack, & D. Sperber (Eds.), *Causal understandings in cognition and culture.* New York: Oxford University Press.

Noesjirwan, J. (1978). A rule-based analysis of cultural differences in social behavior. *International Journal of Psychology, 13,* 305–316.

Oatey, H. (1992). Conceptions of social relations and pragmatics research. Unpublished manuscript, Lancaster University, United Kingdom.

Oyserman, D. (1993). The lens of personhood: Viewing the self and others in a multicultural society. *Journal of Personality and Social Psychology, 65,* 993–1009.

Peabody, D. (1985). *National characteristics.* Cambridge: Cambridge University Press.

Pettigrew, T. F. (1979). The ultimate attribution error: Extending Allport's cognitive analysis of prejudice. *Personality and Social Psychology Bulletin, 5,* 461–476.

Pettigrew, T. F. (1986). The intergroup contact hypothesis. In M. Hewstone & R. Brown (Eds.), *Contact and conflict in intergroup encounters* (pp. 169–195). Oxford: Blackwell.

Pierson, H. D. & Bond, M. H. (1982). How do Chinese bilinguals respond to variations of interviewer language and ethnicity? *Journal of Language and Social Psychology, 1,* 123–139.

Riemann, R., Grubich, C., Hempel, S., Mergl, T., & Richter, M. (1993). Personality and attitudes towards current political topics. *Personality and Individual Differences, 15,* 313–321.

Rokeach, M. (1960). *The open and closed mind.* New York: Basic.

Rosenthal, D. A. & Feldman, S. S. (1992). The nature and stability of ethnic identity in Chinese youth: Effects of length of residence in two cultural contexts. *Journal of Cross-Cultural Psychology, 23,* 214–227.

Ross, L. (1977). The intuitive psychologist and his shortcomings: Distortions in the attribution process. In L. Berkowitz (Ed.), *Advances in experimental social psychology* (Vol. 10, pp. 173–220). New York: Academic.

Sagiv, L. & Schwartz, S. H. (1995). Value priorities and readiness for out-group social contact. *Journal of Personality and Social Psychology, 69,* pp. 437–448.

Sampson, D. L. & Smith, H. P. (1957). A scale to measure world-minded attitudes. *Journal of Social Psychology, 45,* 99–106.

Schwartz, S. H. (1992). Universals in the content and structure of values: Theoretical advances and empirical tests in 20 countries. In M. Zanna (Ed.), *Advances in experimental social psychology* (Vol. 25, pp. 1–65). Orlando, FL: Academic.

Schwartz, S. H. (1994). Beyond individualism/collectivism: New cultural dimensions of values. In U. Kim, H. C. Triandis, C. Kagitçibasi, S-C. Choi. & G. Yoon (Eds.), *Individualism and collectivism: Theory, method, and applications* (pp. 85–119). Thousand Oaks, CA: Sage.

Schwartz, S. H. & Bilsky, W. (1990). Toward a theory of the universal content and structure of values. *Journal of Personality and Social Psychology, 58,* 878–891.

Schwartz, S. H. & Struch, N. (1989). Values, stereotypes and intergroup antagonism. In D. Bar-Tal, C. F. Graumann, A., W. Kruglanski, & W. Stroebe (Eds.), *Stereotyping and prejudice: Changing conceptions* (pp. 151–167). New York: Springer-Verlag.

Scollon, S. (1993). Metaphors of self and communication: English and Cantonese. *Working papers of the Department of English, City Polytechnic of Hong Kong, 5*(2).

Scott, W. A. (1965). Psychological and social correlates of international images. In H. C. Kelman (Ed.), *International behavior: A social—psychological analysis* (pp. 70–103). New York: Holt, Rinehart and Winston.

Sherif, M. (1966). *Group conflict and cooperation: Their social psychology.* London: Routledge and Kegan Paul.

Singelis, T. M. (1994a). Culture, self, and emotional contagion. Manuscript submitted for publication.

Singelis, T. M. (1994b). The measurement of independent and interdependent self-construals. *Personality and Social Psychology Bulletin, 20,* 580–591.

Singelis, T. M., Bond, M. H., Lai, S. Y., & Sharkey, W. F. (1994). Self, self-esteem, and embarrassability in Hong Kong, Hawaii, and Mainland United States. Manuscript submitted for publication.

Singelis, T. M. & Brown, W. J. (1995). Culture, self, and collectivist communication: Linking culture to individual behavior. *Human Communication Research, 21,* 354–389.

Singelis, T. M., & Sharkey, W. F. (1995). Culture, self-construal, and embarrassability. *Journal of Cross-Cultural Psychology, 26,* 622–644.

Singelis, T. M., Triandis, H. C., Bhawuk, D. S., & Gelfand, M. (1994). Horizontal and vertical dimensions of individualism and collectivism: A theoretical and measurement refinement. Manuscript submitted for publication.

Smith, M. B. (1992). Nationalism, ethnocentrism, and the new world order. *Journal of Humanistic Psychology, 32.*

Smith, P. B. & Bond, M. H. (1993). *Social psychology across cultures: Analysis and perspectives.* Hemel Hempstead, England: Harvester/Wheatsheaf.

Smith, P. B., Trompenaars, F., & Dugan, S. (1994). The Rotter locus of control scale in 45 countries: A test of cultural relativity. Unpublished manuscript, University of Sussex, England.

Smith, P. B., Dugan, S., & Trompenaars, F. (1996). National culture and the values of organizational employees: A dimensional analysis across 43 nations. *Journal of Cross-Cultural Psychology, 27,* 231–264.

Solomon, S., Greenberg, J., & Pyszezynski, T. (1991). Terror management theory of self-esteem. In C. R. Snyder & D. Forsyth (Eds.), *Handbook of social and clinical psychology* (pp. 21–40). Elmsford, NY: Pergamon.

Spence-Brown, R. (1993). Japanese exchange students overseas. *Journal of Asian Pacific Communication, 4,* 193–207.

Stangor, C., Sullivan, L. A., & Ford, T. E. (1991).

Affective and cognitive determinants of prejudice. *Social Cognition, 9,* 359–380.

Staub, E. (1988). The evolution of caring and nonagressive persons and societies. *Journal of Social Issues, 44,* 81–100.

Staub, E. (1990). Moral exclusion, personal goal theory, and extreme destructiveness. *Journal of Social Issues, 46,* 47–64.

Stephan, W. G. (1987). The contact hypothesis in intergroup relations. In C. Hendrick (Ed.), *Group processes and intergroup relations* (pp. 13–41). Newbury Park, CA: Sage.

Stephan, W. G., Ageyev, V., Coates-Shrider, L., Stephan, C. W., & Abalakina, M. (1994). On the relationship between stereotypes and prejudice: An international study. *Personality and Social Psychology Bulletin, 20,* 277–284.

Stephan, W. G. & Stephan, C. W. (1985). Intergroup anxiety. *Journal of Social Issues, 41,* 157–176.

Stephan, W. G. & Stephan, C. W. (1989). Antecedent to intergroup anxiety in Asian-American and Hispanic-Americans. *International Journal of Intercultural Relations, 13,* 203–219.

Stephan, W. G., & Stephan, C. W. (1992). Reducing intercultural anxiety through intercultural contact. *International Journal of Intercultural Relations, 16,* 89–106.

Stephenson, G. (1981). Intergroup bargaining and negotiation. In J. Turner & H. Giles (Eds.), *Intergroup behavior* (pp. 168–198). Chicago: University of Chicago Press.

Sumner, W. G. (1906). *Folkways.* Boston: Ginn.

Tajfel, H. (1978). Social categorization, social identity, and social comparison. In H. Tajfel (Ed.), *Differentiation between social groups* (pp. 61–76). London: Academic.

Taylor, D. M. (1981). Stereotypes and intergroup relations. In R. C. Gardner & R. Kalin (Eds.), *A Canadian social psychology of ethnic relations* (pp. 151–171). Toronto: Methuen.

Taylor, D. M., Dubé, L., & Bellerose, J. (1986). Intergroup contact in Quebec. In M. Hewstone & R. Brown (Eds.), *Contact and conflict in intergroup encounters* (pp. 107–118). Oxford: Blackwell.

Thalhofer, N. N. (1993). Intergroup differentiation and reduction of intergroup conflict. *Small Group Research, 24,* 28–43.

Ting-Toomey, S. (1988). Intercultural conflict: A face–negotiation theory. In Y. Kim & W. B. Gudykunst (Eds.), *Theories in intercultural communication* (pp. 213–238). Newbury Park, CA: Sage.

Ting-Toomey, S. (1993). Communicative resourcefulness: An identity negotiation perspective. In R. Wiseman & J. Koester (Eds.), *Intercultural communication competence* (pp. 72–110). Thousand Oaks, CA: Sage.

Trew, K. (1986). Catholic–Protestant contact in Northern Ireland. In M. Hewstone & R. Brown (Eds.), *Contact and conflict in intergroup encounters* (pp. 93–106). Oxford: Blackwell.

Triandis, H. C. (1976). On the value of cross-cultural research in social psychology: Reactions to Fancheux's paper. *European Journal of Social Psychology, 6,* 331–341.

Triandis, H. C. (1978). Some universals of social behavior. *Personality and Social Psychology Bulletin, 4,* 1–16.

Triandis, H. C. (1988). Collectivism vs. individualism. In G. Verma & C. Bagley (Eds.), *Cross-cultural studies of personality, attitudes, and cognition* (pp. 60–95). London: Macmillan.

Triandis, H. C. (1994). *Culture and social behavior.* New York: McGraw-Hill.

Triandis, H. C. (1995). *Individualism–collectivism.* Boulder, CO: Westview.

Triandis, H. C., Bontempo, R., Betancourt, H., Bond, M. H., Leung, K., Brenes, A., Georgas, J., Hui, H. C., Marin, G., Setiadi, B., Sinha, J. B. P., Verma, J., Spangenberg, J., Touzard, H., & de Montmollin, G. (1986). The measurement of the etic aspects of individualism and collectivism across cultures. *Australian Journal of Psychology, 38,* 257–267.

Triandis, H. C., Leung, K., Villareal, M., & Clack, F. (1985). Allocentric versus idiocentric tendencies. *Journal of Research in Personality, 19,* 395–415.

Triandis, H. C., McCusker, C., Betancourt, H., Iwao, S., Leung, K., Salezar, J. M., Setiadi, B., Sinha, J. B., Touzard, H., & Zaleski, Z. (1993). An etic–emic analysis of individualism and collectivism. *Journal of Cross-Cultural Psychology, 24,* 366–383.

Triandis, H. C. & Triandis, L. M. (1960). Race, social class, religion, and rationality as determinants of social distance. *Journal of Abnormal and Social Psychology, 61,* 110–118.

Triandis, H. C., Villareal, M., Asai, M., & Lucca, N. (1988). Individualism and collectivism: Cross-cultural perspectives on self-ingroup relationships. *Journal of Personality and Social Psychology, 54,* 323–338.

Turner, J. C., Shaver, I., & Hogg, M. (1983). Social categorization, interpersonal attraction, and group formation. *British Journal of Social Psychology, 22,* 227–239.

Tzeng, O. C. S. & Jackson, J. W. (1994). Effects of contact, conflict, and social identity on interethnic group hostilities. *International Journal of Intercultural Relations, 18,* 259–276.

Vaughan, G., Tajfel, H., & Williams, J. (1981). Bias in reward allocation in an intergroup and interpersonal context. *Social Psychology Quarterly, 44,* 37–42.

Weinreich, P. (1983). Emerging from threatened identities. In G. Breakwell (Ed.), *Threatened identities* (pp. 149–185). London: Wiley.

Weinreich, P. (1991). Ethnic identities and indigenous psychologies in pluralist societies. *Psychology and Developing Societies, 3,* 73–92.

Weinreich, P., Luk, C. L., & Bond, M. H. (1994). *Ethnic identity: Identification with other cultures, self-esteem, and identity confusion.* Paper presented at the International Conference on Immigration, Language Acquisition and Patterns of Social Integration, Jerusalem, June, 1994.

Wetherell, M. (1982). Cross-cultural studies of minimal groups. In H. Tajfel (Ed.), *Social identity and intergroup relations* (pp. 207–238). Cambridge: Cambridge University Press.

Wheeler, L., Reis, H. T., & Bond, M. H. (1989). Collectivism–individualism in everyday social life: The middle kingdom and the melting pot. *Journal of Personality and Social Psychology, 57,* 79–86.

Wierzbicka, A. (1993). A conceptual basis for cultural psychology. *Ethos, 21,* 205–231.

Williams, J. E., Saiz, J. L., Formy-Duval, D. L., Munick, M. L., Adom, A., Hague, A., Neto, F., & Yu, J. Y. (1994). Cross-cultural variation in the importance of psychological traits. Unpublished manuscript, Wake Forest University, North Carolina.

Williams, T. P. & Sogon, S. (1984). Group composition and conforming behavior in Japanese students. *Japanese Psychological Research, 126,* 231–234.

Wish, M., Deutsch, M., & Kaplan, S. J. (1976). Perceived dimensions of interpersonal relations. *Journal of Personality and Social Psychology, 33,* 409–420.

Witkin, H. A. & Berry, J. W. (1975). Psychological differentiation in cross-cultural perspective. *Journal of Cross-Cultural Psychology, 6,* 4–87.

Wu, D. Y. H. (1979). Cross-cultural interaction in public places. *Journal of Sociology and Psychology, 2,* 28–35.

Yamaguchi, S. (1994). Collectivism among the Japanese. In U. Kim, H. C. Triandis, C. Kagitçibasi, S-C. Choi, & G. Yoon (Eds.), *Individualism and collectivism: Theory, method, and applications* (pp. 175–188). Thousand Oaks, CA: Sage.

Yang, K. S. & Bond, M. H. (1980). Ethnic affirmation by Chinese bilinguals. *Journal of Cross-Cultural Psychology, 11,* 411–425.

Young, R. L. (1980). Social images and interpersonal interaction among Hong Kong and American students. Unpublished master's thesis, Department of Psychology, University of Hawaii.

5

SEX, GENDER, AND CULTURE

DEBORAH L. BEST and JOHN E. WILLIAMS
Wake Forest University
United States

Contents

Introduction

The research to be reviewed in this chapter concerns sex and gender viewed cross-culturally with the levels of analysis extending from the individual person to that of cultures. Within this range, topics include gender roles and stereotypes, relationships between men and women, the roles of biology and socialization, and theories of gender role development. We have not comprehensively reviewed the literature on cultural differences in sexual practices because this topic is adequately covered elsewhere (e.g., Hatfield & Rapson, 1995; Reiss, 1986), nor have we attempted to include every cross-cultural study in which gender was a variable and where gender differences were found, such as studies of spatial abilities in men and women. Rather, our focus is on studies from the general areas of developmental, personality, and social psychology that deal with the manner in which males and females view themselves and one another and the way in which the sexes should and do interact. Also, generally we have not included unicultural, noncomparative studies.[1]

Definitions of Gender-Related Concepts

First, some terms need to be defined because scholars working in this area use terms differently, often leading to some conceptual confusion. In this chapter, we will use the following definitions:

Sex. The term sex is ordinarily used in a biological context to refer to the anatomical and physiological differences between the female and male and the implication of those differences in procreation. Human sexual behavior is elaborated and modified in a great variety of ways, including those related to learning cultural standards and norms. We will also use the term "the sexes" as an alternative way of referring to women and men, collectively.

Gender. The term gender is also used to distinguish the female and male members of the human species but with the emphasis upon social rather than upon biological factors. Implicit is the recognition that what constitutes "women" and "men" may be as much a product of socialization as of biology. Beyond the truly biological level, most of the differences of consequence between women and men are referred to as gender differences.

Gender roles. This term is reserved for the social roles that men and women occupy with differential frequency. These roles may be found in virtually all areas of human endeavor including family, occupation, recreation, and so forth. If something is done primarily by women, such as nursing in the United States, it is a female gender role; if it is done primarily by men, for example truck driving in the United States, it is a male gender role. Cross-culturally, there are substantial variations in the roles considered appropriate for each gender and, thus, gender roles must be defined in terms of place and time. While other scholars (e.g., Bem, 1974) have used the term sex role more broadly to include personality differences between the sexes, we prefer to restrict the meaning of sex role in order to avoid confusing social activities with psychological characteristics.

Sex role ideology. This term, similar to attitude toward women (Spence & Helmreich, 1972), designates beliefs concerning appropriate relationships between the genders. The emphasis is not merely on what men and women do but what they should do, including how they should relate to one another. Sex role ideology is assumed to vary along a dimension ranging from a traditional, male dominant, or anti-female view to a modern or egalitarian view.

Gender stereotypes. This term refers to the psychological traits and behaviors that are believed to occur with differential frequency in the two gender groups, for example, men are more "aggressive," women are more "emotional," and so forth. Assertions about differences in the general psychological makeup of the two gender groups provide support for traditional sex role assignments of women and men and serve as socialization models for children.

Masculinity/femininity. Although widely used in different ways, we will restrict this term to the degree to which men and women have incorporated traits considered to be "womanlike" or "manlike" by their culture into their self perception. Thus, a person whose self description consists primarily of traits that the local gender stereotype identifies as male-associated would be described as "masculine," regardless of the sex of the respondent.

It is important to remember that human males and females are only slightly variant members of the same species; women and men are much more similar than they are different, whether one is speaking biologically or psychologically. It is easy to focus upon differences and unintentionally to magnify their importance. This also occurs when people refer to the "opposite" sex instead of the "other" sex. To properly appreciate the research described in this chapter, one must recognize the highly similar biological and psychological natures of women and men.

Gender at the Individual Adult Level

Sex Role Ideology

There is a high degree of pancultural similarity in the tasks socially assigned to women and to men. In virtually all human groups, women have greater responsibility for "domestic" activities while men have greater responsibility for "external" activities. These pan-cultural similarities may rest, primarily, on biological differences between the sexes, particularly because women bear and, in most societies nurse, the offspring (Williams & Best, 1990b).

Recently, in many societies, duties are often shared so that men engage in more domestic activities and women in more external, particularly economic, activities.

The gender division of labor will be reviewed later in the chapter but here we discuss beliefs and attitudes about the appropriate role behaviors for the two sexes.

Most researchers classify sex-role ideologies along a continuum ranging from traditional to modern.[2] Traditional ideologies hold that men are more "important" than women and it is proper for men to control and dominate women. On the other hand, modern ideologies represent a more egalitarian view, sometimes labeled a feminist position, in which women and men are equally important, and dominance of one gender over the other is rejected.

Because Indian culture juxtaposes traditional and modern ideologies, sex roles have been studied extensively in India. When male and female Indian and American university students were asked what qualities women in their culture should and should not possess, Indian students expressed more traditional sex role ideology than American students, and women in both groups were more modern, or liberal, than were men (Agarwal & Lester, 1992; Rao & Rao, 1985). University women with nontraditional sex role attitudes tended to come from nuclear families, had educated mothers, and were in professional or career-oriented disciplines (Ghadially & Kazi, 1979).

Furnham and Karani (1985) studied English Christians, Indian Hindus, and Indian Zoroastrians and found greater cross-cultural similarity in sex-role attitudes among females than among males, with males being more conservative. Among Hindu and Muslim school children in India, sex prejudice is very high with males being even more prejudiced than females (Jayaswal, 1985). Singh (1980) found that among Indian school students sex prejudice was more dramatic than prejudice toward religion, caste, or class.

Rapoport, Lomski-Feder, and Masalha (1989) found that among high-school-age students in the Arab-Israeli community in Israel, young females opposed the imposition of social constraints upon women more than their male counterparts, but both expressed strong traditional, conservative attitudes regarding the Islamic code of protecting female honor and chastity. Looking more closely at Jewish and Arab-Israeli adolescents' attitudes toward women, Seginer, Karayanni, and Mar'i (1990) found that Jews, females, and older adolescents expressed more liberal views toward women's roles than did Arabs, males, and younger adolescents. The greater liberalism of the older Arab females suggests a shift in gender attitudes during their transition to adulthood, perhaps due to an increase in perceived power among middle-class Arab women in Israel (Friedman & Pines, 1992).

Consistent with the Israeli data, female college students in Japan, Slovenia, and the United States are less traditional than men, with Japanese students the most traditional of the three groups (Morinaga, Frieze, & Ferligoj, 1993). Likewise, Trommsdorff and Iwawaki (1989) reported that Japanese adolescents were more traditional than German adolescents. Using the Scale of Egalitarian Sex Role Attitudes, Suzuki (1991a) found that American women have more modern, egalitarian attitudes than Japanese women, although Japanese women's attitudes have become more egalitarian and individualistic over the past two decades. Education and professional managerial work were strong predictors of sex role attitudes for both Japanese and American women (Suzuki, 1991b). Interestingly, American women with jobs, no matter what sort, had more egalitarian attitudes than women without jobs. Japanese women with career-oriented professional jobs differed from all other women, with or without jobs. Using a novel historical method to examine fluctuations in the number of distinguished women authors in Japan, Simonton (1992) found that both women's and men's successes were negatively associated with male power and aggressive activities.

Similar to the Japanese findings, Chia, Moore, Lam, Chuang, and Cheng (1994) found that Chinese-American university students have more conservative views than Caucasian Americans, and that women in both groups are more liberal than men. Moreover, British working-class women are more conservative than American working-class women, with no difference between groups of upper-middle-class women (Nelson, 1988).

Gibbons, Stiles, and Shkodriani (1991) capitalized on a unique research opportunity and studied attitudes toward gender and family roles among adolescent students from 46 different countries attending schools in The Netherlands. Countries of origin were grouped into two categories based on Hofstede's cultural values: the wealthy, more individualistic countries and the less wealthy, more collectivistic countries. Students from the second group of countries had more traditional attitudes than students from the first group of countries, and girls generally responded less traditionally than boys.

Across the studies examined above, males generally have more traditional sex-role ideologies than women. This is not surprising given that in most countries males benefit in terms of status and privileges from more traditional male-dominant orientations.

In many of the studies just described, Americans were used as a reference group and were usually found to be more liberal, suggesting that Americans may be unusual in this respect. However, Williams and Best (1990b) did not find this to be true in their 14-country study of sex-role ideology and related cultural comparison variables. To date, this study includes the largest number and variety of countries to be examined in a single study.

In their study, university students responded to the 30-item Kalin Sex Role Ideology (SRI) measure (Kalin & Tilby, 1978; e.g., "The husband should be regarded as the legal representative of the family group in all matters of law"). The most modern ideologies were found in Northern European countries (the Netherlands, Germany, Finland, England, Italy), the United States was in the middle of the distribution, and the most traditional ideologies were found in the African and Asian countries (Nigeria, Pakistan, India, Japan, Malaysia). Generally, women had more modern views than men, but not in all countries (e.g., Malaysia and Pakistan). However, there was high correspondence between men's and women's scores in a given country with a correlation of .95 for men and women across the 14 countries. Overall, the effect of culture was greater than the effect of gender.

Before concluding that observed variations between countries are due to cultural factors, the variations must be shown to relate to cultural comparison variables. A substantial relationship was found between men's and women's SRI scores and economic–social development; that is, sex role ideology tended to be more modern in more developed countries. Sex role ideology also was more modern in more heavily Christian countries, in more urbanized countries, and in countries in the high latitudes (i.e., relatively far from the equator).

Gender Stereotypes

Related to sex-role ideology, and often used as justifications for those beliefs, are gender stereotypes, the psychological characteristics believed to be more characteristic of one gender than the other. In addition to the relatively few cross-cultural studies of gender stereotypes conducted by independently-working researchers (e.g., Lii & Wong, 1982; Sunar, 1982), a great number of studies have been conducted by an international group of researchers cooperating in a 32-country project (Best & Williams, 1994a, 1994b; Best, Williams, Cloud, Davis, Robertson, Edwards, Giles, & Fowles, 1977; Bjerke, Williams, & Wathne, 1989; Edwards & Williams, 1980; Haque, 1982; Neto, Williams, & Widner, 1991; Tarrier & Gomes, 1981; Ward, 1982, 1985; Ward & Williams, 1982; Williams & Best, 1982/1990a, 1990b, 1993, 1994; Williams, Best, Haque, Pandey, & Verma, 1982; Williams, Best, Tilquin, Keller, Voss, Bjerke, & Baarda, 1981; Williams, Daws, Best, Tilquin, Wesley, & Bjerke, 1979; Williams, Giles, & Edwards, 1977; Williams, Giles, Edwards, Best, & Daws, 1977). Findings from these studies have been reviewed and integrated by Williams and Best (1982/1990a). Studies conducted with adult subjects are summarized here and those involving young children are discussed later.

In the adult studies, university students in 27 countries were presented with a list of 300 adjectives from the Adjective Check List (ACL; Gough & Heilbrun, 1980) and were asked to indicate whether, in their culture, each adjective was more frequently associated with men, more frequently associated with women, or not differentially associated by gender. These frequencies were converted to an M% score, with high values indicating items that were highly associated with men, low values indicating items that were highly associated with women, and scores in the mid-range indicating items that were associated equally with men and women.

Correlation coefficients computed for M% scores between pairs of countries across all 300 items ranged from .35 for Pakistan versus Venezuela to .94 for Australia versus England. The mean common variance across all 25 countries was 42 percent, indicating a substantial degree of agreement concerning the psychological characteristics differentially associated with men and with women. Male and female stereotypes were the most different in the Netherlands, Finland, Norway, and Germany and least different in Scotland, Bolivia, and Venezuela. The stereotypes of men and women were more different in Protestant than in Catholic countries, in more developed countries, and in countries where Hofstede's male work-related values were relatively high in Individualism (Williams & Best, 1982/1990a, Appendix D).

In each country, the "focused," high agreement male- and female-stereotype items were scored using an affective meaning scoring system, and in all countries the male-stereotype items were more active and stronger than the female-stereo-type items. Interestingly, there was no pan-cultural effect for favorability, with the male stereotype being more positive in some countries (e.g., Japan, South Africa, Nigeria) and the female stereotype in others (e.g., Italy, Peru, Australia). A second scoring system, derived from the five functional ego states of Transactional Analysis Theory (Berne, 1961, 1966), indicated that in all countries the Critical Parent and Adult ego states were more characteristic of men while the Nurturing Parent and Adapted Child ego states were more characteristic of women, with the Free Child ego state not differentially associated. A third scoring system based on 15 psychological needs revealed that across all countries, dominance, autonomy, aggression, exhibition, and achievement were associated with men while nurturance, succorance, deference, and abasement were associated with women. Theoretical discussion of this overwhelming evidence supporting a general pan-cultural sex stereotype is presented elsewhere (Williams & Best, 1982/1990a), but it points to commonalities in the biological and sociological factors with which all human groups must contend.

Within this setting of similarities, there were also some variations between countries. The strength and activity differences between the male and female stereotypes were greater in socioeconomically less developed countries, in countries where literacy was low, and where the percentage of women attending the university was low. Perhaps economic and educational advancement are accompanied by a reduction in the tendency to view men as stronger and more active than women. Interestingly, in Catholic countries the female stereotype appeared relatively more favorable and less weak than in Protestant countries, a finding consistent with the greater role of women in the Catholic tradition. Note, however, that the foregoing effects were merely reduced—not eliminated by cultural and economic factors.

Masculinity/Femininity of Self Concepts

Manlike or womanlike—this is the essential meaning of the twin concepts of masculinity/femininity (M/F). Considered broadly, a person might be masculine or feminine in many different ways including dress, mannerisms, and tone of voice, but we restrict our definition to the self-concepts and the degree to which they incorporate traits that are differentially associated with women or men. Even with this restricted concept of masculinity and femininity researchers have taken different approaches: identifying self-descriptive questionnaire items differentially endorsed by men and women (California Personality Inventory femininity scale; Gough, 1952), examining frequency of endorsement of characteristics considered socially desirable in one gender or the other (Bem, 1974; Spence & Helmreich, 1978), or determining characteristics more frequently associated with one gender or the other without reference to social desirability (Williams & Best, 1990b).

Moreover, cross-cultural studies differ in their attention to emic or culture specific considerations in the definition of masculinity/femininity. At one extreme are pseudo-etic studies (Acosta & Sanchez de Almeida, 1983; Basow, 1984; Gackenbach, 1981; Krampen, Galli, & Nigro, 1992; Maloney, Wilkof, & Dambrot, 1981; Murphy-Berman, Berman, Singh, & Pandy, 1992; Reed-Sanders, Dodder, & Webster, 1985; Ryan, Dolphin, Lundberg, & Myrsten, 1987; Spence & Helmreich, 1978) in which a masculinity/femininity scale developed in one country, most often the United States, is translated into another language and administered to persons in other cultures. Scores are interpreted as if they represent comparative degrees of masculinity/femininity in the different cultures and there is little emic consideration. At the other extreme are studies employing some emic orientation where an effort is made to define masculinity/femininity in culturally relevant terms.

To briefly illustrate the first approach, Spence and Helmreich developed the Personal Attributes Questionnaire (PAQ) from M/F studies conducted in the United States. Self-descriptions of American male university students revealed similar means on the masculinity (M = 21.69) and femininity scales (M = 22.43), whereas the self-descriptions of American female university students revealed lower masculinity scores (M = 19.54) and higher femininity scores (M = 24.37) (Spence & Helmreich, 1978, p. 50). The PAQ was translated into Portuguese and administered to university students in Brazil, where the pattern of female scores in Brazil was found to be similar to that in the United States. However, in contrast to American men, Brazilian men had higher femininity scores (M = 21.61) than masculinity scores (M = 18.98). Can we conclude that Brazilian men are "more feminine" that American men? Hardly. All groups responded to items that had been chosen to be female- and male-associated only in the United States. Only by comparing the self-descriptions of Brazilian men with traits that are associated with women and men in their country would it be possible to obtain findings to permit such a conclusion.

The general problem with using translated scales in cross-cultural studies of masculinity/femininity is that while some items appear to work very well across cultures, others do not (see Gough, 1966, CPI in France, Italy, Turkey, and Spain; Pitariu, 1981, CPI in Romania; Nishiyama, 1975, CPI in Japan; Kaschak & Sharratt, 1983, PAQ and SRI in Costa Rica; Sethi & Allen, 1984, Ward & Sethi, 1986, BSRI in India and Malaysia; Lara-Cantu & Navarro-Arias, 1987, BSRI in Mexico; Harris, 1994, BSRI in USA ethnic groups). Some items may be inappropriate due to content, whereas others may be poorly translated. In either case, scores obtained from persons in different cultures cannot be directly compared to judge the relative masculinity/femininity of persons from different cultures. What is needed are methods for assessing M/F in a given culture in terms of the attributes that are male-associated and female-associated in that culture. Illustrative of culture specific masculinity/femininity tests are: the Singapore Androgyny Scale (Pei-Hui & Ward, 1994); the Bar Ilan Sex Role Inventory for use in Israel (Tzuriel, 1984, 1985); the Masculine-Feminine Personality Traits Scale for use in Mexico (Lara-Cantu, 1989); the Australian Sex Role Scale (Antill, Cunningham, Russell, & Thompson, 1981); the Chinese Sex Role Inventory (Keyes, 1984); and the Latin American Sex Role Inventory (Kaschak & Sharratt, 1983). While generally excellent for intra-cultural comparisons (e.g., to determine the correlates of masculinity/femininity in a given cultural setting), the methodological variations from instrument to instrument make cross-cultural comparisons difficult.

Williams and Best (1990b) employed culture specific measures of masculinity/femininity in 14 countries with the university students in the sex role ideology study discussed above (Williams & Best, 1990b). Subjects first described their actual self ("descriptive of you as you really are") and then their ideal self ("descriptive of the person you would like to be") using the 300 ACL adjectives employed in the previous gender stereotype study. These self-descriptions were scored to obtain a culture-specific mean M% score for each description, employing the M% values for that particular country as determined in the earlier study. These mean M% scores could be considered rough indices of "masculinity–femininity." Self-descriptions with high mean M%s could be considered relatively masculine and self-descriptions with low M%s being relatively feminine. Analyses of the mean M% scores indicated that men in all countries were more masculine than women, hardly surprising. In contrast, for the ideal self, both gender groups wished to be "more masculine" than they thought they were.

This large-scale cross-cultural study of masculinity–femininity with these concepts defined in local, culture-specific terms should have led to interesting findings about cultural variations in masculinity–femininity, but this expectation was largely unrealized. While differences in mean M% of self-concepts were found, there were no substantial associations with cultural comparison variables, such as economic/social development. Across cultural groups, there was no evidence that, relative to their own culture's definition of femininity and masculinity, women in some societies were more feminine than women in other societies or that men in some societies were more masculine than men in others.

In contrast, when a different scoring system was employed, there were substantial differences across countries in the affective meaning scores of the self and ideal self-concepts, and these correlated with the cultural comparison variables. For example, the differences between men's and women's self-concepts were greater in less developed countries than in more developed countries; the differences in the self-concepts of men and women were less when women were employed outside the home, when they constituted a large percentage of the university population, and where a relatively modern sex-role ideology prevailed.

In sum, an interesting paradox occurs. When the masculinity–femininity scoring system, which seems methodologically superior because of its reliance on culture-specific definitions is used, there is scant evidence of true cross-cultural variation and greater evidence of pan-cultural definitions of masculinity–femininity. On the other hand, when using the affective meaning scoring system, which may be culturally biased because it is based on scores from English-speaking persons in the United States, there are a number of robust relationships with cultural comparison variables. This paradox cannot be resolved easily.

Relations Between Women and Men

In this section we summarize cross-cultural studies dealing with the relationships between men and women. While we will touch upon a number of facets of these relations, some of which deal with sexuality, we do not attempt a general summary of cross-cultural variations in human sexual behavior. Readers interested in this topic are referred to books by Reiss (1986) and Hatfield and Rapson (1995) and to the review papers by Davis and Whitten (1987) and Hatfield and Rapson (1993), the latter listing 148 references.

Sexuality

Many studies of sexuality have used the Murdock and White Standard Cross-Cultural Sample from the Human Relations Area Files (HRAF). Broude (1987) conducted a hologeistic study of the patterning of male–female relationships across cultures and found, contrary to expectations, that there was no overwhelming overall consistency in how male-female relationships are related across cultures, i.e., the premise that sexual intimacy, non-sexual marital intimacy, and male sexual orientation would be predictably connected was not supported. Betzig (1989) examined the causes of conjugal dissolution in the Standard Cross-Cultural Sample and found that, cross-culturally, adultery and sterility were the most common reasons for divorce. Using HRAF data, Ember (1978) tested, cross-culturally, the implications of four theories to explain men's fear of sex with women: men may fear sex with women because their wives come from enemy villages; population pressure on resources favors the avoidance of intercourse; males are conflicted about their sexual identity; or males have an exaggerated Oedipus complex. Ember reports that the cross-cultural evidence is generally consistent with all four theories.

Mate Preferences

Related to issues of sexuality are mate preferences. While there are other cross-cultural studies of preferences in mate selection (e.g., DeRaad & Doddema-Winsemius, 1992), the most extensive investigation was conducted by Buss and his associates (1989, in press, Buss et al., 1990) who gathered data from 37 samples of respondents totalling over 10,000 persons from 33 countries located on six continents and five islands. Buss (1994) suggest that while social scientists have long assumed that mate preferences are highly culture-bound and arbitrary, his findings are contrary. On the first of two similar lists of potential mate characteristics (dependable character, chastity, good health, etc.), subjects indicated their preferences by rating the 18 items on a four-point scale, and on the second list the same subjects indicated their preferences by ranking 13 items.

The most striking finding was the remarkable degree of agreement in preference for mate characteristics between men and women. Both genders ranked "kind and understanding" first; "intelligent" second; "exciting personality" third; "healthy" fourth; and "religious" last. The correlation between male and female ranks was +.92. Despite the overall gender similarity, as hypothesized, women generally valued good earning capacity in a potential mate slightly more than men did, whereas men generally valued physical appearance slightly more than women did, providing modest support for the expectation of the sociobiologists (e.g., Wilson, 1975).

The small amount of variance accounted for by gender contrasts with the much greater variation due to culture. Cultural differences were found for virtually every item and great variation was found in the magnitude of the cultural effects. For example, the greatest cultural effect occurred for chastity, with Northern European groups viewing chastity as largely irrelevant or unimportant while groups from China, India, and Iran placed great emphasis on it. Men valued chastity in a prospective mate more than women did.

Buss et al. (1990) concluded that there were substantial commonalities among all samples, suggesting that there is some unity to human mate preferences that may be regarded as "species typical." On the other hand, no sample was exactly like any other sample—each displayed some uniqueness in their mate preference orderings of characteristics, reflecting modest degrees of cultural variation.

Romantic Love and Intimacy

As with mate preferences, romantic love and intimacy are assumed to be influenced by culture. Simmons, Kolke, and Shimizu (1986) used university students from West Germany, Japan, and the United States to assess attitudes toward love and romance. Generally, romantic love is valued highly in less traditional cultures, with few strong extended family ties, and is less valued in cultures where strong family ties reinforce the relationship between marriage partners. Japanese subjects valued romantic love less than did West German subjects, with American subjects between the other two societies. Compared with Swedish young adults, American young adults differentiate love and sex more strongly (Foa, Anderson, Converse, Urbansky, Cawley, Muhlhausen, & Tornblom, 1987) and compared with Mexicans, they employ power relationships differently (Belk, Snell, Garcia-Falconi, Hernandez-Sanchez, Hargrove, & Holtzman, 1988).

Interestingly, Vaidyanathan and Naidoo (1990/1991) found that Asian Indian immigrants to Canada show generational changes in attitudes toward love and marriage. Although 63 percent of first generation immigrants have had arranged marriages, a large proportion of these believed that "love marriages" were an option for their offspring. Moreover, 79 percent of the second generation indicated they wanted more freedom in the selection of a mate and 75 percent supported the notion that love should precede marriage.

Cunningham (1981) presented a sample of self-disclosure topics to women and men university students in the United States and Australia and obtained ratings of intimacy of content. While sex differences were few, Australians rated items in seven categories as less intimate than Americans did, demonstrating a greater willingness for intimacy among Australians. With regard to expressions of intimacy, French and American university students reported a higher degree of love commitment and disclosure maintenance than Japanese students, but French students reported the lowest degree of conflict expression (Ting-Toomey, 1991).

Dion and Dion (1993) examined the concepts of love and intimacy in individualistic (Canada, United States) and collectivistic (China, India, Japan) countries and report some paradoxical findings:

- In societies where individualism is prevalent, greater emphasis is placed on romantic love and on personal fulfillment in marriage. However, some features of individualism at the psychological level make the likelihood of realizing these outcomes more difficult. In contrast, collectivism . . . fosters a receptiveness to intimacy, but at the psychological level, this intimacy is likely to be diffused across a network of family relationships (p. 66).
- Similarly, Broude's (1987) hologeistic study of the relationships of marital intimacy to social environment concluded that intimacy is likely to occur in societies where individuals have no social support systems outside of marriage.
- Buunk and Hupka (1987) surveyed over 2,000 students from seven industrialized nations (Hungary, Ireland, Mexico, the Netherlands, the Soviet Union, the United States, Yugoslavia) with regard to behaviors that elicit sexual jealousy, and they report a general picture of cross-cultural similarities with some interesting differences in particular countries. For example, flirting in Yugoslavia evokes a more negative emotional response than in any other country, but kissing and sexual fantasies elicit the least negative reactions. In the Netherlands, sexual fantasies are less accepted than in any other country, but kissing, dancing, and hugging arouse less jealousy than in most other countries. Culture seems to play a critical role in the interpretation of men's and women's close relationships.

Harassment and Rape[3]

Among the few cross-cultural studies of male harassment and hostility toward women is the study by Kauppinen-Toropainen and Gruber (1993) who examined professional and blue-collar women in the United States, Scandinavia, and the former Soviet Union. Americans reported more woman-unfriendly experiences than the other groups. Scandinavians had fewer woman-unfriendly experiences than Americans, fewer job-related or psychological problems, more autonomy, and better work environments. Former Soviet professionals reported more unfriendly experiences than workers but less than their peers in other regions.

Several scholars have addressed the topic of rape in a cross-cultural perspective. Rozé (1993) examined rape in a random sample of 35 world societies from the Standard Cross Cultural Sample. Rape was found in all the societies, once the definition of rape was broadened to include socially condoned (e.g., ritualistic) rapes. The presence of both normative (condoned) and non-normative (uncondoned) rapes in the majority of societies suggests that, cross-culturally, rape should be viewed as a regulated rather than prohibited behavior.

L'Armand, Pepitone, and Shanmugam (1981) compared attitudes toward rape in India and the United States and found that Indian respondents tended to blame both criminal and victim less than did Americans, emphasizing instead the circumstances surrounding the offense.

The most comprehensive cross-cultural study of attitudes toward rape victims has been conducted by a network of researchers led by Ward from Singapore (Ward, 1995) using the Attitude Toward Rape Victims Scale (ARVS) with university students in 15 countries. Countries with relatively favorable attitudes toward rape victims included United Kingdom, Germany, and New Zealand, while countries with relatively unfavorable attitudes toward rape victims included Turkey, Mexico, Zimbabwe, India, and particularly, Malaysia. In addition, Ward and her colleagues have shown that attitudes toward rape victims mirror attitudes toward women more generally. For example, attitudes toward rape victims were less supportive in countries with a lower percentage of female labor force participation and lower literacy rates. (The present authors also note a substantial relationship between ARVS scores and the sex role ideology scores discussed earlier, with more favorable attitudes toward rape victims found in countries with more modern sex role ideologies.)

Masculine Work-Related Values

In the area of more general values, Hofstede (1980) compared work-related values in 40 countries using attitude survey data collected from thousands of employees of subsidiaries of IBM, a large multinational high-technology business organization (see Kagitçibasi in this volume for more details). One scale derived from Hofstede's factor analysis concerned the extent to which values of assertiveness, money, and things prevail in a society rather than the values of nurturance, quality of life, and people. While the scale might have easily been named "Materialism," Hofstede named the scale "Masculinity" (MAS) because research suggested that male employees assign greater weight to the first set of values whereas females assign greater weight to the second set. Calling the scale Masculinity naturally leads to the expectation that variations on these values might be associated with cross-country variations in other gender-related concepts, such as those discussed earlier in this chapter.

Based on his data, Hofstede computed a masculinity (MAS) index for each of the 40 countries in his study. The five countries with the highest MAS indices were Japan, Austria, Venezuela, Italy, and Switzerland; the five countries with the lowest MAS indices were Sweden, Norway, Netherlands, Denmark, and Finland.

Hofstede (1980) made extensive comparisons with data from other sources and found a large number of relationships between country MAS scores and attitudes, beliefs, and social roles. For example, in high MAS countries there is greater belief in independent decision-making as opposed to group decision-making;

stronger achievement motivation; higher job stress; work is more central in peoples' lives; and so forth. Leung, Bond, Carment, Krishnan, and Liebrand (1990) predicted and found differences in methods of conflict processing between persons from Canada (a high MAS country) and the Netherlands (a low MAS country). Thus, while it is clear that the MAS dimension is significant, the appropriateness of designating this value system as "Masculinity" remains somewhat dubious. For example, Best and Williams (1994b) found no relationship between the cross-country variations in sex stereotypes and masculinity/femininity scores observed in their studies (Williams & Best, 1982/1990a, 1990b) and the cross-country variations in Hofstede's MAS scores. Likewise, Ward (1995) notes that while Attitude Toward Rape scores co-vary with Power Distance scores, they are unrelated to MAS scores.

Developmental Influences

Having seen the influence of gender on the behavior and relationships of adults, it is natural to wonder about the development of gender-related beliefs and behaviors and the role of biological and cultural influences across ontogeny.

Biological Determinism

Researchers studying gender differences in behavior often cite the similarities across cultures as support for the role of genes and hormones, implying complete genetic or biological determinism. Biological determinism assumes that any biological influence or bias always leads to an irreversible sex difference, making biology both the necessary and sufficient cause of sex differences. Biology is neither. The long-standing nature–nurture controversy within developmental psychology has shown that biology does not cause behavior and that such thinking is quite naive.

The classic example in developmental psychology of phenlyketonuria, or PKU, describes how biology is neither necessary nor sufficient to cause mental retardation and how the gene-behavior pathway is bidirectional (Gottlieb, 1983). Similarly, it is clear that sex chromosomes or sex hormones are neither necessary nor sufficient to cause behaviors; they simply change the probability of occurrence of certain behaviors (Hoyenga & Hoyenga, 1993). The individual contributions of nature and nurture to gender differences cannot easily be determined (Johnston, 1987; Stewart, 1988), making the nature versus nurture question a false dichotomy that cannot be answered. One can determine in a particular environment or culture given a particular set of genes how much each contributes, but such findings do not generalize to other environments or to other genes. Indeed, somewhat like people inherit genes, they may "inherit" environments by living close to parents and family.

Sociobiology, Evolutionary Psychology, and Economic Anthropology

Looking at the interplay between biology and environment, sociobiologists (e.g., Daly & Wilson, 1978; Low, 1989; Wilson, 1975), evolutionary psychologists (e.g., Buss, 1990; Nisbett, 1990), and economic anthropologists (Fry, 1987) suggest that behavioral mechanisms evolved in response to selection pressures. Diversity in gender roles reflects the fact that different circumstances trigger different behavioral responses, each of which are biologically prepared.

Gilmore (1990) proposes that the male macho behavior pattern is an adaptation to extreme risk associated with economic necessities. The dramatic difference in gender roles between two South Pacific islands, Truk and Tahiti, illustrate Gilmore's hypothesis. Trukese males are violent fighters, often competing with one another in physical contests, they are expected to have many love affairs, they begin to sire children early, and they are proud of their material possessions. Women are expected to be utterly submissive and protected by the men. In contrast, Tahitian men are not interested in material pursuits or in competition, and they are expected to be passive and submissive, and not expected to defend one's honor. The women are sexually active with the full knowledge of the males of the island. Gilmore (1990) accounts for these differences by describing the dramatic difference in obtaining food. The Tahitians fish in a protected lagoon where there is little risk and fish are plentiful. The Trukese must fish in the open ocean with the genuine possibility of not returning after a day at sea. The macho style is an adaptation to danger and serves to encourage Trukese men to face great peril.

While many of the notions of sociobiology are consistent with the interactive view of nature and nurture, the theory has been criticized on many levels (Gould & Lewontin, 1979). Not only are many of its assumptions not supported by empirical data, but many of its generalizations to human behavior are considered to be implicitly sexist (Travis & Yeager, 1991). Segall, Ember, and Ember, in this volume, provide an alternative account for macho behavior patterns.

Epigenesis

The interactionist view with wide support from developmental psychologists is the epigenetic conception of development that assumes a probabilistic, as opposed to predetermined, interaction of genes and environment throughout the course of development (Gottlieb, 1983; Miller, 1988). Epigenesis occurs because only a few genes are active in each cell at a given time. Which genes are active depends upon the environment of the cell, both the kinds of other cells around the cell and the external environment of the organism. Hormones secreted by the gonads in response to stress become part of a cell's environment (Hoyenga & Hoyenga, 1993). Even though two organisms have identical genes, environmental differences could lead to different expression of those genes.

Evolutionary theory explains how gene frequencies change across generations and how sex chromosomes have come to control, both directly and indirectly, the activity of certain genes at the cell level. Learning theories are related to evolution and explain how developmental environments can affect the adult behaviors of individuals across generations. Evolution also confirms that the human capability to establish rules and customs creates the competence for cultural development (Hoyenga & Hoyenga, 1993).

Sexual Dimorphism

In spite of the caution that biology is not destiny, biological influences are certainly important contributors to the development of gender differences. The term "biological" is often used to refer to genes, in this case sex chromosomes, but biological should also include the influence of an organism's prenatal and postnatal environments, and often the activities in those environments are culturally determined. For example, length of sleep bouts are modified by culturally-determined demands on mothers' time, and the course of infants' sitting and walking are influenced by culturally-defined childcare practices (Super & Harkness, 1982).

Compared with females, at birth males are larger, have a higher activity level (Eaton & Enns, 1986), higher basal metabolism, more muscle development, and a higher pain threshold (Rosenberg & Sutton-Smith, 1972). During the preadolescent years (ages 3–10), there are few gender differences in morphology or hormonal states, but those that are found are consistent with the sexual dimorphism that is found later (Tanner, 1961, 1970). Some of the most reliable indices of sexual dimorphism are based upon measurements of bone, muscle, and fatty tissues in the calf. During preadolescence, boys and girls differ little on these measures, but by age 17 gender classification based upon these indices are accurate 95 percent of the time. Looking at a sport not strongly gender stereotyped in the United States, Amateur Athletic Union swimming records for boys and girls do not differ at 10 years of age, but by 17 the differences are sizable and are proportional to the differences in muscle–bone measurements that are 3 to 4 percent in preadolescents and 10 to 12 percent in adolescents. Because the differential between boys and girls grows and is correlated with muscle to bone ratio, much of the difference can be attributed to physical growth changes that accompany puberty.

By adulthood, males attain greater height, have a more massive skeleton, higher muscle-to-fat ratio, higher blood oxygen capacity, more body hair, and different primary and secondary sex characteristics (D'Andrade, 1966; Tanner, 1961). The first of these differences are related to the greater physical strength and stamina of the male and seem to be related to the longer growth period of boys and the hormonal changes that appear after age eight (Ember, 1981). However, these differences only hold within populations, not between, and they apply only to group means, not individual comparisons (Munroe & Munroe, 1975/1994). Many women are stronger and more active than many men.

Biology has even been related to personality. Twin studies have shown that when looking at the masculine and feminine traits that people choose to describe themselves, individual heredity accounts for 20 to 50 percent of the variability in their descriptions (Loehlin, 1992; Mitchell, Baker, & Jacklin, 1989) while the remainder can be related to environmental factors.

Cultural Influences

Even though biological factors may impose predispositions and restrictions on development, sociocultural factors are important determinants of development (Best & Williams, 1993; Munroe & Munroe, 1975/1994; Munroe, Munroe, & Whiting, 1981; Rogoff, Gauvain, & Ellis, 1984; Triandis & Heron, 1981). Culture has profound effects on behavior, prescribing how babies are delivered, how children are socialized, how they are dressed, what is considered intelligent behavior, what tasks children are taught, and what roles adult men and women will adopt. As noted earlier, the scope and progression of the children's behaviors, even behaviors that are considered biologically determined, are governed by culture. Cultural universals in gender differences are often explained by similarities in socialization practices while cultural differences are attributed to differences in socialization.

Perhaps the best example of cultural diversity in gender-related behaviors is Margaret Mead's classic study of three primitive tribes in New Guinea (Mead, 1935). Mead reported that among the Mundugamor both men and women act aggressively and have little parental orientation. The opposite was true for the Arapesh; both men and women were gentle and nurturant. Among the Tchambuli, stereotypic roles were reversed with men being more nurturant and women more aggressive. From a Western viewpoint, these societies created men and women who are both masculine, feminine, and who reversed the usual gender roles.

The pervasive nature of sex differences in behaviors are poignantly illustrated in the Israeli kibbutz, established in the 1920s, which attempted to develop egalitarian societies (Nevo, 1977; Rosner, 1967; Snarey & Son, 1986; Spiro, 1956; Tiger, 1987). When the *vattikim* [original settlers] first settled on the land, there was no sexual division of labor; women, like men, worked in the fields and drove tractors; men, like women, worked in the kitchen and in the laundry. Men and women, it was assumed, were equal and could perform their jobs equally well. It was soon discovered, however, that men and women were not equal. For obvious biological reasons, some women could not undertake many of the physical tasks of which men were capable; tractor driving, harvesting, and other heavy labor proved too difficult for them. Moreover, women were compelled at times to take temporary leave from that physical labor of which, in theory, they were capable. A pregnant woman, for example, could not work too long, even in the vegetable garden, and a nursing mother had to work near the Infants House in order to be able to feed her child. Hence, as the kibbutz grew older and the birth rate increased, more and more women were forced to leave the "productive" branches of the economy and enter its "service" branches. But as they left the "productive" branches, it was necessary that their places be filled, and they were filled by men. The result was that the women found themselves in the same jobs from which they were supposed to have been emancipated—cooking, cleaning, laundering, teaching, caring for children, and so forth.

Exposing children to the ideology of the kibbutz which stresses equality between the sexes would be expected to lead children to have more egalitarian views of gender roles. However, like the kibbutz attempts at equitable division of labor, the cultural message was not effective for the children. Carlsson and Barnes (1986) found no cultural or sex differences between kibbutz-raised children and Swedish children in regard to how they conceptualized typical female and male sex role behaviors nor in the proportion of traditional and androgynous sex-typed self attributions.

Socialization of Boys and Girls

For boys and girls, many behavioral differences are often attributed to differences in socialization. Using Human Relations Area Files data, Barry, Bacon, and Child (1957) examined socialization practices in over 100 societies and found that boys are generally raised to achieve and to be self-reliant and independent, while girls are raised to be nurturant, responsible, and obedient. Some societies emphasize these behaviors more than others, with the direction of difference consistent, but the magnitude of difference varies according to socialization practices.

Hendrix and Johnson (1985) reanalyzed Barry, Bacon, and Child's (1957) data and found no general dimension of male–female difference in socialization. Indeed, the instrumental–expressive dichotomy popularly used to describe socialization differences were not polar opposites but were orthogonal, unrelated dimensions with similar emphases in the training of boys and girls. In a more recent study, Barber, Chadwick, and Oerter (1992) examined parental socialization practices in Germany and the United States and found that across a number of behaviors, the only sex difference found was that in both cultures adolescent girls reported more physical affection from their fathers than did boys.

In their meta-analysis of 172 studies, Lytton and Romney (1991) found that in the 158 North American studies they reviewed, the only socialization area that displayed a significant effect was the encouragement of sex-typed behaviors. In the 17 additional studies from other Western countries, there was a significant sex difference for physical punishment with boys receiving a greater portion than girls. Differential treatment of boys and girls decreased with age, particularly for disciplinary strictness and encouragement of sex-typed activities.

Overall, these socialization findings suggest that there may be subtle differences in the ways that boys and girls are treated by parents. In research, these differences are only occasionally significant, perhaps due to the categories used to quantify behaviors. Indeed, even if parents do not differentiate between daughters and sons, due to biological differences or preexisting preferences, the same parental treatment may affect girls and boys differently.

Task Assignment

Examination of the learning environments of children in various cultural groups yields a better understanding of how cultural differences in socialization processes affect children's development. Learning environments were investigated in the Six Culture study (Edwards & Whiting, 1974; Minturn & Lambert, 1964; Whiting & Edwards, 1973; Whiting & Whiting, 1975) that examined aggression, nurturance, responsibility, and help and attention seeking behaviors of children aged 3 to 11 in Okinawa, Mexico, the Philippines, India, Kenya, and the United States. Fewer gender differences were found in the three samples (United States, the Philippines, Kenya) where both boys and girls were assigned care for younger siblings and were asked to perform household chores. In contrast, more differences were found in the samples (India, Mexico, Okinawa) where boys and girls were treated dissimilarly and girls were asked to assume more responsibility for siblings and household tasks. Indeed, the fewest gender differences were found in the American sample in which neither girls nor boys were assigned many childcare or household tasks. The relationship of gender differences and the antecedent variable of task assignment would not have been explored if only American, Philippino, or Kenyan samples had been studied.

Bradley (1993) examined children's labor in 91 Standard Cross-Cultural Sample cultures (Murdock & White, 1969) and found that children who are less than six years of age perform little work whereas children more than ten years old perform work much like that of same gender adults. Both boys and girls do women's work (e.g., fetching water) more frequently than men's (e.g., hunting), and children tend to do work that adults consider demeaning or to require little skill, such as herding small animals. Women control children's labor which socializes and controls the children as well as helps the mother. Along with bringing pleasure and care in parents' old age, children's labor is one of the important benefits of having children.

Caretaking

Weisner and Gallimore (1977) reanalyzed Barry and Paxson's (1971) ethnographic sources on 186 sampled societies and found that mothers, female adult relatives, and female children are the primary caretakers of infants, but when those children reach early childhood, responsibilities are shared among both sex peer groups. Sibling caretakers must learn to understand the complex social rules represented by their parents and they must correctly interpret the behaviors of the children for whom they are responsible. While young caretakers may try to imitate their parents' styles, pressures on them often result in their developing different caretaking styles from their parents. These different styles of caretaking may be the predominant source of socialization in societies where two- to four-year-olds spend more than 70 percent of every day in sole charge of and in contact with their child nurses. Mothers in these societies spend a considerable portion of their time in productive activities and are not devoted exclusively to mothering (Greenfield, 1981; Minturn & Lambert, 1964). Nevertheless, children in all cultures see mothers as responsible for children. As they grow up, if they are female, they assume they will take care of children when they are adults, while if they are male, they expect that their wives will do it.

Moreover, Konner and colleagues (Katz & Konner, 1981; West & Konner, 1981) have found that fathers were rarely or never near their infants in 20 percent of the 80 cultures they surveyed. Father–infant relationships were close in only four percent of the cultures, but even when close, fathers spent only 14 percent of their time with their infants and gave only six percent of the actual caregiving. In most societies, play characterized paternal interactions with children (Munroe & Munroe, 1994), though rough or vigorous play found in American culture is not always seen in other cultures, such as Fiji (Katz & Konner, 1981). Societies with significant paternal involvement with routine child care are more likely than father-absent societies to include women in public decision making and in positions of authority (Coltrane, 1988).

Father absence, often a result of polygyny, has been associated with violent or hypermasculine behaviors (Katz & Konner, 1981; Segall & Knaak, 1989; Segall, 1988a, b, c; Whiting, 1965). When fathers are absent for extended periods of time due to war (Stolz, 1954) or lengthy sea voyages (Norwegian sailors: Gronseth, 1957; Lynn & Sawrey, 1959; Tiller, 1957), their sons display effeminate overt behaviors and high levels of dependence coupled with excessive fantasy aggression and overly masculine behaviors. Cross-cultural findings indicate that absence of the father produces cross-sex identification in boys that is either acted out or defended against with exaggerated masculine behaviors (Burton & Whiting, 1961). See a parallel discussion of this issue in Segall, Ember & Ember in this volume.

Fathers also pay less attention to female than to male offspring and encourage sex-typed activities more than mothers (Lytton & Romney, 1991). Rohner and Rohner (1982) examined Murdock and White's (1969) sample of 186 cultures and found that mothers were equally important as caretakers of sons and daughters, but fathers tended to be more important as caretakers of sons than daughters.

Mackey (1985) observed parents and children in public places in ten different cultures and counted the frequency of adult male and female interactions with girls and boys. Girls were more frequently found in groups that had no adult males while boys were frequently found in all male groups, and with age these differences intensified.

Peers

Throughout childhood and adolescence, peers play an important socialization role and their influence increases as children grow older. Peer relations help to structure the transition between childhood and adulthood. Peer relations become important when societies attained the middle level of socioeconomic complexity, characterized by subsistence agriculture or animal husbandry (Edwards, 1992).

Edwards (1992; Edwards & Whiting, 1993) reanalyzed peer interaction data of two- to ten-year-olds from the Six Culture study and additional samples for a total of 12 cultures studied from 1954 through 1975. Similar to other researchers (e.g., Farver & Howes, 1988), Edwards found a cross-culturally universal and robust tendency for both boys and girls to prefer and to associate more frequently with their own gender. Same gender preference emerges sometime after age two and by middle childhood gender segregation and exclusion of the other gender (for example, on the playground) are frequently found. Edwards speculates that the same-gender attraction may be motivated by a desire for self-discovery, making same gender agemates the best mirrors. Agemates resemble the child in abilities and activity preferences, but they also provide the greatest opportunity for competition and conflict.

Adolescent initiation rites found in many cultures were designed to detach the initiate from family, to socialize them to culturally appropriate styles of sexuality, dominance, and aggression, to create peer group loyalty, and to solidify political ties that cut across family lines. Collective rituals are more common for boys than girls and are found more frequently in warrior societies that emphasize gender differences in men's and women's work, leisure, and even in sleeping and eating arrangements (Edwards, 1992). In a few societies, elaborated, collective rites for girls are found along with group instruction in sexuality (Brown, 1981; Ericksen, 1989). Initiation rites serve as the cultural system for resolving gender identity conflict and for symbolically demonstrating womanhood/manhood as the desirable role for the girl/boy to adopt (Edwards, 1992; Munroe, Munroe, & Whiting, 1981; Whiting, 1990; Young, 1965). Although Western education has begun to change initiation rites, vestiges remain.

Education

Educational settings also greatly influence children's behaviors. In at least some societies, teachers seem to spend more time with boys than with girls. Observations of fifth grades in Japan and in the United States indicate that in both academic and social domains, boys are the targets of communication from teachers more often than are girls (Hamilton, Blumenfeld, Akoh, & Miura, 1991). Teachers in both countries paid more attention to boys, particularly negative attention, and the greater attention was not attributable to off-task or bad behavior. Overall, the amount of attention to boys per se was exaggerated in Japan relative to the United States.

Parental beliefs about academic performance can also have profound impact upon children's achievements. Serpell (1993) found that education was considered to be more important for Zambian boys than girls and that fathers assumed more responsibility for arranging schooling even though mothers were primarily responsible for childcare. In China, Japan and the United States, mothers expect boys to be better at mathematics and for girls to be better at reading (Lummis & Stevenson, 1990), although girls and boys perform equally well in some aspects of both disciplines. Mothers' biases certainly have an important impact on their children's academic efforts, especially during elementary school years.

Gender Differences in Male and Female Behaviors

Together, biological and cultural influences lead to differences in the behaviors of males and females. In this section, we will review five areas where gender differences have been found cross-culturally: nurturance, aggression, anxiety, proximity to adults, and self-esteem.

Nurturance

In the Six Culture study, Edwards and Whiting (1980) found that between ages five and twelve, gender differences in nurturance were most consistent in behavior directed to infants and toddlers rather than in behavior directed toward mothers and older children. With further analysis they found that this gender difference was not necessarily due to mothers' assigning more child-care chores to girls but that girls were more willing to comply with such requests. Further, because infants seem to elicit more nurturant behavior than older children, regardless of the gender of the caregiver, girls who spent more time with infants demonstrated more nurturance than boys who were not engaged in as much infant interaction.

Barry, Bacon, and Child (1957) found that girls were socialized more than boys to be nurturant (82 percent of cultures), to be more obedient (35 percent of cultures), and to be more responsible (61 percent of cultures). Boys, on the other hand, were socialized to be more achieving (87 percent of cultures) and more self-reliant (85 percent of cultures) than girls. Welch and Page (1979) and Welch, Page, and Martin (1981) confirmed these findings in 106 cultures examined in five regions. Indeed, they found more pressure for males to conform to their roles than females, with more tolerance for deviation and greater variability in the roles for girls.

Aggression

Cross-cultural studies of prepubertal children has consistently shown that boys have higher levels of aggression, competitiveness, dominance seeking, and rough-and-tumble play than girls (Ember, 1981; Freedman & DeBoer, 1979; Strube, 1981; Rubenstein, Feldman, Rubin, & Noveck, 1987; Segall, Ember, & Ember, this volume). Whiting and Edwards (1988) combined the data from the original Six Culture study with five more African cultures and found sex differences in aggression and dominance. Unlike their earlier reports, aggression did not decrease with age and tended to be more physical among the oldest boys. Omark, Omark, and Edelman (1975) observed children on playgrounds in Ethiopia, Switzerland, and the United States and found that boys were more aggressive than girls, and Blurton Jones and Konner (1973) findings were similar in four !Kung Bushmen villages and in London. The interesting puzzle for the latter study was that there was less behavioral differentiation between !Kung Bushmen boys and girls than among boys and girls in London.

Data from the Six Culture study indicate that mothers generally react similarly to aggression of boys and girls, but there was some evidence of differential aggression training in Okinawa and the United States, suggesting that fathers may play an important role in socializing aggression in boys (Minturn & Lambert, 1964). Acceptance of aggression is similar for males and females in Western European countries, but there are gender differences in the forms of aggressive acts; men may be initially more restrained but when they do act, they are more violent (Ramirez, 1993). Females, on the other hand, use more emotional means of aggressing, such as shouting and verbal attacks (Burbank, 1987).

Moving to the other end of the spectrum, Boehnke and colleagues (Boehnke, Silbereisen, Eisenberg, Reykowski, & Palmonari, 1989) examined the development of prosocial motivation in school children from West Germany, Poland, Italy, and the United States. They found that at age 12, but not before, girls demonstrated more mature motives in their responses to hypothetical situations, which provided opportunity for prosocial action.

Anxiety

Gender differences in self-reported anxiety have been found, with girls reporting higher levels than boys. Girls in Sweden and Hungary report greater anxiety in response to hypothetical anxiety-provoking situations than boys, but no gender differences were found in Japan (Magnusson & Stattin, 1978).

Proximity to Adults and Movement

Observing the play of 5- to 7-year-olds in eight cultures (Australian Aboriginal, Balinese, Ceylonese, Japanese, Kikuyu, Navajo, Punjabi, Taiwanese), Freedman (1976) found that boys ran in larger groups, covered more physical space, and did more physical and unpredictable activities while girls were involved in more conversations and games with repeated movements. Girls are usually found closer to home (Draper, 1975; Munroe & Munroe, 1971; Whiting & Edwards, 1973). Task assignment has been suggested as the reason for these gender differences (Whiting & Edwards, 1973) as have differences in behavioral preferences (Draper, 1975). Boys tend to interact more with other boys and girls to interact with adults (Blurton Jones & Konner, 1973; Omark, Omark, & Edelman, 1975; Whiting & Edwards, 1973).

Children's drawings reflect similar gender segregation as in play, with boys drawing more pictures of boys and girls of girls (Freedman, 1976). Boys in nine cultures drew more vehicles, monsters, and violence themes than did girls, who drew more flowers. Assuming children's pictures represent their interests, these findings suggest gender differences in what children like.

Self-Esteem

Although both gender groups make similar gender role attributions, girls seem to be less satisfied with being girls than boys are with being boys (Burns & Homel, 1986), and boys perceive themselves to be more competent than girls (van Dongen-Melman, Koot, & Verhulst, 1993). However, girls' dissatisfaction does not seem to manifest itself in consistently lower self-esteem than boys' (Calhoun & Sethi, 1987). Compared with boys, young adolescent girls in Nepal, the Philippines, and Australia had lower opinions of their physical abilities and mathematical competence, but in Australia and Nigeria girls felt more competent in reading (Watkins & Akande, 1992; Watkins, Hattie, & Regmi, 1994; Watkins, Lam, & Regmi, 1991) but Nigerian boys believed they were more intelligent than did girls (Olowu, 1985).

In sum, differences between boys and girls in nurturance, aggression, and motility are robust and consistently found across cultures (Ember, 1981), while anxiety and self esteem differences are less consistent. Culture shapes the social behaviors of children by selecting the company they keep and the activities that engage their time. Such experiences can maximize, minimize, or even eliminate gender differences in social behaviors.

Gender Roles and Stereotypes

Within the context of the cultural stereotypes about differences between males and females, gender roles and knowledge develop. Research in the United States indicates that by three to four years of age children accurately assign sex-stereotypic labels to toys, activities, and occupations (Edelbrook & Sugawara, 1978; Guttentag & Longfellow, 1977; Hartley, 1960; Nadelman, 1970). As early as two years of age, American children stereotype objects as masculine or feminine (Thompson, 1975; Weinraub, Clemens, Sockloff, Etheridge, Gracely, & Myers, 1984). Similar gender stereotyping of toys is found in Africa where girls play with dolls and boys construct vehicles and weapons (Bloch & Adler, 1994).

Prosser, Hutt, Hutt, Mahindadasa, and Goonetilleke (1986) found that by age four or five Sri Lankan village children demonstrate gender differences in play, similar to those found with British children. Boys exhibit more negative behaviors and more fantasy object play while girls display more fantasy person and immaterial fantasy play. Even though cultural factors determine the particular content of children's play, the form of only a few behaviors seems to be culturally specific.

Development of Sex-Trait Stereotypes

Research concerning the development of sex-trait stereotypes in the United States indicates that children acquire this knowledge somewhat later than stereotypic knowledge of toys and occupations (Best, Williams, Cloud, Davis, Robertson, Edwards, Giles, & Fowles, 1977; Reis & Wright, 1982; Williams, Bennett, & Best, 1975; Williams & Best, 1982/1990a). The most extensive research on the development of stereotype knowledge was conducted by Williams, Best, and their colleagues. Based upon their research with young adults (Williams & Bennett, 1975; Williams & Best, 1977; Best, Williams, & Briggs, 1980), Williams and Best developed the Sex Stereotype Measure (SSM) for assessing children's knowledge of adult-defined stereotypes (Best et al., 1977; Williams, Bennett, & Best, 1975). The revised SSM II (Best et al., 1977) has 16 stories representing female traits (emotional—"cries a lot") and 16 representing male traits (aggressive—"gets into fights"), presented with a silhouette figure of a male and a female, and the child is asked to select the person described in the story.

Research conducted in the United States with Euro-American children (Best et al., 1977; Williams & Best, 1982/1990a) revealed a consistent pattern of regularly increasing stereotype knowledge from kindergarten through high school, similar to a typical learning curve pattern. At the younger ages, male stereotype items were known somewhat better than female stereotype items, but the difference in knowledge virtually disappeared at the older age levels. The most dramatic increases in stereotype knowledge occurred in the early elementary school years, with scores reaching a plateau in the junior high years.

At the kindergarten level, 57 percent of the responses to the adult-defined female items were stereotyped and 65 percent of the male responses, while at age 15 stereotyped responses increased to 90 percent for the female items and 88 percent for the male items. Certain items, such as emotional, gentle, soft-hearted, affectionate, strong, aggressive and dominant were learned quite early, while items such as frivolous, fussy, flirtatious, steady, jolly, and severe were learned somewhat later.

Third and sixth grade Afro-American children's SSM II scores showed an increase with age but were noticeably lower than those of the Euro-American children, perhaps reflecting subcultural variation in stereotypic knowledge.

Cross-Cultural Findings

Williams and Best and their colleagues (1982/1990a) administered the SSM II to 5-, 8-, and 11-year-old children in 25 countries. Across all countries, the overall percentage of stereotyped responses rose from around 60 percent at the five-year level to around 70 percent at the eight-year level. Strong, aggressive, cruel, coarse, and adventurous were consistently associated with men at both age levels and weak, appreciative, softhearted, gentle, and meek were consistently associated with women. Eleven of the 16 male items and 8 of the 16 female items were associated with the stereotype figure at least 60 percent of the time.

Relative to the other countries, both male and female scores were unusually high in Pakistan and relatively high in New Zealand and England. Scores were atypically low in Brazil, Taiwan, Germany, and France. Although there was variation between countries in the rate of learning, there was a general developmental pattern in which the acquisition of stereotypes begins prior to age five, accelerates during the early school years, and is completed during the adolescent years.

In all countries studied, boys and girls learned the stereotypes at the same rate, though there was a slight tendency for the male-stereotype traits to be learned somewhat earlier than the female traits. In 17 of the 24 countries studied (for example, Taiwan, France, Pakistan, and Ireland), the male stereotype items were better known than the female items. Germany was the only country where there was a clear tendency for the female stereotype to be better known than the male stereotype. In contrast, the female stereotype items seemed to be learned earlier than the male items in some of the Latin/Catholic cultures (Brazil, Chile, Portugal,

Venezuela) where the adult-defined female stereotype is more positive than the male (Neto, Williams, & Widner, 1991; Tarrier & Gomes, 1981). Nevertheless, the stereotypes appeared to be universal models that are modified by specific cultural influences.

In the more urbanized countries where education is emphasized, children appear to learn stereotypes that are perhaps more similar to those in other countries. By the adult level, these stereotypes are refined by the culture such that urban and educational influences seem to have less importance. In predominantly Muslim countries, five-year-olds tend to associate traits with the two sexes in a more highly differentiated manner and they learn the stereotypes, particularly the male stereotype, at an earlier age than in non-Muslim countries. Children in predominantly Catholic or Christian countries are somewhat slower in their initial learning of the stereotypes, and they show a greater increase in knowledge during the five-to-eight-year interval. This slower initial learning may be related to the fact that the adult-defined stereotypes are somewhat less differentiated in Catholic countries.

Using a combined measure of traits and roles, Albert and Porter (1986) examined the gender stereotypes of four- to six-year-olds in the USA and South Africa. Similar to Williams and Best's (1982/1990a) findings, stereotyping increased with age for both groups. South African children stereotyped the male role more than did the United States children, but there were no country differences for the female role. Children from liberal Christian and Jewish backgrounds in South Africa assigned fewer stereotyped traits and roles to the sexes than children from more conservative religious groups, but religious background was not a factor for children in the United States.

The differential rate of learning of the male and female stereotypes is not consistent across cultures. Williams and Best (1982/1990a) found that male items were learned faster than female items in a majority of the countries they sampled. However, the effect was not replicated with Swedish (Carlsson, Andersson, Berg, Jäderquist, & Magnusson, 1984), Korean (Lee & Sugawara, 1982), or German children (Trautner, Sahm, & Stevermann, 1983). Brazilian children (Tarrier & Gomes, 1981), similar to Williams and Best's (1982/1990a) German sample, knew the female stereotype better than the male. Brazilian children also demonstrated more pronounced stereotypes than did American children. Considering the similarities across the diverse countries studied and the differing measures used, sex stereotypes appear to be universal with culture modifying the rate of learning and only minor aspects of their content.

Looking at older children, 11 to 18 years of age, Intons-Peterson (1988) found that Swedish children attributed more instrumental qualities to women than did American children. Stereotypes of males and females were more alike in Sweden than in the United States, reflecting themes of individual independence and commitment to their society, basic tenets of Swedish cultural philosophy. Cross-nationally, similar attributes, such as being kind/nice, trying to do one's best, and never giving up, were considered highly important in both countries. In spite of less gender-typing in Sweden than in America, ideal occupational choices for the two sexes did not overlap in Sweden and reflected the dual labor market. Swedish women were interested in service occupations, such as flight attendant, hospital worker, nanny, and Swedish men were interested in business occupations. In contrast, ideal occupations in the United States showed great overlap between the sexes with both groups listing doctor/dentist/attorney, and business executive as their top choices.

Cross-Cultural Theories of Gender-Related Learning

Even though there is theoretical disagreement about the sources of influence and the course of sex role development, most theories of gender role learning emphasize the gender information readily available in the culture. Most of the current assumptions about gender role learning have been generated by social learning and cognitive developmental theories developed primarily in the United States, but each can be adapted to explain cross-cultural patterns of development.[4] We will briefly review these theories in this section.

Social Learning

Social learning theories (Bandura, 1969; Bussey & Bandura, 1984; Mischel, 1970) consider sex role development to be the result of cumulative experience. Parents, teachers, peers, and other socialization agents shape children's gender-related behaviors through reinforcement and punishment of gender-appropriate and inappropriate behaviors, modeling, expectations, toy choices, and other differential treatment of boys and girls. Research conducted in the United States has shown same-sex and opposite-sex parents react differently to their children, with fathers showing more differential behavior. Boys receive more physical stimulation than girls (Lamb, 1976, 1977), they are given more freedom and independence than girls (Maccoby & Jacklin, 1974), and they are expected to achieve in different areas than are girls (Hess & Shipman, 1967). Interestingly, the few studies conducted in other countries concerning differential treatment of boys and girls (Bronstein, 1984; Russell & Russell, 1987) do not show the same patterns as those found in the United States. For example, Lamb and his colleagues (Lamb, 1976, 1977; Lamb, Frodi, Hwand, Frodi, & Steinberg, 1982; Sagi, Lamb, Shoham, Dvir, & Lewkowicz, 1985) have shown that in contrast to data collected in the United States, observations of Swedish and Israeli kibbutzim parents and children revealed no gender differences for parental play style with infants and toddlers.

Best and her colleagues (Best, House, Barnard, & Spicker, 1991) observed interactions between preschool children and their parents in public parks and playgrounds in France, Germany, and Italy to see if cultural differences that may contribute to children's learning of gender concepts would be found. Parent–child interactions varied across both gender and country. Italian and French parents and children displayed more interactive behaviors than the German parent–child dyads, and French and Italian children showed objects and shared them more with their fathers than mothers, but the pattern was reversed for the German children. These interactional differences may be related to the cultural differences found in sex stereotype learning discussed earlier. That is, unlike the French and Italian children, German children demonstrated greater knowledge of the female stereotype traits than of the male traits. Perhaps the female characteristics are learned earlier by the German children as a result of greater interaction with mothers than fathers, a pattern that was not found in the other countries. Although gender generally influences parent–child behaviors, culture modifies the manifestation of these differences.

While there is substantial cross-cultural evidence indicating that social learning plays a part in gender role learning, it is clear that social learning by itself is not a sufficient explanation. The patterns of differential treatment of boys and girls found cross-culturally demonstrate great variation and are not consistently tied to differential behavior (Bronstein, 1984; Lamb et al., 1982; Sagi et al., 1985; Russell & Russell, 1987). In addition, the imitation process is more complex than choosing a single model to emulate. Tasks assigned to children as well as the models available in the larger culture provide opportunities for them to learn differential roles and encourage distinct behaviors. However, additional cross-cultural research is needed to identify the salient aspects of culture that contribute to children's gender role learning and behaviors.

Cognitive Development

Turning to the other most prominent theory of gender role learning, cognitive developmental theory (Kohlberg, 1966; Kohlberg & Ullman, 1974; Ruble, 1987) emphasizes the role of external forces on children's developing gender-role orientation. The impact of these factors, however, is governed by the emerging cognitive structures of the child. According to cognitive developmental theories, children progress through stages of understanding in acquiring gender knowledge and the degree of understanding structures their experiences.

Slaby and Frey (1975) identified four stages in the development of American children's understanding of gender. In Stage 1 children do not correctly distinguish between the sexes. However, by age 2 to 3 they begin to use gender categories for themselves and others and soon achieve Stage 2, gender identity. Gender identity and labeling, the most rudimentary of the gender concepts that children acquire, are initially based upon superficial physical characteristics, such as clothing and hairstyles. In Stage 3, gender stability, children understand that gender remains constant across time ("When you grow up, will you be a mommy or daddy?"). In the final stage, Stage 4 gender consistency, children understand that gender is unaffected by motives or changes in clothing and activity ("If you played with dolls/trucks (the opposite sex toy), would you be a boy or girl?"). These latter two stages which are achieved by age 4-1/2 to 5, are functionally unrelated to Stage 2.

Munroe, Shimmin, and Munroe (1984) tested cognitive developmental theory in a cross-cultural study of gender understanding and sex role preference. They expected cultural effects to be found in differential rates of development through the gender stages, based upon the degree to which societies emphasize distinctions between males and females. In two of their cultures, the Logoli of Kenya and the Newars of Nepal, childhood experiences were sharply differentiated. However, for the Garifuna of Belize and the Samoans of American Samoa, girls and boys are treated almost equally. They hypothesized that because of sex distinction in socialization practices, gender classification should be more salient for the Kenyan and Nepalese children and the identity stage should be achieved earlier for them. However, because the latter stages of stability and consistency are dependent upon cognitive structural factors, they would be less influenced by culture and should appear at essentially the same time in the four groups.

Overall, they found that children's understanding of gender conformed to the stages discovered for children in the United States, and there was an orderly progression through the stages. However, contrary to expectation, the culture-specific predictions were not supported. Children in the two sex-differentiating cultures, Kenya and Nepal, did not attain Stage 2 at an earlier age than did children in Belize and Samoa. In fact, the Kenyan children reached Stage 2 at an older age than did the Samoan children, and the Nepalese children did not differ from the other groups. The prediction that attainment of Stages 3 and 4 would show little variation across cultures was confirmed.

Consistent with these findings, Dickerscheid, Schwarz, Noir, and El-Taliawy (1988) found that children from a nontraditional culture, the United States, had a higher level of gender identity than those from a more traditional culture, Egypt. Munroe and Munroe (1982) suggest that gender understanding develops more slowly in cultures where young children have little contact with male figures, such as more traditional cultures where child care is almost completely a maternal responsibility.

Bussey (1983) has found that gender constancy, assessed via the traditional Kohlbergian verbal questioning of the child, does not seem to be the important antecedent for the development of sex-typed behaviors. Children appear to learn the most appropriate ways to behave before they can translate these behaviors to words. Indeed, the models for boys and girls seem to differ with a two-process model for boys, acceptance of masculine behavior and rejection of feminine behavior, and a one-process model for girls, acceptance of same-sex behavior without rejection of other-sex behavior.

Taken as a whole, these findings indicate the dominant contribution of cognitive developmental factors and the concomitantly small contribution of culture-specific factors in the development of gender concepts. Moreover, young children are more competent than traditional theories of gender role development suggest.

Gender Schema Theory

Recently, a variant of cognitive developmental theory and social learning theory has evolved, gender schema theory (Bem, 1981, 1983, 1985; Liben & Signorella,

1980, 1987; Martin & Halverson, 1981, 1983; Signorella, Bigler, & Liben, 1993). A schema is a set of ideas used for organizing information, filtering new information, and directing cognitive processing. Gender schema theory deals with the primacy of the gender concept within a particular culture, as opposed to other concepts, as a basis for organizing information. While there is considerable research in the United States documenting the existence of gender schemas (Jacklin, 1989), as yet there is little evidence from other cultures.

The social learning, cognitive developmental, and gender schema theories of gender understanding are consistent with cross-cultural data. However, only a few studies have directly tested their assumptions in a cross-cultural context.

Cultural Practices that Influence Behaviors of Males and Females

Throughout the first portions of this chapter we have focused upon the individual, whether adult or child, and the aspects of gender and sex that are influenced by culture. In this section we will examine the broader cultural influences of gender that have only been alluded to in earlier sections: the status of women, gender division of labor, religious beliefs and values, economic factors, and political participation.

Status of Women

Ethnographic evidence suggests that women's "status" is multidimensional, including economic indicators, power, autonomy, prestige, and ideological dimensions (Mukhopadhyay & Higgins, 1988; Quinn, 1977). Whyte's (1978) study of 93 preindustrial societies identified nine independent indicators of women's status. Various determinants for status asymmetry have been proposed, such as women's reproductive roles, secondary sexual characteristics, greater male aggression and strength, the sexual division of labor, the complexity of the society (Berry, 1976; Ember, 1981), socialization, education, religious beliefs, cultural conceptions of honor, and economic factors.

Gender Division of Labor

While definitions of what is masculine and feminine seem to be culturally variable, examination of the literature suggest two possible cultural universals: At least to some degree, every society assigns traits and tasks on the basis of gender (Munroe & Munroe, 1975/1994); and, in no society is the status of women superior to that of men, but the reverse is quite common (Hoyenga & Hoyenga, 1993; Population Crisis Committee, 1988; Whyte, 1978). D'Andrade (1966) analyzed ethnographic records of 224 different societies and classified jobs and tasks according to whether they were performed by men, women, or both. Men were involved with hunting, metal work, weapon making, and travel further from home while women were responsible for cooking and food preparation, carrying water, making and repairing clothing, and making things used in the home. Women participate in subsistence activities that are consistent with childrearing responsibilities (Brown, 1970; Segal, 1983), but even in industrialized societies women who never marry do not fare much better than married women in their occupational attainments (Roos, 1983). In a survey of 80 cultures, fathers were found to assume major responsibility for child rearing in only 10 percent of the cultures (Katz & Konner, 1981).

Looking at more developed countries, even in the early 20th century, the domain of women's activities were limited. For example in Germany, women were responsible for the three "Ks"—*kinder, küche, kirche* (loosely translated as child care, cooking, churchgoing (Adler, 1993); and even now, fathers only "help out" with these activities that are still the responsibility of the mother.

Rosenblatt and Cunningham (1976) estimate that with the average woman in the world having four children who survive through age two and each is breastfed for an average of two years, the typical woman may have eight years of reduced mobility, a powerful factor in producing gender role differences. Decreases in infant mortality and fertility have reduced the proportion of women's lifespan spent in rearing children, and technology has made it possible to separate childbearing from childrearing (Huber, 1986). Such advances have made it possible for women to move outside the home to participate in the labor force. However, focusing on paid employment does not provide a full picture of women's economic contributions to the family (Dixon, 1978).

Looking at the trends across a 20-year span, from 1960 to 1980, Jacobs and Lim (1992) examined occupational sex segregation in the International Labor Organization data in 56 countries. They found no overall trend in sex segregation, but in most countries, men experienced a greater chance of being employed in the same occupational or industrial group as women, whereas women experienced a decline in occupational opportunities and greater segregation. Surprisingly, measures of modernization, such as per capita GNP and women's education and literacy, were positively related to sex segregation but, as expected, women's labor force participation and fertility rate were inversely related to segregation. Men may perceive that women are making substantial progress but women remain economically disadvantaged when compared with men and continue to be paid less than their male counterparts (Ottaway & Bhatnagar, 1988). Women continue to prefer traditionally feminine jobs and those that offer the greatest possibilities for contact with other people while men prefer jobs judged to offer the highest income and the greatest possibilities for promotion (Loscocco & Kalleberg, 1988; Mullet, Neto, & Henry, 1992).

Even in societies where women have actively moved into the labor force, working outside the home, there has not been a commensurate reduction in their household duties (Population Crisis Committee, 1988). Research in the United States, Switzerland, Sweden, Canada, Italy, Poland, and Romania has shown that the overwhelming majority of household work is performed by women, regardless of the extent of their occupational demands (Calasanti & Bailey, 1991; Charles &

Höpflinger, 1992; Guberman, Maheu, & Maillé, 1992; Vianello, Siemienska, Damian, Lupri, Coppi, d'Arcangelo, 1990; Wright, Shire, Hwang, Dolan, & Baxter, 1992). Presence of children and larger homes requiring more work were associated with less male participation in domestic chores. Traditionality of women's sex role ideology plays a determining role in the household division of labor with less participation by husbands found when their wives place great importance on family. Other studies have pointed to the importance of husbands' gender-role values in determining their contributions to household tasks (Banaszak & Plutzer, 1993; Calasanti & Bailey, 1991; Finley, 1989; Ross, 1987). Indeed, more traditional views of the sexual division of labor in the home are found with blue-collar workers in all countries, suggesting that more egalitarian views are found with increases in education and social class (Vianello et al., 1990).

However, gender inequity does not completely disappear with greater job opportunities for women or with greater education. Looking within four Western countries, United States, Great Britain, West Germany, and Austria, Davis and Robinson (1991) found that well-educated people and women with employed husbands tended to be less favorable toward efforts to reduce gender inequality than were less educated people or women without a male wage earner. Women were more likely to perceive gender inequality and were more supportive of efforts to combat it than were men, but women's employment status had little effect on their consciousness of gender inequality.

Religious Beliefs and Values

Religious beliefs and culturally-based views of family honor may also influence views of women and reactions to women working outside the home (Williams & Best, 1982/1990a; Rapoport, Lomski-Feder, & Masalia, 1989). Youssef (1974) points out the similarity of normative patterns in family organization in the Middle East and Latin America, which perhaps are culturally connected by the Spanish conquistadors who had experienced 800 years or so of Moorish hegemony over Spain prior to their ventures into the New World. Latin America and the Middle East share many of the ideals of personal and family honor that links the manliness of men (*machismo, muruwwa*) and the sexual purity of women (vergnenza, 'ird) and influences the division of roles and labor in the family. The dominant, powerful male is supposed to protect the frail, helpless female and especially to guard her sexual honor. There is strong resentment in both Latin America and the Middle East against the participation of married women in the labor force, and if they do work, they must have few contacts with men in public. Despite similarities in level of economic development and values, female rate of participation in the nonagricultural labor force is strikingly higher in Latin American than in the Middle East. The female activity rate in the least developed of ten countries in Latin America, Honduras, is six times as high as the rate in the most developed of eight countries studied in the Middle East, Iraq. Youssef (1974) suggests that the powerful male-based family kinship structure of social organization in the Middle East, where male kin assume economic responsibility for females, regardless of their marital status, is responsible for the tight control over women's participation in the labor force. The central role of priests in Latin America diffused the power of the male kin. Education sufficient to obtain prestigious position will overcome barriers to women working in both Latin America and the Middle East (Youssef, 1974).

Economic Factors

While males generally receive preferential treatment in most cultures, economic factors appear to influence customs that favor one gender over the other. Based upon his examination of 386 cultures, Heath (1958) found that the bride price paid to the bride's family was a form of compensation for the loss of her economic contributions to her family. Bride price was found more frequently where the female contribution to subsistence was appreciable, and dowry accompanied the bride more often where her economic productivity for her family was relatively small.

Cronk (1993) theorizes that bride price and female status are related to socioeconomic conditions. When parents have high socioeconomic status, males are favored, but when they have low status, females are favored. Cronk studied the Mukogodo in Kenya who until the early part of this century were foragers and beekeepers living in caves within the forest. Within a few years they acquired cattle, sheep, and goats, mostly bridewealth when their daughters married men from neighboring herding groups. The Mukogodo moved out of their caves, which were inconvenient for maintaining livestock, and adopted the language and most of the customs of their neighbors. Thus, they ended up at the bottom of the regional hierarchy of wealth, prestige, and ultimately marital and reproductive opportunities. Due to their low status it is hard for the Mukogodo men to find wives because they do not have bridewealth needed to pay for a bride. Because men can have as many wives as they can afford, women in the area are always in short supply, so Mukogodo women all find husbands, often among the wealthier and higher status neighbors.

Economic conditions also influence sex-biased parental investment of the Mukogodo. While the birth ratio of males to females is typical, the census shows a sex ratio in 1986 of 98 girls and 66 boys under four years of age. There is no evidence of male infanticide, but it is likely that boys are dying at a higher rate because of favoritism shown toward girls, such as taking them to doctors more often, and enrolling them in a baby clinic, a major investment of money and time. Daughters are breast fed longer and are generally well fed, while clear cases of child neglect involving boys are not uncommon. Parents tend to invest more in the offspring that provides the greater economic or reproductive success—rural farming favors boys, and the urban industrial revolution in the 19th century favored girls. In looking at the literature, across human societies those in which girls are favored over boys are strangely abberant but they clearly do exist and provide fascinating insights into sex-bias in parental investment (Cronk, 1993).

Cronk's (1993) findings are consistent with Trivers and Willard's (1973) model that suggests that male reproductive success is both more variable than females' and more likely to be influenced by environmental conditions. When conditions are good, both males and females benefit reproductively, but males benefit more because of greater reproductive potential. When conditions are bad, both suffer but males suffer more. So, in good conditions sons are to be favored; in poor conditions energies should focus on girls in order to have the most grandchildren.

Additional support for Trivers and Willard's model is seen with the Kanjar of Pakistan and northern India, nomads who travel from town to town selling ceramic and papier-maché toys, dancing, begging, and occasionally offering carnival rides and engaging in prostitution (Cronk, 1993). Almost half of these activities are in the female domain, and women provide more than half of the income of most families. Kanjar men are passive, cooperative, subordinate to females, whereas Kanjar women dominate public life, private affairs, and are socialized to be aggressive and independent. Bridewealth payments are high, sometimes ten times the family's annual income. To reduce costs, two families will exchange daughters. Kanjar girls also help their brothers get married. It is easy to see why the birth of a girl is greeted with fanfare but boys are greeted with little interest.

These cultural practices and economic conditions contrast sharply with those found in India, China, Turkey, Korea and other traditional parts of the world where the birth of a boy leads to great rejoicing and males are greatly valued by their families (Kagitçibasi, 1982, 1990). Female infanticide (Krishnaswamy, 1988), wife beating (Flavia, 1988), and bride burning (Ghadially & Kumar, 1988) are all cultural practices found in India that speak to the lack of concern for women in many traditional Indian cultures. Similarly, women in Muslim cultures have little influence in general society; they are customarily confined to domestic roles, they remain secluded in their homes, and they must observe the Purdah (veil) system (Allman, 1978).

Parents in Australia and Malaysia report a preference for having sons over daughters to continue the family name, for old age support, and for the companionship of a son (Callan & Kee, 1981). Though male preference seems to dominate, parents in preindustrial societies experience greater difficulties in socializing male children than female (Welch, Page, & Martin, 1981).

When studying the Mundugumor of New Guinea in the 1930s, Mead and Fortune found that gender preferences were not consistent between parents. Fathers tended to favor daughters and mothers favored sons. Each parent was close to the other gender child and tried to tip the balance of inheritance in his/her favor. They speculated that these preferences may be due to the marriage system that exchanged women between families and pitted fathers against sons for wives. Daughters were used as currency to obtain a wife for the son, but because men could have multiple wives, the sons could be cheated by their fathers.

Preference for daughters has been found in other societies where property is passed down matrilineally or where women were economically highly productive. However, in some of these societies contact with Western culture has changed the economic factors that made girls prized and preference for daughters has declined (Beal, 1994). Preference for boys continues to be strong in the United States (Hamilton, 1991; Macfarlane, 1977; Oakley, 1980; Pooler, 1991) and non-Western countries (Hammer, 1970), even though many of the religious traditions and economic circumstances that created the preference for sons no longer apply to contemporary culture.

Female Political Participation

Cross-cultural data suggest that men are more likely to be involved in political activities and to wield greater power than are women (Ember, 1981; Masters, 1989; Ross, 1986a, b). Ross (1986a) found that female political participation involves at least two independent dimensions, decision-making and the control of positions or organizations of authority. Female political participation has been attributed to the simplicity of the society, to women's participation in subsistence activities, to low male bonding, to conflict and warfare, and to warm and affectionate socialization practices.

Ross (1986a) examined these explanations of female political participation in the ethnographies of a world-wide sample of 90 preindustrial societies. He found that high internal conflict and violence within a society, low external warfare, warm and affectionate childrearing practices, low male gender identity conflict, and weak fraternal interest groups in a society are associated with greater political involvement by women. Women in such societies can solidify coalitions and serve as influential go-betweens. When tensions are low, men sit around and talk, leading to few consequences for women, but when tensions are high and violence is likely to erupt, women get involved as peacemakers. When a society has a high level of conflict with other societies, women have less political involvement, perhaps due to the high status conferred on warriors. Female organizations and positions occur more frequently in societies that are socioeconomically more complex, but this does not automatically lead to greater advantages for women.

The longstanding stereotyped dichotomy of public/male vs. private/female suggests that men are in the public eye, active in business, politics, and culture while women stay at home, taking care of the home and family (Peterson & Runyan, 1993). However, cross-cultural studies suggest that today this dichotomy is a false one. Women in Canada, Italy, Poland, and Romania have experienced work and public life outside the home and today men are more involved with their families (Vianello et al., 1990). Private, family considerations influence both women's and men's career decisions. The barrier confronting most women's advancement in the working world is the lack of connectedness to male-controlled networks or their unwillingness to play the game.

Indeed, Gibbons, Stiles and their colleagues (Gibbons, Lynn, Stiles, Berducido, Richter, Walker, & Wiley, 1993; Gibbons, Stiles, & Shkodriani, 1991) have found that adolescents in a variety of cultures conceptualize the female gender role to encompass both homemaking and employment outside the home. With the increasing interest in adult roles in adolescence and the tremendous change in conditions and attitudes toward women around the world, adolescents' images of women are certain to reflect these changes.

Conclusions

When one considers the amount and variety of material reviewed in this chapter it is clear that any final observations must be of a very general nature. Most striking to the authors is the central finding that in the area of sex and gender, the pancultural similarities greatly outweigh the cultural differences. Earlier in the chapter we noted that the biological differences between the male and female of the human species are, in fact, relatively minor. To this we add the observation that the psychological differences between men and women, boys and girls, are also relatively small in magnitude. Finally, we note that on the social scene, the manner in which the relationships between men and women are organized and the way in which the two sexes relate to one another are remarkably similar in nature across social groups. Indeed, the biological differences between the sexes can be amplified or diminished by cultural practices and socialization, making gender differences in roles and behaviors generally modest but in some cases culturally important.

To use an athletic metaphor, sex and gender do not constitute a new ball game in each culture, but rather some relatively minor variations on a very old ball game. This observation should be comforting to scholars interested in sex and gender on a cross-cultural basis. In many instances, for example, with gender stereotypes, it is reasonable to think in terms of a pan-cultural model with degrees of variation created by various cultural influences. Such a view makes a scholarly approach to the complex matter of cross-cultural variations related to sex and gender an intellectually manageable task.

It is somewhat surprising when reviewing the literature in this domain that much of the gender-related cross-cultural research is not theory driven. For example, few studies have directly tested any of the theories of gender development in a cross-cultural context, although there are some studies that are consistent with various hypotheses generated from those theories. To further refine the existing knowledge of sex and gender, future research should address theoretical concerns relevant to cultural influences on behavior.

Finally, it was somewhat surprising to find that research from the various areas of social and behavioral science seem to have evolved in isolation. Few researchers have studied the relationship between cultural practices such as initiation rites, a typical topic for the anthropologists, and the development of the individual, a topic usually confined to the psychological domain. We close with a plea for anthropologists and psychologists to learn more from each other in their efforts to understand the impact of culture on behavior. Perhaps the growing field of cultural psychology, together with cross-cultural psychology, will provide the bridge between disciplines, recognizing that culture serves as both an independent and an organizing variable.

Endnotes

1. Illustrative of the many excellent studies of the unicultural noncomparative type are: Adler (1991, 1993); Brettell and Sargent (1993); Farley (1985); Goldman and Goldman (1982); Iglitzin and Ross (1976); Jahoda and Lewis (1988); Lupri (1983); Morgen (1989); Rosaldo and Lamphere (1974); Schlegel (1977); and Tripathy and Das (1991).

2. Other ways of classifying sex role ideologies would be along continua defined as hierarchical–equalitarian, conservative–liberal, or patriarchal–feminist. We have chosen to use the terms traditional–modern because these are the terms

used most frequently in the literature.

3. The general phenomenon of men's aggression toward women has been examined from an evolutionary perspective by Smuts (1992) and Thornhill and Thornhill (1992).

4. Psychoanalytic theory was quite influential in early cross-cultural gender differences (see: Burton & Whiting, 1961; Freud, 1939; Mead, 1949; Munroe & Munroe, 1975/1994; Munroe, Munroe, & Whiting, 1981) but has received little recent attention.

References

Acosta, E. A. & Sanchez de Almeida, M. E. (1983). Psychological factors affecting change in women's roles and status: A cross-cultural study. *International Journal of Psychology, 18,* 3–35.

Adler, L. L. (Ed.). (1991). *Women in cross-cultural perspective.* New York: Praeger.

Adler, L. L. (Ed.). (1993). *International handbook on gender roles.* Westport, CT: Greenwood.

Agarwal, K. S. & Lester, D. (1992). A study of perception of women by Indian and American students. In S. Iwawaki, Y. Kashima, & K. Leung (Eds.), *Innovations in cross-cultural psychology* (pp. 123–134). Amsterdam: Swets and Zeitlinger.

Albert, A. A. & Porter, J. R. (1986). Children's gender role stereotypes: A comparison of the United States and South Africa. *Journal of Cross-Cultural Psychology, 17,* 45–65.

Allman, J. (Ed.). (1978). *Women's status and fertility in the Muslim world.* New York: Praeger.

Antill, J. K., Cunningham, J. D., Russell, G., & Thompson, N. L. (1981). An Australian sex role scale. *Australian Journal of Psychology, 33,* 169–183.

Banaszak, L. A. & Plutzer, E. (1993). The social bases of feminism in the European community. *Public Opinion Quarterly, 57,* 29–53.

Bandura, A. (1969). Social learning theory of

identificatory process. In D. A. Goslin (Ed.), *Handbook of socialization theory and research* (pp. 213–262). Chicago: Rand McNally.

Barber, B. K., Chadwick, B. A., & Oerter, R. (1992). Parental behaviors and adolescent self-esteem in the United States and Germany. *Journal of Marriage and the Family, 54,* 128–141.

Barry, H., III, Bacon, M. K., & Child, I. L. (1957). A cross-cultural survey of some sex differences in socialization. *Journal of Abnormal and Social Psychology, 55,* 327–332.

Barry, H., III & Paxson, L. M. (1971). Infancy and early childhood: Cross-cultural codes 2. *Ethnology, 10,* 466–508.

Basow, S. A. (1984). Cultural variations in sex typing. *Sex Roles, 10,* 577–585.

Beal, C. R. (1994). *Boys and girls: The development of gender roles.* New York: McGraw-Hill.

Belk, S. S., Snell, W. E., Jr., Garcia-Falconi, R., Hernandez-Sanchez, J. E., Hargrove, L., & Holtzman, W. H., Jr. (1988). Power strategy use in the intimate relationships of women and men from Mexico and the United States. *Personality and Social Psychology Bulletin, 14*(3), 439–447.

Bem, S. L. (1974). The measurement of psychological androgyny. *Journal of Consulting and Clinical Psychology, 42,* 155–162.

Bem, S. L. (1981). Gender schema theory: A cognitive account of sex-typing. *Psychological Review, 88,* 354–364.

Bem, S. L. (1983). Gender schema theory and its implications for child development: Raising gender-aschematic children in a gender-schematic society. *Signs, 8,* 598–616.

Bem, S. L. (1985). Androgyny and gender schema theory: A conceptual and empirical integration. In T. B. Sonderegger (Ed.), *Nebraska Symposium on Motivation: Psychology of gender* (pp. 179–226). Lincoln: University of Nebraska Press.

Berne, E. (1961). *Transactional analysis in psychotherapy.* New York: Grove.

Berne, E. (1966). *Principles of group treatment.* New York: Oxford University Press.

Berry, J. W. (1976). Sex differences in behaviour and cultural complexity. *Indian Journal of Psychology, 51,* 89–97.

Best, D. L., House, A. S., Barnard, A. E., & Spicker, B. S. (1991). Parent–child interaction in France, Germany, and Italy: The effects of gender and culture. *Journal of Cross-Cultural Psychology, 25,* 181–193.

Best, D. L. & Williams, J. E. (1993). Cross-cultural viewpoint. In A. E. Beall & R. J. Sternberg (Eds.), *Perspectives on the psychology of gender* (pp. 215–248). New York: Guilford.

Best, D. L. & Williams, J. E. (1994a). A cross-cultural examination of self and ideal self descriptions using Transactional Analysis Ego States. In I. R. Lagunes & Y. H. Poortinga (Eds.), *From a different perspective: Studies of behavior across cultures* (pp. 213–220). Lisse, The Netherlands: Swets and Zeitlinger.

Best, D. L. & Williams, J. E. (1994b). Masculinity/femininity in the self and ideal self descriptions of university students in fourteen countries. In A-M. Bouvy, F. J. R. van de Vijver, P. Boski, & P. Schmitz (Eds.), *Journeys into cross-cultural psychology* (pp. 292–306). Amsterdam: Swets and Zeitlinger.

Best, D. L., Williams, J. E., & Briggs, S. R. (1980). A further analysis of the affective meanings associated with male and female sex-trait stereotypes. *Sex Roles, 6,* 735–746.

Best, D. L., Williams, J. E., Cloud, J. M., Davis, S. W., Robertson, L. S., Edwards, J. R., Giles, H., & Fowles, J. (1977). Development of sex-trait stereotypes among young children in the United States, England, and Ireland. *Child Development, 48,* 1375–1384.

Betzig, L. (1989). Causes of conjugal dissolution: A cross-cultural study. *Current Anthropology, 30,* 654–676.

Bjerke, T., Williams, J. E., & Wathne, P. H. (1989). Sex stereotypes in Norway revisited: 1977–87. *Scandinavian Journal of Psychology, 30,* 266–274.

Bloch, M. N. & Adler, S. M. (1994). African children's play and the emergence of the sexual division of labor. In J. L. Roopnarine, J. E. Johnson, & Frank H. Hooper (Eds.), *Children's play in diverse cultures* (pp. 148–178). Albany: State University of New York Press.

Blurton Jones, N. B. & Konner, M. (1973). Sex differences in behavior of London and Bushman children. In R. P. Michael & J. H. Crook (Eds.), *Comparative ecology and behavior of primates* (pp. 690–749). London: Academic.

Boehnke, K., Silbereisen, R. K., Eisenberg, N., Reykowski, J., & Palmonari, A. (1989). Developmental pattern of prosocial motivation: A cross-national study. *Journal of Cross-Cultural Psychology, 20,* 219–243.

Bradley, C. (1993). Women's power, children's labor. *Cross-Cultural Research, 27,* 70–96.

Brettell, C. B. & Sargent, C. F. (Eds.). (1993). *Gender in cross-cultural perspective.* Englewood Cliffs, NJ: Prentice Hall.

Bronstein, P. (1984). Differences in mothers' and fathers' behaviors toward children: A cross-cultural comparison. *Developmental Psychology, 20,* 995–1003.

Broude, G. J. (1987). A hologeistic study of the patterning of male–female relationships. In C. Kagitçibasi (Ed.), *Growth and progress in cross-cultural psychology.* Lisse, Netherlands: Swets and Zeitlinger.

Broude, G. J. (1987). The relationships of marital intimacy and aloofness to social environment: A hologeistic study. *Behavior Science Research, 21,* 50–69.

Brown, J. K. (1970). A note on the division of labor by sex. *American Anthropologist, 72,* 1073–1078.

Brown, J. K. (1981). Cross-cultural perspective on the female life cycle. In R. H. Munroe, R. L.

Munroe, & B. B. Whiting (Eds.), *Handbook of cross-cultural human development* (pp. 581–610). New York: Garland.

Burbank, V. K. (1987). Female aggression in cross-cultural perspective. *Behavior Science Research, 21*(1-4), 70–100.

Burns, A. & Homel, R. (1986). Sex role satisfaction among Australian children: Some sex, age, and cultural group comparisons. *Psychology of Women Quarterly, 10,* 285–296.

Burton, R. V. & Whiting, J. W. M. (1961). The absent father and cross-sex identity. *Merrill-Palmer Quarterly, 7*(2), 85–95.

Buss, D. (1990). Evolutionary social psychology: Prospect and pitfalls. *Motivation and Emotion, 14,* 265–286.

Buss, D. M. (1989). Sex differences in human mate preferences: Evolutionary hypotheses tested in 37 cultures. *Behavioral and Brain Sciences, 12,* 1–49.

Buss, D. M. (1994). Mate preference in 37 cultures. In W. J. Lonner & R. Malpass (Eds.), *Psychology and culture* (pp. 197–201). Boston, MA: Allyn and Bacon.

Buss, D. M. (1994). *The evolution of desire.* New York: Basic.

Buss, D. M. et al. (1990). International preferences in selecting mates. *Journal of Cross-Cultural Psychology, 21,* 5–47.

Bussey, K. (1983). A social–cognitive appraisal of sex-role development. *Australian Journal of Psychology, 35,* 135–143.

Bussey, K. & Bandura, A. (1984). Influence of gender constancy and social power on sex-linked modeling. *Journal of Personality and Social Psychology, 47,* 1292–1302.

Buunk, B. & Hupka, R. B. (1987). Cross-cultural differences in elicitation of sexual jealousy. *The Journal of Sex Research, 23,* 12–22.

Calasanti, T. M. & Bailey, C. A. (1991). Gender inequality and the division of household labor in the United States and Sweden: A socialist–feminist approach. *Social Problems, 38,* 34–53.

Calhoun, G., Jr. & Sethi, R. (1987). The self-esteem of pupils from India, the United States, and the Philippines. *The Journal of Psychology, 121,* 199–202.

Callan, V. J. & Kee, P-K. (1981). Sons or daughters? Cross-cultural comparisons of the sex preferences of Australian, Greek, Italian, Malay, Chinese, and Indian parents in Australia and Malaysia. *Population and Environment, 4,* 97–108.

Carlsson, M., Andersson, K., Berg, E., Jäderquist, P., & Magnusson, E. (1984). Opinions of typical female and male sex-role behavior in Swedish children. *Scandinavian Journal of Psychology, 25,* 276–283.

Carlsson, M. & Barnes, M. (1986). Conception and self-attribution of sex-role behavior: A cross-cultural comparison between Swedish and kibbutz-raised Israelian children. *Scandinavian Journal of Psychology, 27,* 258–265.

Charles, M. & Höpflinger, F. (1992). Gender, culture, and the division of household labor: A replication of U.S. studies for the case of Switzerland. *Journal of Comparative Family Studies, 23,* 375–387.

Chia, R. C., Moore, J. L., Lam, K. N., Chuang, C. J., & Cheng, B. S. (1994). Cultural differences in gender role attitudes between Chinese and American students. *Sex Roles, 31,* 23–30.

Coltrane, S. (1988). Father–child relationships and the status of women: A cross cultural study. *American Journal of Sociology, 93,* 1060–1095.

Cronk, L. (1993). Parental favoritism toward daughters. *American Scientist, 81,* 272–279.

Cunningham, J. D. (1981). Self-disclosure intimacy: Sex, sex-of-target, cross-national, and "generational" differences. *Personality and Social Psychology Bulletin, 7*(2), 314–319.

Daly, M. & Wilson, M. (1978). *Sex, evolution, and behavior.* North Scituate, MA: Duxbury.

D'Andrade, R. G. (1966). Sex differences and cultural institutions. In E. E. Maccoby (Ed.), *The development of sex differences* (pp. 174–204). Stanford, CA: Stanford University Press.

Davis, D. L. & Whitten, R. G. (1987). The cross-cultural study of human sexuality. *Annual Review of Anthropology, 16,* 69–98.

Davis, N. J. & Robinson, R. V. (1991). Men's and women's consciousness of gender inequality: Austria, West Germany, Great Britain, and the United States. *American Sociological Review, 56,* 72–84.

DeRaad, B. & Doddema-Winsemius, M. (1992). Factors in the assortment of human mates:

Differential preferences in Germany and the Netherlands. *Personality and Individual Differences, 13,* 103–114.

Dickerscheid, J. D., Schwarz, P. M., Noir, S., & El-Taliawy, M. S. T. (1988). Gender concept development of preschool-aged children in the United States and Egypt. *Sex Roles, 18,* 669–677.

Dion, K. K. & Dion, K. L. (1993). Individualistic and collectivistic perspectives on gender and the cultural context of love and intimacy. *Journal of Social Issues, 49,* 53–69.

Dixon, R. B. (1978). *Rural women at work: Strategies for development in South Asia.* Baltimore: Johns Hopkins University Press.

Draper, P. (1975). Cultural pressure on sex differences. *American Ethnologist, 2*(4), 602–616.

Eaton, W. O. & Enns, L. R. (1986). Sex differences in human motor activity level. *Psychological Bulletin, 100,* 19–28.

Edelbrook, C. & Sugawara, A. I. (1978). Acquisition of sex-typed preferences in preschool-aged children. *Developmental Psychology, 14,* 614–623.

Edwards, C. P. (1992). Cross-cultural perspectives on family-peer relations. In R. D. Parke & G. W. Ladd (Eds.), *Family-peer relationships: Modes of linkage* (pp. 285–316). Hillsdale, NJ: Lawrence Erlbaum.

Edwards, C. P. & Whiting, B. B. (1974). Women and dependency. *Politics and Society, 4,* 343–355.

Edwards, C. P. & Whiting, B. B. (1980). Differential socialization of girls and boys in light of cross-cultural research. *New Directions for Child Development, 8,* 45–57.

Edwards, C. P. & Whiting, B. B. (1993). "Mother, older sibling, and me": The overlapping roles of caretakers and companions in the social world of 2–3-year-olds in Ngeca, Kenya. In K. MacDonald (Ed.), *Parent–child play: Descriptions and implications* (pp. 305–329). Albany: State University of New York Press.

Edwards, J. R. & Williams, J. E. (1980). Sex-trait stereotypes among young children and young adults: Canadian findings and cross-national comparisons. *Canadian Journal of Behavioral Science, 12,* 210–220.

Ember, C. R. (1978). Men's fear of sex with women: A cross-cultural study. *Sex Roles, 4*(5), 657–678.

Ember, C. R. (1981). A cross-cultural perspective on sex differences. In R. H. Munroe, R. L. Munroe, & B. B. Whiting (Eds.), *Handbook of cross-cultural human development* (pp. 531–580). New York: Garland.

Ericksen, K. P. (1989). Female genital mutilations in Africa. *Behavior Science Research, 23,* 182–204.

Farley, J. (Ed.). (1985). *Women workers in fifteen countries: Essays in honor of Alice Hanson Cook.* Ithaca: ILR Press.

Farver, J. A. M. & Howes, C. (1988). Cross-cultural differences in social interaction: A comparison of American and Indonesian children. *Journal of Cross-Cultural Psychology, 19,* 203–215.

Finley, N. J. (1989). Theories of family labor as applied to gender differences in caregiving for elderly parents. *Journal of Marriage and the Family, 51,* 79–86.

Flavia. (1988). Violence in the family: Wife beating. In R. Ghadially (Ed.), *Women in society: A reader* (pp. 151–166). New Delhi, India: Sage.

Foa, U. G., Anderson, B., Converse, J., Jr., Urbansky, W. A., Cawley, M. J., III, Muhlhausen, S. M., & Tornblom, K. Y. (1987). Gender-related sexual attitudes: Some cross-cultural similarities and differences. *Sex Roles, 16,* 511–519.

Freedman, D. G. (1976). Infancy, biology and culture. In L. P. Lipsitt (Ed.), *Developmental psychobiology* (pp. 34–54). New York: Halsted, Wiley.

Freedman, D. G. & DeBoer, M. M. (1979). Biological and cultural differences in early child development. *Annual Review of Anthropology, 8,* 579–600.

Freud, S. (1939). *Moses and monotheism.* New York: Vintage Books.

Friedman, A. & Pines, A. M. (1992). Increase in Arab women's perceived power in the second half of life. *Sex Roles, 26,* 1–9.

Fry, D. P. (1987). What human sociobiology has to offer economic anthropology and vice versa. *Journal of Social and Biological Structures, 10,* 37–51.

Furnham, A. & Karani, R. (1985). A cross-cultural study of attitudes to women, just world, and locus of control beliefs. *Psychologia, 28,* 11–20.

Gackenbach, J. (1981). Sex-role identity across two cultures. *Psychological Reports, 49,* 677–678.

Ghadially, R. & Kazi, K. A. (1979). Attitudes toward sex roles. *Indian Journal of Social Work, 40,* 65–71.

Ghadially, R. & Kumar, P. (1988). Stress, strain and coping styles of female professionals. *Indian Journal of Applied Psychology, 26*(1), 1–8.

Gibbons, J. L., Lynn, M., Stiles, D. A., de Berducido, E. J., Richter, R., Walker, K., & Wiley, D. (1993). Guatemalan, Filipino, and U.S. adolescents' images of women as office workers and homemakers. *Psychology of Women Quarterly, 17,* 373–388.

Gibbons, J. L., Stiles, D. A., & Shkodriani, G. M. (1991). Adolescents' attitudes toward family and gender roles: An international comparison. *Sex Roles, 25,* 625–643.

Gilmore, D. D. (1990). *Manhood in the making.* New Haven: Yale University Press.

Goldman, R. & Goldman, J. (1982). *Children's sexual thinking: A comparative study of children aged 5 to 15 years in Australia, North America, Britain, and Sweden.* Boston: Routledge and Kegan Paul.

Gottlieb, G. (1983). The psychobiological approach to developmental issues. In P. H. Mussen (Series Ed.) & M. M. Harth & J. J. Campos (Vol. Eds.), *Handbook of child psychology. Vol. II. Infancy and developmental psychobiology* (pp. 1–26). New York: Wiley.

Gough, H. G. (1952). Identifying psychological femininity. *Educational and Psychological Measurement, 12,* 427–439.

Gough, H. G. (1966). A cross-cultural analysis of the CPI femininity scale. *Journal of Consulting Psychology, 30,* 136–141.

Gough, H. G., & Heilbrun, A. B., Jr. (1980). *The Adjective Check List manual.* Palo Alto: Consulting Psychologists Press.

Gould, S. J. & Lewontin, R. C. (1979). The spandrels of San Marco and the Panglossian paradigm: A critique of the adaptationist programme. *Proceedings of the Royal Society of London, B, 205,* 581–598.

Greenfield, P. M. (1981). Child care in cross-cultural perspectives: Implications for the future organization of child care in the United States. *Psychology of Women Quarterly, 6,* 41–54.

Gronseth, E. (1957). The impact of father absence in sailor families upon the personality structure and social adjustment of adult sailor sons. Part I. In N. Anderson (Ed.), *Studies of the family* (Vol. 2, pp. 97–114). Gottingen, Germany: Vandenhoeck and Ruprecht.

Guberman, N., Maheu, P., & Maillé, C. (1992). Women as family caregivers: Why do they care? *The Gerontologist, 32,* 607–617.

Guttentag, M. & Longfellow, C. (1977). Children's social attributions: Development and change. In C. B. Keasey (Ed.), *Nebraska Symposium on Motivation* (pp. 305–341). Lincoln: University of Nebraska Press.

Hamilton, M. C. (1991). Masculine bias in the attribution of personhood. *Psychology of Women Quarterly, 15,* 393–402.

Hamilton, V. L., Blumenfeld, P. C., Akoh, H., & Miura, K. (1991). Group and gender in Japanese and American elementary classrooms. *Journal of Cross-Cultural Psychology, 22,* 317–346.

Hammer, J. (1970). Preference for a male child: Cultural factors. *Journal of Individual Psychology, 26,* 54–56.

Haque, A. (1982). Sex stereotypes among adults and children in Pakistan. In R. Rath, H. S. Asthana, D. Sinha, & J. B. H. Sinha (Eds.), *Diversity and unity in cross-cultural psychology* (pp. 238–249). Amsterdam: Swets and Zeitlinger.

Harris, A. C. (1994). Ethnicity as a determinant of sex role identity: A replication study of item selection for the Bem Sex Role Inventory. *Sex Roles, 31,* 241–273.

Hartley, R. E. (1960). Children's concepts of male and female roles. *Merrill-Palmer Quarterly of Behavior and Development, 6,* 83–91.

Hatfield, E. & Rapson, R. L. (1993). Historical and cross-cultural perspectives on passionate love and sexual desire. *Annual Review of Sex Research, 4,* 67–97.

Hatfield, E. & Rapson, R. L. (1995). *A world of passion: Cultural perspectives on love and sex.* Boston: Allyn and Bacon.

Heath, D. B. (1958). Sexual division of labor and cross-cultural research. *Social Forces, 37,* 77–79.

Hendrix, L. & Johnson, G. D. (1985). Instrumental and expressive socialization: A false dichotomy. *Sex Roles, 13,* 581–595.

Hess, R. D. & Shipman, V. C. (1967). Cognitive elements in maternal behavior. In J. P. Hell (Ed.), *Minnesota symposia on child psychology* (pp. 57–81). Minneapolis: University of Minnesota Press.

Hofstede, G. (1980). *Culture's consequences: International differences in work-related values.* Beverly Hills: Sage.

Hoyenga, K. B. & Hoyenga, K. T. (1993). *Gender-related differences: Origins and outcomes.* Boston: Allyn and Bacon.

Huber, J. (1986). Trends in gender stratification, 1970–1985. *Sociological Forum, 1,* 476–495.

Iglitzin, L. B. & Ross, R. (Eds.). (1976). *Women in the world: A comparative study.* Santa Barbara: Clio.

Intons-Peterson, M. J. (1988). *Gender concepts of Swedish and American youth.* Hillsdale, NJ: Lawrence Erlbaum.

Jacklin, C. N. (1989). Female and male: Issues of gender. *American Psychologist, 44,* 127–133.

Jacobs, J. A. & Lim, S. T. (1992). Trends in occupational and industrial sex segregation in 56 countries, 1960–1980. *Work and Occupations, 19,* 450–486.

Jahoda, G. & Lewis, I. M. (Eds.). (1988). *Acquiring culture: Cross-cultural studies in child development.* New York: Croom Helm.

Jayaswal, M. (1985). *Sex and sex prejudice.* Unpublished manuscript, Department of Psychology, Ranchi University, Ranchi, India.

Johnston, T. D. (1987). The persistence of dichotomies in the study of behavioral development. *Developmental Review, 7,* 149–182.

Kagitçibasi, C. (1982). Old-age security value of children: Cross-national socioeconomic evidence. *Journal of Cross-Cultural Psychology, 13,* 29–42.

Kagitçibasi, C. (1990). Family and socialization in cross-cultural perspective: A model of change. In J. Berman (Ed.), *Cross-cultural perspectives: Nebraska Symposium on Motivation, 1989* (Vol. 37, pp. 135–200), Lincoln: University of Nebraska Press.

Kalin, R. & Tilby, P. (1978). Development and validation of a sex-role ideology scale. *Psychological Reports, 42,* 731–738.

Kaschak, E. & Sharratt, S. (1983). A Latin American sex role inventory. *Cross-Cultural Psychology Bulletin, 18,* 3–6.

Katz, M. M. & Konner, M. J. (1981). The role of the father: An anthropological perspective. In M. E. Lamb (Ed.), *The role of the father in child development* (pp. 155–185). New York: Wiley.

Kauppinen-Toropainen, K. & Gruber, J. E. (1993). Antecedents and outcomes of woman-unfriendly experiences. *Psychology of Women Quarterly, 17,* 431–356.

Keyes, S. (1984). Measuring sex-role stereotypes: Attitudes among Hong Kong Chinese adolescents and the development of the Chinese Sex Role Inventory. *Sex Roles, 10,* 129–140.

Kohlberg, L. (1966). A cognitive–developmental analysis of children's sex role concepts and attitudes. In E. E. Maccoby (Ed.), *The development of sex differences* (pp. 82–173). Stanford, CA: Stanford University Press.

Kohlberg, L. & Ullman, D. Z. (1974). Stages in the development of psychosexual concepts and attitudes. In R. C. Friedman, R. M. Richart, & R. L. Van de Wiele (Eds.), *Sex differences in behavior* (pp. 209–223). New York: Wiley.

Krampen, G., Galli, I., & Nigro, G. (1992). Sex-role orientations and control orientations of southern Italian and West German university students. *Journal of Cross-Cultural Psychology, 23*(2), 240–250.

Krishnaswamy, S. (1988). Female infanticide in contemporary India: A case study of Kallars of Tamilnadu. In R. Ghadially (Ed.), *Women in Indian society: A reader* (pp. 186–195). New Delhi, India: Sage.

Lamb, M. E. (1976). Twelve-month-olds and their parents: Interactions in a laboratory playroom. *Developmental Psychology, 12,* 435–443.

Lamb, M. E. (1977). Father–infant and mother–infant interaction in the first year of life. *Child Development, 48,* 167–181.

Lamb, M. E., Frodi, A. M., Hwang, C. P., Frodi, M., & Steinberg, J. (1982). Mother– and father–infant interaction involving play and holding in traditional and nontraditional

Swedish families. *Developmental Psychology,* 18, 215–221.

Lara-Cantu, M. A. (1989). A sex role inventory with scales for "machismo" and "self-sacrificing woman." *Journal of Cross-Cultural Psychology,* 20(4), 386–398.

Lara-Cantu, M. A. & Navarro-Arias, R. (1987). Self-descriptions of Mexican college students in response to the Bem Sex Role Inventory and other sex role items. *Journal of Cross-Cultural Psychology,* 18(3), 331–344.

L'Armand, K., Pepitone, A., & Shanmugam, T. E. (1981). Attitudes toward rape: A comparison of the role of chastity in India and the United States. *Journal of Cross-Cultural Psychology,* 12(3), 284–303.

Lee, L. Y. & Sugawara, A. (1982). Awareness of sex trait stereotypes among Korean children. *Journal of Social Psychology,* 117, 161–170.

Leung, K., Bond, M. H., Carment, D. W., Krishnan, L., & Liebrand, W. B. G. (1990). Effects of cultural femininity on preference for methods of conflict processing: A cross-cultural study. *Journal of Experimental Social Psychology,* 26, 373–388.

Liben, L. S. & Signorella, M. L. (1980). Gender-related schemata and constructive memory in children. *Child Development,* 51, 11–18.

Liben, L. S. & Signorella, M. L. (Eds.). (1987). *Children's gender schemata.* San Francisco: Jossey-Bass.

Lii, S-Y. & Wong, S-Y. (1982). A cross-cultural study on sex-role stereotypes and social desirability. *Sex Roles,* 8, 481–491.

Loehlin, J. C. (1992). *Genes and environment in personality development.* Individual differences and development series, Vol. 2. Newbury Park, CA: Sage.

Loscocco, K. A. & Kalleberg, A. L. (1988). Age and the meaning of work in the United States and Japan. *Social Forces,* 67, 337–356.

Low, B. S. (1989). Cross-cultural patterns in the training of children: An evolutionary perspective. *Journal of Comparative Psychology,* 103, 311–319.

Lummis, M. & Stevenson, H. W. (1990). Gender differences in beliefs and achievement: A cross-cultural study. *Developmental Psychology,* 26, 254–263.

Lupri, E. (Ed.). (1983). *The changing position of women in family and society: A cross-national comparison.* Leiden: Brill.

Lynn, D. B. & Sawrey, W. L. (1959). The effects of father-absence on Norwegian boys and girls. *Journal of Abnormal Social Psychology,* 59, 258–262.

Lytton, H. & Romney, D. M. (1991). Parents' differential socialization of boys and girls: A meta-analysis. *Psychological Bulletin,* 109, 267–296.

Maccoby, E. E. & Jacklin, C. N. (1974). *The psychology of sex differences.* Stanford, CA: Stanford University Press.

Macfarlane, A. (1977). *The psychology of childbirth.* Cambridge, MA: Harvard University Press.

Mackey, W. C. (1985). *Fathering behaviors: The dynamics of the man–child bond.* New York: Plenum.

Magnusson, D. & Stattin, H. (1978). A cross-cultural comparison of anxiety responses in an interactional frame of reference. *International Journal of Psychology,* 13, 317–332.

Maloney, P., Wilkof, J., & Dambrot, F. (1981). Androgyny across two cultures: United States and Israel. *Journal of Cross-Cultural Psychology,* 12(1), 95–102.

Martin, C. L. & Halverson, C. F., Jr. (1981). A schematic processing model of sex typing and stereotyping in young children. *Child Development,* 52, 1119–1134.

Martin, C. L. & Halverson, C. F., Jr. (1983). The effects of sex-typing schemas on young children's memory. *Child Development,* 54, 563–574.

Masters, R. D. (1989). Gender and political cognition: Integrating evolutionary biology and political science. *Political and Life Sciences,* 8, 3–39.

Mead, M. (1935). *Sex and temperament in three primitive societies.* New York: Morrow.

Mead, M. (1949). *Male and female.* New York: New American Library.

Miller, D. B. (1988). Development of instinctive behavior: An epigenetic and ecological approach. In E. M. Blass (Ed.), *Handbook of behavioral neurobiology.* Vol. 9. *Developmental psychobiology and behavioral ecology* (pp. 415–444). New York: Plenum.

Minturn, L. & Lambert, W. W. (1964). *Mothers of six cultures: Antecedents of child rearing*. New York: Wiley.

Mischel, W. (1970). Sex-typing and socialization. In P. H. Mussen (Ed.), *Carmichael's manual of child psychology* (pp. 3–72). New York: Wiley.

Mitchell, J. E., Baker, L. A., & Jacklin, C. N. (1989). Masculinity and femininity in twin children: Genetic and environmental factors. *Child Development, 60*, 1475–1485.

Morgen, S. (Ed.). (1989). *Gender and anthropology: Critical reviews for research and teaching*. Washington, DC: American Anthropological Association.

Morinaga, Y., Frieze, I. H., & Ferligoj, A. (1993). Career plans and gender-role attitudes of college students in the United States, Japan, and Slovenia. *Sex Roles, 29*, 317–334.

Mukhopadhyay, C. C. & Higgins, P. J. (1988). Anthropological studies of women's status revisited: 1977–1987. *Annual Review of Anthropology, 17*, 461–495.

Mullet, E., Neto, F., & Henry, S. (1992). Determinants of occupational preferences in Portuguese and French high school students. *Journal of Cross-Cultural Psychology, 23*, 521–531.

Munroe, R. H. & Munroe, R. L. (1982). The development of sex-gender constancy among children in four cultures. In R. Rath, H. S. Asthana, D. Sinha, & J. B. P. Sinha (Eds.), *Diversity and unity in cross-cultural psychology* (pp. 272–280). Lisse, Netherlands: Swets and Zeitlinger.

Munroe, R. H. & Munroe, R. L. (1994). Behavior across cultures: Results from observational studies. In W. J. Lonner & R. Malpass (Eds.), *Psychology and culture* (pp. 107–111). Boston: Allyn and Bacon.

Munroe, R. H., Shimmin, H. S., & Munroe, R. L. (1984). Gender understanding and sex role preference in four cultures. *Developmental Psychology, 20*, 673–682.

Munroe, R. L. & Munroe, R. H. (1971). Effect of environmental experiences on spatial ability in an East African society. *Journal of Social Psychology, 83*, 3–10.

Munroe, R. L. & Munroe, R. H. (1975/1994). *Cross-cultural human development*. Prospective Heights, IL: Waveland.

Munroe, R. L., Munroe, R. H., & Whiting, J. W. M. (1981). Male sex-role resolutions. In R. H. Munroe, R. L. Munroe, & B. B. Whiting (Eds.), *Handbook of cross-cultural human development* (pp. 611–632). New York: Garland.

Murdock, G. P. & White, D. R. (1969). Standard cross-cultural sample. *Ethnology, 8*, 329–369.

Murphy-Berman, V. A., Berman, J. J., Singh, P., & Pandy, J. (1992). Cultural variations in sex typing: A comparison of students in the United States, Germany, and India. *Journal of Social Psychology, 132*, 403–405.

Nadelman, L. (1970). Sex identity in London children: Memory, knowledge, and preference tests. *Human Development, 13*, 28–42.

Nelson, M. G. (1988). Reliability, validity, and cross-cultural comparisons for the Simplified Attitudes Toward Women Scale. *Sex Roles, 18*, 289–296.

Neto, F., Williams, J. E., & Widner, S. C. (1991). Portuguese children's knowledge of sex stereotypes: Effects of age, gender, and socioeconomic status. *Journal of Cross-Cultural Psychology, 22*, 376–388.

Nevo, B. (1977). Personality differences between kibbutz born and city born adults. *Journal of Psychology, 96*, 303–308.

Nisbett, R. E. (1990). Evolutionary psychology, biology, and cultural evolution. *Motivation and Emotion, 14*, 255–263.

Nishiyama, I. (1975). Validation of the CPI femininity scale in Japan. *Journal of Cross-Cultural Psychology, 5*, 482–489.

Oakley, A. (1980). *Becoming a mother*. New York: Schocken.

Olowu, A. A. (1985). Gender as a determinant of some Nigerian adolescents' self-concepts. *Journal of Adolescence, 8*, 347–355.

Omark, D. R., Omark, M., & Edelman, M. (1975). Formation of dominance hierarchies in young children: Action and perspective. In T. Williams (Ed.), *Psychological anthropology* (pp. 289–315). Monton: The Hague.

Ottaway, R. N. & Bhatnagar, D. (1988). Personality and biographical differences between male and female managers in the United States and India. *Applied Psychology: An International Review, 37*, 201–212.

Pei-Hui, R. A. & Ward, C. (1994). A cross-cultural

perspective on models of psychological androgyny. *The Journal of Social Psychology, 134*(3), 391–393.

Peterson, V. S. & Runyan, A. S. (1993). *Global gender issues.* Boulder, CO: Westview.

Pitariu, H. (1981). Validation of the CPI femininity scale in Romania. *Journal of Cross-Cultural Psychology, 12*(1), 111–117.

Pooler, W. S. (1991). Sex of child preferences among college students. *Sex Roles, 25,* 569–576.

Population Crisis Committee. (1988). *Country rankings of the status of women: Poor, powerless, and pregnant* (Issue Brief No. 20, June). Washington, DC: Population Crisis Committee.

Prosser, G. V., Hutt, C., Hutt, S. J., Mahindadasa, K. J., & Goonetilleke, M. D. J. (1986). Children's play in Sri Lanka: A cross-cultural study. *British Journal of Developmental Psychology, 4,* 179–186.

Quinn, N. (1977). Anthropology studies of women's status. *Annual Review of Anthropology, 6,* 181–225.

Ramirez, J. M. (1993). Acceptability of aggression in four Spanish regions and a comparison with other European countries. *Aggressive Behavior, 19,* 185–197.

Rao, V. V. P. & Rao, V. N. (1985). Sex-role attitudes across two cultures: United States and India. *Sex Roles, 13,* 607–624.

Rapoport, T., Lomski-Feder, E., & Masalha, M. (1989). Female subordination in the Arab-Israeli community: The adolescent perspective of "social veil." *Sex Roles, 20,* 255–269.

Reed-Sanders, D., Dodder, R. A., & Webster, L. (1985). The Bem Sex Role Inventory across three cultures. *Journal of Social Psychology, 125,* 523–525.

Reis, H. T. & Wright, S. (1982). Knowledge of sex-role stereotypes in children aged 3 to 5. *Sex Roles, 8,* 1049–1056.

Reiss, I. L. (1986). *Journey into sexuality: An exploratory voyage.* Englewood Cliffs, NJ: Prentice Hall.

Rogoff, B., Gauvain, M., & Ellis, S. (1984). Development viewed in its cultural context. In M. H. Bornstein & M. E. Lamb (Eds.), *Developmental psychology: An advanced textbook* (pp. 533–571). Hillsdale, NJ: Lawrence Erlbaum.

Rohner, R. P. & Rohner, E. C. (1982). Enculturative continuity and the importance of caretakers: Cross-cultural codes. *Behavior Science Research, 17,* 91–114.

Roos, P. A. (1983). Marriage and women's occupational attainment in cross-cultural perspective. *American Sociological Review, 48,* 852–864.

Rosaldo, M. Z. & Lamphere, L. (Eds.). (1974). *Woman, culture, and society.* Stanford, CA: Stanford University Press.

Rosenberg, B. G. & Sutton-Smith, B. (1972). *Sex and identity.* New York: Holt, Rinehart, and Winston.

Rosenblatt, P. C. & Cunningham, M. R. (1976). Sex differences in cross-cultural perspective. In B. Lloyd & J. Archer (Eds.), *Exploring sex differences* (pp. 71–94). New York: Academic.

Rosner, M. (1967). Women in the kibbutz: Changing status and concepts. *Asian and African Studies, 3,* 35–68.

Ross, C. E. (1987). The division of labor at home. *Social Forces, 65,* 816–833.

Ross, M. H. (1986a). Female political participation: A cross-cultural explanation. *American Anthropologist, 88,* 843–858.

Ross, M. H. (1986b). The limits to social structure: Social structural and psychocultural explanations for political conflict and violence. *Anthropological Quarterly, 59,* 171–176.

Rozée, P. D. (1993). Forbidden or forgiven? Rape in cross-cultural perspective. *Psychology of Women Quarterly, 17,* 499–514.

Rubenstein, J., Feldman, S. S., Rubin, C., & Noveck, I. (1987). A cross-cultural comparison of children's drawings of same- and mixed-sex peer interaction. *Journal of Cross-Cultural Psychology, 18,* 234–250.

Ruble, D. N. (1987). The acquisition of self-knowledge: A self-socialization perspective. In N. Eisenberg (Ed.), *Contemporary topics in developmental psychology* (pp. 243–270). New York: Wiley.

Russell, G. & Russell, A. (1987). Mother–child and father–child relationships in middle childhood. *Child Development, 58,* 1573–1585.

Ryan, G., Dolphin, C., Lundberg, U., & Myrsten, A-L. (1987). Sex role patterns in an Irish student sample as measured by the Bem Sex Role Inventory (comparisons with an American sample). *Sex Roles, 17,* 17–29.

Sagi, A., Lamb, M. E., Shoham, R., Dvir, R., & Lewkowicz, K. (1985). Parent–infant interaction in families on Israeli kibbutzim. *International Journal of Behavioral Development, 8,* 273–284.

Schlegel, A. (Ed.). (1977). *Sex stratification: A cross-cultural view.* New York: Columbia University Press.

Segal, E. S. (1983). The structure of division of labor: A tentative formulation. *Behavior Science Research, 18,* 3–25.

Segall, M. H. (1988a). Cultural factors, biology and human aggression. In J. Groebel & R. Hinde (Eds.) *Aggression and war: Their biological and social bases* (pp. 173–185). New York: Cambridge University Press.

Segall, M. H. (1988b). Cultural roots of aggressive behavior. In M. Bond (Ed.), *The cross-cultural challenge to social psychology* (pp. 208–217). Newbury Park, CA: Sage.

Segall, M. H. (1988c). Psycho-cultural antecedents of male aggression: Some implications involving gender, parenting, and adolescence. In P. Dasen, J. W. Berry & N. Sartorius (Eds.), *Health and Cross-cultural Psychology* (pp. 71–92). Beverly Hills: Sage.

Segall, M. H. & Knaak, F. (1989). Un théorie de machisme compensatoire. In *Socialisations et Cultures* (pp. 357–358). Interculturels Presses Universitaires de Murail: ARIC.

Seginer, R., Karayanni, M., & Mar'i, M. M. (1990). Adolescents' attitudes toward women's roles: A comparison between Israeli Jews and Arabs. *Psychology of Women Quarterly, 14,* 119–133.

Serpell, R. (1993). *The significance of schooling: Life-journeys in an African society.* New York: Cambridge University Press.

Sethi, R. R. & Allen, M. J. (1984). Sex-role stereotypes in Northern India and the United States. *Sex Roles, 11,* 615–626.

Signorella, M. L., Bigler, R. S., & Liben, L. S. (1993). Developmental differences in children's gender schemata about others: A meta-analytic review. *Developmental Review, 134,* 147–183.

Simmons, C. H., Kolke, A. V., & Shimizu, H. (1986). Attitudes toward romantic love among American, German, and Japanese students. *The Journal of Social Psychology, 126,* 327–336.

Simonton, D. K. (1992). Gender and genius in Japan: Feminine eminence in masculine culture. *Sex Roles, 27,* 101–119.

Singh, A. K. (1980). Women: The most disliked group—ranking of prejudices. *Social Change, 10,* 3–9.

Slaby, R. G. & Frey, K. S. (1975). Development of gender constancy and selective attention to same-sex models. *Child Development, 46,* 849–856.

Smuts, B. (1992). Male aggression toward women: An evolutionary perspective. *Human Nature, 3,* 1–44.

Snarey, J. & Son, L. (1986). Sex-identity development among kibbutz-born males: A test of the Whiting hypothesis. *Ethos, 14,* 99–119.

Spence, J. T. & Helmreich, R. (1972). The Attitudes Towards Women Scale: An objective instrument to measure attitudes towards the rights and roles of women in contemporary society. *JSAS Catalog of Selected Documents in Psychology, 2,* 66.

Spence, J. T. & Helmreich, R. L. (1978). *Masculinity and femininity: Their psychological dimensions, correlates, and antecedents.* Austin: University of Texas Press.

Spiro, M. (1956). *Kibbutz: Venture in utopia.* New York: Schocken.

Stewart, J. (1988). Current themes, theoretical issues, and preoccupations in the study of sexual differentiation and gender-related behaviors. *Psychobiology, 16,* 315–320.

Stolz, L. M. (1954). *Father relations of warborn children.* Stanford: Stanford University Press.

Strube, M. J. (1981). Meta-analysis and cross-cultural comparison. *Journal of Cross-Cultural Psychology, 12,* 3–20.

Sunar, D. G. (1982). Female stereotypes in the United States and Turkey: An application of functional theory to perception in power relationships. *Journal of Cross-Cultural Psychology, 13,* 445–460.

Super, C. M. & Harkness, S. (1982). The infants' niche in rural Kenya and metropolitan America. In L. L. Adler (Ed.), *Cross-cultural research at issue* (pp. 47–55). New York: Academic.

Suzuki, A. (1991a). Egalitarian sex role attitudes: Scale development and comparison of American and Japanese women. *Sex Roles, 24,* 245–259.

Suzuki, A. (1991b). Predictors of women's sex role attitudes across two cultures: United States and Japan. *Japanese Psychological Research, 33*(3), 126–133.

Tanner, J. M. (1962). *Growth at adolescence* (2nd ed). Oxford: Blackwell.

Tanner, J. M. (1970). Physical growth. In P. H. Mussen (Ed.), *Carmichael's manual of child psychology* (Vol. 1, pp. 77–155). New York: Wiley.

Tarrier, N. & Gomes, L. (1981). Knowledge of sex-trait stereotypes: Effects of age, sex, and social class on Brazilian children. *Journal of Cross-Cultural Psychology, 12,* 81–93.

Thompson, S. K. (1975). Gender labels and early sex role development. *Child Development, 46,* 339–347.

Thornhill, R. & Thornhill, N. W. (1992). The evolutionary psychology of men's coercive sexuality. *Behavioral and Brain Sciences, 15,* 363–421.

Tiger, L. (1987). Alienated from the meanings of reproduction? In J. M. Reinisch, L. A. Rosenblum, & S. A. Sanders (Eds.), *Masculinity/femininity: Basic perspectives.* New York: Oxford University Press.

Tiller, P. O. (1957). Father absence and personality development in children in sailor families: A preliminary research report. Part II. In N. Anderson (Ed.), *Studies of the family* (Vol. 2, pp. 115–137). Gottingen, Germany: Vandenhoeck and Ruprecht.

Ting-Toomey, S. (1991). Intimacy expressions in three cultures: France, Japan, and the United States. *International Journal of Intercultural Relations, 15,* 29–46.

Trautner, H. M., Sahm, W. B., & Stevermann, I. (1983). *The development of sex-role stereotypes and classificatory skills in children.* Paper presented at the Seventh Biennial Meeting of the International Society for the Study of Behavioural Development in Munich August, 1983.

Travis, C. B. & Yeager, C. P. (1991). Sexual selection, parental investment, and sexism. *Journal of Social Issues, 47,* 117–129.

Triandis, H. C. & Heron, A. (Eds.). (1981). *Handbook of cross-cultural psychology,* Vol. 4. Boston: Allyn and Bacon.

Tripathy, S. N. & Das, S. (1991). *Informal women labour in India.* New Delhi, India: Discovery.

Trivers, R. L. & Willard, D. E. (1973). Natural selection of parental ability to vary the sex ratio of offspring. *Science, 179,* 90–92.

Trommsdorff, G. & Iwawaki, S. (1989). Students' perceptions of socialisation and gender role in Japan and Germany. *International Journal of Behavioral Development, 12*(4), 485–493.

Tzuriel, D. (1984). Sex role typing and ego identity in Israeli, Oriental, and Western adolescents. *Journal of Personality and Social Psychology, 46,* 440–457.

Tzuriel, D. (1985). Sex-role typing and ego identity components: A comparison of Israeli, Jewish, and Arab adolescents. In I. R. Lagunes & Y. H. Poortinga (Eds.), *From a different perspective: Studies of behavior across cultures* (pp. 222–227). Amsterdam: Swets and Zeitlinger.

Vaidyanathan, P. & Naidoo, J. (1990/1991). Asian Indians in Western countries: Cultural identity and the arranged marriage. In N. Bleichrodt & P. J. D. Drenth (Eds.), *Contemporary issues in cross-cultural psychology* (pp. 37–49). Amsterdam: Swets and Zeitlinger.

Vianello, M., Siemienska, R., Damian, N., Lupri, E., Coppi, R., d'Arcangelo, E., & Bolasco, S. (1990). *Gender inequality: A comparative study of discrimination and participation.* Newbury Park, CA: Sage.

van Dongen-Melman, J. E. W. M., Koot, H. M., & Verhulst, F. C. (1993). Cross-cultural validation of Harter's self-perception profile for children in a Dutch sample. *Educational and Psychological Measurement, 53,* 739–753.

Ward, C. (1982). Sex trait stereotypes of males and females in Malaysia. *Psychologia, 25,* 220–227.

Ward, C. (1985). Sex-trait stereotypes in Malaysian children. *Sex Roles, 12,* 35–45.

Ward, C. (1995). *Blaming victims: Feminist and social psychological perspectives on rape.* London: Sage.

Ward, C. & Sethi, R. R. (1986). Cross-cultural validation of the Bem Sex Role Inventory: Malaysian and South African research. *Journal of Cross-Cultural Psychology, 17,* 300–314.

Ward, C. & Williams, J. E. (1982). A psychological needs analysis of male and female sex trait stereotypes in Malaysia. *International Journal of Psychology, 17*, 369–381.

Watkins, D. & Akande, A. (1992). The internal structure of the self description questionnaire: A Nigerian investigation. *British Journal of Educational Psychology, 62*, 120–125.

Watkins, D., Hattie, J., & Regmi, M. (1994). The structure of self-esteem of Nepalese children. *Psychological Reports, 74*, 832–834.

Watkins, D., Lam, M. K., & Regmi, M. (1991). Cross-cultural assessment of self esteem: A Nepalese investigation. *Psychologia, 34*, 98–108.

Weinraub, M., Clemens, L. P., Sockloff, A., Etheridge, T., Gracely, E., & Myers, B. (1984). The development of sex-role stereotypes in the third year: Relationships to gender labeling, gender identity, sex-typed toy preference, and family characteristics. *Child Development, 55*, 1493–1503.

Weisner, T. S. & Gallimore, R. (1977). My brother's keeper: Child and sibling caretaking. *Current Anthropology, 18*, 169–190.

Welch, M. R. & Page, B. M. (1979). Sex differences in socialization anxiety. *Journal of Social Psychology, 109*, 17–23.

Welch, M. R., Page, B. M., & Martin, L. L. (1981). Sex differences in the ease of socialization: An analysis of the efficiency of child training processes in preindustrial societies. *The Journal of Social Psychology, 113*, 3–12.

West, M. M. & Konner, M. J. (1981). The role of the father: An anthropological perspective. In M. E. Lamb (Ed.), *The role of the father in child development* (2nd Ed) (pp. 155–186). New York: Wiley.

Whiting, B. & Edwards, C. P. (1973). A cross-cultural analysis of sex differences in the behavior of children aged 3 to 11. *Journal of Social Psychology, 91*, 171–188.

Whiting, B. B. (1965). Sex identity conflict and physical violence: A comparative study. *American Anthropologist, 67*, (Special publication), 123–140.

Whiting, B. B. & Edwards, C. P. (1988). *Children of different worlds: The formation of social behavior.* Cambridge, MA: Harvard University Press.

Whiting, B. B. & Whiting, J. W. M. (1975). *Children of six cultures: A psychocultural analysis.* Cambridge, MA: Harvard University Press.

Whiting, J. W. M. (1990). Adolescent rituals and identity conflicts. In J. Stigler, R. A. Shweder, & G. Herdt (Eds.), *Cultural psychology* (pp. 357–365). New York: Cambridge University Press.

Whyte, M. K. (1978). *The status of women in preindustrial societies.* Princeton: Princeton University Press.

Williams, J. E. & Bennett, S. W. (1975). The definition of sex stereotypes via the adjective check list. *Sex Roles, 1*, 327–337.

Williams, J. E., Bennett, S. M., & Best, D. L. (1975). Awareness and expression of sex stereotypes in young children. *Developmental Psychology, 11*, 635–642.

Williams, J. E. & Best, D. L. (1977). Sex stereotypes and trait favorability on the adjective check list. *Educational and Psychological Measurement, 37*, 101–110.

Williams, J. E. & Best, D. L. (1982/1990a). *Measuring sex stereotypes: A multination study.* Newbury Park, CA: Sage.

Williams, J. E. & Best, D. L. (1990b). *Sex and psyche: Gender and self viewed cross-culturally.* Newbury Park, CA: Sage.

Williams, J. E. & Best, D. L. (1993). Cross-cultural views of men and women. In W. J. Lonner & R. S. Malpass (Eds.), *Readings in psychology and culture* (pp. 191–196). Boston: Allyn and Bacon.

Williams, J. E. & Best, D. L. (1994). Masculinity/femininity in the self and ideal self descriptions of university students in fourteen countries. In A-M. Bouvy, F. J. R. van de Vijver, P. Boski, & P. Schmitz (Eds.), *Journeys into cross-cultural psychology* (pp. 297–306). Amsterdam: Swets and Zeitlinger.

Williams, J. E., Best, D. L., Haque, A., Pandey, J., & Verma, R. K. (1982). Sex-trait stereotypes in India and Pakistan. *Journal of Psychology, 111*, 167–181.

Williams, J. E., Best, D. L., Tilquin, C., Keller, H., Voss, H. G., Bjerke, T., & Baarda, B. (1981). Traits associated with men and women: Attribution by young children in France, Germany, Norway, the Netherlands, and Italy. *Journal of Cross-Cultural Psychology, 12*, 327–346.

Williams, J. E., Daws, J. T., Best, D. L., Tilquin, C., Wesley, F., & Bjerke, T. (1979). Sex-trait stereotypes in France, Germany, and Norway. *Journal of Cross-Cultural Psychology, 10,* 133–156.

Williams, J. E., Giles, H., & Edwards, J. R. (1977). Comparative analysis of sex-trait stereotypes in the United States, England, and Ireland. In Y. H. Poortinga (Ed.), *Basic problems in cross-cultural psychology* (pp. 241–246). Amsterdam: Swets and Zeitlinger.

Williams, J. E., Giles, H., Edwards, J. R., Best, D. L., & Daws, J. T. (1977). Sex-trait stereotypes in England, Ireland, and the United States. *British Journal of Social and Clinical Psychology, 16,* 303–309.

Wilson, E. O. (1975). *Sociobiology: The new synthesis.* Cambridge, MA: Harvard University Press.

Wright, E. O., Shire, K., Hwang, S-L., Dolan, M., & Baxter, J. (1992). The non-effects of class on the gender division of labor in the home: A comparative study of Sweden and the United States. *Gender and Society, 6,* 252–282.

Young, F. W. (1965). *Initiation ceremonies: A cross-cultural study of status dramatization.* New York: Bobbs-Merrill.

Youssef, N. H. (1974). *Women and work in developing societies.* Berkeley, CA: Institute of International Studies.

6

AGGRESSION, CRIME, AND WARFARE

MARSHALL H. SEGALL
Syracuse University
United States

CAROL R. EMBER and MELVIN EMBER
Human Relations Area Files
United States

Contents

Introduction

Aggression and violence are, arguably, human universals (cf. Lonner, 1980).[1] It is indisputable that the species that is capable, everywhere in the world, of heart-rending deeds of love, nurturance, caring, and altruism, also commits heart-breaking acts of violence. Although many people would go to great lengths to sustain the lives of others, some may readily commit murder. One suspects that many of us are capable of both great good and unspeakable evil. How do these capacities play out in different societies? How do cultural variables manifest themselves in aggressive behavior?

In any society, when aggression is committed, the perpetrators and victims may be unknown to each other, or may have a history of personal competition and conflict. They may even be intimates, such as spouses, lovers, parents, and offspring. The particular violent acts may be negatively sanctioned, (as in "criminal" violence), tolerated (as in playful jostling by children), encouraged (as in some forms of organized "sport") or even positively sanctioned by law (as in capital punishment). The acts may be premeditated or impulsive; they may be followed by rejoicing or remorse. They may go relatively unnoticed or they may unleash vengeful acts no less violent than the actions to which they are a reaction. Or, in some places, they may hardly ever occur. Thus, human aggression is displayed in many varieties and to varying degrees.

Is there a society where no one *ever* inflicts physical or psychological harm to another? Probably not, despite occasional, unsubstantiated claims to the contrary, typically in journalistic accounts of a "discovery" of a pacific society, heretofore unknown to anthropology. On the other hand, as has cogently been argued (e.g., Montagu, 1976) and amply shown by research to be reviewed, there is considerable variation across cultures in the nature and magnitude of aggressive interpersonal behavior.

General Understanding, Beliefs, and Myths

Campbell (1975) saw belief in the pervasiveness of aggression as a cultural universal. But, he also noted, all cultures have developed traditions (ethical, religious, political, etc.) to *control* aggression. There are cultural variations in the manner and degree of these traditions. Prevailing political ideologies regarding individual freedom (Skinner, 1971) and psychological ethno-theories (e.g., popular beliefs in negative implications of "repressing" aggression) can derail efforts to control aggression and even lead to practices which inadvertently contribute to it. Punishment of aggression, to be discussed, is a case in point. It does not usually have the intended effect. It is analogous to old medical practices, finally discarded in most if not all societies, of treating ill heath by bleeding the patients. For centuries, few doubted *its* efficacy, either.[2]

Then there is aggression and violence *between and among* societies, both smaller ones popularly called "tribes" or, preferably, ethnic groups, and much larger and more powerful ones, more recent arrivals on the scene, called "nation-states."

Intergroup relations,[3] much of the time harmonious, often involve intergroup conflicts, which all too often evolve into full-blown warfare. Lonner (1980) noted that ethnocentrism has been a postulated universal from at least Sumner (1906) onward. Lonner also described ethnocentrism as either a variant of aggression or one of its major causes. Later, we will see that Campbell in a number of publications (e.g., 1975, 1991)[4] and LeVine and Campbell (1972), in their classic treatise on ethnocentrism, see intergroup conflict, including warfare, as separate from interpersonal aggression. If there is a relationship between the two, following Sumner, it is a reciprocal one.

So, human aggressive acts are diverse; they occur both within and across borders and are ubiquitous, possibly universal. Little wonder, then, that human biology (often loosely dubbed "human nature") is considered by many to hold the key to the etiology and control of aggression. Laypersons often uncritically accept the notion that aggression is "natural," if not "instinctive", and hence, unlikely ever to be controlled, much less eliminated. In his thought-provoking essay on biological and social evolution, psychological theory, and moral traditions, Campbell (1975) suggested that in all cultures there is a deeply embedded conviction that humans are necessarily aggressive. In the same vein, Lore and Schultz (1993), in a discussion of the "unacceptably high" incidence of violence and aggression in the United States,[5] argued that the major cause of the apparent "inability to deal with" violence is "the prevailing view of the nature of human aggression and its control" (p. 16).

Lore and Schultz, who are primarily comparative, *inter-species* psychologists, dispute this prevailing view and argue, to the contrary, that aggression at the human level can indeed be controlled. They view culture as crucial in determining whether it will or not. They attribute "striking between-culture differences in the use of violence"[6] to cultural "convictions about the potential effectiveness and desirability of controlling aggression" (p. 16).

A prevalent myth about aggression, namely, that punishment is an effective control, takes the form in some parts of the world of a belief that capital punishment deters the crimes to which it is applied as a threat (Young, 1992). Where this belief prevails, (for example, in the United States, one of the very few industrialized nations in the world that still allows executions) all available evidence, consisting primarily of a positive correlation between murder rates and numbers of executions, rather than the negative correlation that a deterrence theory requires, points in the very opposite direction.[7] Ellsworth and Gross (1994) note that American support for the death penalty has steadily increased from 1966, to reach record highs in the mid 1990s. Worse, they add, "Factual information (e.g., about deterrence and discrimination) is generally irrelevant to people's attitudes, and they are aware that this is so" (p. 19).

In a book that discusses both interpersonal aggression and warfare, Groebel and Hinde (1989) pleaded that scholars working on these topics should try to dispel the widely held myths that they consider to be largely responsible for both individual aggression and war, namely, that aggression is an innate drive, that violence follows some natural law, that individual aggression, group violence, and war are completely analogous, and that wars are a necessary (and hence not preventable) part of human life. Earlier, Hinde (1982), in a challenge to older ethology theorists like Lorenz (1966), emphasized that environmental conditions (such as exposure to aggressive acts and frustrations) stimulate violence, and that factors in the socialization of individuals play an important role. Later, Schwartz (1986) also effectively questioned some popular "human nature" myths.

Many of the most enduring literary works produced in diverse societies attests to the ubiquitousness of aggressive acts through all of recorded time. Illustrations of aggression even appear in prehistoric rock paintings (Woodhouse, 1987). Many literary works attest also to stirring acts of self-sacrifice and kindness.

Another less venerable "literature," that of the social sciences, comprising empirical research in many settings and employing diverse methods of inquiry, confirms the picture created by the great novels, plays, and epic poems that have come down to us through the ages, namely, that in every society, we are capable of violence ranging from the putatively glorious to the apparently senseless.

Literary artists at their best surpass social scientists in conveying the emotions, the hatred, the ugliness, and the pain and suffering that accompany aggression and violence. Descriptions in literature may rival reality in their vividness and when violence is presented theatrically—on the stage and, more importantly, on the screen—the effect on the audience may be sickening, arousing, or cathartic.[8] But while such artistic, ideographic, literature describes, depicts and recreates, it seldom *explains* with the force of empirical data, dispassionately analyzed. Although artists may explicate a fictional perpetrator's motivations and other contributing factors, the artist's inferences may not stand up to the light of nomothetic, social scientific, inquiry.

To explain human aggression is the aim of social science research on the topic. And social scientists at *their* best try to do it by collecting data both within and across societies, and organize their findings into testable theories about its etiology and control. In this chapter, we ask fundamental questions about aggression and culture. We note intersocietal variation in characteristic levels of aggression and ask how this variation is systematically related to cultural variables. The goal of cross-cultural research on aggression is to understand why human beings, in whatever society, sometimes and under certain conditions, behave aggressively, which is to say, behave in ways that inflict harm on other persons.[9] For many social scientists, this goal serves another—to control and prevent aggression.

A state-of-the-art review of scholarly research on aggression is obviously appropriate for a chapter in a *Handbook* volume devoted to social behavior and applications. Yet, in the earlier edition of this *Handbook* (Triandis, et al., 1980), the volume devoted to social psychology (Volume 5, edited by Triandis & Brislin) had no such chapter. Indeed, the word "aggression" is not in the subject index of that entire volume. Aggression did not figure in Volume 4, devoted to developmental psychology, either, except for a brief discussion by Sutton-Smith and Roberts (1981) of the relationship of games and sport to aggression. Aggression was, however, discussed in several other volumes of the first edition of the *Handbook*. As we saw earlier, Lonner (1980) explored its possible status as a psychological universal in

Volume 1. In that same volume, Munroe and Munroe (1980) in their chapter entitled "Perspectives Suggested by Anthropological Data," noted that "aggressive behavior is found in every society, but its range of expression is enormous" (p. 283). In Volume 3 of the first edition, in what is that edition's most thorough treatment of the topic, Kornadt, Eckensberger, and Emminghaus (1980) discuss aggression "as a motive," which they conclude is a "universal . . . motive, with an essential root in the innate anger–affect reactions to certain instigating situations" (p. 272). They also cited both biological and social components in this "motive." Accordingly, while we will emphasize here post-1980 social science literature, earlier publications will often be referred to as well.

The years since 1980 did not yield much cross-cultural research on aggression either. During those 15 years, the *Journal of Cross-Cultural Psychology* published only a handful of articles dealing explicitly with aggression; it was disconcertingly easy to consult them all during the preparation of this chapter.

In contrast, a computerized search, using only one key word (aggression) of the social science literature for the six years 1989–1994 in one American university library, yielded some 500 references![10] Most were single country studies, many in journals not regularly consulted by cross- cultural psychologists. Many were clinical reports, many dealt with biological correlates of aggression, some were experimental social psychology experiments, others were ethnographic reports. Some dealt with crime in America and, less often, elsewhere, and several were studies of warfare. Although in most cases these studies were not authored by cross-culturalists, they provide information that belongs in a review such as this. Accordingly, a few of these 500 works are included in this chapter.

Among works that are deliberately cross-cultural or cross-national research, Goldstein and Segall (1983) provided broad geographic coverage (16 modern nation-states from various regions of the world including Holland, Israel, Italy, France, Ireland, Hungary, China, Japan, Finland, India, Brazil, Germany, Peru, Turkey, Nigeria, Hawaii, and the United States), but for only some were cultural antecedents and consequences of aggression dealt with. Most of the chapters stood alone, describing rather than comparing across societies. And, this book said little about aggression between states, which neither "mainstream" nor cross-cultural psychological research has thoroughly treated, even to date. Draguns (1985), in a review of this book, noted (p. 513), "In view of its importance as a social phenomenon, it is baffling that aggression has received so little attention from cross-cultural psychologists."

Both interpersonal aggression and group aggression, especially warfare, were addressed in the Groebel and Hinde (1989) volume by many contributors from the United States, the United Kingdom, Germany, the Netherlands, Finland, and Turkey. To explain the relevant phenomena at either level, the editors argue, requires multicausal theorizing. No single factor, whether biological, psychological, societal, or cultural, is by itself determinant. Moreover, they argued, the phenomena at various levels require separate and probably different explanations. Thus, when Groebel and Hinde consider war, they argue that "the behaviour of individuals in modern war is for the most part influenced by their [individual] aggressive propensities only indirectly" (Groebel & Hinde, 1989, p. 226). "But," they add, "individual behavioural propensities enter more directly into the maintenance of the institution of war" (p. 227). We will also address both interpersonal and intersocietal aggression in this chapter and, later, we will re-open the question of possible relationships across the two levels.

In a thorough review of several alternative theoretical perspectives on aggression, Siann (1985) discusses psychoanalytic, biological, and social-learning approaches. Some parts of all of these approaches are employed in this chapter, but we stress ecocultural forces in linkage with socialization practices, combining to produce some kinds of aggression, including both interpersonal and intergroup violence.

One point of view is reflected in a conceptual framework that first appeared as a diagram in Segall (1983) and subsequently reproduced, in slightly modified form, in Segall (1988) and Segall, Dasen, Berry, and Poortinga (1990).[11] The framework points to the need to study many factors contributing to an individual's probability of behaving aggressively. These factors are imbedded in a complex system with links between ecocultural forces, socialization practices, individual experiences, and individual behavioral dispositions (learned habits and possibly genetic predispositions as well) when they find themselves in situations in which frustrations need to be overcome or conflicts need to be resolved.

Other overviews of theories of aggression include Geen and Donnerstein (1983), who provide a series of reviews dealing with effects of the physical environment, mass media, drugs, pornography, as well as "sex "and "race" differences. An update of the frustration–aggression hypothesis . . . namely, that frustration leads to aggression (Dollard et al., 1939) was provided by Berkowitz (1989). Theories are discussed also in Blanchard and Blanchard (1984, 1986), in related volumes, with some emphasis in both on the role of biological factors, as inferred from animal studies, as well as more "social" theories, reflecting human studies. Excellent classic treatments of the role of learning in the development of aggressive behavioral tendencies may be found in Bandura (1973) and in Berkowitz (1962), both of whose work continues to inform cross-cultural research.

Our central theme in this chapter is that aggression, albeit rooted in human biology, has multiple causes, most of which are enmeshed in culture and hence can be discerned best by doing cross-cultural research. We believe that cross-cultural research, both of the psychological variety and of the hologeistic mode (using the ethnographic record)[12] demonstrates that any genetically based dispositions to aggression (rooted, of course, in human evolution) interact with experience-based dispositions to produce aggression as one of several possible reactions to frustration or as a conflict resolution strategy. Because so little is known about the precise nature of potentially relevant genetic factors, we shall concentrate in this chapter on relevant experiences, and the cultural contexts that shape them.

Definition and Measurement of Aggression-Related Concepts

Cross-cultural studies of aggression, violence, and war are obliged to deal with two issues that investigators working within a single culture do not have to confront (although they may). First, can we define "aggression, violence, and war" and related concepts in a cross-culturally valid way? Second, can we operationalize our theoretical definitions and devise measures that can be applied to most, if not all, cultures?

In their hologeistic research on "interpersonal violence" (mainly focusing on homicide and assault), C. R. Ember and M. Ember (1993, 1994) talk about violence behaviorally; thus, they avoid using the word "crime" because definitions of crime vary so widely from one society to another. In many societies, killing an infant intentionally is called a "homicide." But in others, including many societies described in the Human Relations Area Files (HRAF), infanticide is an accepted practice. Minturn and Shashak (1982) found infanticide in 53 percent of the cases in their sample of mostly non-industrial societies. They suggest that infanticide is best defined as "terminal abortion," because the reasons given for it are very similar to those given for abortion (e.g., illegitimacy, excess children). An infanticide almost always occurs before the ceremony that socially marks or announces a birth. So, when a society socially recognizes a new person (before, at, or after birth) is related to whether or not infanticide is considered a crime.[13]

Similarly, the killing of an adult means different things in different societies, depending generally on the adult's origin. For example, among the Kapauku of New Guinea, punishment for killing a person varied according to whether or not the killing occurred within the polity ("country" or "nation"); intention did not count. Killing within the village and the *confederacy* (comprising a few villages) was punishable; killing outside those political units was not punishable because it was "war" (Pospisil, 1958, as referred to in Ember and Ember, 1993). Because the biggest political unit in many societies (Ember and Ember, 1992a) is the band or village, it is not surprising that killing a person is interpreted differently in different societies. In most industrialized nations, killing in the context of war is considered to be legitimate because those who are targeted for killing belong to another polity. Further, in these societies, execution may be considered legitimate not just because of what the "criminal" did, or because justice is administered by constituted authority, but because murderers (and traitors too) put themselves "outside the law," which would otherwise protect their right to live.

In most societies known to anthropology, the killing of some people is considered a "crime." But some acts called crimes in some societies have no analogs in others. In a society with no concept of private property in land, the concept of trespass may not have any meaning (see Rudmin, 1992). In societies where physical punishment is considered an appropriate form of discipline, severe beatings of a family member will not be considered assault if they are administered by someone who is considered to have that right.

For example, in many societies, wife beating was (and is) not considered a crime. In the United States today, where it is a "crime," newspaper accounts often note that policemen don't always take spousal abuse very seriously. In the ethnographic record, there are many accounts of people believing that a husband had the right to beat his wife for any reason. Levinson (1989, citing Erlich, 1966) mentions many such groups.

When meanings vary, it is difficult to use a concept like "crime" in a cross-cultural study. In anthropological discourse, the cultural or local meaning is the "emic" meaning. But the emic meaning may be too difficult to discover in an ethnographic document, precluding easy hologeistic comparison. So we usually define variables in "etic," or observable, terms and try to measure the frequency of killing a person or of wife beating, rather than the "meaning" inherent in terms like murder and assault. For example, in a hologeistic study of family violence, Levinson (1989) examined the relative frequency of wife-beating (measured ordinally) in societies where it is considered appropriate and where it is not.

Units of Analysis

For wife beating, one obviously focuses on the husband–wife dyad. But what level of social unit is appropriate for homicide? In their hologeistic research on war and aggression employing the ethnographic record (mainly as represented in the Human Relations Area Files), Ember and Ember (1992a) define war as socially organized armed combat *between* local communities (bands, villages) or larger territorial units. This decision largely reflected the fact that, as of the time of earliest description, half the societies in the ethnographic record had no political organization beyond the community. Given this definition of war, Ember and Ember chose to focus on a smaller unit . . . the face-to-face community . . . to assess the frequency of homicide and assault.[14]

These definitions were driven by empirical realities. If all societies had large political entities, killings within the larger polity would be homicides (not war, unless the war were what is called "civil war" [sic]). Similarly, if all or most societies considered infanticide a crime, they would not have excluded it. Still, their decisions could have been otherwise. They could have chosen something close to their own culture's emic definition and used it as an imposed etic. Or they could have focused on each society's largest political unit as the unit of analysis.[15] The choice of focus in a cross-cultural study is arbitrary, but one focus may be easier or more heuristic than another.[16]

Levels of Measurement

Ethnographically based studies measure their variables in terms of ordinal scales at best, because ethnography rarely provides quantitative information over time. Ethnographers rarely spend more than a year in the field, and field sites often lack a historical record. As regards frequency of violence, ethnographies hardly ever allow a rate computation.[17] For example, with reference to the Lepcha of the Indian Himalayas, the ethnographer Gorer (who worked there in 1937) stated that the only authenticated murder in the area occurred two centuries before (Gorer, 1938). The Embers' scale for frequency allowed only for ratings of "low," "moderate," and "high." (The coding assistants did reliably code the Lepcha as having a low rate of homicide; see Ember & Ember, 1992b.)

Coders can often draw reliable inferences about frequency from other kinds of information. For example, Turnbull (1965) described numerous quarrels and disputes among individual Mbuti Pygmies. Although those individuals were often verbally abusive and sometimes assaulted each other, no case resulted in a homicide. Given Turnbull's interest in quarrels and disputes, it is reasonable to infer that he would have mentioned homicides had they occurred. (Hence the Embers' coders again judged the frequency of homicide to be low.) Because ethnographies commonly have the problems we have mentioned, we recommend developing codes to assess data quality on a case-by-variable basis.[18]

Of course, using ethnographic data to measure aggression variables in a sample of societies is not the only way to do cross-cultural research. Other types of comparative study might provide data not generally available in the ethnographic record. One could compare cultures for which homicide and other violence rates are available. Or one could ask informants what they remember about the frequency of various kinds of violence in the recent past. In addition, while collecting geneologies, one could ask for causes of death. Such comparative field studies could be designed from the outset to allow for intra-cultural as well as cross-cultural testing of hypotheses concerning violence and aggression.

With these preliminary concerns for definition and method behind us, we turn now to a discussion of theories and findings from cross-cultural research that contribute to our understanding of the complex "causes" of human aggression, in its various forms.

The Biological Basis of Aggression

All behavior has a biological basis; aggressive behavior is no exception. For aggression at the human level, there is much that is known about the implication of genes and hormones, such as androgen or testosterone. Other biological factors may also play a role, like hypoglycemia, found by Bolton (1973, 1984) to be linked with homicide among the Qolla, an Amerindian society living in the Andes. Booth (1993) reports a relationship in the United States between testosterone and deviance in adulthood, and Constantino (1993) discusses testosterone and aggression in problem boys, also in the United States. In studies of male sexual behavior and aggression, of which Loosen (1994) is an example, hormones and gonadal function are implicated. The only question to be asked about the role of biology in aggression is *to what extent* does it explain aggression. The cross-cultural evidence, as we are about to show, makes it clear that only by *combining biological factors with cultural ones* can the documented variations across cultures, across genders, and even across age groups in aggression be understood.

This position has been summarized in the ecocultural framework first presented by Berry (1971) and more recently elaborated in Segall et al. (1990) and Berry, Poortinga, Segall, and Dasen (1992). The position was also articulated by Boyd and Richerson (1985) who point out how human evolution involves both genetic transmission and cultural transmission. Earlier, Campbell (1965b, 1975) had also argued that cultural evolution, like biological evolution, proceeds in a nonprescient manner, involving random variation and environmental selection. These sources deal with human behavior generally; their perspective applies as much to aggressive behavior as to any other.

If some social scientists in the past gave short shrift to biological factors implicated in the story of human aggression, it may partly have been a reaction to the unjustified public acceptance in many societies of biological-deterministic accounts of human aggression, earlier by instinct theorists (e.g., Lorenz, 1963; Ardrey, 1966; Morris, 1967; Storr, 1968) and later by some sociobiologists (e.g., Wilson & Herrnstein, 1985, who conceived of criminal behavior as reflecting "criminality," a syndrome of traits reflecting genetic and biopsychological variables that predispose certain individuals to become "criminal"). They cited low intelligence as a prime predisposing factor, claiming that individuals of low intelligence (usually measured by IQ) are less aware of long-range consequences, less willing to delay gratification, and less able to restrict impulsivity. This argument assumes that "intelligence" is, simply, a genetically determined trait. That IQ and crime are correlated in some, if not all, societies, has several possible explanations, some having nothing to do with genetics. And, there is Rushton (1995), whom we hesitate to cite, except to show that even as we write this chapter, some still link "race" to "traits." In this particularly glaring example, Rushton (1995), speaks of "Mongoloids," Caucasoids" and "Negroids," and explains "lawabidingness" as "racially determined."[19]

Surely certain biological factors, including, but not only, genetic ones, predispose individuals to react in certain ways to particular experiences they might have in their lifetimes. We will look again at biological factors when we consider sex differences in aggression. However, aggression cannot be attributed to biological factors in any simple, direct way. Rather, our review points to the need to examine different experiences as they interact with biological factors; arguably, cross-cultural research provides a fruitful way to do this.

Societal Reactions to Aggressive Behavior

One important issue pertaining to aggression in recent cross-cultural research concerns attitudes toward and reactions to acts of aggression. Numerous studies focus on punishment, which may well be the most popularly-supported type of attempted aggression control, despite its being consistently deplored by child-development scholars (e.g., Kurz, 1991; McCord, 1991; Weiss, 1992). Some of these cross-cultural studies in recent years have dealt with childrearing practices, especially discipline. Some cross-national studies found differences (e.g., Conroy et al., 1980, comparing Japanese and American maternal strategies), but because so many variables are confounded with parental discipline in a two-nation comparison, little can be concluded from such studies. With a larger sample of societies, such as 110 in a hologeistic study by Zern (1984), one is more impressed when finding that parents differ across societies in how they respond to aggression in their children.

Using a similar sample (90 small-scale societies described in the HRAF), Levinson (1989) uncovered correlates of four types of family violence (wife beating, husband beating, sibling aggression, and physical punishment of children). Punishment was found to be less common in societies with extended family residence patterns. Child beating in particular was correlated with cultural complexity.[20]

According to Schlegel and Barry (1991), "Generally lower permissiveness toward infants and children is associated with adolescent misbehavior, particularly physical aggression" (p. 154). And, "Severe punishment also characterizes the societies in which violence is expected of at least some adolescent boys" (p. 155). They also commented, "Unsurprisingly, antisocial behavior occurs among adolescents when it occurs among adults" . . . "Adolescent violence, a physically impulsive form [of antisocial behavior] is likely to be found along with adult sexual license, also physically impulsive" (Schlegel & Barry, 1991, p. 154).

One thorough cross-national study, albeit with only two nations involved, was reported by Pinto, Folkers, and Sines (1991), who administered culturally appropriate, comparable questionnaires dealing with children's behaviors and various responses elicited by them to 681 mothers of school-aged children in a midwestern part of the United States and to 419 mothers in the cities of Bangalore and Mangalore in India. In these rather contrasting settings, some striking similarities in patterns of findings occurred. In both settings, there was a significant sex difference in reported aggression while measures of parental rejection (reminiscent of the work of Rohner, 1975) and rejection by peers outside the home were both positively correlated with aggression for children of both sexes. Parental affection was negatively correlated with children's aggression, again both in the United States and India, and for both sexes.

A number of within-country studies of diverse ethnic groups have also been reported. Lambert (1987) studied Canadian parents of Italian, Greek, Japanese, Portuguese, and Anglo origins, and found no large differences in parental disciplinary techniques. In contrast, several studies found differences. In India, Singh et al. (1986) found differences in parental discipline between two religious communities (Santals and Hindus). In Australia, Papps et al. (1995) compared disciplinary practices by mothers in four ethnic groups and found that assertion of parental power, by physical or verbal means, was most frequently used in reaction to "bad behavior" by Anglo, Greek, Lebanese, and, to a lesser extent, Vietnamese mothers. Some of the "bad behavior" vignettes used in this questionnaire study referred to aggressive behaviors, but the authors did not specify which discipline was applied to which behavior, so how aggressive behavior per se was reacted to is not clear from the published report. (We mention this study here, however, because parental discipline elicited by whatever their children may do when "misbehaving" can incite anger and aggression in their children.) Earlier, Ross (1984) had found that Australian parents (Anglo) rely on reasoning and persuasion more than power assertion, but his research methods were criticized by Papps et al. and his results considered to be more in keeping with their own. We tentatively conclude, therefore, that there is some cross-cultural evidence that discipline involving physical force by parents has a relatively high frequency. In a very real sense, studies such as these are studies of parental aggression.

Spiro and Swartz (1994) interviewed 60 mothers of preschool children in various clinic settings in Cape Town, of "African," "Malay," and "White" ethnicity, about various "behaviour problems." Although these children were only about four years old, a larger proportion of mothers in all three groups cited temper tantrums as a problem more than nearly any other, and temper tantrums as a category of complaint was exceeded in frequency only by "feeding dependency" and "dress dependency." There was no difference in general frequencies of problems across the three groups, but there were some significant differences in particular categories, including a tendency for Malay mothers to be very concerned with temper tantrums, which the authors explained as possibly "due to the premium on discipline, in keeping with Muslim tradition, that is characteristic of Malay homes . . ." (Spiro & Swartz, 1994, p. 348). Also worth noting is the authors' observation that while many African and White mothers ignored "conduct disorders," " Malay mothers physically punished the child" (p. 349).

Of course, in such studies as those just reviewed, the precise "cultural" factors responsible for a given level of aggressive behavior by parents or by their children can seldom be specified. Indeed, in many such studies, economic disadvantage (rather than "cultural" factors) may be in play. There are numerous examples of studies relating aggression to disadvantaged circumstances in the United States; for example, Bernard (1990) discusses subcultural differences in criminal behavior in these terms, Keenan (1994) focuses on the low-income status of aggressive toddlers, and Skinner (1992) links economic hardship to adolescent aggression. Young (1991), among other students of Native Americans, finds poverty related to aggression within this group. So, we must be vigilant about studies in which apparent ethnic group differences may be confounded with socio-economic group differences. In all such studies, either ethnicity or social class may contain, as "packaged variables," factors which contribute to aggression.

Related to parental reactions to children's aggression and other "bad behavior" is the prevailing set of attitudes toward aggressive acts committed by adults. Some research done in Europe shows that in some settings, at least, different kinds of aggression are differently assessed. In Finland, Lagerspetz and Westman (1980) found that 83 adult subjects (who lived in a university town, but were mostly not students) were more likely to approve of aggressive acts motivated by altruism than by self-interest, and suggested that in European culture the presence or absence of provocation shapes a people's attitude toward aggression. With it, approval is likely; without, there is disapproval.

In Poland and Finland, Fraczek (1985) inventoried approval/disapproval of various kinds of aggressive acts among 64 extramural university students, of both genders, about 30 years old, and found for both samples that violent aggressive behaviors to benefit others or for self-defense were the most approved kinds. Generally, however, the Polish sample gave higher approval to more violent forms of aggression than did the Finnish sample. The author attributed these attitudes to various so-called "socialization experiences." Fraczek cited legal codes suggesting that Polish society is highly punitive and approves of severe punishment. Notable is the fact that Poland uses capital punishment, which Finland long ago abandoned. (Paradoxically, however, as noted earlier in this chapter, Finland was cited by Lore and Schultz (1993) as having the highest murder rate in Europe. This is difficult to reconcile with Fraczek's argument.)

The studies reviewed in this section do not explicitly link social variables to aggressive behavior as often as we might wish, but the set of studies does support the view that there are cultural differences in aggressive behaviors of both children and adults and in various circumstances surrounding them. More attention to the linkages that social theorists expect would be a useful cross-cultural research emphasis.

Cross-Cultural Studies of Gender Differences in Aggression

Biologically oriented students of aggression have found the empirically documented and well known "sex-differences" in aggressive behavior to be of particular interest. But so have theorists more interested in the effects of experience. So, what do we know, *cross-culturally* about these differences, and how best to interpret them?[21]

On the average around the world, males quite consistently display more aggression than do females. C. Ember (1981) noted, "the most consistent and most documented cross-cultural difference in interpersonal behavior appears to be that boys exhibit more aggression [than girls] after age 3 or so" (p. 551). This is true in the United States (Maccoby, 1966; Maccoby & Jacklin, 1974, 1980), and among children in the several societies studied in the Six Cultures study (Whiting & Edwards, 1973; Whiting & Whiting, 1975). Natural observations were made in Kenya (Nyansongo), Mexico (Juxtlahuaca), Philippines (Tarong), India (Khalapur), Okinawa (Taira), and the United States ("Orchard Town"). Other observations, consistent with the prevailing sex differences, were reported from Kenya (Luo) by Ember (1973), from an Israeli kibbutz by Spiro (1965) and among the !Kung in southwestern Africa by Blurton-Jones and Konner (1973).

Across the six cultures, rough and tumble play as well as insulting were significantly higher in boys. (A discussion of rough-and-tumble play, fighting, and chasing in nursery school children in England appears in Smith and Lewis [1985].) In the Six Cultures study, assaulting was higher in boys but not significantly. (However, Whiting and Edwards [1973] comment that assaulting occurred rarely in their samples.)

There was a puzzling exception to the finding that boys are more aggressive than girls. The "Orchard Town" (USA) observation showed no sex difference, even while most studies and meta-analyses show generally robust differences in the United States. This might be due to the fact that the observations were done outside of school settings and involved relatively small numbers of peers available to elicit aggressive behavior.

C. Ember (1973) found significantly more egoistic aggression in boys. In 14 societies for which ethnographic reports on aggression by young children (2-6 years) were examined by Rohner (1976) , either males clearly out-aggressed females or no difference was detectable.[22]

More recent natural observations were conducted in a four culture project (Munroe & Munroe, 1994) among the Logoli (Kenya), Garifuna (Belize), Newars (India), and Samoans (American Samoa). They found that countering aggression with aggression was significantly higher in 7- to 11-year-old boys. The Munroe's (1994) four-culture comparison shows less consistency with regard to verbal aggression, but boys in the four cultures show more overall aggression.

It is virtually impossible to find a society in which young girls are more aggressive than young boys.[23] This is not to say, of course, that females do not aggress. In a single journal issue devoted to cross-cultural perspectives on aggression in women and girls, Burbank (1994) and several colleagues[24] discussed various customs relating to sex differences in aggression, especially as applied to females. In the same journal, Bjorkqvist (1994) reviewed recent research on sex differences in physical, verbal, and indirect aggression and suggested that "since females are physically weaker than males, they may early in life learn to avoid physical aggression, and instead develop other means" (p. 185). This is consistent with Fry's (1990) findings of indirect aggression among females in non-Western societies, including Zapotec Indians, and those of Hines and Fry (1994) concerning women in Buenos Aires, Argentina.

With regard to criminal behavior, the findings are consistent. Bacon, Child, and Barry (1963) showed that males commit the preponderance of criminal acts in 48 nonindustrialized societies. The same appears to be the case in large industrialized societies. In the United States, for example, the best predictor of fluctuations in crime rates has long been the proportion of the population composed of adolescent males. As Goldstein (1983) has noted, "The 1960–1975 increase in violent crime and the stabilization of the crime rate since 1975 parallel directly the number of 14–24 year-old males in the United States" (1983, p. 439). By the mid-1990s, a decline in that cohort in the United States has been paralleled by a decline in violent crimes.

So, the correlation between sex and aggression exists across most societies, as does one between age and aggression. Schlegel and Barry (1991) report, in a study using the Standard Cross-Cultural Sample,[25] "For boys but not for girls, adolescence tends to be the stage during which antisocial behavior most often occurs, if it occurs at all" (p. 39). Turning to large scale contemporary societies, Goldstein (1983) singles out a particular age group—18–24 year olds . . . as the perpetrators of most crimes in the United States. In Japan, from 1966 through 1979, 14–24 year olds outnumbered 25–39 year olds by almost 4–1 in arrests (Goldstein & Ibaraki, 1983, p. 317). In other industrialized societies, Newmann's (1979) profile of the most typical violent individuals shows they are 15–30 year-old males, with lower socioeconomic status, living in urban areas, and disproportionately likely to be members of an ethnic group that is low in the social hierarchy in the country. Naroll (1983) compiled "Juvenile Criminal Ratios" for 42 such societies (e.g., West Germany, New Zealand, Australia, etc.). In all of them, at least a quarter and as many as half of *all reported crimes* were committed by adolescent males, who surely constitute less than a quarter of the population in nearly every society (Naroll, 1983, p. 389).

Focusing on age, Lore and Schultz (1993) cite Blum's (1987) survey that showed homicides among youth having increased threefold in the United States over the past 30 years to become the number-two killer, after accidents (many of them the result of aggressive driving), of 15–24 year olds. Cross-culturally, homicide, a relatively rare aggression, is higher in the twenties than earlier ages. Its relationship to age is probably curvilinear, with declines later in life (Daly & Wilson, 1988, p. 169). For aggravated assault, a more common form in the United States, FBI data cited by Lore and Schultz (1993) show a peak at age 21 with a gradual decline thereafter, reaching 50 percent of the 21 year olds' rate by age 36. Daly and Wilson show that males are by far responsible for most of the lethal violence cross-culturally. Daly and Wilson (1988, pp. 147–148) present comparisons of the proportion of homicides where the perpetrator and victim were the same sex for 22 different societies. The smallest ratio of male–male homicide to female–female was 11 to 1! The numbers underrepresent the proportion of homicides committed by men if we add male–female homicides, many of which seem to occur over issues of sexual jealousy. Schlegel and Barry (1991) present considerable evidence of more antisocial behavior, including physical aggression, on the part of boys than of girls. And, we have not even considered rape, which is rated as occurring "commonly" in 41 percent of the societies that had information on the subject (Broude & Green, 1976).[26]

Hyde (1986) conducted a meta-analysis of sex-difference studies previously reviewed by Maccoby and Jacklin (1974, 1980), as well as additional ones conducted in the interim (clinical studies were omitted).[27] Hyde's meta-analysis, which was based mostly on studies done in the United States and Canada, confirms that one of the most consistent sex differences in behavior occurs for aggression. First, there is no age at which females are more aggressive than males. Second, almost all kinds of aggression show significant differences. Third, the average effect size is one-half a standard deviation (which Hyde calls a "moderate" effect). Fourth, contrary to some previous assumptions, males display more verbal as well as physical aggression, with nonsignificant difference between the two types.[28]

Gender differences in aggression may be so pervasive that they show up in dreams. One such finding in an East African sample was reported by Munroe (1989). In studies of dreams in East Africa, men dream more about outdoor scenes, and express less emotion, but both males and females express roughly equal amounts of aggression in dreams. But, subsequent analysis suggests that the relatively high content of aggression in female dreams expresses concern with their being victims, a concern that may reflect reality.[29]

Thus we have cross-cultural evidence that human males perform most aggressive acts and are most apt to do so as they move toward adulthood. This consistent gender difference within most cultures studied makes it tempting to see biology as the key to its explanation. But masculine identity (how manly a male considers himself to be) may also relate to aggression. Social learning that leads to gender identity involves possible linkages between gender and aggression.

In looking for explanations, many researchers tend to look *either* for biological explanations *or* social ones—rarely is more than one type of explanation examined at the same time, a pattern that we consider unfortunate. C. Ember (1981) noted that studies of gender differences were devoted mostly to documenting their nature and extent (what she called "distributional evidence") rather than to testing causal hypotheses. Distributional evidence *per se* does not point to one theory rather than another.

It is misleading simply to assume that if a sex difference appears early and is nearly universal, it must be biologically determined, because the two human sexes are treated differently from birth. There are cultural universals such as marriage, incest taboos, and kinship systems, but these are clearly not biologically determined. Timing is also irrelevant; late-appearing sex differences are not necessarily better candidates for experiential explanations, because some biologically determined factors are not expressed until later in life. So, we must look carefully at the evidence relating to biology and gender differences.

Biological Explanations for Sex Differences

Two types of biological explanation have been offered for the difference in aggression. The first is that the hormone androgen may be implicated in producing more aggression (cf. Benton, 1992). The second is that aggression in males may be functional and is part of a reproductive strategy favored by natural selection.

Testosterone

Mazur (1976) reported that the androgen "circulating testosterone" is related to dominance behavior. Mazur (1985) explicitly linked testosterone to male adolescent behavior: "As young primate males pass through adolescence, they often become more assertive with posturing and strutting that may be labeled "macho" in human terms. . . . These changes may be a consequence of the massive increase in testosterone production that occurs during puberty." (p. 383). Because there is a surge of male testosterone at adolescence, then a sex-linked, age-related hormonal phenomenon could account for male adolescent aggression. Mazur's (1976) review included some evidence that testosterone-produced differences in early development made males both more dominant and more aggressive, but Mazur (1985) concluded that dominance and aggression are not inextricably linked. Mazur (1985) noted that the literature links testosterone and *dominance* behavior and that it is important to distinguish dominance behavior from aggressive behavior, a distinction which is particularly important for humans, "who often assert their dominance without any intent to cause injury" (p. 382).[30] Whether dominance-striving by male adolescents includes aggressive acts probably depends, in the end, on cultural norms. In this view, culture acts on an organism already primed for the sex difference.

Concerning modes of communicating dominance, Mazur notes that among humans, "violent threat and attack is discouraged in most modern societies as a mode of allocating status, but it is still common among certain subgroups, such as adolescent males, where there are culturally specific norms that govern fights" (1985, p. 390). In any event, whether testosterone produces both dominance and aggression or merely dominance is not clarified by these two papers, nor by the literature generally.

Some early laboratory studies of nonhuman animals suggested that androgen, particularly if introduced during the critical time of sexual differentiation (prenatally in guinea pigs and primates, early in the postnatal period in rats) may predispose females to exhibit more aggression. And early castration of male rodents (which reduces androgen) seems to lower aggression. In humans, some studies suggest that sex-hormone abnormalities (for example, those caused by drugs during pregnancy) show parallel effects. While the evidence is certainly consistent with the view that prenatal androgen may be implicated in causing more aggression in males, there are other possibilities that cannot yet be ruled out. First, androgen generally causes females to look like males (they acquire male genitalia) and they may smell like males (in those species that depend on olfactory cues), which means that others may treat them like males (e.g., they may be attacked more). Second, in the case of humans, the affected individuals (and the parents) usually know they have an abnormality, which may alter parental behavior. Thus, possible effects of social learning cannot be discounted (Ember, 1981).

Reports presented at the 1995 annual meeting of the (American) Endocrine Society led a prominent science writer, Natalie Angier, to state, "As it turns out, testosterone may not be the dread "hormone of aggression" that researchers and the popular imagination have long had it. . . . [New studies suggest that] it was a deficiency of testosterone, rather than its excess, that could lead to all the negative behaviors normally associated with the androgen" (Angier, 1995, p. A1). These reports included one from a UCLA research team headed by Christina Wang of a study of 54 hypogonadal men, low in testosterone, who, prior to any treatment described feelings of anger and irritability; when given testosterone replacement therapy for two months, their general sense of well-being (self-reported) improved markedly over the treatment period. The Wang findings suggest that the commonly held belief that testosterone produces antisocial behavior "may be a misconception." Other reports are summarized by Angier, who commented, "Considered together, the new work underscores how primitive is scientists' understanding of the effects of hormones on human and even animal behavior" (Angier, 1995, p. C3).

Evolution

Recent evolutionary theorizing about sex differences comes from sociobiology and behavioral ecology. (See the chapter by Keller in Volume 1 of this *Handbook.*) For example, Low (1989) suggests that: (1) humans are basically a polygynous species since most human societies allow polygyny; (2) with polygyny, males have more variance in reproductive success than females—some males reproduce little, others (with many wives) reproduce more; (3) the more variance, the more the selection for competitive behavior to get resources to attract mates. Many hypotheses follow from these assumptions; some less obvious predictions are: (1) the more polygynous the society, the more emphasis there should be on male competition; (2) in stratified societies (where resources are more controlled by those who inherit wealth and status), sex differences in training for aggressiveness should be muted.

However, the relationship between polygyny and training for aggressiveness of males can be explained in more social terms. In a hologeistic study, M. Ember (1974) has found that polygyny is more likely in societies with high male mortality in warfare. If war (and high male mortality) is causally prior to polygyny (not a result of male–male competition), then polygyny may simply be a response to an unequal sex-ratio. In other research, C. Ember and M. Ember (1994) have presented evidence consistent with the idea that the presence of war increases the likelihood that parents will increase their socialization for aggression in boys, perhaps as a way of trying to produce effective and unambivalent warriors. This idea is still speculative, because determining the direction of causality that may underlie the correlation between polygyny and war requires research methods other than correlational.

Social Explanations for Sex Differences

What evidence is there for social learning? Because experiments with humans are unethical, we do not have direct evidence linking social treatment differences to ultimate behavior differences. What we mostly have are documented differences in the ways boys and girls are treated. Cross-culturally, where there are reported gender differences in socialization, boys receive more pressure than girls to be aggressive (data from Barry et al., 1976, as tabulated by C. Ember, 1981, p. 555). While these different socialization pressures do correspond to observed behavior differences in aggression, it is important to note that these socialization pressure differences are far from universal—surprisingly, perhaps, most societies in these studies show no obvious differences in socialization for aggression of boys and girls (80 percent of those studied for early childhood and 73 percent for later childhood), at least as reported by ethnographers. Learning, however, may take place through much more subtle mechanisms, such as the assignment of chores, the encouragement of certain kinds of games, the rough or gentle handling of a child, the kind of attention a parent gives to a child, or the amount of time a child spends in different settings requiring different behaviors. Social learning also comes from other children. As long as there are gender role differences, boys and girls may observe and cognize differently about how they are expected to behave. Because, as mentioned earlier, children watch their own sex more, this fact may contribute to a maintenance of sex differences in behavior. Indeed, by the age of four or five in the United States, girls and boys generally have very clear and different gender stereotypes (Ember, 1981). See Best and Williams (this volume of the *Handbook*) for similar evidence from other industrialized and developing nations.

Some evidence links differential task assignment to aggressive behavior. In a study conducted in Kenya, C. Ember (1973) found that boys assigned girls' work (e.g., babysitting, household chores) were significantly less aggressive than other boys, even when not doing chores. These boys, who did not do as much "girls' work" as girls, were intermediate in their social behavior between other boys and girls, suggesting that "feminine" task assignment had something to do with the behaviors they developed. Self-selection was not apparently at issue because the assignment of girls' work to boys was predicted by whether or not an older sister was at home.

A major influence on children may also be the company they keep. Findings from the Six Cultures project (Whiting & Whiting, 1975) suggest that the individuals in a child's setting play an important role in eliciting or evoking certain behaviors. For example, being around peers seems to evoke aggressive and sociable behavior, while being around adults seems to eliminate aggressive behavior. If boys generally have less work around the home (where adults are more apt to be) and more time to play with peers, then we might expect more aggressive behavior for those reasons alone.

What can we conclude about the causes of gender differences in aggression? Unfortunately, little as yet. We think this is because, with few exceptions, research has not been designed explicitly to test theories about specific causes and specific effects, and most lack designs that attempt to evaluate alternative theories. Moreover, few have attempted to test the effects of subtle socialization (such as the role of task assignment, toys, rough play with parents, and time allowed with large groups of peers) on the development of aggressive behaviors. An exception is the effort by Schlegel and Barry (1991), who examined many patterns of variables pertaining to adolescent males and females in a hologesitic study employing the Standard Cross-Cultural Sample of 186 societies (Murdock & White, 1969).

In one part of their study, Schlegel and Barry examined anew the issue of differences across the sexes in inculcation of various traits. Using an 11-point scale, they found a less than one point difference across the sexes on inculcation of most traits, including obedience, sexual expression, sexual restraint, conformity, trust, responsibility, and achievement. In short, males and females were given essentially the same degree of encouragement in these domains. In the context of this lack of sex difference, however, there were greater differences across the sexes in inculcation of aggressiveness, self-reliance, and competitiveness, "with boys receiving higher mean scores in all cases" (Schlegel & Barry, 1991, p. 41).

Another part of their study dealt with family structure and antisocial behavior including violence. Some findings include "an association between violence and a lesser degree of early contact with both the mother and the father than usual for the sample" (p. 155) and "extensive involvement with adults seems to dampen boys' aggressiveness" (p. 163). The latter finding involved a comparison between multigenerational "stem families" with nuclear or extended families. In the stem families, where the ratio of adults to children is higher than in in the other two types, there was found to be lower inculcation of aggression for boys.

Father Absence and Aggression

Studies conducted in the United States suggest that juvenile delinquents (usually boys) are more likely than nondelinquents to come from broken homes, with the father absent for much of the time the boy is growing up (Burton & Whiting, 1961; Munroe, Munroe, & Whiting, 1981). The conclusion often drawn is that father absence somehow increases the likelihood of delinquency and adult forms of physical violence. However, other conditions associated with broken homes in the United States (not father absence by itself) may be the real causes of delinquency. Therefore, as B. Whiting (1965) has noted, it is necessary to investigate situations in which father absence does not occur in concert with other possible causal factors, in order to avoid confounding with those other factors. Clearly, cross-cultural research provides appropriate opportunities.[31]

For example, in many societies with an appreciable incidence of polygyny, children often grow up in a "mother–child" household; the father eats and sleeps separately most of the time (in a nearby house, in a men's house, or in a distant town where he works for wages) and is hardly ever around the child. Does the "father absence" explanation of delinquency and violence fit such societies? The answer apparently is yes. Societies in which children are reared in mother-child households, where the father spends little or no time in child care, tend to have more physical violence by males (Bacon, Child, & Barry 1963). Furthermore, using primary data from a set of comparative field studies in the "Six Cultures Project," B. Whiting (1965) also found more interpersonal violence where fathers are relatively absent. Following the "status-envy" theory of J. Whiting, B. Whiting's hypothesis is that "father-absent" boys unconsciously identify early in life with their mothers, because mothers are perceived to control access to resources. Later the boys want to be like their fathers, because they finally realize that males (not females) actually control resources in their usually patrilocal and patrilineal societies. The result is a conflict in sex identity that gets expressed, B. B. Whiting suggests, in the form of "protest masculinity" or hypermasculine behavior (otherwise known as machismo). To paraphrase Shakespeare, father-absent boys may "protest too much."

Segall (1988), Segall and Knaak (1989) and Segall et al. (1990) presented a similar argument, built around the concept of "compensatory machoism." They, too, treated father absence and mother dominance in early childrearing (both of which are likely in societies with sharply defined division of labor by sex) as leading to a need for stamping in of masculinity. In societies with initiation ceremonies, the process is institutionalized. In societies without, adolescent males may be expected to assert their masculinity on their own, in a variety of ways, some of them involving shows of aggressive behavior. However, C. Ember and M. Ember (1994) identified ten conditions of socialization that theoretically would make expressions of masculinity more likely and only two of the ten (infrequent interaction of fathers and infants, and a long postpartum sex taboo) significantly, but weakly, predicted warfare frequency. With respect to homicide and assault, only 1 out of 20 was significant (mother sleeps closer to baby than to father). These observations suggest that "protest masculinity" is a cause neither of war nor of homicide/assault.

Still, it may contribute to other forms of interpersonal aggression, particularly as displayed by insecure male adolescents. Schlegel and Barry (1991), in their hologeistic study of adolescence, found that boys' contact with men was inversely related to aggressiveness, but in a non-statistically significant way. However, additional details, as revealed in the next paragraph, quoted verbatim, are intriguing.

> *Judging from the finding that aggression is lower in households with a higher adult–child ratio, it seems that it is not mere contact with men that inhibits aggression (as it does [other] antisocial behavior) but rather level of involvement. It stands to reason that men will not tolerate aggressive boys if they have to be involved with them a good part of the time. The argumentative adolescent is very tiring in large doses. However, there is a trend toward an association between high inculcation of aggression in adolescence and infrequent contact with the father in childhood ($p = .07$). This association supports the position (Burton & Whiting, 1961) that aggression can be a form of masculine protest, engaged in by boys as a way of asserting a masculinity about which they are in doubt. Their weakness of masculine identity results from an absent or uninvolved father in childhood (Schlegel & Barry, 1991, p. 164.)*

More research is clearly needed, however, before the notion of "protest masculinity" or "compensatory machoism" can claim adequate empirical support.

Alternative theories of adolescent aggressiveness, particularly of the type dubbed "delinquency," of course abound. For example, Kaplan (1980) provides a theory of such deviant behavior, developed primarily in the light of circumstances in the United States. The theory implies that low self-esteem, rooted in such experiences as parental and peer rejection, perceived lack of competence, and school failure, predisposes young people to commit delinquent behavior. Such behavior conceivably involves actions which serve a self-enhancing function, despite being deviant from normative patterns. Leung and Drasgow (1986) examined relationships between self-esteem and delinquent behavior in three groups totaling over 12,000 male youths, aged 14 to 21 years (Whites, Blacks, and Hispanics) in a U.S. national survey and found: (1) significantly lower self-esteem among the Hispanics (with no difference between the other two groups), (2) significantly higher frequency of reported delinquent behavior among Whites (again with no difference between the other two groups), and (3) the kind of relationship predicted by Kaplan (1980), namely, a negative relationship between self-esteem and self-reported delinquency *only* for Whites. The authors suggest the intriguing possibility that in the United States, Black and Hispanic cultures, for whatever reasons, may not consider various acts that are defined as delinquent by Whites as counter-normative or worthy of disapproval and indignation.

In the Camilleri and Malewska-Peyre chapter in Volume 2 of this *Handbook*, there is a thought-provoking discussion of the disproportionately high numbers of Arab immigrants in French prisons, which might be explainable as a reflection of discrimination within the criminal justice system in France (and in French society generally), or, simply, attributable to higher rates of criminal (including aggressive and violent) behavior in the immigrant population. Camilleri and Malewska-Peyre have concluded that both explanations hold, but that they are linked, with discrimination causing "negative identity" (or low self-esteem) in the immigrant group, which in turn induces criminal behavior. This line of argument is consistent with the analyses by Leung and Drasgow (1986) and Kaplan (1980) of delinquent behavior in groups discriminated against in the United States.

Effects of the Mass Media

Wherever in the world the mass media, especially television and cinema, now extend—and that's practically everywhere, and still spreading—audiences of viewers, including children, are exposed frequently to fictionalized violence. For several decades, a debate has raged over its impact, with media producers in the main arguing that there is either no effect, an insignificantly small effect, or even a cathartic effect on viewers, while social scientists repeatedly have documented negative effects (namely, incitement to aggress among some, especially younger viewers, following a viewing experience). Research in the United States has been done experimentally in laboratories, and correlationally in field studies, some of them very large scale and long term. Many summaries of this research are available, for example, Geen (1983), which summarizes both experimental and correlational studies done over two decades, nearly all in the United States. These, he argued, "strongly support the hypothesis that observation of violence is the cause . . . and aggression the effect" (p. 121). A meta-analysis by Paik (1994) also supports this view.

The question seems not to be if media violence spawns aggression, but rather *how*. Geen offered four hypotheses for the relationship between mass media violence and aggressive behavior: (1) elicitation of aggressive impulses, (2) modeling, (3) desensitization, and (4) changes in attitudes and beliefs about aggression. Heusmann (1983) came to similar conclusions, updating a classic study authorized a decade earlier by the United States Surgeon General's Office.

Eron, along with Heusmann and other colleagues, were responsible for two longitudinal studies of the long-term effects among American children of their early childhood television viewing, one done in New York State and the other in and near Chicago, Illinois. Both showed long-term effects, with early viewing correlated positively with later aggressing.[32] Following the second American study, discussed in Eron, Huesmann, Brice, Fischer, and Mermelstien (1983) and Heusmann, Eron, Klein, Brice, and Fischer (1983), replications occurred in Finland, Poland, Australia, the Netherlands, and Israel. These are reported in Heusmann, Lagerspetz, and Eron (1984), Fraczek (1983), and Sheehan (1983) and were summarized as a coherent set of studies in Eron and Heusmann (1984). Here it is made clear that the oft-replicated American finding (namely, that violence in the media contributes to aggression in the real world) is a phenomenon common to several nations. There were differences across these several nations in the age at which the malicious effect of media violence is most likely to occur; for example, in Australia, Sheehan found that the effect of viewing violent televison peaked in primary grade 4 for boys, which is earlier than in some other countries. Eron and Heusmann commented that ". . . one effect of the specific socialization processes employed in a culture may be to alter the time of the sensitive period when television can have its greatest effect" (1984, p. 143). In all cases, however, there were effects.

However, the effects are not independent of viewer characteristics. Harris (1992) cites sex, ethnicity, and "race" as variables in viewer's reactions to American television and Groebel, working in Germany, reported interactions involving personality variables, especially anxiety, resulting in enhancement or reduction of media effects (Groebel, 1983). Heusmann, Lagerspetz, and Eron (1984) found both in Finland and the United States that boys are more affected by television viewing than girls, but the girls who happened to be among the very aggressive children were those who prefered boys' activities.

Another of the Heusmann, Lagerspetz, and Eron (1984) findings was that viewing violence and aggressivity had bidirectional effects; namely, each could lead to the other. Space constraints preclude our expanding on these effects here, but suffice it to say that around the world, fictional and real violence appear to be interrelated.

Ethnic Conflict

Among ethnic groups within a society, there is sometimes harmony but sometimes tension, even hostility and overt conflict. A broad range of topics pertaining to intergroup relations is provided by Gudykunst and Bond, in this volume. But we need to say a few words about interethnic relations when they go sour, as they so often seem to do. As this chapter is being written, the world seems subject to both centrifugal and centripetal forces, with perhaps both in mutual, reciprocal, reaction. Just as regional economic and political supranational organizations grow and strengthen (e.g., the European Union and the former General Agreement of Tariffs and Trade, now the World Trade Organization), some *intra*national groups, some so small as to be viewed, popularly, as "tribes," are defining themselves as nations. Many of these groups are seeking independent-nation status, a quest which often leads to warfare with the larger nation, or other parts thereof, with which these groups were affiliated. Characterized by the language they speak, the religion they profess, or a revisionist history of prior national glory, they are victimized by, or themselves aggress against, groups who speak different languages, worship different gods, or worship the same ones in different ways.[33] And people are raped, hung, shot, bombarded, and otherwise debased. Ironically, however, there is not a lot of recent cross-cultural psychological research on this topic to report here. But, see Ross (1993a) for the results of an extensive study of conflict and violence in both the anthropological record and in the modern world.

A useful collection of papers covering theories of interethnic conflicts, their causes, and variables that affect the probability of their occurrence may be found in Boucher, Landis, and Clark (1987). Geographical/cultural coverage in this edited volume includes the United States (American Indians, Hawaii, Puerto Rico, and the state of Mississippi), Asia (Sri Lanka, Hong Kong, China, Malaysia, the Philippines, the Solomon Islands, and New Zealand), and a single example from Europe (Basque). A volume edited by Giliomee and Gagiano (1990) focused on three long-term conflicts, those in South Africa, Israel, and Northern Ireland.[34] Many journal articles on interethnic conflict can be found; the following papers are representative. Jaffe, Shapir, and Yinon (1981) discussed intergroup aggression between Arabs and Jews in Israel. Nevo (1984), working in the same country, studied appreciation of, and production of, humor as aggression and found that the Arab sample used aggressive humor less than the Jewish sample, casting doubt, according to the author, on a catharsis theory of aggressive joking because, presumably, the Arabs had sufficient cause to be at least as angry as the Jews. Toelken (1985) reports research done in Germany on aggressive humor directed against Turkish guestworkers. Kanekar and Merchant (1982) studied intergroup aggression between Hindus and Moslems in India, groups long known to be mutually hostile in expression of their respective religions, both before and after Ghandi.

In the domain of interethnic conflict, perhaps the most interesting and worthwhile category of research, inspired by the Ghandians, is called "Peace Studies," or "Studies in Non-Violent Conflict Resolution."[35] Many successes (as well as many failures) have been recorded by researchers in this tradition, which includes some earlier applied research by cross-cultural psychologists such as Doob (1981) and Kelman (1965). Mostly non-psychologists, however, have been responsible for the more recent efforts in this regard. The sociologist Kriesberg (1993) describes in a cogent argument psychological forces (e.g., identity) that contribute to intercommunal conflicts, as well as ways to prevent them from developing or escalating. Political scientists Gurr and Harff (1994) discuss post-Cold War international politics, covering numerous ethnic conflicts occurring in the context of "the changing world order," with particular attention to Kurds in Europe and Asia Minor, Miskitos in Latin America, Chinese in Malaysia and various immigrant minorities in Europe, and review a number of "measures that may enable policy-makers to anticipate and restrain ethno-political conflicts" (p. 151). In another book, Gurr (1993) mentions 233 "politically active" communal groups, describes ethnic tensions on several continents, and assesses various strategies for reducing ethnic conflict. A good comparative politics approach to the study of interethnic conflict may be found in Giliomee and Gagiano (1990), referred to earlier. The authors call for "acceptable accommodations" in these cases. That surprising progress has been made in all three since this volume was produced makes it all the more important to consult. McGarry and O'Leary (1993), whose own disciplines include history, political science, and public administration, provide in another edited volume case studies of ethnic conflicts, and their diverse forms of management, in Canada, the former Soviet Union, India, Malaysia, Northern Ireland, Burundi, ex-Yugoslavia, Spain, South Africa, Fiji, and Belgium.

Warfare

Challenging "the prevailing view" of a sample of Americans and others that "aggression either cannot or should not be controlled," Lore and Shultz (1993) addressed a number of public policy options that would, in their view, affect levels of aggression, in either direction. In one example, they cited nation–state efforts to legitimize violence toward "enemies" during wartime as possible provocation for postwar aggression by its citizens, an idea that they acknowledge was broached as early as the Renaissance by Erasmus (1514/1975). This idea was tested by Archer and Gartner (1967, 1984), who reported, among other findings, more increases in homicide rates in the first five postwar years in nations that had engaged in it than in nations not involved. Moreover, the phenomenon was no greater for victors than for the vanquished. An interpretation of this finding is that a country legitimizes violence during wartime. If it is permissible to kill enemies during wartime, inhibitions against killing may have consequently been relaxed, in turn causing homicide rates to go up.

In Israel, Landau and Beit-Hallahmi (1983) report that, during war, rates of civilian aggression go down, primarily, they argue, because of an increase in numbers mobilized and a strong sense of solidarity among the remaining civilians.[36] Nevertheless, they argue that there is no "cathartic" effect of war, and that war "may be an instigator of individual aggression toward ingroup targets" (p. 279).

That war legitimizes violence is also consistent with data provided by Gurr (1989, pp. 47–48). Although there seems to be a long-term downtrend in crime in Western countries, which, viewed optimistically, implies some emphasis on humanistic values and the nonviolent achievement of goals, people may behave and feel otherwise during (and immediately after) wartime. In the United States, for example, surges in violent crime rates occurred during the 1860s and 1870s (during and after the Civil War), after World War I, after World War II, and during the Vietnam War.

Despite the fact that the cross-cultural data on violence rates are not originally quantitative, it is striking that the hologeistic results (Russell, 1972; Eckhardt, 1973; C. R. Ember & M. Ember, 1994) are consistent with the cross-national results. More war is clearly associated with more "crime" (defined more narrowly as homicide and assault in the Embers' research), in the ethnographic record just as in recent history.

War in the ethnographic record is associated with other kinds of aggression as well. Societies with more war tend to have more warlike sports (Sipes, 1973), beliefs in malevolent magic (Palmer, 1970; Sipes & Robertson, 1975), and severe punishment for all kinds of crime (Palmer, 1965; Sipes & Robertson, 1975). Violent feuding is associated with war between polities (Otterbein & Otterbein, 1965); family violence is associated with other kinds of violent conflict-resolution (Levinson, 1989), including war (Erchak & Rosenfeld, 1994; Erchak, 1994); and some societies (at least among small-scale societies) are generally more violent than others (Ross, 1985, 1986). Ember and Ember (1992a), in their examination of 186 mostly preindustrial societies showed that while war involving such societies appears to be caused mostly by a fear of nature (assessed in their research as threat of resource unpredictability), it may also be partially a result of fear of others (assessed as socialization for mistrust). Whether or not war is causally central to all forms of violence is still an unanswered question, but one set of results (C. R. Ember & M. Ember, 1994) suggests (as will be explained in the next section) that war is the main *cause* of homicide and assault.

The Interrelatedness of Forms of Aggression

In this section, we present two opposing arguments about the relationship between warfare (intergroup) and violence (intragroup). The first argument is that threat from an out-group increases in-group solidarity; if this is so, we would expect a negative relationship between warfare and violence. The second argument is that warfare and violence are positively related because some cultures are generally more violent than others, and therefore groups with a lot of war should also have a lot of in-group violence.

The argument for a negative relationship between war (intergroup conflict) and violence (interpersonal aggression) was presented by Donald Campbell, among others. A seminal theorist in social psychology and an early advocate of cross-cultural research as a method essential to general psychology, Campbell, beginning in 1965 and continuing into the 1990s, developed a position regarding intergroup conflict that transcends the social and biological sciences. A brief exposition here will, we trust, encourage our readers to consult the Campbell papers on intergroup conflict; they are, in our opinion, profoundly significant.

Campbell (1965a), rejected "psychologizing in the explanation of intergroup conflict" (p. 286) and espoused "realistic-group-conflict theory" described in a series of propositions (pp. 287–291) that began with the straightforward assertion that "real conflict of group interests causes intergroup conflict" (pp. 287–288). Campbell attributed perception of threat to *real* threat, as may be found in "the presence of hostile, threatening, and competitive outgroup neighbors" (p. 288).

The Sumnerian dictum, namely, "The exigencies of war with outsiders are what make peace inside, lest internal discord would weaken the we-group for war" (Sumner, 1906, p. 12), was cited by Campbell as the source of "the most recurrent and explicit proposition of the [realistic-group-conflict] theory," namely that "real threat causes ingroup solidarity" (p. 288). A thorough exposition of this dictum, buttressed with many citations and empirical research, may be found in LeVine and Campbell (1972, p. 31 onward). This notion clearly implies that the relationship between interpersonal aggression *within* a society and its participation in a war is negative, not positive.[37] In brief, this 1965 paper argues that intergroup conflict (a social process) is not shaped by individual, psychological, mechanisms, but that the intergroup conflict has implications for psychological processes. The direction of influence is from social to individual.

Schlegel and Barry (1991) tested a similar hypothesis that "when adolescents unite in achieving some common end, be it religious, military, or community service, there is a lesser tendency to misbehave." They found, to the contrary, that "antisocial behavior is significantly present when peer groups engage in religious or military activities" (p. 80). So, whether war causes more or less internal violence is still an open question. But it seems safe to argue that levels of internal violence do not influence the probability of a society's going to war.

That war is associated with higher rates of interpersonal violence is one of the most replicated findings to emerge from cross-national and hologeistic studies. However, this may be a particular aspect of the more general fact that many kinds of aggression go together, that some cultures are more violent generally than others.[38]

C. R. Ember and M. Ember (1994) specify a mechanism for the linkage between some forms of interpersonal violence (homicide/assault) and war. That mechanism is the socialization for aggression (i.e., encouragement of aggression) in boys. They suggest that "war mainly causes socialization for aggression" (p. 621) because parents will want their sons to be courageous warriers. Once people learn to kill an enemy, they may find it easier to hurt or kill anyone. Thus socialization for aggression inadvertently "causes high rates of interpersonal aggression" (pp. 621, 643). This argument was supported by regression analyses and path analyses.

In their comparative perspective on aggression (which they applied both across species[39]—including humans—and across cultures), Lore and Schultz (1993) attended to many forms, including homicide, assault, forcible rapes, warfare, wife beating, childhood violence, and others, and argued that these tend to vary together across societies. They reason that this is so because of varying cultural "convictions about the potential effectiveness and desirability of controlling aggression" (p. 16). Applying this idea to the United States, they state that most Americans hold "antiquated views about the nature of human violence" and are convinced that aggression cannot be controlled. This conviction is attributed to a prior belief in the "naturalness" of aggressive "drives" and "instincts," concepts fostered, they say, by influential works by Lorenz (1966) and "the pervasive influence in the United States of Freudian psychology" (Lore & Schultz, 1993, p. 17).

Segall et al. (1990) suggested that theories dominated by such concepts as instinct and drive enjoy continuing popularity because of the justification they offer both to perpetrators of aggression ("I couldn't help myself"), as well as for an ideology that precludes social programs that promise prevention, in favor of punitive policies (p. 267).[40]

The supposed effect of capital punishment may be relevant in this context. It seems to be commonly believed that would-be murderers are deterred by the prospect of capital punishment. Yet cross-national research suggests otherwise. Instead of increasing after capital punishment is abolished, murder rates generally go down (Archer & Gartner, 1984, pp. 118–139). Why? Perhaps capital punishment, which of course is homicide committed on behalf of society, legitimizes violence just as war may.

Conclusions

Our review has suggested several generalizations which can confidently be made.

1. Human aggression is ubiquitous. It is found in all societies, in which, quite generally, it is enveloped in popular myths that research to date, including cross-cultural research, has done little to dispel.
2. In all societies, there are efforts to control, reduce, or manage aggression. These efforts vary in type and degree, but, among them, strict discipline and punishment generally predominate. But, as was long ago made abundantly clear by Skinner (1971), punished behavior usually reappears when the punishment or punisher is not present. But the illusion of the effectiveness of punishment is compelling; because punishers see a diminution in the behavior they believe they are affecting, their own behavior, that is to say, the acts of punishing, is reinforced and thus, ironically, if not tragically, that behavior is very tenacious. This psychological mechanism appears to be general, if not universal, because punishment is so pervasive cross-culturally.
3. Because most social scientists assign a major role in the etiology of aggression to socially rooted experiences occurring in cultural context, much attention to aggression might have been expected from cross-cultural psychologists and comparative anthropologists; this expectation was not borne out by our literature search. Cross-cultural research constitutes a very small proportion of the social science literature on aggression, violence, and warfare.
4. Biology remains a domain wherein great concern for, and research on, aggression takes place. Much of the research is with animals other than human, but some is done with humans as well, most often in clinical and laboratory settings. Focus on hormones continues apace, often linked with an interest in sex differences (found both consistently and with variations in degree across cultures), but definitive understanding of the role of hormones in human aggression is not yet in our grasp.
5. Sociobiology, with a focus on evolutionary ideas about the possible functions of human aggression, continues to offer intriguing ideas, and must be examined critically by cross-cultural psychologists. (One idea, for example, is that male–male competition enhances the reproductive success of the victors.) Even if many of these sorts of ideas are untestable, we should search for the testable ones, and try to design cross-cultural research that could demonstrate the degree to which such functional hypotheses need to be factored into our conceptual framework for understanding aggression.

6. Despite evidence from Europe and America that supports the hypothesis that attending to fictional violence, particularly in the visual media, contributes to the commission of real aggression, the content of fiction in all media is surely no less violent than it was some years ago. How social scientists, including cross-cultural psychologists, can contribute to efforts to combat the spread of violent content is a question the present authors cannot answer.

7. Cross-culturally, in the kinds of societies described in the Human Relations Area Files, a high frequency of warfare is strongly predicted by resource unpredictability. In the contemporary world of large and small nation states, many other causes of warfare may be discerned, including conflicts over territory and interethnic (including interreligious) rivalries. Warfare, or socially organized aggression between communities and larger territorial units, is cross-culturally related to many other forms of aggression, including more warlike sports, severe punishment for wrongdoing, and family violence. Many cross-cultural and cross-national results also suggest that rates of violent interpersonal behavior increase as a result of war. Socialization for aggression may be the mechanism linking war to other forms of aggression as societies that engage in war try to rear boys to be unambivalent warriers and inadvertantly encourage other forms of aggression. To complicate matters, a Sumnerian view, advocated by Campbell, predicts that participation in a war (an intergroup event) will reduce intragroup violence, and some findings, such as the decline in civilian violence in some countries during warfare, can be cited to support this view as well.

8. Regarding methods of cross-cultural research on aggression, we advocate more multi-cultural studies, both psychological and hologeistic. For the latter, we ask sometime skeptical colleagues to recognize that despite the fact that many societies in HRAF are small scale and were first described years ago, comparisons across ethnographic cases have some advantages. Cultural variables, often merely assumed in cross-cultural psychology studies, can be explicitly isolated and tested for their predicted effects. Also, hologeistic studies increasingly include both simple and complex societies, so relationships that emerge are more generalizable than those derived from a narrower range of societies, such as modern nation states.

   That a society may have been described decades ago and no longer exists as it was at that time is not the problem some critics suggest, for any case, whenever described, is a bona fide case. The Banyankole in 1890 and the Banyankole in 1996 could comprise two separate cases; either one would be a legitimate instance of a society and, in fact, both could conceivably be included in a single holgeistic study.

   Moreover, any hypothesis that receives support from a hologeistic study can subsequently be retested on a contemporary sample of societies, of whatever scale. So, we urge more cross-fertilization between the cross-cultural psychological tradition and the hologeistic, comparative anthropology tradition.

On the Need for Multidisciplinary Attention

To understand human aggression, we need not only study it cross-culturally, we need better to understand the world as it is and as it will be, and to do this, we need the insights of many disciplines other than psychology. So, we urge our readers who are psychologists to reach out to other social sciences, especially anthropology and political science, from which several works described in this chapter were drawn. Other social sciences are relevant, too, like sociology and economics, for their descriptions of the real-world context in which competition over scarce resources occur, often involving groups of varying socioeconmic status. Recommended works in this domain are Reich (1992) and Kennedy (1993), both of which describe critically important aspects of the emerging global economy, including ways it will both unite and divide us.

Applications of Cross-Cultural Aggression Research—Some Decidedly Unfinished Business

Aggression, violence, and warfare constitute a category of research for which real-world implications and potential applications cry out for articulation. The world that is on the threshold of a new millennium (at least according to the calendar most widely used) is awash in blood. Journalistic accounts in more than one nation paint gory pictures of schools equipped with metal detectors in vain efforts to deter weapons, of adolescent gang warfare, of "mafias" springing up in the new democracies, of innocent victims obliterated by terrorist bombings, of hostage taking, of ethnic cleansing, of spouse abuse to the point of murder, of the continuing spread of hate messages on the airwaves and the internet, and of growing support for mean-spirited policies in many nations, including some of the old democracies, directed against minority groups defined by skin color, religion, sex, sexual preference, economic powerlessness, and immigrant status, among other perceived "failings." In some industrialized nations, programs designed to prevent violence are being abandoned in favor of programs designed to punish it, however lacking the evidence that punishment deters. Funding for schools dries up while funding for prisons and the installation of technologically sophisticated instruments of execution is allocated enthusiastically.

None of this human misery is new. Recall Voltaire's *Candide* (1759/1963), its accounts of religious fanatacism, class conflict, brutal warfare, and its ridicule of the Panglossian dictum that "all is for the best in this best of all possible worlds." But one may be forgiven if one perceives that, for the present at least, the world is a very messy place indeed. Must we despair? Must we endorse the fatalistic optimism of Dr. Pangloss?

It would be comforting if we could say "no." But our review of the relevant research does not leave us optimistic. Cross-cultural psychologists in the main have contributed very little of practical significance to a search for a less violent world. Those few cross-culturalists who have explicitly addressed topics relating to aggression, violence, and warfare have contributed some insights into the possibilities of minimizing aggression by pointing to causal factors that are potentially manipulable by governments, international organizations, moral and political leaders, policymakers, and influential directors of relevant institutions. But few researchers have clearly drawn for their readers the how-to-do-it lessons and the guidelines for finding the political courage and will to put potentially useful programs into practice.

There are some rare exceptions. M. Ember and C. Ember (1994), for example, citing the "robust relationship between democracy and peace in the ethnographic as well as recent historical records, as detailed by C. Ember, M. Ember, and Russett (1992)" suggest that "it is counterproductive to support any undemocratic regimes, even if they happen to be the enemies of our enemies" (p. 348). In the same article, they recall the warfare research finding reviewed in this chapter (namely, that war is more likely given a history of unpredictable disasters that destroy food supplies, and, by implication, other important resources) and advocate international cooperation to mitigate such disasters. They argue, ". . . the fear of disasters and the fear of others (and the consequent risk of war) could be reduced by the assurance that the world would share with those in need" (p. 348). Finally, referring to their results on the relationship between war and homicide and assault, with war possibly an important cause of internal violence (see above), they conclude, "If we want to rid the world of violence, we may first have to rid the world of war" (p. 349).

Campbell (1972), as an exponent of the view that man's capacity for military heroism is based in culturally transmitted dispositions, not genetic ones, is optimistic about the possibilities of social inventions that might eliminate war, but he worries about "those societies which are first to lose the archaic capacity to fight wars" (1972, p. 35).

A long-time student of animal aggression, Scott (1992) turned his attention to human violence and, focusing primarily on the United States, offered several recommendations for societal innovations to reduce it. Expressing the belief that "scientific research can solve the problems of human destructive violence" (p. 19), he suggested changes in public policy to encourage full employment and to enhance social deference (a sense of community and concern for others), among other steps. His ideas were also cited by Lore and Schultz (1993), giving them exposure to a very broad audience.

Regarding interethnic or communal violence, Kriesberg (1993) addressed a variety of policies which, he said, "may prevent communal conflicts from destructively deteriorating" (p. 1), none of which could be used under all circumstances, but many of which seem eminently suitable for particular circumstances. The policies include familiar social–scientific, including psychological, ideas such as reducing inequalities, improving economic and social conditions, improving dialogue among different peoples, and enhancing shared identities.

Described by a committee of the American Psychological Association in 1987 as "a social statement designed to eliminate unfounded stereotypic thinking on the inevitability of war," The Seville Statement on Violence was drafted by a committee of 20 scholars at a colloquium dealing with "brain and aggression" in Spain in 1986, and was endorsed by UNESCO in Paris in 1989. Printed widely and frequently since 1990, it is, rarely, criticized (e.g., Beroldi, 1994) and frequently and widely supported (e.g., Scott & Ginsburg, 1994). The latter paper provides us with a coda to our own chapter, noting that the Seville Statement "calls attention to the most pressing behavioral problems of our society—violence and war—and addresses these in terms of the nature of human nature, [shifting] the emphasis from biology to psychology" (p. 849). Here, we have noted that these are behavioral problems in all societies, and that only by studying both the similarities and differences across societies in aggression and its control, can we hope to understand and, possibly someday, solve them.

Endnotes

1. Lonner (1980, p. 158), in his chapter entitled "The Search for Psychological Universals" in the first edition of this *Handbook*, cited "aggression," along with mating behavior, as a good but "slippery" example of a variform universal. In another part of his chapter, Lonner (p. 177) referred to "unbridled and barbarous aggression" as one pole of a (likely) universal dimension, with sexuality (including love) as its other pole.

2. Despite recent suggestions that leeches may have beneficially removed excess iron under certain conditions, the point about its uncritical acceptance in the past still holds.

3. See the chapter entitled "Intergroup Relations Across Cultures," by Gudykunst and Bond, in this volume of the *Handbook*.

4. Campbell (1991) takes into account the views of Boyd and Richerson (1985) in this later version of his thinking on ethnocentrism, as he continues to seek answers to the question, "What is functional about going to war?"

5. Blum (1987) presents a survey showing that violence in the United States had replaced communicable diseases as the primary cause of death in young people and that homicides increased three-fold over 30 years, exceeded only by accidents, in killing 15- to 24-year-olds.

6. As an example, Lore and Schultz note that the "risk of being murdered in the United States is 7 to 10 times that in most European countries" and "3 times that of Finland," which is the "closest European competitor" (p. 17).

7. Of course, correlation does not imply causation, but it is chilling to note that in the United States, where each state may or may not allow executions, those states that have performed the most executions have well above average murder rates, as revealed in a series of articles in the *New York Times* during 1995.

8. The real-world impact on the reader or viewer of fictionalized violence is discussed later in this chapter.

9. This definition of aggression is deliberately behavioral, to avoid the stick problem of intentionality. It is distanced, again deliberatively, from usages denoting "drives" or "instincts." The need to be behavioral when studying aggression cross-culturally will become apparent, as discussed later in this chapter.

10. Other key words—violence, crime, warfare—provide additional hundreds of references. Aggression in its several forms is an exceedingly popular topic for social scientists, if not yet evident in the cross-cultural psychology literature.

11. Space constraints preclude its reproduction here, but it is easily accessible in the cited sources.

12. Hologeistic research tests hypotheses on a worldwide sample of societies. Modern nation states often contain many societies and therefore many cultures (e.g., more than 50 in China, many in Nigeria, and there were several in the former Yugoslavia and the former Soviet Union, while, in contrast, perhaps only one in Japan). The results of a hologeistic study of "cultures" are generalizable to a wider universe than a cross-national study. Further, nations usually have historical documents ranging over lengthy time periods, but ethnographic materials pertaining to

societies used in holgeistic research typically relate to only one or a few points in time. So, in hologeistic research, one examines relationships between presumed causes and effects syncronically, focusing on variables measured at a particular time in each case. It is assumed that regardless of different time foci for sample cases, a significant result should be obtained if there is a systematic relationship between measured variables. Unable to prove causation, this research strategy does provide a way to falsify hypotheses that have no predictive, hence presumably causal, value.

13. Consider how the debate over abortion rights in some Western societies hinges on when a fetus is considered human or a person, and deserving of the "right to life."

14. They excluded infanticide from their definition of homicide because infanticide is so commonly accepted cross-culturally, particularly in small-scale societies of the kind covered in the HRAF.

15. Compare their definition of war with those of Otterbein (1970) and Ross (1983, 1985).

16. They focused on the local community first because it was the most inclusive unit in about half the known societies. Second, most societies have a local multifamily set of people who interact daily (be it in a band, village, town, or neighborhood). If people feared frequent violence within such units, their quality of life would be affected by their perception of danger, just as persons in a small town, which might have higher homicide rates than some big cities, nonetheless feel safer thanks to the low frequency of violence. Thus, frequency is the psychologically operative measure. Third is a practical reason: Ethnographers live typically in particular communities and described their experiences there, so even alleged descriptions of whole societies are likely to be about local communities known to the ethnographer.

17. Indeed, they may not even provide a qualitative frequency statement (e.g., "homicide is rare"). Even when numbers of cases observed are reported, there is usually no total population number to permit a rate calculation (homicides per capita).

18. See Ember and Ember (1993) for procedural details.

19. The pernicious social and political implication of biological–deterministic arguments suffices to make us wary, but to rebut such arguments convincingly, we need far more data than cross-cultural research has thus far provided.

20. Incidentally, in this sample of 90 societies, physical punishment of children occurred less frequently than wife beating.

21. For more information on sex differences in various behavioral domains, including aggression, see chapter by Best and Williams, this volume.

22. Although ethnographers rarely provide enough data to allow assessment of sex differences in aggression, Rohner was able to make ordinal judgments in ten cases, nine of them different from any mentioned above. Rohner found no cases where 2- to 6-year-old girls displayed more aggression than boys. Across the ten societies, there were significant differences in aggression for boys and girls. Rohner also noted that gender differences in aggressive behavior narrow in adulthood, which is also true in the United States (when one excludes participation in war and the relatively rare act of homicide).

23. Because "rough and tumble play" is *play* and not truly aggressive behavior, it is not surprising that the usual sex difference is sometimes absent when this behavior is observed.

24. Olson (1994) described female aggression in Tonga, Frey (1994) dealt with Brazil, Glazer (1994) described a case of aggression for family honor in Israel, and Harris (1994) described Mexican-American gang behavior.

25. This sample (described in detail by Murdock & White, 1969) includes 186 mostly preindustrial societies distributed widely among cultural regions of the world.

26. Broude and Greene looked for information on rape in the Standard Cross-Cultural Sample. They were able to code 34 societies for rape frequency.

27. Meta-analysis not only allows a synthesis across studies, it also permits an assessment of effect size.

28. Further analysis suggests that naturalistic/correlational studies show larger differences than experimental studies and that sex differences in aggression decline with age (preschoolers show the most difference; college students the least).

Because most of the adult studies were done with American college students, age is unfortunately confounded with socioeconomic class.

29. Analysis of dreams in the United States (Hall & Van de Castle, 1966; Brenneis & Roll, 1975) suggests that men dream more about physical aggression while women describe more emotion than men. These studies also suggest that women dream more about indoor scenes, and that men dream about outdoor scenes.

30. Mazur also notes that at present there are no firm data on the effect of testosterone on dominance in humans. Also, the causal link between testosterone and dominance behavior may be in the opposite direction, with success in status competition producing increase in testosterone. So, he refers to the relationship between testosterone and dominance behavior as "reciprocal" (1985, p. 383).

31. See the discussion of the unconfounding function of cross-cultural research in Campbell and Naroll, 1972. A summary of this fundamental Campbellian principle may be found in Segall et al., 1990, pp. 35–37.

32. Eron et al. (1987) and others who have done longitudinal research in the United States also show that children who behave in antisocial ways tend to become adults with many problems, including alcoholism, criminality, and a history of violent acts. This is quite apart from, but in addition to, the effects of television viewing.

33. So as not to offend any such group, none will be named here. Each reader can surely call to mind a long list of such names, however, for they clog the journalistic media.

34. Conflicts during the 1990s in Rwanda and former Yugoslavia captured much attention in the popular media and in numerous social scientific articles, but were virtually ignored by cross-cultural psychologists.

35. A related, newer, tradition, might be termed "conflict management."

36. This is not inconsistent with the Archer and Gartner (1984) findings, because they excluded wartime *per se* from their study precisely because of the absence of so many young men.

37. In a personal communication (letter to M. Segall, August 25, 1995) Campbell expressed the belief that the most effectively warlike nations (for example, Germany and Japan during the first half of the 20th century) had extremely low rates of internal, interpersonal, violence.

38. It may be more than coincidence that aggressive games like football and hockey are so popular in the United States, which has a higher homicide rate and has been involved in more military episodes than most other countries in recent history. Of course, similar games are popular elsewhere, and in many of these societies, various forms of aggressive behavior occur with some frequency also. Soccer games in some European countries have often been accompanied by violence in the stands and beyond, in the cities hosting the games, and in public conveyances carrying fans to and from them.

39. A conclusion from numerous nonhuman studies is that "all organisms have evolved strong inhibitory mechanisms that enable animals to suppress aggression when it is in their interest to do so" (Lore & Schultz, 1993, p. 18).

40. An earlier, and more complete, discussion of the pernicious effect on societies of the instinct doctrine applied to aggression may be found in Segall, 1976, pp. 193–200.

References

Angier, N. (1995). Does testosterone equal aggression? Maybe not. *New York Times*, June 20, 1995, A1, C3.

Archer, D. & Gartner, R. (1967). Violent acts and violent times: A comparative approach to postwar homicide rates. *American Sociological Review, 41,* 937–963.

Archer, D. & Gartner, R. (1984). *Violence and crime in cross-national perspective*. New Haven: Yale University Press.

Ardrey, R. (1966). *The territorial imperative*. New York: Atheneum.

Bacon, M. K., Child, I. L., & Barry, H. III., (1963). A cross-cultural study of correlates of crime.

Journal of Abnormal and Social Psychology, 66, 291–300.

Bandura, A. (1973). *Aggression: A social learning analysis.* Englewood Cliffs, NJ: Prentice Hall.

Barry, H., III, Josephson, L., Lauer, E., & Marshall, C. (1976). Traits inculcated in childhood: Cross-cultural codes V. *Ethnology, 15,* 83–114.

Benton, D. (1992). Hormones and human aggression. In K. Bjorkqvist & P. Niemela (Eds.), *Of mice and women: Aspects of female aggression* (pp. 37–48). San Diego: Academic.

Berkowitz, L. (1962). *Aggression: A social psychological analysis.* New York: McGraw-Hill.

Berkowitz, L. (1989). Frustration–aggression hypothesis: Examination and reformulation. *Psychological Bulletin, 106,* 59–73.

Bernard, T. J. (1990). Angry aggression among the "truly disadvantaged." *Criminology, 28,* 73–96.

Beroldi, G. (1994). Critique of the Seville Statement on Violence. *American Psychologist, 49,* 847–848.

Berry, J. W. (1971). Ecological and cultural factors in spatial perceptual development. *Canadian Journal of Behavioral Science, 3,* 324–336.

Berry, J. W., Poortinga, Y. H., Segall, M. H., & Dasen, P. R. (1992). *Cross-cultural psychology: Research and applications.* Cambridge: Cambridge University Press.

Bjorkqvist, K. (1994). Sex differences in physical, verbal, and indirect aggression: A review of recent research. *Sex Roles, 30,* 177–188.

Blanchard, D. C. & Blanchard, R. J. (Eds.). (1986). *Advances in the study of aggression*, Vol. 2. Orlando: Academic Press.

Blanchard, R. J. & Blanchard, D. C. (Eds.) (1984). *Advances in the study of aggression.* Vol. 1. Orlando, FL: Academic.

Blum, R. (1987). Contemporary threats to adolescent health in the United States. *Journal of the American Medical Association, 257,* 3390–3395.

Blurton-Jones, N. G. &. Konner, M. (1973). Sex differences in behavior of London and Bushman children. In R. P. Michael & J. H. Crook (Eds.), *Comparative ecology and behaviour of primates* (pp. 690–750). London: Academic.

Bolton, R. (1973). Aggression and hypoglycemia among the Qolla: A study in psychobiological anthropology. *Ethnology, 12,* 227–257.

Bolton, R. (1984). The hypoglycemia–aggression

hypothesis: Debate versus research. *Current Anthropology, 25,* 1–53.

Booth, A. (1993). The influence of testosterone on deviance in adulthood: Assessing and explaining the relationship. *Criminology, 31,* 93–117.

Boucher, J., Landis, D., & Clark, K. A. (Eds.). (1987). *Ethnic conflict: International perspectives.* Newbury Park, CA: Sage.

Boyd, R. & Richerson, P. J. (1985). *Culture and the evolutionary process.* Chicago: University of Chicago Press.

Brenneis, C. B. & Roll, S. (1975). Ego modalities in the manifest dreams of male and female Chicanos. *Psychiatry, 38,* 172–185.

Broude, G. J. & Green S. J. (1976). Cross-cultural codes on twenty sexual attitudes and practices. *Ethnology, 15,* 409–429.

Burbank, V. K. (1994). Cross-cultural perspectives on aggression in women and girls: An introduction. *Sex Roles, 30,* 169–176.

Burton, R. V. & Whiting, J. W. M. (1961). The absent father and cross-sex identity. *Merrill-Palmer Quarterly of Behavior and Development, 7,* 85–95.

Campbell, D. T. (1965a). Ethnocentric and other altruistic motives. In David Levine (Ed.), *Nebraska Symposium on Motivation, 1965* (pp. 283–311). Lincoln: University of Nebraska Press.

Campbell, D. T. (1965b). Variation and selective retention in sociocultural evolution. In H. R. Barringer, G. I. Blanksten, & R. W. Mack (Eds.), *Social change in developing areas: A reinterpretation of evolutionary theory* (pp. 19–49). Cambridge: Schenkman.

Campbell, D. T. (1972). On the genetics of altruism and the counter-hedonic components in human culture. *Journal of Social Issues, 28,* 21–37.

Campbell, D. T. (1975). On the conflicts between biological and social evolution and between psychology and moral tradition. *American Psychologist, 30,* 1103–1126.

Campbell, D. T. (1991). A naturalistic theory of archaic moral orders. *Zygon, 26,* 91–114.

Campbell, D. T. & Naroll, R. (1972). The mutual methodological relevance of anthropology and psychology. In F. L. K. Hsu (Ed.), *Psy-*

chological anthropology, Rev. ed. (pp. 435–463). Cambridge, MA: Schenkman.

Conroy, M., Hess, R. D., Azuma, H., & Kashiwagi, K. (1980). Maternal strategies for regulating children's behavior: Japanese and American families. *Journal of Cross-Cultural Psychology, 11,* 153–172.

Constantino, J. N. (1993). Testosterone and aggression in children. *Journal of the American Academy of Child and Adolescent Psychiatry, 32,* 1217–1222.

Daly, M. & Wilson, M. (1988). *Homicide.* New York: Aldine de Gruyter.

Dollard, J., Doob, L. W., Miller, N. E., Mowrer, O. H., & Sears, R. R. (1939). *Frustration and aggression.* New Haven: Yale University Press.

Doob, L. (1981). *The pursuit of peace.* Westport, CT: Greenwood.

Draguns, J. (1985). Book review of Goldstein, A. P. & Segall, M. H. (Eds.). (1983). *Aggression in global perspective.* Elmsford: Pergamon. In *Journal of Cross-Cultural Psychology, 16,* 513–515.

Eckhardt, W. (1973). Anthropological correlates of primitive militarism. *Peace Research, 5,* 5–10.

Ellsworth, P. C. & Gross, S. R. (1994). Hardening of the attitudes: Americans' views on the death penalty. *Journal of Social Issues, 50,* 19–52.

Ember, C. R. (1973). Feminine task-assignment and the social behavior of boys. *Ethos, 1,* 424–439.

Ember, C. R. (1981). A cross-cultural perspective on sex differences. In R. H. Munroe, R. L. Munroe, & B. B. Whiting (Eds.), *Handbook of cross-cultural human development* (pp. 531–580). New York: Garland STPM.

Ember, C. R. & Ember, M. (1992a). Resource unpredictability, mistrust, and war: A cross-cultural study. *Journal of Conflict Resolution, 36,* 242–262.

Ember, C. R. & Ember, M. (1992b). Warfare, aggression, and resource problems: Cross-cultural codes. *Behavior Science Research, 26,* 169–226.

Ember, C. R. & Ember, M. (1993). Issues in cross-cultural studies of interpersonal violence. *Violence and Victims, 8,* 217–233.

Ember, C. R. & Ember, M. (1994). War, socialization, and interpersonal violence: A cross-cultural study. *Journal of Conflict Resolution, 38,* 620–646.

Ember, C. R., Ember, M., & Russett, B. (1992). Peace between participatory polities: A cross-cultural test of the "democracies rarely fight each other" hypothesis. *World Politics, 44,* 573–599.

Ember, M. (1974). Warfare, sex ratio, and polygyny. *Ethnology, 13,* 194–206.

Ember, M. & Ember, C. R. (1994). Prescriptions for peace: Policy implications of cross-cultural research on war and interpersonal violence. *Cross-Cultural Research, 28,* 343–350.

Erasmus, D. (1514/1975). Letter to Antoon van Bergen, Abbot of St. Bertin, dated London, 14 March 1514. In R. A. Mynors & D. F. S. Thomson (Trans.) & W. K. Fergusen (Ed.), *The correspondence of Erasmus, Letters 142 to 297* (No. 288, p. 422). Toronto: University of Toronto Press.

Erchak, G. M. (1994). Family violence. In C. R. Ember & M. Ember (Eds.), *Research frontiers in anthropology.* Englewood Cliffs, NJ: Prentice Hall.

Erchak, G. M. & Rosenfeld, R. (1994). Societal isolation, violent norms, and gender relations: A re-examination and extension of Levinson's model of wife beating. *Cross-Cultural Research, 28,* 11–133.

Erlich, V. (1966). *Family in transition: A study of 300 Yugoslav villages.* Princeton: Princeton University Press.

Eron, L. D. & Heusmann, L. R. (1984). The control of aggressive behavior by changes in attitudes, values, and the conditions of learning. In R. J. Blanchard & D. C. Blanchard (Eds.), *Advances in the study of aggression* (Vol. 1, pp. 139–171). Orlando, FL: Academic .

Eron, L. D., Heusmann, L. R., Brice, P., Fischer, P., & Mermelstein, R. (1983). Age trends in the development of aggression, sex typing and related television habits. *Developmental Psychology, 19,* 71–77.

Eron, L. D., Huesmann, L. R., Romanoff, E., & Yarmel, P. W. (1987). Aggression and its correlates over 22 years. In D. H. Crowell, I. M. Evans, & C. R. O'Donnel (Eds.), *Childhood aggression and violence: Sources of influence, prevention and control* (pp. 249–262). New York: Plenum.

Fraczek, A. (1983). Age and sex related trends in patterns of TV violence viewing and interpersonal aggression in children. *Polish Psychology Bulletin*, Whole No. 1.

Fraczek, A. (1985). Moral approval of aggressive acts: A Polish–Finnish comparative study. *Journal of Cross-Cultural Psychology, 16,* 41–54.

Frey, C. (1994). Serious and playful aggression in Brazilian girls and boys. *Sex Roles, 30,* 249–268.

Fry, D. (1990). Play aggression among Zapotec children: Implications for the practice hypothesis. *Aggressive Behavior, 16,* 321–340.

Geen, R. G. (1983). Aggression and television violence. In R. G. Geen & E. I. Donnerstein (Eds.), *Aggression: Theoretical and empirical reviews.* Vol. 2, *Issues in research* (pp. 103–125). New York: Academic.

Geen, R. G. & Donnerstein, E. I. (Eds.). (1983). *Aggression: Theoretical and empirical reviews.* Vol. 2. *Issues in research.* New York: Academic.

Giliomee, H. & Gagiano, J. (1990). *The elusive search for peace.* Capetown: Oxford University Press.

Glazer, I. M. (1994). On aggression, human rights, and hegemonic discourse: The case of a murder for family honor in Israel. *Sex Roles, 30,* 269–288.

Goldstein, A. P. (1983). United States: Causes, controls, and alternatives to aggression. In A. P. Goldstein & M. H. Segall (Eds.), *Aggression in global perspective* (pp. 435–474). Elmsford, NY: Pergamon.

Goldstein, S. B. & Ibaraki, T. (1983). Japan: Aggression and aggression control in Japanese society. In A.P. Goldstein & M. H. Segall (Eds.), *Aggression in global perspective* (pp. 313–324). Elmsford, NY: Pergamon.

Goldstein, A. P. & Segall, M. H. (Eds.). (1983). *Aggression in global perspective.* Elmsford, NY: Pergamon.

Gorer, G. (1938). *Himalayan village: An account of the Lepchas of Sikkim.* London: M. Joseph.

Groebel, J. (1983). Federal Republic of Germany: Aggression and aggression research. In A. P. Goldstein & M. H. Segall (Eds.), *Aggression in global perspective* (pp. 75–103). Elmsford, NY: Pergamon.

Groebel, J. & Hinde, R. A. (Eds.). (1989). *Aggression and war: Their biological and social bases.* Cambridge: Cambridge University Press.

Gurr, T. R. (1989). Historical trends in violent crime: Europe and the United States. In T. R. Gurr (Ed.), *Violence in America.* Vol. I. *The history of crime* (pp. 21–49). Newbury Park, CA: Sage.

Gurr, T. R. (1993). *Minorities at risk: A global view of ethnopolitical conflicts.* Washington, DC: United States Institute of Peace.

Gurr, T. R. & Harff, B. (1994). *Ethnic conflict in world politics.* Boulder, CO: Westview.

Hall, C. S. & Van de Castle, R. L. (1966). *The content analysis of dreams.* New York: Appleton-Century-Crofts.

Harris, M. B. (1992). Television viewing, aggression, and ethnicity. *Psychological Reports, 70,* 137–138.

Harris, M. G. (1994). Cholas, Mexican-American girls, and gangs. *Sex Roles, 30,* 289–301.

Heusmann, L. R. (1983). Television violence and aggressive behavior. In D. Pearl, L. Bouthilet, & J. Lazar (Eds.), *Television and behavior: Ten years of scientific progress and implications for the 80's.* Vol. II. *Technical reviews* (pp. 126–137). Washington, DC: U. S. Government Printing Office.

Heusmann, L. R., Eron, L. D., Klein, R., Brice, P., & Fischer, P. (1983). Mitigating the imitation of aggressive behaviors by changing children's attitudes about media violence. *Journal of Personality and Social Psychology, 44,* 899–910.

Heusmann, L. R., Lagerspetz, K., & Eron, L. D. (1984). Intervening variables in the television violence–aggression relation: Evidence from two countries. *Developmental Psychology, 20,* 746–775.

Hinde, R. A. (1982). *Ethology: Its nature and relations with other sciences.* Oxford: Oxford University Press.

Hines, N. J. & Fry, D. P. (1994). Indirect modes of aggression among women of Buenos Aires, Argentina. *Sex Roles, 30,* 213–236.

Hyde, J. S. (1986). Gender differences in aggression. In J. S. Hyde & M. C. Linn, *The psychology of gender: Advances through meta-analysis* (pp. 51–66). Baltimore: Johns Hopkins University Press.

Jaffe, Y., Shapir, N., & Yinon, Y. (1981). Aggression and its escalation. *Journal of Cross-Cultural Psychology, 12,* 21–36.

Kanekar, S. & Merchant, S. M. (1982). Aggression,

retaliation, and religious affiliation. *Journal of Social Psychology, 117*, 295–296.

Kaplan, H. B. (1980). *Deviant behavior in defense of self.* New York: Academic Press.

Keenan, K. (1994). The development of aggression in toddlers: A study of low-income families. *Journal of Abnormal Child Psychology, 22*, 53–77.

Kelman, H. (Ed.). (1965). *International behavior: A social–psychological analysis.* New York: Holt, Rinehart, and Winston.

Kennedy, P. (1993). *Preparing for the twenty-first century.* New York: Random House.

Kornadt, H-J., Eckensberger, L. H., & Emminghaus, W. B. (1980). Cross-cultural research on motivation and its contribution to a general theory of motivation. In H. C. Triandis & W. J. Lonner (Eds.), *Handbook of cross-cultural psychology* (Vol. 3, pp. 223–321). Boston: Allyn and Bacon.

Kriesberg, L. (1993). *Preventive conflict resolution of inter-communal conflicts.* Syracuse: Syracuse University PARC Working Papers, No. 29.

Kurz, D. (1991). Corporal punishment and adult use of violence: A critique of "discipline and deviance." *Social Problems, 38*, 155–161.

Lagerspetz, K. & Westman, M. (1980). Moral approval of aggressive acts: A preliminary investigation. *Aggressive Behavior, 6*, 119–130.

Lambert, W. E. (1987). The fate of old-country values in a new land: A cross-national study of child rearing. *Canadian Psychology, 28*, 9–20.

Landau, S. F. & Beit-Hallahmi, B. (1983). Israel: Aggression in psychohistorical perspective. In A. P. Goldstein & M. H. Segall (Eds.), *Aggression in global perspective* (pp. 261–286). Elmsford, NY: Pergamon.

Leung, K. & Drasgow, F. (1986). Relation between self-esteem and delinquent behavior in three ethnic groups: An application of item response theory. *Journal of Cross-Cultural Psychology, 17*, 151–167.

LeVine, R. A. & Campbell, D. T. (1972). *Ethnocentrism: Theories of conflict, ethnic attitudes, and group behavior.* New York: Wiley.

Levinson, D. (Ed.). (1989). *Family violence in cross-cultural perspective.* Newbury Park, CA: Sage.

Lonner, W. J. (1980). The search for psychological universals. In H. C. Triandis & W. W. Lambert (Eds.), *Handbook of cross-cultural psychol-*ogy (Vol. 1, pp. 143–204). Boston: Allyn and Bacon.

Loosen, P. T. (1994). Effects on behavior of modulation of gonadal function in men with gonadotropin-releasing hormone antagonists. *The American Journal of Psychiatry, 151*, 271–273.

Lore, R. K. & Schultz, L. A. (1993). Control of human aggression: A comparative perspective. *American Psychologist, 48*, 16–25.

Lorenz, K. (1966). *On aggression.* New York: Harcourt Brace Jovanovich.

Low, B. S. (1989). Cross-cultural patterns in the training of children: An evolutionary perspective. *Journal of Comparative Psychology, 103*, 311–319.

Maccoby, E. E. (Ed.). (1966). *The development of sex differences.* Stanford, CA: Stanford University Press.

Maccoby, E. & Jacklin, C. N. (1974). *The psychology of sex differences.* Stanford, CA: Stanford University Press.

Maccoby, E. & Jacklin, C. N. (1980). Sex differences in aggression: A rejoinder and reprise. *Child Development, 51*, 964–980.

Mazur, A. (1976). Effects of testosterone on status in face-to-face primate groups. *Folia Primatologica, 26*, 214–226.

Mazur, A. (1985). A biosocial model of status in face-to-face primate groups. *Social Forces, 64*, 377–402.

McCord, J. (1991). Questioning the value of punishment. *Social Problems, 38*, 167–179.

McGarry, J. & O'Leary, B. (1993). *The politics of ethnic conflict regulation.* London: Routledge.

Minturn, L. & Shashak, J. (1982). Infanticide as a terminal abortion procedure. *Behavior Science Research, 17*, 70–90.

Montagu, A. (1976). *The nature of human aggression.* New York: Oxford University Press.

Morris, D. (1967). *The naked ape.* New York: McGraw-Hill.

Munroe, R. H. (1989). Sex differences in East African dreams of aggression. *Journal of Social Psychology, 129*, 727–728.

Munroe, R. H. & Munroe, R. L. (1994). Behavior across cultures: Results from observational studies. In W. J. Lonner & R. Malpass (Eds.), *Psychology and culture* (pp. 107–111). Boston: Allyn and Bacon.

Munroe, R. L. & Munroe, R. H. (1980). Perspectives suggested by anthropological data. In H. C. Triandis & W. W. Lambert (Eds.), *Handbook of cross-cultural psychology* (Vol. 1, pp. 253–317). Boston: Allyn and Bacon.

Munroe, R. L., Munroe, R. H., & Whiting, J. W. M. (1981). Male sex-role resolutions. In R. H. Munroe, R. L. Munroe, & B. B. Whiting (Eds.), *Handbook of cross-cultural human development* (pp. 611–632). New York: Garland STPM.

Murdock, G. P. & White, D. (1969). Standard cross-cultural sample. *Ethnology, 8*, 329–369.

Naroll, R. (1983). *The moral order: An introduction to the human situation*. Beverly Hills: Sage.

Nevo, O. (1984). Appreciation and production of humor as an expression of aggression: A study of Jews and Arabs in Israel. *Journal of Cross-Cultural Psychology, 15*, 181–198.

Newman, G. (1979). *Understanding violence*. New York: Lippincott.

Olson, E. (1994). Female voices of aggression in Tonga. *Sex Roles, 30*, 237–248.

Otterbein, K. (1970). *The evolution of war*. New Haven: HRAF.

Otterbein, K. & Otterbein, C. S. (1965). An eye for an eye, a tooth for a tooth: A cross-cultural study of feuding. *American Anthropologist, 67*, 1470–1482.

Paik, H. (1994). The effects of television violence on antisocial behavior: A meta-analysis. *Communication Research, 21*, 516–546.

Palmer, S. (1965). Murder and suicide in forty nonliterate societies. *Journal of Criminal Law, Criminology and Police Science, 56*, 320–324.

Palmer, S. (1970). Aggression in fifty-eight non-literate societies: An exploratory analysis. *Annales Internationales de Criminologie, 9*, 57–69.

Papps, F., Walker, M., Trimboli, A., & Trimboli, C. (1995). Parental discipline in Anglo, Greek, Lebanese, and Vietnamese cultures. *Journal of Cross-Cultural Psychology, 26*, 49–64.

Pinto, A., Folkers, E., & Sines, J. O. (1991). Dimensions of behavior and home environment in school-age children. India and the United States. *Journal of Cross-Cultural Psychology, 22*, 491–508.

Pospisil, L. (1958). *Kapauku Papuans and their law*.

New Haven: Yale University Publications in Anthropology, No. 54.

Reich, R. B. (1992). *The work of nations*. New York: Vintage Books.

Rohner, R. P. (1975). *They love me, they love me not: A worldwide study of the effects of parental acceptance and rejection*. New Haven: HRAF.

Rohner, R. (1976). Sex differences in aggression: Phylogenetic and enculturation perspectives. *Ethos, 4*, 58–72.

Ross, G. F. (1984). Styles of discipline: Reported responses to a variety of child behaviours. *Australian Journal of Sex, Marriage and the Family, 5*, 215–220.

Ross, M. H. (1983). Political decision-making and conflict: Additional cross-cultural codes and scales. *Ethnology, 22*, 169–192.

Ross, M. H. (1985). Internal and external conflict and violence: Cross-cultural evidence and a new analysis. *Journal of Conflict Resolution, 29*, 547–579.

Ross, M. H. (1986). A cross-cultural theory of political conflict and violence. *Political Psychology, 7*, 247–269.

Ross, M. H. (1993a). *The culture of conflict: Interpretations and interests in comparative perspective*. New Haven: Yale University Press.

Ross, M. H. (1993b). *The management of conflict: Interpretations and interests in comparative perspective*. New Haven: Yale University Press.

Rudmin, F. W. (1992). Cross-cultural correlates of the ownership of private property. *Social Science Research, 21*, 57–83.

Rushton, J. P. (1995). *Race, evolution, and behavior*. New Brunswick, NJ: Transaction.

Russell, E. W. (1972). Factors of human aggression: A cross-cultural factor analysis of characteristics related to warfare and crime. *Behavior Science Notes, 7*, 275–312.

Schlegel, A. & Barry, H., III. (1991). *Adolescence: An anthropological inquiry*. New York: Free Press.

Schwartz, B. (1986). *The battle for human nature*. New York: Norton.

Scott, J. P. & Ginsburg, B. E. (1994). The Seville Statement on Violence revisited. *American Psychologist, 49*, 849–850.

Scott, P. (1992). Aggression: Functions and control in social systems. *Aggressive Behavior, 18*, 1– 20.

Segall, M. H. (1976). *Human behavior and public policy*. Elmsford, NY: Pergamon.

Segall, M. H. (1983). Aggression in global perspective: A research strategy. In A. P. Goldstein, & M. H. Segal (Eds.), *Aggression in global perspective* (pp. 1–43). Elmsford, NY: Pergamon.

Segall, M. H. (1988). Psychocultural antecedents of male aggression: Some implications involving gender, parenting, and adolescence. In P. R. Dasen, J. W. Berry, & N. Sartorius (Eds.), *Health and cross-cultural psychology: Towards applications* (pp. 71–92). Newbury Park, CA: Sage.

Segall, M. H., Dasen, P. R., Berry, J. W., & Poortinga, Y. H. (1990). *Human behavior in global perspective*. Boston: Allyn and Bacon.

Segall, M. & Knaak, F. (1989). Une theorie du machisme compensatoire. In *Socialisations et cultures* (pp. 357–358). Presses Universitaires du Murail: ARIC.

Sheehan, P. (1983). Age trends and correlates of children's television viewing. *Australian Journal of Psychology, 35,* 417–431.

Siann, G. (1985). *Accounting for aggression: Perspectives on aggression and violence*. Boston: Allen and Unwin.

Singh, L. B., Sinha, B., Singh, C. B., & Kumari, R. (1986). Modes of parental discipline among Santals and Hindus: Assessment across communities. *Indian Journal of Social Work, 47,* 315–322.

Sipes, R. G. (1973). War, sports, and aggression: An empirical test of two rival theories. *American Anthropologist, 75,* 64–86.

Sipes, R. G. & Robertson, B. A. (1975). *Malevolent magic, mutilation, punishment, and aggression*. Paper presented at the Annual Meeting of the American Anthropological Association, San Francisco, November, 1975.

Skinner, B. F. (1971). *Beyond freedom and dignity*. New York: Knopf.

Skinner, M. L. (1992). Linking economic hardship to adolescent aggression. *Journal of Youth and Adolescence, 21,* 259–276.

Smith, P. K. & Lewis, K. (1985). Rough-and-tumble play, fighting, and chasing in nursery school children. *Ethology and Sociobiology, 6,* 175–181.

Spiro, M. (1965). *Children of the kibbutz*. New York: Schocken.

Spiro, M. & Swartz, L. (1994). Mothers' reports of behaviour problems in three groups of South African preschool children. *Journal of Cross-Cultural Psychology, 25,* 339–352.

Storr, A. *Human aggression*. New York: Atheneum.

Sumner, W. G. (1906). *Folkways*. Boston: Ginn.

Sutton-Smith, B. & Roberts, J. M. (1981). Play, toys, games, and sports. In H. C. Triandis & A. Heron (Eds.), *Handbook of cross-cultural psychology* (Vol. 4, pp. 425–471). Boston: Allyn and Bacon.

Toelken, B. (1985). "Turkenrein" and "Turken, raus": Images of fear and aggression. In I. Basgoz & N. Furniss (Eds.), *Turkish workers in Europe* (pp. 151–164). Bloomington: Indiana University Press.

Triandis, H. C., Lambert, W. W., Berry, J. W., Lonner, W. J., Heron, A., Brislin, R. W., & Draguns, J. (Eds.). (1980). *Handbook of cross-cultural psychology*. Boston: Allyn and Bacon.

Triandis, H. C. & Brislin, R. W. (Eds.). (1980). *Handbook of cross-cultural psychology*. Vol. 5. *Social psychology*. Boston: Allyn and Bacon

Triandis, H. C. & Lambert, W. W. (Eds.). (1980). *Handbook of cross-cultural psychology*. Vol. 1. *Perspectives*. Boston: Allyn and Bacon.

Triandis, H. C. & Lonner, W. J. (Eds.). (1980). *Handbook of cross-cultural psychology*. Vol. 3. *Basic processes*. Boston: Allyn and Bacon.

Turnbull, C. M. (1965). *Wayward servants: The two worlds of the African Pygmies*. Garden City, NY: The Natural History Press.

Voltaire. (1759/1963). *Candide*. (Bilingual edition.) New York: St. Martin's.

Weiss, B. (1992). Some consequences of early harsh discipline: Child aggression and a maladaptive social information processing style. *Child Development, 63,* 1321–1335.

Whiting, B. B. (1965). Sex identity conflict and physical violence: A comparative study. *American Anthropologist, 67,* 123–140.

Whiting, B. B. & Edwards, C. P. (1973). A cross-cultural analysis of sex differences in the behavior of children aged 3–11. *Journal of Social Psychology, 91,* 171–188.

Whiting, B. B. & Whiting, J. W. M. (1975). *Children of six cultures: A psycho–cultural analysis*. Cambridge, MA: Harvard University Press.

Wilson, E. O. & Herrnstein, R. J. (1985). *Crime

and human nature. New York: Simon & Schuster.

Woodhouse, H. C. (1987). Inter- and intra-group aggression illustrated in the rock paintings of South Africa. *Ethnologie, 10,* 42–48.

Young, T. J. (1991). Poverty and aggression management among Native Americans. *Psychological Reports, 69,* 609–610.

Young, T. J. (1992). Myths about aggression and attitudes about the death penalty. *Psychological Reports, 71,* 1337–1338.

Zern, D. S. (1984). Relationships among selected child-rearing variables in a cross-cultural sample of 110 societies. *Developmental Psychology, 20,* 683–690.

7

ENVIRONMENTAL PSYCHOLOGY[1]

CAROL M. WERNER, BARBARA B. BROWN, and IRWIN ALTMAN
University of Utah
United States

Contents

Introduction

This chapter examines ways in which humans understand, alter, and act in the built and natural environment, with emphasis on cross-cultural work from 1980 to the present. The physical environment is often neglected in psychological research, and we have selected topics that reveal its multifaceted roles in human behavior. The physical environment does not provide simply a passive backdrop to human behavior but is the basis of life, the source of water, food, and resources; it is used in ways that reflect individual and cultural aspects of identity and that shape and channel human interactions and understandings of their culture. Furthermore, cultural variations in use of the physical environment can often illuminate its significance.

Although environment and behavior research is rarely explicitly cross-cultural in design, the presence of scholars on all continents gives an increasingly international flavor to this research domain. In addition, changes around the globe in environmental quality have prompted research on problems that accompany increased urbanization, density, and population size. Worldwide, scholars from many disciplines are addressing the needs of growing human populations amid concerns for environmental preservation and cultural continuity.

Transactionalism and Dialectics

We adopt a transactional/dialectical perspective (Altman & Rogoff, 1987) that presumes that human behavior is inseparable from sociophysical contexts and that opposition and change are integral to events.

Transactionalism

A transactional approach involves several related assumptions.

1. *All human behavior occurs in context.* Behavior contributes to and reflects the operation of temporal, cultural, social, and physical aspects of context. Thus the physical environment is more than a passive backdrop to or static symbol of societal values. "One's daily movements through space, with the attendant activities and people associated with various spaces, are integral parts of the dynamic process by which one continually learns and revises the values of society. . . . The built environment . . . is actively implicated in the entire enculturation process, enabling and constraining changing behaviors" (Pader, 1994, p. 78).

2. *Sociophysical contexts exist at many levels of scale.* One can examine very microscopic levels of a setting—such as the use of space and furniture arrangements in one room—or very macroscopic levels of a setting — such as the way in which social (e.g., status hierarchies) or economic and biological systems (e.g., agriculture or hunting and gathering systems) are related to human settlement patterns. In this present chapter we will develop our earlier ideas that it is useful to acknowledge both micro and macro levels of analysis within any particular setting (Brown, Altman, & Werner, 1992). For example, a decision to marry is a micro-level event that not only connects a man and woman to the immediate context of family and friends but also ties them to broader issues of history and economics, as well as societal patterns of the division of labor, degrees of urbanization, technological development, and the like.

Other analyses illustrate how at both micro and macro levels, the physical environment reflects social roles and relationships. For example, in many groups, where newlyweds live reflects and supports the relative strength of their ties to their families. The decision of where to live can be culturally determined, but can change with economic and resource hardship, which may result in living arrangements that undermine traditional levels of contact and fealty. Inside the home, what settings and implements are used, who is invited to visit and what their roles are, can all serve to reflect or sustain power and role relationships, affective ties, and familial relationships (Altman, Brown, Staples, & Werner, 1992). At a broader level of scale, settlement patterns of a group can reflect power hierarchies among group members. During historic and prehistoric times, North American Cheyenne peoples lived apart in winter to take better advantage of resource availability. They gathered together every spring to celebrate the end of winter. Tents were arranged to indicate clan membership, the owner's status within the clan, and the clan's relationship to the larger tribe (see Werner, Altman, & Oxley, 1985, for review).

3. *Both change and continuity are intrinsic.* In contrast to perspectives that assume stability, this view holds that change and continuity are necessary and ongoing aspects of human experience. Furthermore, temporal qualities such as pace and rhythm are integral to phenomena. Analyses of a Zuni Shalako ceremony and life among French farmers revealed that behaviors across the year ebbed and flowed in accord with seasonal weather changes and socially prescribed activities. Especially among the French families, changing events and the settings in which they occurred bespoke changing relationships among family members (Werner, Altman, & Oxley, 1985).

4. *A goal of transactional analysis is to elucidate the patterned nature of behavior.* A transactional analysis avoids separating phenomena into component parts and does not necessarily search for cause-effect relationships. Instead, transactional analyses seek to provide holistic descriptions or illuminate patterns and coherent sequences of behavior. For example, Oxley et al. (1986) studied a single neighborhood and compared patterns of association between social relationships and environmental practices in the summer and during the Christmas season. Whereas in summer, front yard decoration and upkeep reflected individual qualities such as being retired or having time available for yard work, at Christmas, the decorations took on a more social meaning and were related to group spirit and cohesiveness.

5. *Within a transactional perspective, a focus on the environment does not begin and end with the environment per se.* Focusing on the environment forces researchers to avoid the tendency to treat social processes in the abstract, without examining the range of contextual features that are intrinsic to the substance and execution of social processes. Thus, a phenomenon—a social, physical, and temporal reality— becomes the unit of analysis, not just an abstract process such as motivation, or spousal interactions, or economic exchange. To understand how a society lives in homes, for example, the focus must go beyond the walls of the home to encompass historical and cultural traditions and changes in the society and in the availability of resources. It may require understanding how work and home life are related, how food is obtained and how cooking gets done, what inheritance patterns exist, what community planning parameters exist in the neighborhood, and so forth. Thus, beginning with the environment is just one step into a journey that can involve explorations of history, architecture, psychology, sociology, planning, political science, and theology.

Although this chapter focuses specifically upon the assumptions of a transactional approach, many other approaches in psychology also emphasize the interdependence of behavior and the physical environment. Social production theorists (summarized in Lawrence & Low, 1990), for example, argue that everyday activities in micro-level settings give substance and reality to larger scale social or political structures. Behavior-setting theorists (Wicker, 1979) examine the contribution of both human and physical features to the coherent creation of a setting with its own regulating and dynamic features. In this view, the only tangible connection to larger, abstract, social processes and institutions is through the range and nature of behavior settings available to individuals. Similarly, personality psychologists often adopt a person–environment psychology that connects individuals within their sociophysical context (Walsh, Craik, & Price, 1992). Systems approaches (e.g., Bronfenbrenner, 1979) recognize that behavior is a function of a variety of physical and cultural forces acting on the individual in fairly concrete ways over time. And finally, cross-cultural scholars such as Segall et al. (1990) and Berry et al. (1992) also argued that human behaviors always occur in an ecocultural context. Thus, although a transactional approach is a specific one, its goals are in keeping with many allied approaches that view behavior as integral with the socioenvironmental context.

Dialectics

Kagitçibasi addresses individualism/collectivism in a chapter in this volume. We, too, find it useful to adopt a dialectic perspective that assumes that both individualistic and communal forces are always at play in human behavior. Too much emphasis on the individual or subgroup can destroy the collective, and too much emphasis on the collective may undermine the individual or subgroup. At a broader level of scale is a species/ecosystem dialectic with the same theme: too much domination or consumption by an individual species can destroy the ecosystem, and too much pressure from the system on the species can undermine its individual viability.

Our conception of dialectics is similar to those emerging in studies of social relationships (Altman, Vinsel, & Brown, 1981; Baxter, 1993; Werner & Baxter, 1994), which emphasize that relationships involve an ever-present interplay of oppositional processes rather than any attempt to achieve a single, ideal, balanced end-state. In our perspective, an individual/society or autonomy/connection dialectic can involve individuals or clusters at many levels of scale, such as a single individual in opposition to a dyad, a nuclear family, an extended family, a social or religious group, and so on; it can involve any size collective in opposition to another, such as a dyad in opposition to the nuclear family, extended family, social group, and so on. And finally, we see dialectics as complementary to a transactional worldview, as an essential "motor" that defines and shapes ongoing processes in phenomena (cf. Reice, 1994, on ecosystems as nonhomeostatic).

The relationship between individuals and society may be seen as both oppositional and complementary. For example, Northern Athapaskan and Algonquian hunters are described as belonging to a highly individualistic society (Ridington, 1988). Yet individualism is "sustained by their closely contexted communities" (p. 108) in which essential knowledge about social and natural conditions are shared. That is, individuals can be autonomous precisely because they have learned the society's repertoire of survival techniques. Furthermore, forces toward individuality and community shift and change in potency over time. Thus, individualism waxes during solitary hunts and times when bands are moving; community orientation predominates during times of socialization, ceremony, or sharing.

Chapter Overview

The chapter begins with an examination of humans' worldviews and relationships to nature and how those guide behaviors in the environment; the issues are largely about resource consumption, and dialectic tensions between individuals and groups and involving humans and nature are salient. The subsequent section examines how a variety of social and interpersonal processes are managed or change under changing physical and social circumstances. We focus in particular on how people cope with changes in personal and social identities and with changing levels of openness and social density. Throughout, we illustrate the transactional perspective that behaviors at multiple levels of functioning—including the physical environment—combine in holistic ways as people adapt their ways of behaving to changing circumstances.[2]

Environment and Consumptive Processes

World Views of Nature

History, philosophy, and mythology are all concerned with the relationship of people to nature. Both oral and written histories indicate that people have been concerned with the physical environment, sometimes viewing it as hostile, sometimes as nurturant, sometimes seeing themselves as part of the environment, and sometimes believing themselves to be separate from (and often above) nature. Indeed, most anthropologists agree that human societies originally developed religion, magic, and rituals in order to gain a sense of control over an uncertain environment on which they depended for food, water, and shelter, but which also brought catastrophic events such as earthquakes, hurricanes, mudslides, and so on.

Scholars and environmental writers from several disciplines have explored human/nature relationships (e.g., Altman & Chemers, 1980a, 1980b; Devall & Sessions, 1985; Joranson & Butigan, 1984; Nash, 1990). Most descriptions are at least partly consistent with Kluckhohn's (1953) analysis that cultures can be characterized as to whether they believe that (1) people are subjugated to nature and live at the whim of powerful and uncompromising natural forces, (2) people are an inherent part of nature, like animals, trees and rivers, and should live in harmony with their environment, or (3) people are separate from nature and have the power, right, and even the obligation to control the natural world. Of course, these are general characterizations, and both individuals and societies may include a mix of the three perspectives, with the strength of worldviews shifting in response to circumstances.

Humans Subordinate to Nature

Altman and Chemers (1980b) provided several examples of societies whose dominant belief is that they live at the whim of an unpredictable and uncontrollable nature. They suggested that this view was most typical of groups having little industrial technology or who lived in particularly harsh climates; they also stressed that this view was likely to emerge during periods of natural disasters or atypical weather patterns. Many societies have myths and beliefs about monsters, witches, vampires, or other creatures that live in woods, water, and forests ready to attack any unsuspecting passerby. Natural areas are often contrasted with urban areas, especially homes, which are seen as places of refuge against a dangerous outer world. Although this worldview has not been as well documented or widespread as the other two, there is some evidence that people view nature as powerful and uncontrollable and view themselves as passive recipients of both good and bad events.

Humans in Harmony with Nature

Many no-Western groups, especially before encounters with Europeans, held the view that they were integral with nature, a view that was evident in many aspects of their beliefs and practices, such as annual planting and harvesting ceremonies, hunting and fishing rituals, daily prayers, and many other aspects of their spiritual and survival behaviors (see for example, Goodwin, 1977; McCay & Acheson, 1987; and Suzuki & Knudtson, 1992). By balancing consumption with available resources or relocating to allow a degraded environment to restore itself, humans and their environments survived and prospered for many thousands of years. Suzuki and Knudtson (1992) suggested that traditional peoples developed a sophisticated understanding of the interdependency of species as reflected in their songs, stories, and myths.

Research suggests that practices acknowledging interdependency have helped preserve ecosystem health. Goodwin (1977) reviewed behaviors of the Cherokee peoples in the United States before and after European settlement. He argued that, before Europeans arrived, the Cherokee actively managed their environment to shape a healthy ecosystem in which they could flourish. Thus, they changed their environment to suit their needs, but did so without undermining general ecosystem functioning. For example, although they might start a fire to regulate plant species or drive game into the open, they used this practice judiciously in order to preserve other food sources. Post-settlement, however, the Cherokee engaged in more devastating behaviors such as harvesting larger numbers of fur-bearing species in order to use them for trade, ultimately decimating their food supply and undermining their own viability. They adopted European cultivation and animal farming practices that degraded the environment and eliminated natural sources of food, again altering the local habitat and undermining their traditional practices, health, and viability.

Berkes (1987), comparing fishing practices of Cree people in subarctic Canada with harvesting recommendations of modern scientific management, found that the Cree violated several key scientific principles, yet the populations of fish over which they had control were high and had been so for at least 40 years. Berkes noted that many of the Cree practices were self-limiting, having minimal impact on the ecosystem in which the Cree were interdependent (e.g., harvesting only what they needed and giving away rather than storing excess; catching fish of mixed sizes, thereby leaving a population of mixed-age fish that maintained both general ecosystem balance and the fishes' potential for reproductive success). Thus, a common theme in the world views and practices of many pre-industrial peoples is that by taking only what they needed and with minimum impact, they lived in harmony with and were an integral part of nature.

This view has been challenged by anthropologists. One line of thought holds that even in ancient times some people opted for short-term human benefits at long-term environmental costs; another challenges whether self-limiting behaviors represent genuine conservation and harmonious values or are simply side effects of other processes, including lack of technology; and a third suggests that living in harmony only evolved after widespread ecosystem devastation. We consider each in turn.

Advocates of the first challenge suggest that living in harmony with nature may be true of small groups with diverse economies, but is inconsistent with archeological evidence from large-scale civilizations (Jacobsen & Firor, 1992). The argument is that all societies have had an impact on the environment and major environmental destruction has occurred when people use technologies that provide short-term gains at long-term environmental costs. Environment-sustaining mechanisms were not implemented because the long-term costs could not be anticipated and because emerging technologies gave the appearance that high consumption patterns could be sustained. For example, Redman (1992; see also Lowe, 1985) reviewed archeological evidence from Ancient Greece, Mesopotamia, and the southwestern United States indicating that when people learned how to farm more efficiently (e.g., with massive irrigation systems) there were resulting rapid rises in population; eventually, the numbers of people exceeded technology's ability to provide food and clean water, and the population declined. In fact, archeologists speculate that Ancient Mesopotamia experienced ground salinization problems such as are occurring today in parts of the United States, precluding further use of the land for agriculture. In Greece, farming and then overgrazing of marginal agricultural lands is blamed for large-scale soil erosion and the restriction of population to smaller arable land. A similar pattern has been implicated in the rise and fall of civilization in the Copan Valley of Central America (Lowe, 1985).

The second challenge asks whether indigenous peoples really "conserve" or whether conservation is simply a fortuitous side effect of other practices or constraints (including lack of technology, Brightman, 1987). This view is still being developed, but generally takes the position that people *have* evolved within their ecosystem and many *have* developed practices that avoid overharvesting; the question is whether conservation or some other purpose (such as hunting efficiency) drives the process (Hames, 1987). Although he was not an advocate of this position, Goodwin (1977) observed that the Cherokee nation resisted European cultivation equipment (especially the plow) not because it was harmful to the environment, but rather because it required fewer workers, disrupting traditional group farming practice.

The final challenge takes a more mixed view of traditional peoples. In this view, conservation practices only occurred after ecological disasters. That is, in ancient times, some groups did overharvest to the point that one or more prey species became extinct, threatening the society's health; only then did the group develop practices to moderate their environmental impact and live integral to their ecosystem. Thus, these approaches argue that traditional people should not be romanticized, are capable of destroying their environment, but are also capable of learning from the experience (e.g., Brightman, 1987).

A reconciliation of these positions is difficult: Do groups hold and practice a value that it is important to live in harmony with nature? One response is to gather additional evidence from ancient songs and myths that express native people's intuitive understandings of human's interconnectedness with nature (e.g., Suzuki & Knudtson, 1992, pp. 66–67). Another argument is that practice is more important than underlying values or attitudes. That is, if groups do not overharvest and in other ways maintain ecosystem viability, these very practices constitute living in harmony with nature and it doesn't matter what their cognitive or attitudinal base is or why they developed.

Humans Dominant over Nature

Kluckhohn's (1953) third orientation partly fits with Western, Judeo-Christian world views of the environment (see Devall & Sessions, 1985, for review). White (1967/ 1974) traced changes in Christian theology during the Middle Ages as technology gave increasing control over nature and Christian world views changed from an emphasis on harmony with nature to an emphasis on humans as separate from and dominant over nature. People were not just another object in the world, but were special beings of divine origin who were put on earth to do God's will. In addition, a cause and effect perspective grew that emphasized a chain of events rather than an appreciation of living, holistic systems. As Altman and Chemers (1980a, 1980b) and Nash (1990) have shown, the duality of people and nature and emphasis on causality was manifested in multiple ways in art, literature, recreation, and science.

This worldview suggests a competition/cooperation dialectic between humans and nature. That is, although Judeo-Christian theologies emphasize a need to balance cooperation and competition (e.g., share one's bounty with others) among people, there is no similar concern expressed about nature, which is there to be consumed. It is rare for their societies to hold back in harvesting of a resource or giving aid to nonhuman species until that species or its predator is endangered, and even then species' safety is not assured. Thus, although there is evidence of dialectic forces operating to increase sharing and mutual aid and protection among humans, there is little evidence that these forces impinge on human behaviors vis à vis other species until human welfare is threatened or until there is a clear crisis for a species.

These values still predominate in Western culture, as reflected in "multiple use management" of public lands, predator control and game management programs, large-scale agriculture with its use of chemical pesticides and fertilizers and genetically engineered plants and animals, and in dikes and dams and seawalls (even though these are destroyed periodically by "century" storms). In a small yet significant example of this view, Jenkins (1994) reviewed the history of lawns in the United States and argued that they represent one form of this "war" on nature, that is, the United States tendency to attempt to dominate and control nature with non-native plantings, chemicals, and mechanized equipment.

At the same time, there is evidence of changing values and practices, such as Alfred North Whitehead's efforts to bring a systems view to Western thought (Joranson & Butigan, 1984; Spring & Spring, 1974) and other efforts to reinterpret biblical passages and humans' role in the world to emphasize harmony with and protection of nature (Carmody, 1983; Ehrenfeld, 1978). These scholars decry the destruction of nature and the use of biblical passages to justify it; they urge a new look at Christianity and modern humanity's fundamental values. Philosophers (many of them self-proclaimed "eco-ethicists") are exploring the ethical implications of reframing social philosophy to be less anthropocentric and more geocentric (Scherer, 1990). For example, Schrader-Frechette (1990) argued that mathematical models of environmental impact are often inadequate for predicting long-term consequences, leading to environmental disasters; she implied that society should not be willing to accept this level of uncertainty in its decision-making. Other writers and scholars simply sidestepped the Judeo-Christian and social contract philosophies, and proposed Eastern and other non-Western philosophies as more appropriate guides to human-environment relations (e.g., Corrington, 1992; Devall & Sessions, 1985; Nash, 1990; Suzuki & Knudtson, 1992). As manifestations of these value shifts, U.S., Australian, and European activists, such as the Green Party, have engaged in direct confrontations as well as secret assaults to protect natural environments.

Indeed, all around the world, there has been increasing concern about the health of ecosystems on which humans depend, especially with the use of increasingly destructive technologies (Calthorpe, 1993; Schnaiberg & Gould, 1994; Thayer, 1994). There has been considerable tension and debate around whether development can be sustained, whether we can continue to use manufactured chemicals in food production, whether we can continue to produce toxic chemicals and tolerate harmful spills, how we decide whether and what technology to use, whether Euro-Americans can continue the rich lifestyles that so many take for granted, and what will happen when people all around the globe achieve similar levels of consumption and waste (see, for example, Kagitçibasi, 1991; Pawlik, 1991).

There is social and political pressure to preserve natural habitats by limiting and even reducing the size of the human population as well as reducing our consumption of resources and our destruction of natural environments all around the globe. Advocates of this position argue that if we do not act quickly and dramatically to save the earth's total ecosystem there will be a widespread decline, and many of the individuals that it supports—including humans—will die. Others argue that the problem is not serious and can be solved with improved technologies; they note that if we do not cultivate new land or harvest the available animals, people will die, and people should not be expected to die in order to preserve other species. These are very difficult issues without easy solutions, and they pose a number of psychological questions beyond the scope of the present chapter, including: Is it possible to live in harmony with nature given human population size? What are the individual and social reasons for having children? What are the individual and social reasons for high levels of consumption? What are the implications of short- and long-term views of resource consumption? Some insights into these issues may be gained by examining the Tragedy of the Commons dilemma.

Commons Dilemmas and Resource Conservation

The Tragedy of the Commons has been used to illustrate fundamental questions of human social and economic systems: How do users share a natural resource without overusing it and ultimately destroying it (Roberts & Emel, 1992)? How do individuals maximize their individual gains and yet maintain the health of the whole? Hardin's (1968) popularization of the problem first brought it to psychologists' attention, although it had been used for many years to illustrate the fundamental conflict underlying individual and group needs.

Whereas the problem is defined typically as an either/or proposition, we believe that it is fruitful to cast it as a dialectic in which both individuals and collectives must achieve adequate outcomes. Indeed, as we will describe, the traditional economic assumption that humans always act competitively is inconsistent with ethnographic evidence. Furthermore, and in accord with a transactional view, ethnographic analyses also indicate that groups use a complex and interconnected array of mechanisms for managing resource consumption.

The problem is posed as farmers grazing their cattle on a Commons, or shared field. Each farmer would benefit by putting more and more cattle on the Commons, but if they all put on too many cattle, the area would be destroyed by overgrazing and the cattle and farmers would die of starvation. There has been considerable laboratory research on this question, and although explicitly cross-cultural comparisons are rare, research has been conducted in diverse countries including the United States, Canada, Japan, Germany, Netherlands, and Israel, among others. The work generally shows that individuals in these countries act in self-interested ways unless the group's or ecosystem interests are made clear to them, in which cases they usually act for the good of all. This also implies that the Commons Dilemma is not a dilemma if participants appreciate their interdependency with the group and the ecosystem (and as long as population size does not exceed carrying capacity). The typical laboratory scenario is to let groups of individuals cycle through a series of decisions about how much of a resource to harvest; after each harvest, the resource is replenished partially or completely; if at any point, the group overharvests and draws more of the resource than exists, the ecosystem is destroyed and the game ends (resource renewability distinguishes commons dilemmas from prisoners' dilemmas). For example, allowing a group of competitors to talk, preventing anonymity, increasing the visibility of the resource being consumed, delivering moral appeals, and increasing the levels of trust have all increased the levels of cooperation and extended the resource (see Gifford, 1987, for review; see also Sato, 1989; Van-Lange & Liebrand, 1991).

Research in natural settings also suggests that people may balance both individual and group needs to preserve a resource, although the issue is a controversial one and control mechanisms do break down when environments are stressed by high populations, unusual weather conditions, toxic contaminants, and the like (Feeny et al., 1990; McCabe, 1990; McCay & Acheson, 1987). In studies of lobstermen on the East coast of the United States, Acheson (1987) compared the health of lobster beds under a loosely territorial versus a strongly territorial system. Lobstermen in the strongly territorial system used a variety of mechanisms for protecting their territories, and their lobster beds were in fact healthier. They had agreed only to trap in their own area; newcomers were rarely admitted into the group; and interlopers were warned away. Acheson noted that other groups used local laws as an additional mechanism for assuring lobster abundance. So—as anticipated by a transactional perspective—in a variety of interconnected and mutually supportive ways including legal, interpersonal, and social mechanisms, some lobstermen have been able to maintain healthy lobster beds and a healthy lobster industry.

Peoples' ability to work out collective arrangements (in contrast to the assumed competitiveness) has also been noted in numerous ethnographic studies and econometric analyses. Several authors (e.g., Feeny, Berkes, McCay, & Acheson, 1990; Larson & Bromley, 1990; McCabe, 1990) described societies with well-developed, complex and culturally/environmentally suited methods for moderating overgrazing. McCabe's (1990) research among the Ngisonyoka Turkana in northwestern Kenya showed that—rather than overgrazing—livestock owners actually held fewer animals than the ecosystem could support. Numerous mechanisms contributed to this, including territorial boundaries between this group and adjacent tribes that clearly defined the amount of grazing space available, strong leaders who mediated disputes, private and therefore clearly predictable water supplies, and livestock diversity to buffer against varied conditions, among other things. Thus, in multiple and interconnected ways, these people effectively managed their commons. Feeny and colleagues (1990) also reviewed cases around the globe in which groups had used combinations of private and public access, social pressure, and so on, to moderate consumption. Thus, much research indicates that resource utilization is part of a complex social and ecological system, and that, over time, many peoples have been able to work out cooperative ways of optimizing their own and the group's outcomes.

Hardin (1968) also cast other environmental behaviors as commons dilemmas, such as childbearing and overpopulation, and energy consumption and resource depletion. Thus, to the extent that a family satisfied its desire to have many children or to use a lot of energy, it depleted those opportunities for other members of the system. Gifford (1987) extended this reasoning to other environmental behaviors including recycling, water conservation, and polluting. He noted, for example, that if a company could discharge its effluent into a commons area without cost, the company would realize higher profits, although it would undermine the health of the ecosystem.

Despite an extensive literature on environmental behaviors, it is rare to see these behaviors studied from an explicitly dialectic perspective or to see them put into the context of a total holistic system. Recycling and energy conservation experiments, for example, tend to examine the impact of individual-oriented appeals (e.g., individual costs and rewards) without invoking any broad societal and ecological values and without understanding the social context in which the appeal is made. Survey research, on the other hand, indicates that people who conserve are aware of both their own and social/ecological aspects of conservation behaviors (Gamba & Oskamp, 1994; Vining & Ebreo, 1990; Stern, Dietz, & Kalof, 1993), suggesting that in the real world, people can make behavioral choices that may embrace both sides of the self/society and species/ecosystem dialectics.

Analyses also suggest that researchers need to consider time and change. Motives for conservation that operate in one time and place may not be relevant in different contexts. For example, some recycling researchers find economic or self-interested motives are salient, whereas others identify altruistic nature-centered or future-oriented motives as the driving force behind recycling (Hopper & Nielsen, 1991). And in settings where people are legally obligated to recycle, upwards of 90 percent of the people recycle, rendering irrelevant either economic or altruistic motives. Thus, as suggested by transactional and dialectical perspectives, it is important to understand phenomena in holistic ways; at multiple levels of behavior, and in particular, social and temporal contexts; and to examine how oppositional forces are operating.

Summary

We reviewed three world views with different implications for human–nature relationships. Societies and individuals vary in the extent to which they embrace each worldview and adherence to any one can wax and wane with changing historical and environmental circumstances. We illustrated how these worldviews were manifested in human behaviors at many levels of scale and with varying implications for ecosystem functioning. Our analysis of the Commons Tragedy as a dialectic process suggested that humans can moderate their consumption practices in order to maintain their own viability in a well-functioning ecosystem. However, rapid changes, including increased population, consumption, and use of highly damaging technologies, are putting increased demands on nature that may result in long-term crises. In the next section, we will examine how people have begun to cope with numerous additional challenges such as changing social systems, new technologies, and high density and crowding.

Social Processes and Change

Change is pervasive in human experience, whether one considers the development of an individual, a relationship, a family, or a whole society. Changing circumstances can provide an opportunity to observe the functions of the physical environment as people create and respond to new experiences. How is the confluence of social, physical, and cultural aspects of settings reconfigured in the face of ongoing change? How do people manage dialectic processes of autonomy and connectedness in these circumstances?

We will examine social/environmental processes and change in five domains: (1) rituals and ceremonies that create and reflect both tradition and change; (2) changing population and urbanization pressures; (3) changing social roles and opportunities of men and women; (4) changing political, economic, and technological environments; and (5) social and environmental disruptions. These represent rather different sources of change, but all illustrate our general theme that changes arise and are manifested in multiple and interconnected aspects of phenomena, including the physical environment.

Rituals and Ceremonies: Creating and Reflecting Tradition and Change

Rituals and ceremonies are pervasive in societies, yet they have long been neglected by psychologists. They can range from small-scale events such as birth and naming ceremonies, and birthdays and wedding anniversaries, to widespread annual celebrations, such as planting and harvesting ceremonies, Christmas, Channukah, Ramadan, and so on. As Manning (1983) and Roberts (1988) said, celebrations contain paradox: they can both reflect and create change; they allow the expression of old, new, and temporary identities; and they allow the expression of individual, family, and community values and identities (all, we note, psychologically important constructs). These multiple facets can occur simultaneously, but more typically each is emphasized at a different stage or in different aspects of the ceremony. Of particular relevance to the present chapter, the physical environment is integral to the actions and meanings of these events.

Wolin and Bennett (1984) studied how rituals support and affirm social relationships, especially family and cultural bonding. They used the term "ritual" as a broad term that encompasses festivals, celebrations, holidays, family traditions, and other celebratory or ritualized practices. Highly ritualized events are those with precise rules and expectations about who is involved, what objects are used and for what purpose, where and when events occur, and their timing, sequence, and duration; examples are High Holy Mass, Jewish circumcision, and formal inauguration ceremonies. However, as Manning (1983) has shown, even informal, playful ceremonies can support individual and societal goals. For example, at Muslim and Christian festivals in Sierra Leone, preadolescent males dress up as mythical figures and dance in the street. Some characters give the children temporary power to assert their authority over adults; this enables children to cope with their subordinate status, reminds adults of their own weakness and mortality, and also gives families an opportunity to acknowledge and cope with the stresses and conflicts of rapid modernization (Cannizzo, 1983).

Thus, formal and informal ceremonies can serve multiple purposes. In the following overview, we illustrate how ceremonies allow the expression of macro-level values in individual behaviors, how ceremonies support individual and collective identities, how ceremonies support and construct continuity and change, and how they involve the physical environment. We begin with descriptions of community-wide celebrations that contain continuity and change, and then examine practices at individual and family levels that support and recognize transitions from one life phase to the next.

Community-Wide Celebrations

By involving people of all ages, festivals as diverse as Carnival in Rio de Janeiro, the Alikali devils of Sierra Leone, and the Calgary Stampede in Canada give young and old an opportunity to be a part of the larger society and also to celebrate their unique identities as children, adolescents, elders, and so on (see Manning, 1983). Typically, festivals contain multiple events, each of which emphasizes different identities or different values, or different identities may be salient at different times of year during different kinds of festivals. A small town in Ontario Province, Canada, holds several festivals each year. In one, there are two different parades, one to celebrate the town's identity and the other—held in a different place and at a different time—celebrate its identity as part of the nation of Canada (Farber, 1983). An analysis of "Christmas Street" in the United States reveals a similar pattern. The street has a 40-year history of decorating for and celebrating the Christmas holidays (Oxley, Haggard, Werner, & Altman, 1986; Werner, Haggard, Altman, & Oxley, 1988). Residents reported an increase in community spirit and group identity during the festivities. Several events highlighted one group or another, such as the communally decorated Christmas tree that symbolized group unity, and the children's parade and party that highlighted youngsters' individual identities. By inviting relatives and former residents of the street, members of Christmas Street also took this opportunity to connect themselves to the past and to reaffirm their ties to the larger community.

Especially in a changing world, celebrations can be used to acknowledge changing power relationships among residents and changing values and circumstances while simultaneously reaffirming traditional values. Manning (1983) discussed community festivals that honored town founders while at the same time recognizing the new opportunities that could revitalize the town's economy. Festivals also link macro-level cultural values and beliefs to the individual level. In Farber's (1983) study, the people who organized a town's decennial festival were the same core group of people who owned the stores and held political office; their families had been the town founders and early leaders. It is not surprising then, that many of the events during "Old Home Week" celebrated and reaffirmed traditional social and economic structures and aspects of individual identities, such as schools, churches, and local businesses. Parade awards emphasized traditional values, such as the "Best Patriotic Float" and "Best Historic Float." In celebrations at other times of year, traditional values were also highlighted; however, there was greater acknowledgement of the changing nature of the people and economic base of the town. Thus, community celebrations capture the themes of the present chapter: behaviors occur at multiple levels of functioning and are parts of an interconnected whole; celebrations provide opportunities to play out tensions between individual and societal identities; and they highlight aspects of the past, present, and future.

Individual Role Transitions

Individual role transitions are frequent events in all societies, as society members change from child to adult, from unmarried to married, or other roles. Often, these transitions are ritualized in order to clearly mark the change and underscore individuals' new identities, role relationships, and status. And, from a holistic, transactional perspective, it is useful to examine how role transitions involve the physical environment, typically requiring an array of meaningful objects and places, participants, and activities for their enactment.

Many societies have manhood ceremonies that often coincide with a major change in use of the physical environment. In seminal work, Whiting and Whiting (1975) found that manhood ceremonies often involve special and complex treatment in societies where children sleep in the same dwelling as their mother but apart from their father. Many societies use elaborate and frequently painful ceremonies to transfer socialization of boys from the realm of women to the realm of men. Boys are removed from the dwelling of their mothers and move into a dwelling with their fathers, often a men's house erected next to a source of wealth that needs to be guarded. Thus, the physical aspects of the society underscore and support the change in identity and also illuminate the importance the society places on differentiating boys (who associate with their sisters and mothers) from men (who associate with other men). The chapter by Segall, Ember, and Ember (this volume) discusses the possible role of manhood ceremonies in controlling male aggressiveness.

In our own research we have examined how weddings are events where the physical environment helps to communicate the nature of the transition from single to married life (Altman, Brown, Staples, and Werner, 1992). Not only does a wedding join a husband and wife in a legal or religious sense, but features of the wedding and early marriage also speak to the changed nature of the couple's relationship with each other, their kin, and their past and future. Wedding ceremonies fit with our themes that change is ongoing and continuous; that dialectic tensions can involve individuals, dyads, and groups of many sizes; that behaviors at multiple levels of functioning fit together in coherent patterns; and that macro-level values find expression in micro-level behaviors.

Historically, Taiwanese marriages created strong ties between families, so strong, in fact, that the relationship between the bride and mother-in-law assumed more significance than the relationship between the bride and groom. The severing of the bride's ties to her family and establishment of her new connection to the groom's family are richly illustrated through actions, objects, and physical settings during the courtship and wedding.

The courtship phase clearly portrays the Taiwanese view of marriage as a merger of two families rather than a joining of two individuals. A matchmaker proposes the initial match, which is then proposed to the ancestors, who might signal displeasure with the match by creating an accident or sickness. If signs of displeasure are not seen, the parents of the couple visit in the bride-to-be's home and exchange cakes, which are placed at an ancestral altar as a form of wedding announcement. After betrothal and during the wedding ceremony itself, the bride sits on a stool, facing the door and with her back to her family's shrine, symbolically reflecting her upcoming separation from her family. When preparing to leave for her new home, the bride makes a final bow to her ancestral shrine. As she leaves, her family slams the door and spits on her marital carriage to show that, "just as spilled water cannot be returned to the container so the bride cannot return to her natal home" (cited in Altman et al., 1992). At her husband's home she drops a fan of her family and picks up the fan of his family. A few days later she visits back home, where she is treated like a guest, reinforcing her split from her family. The repetition of the theme of the bride leaving her home and the reality of her situation of living in one room of the groom's family's home, reinforce the view that marriage splits women from their natal families and ties them to the groom's family, and that the marriage reflects bonds between families rather than individual attraction between husband and wife.

In contrast, Welsh weddings of the late 1960s reveal how personal choice and love were supposed to provide the basis for marriage, with families having much less voice in the relationship (Leonard, 1980). The physical environment provided concrete and symbolic evidence of cultural values. Teens were expected to go out to public places like dance halls and pubs, generally with the same sex friends, but with the goal of meeting a dating partner. When a couple formalized their choice to marry through engagement, the man might ask the bride's father for permission to marry but his approval was expected. The wedding ceremony involved actions that suggested the voluntary coming together of bride and groom, with vows exchanged that referred to personal commitment and dedication to each other (not the family), and the physical environment reinforcing these beliefs. Activities during the wedding and subsequent celebration highlighted both the bride's and groom's families and their friendship networks, indicating that all of them—not just one or the other family—would be important to the couple in their new life.

After the wedding, the couple usually lived on its own, though close to her parents. The relationship between the bride and her mother remained close, but changed to reflect her new identity as a wife, reinforcing the importance of the marital bond. Mother–daughter visits were conducted in each other's homes, the conversations were often about domestic skills intended to please the husband. Thus the entire context of Welsh life —laws and wedding ceremonies, gift giving traditions, public and private settings—provide opportunities for individuals to experience and sustain the Welsh form of marriage. Individuals also maintain their own unique identities, which is supported by the independence of their own home; they are simultaneously tied to the larger society as they engage in the micro-behaviors that sustain and manifest this view of marriage.

Summary

Celebrations are holistic events that involve people, places, things, and actions in specific ways; they hold dialectical contradictions of individual and collective identities; they both illuminate and underscore changing circumstances and changing relationships, but also contribute to stability. We described the courtship, wedding, and placemaking practices of two groups, one emphasizing communal qualities of marriage, and the other emphasizing more individualistic and dyadic significance to marital bonds. In both cases, behaviors at several stages of the relationship and involving particular people, places, and things reflected and supported the particular meaning of marriage in that society and the changing relationships among bride and groom and their families and friends. This section has examined changes integral to society; we next turn to changes imposed on societies from the outside.

Changing Population or Urbanization Pressures

In 1980, when the original version of this chapter was published, human population worldwide was estimated to be 4.4 billion; the population had approximately doubled in the previous 46 years as improved health care and food supplies decreased infant mortality and extended the lives of adults into old age (Bennett, 1984; Johnson, 1987). Current estimates put the human population at 5.6 billion; modest U.N. projections estimate that birth/mortality rates will not decline to replacement level (no increased growth) until 2035, resulting in a total population of 11.6 billion in the early part of the 2100s (Hargreaves, Eden-Green, & Devaney, 1994).

In many settings, living arrangements have become extremely dense as human numbers outstripped available housing. Rapid migration from rural to urban areas often resulted in severe poverty and makeshift housing, including squatter settlements. Although there has been a long history of high urban densities in Europe, the United States, and other regions of the world, the worldwide explosion in densities raised alarms, especially in light of animal research suggesting severe negative effects of high density living arrangements and competition for scarce resources. Psychological research on human crowding has emphasized interpersonal processes independent of competition for food and other scarce resources (although see Ember & Ember, 1992, and Segall, Ember, & Ember, this volume, for analyses that link population density, psychosocial factors, resource uncertainty, and aggression).

Psychological Processes underlying Crowding

Altman (1975) suggested that people experience crowding when more social contact occurs than was originally desired. Altman and Chemers (1980a, 1980b) added that every society has different levels of desired contact and social density, so what is considered high density in one group would not be in another. In crowding, stress occurs, motivating a person or group to make or renew attempts at achieving a desired level of interaction. As this happens certain "costs" may occur. These can take various forms, such as physical (energy expenditure, heightened adrenal and cardiovascular functioning, disease, etc.) and psychological (stress, conflict, social disorganization, etc.). Thus, as people handle situations of crowding, negative outcomes may occur if coping requires extensive mobilization of personal and group resources.

Baum and Paulus (1987) provided a review of crowding research that effectively integrated many theoretical approaches and lines of research. Drawing on Stokols' (1972) analysis, they noted that research with Euro-Americans consistently showed that density and crowding are distinct constructs, with density a necessary but not sufficient precondition of crowding. Baum and Paulus suggested that density could lead to four experiences, and that the individual's appraisal of these experiences would determine whether or not the experience was described as crowded. First was simple social stimulation: As the number of people increases so does the amount of sound, visual movement, and so on. If this is desirable, one would describe this as "stimulating"; if not, one would complain about being crowded. Second is the level of intimacy: Are people too close, is behavior too public, or is the situation desirable? The third experience is behavioral constraint: To what extent does the presence of others interfere with achieving one's goals? Do people bump you or get in your way as you attempt to traverse a densely packed waiting room? These would be considered "crowded," whereas the same numbers of people without the disruptions or competition would not be. And fourth is a threat to personal control. People who have or are given a sense of control in highly dense settings do not describe the situation as "crowded" and do not experience negative psychological outcomes compared to people in the same situation without the perception of control.

This fourth category, perceived control, has received considerable research in part because control has been a central factor in other research on stress, such as research on environmental disasters, commuting, noise, and job-related stress. For example, studies in Sweden indicated that overall, being on a densely populated commuter train was stressful, even though not all seats were occupied (Singer, Lundberg, & Frankenhaeuser, 1978). However, people who entered the trains early on reported less distress and had lower epinephrine levels (a physiological indicator of stress) even though by riding longer, they were exposed to the high density for longer periods of time. The implication is that selecting seats and seatmates increased their sense of control and resulted in lower perceived crowding.

Extensive research with U.S. college students affirms the importance of control in high density situations. Grades, housing satisfaction, and interpersonal relationships suffered; however, the situation could be improved simply by introducing a door into a long hallway to create two smaller and separate domains where students could have more control over interactions (Baum, Aiello, & Calesnick, 1978). Research in prisons showed that providing prisoners with a modicum of control over their sleeping area (e.g., with partial walls) reduced perceived crowding and interpersonal hostility, and improved mental and physical health (Paulus, 1988).

Recent research complements the perceived control perspective by examining what happens to social support, a typical stress buffer, under residential crowding. In research conducted in both India and the United States, Evans and his colleagues (Evans, Palsane, Lepore, & Martin, 1989; Lepore, Evans, & Schneider, 1991, 1992), found that people who moved into relatively dense situations experienced more stress and negative physical and psychological symptoms than did those who moved into lower density apartments. Those in dense settings did not call on roommates for advice and support about daily hassles, whereas those in normal density apartments did so. Thus, people in dense settings lost access to the very people who ordinarily would have helped them cope with the day-to-day stresses of life.

Cross-Cultural Responses to Crowding

This section builds on Altman and Chemers' (1980a, 1980b) thesis that societies differ in their preference for and tolerance of density. It should be noted that there are relatively few direct cultural comparisons in existing research; most are single-culture studies that allow some qualitative comparisons.

Two of the most well-established findings are that (1) different cultural groups have different criteria for what is considered high density and different responses to high density, and (2) as previously suggested, the perception of control mediates between high density and perceptions of crowding. Altman and Chemers (1980a) drew on research indicating that numerous groups prefer or tolerate high density compared to Euro-Americans. Draper (1973) described the !Kung Bushmen of southern Africa as living in dense settlements, in constant contact throughout the day, but as seeming to enjoy the contact and to live harmoniously. And research among several Asian groups suggests that individuals from these societies tolerate and perhaps prefer relatively high density living arrangements (Altman & Chemers, 1980a, 1980b; Ruback & Pandey, 1991). Brolin (1976) added that density preferences are person specific; his observations suggested that—compared to Europeans and Americans—natives of India prefer close contact within the family, but greater distance between the family and outsiders.

Our thesis is that part of the reason for these findings is that over the years, these groups have developed effective privacy management skills that provide a needed sense of control. A comparison of U.S. and Asian college students living in similar apartments supports this view; Asian (mostly Korean and Taiwanese) students reported greater ability to avoid their family members when necessary (Harris, Werner, Brown, & Ingebritsen, 1996). In a study conducted in India, increasing density alone did not predict negative outcomes but perceived control did (Ruback & Pandey, 1991); in another in India, students who reported high density at home—who presumably had developed effective privacy management skills—showed more tolerance for high density than did students without such backgrounds (Nagar, Pandey, & Paulus, 1988). Several studies in India suggest that density levels in excess of acceptable standards resulted in negative moods and behaviors, suggesting a limit to the ability of privacy regulation skills to buffer against all crowding stressors (Nagar & Pandey, 1987; Nagar, Pandey, & Paulus, 1988; Ruback & Pandey, 1991; Ruback & Patnaik, 1989; Sinha & Sinha, 1991).

Many groups use a complex array of cultural mechanisms to achieve needed levels of inaccessibility and interpersonal control. Case studies of Chinese Malaysians, Japanese and residents of Hong Kong also identify specific cultural practices consistent with easing privacy regulation under conditions of high density (see Altman & Chemers, 1980a, 1980b, for review). The Taos Pueblo in the southwestern United States provide an interesting example (Katz, 1974). The Pueblos consist of multi-storied, closely packed dwellings, with about six family members occupying one or two small rooms per household. Cultural values idealize restraint, modesty, and noncompetitiveness, features that would ease privacy regulation. In addition, complex dispersing mechanisms exist, including such customs as people rarely acknowledging one another's presence and feeling no obligation to chat when together in a room, entering and leaving rooms without greetings and leavetaking, regularly sitting alone up on the roof for extended periods, and traveling long distances to achieve change. So although the Taos are in close contact, they use mechanisms in multiple domains and varying over time to achieve acceptable levels of openness and closedness. Indeed, the Taos do not have a word for "crowding." When pushed to describe how they would feel about having a large number people in their home, informants said that they would only be concerned about not having enough food to serve everyone.

These analyses focused on societies in rather steady states; we next turn to literature that examines how people cope with population densities and living arrangements that are unusual for their cultural practices, and examine how change reverberates through many aspects of their lives and day to day experiences.

Changing Urban Configurations and Densities

Among the Hausa in Ghana observed by Pellow (1988), population pressures meant that the culture needed to resolve how to fit old traditions with new spatial limitations. The old traditions required strict separation between women's and men's spaces. Inside the home, women spent time in the courtyard, which was buffered from visitors by the husband's area. Men and women showed respect for each other by refusing to eat together, interact, or call each other by name. Pellow reported that the town had grown from 150 to 12,000 over 70 years. Consequently, space was at a premium and the compounds had been divided up to house many families of differing ethnicities. Spatial pressures made the customary isolation of women impossible, so instead, women used symbolic gestures (e.g., carrying a veil; requesting permission to go out) and shared space with other women. Hence, population pressures created the necessity for cultural change and adaptation, and, consistent with a transactional view, these changes occurred at verbal, nonverbal, and spatial levels.

In Tunisia, urban densities have altered house forms but not expectations that women should spend most of their time in the home. By moving to small, Western-style apartments, women lost the rural courtyard house that had allowed shared labor, informal social contacts, safe child play areas, and access to light and air. Women were expected to stay at home, but men still had access to their community spaces of streets, cafes, and shops (Waltz, 1988). In Egypt, similar population pressures in middle-class communities resulted in decreased housing space. However, in this society, accommodation involved shrinking but maintaining a private entry for greeting guests. Thus, the traditional separation between women and outsiders was maintained (El-Rafey, 1992). In Japan, population pressures combined with post-war reconstruction and resulted in the disappearance of guest rooms and a new practice of entertaining guests outside of the home (Hagino, Mochizuki, & Yamamoto, 1987). In Columbia, the spatial restrictions of high-density housing meant that childrens' play space moved from indoors to outside in the street (Sanchez, Wiesenfeld, & Cronick, 1987, p. 1345). So each society responded to changing physical constraints in different ways, but in ways that maintained some aspects of social roles and relationships, and some aspects of traditional customs.

Not all consequences of urbanization and population growth involve decreasing the amount of space. In many places, communities are adopting an American-style suburbanization pattern that increases private space but may decrease community space. Lawrence (1988) described how newer housing forms in a Portuguese town altered relationships between and within households. In the traditional design, a large interior room oriented around a hearth served as living, dining, and kitchen area; men were rarely home, so women and children controlled the area. Outside, women socialized or shared chores with their neighbors such as gardening, whitewashing or painting the exterior, sweeping or weeding the street, knitting, or preparing food. These activities provided plenty of opportunities for spontaneous and informal visits among the women, and women were accused of laziness or family problems if they did not make regular appearances. Thus, women were expected to maintain strong ties to the sidewalk community of women, whereas men socialized and cultivated political and economic ties at cafes outside of the home.

Lawrence then contrasted these traditional community ties with social practices in the same town but in an urban revitalization area with suburban housing. Women no longer congregated outside and visitation no longer occurred in the street, but became a more formal and planned affair inside the home. More bedrooms allowed childrens' play to move from the multipurpose room to the bedroom. Men commuted to steady jobs so they did not need to maintain their community standing through regular appearances at a now distant cafe. Men consequently spent more time at home watching television or visiting with family. As Lawrence concluded, "residents have secured their exterior privacy at the expense of traditional neighborhood sociability" (p. 210). Thus changes in the physical configuration of the home and its relation to other social settings led to widespread changes in social relations within and between families.

Summary

Societies have developed different ways of managing interactions; however, sometimes, especially under increasing population density, these processes break down and crowding occurs. In addition, changing living arrangements can disrupt traditional interaction patterns, and people attempt to adapt to these changes in multiple ways and with more or less success. It may be that with sufficient time, emerging cultural practices will enable people to manage their relationships satisfactorily, even in the new social and physical milieu. In some cases, the changing densities or housing configurations had more impact on women than men, a theme that is explored further in the next section on changing social roles.

Gendered Places and Changing Social Roles

Many societies are witnessing the movement of women into work systems outside the home, as well as a general lengthening of the lifespan. Often, traditional women's tasks of caregiving and unpaid domestic labor are renegotiated when economic obligation or personal preferences lead women to participate in the more public world of paid employment. Yet these social and economic changes are happening quite rapidly, without corresponding changes in the provision of appropriate housing or needed child or elder care.

Changes in sex roles are embedded within other changes, such as modernization trends. These changes often involve transitions in the power and authority given to family members, in the amount of time family members work and spend leisure time together, and even in who is considered to be a part of the family. Dwelling units play a special role in determining who belongs to a family and the proper ways members contribute to family life.

Before examining changing sex roles, it is useful to examine how places have been instrumental in providing substance and stability to sex roles. The gendered nature of places has received much attention over the last decade or two (see Altman & Churchman, 1994; Spain, 1992; Weisman, 1992). Much of the research focuses on the ways in which places reinforce sex roles: "We see the realization of women's relationships to one another, to men, to children, to society at large, in their placing in space" (Pellow, 1988, p. 215). Sebba (1991) traced across history and society how the physical environment has been used to separate boys from girls, with boys given more opportunities and power in the bargain; she argued that the physical separation corresponded to status distinctions, and that the physical environment was deliberately used to achieve this differentiation.

In a cross-cultural analysis of 79 societies from the Human Relations Area Files, supplemented by historical analyses of Euro-American cultures, Spain (1992) traced the patterns of opportunity associated with spatial segregation of men from women in homes, communities, workplaces, and schools. In homes, Spain found that spatial segregation is often reinforced with religious belief. Of the 79 societies examined, 22 divided homes into men's and women's spaces, and in general, these societies held religious beliefs that reinforced the correctness of these divisions. For example, Mongolian tents are divided into the religiously pure male side and the impure female side. A ritual is needed to purify householders if they move objects to the wrong side of the tent. Amongst the Barasana Indians of Columbia, the ceremonies that celebrate initiation rites or the ripening of fruit involve actually closing off the side of the house for men from the side of the house for women, children, and pets.

A transactional/dialectical analysis of such societies would emphasize that the physical division of space is integral to the ways in which men and women develop distinct identities and patterns of interaction, both as individuals and members of groups. So the physical environment is used in ways that support some kinds of contacts but discourages others, celebrates some relationships but not others, signifies changing relationships, and so on.

Spain makes the additional point that such divisions also reflect one's status in the group and even structure opportunities for enhancing one's standing or power in society. In general, Spain found that in societies where men are viewed as superior to women, household spatial segregation reinforced women's subordination by closing off their access to ways to improve their position through labor or education. Furthermore, Spain found statistically significant relationships such that women having low power was associated with segregated spaces in the home. In contrast, societies such as the Navajo that have more egalitarian sex role beliefs use segregated spaces without closing off opportunities for advancement. The Navajo house, the hogan, is symbolically separated into male and female spaces, but the culture provides opportunities for women to participate in valued medicinal and religious ceremonies and has a religion that includes as important figures a First Man and First Woman.

Outside the home, Spain also found that spatial segregation facilitates a segregation of opportunities and status. In 27 of 81 societies with exclusive men's huts, women generally have low power over the fruits of their own labor, their position in kin networks, and the inheritance of property and wealth. In particular, the privacy of men's huts can allow them to pass on valued knowledge that reinforces male power. Many societies exclude women from formal educational settings, thereby restricting their opportunities for socially valued advancement. Spain noted that historically in the United States, girls were first excluded from public schools, although sometimes they were allowed to stand outside and look in the window or to sit behind a curtain to eavesdrop on education. Similarly, jobs that were reserved for women provided low pay, low respect, and little opportunity for advancement.

The view that space usage can reinforce patterns of inequality in society by tying activities to places that are more or less economically valued illustrates our theme of transactionalism. The value of settings is intrinsically tied to physical arrangement of space, cultural traditions and religious values, work patterns, differential expectations for women and men, and women's and men's economical and educational well-being. For example, in African societies, men receive pay and respect for laying water lines but women receive neither pay nor respect for spending five hours a day hauling water by hand (Bergom-Larsson, 1982). Similarly, a study of leisure settings in a small Australian town (Dempsey, 1989) showed that public leisure settings—pubs, sports clubs, voluntary groups—were only open to or controlled by men, providing them ample opportunities for leisure, whereas women were expected to be supportive spectators or use their domestic skills to raise money for the men's organizations. And Christensen (1994) reviewed research indicating that women's home-based work created tensions between women's family demands and their desires for successful employment. For example, Christensen found that children often interrupt their mothers and don't fully appreciate that mother is working.

Horelli and Vespa (1994) detailed how many societies are coming to grips with multiple social changes simultaneously and how these changes are played out in the use of space both in macro-level policies and in micro-level behaviors. In many industrialized societies, women's unpaid household work has supported the economy for a long time. But in the transition to paid employment, many tasks formerly done by full-time homemakers become problematic. Women are now struggling to do former tasks—housekeeping, running errands, shopping—while adding paid employment and the accompanying commute and management of day care. Horelli and Vespa argued that "by compelling women to find individual solutions to collective problems, a situation is created where the women themselves assist in making the causes of the problem invisible and therefore unresolved" (p. 203). In dealing with the new stresses, some societies are renegotiating the lines between public and private domains. In Finland, a community "living room" (so named to stress its similarity to the social room in a home) was built so that residents would have a place to gather and socialize. It contained a cafe, game or craft rooms, and meeting rooms; social programs were designed to attract all ages and particularly seemed to benefit those who would otherwise feel isolated in their private homes.

Consciously providing for more community-oriented space echoes the concerns of Hayden (1984) who criticized suburban developments in the United States for isolating women and separating them from others with similar needs and concerns. In the United States, low-income women have responded by trying to create supportive relationships outside the home, whether that involves working with neighbors to reclaim landlord abandoned buildings (Leavitt & Saegert, 1990) or to provide community resources for laundromats or other necessities (Feldman & Stall, 1994). In the Netherlands, the woonerf—the transformation of public street into semiprivate "play street"—provides more public space by extending the home-like qualities of play space and safety beyond the confines of the individual home (Stringer & Kremer, 1987). However prevalent these new movements may be, Dempsey (1989) notes that changes are difficult when they must overcome the spatial separation of households and other strong traditions of space allocation.

Summary
This section focused on how men's and women's roles and power differences are reflected and reified via spatial location. In many societies, females of all ages are restricted in their movements, and often these restrictions correspond to restrictions in power and advancement. With substantial changes in social structure and corresponding changes in the physical environment, these barriers are being broken down. (see Best & Williams, this volume, for an overview of research on sex and gender.)

Changing Political, Economic, or Technological Environments

Changes in political, economic, or technological environments often happen gradually and outside the control and awareness of individuals. In these instances, it is common to see an evolving rearrangement of interpersonal connections at a micro-level that is often supported and even fostered at a macro-level by new housing or community forms.

Kent (1991) reviewed 73 different societies world wide and found a pattern of changes in society whereby those societies that became more sedentary, more highly populated, or more aggregated in space developed customs of segregated and specialized behavior, use of spaces, and use of the material environment. So, for example, people in highly settled and complex societies, such as Euro-Americans, Zulu, or Javanese, actively separate spaces in homes and elsewhere for different genders and sometimes for different ages, with separate toys for boys and girls, and separate roles for men and women. Conversely, in more traditionally nomadic and/or simply organized societies, such as the Basarwa of the Kalahari, the Hazda or the Mbuti Pygmies, men and women tend to be more flexible about role assignments and material culture is less clearly divided into men's and women's objects. She noted that when nomadic societies such as the !Kung become more sedentary, researchers have reported increased socialization differences between girls and boys, a wider range of possessions that requires rules about ownership and dispersal of goods, and a tendency to divide labor into female domestic and male public realms.

Thus, large-scale patterns of wealth accumulation, population aggregation, or housing type often require cultural-level accommodations that relate to individual-level processes and interactions. Once again the physical environment, by providing or failing to provide places and things that belong to certain members of society, helps to define, enhance, or undermine the rules of authority and affiliation.

In Botswana, the move from thatched houses to brick or concrete and galvanized metal houses involved changes that went beyond the provision of shelter (Larsson, 1989). One change involved the disconnection between housing and women's identity in multiple domains. Women were integral to the traditional homes; they gathered the building materials, built the dwellings, bore their children in and buried the afterbirth underneath the house, and gave their name to the home. Newer house forms totally disrupted this pattern. Newer housing materials were purchased, not gathered, and the monetary economy was open primarily to men. So men needed to work to afford the new materials, and the actual building was done by other men who had the needed equipment and expertise. The expense kept new housing small and sometimes prompted families to open up space to renters; the disappearance of firewood moved cooking indoors to paraffin stoves. These spatial, temporal, and social changes in households meant that families were now crowding more activities into smaller spaces, altering the rhythm and pattern of daily life. Participating in the money economy, hiring professional builders, taking in renters, and buying Western furniture and cooking implements all involved importing public qualities into the formerly private household domain. Men's activities became more crucial to the provision of housing and women lost traditional sources of power and identity; both men and women gained more cramped living quarters over which they had less control.

In a small Brazilian community, Robben (1989) examined how the introduction of motorized fishing boats—an economic and technological innovation—created a range of reverberating consequences for daily life. Motorboat fishing, compared with traditional canoe fishing, required more capital investment, regular payments, and involved longer trips from home. Traditional canoe fishermen were highly involved in daily life of the household and frequently used the living room to entertain their men friends. Motorboat fishermen were gone for days at a time, leaving the women more in charge of daily life and the use of the home; the men were also drawn away from home to socialize with the boat owner in order to remain in his good graces. Thus the technological changes in how fishing was done had implications for the rhythm of daily life, the degree of autonomy experienced by husbands and wives, and their degree of dependence upon others in the community and how this was manifested in many aspects of environmental usage.

Summary
Sociopolitical and technological changes often reverberate throughout a society. As illustrated in this section, a change from a nomadic to a sedentary lifestyle

seems to correspond to changes in the degrees of social segregation and spatial differentiation. Similarly, simple changes, such as the kind of boat one uses or the construction materials used in one's home, can set one on a path that leads to changes in social and marital relationships, family interaction patterns, and economic obligations and opportunities. As in the other case studies in this chapter, we observed an individual/society tension, with macro-level social and technological changes reflected in multiple complex ways at the individual household level.

Social and Environmental Disruptions

Disruptions in human settlements appears to be on the increase as natural disasters leave people homeless, economic pushes and pulls lead to migration, and development projects lead to population displacement. Brown and Perkins (1992) found that disruptions often illuminated the taken-for-granted bonds between people and places. They suggested that *place attachment*—the cognitive, affective, and behavioral bonds forged between inhabitants and their individual homes and communities—had provided residents with a sense of individual and communal identity that needed to be both recognized and reworked before victims could regain a sense of a normal and meaningful life.

Anthropologist Oliver-Smith (1986) conducted fieldwork before and after the small town of Yungay, Peru, was devastated when an earthquake-rocked glacier raced down the mountain and covered the town with five meters of mud. He recognized a grieving process in the 200 survivors which acknowledged the value of what was lost yet committed themselves to a meaningful future. The grieving process took the form of regular visits to the "scar" left by the slide, where mourners felt free to cry and to place markers to honor the dead. They also reminisced about past activities and places—the stroll in the community's plaza, the chapel, their home and belongings.

The ability to commit to a meaningful future was enhanced by the use of traditional ceremonies, such as the Day of the Dead, as well as new ones, such as the anniversary of the disaster. These activities allowed residents to focus and contain their grief and collectively to envision a brighter future. As the plaza had been the heart of the community, it was fitting that they planted new palm trees to mark the corners of the new plaza where they planned to rebuild Yungay.

The generally positive recovery of the town of Yungay was contrasted with the continued loss of personal and community identity for residents of Buffalo Creek, West Virginia, where a flood had devastated the small mining town. A pervasive difference between the two disasters involves the role of the victims in aiding their own recovery and rebuilding the community. In Buffalo Creek, experts arrived quickly, herding survivors into shelters, roping off areas hit by the flood, and bulldozing houses that were too dangerous to enter. Later, expert lawyers arrived to carry on a protracted fight between the miners and their employer, the creator of the dam that failed. In Yungay, help was delayed so that survivors had to scavenge the disaster area for food and shelter, seeking out other victims to share the recovery effort. Later, residents took an active role in rebuilding their community, resisting the work of government experts who wanted to rebuild the town in a safer place. Their rebuilding efforts involved many of the community settings that had been meaningful before the disaster. They reinitiated the soccer league, created church-related aid groups, and developed parents' associations to rebuild the school. The problems created by a disaster are of such great magnitude that it is likely that shared efforts are needed. Consequently, the rebuilding of community becomes the focus, yet personal achievements and esteem also rise along with the new community.

Other relocation problems can occur when people choose or are forced to migrate. Pader (1994) described the experiences of Mexican immigrants from La Chaneja, a small town in rural Mexico, to southern California, in the United States. Their traditional homes had supported a lifestyle of openness and accessibility among the mother, her children, and neighbors; however, California homes did not support these practices. California homes had no central courtyard where families had traditionally gathered; noisy U.S. appliances interfered with the traditional practice of chatting with neighbors while doing housework; California law prevented women from earning money by selling food in their front rooms; long distances and fear of crime precluded the women's and children's traditional daily walks to the store. So in many ways, at multiple levels of behavior and times of day, women became isolated from their communities. Pader reported that families attempted to cope with these changes; some women adapted and even preferred living in the United States, but others never acclimated and even became discouraged and depressed about their circumstances.

Gauvain, Altman, and Fahim (1983) examined how normal patterns of social interaction were disrupted when the Egyptian Nubians were forced to relocate because of rising waters behind the Aswan Dam. The government-provided housing did not support Nubian's traditional ways of withdrawing and discretely avoiding neighbors; homes were closer together than was customary, and exterior doors were across from neighbors' doors, allowing visual access into each others' homes. Nor did the new homes support traditional methods for achieving contact with neighbors; the traditional front stoop or "mustaba" was not provided, and families could no longer sit outside comfortably in the evenings to chat with passersby. More serious were family separations from their close relatives. Whereas traditional homes were clustered into kin groups, in the new city, people were assigned to homes randomly. This was particularly a problem for women and children, who were reluctant to walk across town with its potential dangers, and therefore lost social contacts and social supports with relatives. Over time, the Nubians began restructuring their homes and their social relationships in ways that restored some traditional patterns of interaction. Some built mastabas so they could interact with neighbors; others moved to be closer to family members; and others attempted to remodel their homes to provide more traditional spatial separations. So over time, and in varied ways, they attempted to regain their previous levels of accessibility and inaccessibility with family and friends.

Summary

Disruptions are particularly difficult to deal with because they are usually sudden, dramatic, and all encompassing. These are not subtle changes that build up over time, but rather major events that disturb all aspects of daily life. Our analyses suggested that people have strong ties to their physical and social settings, that often the physical environment and human community are inextricably intertwined so that disruptions in the physical environment correspond to disruptions in social relations and in daily patterns of activity. These examples also illustrated the resilience of these people, and their abilities to rebuild their lives after disruptions. As in the previous sections of this chapter, this analysis of disruptions supported the argument that phenomena are composed of multiple kinds of behaviors, and changes in one facet of a system extend far into other areas of behavior.

Summary and Discussion

This chapter adopted a holistic, transactional/dialectical approach in reviewing environment behavior relationships in societies across time and setting. We described three worldviews and how those are manifested in consumption behaviors; we also explored problems of overburdening the natural environment. Then we examined social and role relationships, how they are integrally connected to the physical environment, and how complex patterns of behavior are changed under changing social, physical, and technological circumstances.

We developed several themes, although not all were equally relevant for each section of the chapter. First, we outlined five key aspects of a transactional worldview: (1) all human behavior involves behavior in context; (2) sociophysical contexts exist at many levels of scale; (3) change and continuity are intrinsic to human behavior and transactional approaches explicitly assume that human behavior will show both change and continuity; (4) human behavior is patterned, and behaviors fit together in complex but coherent ways; and (5) a focus on the environment forces researchers to examine the range of contextual features that are intrinsic to the substance and execution of social processes. Second, we explored dialectical tensions involving individuals or groups and larger social entities, from the perspective of an individual/society or autonomy/connection dialectic. We argued that these dialectic processes are essential to effective social functioning, and showed how dialectic tensions encourage groups to satisfy their individual needs without ignoring the needs of the group or total system; how dialectic tensions encourage recently married couples to develop strong dyadic or familial ties, whichever is most appropriate for their society; how dialectic tensions of continuity/change and old/new can be expressed in rituals and celebrations so that people can explore and express their changing values and identities in a controlled and managed way; and how dialectic tensions of autonomy and connection between husbands and wives and between individuals and their friends and neighbors are played out and adjusted as technological and social systems change around them.

Thus, these dialectic tensions are integral parts of ongoing patterns of behavior, and they may provide an invisible sinew or webbing that holds relationships together through times of dramatic change.

Although these processes are essential to effective functioning, they are also easily disrupted by outside forces. Throughout the chapter, we illustrated how traditional ways of connecting or maintaining independence, of cooperating or engaging in competition, were disturbed by changing population sizes, resource loss, sociopolitical pressures including male and female power relationships, and technological changes or physical disruptions. In most cases, groups that were described as functioning effectively and having well-established modes of interacting experienced widespread disturbances during externally-imposed changes. In some cases, the researchers described how the group responded to restore effective social or economic functioning.

An additional underlying theme—and one that is consistent with a transactional approach—is a tension between continuity and change: change is expected, but in the context of continuity (see also the Berry and Sam chapter on acculturation in this volume). In some of the societies we described, it was clear how groups were maintaining some degree of cultural continuity despite widespread changes in daily practices and ways of relating. In other cases, it was not clear what core aspects of the culture might be retained and how the group would maintain its cultural identity. Sometimes, the changes were too recent to allow a firm understanding of what practices would be restored and which would be lost. And in other cases, the researchers did not provide sufficient information to know what the society would be like in future years.

And finally, we have argued throughout this chapter that the physical environment is integral to phenomena; it is not a passive backdrop, but is a crucial context of behavior. In addition to being an essential source of resources necessary for life, the physical environment suggests, supports, encourages, and provides opportunities and possibilities for a host of behaviors, including the economic and interpersonal behaviors that were our focus. Future analyses are needed to establish its significance in other domains of behavior.

Endnotes

1. The present chapter builds on the original *Handbook of Cross Cultural Psychology* chapter by Altman and Chemers (1980a); we have taken their interest in a systems approach and expanded it into a transactional/dialectical one, and we continue their focus on linkages between psychological processes and the physical environment. Our treatment of privacy regulation and crowding is shortened in order to include additional material; a reading of that chapter will provide useful background to this one.

2. A transactional and dialectical perspective emphasizes how all aspects of a context work together over time. In a sense, such a perspective makes it difficult to describe transactional unities because there are no natural beginning or ending points; one wonders how to enter a phenomenon. In the present case, because change is and has been so common in many places around the globe, a central theme and our point of entry will be transition and change. Especially in later parts of the chapter, we will explore traditional practices and

show how people modify or change them in multifaceted ways in response to changing social and environmental circumstances. Thus, in accord with a transactional perspective, we examine phenomena as holistic and dynamic processes.

References

Acheson, J. M. (1987). The lobster fiefs, revisited: Economic and ecological effects of territoriality in the Maine lobster industry. In B. J. McCay, & J. M. Acheson (Eds.), *The question of the commons* (pp. 37–65). Tucson: University of Arizona Press.

Altman, I. (1975). *Environment and social behavior: Privacy, personal space, territory, and crowding.* Monterey, CA: Brooks/Cole. (Reprinted by Irvington Press, New York, 1981.)

Altman, I., Brown, B. B., Staples, B., & Werner, C. M. (1992). A transactional approach to close relationships: Courtship, weddings and placemaking. In B. Walsh, K. Craik, & R. Price (Eds.), *Person–environment psychology* (pp. 193–241). Hillsdale, NJ: Lawrence Erlbaum.

Altman, I. & Chemers, M. M. (1980a). Cultural aspects of environment–behavior relationships. In H. C. Triandis & R. W. Brislin (Eds.), *Handbook of cross-cultural psychology: Social psychology* (Vol. 5, pp. 335–393). Boston: Allyn and Bacon.

Altman, I. & Chemers, M. M. (1980b). *Culture and environment.* Monterey, CA: Brooks/Cole.

Altman, I. & Churchman, A. (Eds.). (1994). *Women and the environment: Human behavior and the environment: Advances in theory and research* (Vol. 13). New York: Plenum.

Altman, I. & Rogoff, B. (1987). World views in psychology: Trait, interactional, organismic, and transactional perspectives. In D. Stokols & I. Altman (Eds.), *Handbook of Environmental Psychology.* (Vol. 1, pp. 1–40). New York: Wiley.

Altman, I., Vinsel, A., & Brown, B. B. (1981). Dialectic conceptions in social psychology: An application to social penetration and privacy regulation. In L. Berkowitz (Ed.), *Advances in Experimental Social Psychology* (Vol. 14, pp. 107–160). New York: Academic.

Baum, A., Aiello, J., & Calesnick, L. E. (1978). Crowding and personal control: Social density and the development of learned helplessness. *Journal of Personality and Social Psychology, 36,* 1000–1011.

Baum, A. & Paulus, P. (1987). Crowding. In D. Stokols & I. Altman (Eds.), *Handbook of environmental psychology* (Vol. 1, pp. 533–570). New York: Wiley.

Baxter, L. (1993). The social side of personal relationships: A dialectical perspective. In S. Duck (Ed.), *Social context and relationships: Understanding relationship processes* (Vol. 3, pp. 139–165). Newbury Park, CA: Sage.

Bennett, D. G. (1984). *World population problems.* Champaign, IL: Park.

Bergom-Larsson, M. (1982). Women and technology in the industrialized countries. In P. M. D'Onofrio-Flores & S. M. Pfafflin (Eds.), *Scientific-technological change and the role of women in development* (pp. 29–75). Boulder, CO: Westview.

Berkes, F. (1987). Common-property resource management and Cree Indian fisheries in Subarctic Canada. In B. J. McCay & J. M. Acheson (Eds.), *The question of the commons: The culture and ecology of communal resources* (pp. 66–91). Tucson: University of Arizona Press.

Berry, J. W., Poortinga, Y. H., Segall, M. H., & Dasen, P. R. (1992). *Cross-cultural psychology: Research and applications.* New York: Cambridge University Press.

Brightman, R. A. (1987). Conservation and resource depletion: The case of the Boreal Forest Algonquians. In B. J. McCay & J. M. Acheson (Eds.), *The question of the commons: The culture and ecology of communal resources* (pp. 121–141). Tucson: University of Arizona Press.

Brolin, B. (1976). *The failure of modern architecture.* New York: Van Nostrand Reinhold.

Bronfenbrenner, U. (1979). *The ecology of human development*. Cambridge, MA: Harvard University Press.

Brown, B. B., Altman, I., & Werner, C. M. (1992). Close relationships in the physical and social world: Dialectic and transactional analyses. In S. Deetz (Ed.), *Communication Yearbook 15* (pp. 509–522). Newbury Park, CA: Sage.

Brown, B. B. & Perkins, D. D. (1992). Disruptions in place attachment. In I. Altman & S. M. Low (Eds.), *Place attachment* (pp. 279–304). New York: Plenum.

Calthorpe, P. (1993). *The next American metropolis: Ecology, community, and the American dream*. Princeton: Princeton Architectural Press.

Cannizzo, J. (1983). The shit devil: Pretense and politics among West African urban children. In F. E. Manning (Ed.), *The celebration of society: Perspectives on contemporary cultural performance* (pp. 125–141). Bowling Green, KY: Bowling Green State University Popular Press.

Carmody, J. (1983). *Ecology and religion: Toward a new Christian theology of nature*. Mahwah, NJ: Paulist Press.

Christensen, K. (1994). Working at home: Frameworks of meaning. In I. Altman & A. Churchman (Eds.), *Women and the environment: Human behavior and the environment: Advances in theory and research* (Vol. 13, pp. 133–166). New York: Plenum.

Corrington, R. S. (1992). *Nature and spirit: An essay in ecstatic naturalism*. New York: Fordham University Press.

Dempsey, K. (1989). Women's leisure, men's leisure: A study in subordination and exploitation. *Australian and New Zealand Journal of Sociology, 25*, 27–45.

Devall, B. & Sessions, G. (1985). *Deep ecology: Living as if nature mattered*. Salt Lake City: Peregrine Smith Books.

Draper, P. (1973). Crowding among hunter-gatherers: The !Kung bushmen. *Science, 182*, 301–303.

El-Rafey, M. (1992). Housing and women's needs: Emerging trends in the Middle East. *Architecture and Comportement, 8*, 181–196.

Ehrenfeld, D. (1978). *The arrogance of humanism*. New York: Oxford University Press.

Ember, C. R. & Ember, M. (1992). Resource unpredictability, mistrust, and war. *Journal of Conflict Resolution, 36*, 242–262.

Evans, G. W., Palsane, M. N., Lepore, S. J., & Martin, J. (1989). Residential density and psychological health: The mediating effects of social support. *Journal of Personality and Social Psychology, 57*, 994–999.

Farber, C. (1983). High, healthy, and happy: Ontario mythology on parade. In F. E. Manning (Ed.), *The celebration of society: Perspectives on contemporary cultural performance* (pp. 33–50). Bowling Green, KY: Bowling Green State University Popular Press.

Feeny, D., Berkes, F., McCay, B. J., & Acheson, J. M. (1990). The tragedy of the commons: Twenty-two years later. *Human Ecology, 18*, 1–19.

Feldman, R. M. & Stall, S. (1994). The politics of space appropriation: A case study of women's struggles for home placement in Chicago public housing. In I. Altman & A. Churchman (Eds.), *Women and the environment: Human behavior and the environment: Advances in theory and research* (Vol. 13, pp. 167–199). New York: Plenum.

Gamba, R. J. & Oskamp, S. (1994). Factors influencing community residents' participation in commingled curbside recycling programs. *Environment and Behavior, 26*, 587–612.

Gauvain, M., Altman, I., & Fahim, H. (1983). Homes and social change: A cross-cultural analysis. In N. R. Feimer & E. S. Geller (Eds.), *Environmental psychology: Directions and perspectives* (pp. 180–218). New York: Praeger.

Gifford, R. (1987). *Environmental psychology: Principles and practice*. New York: Allyn and Bacon.

Goodwin, G. C. (1977). *Cherokees in transition: A study of changing culture and environment prior to 1775* (Research paper #181). Chicago: University of Chicago, Department of Geography.

Hagino, G., Mochizuki, M., & Yamamoto, T. (1987). Environmental psychology in Japan. In D. Stokols & I. Altman (Eds.), *Handbook of environmental psychology* (Vol. 2, pp. 1155–1170). New York: Wiley.

Hames, R. (1987). Game conservation or efficient

hunting? In B. J. McCay & J. M. Acheson (Eds.), *The question of the commons: The culture and ecology of communal resources* (pp. 92–107). Tucson: University of Arizona Press.

Hardin, G. (1968). The tragedy of the commons. *Science, 162.* 1243–1248.

Hargreaves, D., Eden-Green, M., & Devaney, J. (1994). *World index of resources and population.* Brookfield: Dartmouth.

Harris, P. B., Werner, C. M., Brown, B. B., & Ingebritsen, D. (1996). Relocation and privacy regulation: A cross-cultural analysis. *Journal of Environmental Psychology, 15,* 311–320.

Hayden, D. (1984). *Redesigning the American dream: The future of housing, work, and family life.* New York: Norton.

Hopper, J. R. & Nielsen, J. M. (1991). Recycling as altruistic behavior: Normative and behavioral strategies to expand participation in a community recycling program. *Environment and Behavior, 23,* 195–220.

Horelli, L. & Vepsa, K. (1994). In search of supportive structures for everyday life. In I. Altman & A. Churchman (Eds.), *Woman and the environment: Human behavior and environment advances in theory and research* (Vol. 13, pp. 201–226). New York: Plenum.

Jacobsen, J. E. & Firor, J. (1992). *Human impact on the environment: Ancient roots, current challenges.* Boulder, CO: Westview.

Jenkins, V. S. (1994). *The lawn: A history of an American obsession.* Washington, DC: Smithsonian Institution Press.

Johnson, S. P. (1987). *World population and the United Nations: Challenge and response.* New York: Cambridge University Press.

Joranson, P. N. & Butigan, K. (1984). *Cry of the environment: Rebuilding the Christian creation tradition.* Santa Fe: Bear & Company.

Kagitçibasi, C. (1991). Decreasing infant mortality as a global demographic change: A challenge to psychology. *International Journal of Psychology, 26,* 649–664.

Katz, P. (1974). Adaptations to crowded space: The case of Taos Pueblo. In M. Richardson (Ed.), *The human mirror: Material and spatial images of man* (pp. 300–316). Baton Rouge: Louisiana State University Press.

Kent, S. (1991). Partitioning space: Cross-cultural factors influencing domestic spatial segmentation. *Environment and Behavior, 23,* 438–473.

Kluckhohn, F. R. (1953). Dominant and variant value orientations. In C. Kluckhohn, H. A. Murray, & D. M. Schneider (Eds.), *Personality in nature, society, and culture* (pp. 342–357). New York: Knopf.

Larson, B. A. & Bromley, D. W. (1990). Property rights, externalities, and resource degradation: Locating the tragedy. *Journal of Development Economics, 33,* 235–262.

Larsson, A. (1989). Traditional versus modern housing in Botswana: An analysis from the user's perspective. In J. Bourdier & N. Alsayyad (Eds.), *Dwellings, settlements, and tradition* (pp. 503–525). New York: University Press of America.

Lawrence, D. L. (1988). Suburbanization of house form and gender relations in a rural Portuguese agro-town. *Architecture and Behavior, 4,* 197–212.

Lawrence, D. L. & Low, S. M. (1990). The built environment and spatial form. *Annual Review in Anthropology, 19,* 453–505.

Leavitt, J. & Saegert, S. (1990). *From abandonment to hope: Community households in Harlem.* New York: Columbia University Press.

Leonard, D. (1980). *Sex and generation.* London: Tavistock.

Lepore, S. J., Evans, G. W., & Schneider, M. L. (1991). Dynamic role of social support in the link between chronic stress and psychological distress. *Journal of Personality and Social Psychology, 61,* 899–909.

Lepore, S. J., Evans, G. W., & Schneider, M. L. (1992). Role of control and social support in explaining the stress of hassles and crowding. *Environment and Behavior, 24,* 795–811.

Lowe, J. W. G. (1985). *The dynamics of Apocalypse: A systems simulation of the classic Maya collapse.* Albuquerque: University of New Mexico Press.

Manning, F. E. (1983). Cosmos and chaos: Celebration in the modern world. In F. E. Manning (Ed.), *The celebration of society: Perspectives on contemporary cultural performance* (pp. 3–30). Bowling Green, KY: Bowling Green State University Popular Press.

McCabe, J. T. (1990). Turkana pastoralism: A case against the tragedy of the commons. *Human Ecology, 18,* 81–103.

McCay, B. J. & Acheson, J. M. (1987). *The question of the commons: The culture and ecology of communal resources.* Tucson: University of Arizona Press.

Nagar, D. & Pandey, J. (1987). Affect and performance on cognitive tasks as a function of crowding noise. *Journal of Applied Social Psychology, 17,* 147–157.

Nagar, D., Pandey, J., & Paulus, P. B. (1988). The effects of residential crowding experience on reactivity to laboratory crowding and noise. *Journal of Applied Social Psychology, 18,* 1423–1442.

Nash, R. F. (1990). *American environmentalism readings in conservation history* (3d ed.). New York: McGraw-Hill.

Oliver-Smith, A. (1986). *The martyred city: Death and rebirth in the Andes.* Albuquerque: University of New Mexico Press.

Oxley, D., Haggard, L. M., Werner, C. M., & Altman, I. (1986). Transactional qualities of neighborhood social networks: A case study of "Christmas Street." *Environment and Behavior, 18,* 640–677.

Pader, E. J. (1994). Sociospatial relations of change: Rural Mexican women in Urban California. In I. Altman & A. Churchman (Eds.), *Women and the environment: Human behavior and environment advances in theory and research* (Vol. 13, pp. 73–103). New York: Plenum.

Paulus, P. B. (1988). *Prison crowding: A psychological perspective.* New York: Springer- Verlag.

Pawlik, K. (1991). *International Journal of Psychology: Special Issue on the Dimensions of Global Change, 26,* 545-674.

Pellow, D. (1988). What housing does: Changes in an Accra community. *Architecture and Behavior, 4,* 213–228.

Redman, C. L. (1992). The impact of food production: Short-term strategies and long-term consequences. In J. E. Jacobsen & J. Firor (Eds.), *Human impact on the environment: Ancient roots, current challenges* (pp. 35–49). Boulder, CO: Westview.

Reice, S. R. (1994). Nonequilibrium determinants

of biological community structure. *American Scientist, 82,* 424–435.

Ridington, R. (1988). Knowledge, power, and the individual in Subarctic hunting societies. *American Anthropologist, 90,* 98–110.

Robben, A. C. (1989). Habits of the home: Spatial hegemony and the structuration of house and society in Brazil. *American Anthropologist, 91,* 570–588.

Roberts, J. (1988). Setting the frame: Definition, functions, and typology of rituals. In E. Imber-Black, J. Roberts, & R. A. Whiting (Eds.), *Rituals in families and family therapy* (pp. 3-46). New York: Norton.

Roberts, R. S. & Emel, J. (1992). Uneven development and the tragedy of the commons: Competing images for the nature–society analysis. *Economic Geography, 68,* 249–271.

Ruback, R. B. & Pandey, J. (1991). Crowding, perceived control, and relative power: An analysis of households in India. *Journal of Applied Social Psychology, 21,* 315–344.

Ruback, R. B. & Patnaik, R. (1989). Crowding, perceived control, and the destruction of property. *Psychological Studies, 34,* 1–14.

Sanchez, E., Wiesenfeld, E., & Cronick, K. (1987). Environmental psychology from a Latin American perspective. In D. Stokols & I. Altman (Eds.), *Handbook of environmental psychology* (Vol. 2, pp. 1337–1358). New York: Wiley.

Sato, K. (1989). Trust and feedback in a social dilemma. *Japanese Journal of Experimental Social Psychology, 29,* 123–128.

Scherer, D. (Ed.). (1990). *Upstream/downstream: Issues in environmental ethics.* Philadelphia: Temple University Press.

Schnaiberg, A. & Gould, K. A. (1994). *Environment and society: The enduring conflict.* New York: St. Martin's.

Schrader-Frechette, K. (1990). Models, scientific method, and environmental ethics. In Scherer, D. (Ed), *Upstream/Downstream: Issues in environmental ethics* (pp. 90–120). Philadelphia: Temple University Press.

Sebba, R. (1991). The role of the home in environment in cultural transmission. *Architecture and Behavior, 7,* 223–242.

Segall, M. H., Dasen, P. R., Berry, J. W., & Poortinga, Y. H. (1990). *Human behavior in global perspec-*

tive: An introduction to cross-cultural psychology. New York: Pergamon.

Singer, J. E., Lundberg, U., & Frankenhaeuser, M. (1978). Stress on the train: A study of urban commuting. In A. Baum, J. E. Singer, & S. Valins (Eds.), *Advances in environmental psychology* (Vol. 1), pp. 41–56). Hillsdale, NJ: Lawrence Erlbaum.

Sinha, S. P. & Sinha, S. P. (1991). Personal space and density as factors in task performance and feeling of crowding. *The Journal of Social Psychology, 131,* 831–837.

Spain, D. (1992). *Gendered spaces.* Chapel Hill: University of North Carolina Press.

Spring, D. & Spring, E. (Eds.). (1974). *Ecology and religion in history.* New York: Harper Torchbooks.

Stern, P. C., Dietz, T., & Kalof, L. (1993). Value orientations, gender, and environmental concern. *Environment and behavior, 25,* 322–348.

Stokols, D. (1972). On the distinction between density and crowding: Some implications for future research. *Psychological Review, 79,* 275–277.

Stringer, P. & Kremer, A. (1987). Environmental psychology in the Netherlands. In D. Stokols & I. Altman (Eds.), *Handbook of environmental psychology* (Vol. 2, pp. 1227–1242). New York: Wiley.

Suzuki, D. & Knudtson, P. (1992). *Wisdom of the elders: Honoring sacred native visions of nature.* New York: Bantam Books.

Thayer, R. L., Jr. (1994). *Gray world, green heart: Technology, nature and the sustainable landscape.* New York: Wiley.

Van-Lange, P. A. & Liebrand, W. B. (1991). The influence of others' morality and own social value orientation on cooperation in the Netherlands and the USA. *International Journal of Psychology, 26,* 429–449.

Vining, J. & Ebreo, A. (1990). What makes a recycler? A comparison of recyclers and nonrecyclers. *Environment and Behavior, 22,* 55–73.

Walsh, W. B., Craik, K. H., & Price, R. H. (1992). *Person–environment psychology: Models and perspectives.* Hillsdale, NJ: Lawrence Erlbaum.

Waltz, S. E. (1988). Women's housing needs in the Arab cultural context of Tunisia. In W. van Vliet (Ed.), *Women, housing, and community* (pp. 171–183). Brookfield, IL: Gower.

Weisman, L. (1992). *Discrimination by design: A feminist critique of the man-made environment.* Urbana: University of Illinois Press.

Werner, C. M., Altman, I., & Oxley, D. (1985). Temporal aspects of homes: A transactional perspective. In I. Altman & C. M. Werner (Eds.), *Home environments: Human behavior and the environment* (Vol. 8, pp. 1–32). New York: Plenum.

Werner, C. M. & Baxter, L. A. (1994). Temporal qualities of relationships: Organismic, transactional, and dialectical views. In M. L. Knapp & G. R. Miller (Eds.), *Handbook of interpersonal communication,* 2d ed. (pp. 323–379). Newbury Park, CA: Sage.

Werner, C. M., Haggard, L. M., Altman, I., & Oxley, D. (1988). Temporal qualities of rituals and celebrations: A comparison of Christmas Street and Zuni Shalako. In J. E. McGrath (Ed.), *The social psychology of time: New perspectives* (pp. 203–232). Beverly Hills: Sage.

White, L., Jr. (1967/1974). The historical roots of our ecologic crisis. In D. Spring & E. Spring (Eds.), Ecology and religion in history (pp. 15–31). New York: Harper Torchbooks. (Reprinted from *Science, 155,* 1203–1207.)

Whiting, J. W. M. & Whiting, B. B. (1975). Aloofness and intimacy of husbands and wives: A cross-cultural study. *Ethos, 3,* 183–208.

Wicker, A. W. (1979). *An introduction to ecological psychology.* Monterey, CA: Brooks/Cole.

Wolin, S. J. & Bennett, L. A. (1984). Family rituals. *Family Process, 23,* 401–420.

8

ACCULTURATION AND ADAPTATION

J. W. BERRY
Queen's University
Canada

D. L. SAM
University of Bergen
Norway

Contents

Introduction

Much of the field of cross-cultural psychology has been concerned with understanding the development and display of human behavioral diversity in adaptation to the cultural contexts in which the behaviors occur. This approach, while valid for many purposes, can be criticized as viewing cultural contexts as relatively static. In recent years a second major line of enquiry has come to the fore in cross-cultural psychology, one that views cultures as *changing* contexts, due to both their own internal dynamics, and due to contacts with other cultures (Berry, 1980a). These two branches of cross-cultural psychology correspond to the two main features of the ecocultural framework that has guided previous attempts to review and systematize the field (Berry, Poortinga, Segall, & Dasen, 1992; Segall, Dasen, Berry, & Poortinga, 1990). Within that framework, cultural adaptation to ecological context and contacts with other cultures provide the two main sets of explanatory variables for human behavioral diversity.

This chapter focuses on the second of these branches: how individuals, who have developed in one cultural context, manage to adapt to new contexts that impinge on them as a result of migration, colonization, or other forms of intercultural encounters. The concept of *acculturation* is employed to refer to the cultural changes resulting from these encounters, while the concepts of *psychological acculturation* and *adaptation* are employed to refer to the psychological changes and eventual outcomes that occur as a result of individuals experiencing acculturation (Berry, 1980b).

Because this is a massive and rapidly changing field, our chapter is necessarily selective, and possibly biased, in its coverage and perspectives. The authors' experiences and interests have led us to emphasize literatures pertaining to immigrants, refugees, and indigenous peoples, especially in adaptation to North America, Australia, and to a lesser extent Europe; largely absent are studies done in Asian, African, and South American settings (where, in fact, most acculturation has taken place). This bias reflects the availability of literature for some peoples of the world but not for others.

Theoretical and Conceptual Issues

Many theoretical perspectives have been advanced in the acculturation literature. However, some common meanings have emerged, and are now widely shared.

Acculturation

The classical definition of *acculturation* was presented by Redfield, Linton and Herskovits (1936, p. 149): "Acculturation comprehends those phenomena which result when groups of individuals having different cultures come into continuous first-hand contact with subsequent changes in the original culture patterns of either or both groups." While acculturation is a neutral term in principle (that is, change may take place in either or both groups), in practice acculturation tends to induce more change in one of the groups (termed the *acculturating group* in this chapter) than in the other (Berry, 1990a).

A distinction has been made by Graves (1967) between acculturation as a collective or group-level phenomenon, and *psychological acculturation*. In the former (and original level of the concept) acculturation is a change in the culture of the group; in the latter, acculturation is a change in the psychology of the individual. This distinction between the set of cultural variables that influence the individual on the one hand, and the psychological outcomes of these influences, on the other, is important in order to examine the systematic relationships between these two sets of variables. Moreover, in acculturation research we need to attend to this distinction because not all individuals participate to the same extent in the general acculturation being experienced by their group. While the general changes may be profound in the group, individuals may vary greatly in the degree to which they participate in these community changes. The concept of acculturation has become widely used in cross-cultural psychology and has also been the subject of criticism. One difficulty has been the gradual erosion of the original meaning of the concept so that it became synonymous with only one possible outcome of acculturation. According to a number of critics (e.g., Vasquez, 1984), the concept came to mean *assimilation,* even though in the original definition this outcome was identified as only one of the many possible varieties of acculturation (see following discussion). There are two possible ways to deal with this criticism: to discard the concept because of this confusion, or to emphasize clearly the original meaning; in this chapter we adopt the latter approach.

A parallel conceptualization has been developed, mainly among French-language scholars: *interculturation* (see Camilleri, 1990; Camilleri & Malewska-Peyre, Volume 2, this *Handbook*; Clanet, 1990). This concept is defined as "the set of processes by which individuals and groups interact when they identify themselves as culturally distinct" (Clanet, 1990, p. 70, our translation). A more extended description of this approach emerged from recent conference discussions (Bouvy et al., 1994): interculturation "refers to the construction of cultural diversity in the context of intercultural contacts.... Intercultural psychology has a specific research field (intercultural encounters), a specific research object (cultural distinctiveness), and a specific mechanism ('interculturation,' i.e., the formation of a new culture on the basis of these encounters)" (p. 2).

There are evident similarities between the *acculturation* and *interculturation* approaches, and it is often difficult in practice to distinguish the research done, or the conclusions drawn from the two approaches. One distinguishing feature, however, is the interest in the formation of new cultures in the interculturation, more than in the acculturation, approach. Given these rather broad similarities, this chapter will employ the term acculturation to refer to the general processes and outcomes (both cultural and psychological) of cultural contact.[1]

Plural Societies

Often, during the process of acculturation, societies become *culturally plural*. That is, people of many cultural backgrounds come to live together in a diverse society, forming a multicultural society. In many cases they form cultural groups that are not equal in power (numerical, economic or political); these power differences have given rise to popular and social science terms such as "mainstream," "minority," "ethnic group," and so forth. In this chapter, while recognizing the unequal influences and changes that exist during acculturation, we employ the term *cultural group* to refer to all groups, and the terms *dominant* and *non-dominant* to refer to their relative power where such a difference exists and is relevant to the discussion. In this way, we attempt to avoid a host of political and social assumptions that have distorted much of the work on psychological acculturation. Principally, we are concerned with the widespread view that "minorities" are inevitably (or should be in the process of) becoming part of the "mainstream" culture. While this does occur in many plural societies, it does not always occur, and in some cases it is resisted by either or both the dominant and non-dominant cultural groups, resulting in the continuing cultural diversity of so many contemporary societies. In this way, our concepts and measures allow us to avoid prejudging this issue.

Acculturating Groups

Many kinds of cultural groups may exist in plural societies and their variety is primarily due to three factors: mobility, voluntariness, and permanence (see Figure 8–1). Some groups are in contact because they have moved to a new location (e.g., immigrants and refugees), while others have had the new culture brought to them (e.g., indigenous peoples). Second, some have entered into the acculturation process voluntarily (e.g., immigrants) while others experience acculturation without having sought it out (e.g., refugees, indigenous peoples). And third, among those who have migrated, some are relatively permanently settled into the process (e.g., immigrants), while for others the situation is a temporary one (e.g., so-

Mobility	Voluntariness of contact	
	Voluntary	**Involuntary**
Sedentary	Ethnocultural groups	Indigenous peoples
Migrant Permanent Temporary	Immigrants Sojourners	Refugees Asylum seekers

FIGURE 8–1   Types of acculturating groups

journers such as international students and guest workers, or asylum seekers who may eventually be deported).

These three factors, when interacting as in Figure 8–1, correspond to six relatively independent research literatures on acculturating peoples. In this chapter we take the position that despite these substantial variations in the life circumstances of these acculturating groups, and despite the large variation in cultural groups that experience acculturation, the psychological processes that operate during acculturation are essentially the same for all groups; that is, we adopt a *universalist* perspective on acculturation (Berry et al., 1992). A framework that attempts to show these commonalities will follow this section on theory.

Acculturation Strategies

In all plural societies, cultural groups and their individual members must deal with the issue of *how* to acculturate (see also chapter by Camilleri & Malewska-Peyre, Volume 2, this *Handbook*). Strategies with respect to two major issues are usually worked out by groups and individuals in their daily encounters with each other. These issues are: *cultural maintenance* (to what extent are cultural identity and characteristics considered important by individuals, and their maintenance strived for) and *contact and participation* (to what extent should individuals become involved in other cultural groups, or remain primarily among themselves) (Berry, 1970).

When these two central issues are considered simultaneously, a conceptual framework (Figure 8–2) is generated which posits four acculturation strategies. These two issues can be responded to on attitudinal dimensions, represented by bipolar arrows. For purposes of presentation, generally positive or negative ("yes"

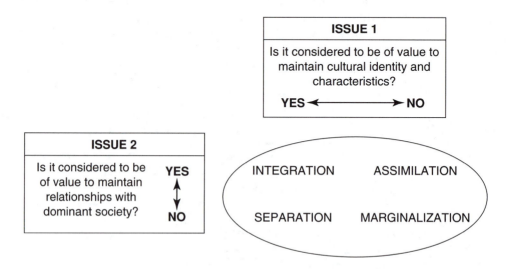

FIGURE 8–2   Acculturation strategies

or "no") responses to these issues intersect to define four strategies. When individuals do not wish to maintain their cultural identity and seek daily interaction with other cultures, then the Assimilation strategy is defined. In contrast, when the non-dominant group places a value on holding onto their original culture, and at the same time wishes to avoid interaction with others, then the Separation alternative is defined. (When this mode of acculturation is pursued by the dominant group with respect to the non-dominant group, then Segregation is the appropriate term.) When there is an interest in both maintaining one's original culture while in daily interactions with other groups, Integration is the option; here, some degree of cultural integrity is maintained, while at the same time the individual seeks to participate as an integral part of the larger social network of a multicultural society. Finally, when there is little possibility or interest in cultural maintenance (often for reasons of enforced cultural loss), and little interest in having relations with others (often for reasons of exclusion or discrimination), then Marginalization is defined. *Attitudes* towards these four alternatives, and actual *behaviors* exhibiting them, together constitute an individual's acculturation *strategy* (Berry et al., 1989).

Other terms than those used here have been proposed by acculturation researchers (e.g., Gordon, 1964). In particular, the term "bicultural" has been employed to refer to acculturation that involves the individual simultaneously in the two cultures that are in contact (Szapocznik & Kurtines, 1993; LaFromboise, Coleman, & Gerton, 1993; Padilla, 1994); this concept corresponds closely to the Integration strategy as defined here. Similarly, Gordon (1964) refers to two forms of incorporation: cultural assimilation and structural assimilation. In our terms, when both forms occur, complete assimilation is likely to result; however, when structural assimilation is present (a high degree of contact and participation) combined with a low degree of cultural assimilation (a high degree of cultural maintenance), then an outcome similar to Integration is likely.

Three other issues require commentary before proceeding, because preferences for one acculturation strategy over others are known to vary, depending on context and time period. First, although there is usually an overall coherent preference for one particular strategy, there can also be variation according to where one is. In more private spheres or domains (such as the home, the extended family, the ethnic community) more cultural maintenance may be sought than in more public spheres (such as the work place, or in politics); and there may be less intergroup contact sought in private spheres than in the more public ones. Moreover, the broader national context may affect acculturation strategies, such that in explicitly multicultural societies individuals may match such a policy with a personal preference for integration; or, in assimilationist societies, acculturation may be easiest by adopting the assimilation strategy. That is, individuals may well be constrained in their choice of strategy, even to the point where there is a very limited role for personal preference (acculturation attitudes).

Second, there is evidence that during the course of development (and even in later life) individuals explore various strategies, eventually settling on one that is more useful and satisfying than the others; however, as far as is known, there is no set sequence or age at which different strategies are used.

Third, an individual's or group's preferred acculturation strategy may or may not be permitted by the dominant group. For example, in societies that are explicitly assimilationist, the adoption of the Integration strategy may be constrained because of a national ideology that promotes a single culture and identity in the nation state. However, there is some evidence (e.g., Berry & Kalin, 1995; see also chapter by Gudykunst & Bond, this volume) that retaining one's cultural identity does not diminish one's commitment to the larger national entity. Similarly, attempts to restrict cultural maintenance may stem from a confusion in the dominant society between the integration and separation strategies. Emphasizing that Integration involves contact and participation, rather than isolation or self-segregation (as clearly illustrated in Figure 8–2), can reduce this confusion and the associated sense of threat to the culture of the dominant society. Creating greater understanding and acceptance of the integration strategy is an important goal, because evidence (to be presented) strongly supports a positive correlation between the use of this strategy and good psychological adaptation during acculturation.

Psychological Acculturation

Three main points of view can be identified in acculturation research, each suggesting a different level of difficulty for the individual. The first one considers that psychological changes are rather easy to accomplish; this approach has been referred to variously as "behavioral shifts" by Berry (1980a), "culture learning" by Brislin, Landis, and Brandt (1983), and "social skills" acquisition by Furnham and Bochner (1986). Here, psychological adaptations to acculturation are considered to be a matter of learning a new behavioral repertoire that is appropriate for the new cultural context. Of course, some "culture shedding" (Berry, 1992) may also have to occur (the *un*learning of aspects of one's previous repertoire that are no longer appropriate); this may be accompanied by some "culture conflict" (where incompatible behaviors create difficulties for the individual and have to be sorted out).

In cases where conflict exists, then a second point of view is appropriate. Here individuals may experience "culture shock" (Oberg, 1960) or "acculturative stress" (Berry, 1970; Berry et al., 1987) if they cannot easily change their repertoire. While the "culture shock" concept is older and has wide popular acceptance, we prefer the "acculturative stress" conceptualization, because it is closely linked to psychological models of stress as a response to environmental stressors (which, in the present case, reside in the experience of acculturation). In most cases, only moderate difficulties are experienced (such as psychosomatic problems) because other psychological processes (such as problem appraisal and coping strategies) are available to the acculturating individual.

When major difficulties are experienced, the "psychopathology" or "mental disease" perspective is most appropriate (Malzberg & Lee, 1956; Murphy, 1965). Here, changes in the cultural context exceed the individual's capacity to cope, because of the size, speed or some other aspect of the change, leading to serious psychological disturbances, such as clinical depression and incapacitating anxiety.

Adaptation

For most acculturating individuals, after a period of time, some adaptation to the new cultural context usually takes place. Depending on a variety of factors, these adaptations can take many different forms. Sometimes there is increased "fit" between the acculturating individual and the new context (e.g., when the assimilation or integration strategies are pursued, and when attitudes in the dominant society are accepting of the acculturating individual and group). Sometimes, however, a "fit" is not achieved (as in separation/segregation and marginalization) and the groups settle into a pattern of conflict, and with resultant acculturative stress or psychopathology.

In the recent literature on psychological adaptation to acculturation, a distinction has been drawn between *psychological* and *sociocultural* adaptation (Searle & Ward, 1990). The first refers to a set of internal psychological outcomes including a clear sense of personal and cultural identity, good mental health, and the achievement of personal satisfaction in the new cultural context; the second is a set of external psychological outcomes that link individuals to their new context, including their ability to deal with daily problems, particularly in the areas of family life, work, and school. Although these two forms of adaptation are usually related empirically, there are two reasons for keeping them conceptually distinct. One is that factors predicting these two types of adaptation are often different; the other is that psychological adaptation may best be analyzed within the context of the stress and psychopathology approaches, while sociocultural adaptation is more closely linked to the social skills framework (Ward & Kennedy, 1993a).

Acculturation Framework

The complex literature on acculturation has been the subject of numerous frameworks; these have attempted to systematize the process of acculturation and to illustrate the main factors that affect an individual's adaptation. In Figure 8–3, one such framework (Berry, 1992) is presented (see also Olmedo, 1979; Rogler, 1994).

On the left are shown group-level acculturation phenomena, while on the right are individual or psychological phenomena. Along the top are features that exist prior to acculturation, while along the bottom are those that arise during the process of acculturation. Through the middle of the framework are the main group- and psychological-level acculturation phenomena; these flow from left to right beginning with the cultural groups in contact bringing about changes in many of their collective features (e.g. political, economic, social structures), then affecting the individual who is experiencing acculturation (resulting in a number of possible changes including behavioral shifts, acculturative stress and psychopathology), leading finally to a person's adaptation (both psychological and sociocultural). The studies to be reviewed in the following sections show that this central flow is highly variable: the nature of a person's psychological acculturation and eventual adaptation depends on specific features of the group-level factors (on the

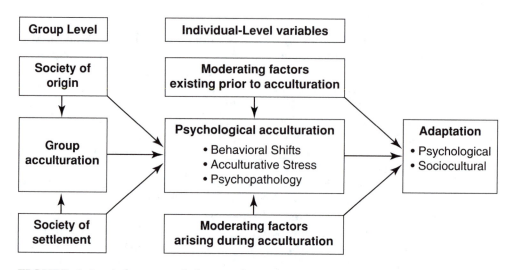

FIGURE 8–3   A framework for acculturation research

left) and of the moderating influence of individual factors that are prior to, or arise during, acculturation (at the top and bottom).[2]

The main point of the framework is to show the key variables that should be attended to when carrying out studies of psychological acculturation. We suggest that any study that ignores any of these broad classes of variables will be incomplete, and be unable to comprehend individuals who are experiencing acculturation. For example, research that does not attend to the cultural and psychological characteristics that the focal individuals bring to the process, merely characterizing them by name (e.g., as "Vietnamese," or "Somali," or even less helpfully as "minorities" or "immigrants"), cannot hope to understand their acculturation or adaptation. Similarly, research that ignores key features of the dominant society (such as their demography, immigration policies, and attitudes towards immigrants) is also incomplete. However, it is important to note that there is no single study that has incorporated or verified all aspects of the framework in Figure 8–3; it is a composite framework, assembling findings from numerous smaller-scale studies.

To expand on Figure 8–3, Tables 8–1 and 8–2 provide a listing of these broad classes of variables that can be found in the literature, using the case of Immigrants. Examples employing other groups and phenomena could serve the purpose equally well. Indeed, given our earlier expressed view that many of the phenomena are shared across acculturating groups, the list of factors affecting acculturation in Table 8–1 may be taken as a more general guide, one that is relevant to most acculturating groups and phenomena. Table 8–2 outlines many of the variables that are typically studied as part of the individual-level phenomena constituting psychological acculturation and adaptation. These are only examples of the large range that will be identified in the review of studies that follows.

TABLE 8–1   Specific factors affecting the process of acculturation and adaptation

Variable	*Specific features*
Society of origin	Ethnographic characteristics (e.g., language, religion, values) Political situation (e.g., conflict, civil war, repression) Economic conditions (e.g., poverty, disparity, famine) Demographic factors (e.g., crowding, population explosion)
Society of settlement	Immigration history (longstanding vs. recent) Immigration policy (intentional vs. accidental) Attitudes towards immigration (favorable–unfavorable) Attitudes towards specific groups (favorable–unfavorable) Social support (availability, usefulness)
Group acculturation	Changes in acculturating group: 　　Physical (e.g., rural to urban) 　　Biological (e.g., nutrition, disease) 　　Economic (e.g., loss of status) 　　Social (e.g., isolation) 　　Cultural (e.g., dress, food, language)
Moderating factors prior to acculturation	Demographic (e.g., age, gender, education) Cultural (e.g., language, religion, distance) Economic (e.g., status) Personal (e.g., health, prior knowledge) Migration motivation (e.g., push vs. pull) Expectations (e.g., excessive vs. realistic)
Moderating factors arising during acculturation	Acculturation strategies (Assimilation, Integration, 　　Separation, Marginalization) Contact/participation Cultural maintenance Social support (appraisal and use) Coping strategies and resources Prejudice and discrimination

TABLE 8–2   Specific features of psychological acculturation and adaptation

Variable	*Specific features*
Behavioral shifts	Culture learning (e.g., language, food, dress, social norms) Culture shedding (e.g., changing social norms, gender attitudes) Culture conflict (e.g., incompatibility, intergroup difficulties)
Acculturative stress	Problem appraisal Stressors Stress phenomena (e.g., psychological, psychomatic, anxiety)

(Cont.)

TABLE 8–2   *(Continued)*

Variable	Specific features
Psychopathology	Problems Crises Pathological phenomena (e.g., depression, schizophrenia)
Psychological adaptation	Self-esteem Identity consolidation Well-being/satisfaction
Sociocultural adaptation	Cultural knowledge, social skills Interpersonal and intergroup relations Family and community relations

Review of Empirical Studies

Given the large and diverse research literature on psychological acculturation, it is not possible to present more than a review that illustrates the kind of work and findings that exist. The previous section painted the broad picture, while the theory section identified the key concepts in the field. Both of these provide us with a "sampling frame" that will guide the selective presentation that follows. Specifically, we will review studies according to the main types of acculturating groups, and within these categories, we will attend to most of the key concepts and variables that were outlined earlier, and that are used in many of the studies.

Immigrants

In our introductory section, two kinds of migrants were identified (sojourners and immigrants) distinguished by the permanence of their contact with the new society. This section focuses on immigrants, whom we characterized as the group of acculturating individuals who voluntarily move from one society to another, and who tend to have a relatively permanent residence in the new society. While these three key words may be essential in distinguishing this group from sojourners and other acculturating groups, some terminological difficulties have been pointed out by Berry and Kim (1988). Of relevance here are the issues of relative permanent residence status and mobility, and how these respectively distinguish immigrants from sojourners and ethnic groups. Sojourners (see next section) are viewed as having a short-term stay, but some guestworkers in Germany are still viewed as sojourners after living in the country for over 30 years, and are de facto immigrants. Even children of these guestworkers who have been born and raised there are thought of as sojourners (Asoyek, 1991). As Cohon (1981) has pointed out, different terms are used to refer to the same group of people in different countries, and this may be dependent on such factors as a "government's perception of the 'mood' of the host country populace toward new arrivals" (p. 256).

In light of the definitional difficulties associated with "immigrants," it is not surprising that studies on immigrants have problems finding a "pure" sample. Some studies of "immigrants" have included sojourners, ethnic groups, and even refugees in their samples, (see, e.g., Krishnan & Berry, 1992; Sam, 1994; Schmitz, 1994).

Due to the voluntary nature of immigrants' cultural contact with new societies, one should expect a relatively easy acculturation experience and positive adaptation outcomes, at least in comparison to refugees (see e.g., Garza-Guerrero, 1974; Krupinski, Stoller, & Wallace., 1973). However, immigrants are sometimes reported to encounter more problems than their voluntary status would suggest (Naidoo, 1992). The number of studies done in the area of migration and mental health bear witness to the problems immigrants are alleged to experience (Burvill, 1984). Moreover, Rogler (1994) points out that the psychological changes individuals undergo as a result of migration go far beyond mental health; problems relating to changes in socioeconomic status, social networks, and the migration experience itself should be areas of interest to psychologists.

As immigrants normally do not intend to return to their countries of origin, they may burn their bridges on emigration, and this may make it more difficult for them to return when it turns out that their acculturation experiences fall short of expectations. The desire for better social conditions and quality of life are probably the main factors motivating migration (Furnham & Bochner, 1986). The motive to migrate is thought to include such factors as relative deprivation of full employment opportunities, education, health and housing facilities, climate, and social and community ties. These factors have been found to be prevalent in Portugal (Neto, 1988), a country where about 50 percent of the adolescent population intends eventually to emigrate. In this study employment, wages, education, and limited opportunities for success in Portugal were the main reasons for plans to emigrate.

In a number of countries immigrants tend to be downwardly mobile in occupation; in many cases they do not get jobs for which they have been trained (Aycan & Berry, 1996; Beiser et al., 1988; Lane, 1992; Stewart, 1983). Many of them tend to undertake jobs of lower social status and prestige. The stressors associated with downward mobility may lead to an increase in psychological problems (Dohrenwend & Dohrenwend, 1978), while upward mobility may reduce them (Moghaddam, 1988). However, it is also known that many immigrants are not as frustrated as might be expected from their downward mobility (Ip, 1993). Suarez-Orozco (1991) has argued that immigrants have a "dual frame of reference" which attenuates the potentially negative effects that their poorer socioeconomic situation might cause. Immigrants make comparisons between "here" (settlement society) and "there" (country of origin), and come to the realization that their living conditions "here" are better than they were "there."

Personal predispositions are the pre-acculturation factors that have had the longest tradition in the study of immigrant adaptation. In a classic study among

Norwegian-born immigrants and native-born Americans in Minnesota, and an examination of hospital rates from the general Norwegian population, Odegaard (1932) found that there was higher mental-hospital admission for schizophrenia among the Norwegian immigrants than native-born Americans and Norwegian natives who did not migrate. He concluded that people who were predisposed to mental health problems were those who migrated. Subsequent studies in this area (Malzberg & Lee, 1956; Murphy, 1965) also found that there is a higher incidence of hospital admission among immigrants than among native-born. Differences in admission rates between the two groups, however, become less when age and gender are controlled for.

More recent investigations have cast doubt on the association between migration and poor mental health. Burnam et al. (1987) found in a study of the prevalence of different psychiatric disorders among Mexican immigrants in Los Angeles that the immigrants had a lower risk factor for different disorders than their native-born peers. They attributed this difference to a stronger sense of self and coping ability among the Mexicans who migrated, a suggestion that is the opposite of that of Odegaard. This conclusion is not an isolated one. Among Mexican-born immigrants in Los Angeles, and U.S.-born Mexican Americans, Golding and Burnam (1990) found that the immigrants had lower depressive symptoms. In a study among Asian (mostly Indians and Pakistani) immigrants in the greater London area, Furnham and Shiekh (1993) found that female immigrants had higher levels of psychological symptomatology than their male counterparts. They found evidence linking social support to mental health, but no difference was noted between the first and second generation immigrants in their level of symptomatology.

In view of the inconclusive evidence that immigrants have more mental health problems than native-born (Burvill, 1984), especially when demographic and cultural factors influencing hospital admission are controlled for, Murphy (1977) suggested that instead of asking why migrants have higher rates of mental disorders, it might be better to ask under what circumstances they have higher rates; that is, we should seek to understand how the many variables involved in the process of migration interact to affect people's adaptation outcome (Aronowitz, 1992) .

In addition to psychiatrists' and psychologists' early concern with migration and mental health outcomes, sociologists were particulalry interested in immigrants' "assimilation," the extent to which immigrants conformed to the norms and values of the society of settlement (Sayegh & Lasry, 1993). It is known that not all immigrants assimilate in the settlement society (Glazer & Moynihan, 1970; Olzak, 1983) and, as outlined earlier, there are a variety of ways an individual may seek to acculturate.

Studies that have focused on immigrants' acculturation strategies have inevitably concluded that integration is most preferred. A preference for integration has been demonstrated for both adults (Krishnan & Berry, 1992) and adolescents (Sam, 1995), in a multicultural society (Berry et al., 1989), and in a relatively monocultural society (Partridge, 1988). Differences, however, exist among immigrant groups in their next most preferred acculturation strategy. In a series of studies in Canada involving samples of different immigrant groups, and involving the use of scales tailored for each group, Berry et al. (1989) found integration to be the most preferred mode. It was noted, however, that among first-generation Hungarian-Canadians, separation is the second most preferred acculturation strategy, while assimilation is the second most preferred mode among the second generation. Among Korean and Portuguese immigrants in Canada, the other three modes of acculturation were not at all desirable. Among Westerners living in Japan, and immigrants from developing countries living in Norway, separation was the second most preferred acculturation strategy (Partridge, 1988; Sam, 1995). The general preference given to separation and integration suggests that many immigrants actually desire to maintain a substantial part of their cultural heritage and identity in the society of settlement.

The general preference for integration over the other strategies raises the question of a possible problem in the measurement of acculturation strategies. While criticizing the operationalization of Berry et al.'s, (1989) acculturation strategies Sayegh and Lasry (1993) nevertheless also found integration to be the most preferred acculturation strategy among a group of Lebanese immigrants to Montreal.

Some studies have looked at other factors that may be related to acculturation strategies themselves. Using the Grossarth-Maticek and Eysenck (1990) Psycho-Social Stress Inventory, Schmitz (1994) found among a group of immigrants to Germany that their personality types were related to the kind of acculturation strategy they preferred. Schmitz found that people with a conformistic dependency on a withdrawing object (i.e., people who persistently and intensively try to attain highly valued targets even when these are inaccessible to them) preferred the assimilation strategy and had heightened psychosomatic complaints. In another study involving young Third World immigrants in Norway, about 20 percent of adolescents' acculturation strategies (specifically assimilation, integration and separation) could be accounted for by their perception of their parents' attitudes to cultural change (Sam, 1995). In the same study, boys were found to be more in favor of assimilation than girls. In contrast, Ghuman (1991) found Asian girls in the United Kingdom to be more in favor of assimilation than boys.

In two separate studies each using over 500 young immigrants in France and Norway, marginalization was found to be negatively correlated with expressed satisfaction with life (Neto, 1994) and positively with psychological and somatic symptoms (Sam, 1994). Integration, on the other hand, was found to contribute negatively to acculturative stress (Krishnan & Berry, 1992; Sam & Berry, 1995). Although integration has been found to correlate positively with psychological well-being, it has been noted in two British studies among Asians (particularly Indians and Pakistanis) that they adjust psychologically very well in spite of poor integration into British society (Aslam et al., 1978; Cochrane, Hashmi, & Stopes-Roe, 1977). This inconsistency may be due to the buffering effect of the extended family and social support system Indians and Pakistanis have. Furnham and Shiekh (1993) found social support to be positively related to mental health outcomes; however, marital status was not linked to psychological distress, a finding which contradicts other studies (see, e.g., Golding & Burnam, 1990). Perhaps the social support provided by spouses may not be as important as that provided by the close-knit family structure made up of many relatives, which is frequently the case for Indians and Pakistanis in Britain (see Rack, 1982).

Sojourners

Members of this acculturating group are short-term visitors to new cultures where permanent settlement is not the purpose of the stay. The group is heterogeneous in composition, and their acculturation experience is usually voluntary and for a specific purpose. Included in this category are international students and scholars, guestworkers, diplomats, business and technical aid personnel, troops stationed in another country, and missionaries. In spite of the group's heterogeneity, the bulk of the sojourner studies have been done with international students (Church, 1982), with some carried out with guestworkers in Europe (e.g., Eldering & Kloprogge, 1989) and in the Gulf States (e.g., Gulati, 1993).

From a psychological point of view, sojourners should have a relatively easy adaptation due to their voluntary contact. In addition, their contact is goal-oriented, and many of them have the basic background "qualifications" needed to achieve their intended goals (Myambo & O'Cuneen, 1988). However, due to the temporary nature of their stay and their intention to return home, some sojourners may underplay the importance of various moderating factors (e.g., acquiring language competence and establishing interpersonal relationships) known to enhance positive adaptation. Selby and Wood (1966), for instance, found that some foreign students in the United States were not interested in establishing friendships with Americans because the purpose of their sojourn was to obtain an academic degree and return home.

Klineberg (1980) identified four main areas of research with international students: selection, preparation (including language competence, and knowledge of the university and the host culture), actual sojourn experiences (including academic work, contacts with the host nationals), and the return home. The first two of these four areas deal with pre-acculturation issues, the third with acculturation and adaptation, and the fourth with post-acculturation, or the long-term effect of acculturation. Among the factors prior to acculturation that have been studied are gender (Fong & Peskin, 1969), age of the student (Hull, 1978), personality (Basu & Ames, 1970), and previous sojourns (Klineberg & Hull, 1979). These factors were all found to moderate acculturation experience and adaptation. Fong and Peskin (1969) found sex differences in the adaptation of foreign students, where female foreign students had a greater number of problems than males. They further reported that special problems may exist for women from more traditional cultures where special gender roles are defined. Marville (1981) has also found that female foreign students in the United States tended to have more academic problems than their male counterparts, and that these problems become compounded when husbands do not support their aspirations.

Younger foreign students and undergraduates have more social contacts with host nationals, and are satisfied with them, while graduate and older students express greater academic and general satisfaction with the outcome of the sojourn (Hull, 1978). These findings may be due to differences in motivation, because younger foreign students and undergraduates had personal goals as their motivating ambition, but older and graduate students had professional goals as their ambition (United States Advisory Commision, 1966). It is difficult to know from the available literature whether level of studies (graduate/undergraduate) or age account for variations in adaptation.

Personality traits have generally been poor predictors of adaptation among sojourners, possibly because of the absence of well-defined personality traits (Kealey & Ruben, 1983). In a study where a clear distinction was made between situational and personal factors, Kealey (1989) found among a group of Canadian technical personnel working in developing countries, evidence for an interaction between situational and personal factors in predicting adaptation outcomes. Personal factors were, however, more important than the situational ones. Basu and Ames (1970) found that foreign students high on authoritarianism were socioculturally more alienated and poorly adjusted. However, level of authoritarianism appears to decline during the sojourn experience (Kagitçibasi, 1978), along with other attitude changes that may facilitate the sojourn.

The effects of age, gender, marital status, and personality found among foreign students have also been found among missionaries. Gish (1983) found that 15 different areas of life were rated as stressful by over 50 percent of respondents, including confronting others when necessary, communication across cultural barriers, work priorities, and making decisions affecting others. These stressful areas were significantly related to gender, age, marital status, nationality, and years of service. In another study with missionaries, Britt (1983) found that personality factors involving self-control and being less moody were important predictors of adaptation.

A number of studies have examined the psychological, sociocultural (e.g., Furnham & Bochner, 1982; Sam & Eide, 1991), and academic adaptations (e.g., Bie, 1976; Raaheim, 1987) of international students. One aspect of sociocultural adaptation that has received a great deal of attention is the interpersonal or social skills used in negotiating everyday social encounters in the new society. Furnham and Bochner (1982) argued that the more competent one is in the social skills, the better the sociocultural adaptation. Social skills were assessed by a scale of difficulties experienced in different social situations. Using 150 foreign students from 29 different countries together with a control group of British students, Furnham and Bochner found that the greater the difference in religion, language, and climate between the host community and the students' native community (referred to as *cultural distance*), the more difficulties the students experienced. The social situations described as most diffcult involved establishing and maintaining interpersonal relationships. Using a slightly modified version of Furnham and Bochner's social skills scale, Ward and Kennedy (1993b) found that Malaysian and Singaporean students in New Zealand faced more sociocultural difficulties than Malaysian students in Singapore, pointing to the role of cultural distance in sociocultural adaptation.

Regarding interpersonal relationships, co-nationals are the most preferred group of friends for foreign students (Furnham & Alibhai, 1985). In contrast, Myambo and O'Cuneen (1988) found among diplomatic wives in Zimbabwe that their primary social network was with host nationals. In a study involving 2,536 foreign students from 139 different countries and studying in 11 different countries, Klineberg and Hull (1979) found that students who made satisfactory social contacts and established relationships with local people during their overseas stay reported broader and more general satisfaction with their academic experience. It is unclear from the study, however, where the causal direction goes, whether satisfactory social contacts facilitate satisfactory academic work or vice versa.

In the same study by Klineberg and Hull, it was found that students who had made a previous adjustment to a foreign culture were significantly better adjusted during their sojourn in a new foreign country. Previous adjustment was defined as having stayed in another culture for a continuous period of one or more months. There is, however, a lack of systematic studies on how such short-term prior acculturation may moderate psychological adaptation.

In a longitudinal study designed in the acculturative stress framework, Zheng and Berry (1991) found that Chinese sojourners in Canada experienced more problems (including communication, making friends, discrimination, work and family) but had no greater stress than a control group of Chinese-Canadians (Chinese settled in Canada) and non-Chinese Canadians. Longitudinal analysis showed that the Chinese sojourners had poorer psychological health three months after arrival than before departure, but among those with longer residence (2 to 5 years) health was as good as pre-departure levels. This study gave support to Lysgaard's U-curve hypothesis (Lysgaard, 1955).

In another longitudinal study involving Taiwan students in the United States, Ying and Liese (1991) found that over half of the participants reported a decline in their emotional well-being, and this change was found to be related to pre-departure mood level, continuation of pre-departure relationships, minimal interpersonal contacts with the host society, and general academic problems. Those whose mood improved were those with high pre-departure depression and high preparation level. In a cross-sectional study involving foreign students from over 50 different countries studying in Norway, Sam and Eide (1991) also found that the students reported more health problems (in the area of anxiety, depression, somatic symptoms, and paranoia) during their overseas sojourn than prior to it. These psychological problems were found to be related to knowledge about study opportunities in Norway and social contacts with host society students in the halls of residence. Overall, a large proportion of the studies with international students suggests that they experience a good deal of acculturative stress. While it is difficult to give the precise number of those who fail to cope, Church (1982) has suggested that about 80 percent of the students make reasonable adaptations to their new cultures and institutional demands.

However, among sojourners who have returned home, Tamura and Furnham (1993) found the returnees to be more dissatisfied with their lives in their native countries than in the foreign country. This study was conducted among Japanese children aged 6 to 18 who had returned from an overseas sojourn of at least one year, with a matched control group from the same schools who had no overseas sojourn. The returnee children also had a more critical image of Japan and its people than the control group. There was, however, no indication that returnees had more adjustment problems than their counterparts. The returnee children were also found to be less worried about their academic achievements and interpersonal relationships. In another study involving Turkish returnee children from Germany, Wolbert (1991) found the children to be predominantly concerned about their academic achievement, a finding that may seem contradictory to that of Tamura and Furnham (1993). It should be noted that the Japanese returnees were mostly children of diplomats, or employees of large corporations and research institutions, while the Turkish sample were children of guestworkers; the two groups probably had very different social lives and length of residence during their overseas sojourn, leading to different experiences on reentry.

Refugees and Asylum Seekers

This group of acculturating persons faces the greatest risks during the process of adaptation according to the three risk factors identified in Figure 8–1: they are involuntary, migratory, and in many cases temporary. In addition, they have likely experienced the most difficult pre-acculturation situations, including war, famine, deprivation, torture, and humiliation (at the individual level), and massive exclusion or domination (at the group level).

At the present time, there are approximately 20 million refugees and asylum seekers in the world. The vast majority (around 80%) are in Asia and Africa. While only a small proportion is eventually settled in Western countries, most of the research literature dealing with refugee adaptation has been done in the West, giving a very biased view of the refugee experience (Leopold & Harrell-Bond, 1994). Psychological knowledge about refugees in countries of first asylum and in camps is very limited, due to a number of factors. One is that the main refugee agency (United Nations High Commission for Refugees, UNHCR) was initially concerned only with the protection of refugees, not with their psychological well-being; mental health issues have not been a priority. A second reason is that psychological work in camps and first settlements is hazardous, and permission to do research or provide service is usually difficult to obtain. The review that follows is only the "tip of the iceberg," providing only a glimpse of the character of psychological adaptation being achieved by refugees. More comprehensive treatments can be found in books edited by Williams and Westermeyer (1986) and Holtzman and Bornemann (1990).

Perhaps the most important pre-acculturation factor identified in the literature is that of traumatic stress, usually involving various forms of violence. Trauma has been defined as an event that an individual has experienced, or witnessed, "that involves actual or threatened death or injury, or threat to the physical integrity of others" (Friedman & Jaranson, 1994, p. 208). Some of these events are specifically related to the origin of one's refugee status (e.g., warfare, ethnic conflict, torture) while others may not be unique but have higher incidence among refugees (such as starvation and rape). Nevertheless, collectively they may constitute a set of "protracted, complex and catastrophic stressors" (ibid, p. 209) that may give rise to *post-traumatic stress*; this is a syndrome involving intrusive recollections of the stressor events, which evoke panic, terror, grief, or despair, and are manifested in daytime fantasies, traumatic nightmares, and psychotic reenactments ("flashbacks"). In addition, there may be coping strategies that involve avoidance of stimuli that are similar to the original stressors, the avoidance of certain situations, and amnesia (ibid, p. 210). While there is some controversy concerning the definition and treatment of trauma, it is clear that such a set of stressors constitutes a risk to good psychological and sociocultural adaptation, (Beiser et al., 1988), and may occur along with serious problems (such as depression and substance abuse). This type of outcome clearly belongs to the psychopathology point of view on the psychological consequences of acculturation.

Some of the clearest evidence of the long term negative consequences of traumatic stress come from a study in the United States by Chung and Kagawa-Singer (1993). Despite evidence of some short-term ability to cope with such experiences (e.g., Beiser, Turner, & Ganesan, 1989; Rumbaut, 1991), these traumatic events appear to affect longer term adaptation. In a large sample of Indochinese refugees (made up of subsamples of Vietnamese, Cambodians, and Lao) in the Los Angeles area, the number of trauma events was a significant predictor of both depression and anxiety; this was true regardless of ethnicity or the number of years refugees had been settled (Chung & Kagawa-Singer, 1993).

Among risk factors arising during acculturation is the widely held view that all refugees are in need of constant control, monitoring, or support; this can well lead to a sense of dependency and a limit on the acquisition of the social skills necessary for good sociocultural adaptation (von Buchwald, 1994). Whether for positive (e.g., "assistance") or negative (e.g., "containment") motives, the outcome can be the development of excessive dependency, involving a loss of a sense of personal control and self-confidence, eventually giving way to numbness and apathy. The psychological consequence of this dependency are similar to those of "learned helplessness" (Seligman, 1975) in which passivity takes over from more active coping strategies, and may become a relatively permanent part of one's behavior. The sociocultural consequences of this dependency and helplessness may be minimal participation in the daily activities of either society, including school, work, and community involvement (Rangaraj, 1988).

Despite these numerous risk factors, the research now available indicates that many refugees eventually make successful adaptations. The most frequently researched group (Vietnamese) have provided much of the evidence for this conclusion. For example, a comprehensive longitudinal project (Beiser, 1994) included a representative group of "boat people" in Vancouver, interviewed in 1981, 1983, and 1992. After ten years in Canada, unemployment rates were below the national average, educational attainment was at or above the national norms, and a variety of mental health indicators (anxiety, depression, and psychosomatic symptoms) revealed no heightened problems. Almost all had become Canadian citizens, and the vast majority indicated that they felt "at home" in their new country.

Not all studies of Vietnamese refugee adaptation, however, show satisfactory adaptation. In Norway, Hauff and Vaglum (1993) found that unemployment rates were high three years after arrival. This problem was higher for those who were single, who had relatively low education, who had lost social status, and who had experienced relatively high pre-departure trauma. Also in Norway, Knudsen (1991) found that Vietnamese had to cope not only with the stressors of the refugee experience, but also with relief and therapeutic programs that had been set up to assist them (cf. earlier discussion of dependency and helplessness).

Another factor posing risk is age (being elderly or a youth). For elderly Vietnamese, substantial difficulty may be experienced (e.g., in Australia; Thomas & Balnaves, 1993), and for youth, problems may increase for some period after arrival (e.g., in Finland; Liebkind, 1993). More generally, being an adolescent, or elderly, have been identified as posing specific risks in a number of reviews of the field (e.g., Beiser et al., 1988; Ahearn & Athey, 1991; Ager, 1993). It is not clear why these two age groups may be more vulnerable. Perhaps general adaptability is lower among elderly acculturating people generally, but that the disruption in one's life due to involuntary migration exacerbates this problem; and perhaps the "double transition" (of adolescence and acculturation) reinforce each other, creating enhanced risk for youth.

Numerous studies have shown the importance of many other factors in refugee adaptation. Evidence suggests that acculturation strategies are as relevant for refugees as for other acculturating peoples. For example, Doná and Berry (1994) found a significantly lower level of acculturative stress among Central American refugees settled in Canada who were pursuing integration compared to those pursuing assimilation or separation. In a study among Guatemalan refugees in camps in Mexico (Doná, 1993), once again, those pursuing integration were happier and reported better satisfaction and quality of life than those pursuing separation (assimilation and marginalization were not pursued by any in these refugee settlements).

Social support has also been shown to be a protective factor. While for many refugee groups there is no prior like-ethnic settlement to serve as a supportive community, culturally similar groups can serve this role well. For example, in one study in Canada, those ethnic Vietnamese who could speak Chinese were found to have better mental health than those who could not (Berry & Blondel, 1982); supplementary interviews revealed that Chinese-speakers were more likely to be employed and advised by the Chinese community who had been settled for several generations. Social support has been found by Beiser, Turner, and Ganesan (1989, with Vietnamese refugees in Canada) to buffer stressors encountered during settlement, but had no effect in reducing the impact of trauma experienced prior to settlement. Similarly, Shisana and Celentano (1985, with Namibian refugee adolescents in various African cities) found that social support was especially important in lessening the intensity of chronic stress resulting from war experience.

Indigenous Peoples

The process of colonization has been underway for centuries, leading to contact with, and domination of, indigenous or aboriginal peoples everywhere. While a considerable amount of acculturation research has focussed on these peoples in the Western Hemisphere (indeed such research had its origins there; see Linton, 1940), a good deal of the impact of acculturation on indigenous peoples is to be found in Asia, Africa, and Oceania. And in some cases there is substantial *secondary acculturation* in which those originally affected by foreign colonial powers now influence smaller indigenous groups that remain with their own countries. For example, Bantu-speaking peoples in the Central African Republic are the major source of acculturation for the Biaka Pygmy peoples with whom they are in daily contact (Berry et al., 1986).

The hallmark of all these situations is that contact was initially involuntary on the part of indigenous peoples, while usually remaining in their original territories. From the point of view of Figure 8–1 then, indigenous peoples are likely to be at moderate risk for acculturative problems. However, a number of other pre-contact factors seem to have placed them at greater risk: they were often much less powerful (militarily, economically, politically) than those who came to dominate them, and the goal of colonization was often explicitly to change their culture and behavior (e.g., their religious beliefs, values, and educational practices). The consequences have thus usually been more devastating than earlier supposed. However, it is among indigenous peoples worldwide that resistance and cultural survival have been the most remarkable, demonstrating most clearly that assimilation is not the only, or inevitable, outcome of acculturation.

Prior to contact, indigenous peoples were extremely varied in cultural adaptations, ranging from sedentary, stratified, and complex societies (e.g., in much of Africa, Asia, and in Meso-America) to nomadic, egalitarian and loosely structured societies (e.g., in much of North and South America and Australia, and occasionally in Africa and Asia). Because many colonizing powers were highly structured societies, and because they often imposed such hierarchical structures on indigenous peoples, it has been hypothesized that indigenous groups who were more similar to them (i.e., hierarchical) would experience relatively fewer problems; conversely, those who were most dissimilar were likely to face greater change, and consequently experience greater acculturative stress. At the cultural level, there is indeed some evidence that egalitarian and loosely-structured societies have been the most vulnerable to the problems brought by colonization (e.g., Mead, 1956; Honigmann, 1972), and at the psychological level these nomadic, hunting- and gathering-based groups have been shown to experience higher levels of acculturative stress than comparable agricultural groups (Berry, 1976; Sinha, Mishra, & Berry, 1992). Various specific reasons have been proposed for these problems, including enforced relocation and sedentarization, increased population density and crowding (leading to social conflict), and new levels of authority that contravene traditional values of personal autonomy and independence (Chance, 1965; Trimble, 1980).

Among other pre-contact factors affecting the acculturation of indigenous peoples have been the lack of warning or preparation for their colonization, and the suddenness with which it occurred. This was particularly true in the Western Hemisphere and in Oceania, where contact was rarely presaged, and where colonial settlement often took place within a few years. In contrast, other acculturating groups (particularly immigrants and sojourners) are often aware of future experiences by way of formal orientation programs, or by informal knowledge through international media. While there are no research studies on the role of this unique situation (and such studies are probably not possible), the lack of foreknowledge and the speed of onset remain a plausible explanation of why indigenous peoples had initially (and perhaps why they continue to have) relatively great difficulty with acculturation.

Like refugees, indigenous peoples also face risks due to their dependency on the colonizing society (once their original means of subsistence, social support, and political organization have been eliminated). Extensive work (reviewed by Freeman, 1988) has revealed how Inuit (Eskimo) in Alaska, Canada, and Greenland were considered as "people under tutelage" (Honigmann & Honigmann, 1965) by colonial authorities, who had to have missionaries, teachers, traders, and police (even researchers) in order to live acceptable lives (Berry & Hart Hansen, 1985; O'Neil, 1986). Indeed, at one time, the colonial policy of France was "to gently polish and reclaim for humanity the savages of the world" (Jaenen, 1976, quoting Montaigne).

During acculturation, indigenous peoples have typically been subjected to contradictory policies of segregation and assimilation. Reservations, homelands, and other areas were often set aside for the exclusive use of indigenous peoples, sometimes with requirements that they reside only there. At the same time, missionaries, school teachers, and government officials came to dominate their day-to-day lives in attempts to alter their beliefs, values, and behaviors. The most common result of these policies was the marginalization of large numbers of indigenous peoples: through attempts at assimilation they became deculturated, losing essential features of their heritage (language, identity, and survival skills); through segregation, they were kept from full participation in the larger society, not acquiring the values or skills necessary to live successfully there (Wintrob & Sindell, 1972; Blue & Blue, 1983).

Not infrequently, indigenous peoples have experienced severe territorial loss, sometimes involving forced relocation. For example, among various Indian peoples in Northern Canada, anthropological and psychological studies of the effects of relocation and loss of territory (due to hydroelectric dam construction and flooding) have shown massive cultural disruption, and high levels of acculturative stress (Berry et al., 1982; Matthiasson & Waldram, 1983; Niezen, 1993). Similar effects have been noted elsewhere (e.g., in India; Sinha et al., 1992). These findings suggest that forced relocation adds to the risks usually experienced by indigenous peoples, making their situation akin to that faced by refugees.

Considerable psychological difficulty has been reported for indigenous peoples worldwide. In Australia (Cawte et al., 1968) and the Arctic (Berry & Hart Hansen,

1985) in particular, rates of suicide, spousal and child abuse, and substance abuse are very high. It has been argued (e.g., by Berry, 1994) that such pathologies are not inherent in either of the two societies in contact (the indigenous or the colonial); instead, evidence clearly shows that feelings of marginalization, identity loss, acculturative stress, and the negative social consequences all reside in the character of the relationships between the two societies, both historically and at the present time. The resolution of these difficulties appears to depend on restructuring these relationships: this requires the joint removal of the colonial pressures by the dominant society, and the reestablishing of a sense of control over their own lives by indigenous peoples.

Ethnocultural Groups

These are groups that have maintained distinct cultures over time while living along with other groups in culturally plural societies. In some cases, they have been established for long periods (e.g., Bretons in France, Basques in Spain), and in other cases they are the descendants of earlier waves of immigrants that have managed to maintain themselves (e.g., French in Canada, Hispanics in the United States). In these latter cases, the groups may be sustained by continuing migration, but most groups have a life of their own, and do not depend on migrant flows for their existence. However, because of this link to migration, much of the acculturation literature on ethnocultural groups overlaps with that of Immigrants (e.g., Jayasuriya, Sang, & Fielding, 1992; Rogler, Cortes, & Malgady, 1991).

Of all types of acculturating groups considered in this chapter, ethnocultural groups should experience the fewest problems of adaptation, because they are sedentary, and usually voluntarily and permanently in contact. Moreover, most members have grown up in an acculturative arena, and have a life-long experience of dealing with the two cultures. Because of this, there are no "pre-acculturation" experiences that need to be taken into account when considering which variables are important influences on adaptation.

However, national policies about group relations have historically set the stage for contemporary acculturation. In terms of the four forms of acculturation outlined in Figure 8–2, national policies can be identified as being assimilationist, integrationist, segregationist, or seeking to marginalize their constituent ethnocultural groups (Berry, 1990b). When integration is the national policy (for example, in explicitly multicultural societies), the terms "cultural communities," "nationalities," or "ethnocultural groups" tend to be used. Because integration involves some degree of heritage culture maintenance, there is some chance that such policies may unintentionally result in moves toward separation; to avoid this, integration policies need also to have elements that encourage cultural communities to involve themselves in the larger society, and that also encourage the larger society to make room for those who are culturally different.

When national policies are assimilationist, the notion of "minorities" is commonly employed. In this case, the process of acculturation is usually accompanied by the process of "minoritization" and this in itself may be a risk factor. Moreover, assimilation involves heritage culture loss, bringing with it some chance of eventual marginalization; to avoid this, assimilation policies need also to encourage the larger society to accept others as full members. Murphy (1965) has argued that in societies that value their cultural pluralism and seek to sustain it (i.e., explicitly multicultural societies), acculturation may present fewer risks for two reasons. First, there is less pressure on groups to change towards cultural homogeneity, and second, there are likely to be cultural communities of sufficient size and vitality to provide social support for acculturating persons (also referred to as "group concentration," by Halpern, 1993). In societies with assimilationist policies, cultural change is usually insisted upon, and social support may be less available. An examination of the literature on acculturation and mental health in assimilationist societies reveals that researchers generally adopt the "minority" paradigm (for reviews, see Littlewood & Lipsedge, 1989; Vega & Rumbaut, 1991).

Because of the sedentary character of ethnocultural groups (as for Indigenous Peoples), the issues of territory, autonomy, language rights, and self-determination frequently arise and become sources of tension and conflict between the groups in contact (UNESCO, 1985). For example, in the case of Swedish people in Finland (Liebkind, 1984), a good deal of the problems of adaptation are associated with their sense of themselves as "a people," with a collective history, a geographical place in Finland, a language, and a distinct identity. Similarly, for French people in Canada (especially in Québec, where the vast majority live) the same feelings have been increasingly articulated (Bourhis, 1994). Outside Québec, where French peoples are less concentrated, there are no territorial claims, but a sense of peoplehood with linguistic and cultural rights is clearly being asserted (Breton, 1985; Clément & Noels, 1991).

The existence of these views is a feature of many ethnocultural groups in plural societies, and is likely to give rise to acculturation attitudes of separation, rather than integration or assimilation. Indeed in one study (Berry et al., 1989) with a sample of French-Canadians living outside Québec, separation attitudes were highest, followed by integration, assimilation, and marginalization. Separation preference was particularly high for those who identified as "Français" rather than "Canadien" or "Canadien-Français." In a related study (Clément, Gauthier, & Noels, 1993), French-Canadians living outside Québec generally preferred integration, but a "French" linguistic identity predicted a preference for separation, and an "English" linguistic identity predicted a preference for assimilation. To the extent that separation is the preferred acculturation strategy among some portion of these ethnocultural populations, this would be predictive of intergroup conflict and acculturative stress. However, no formal psychological studies of the extent of adaptation problems has been carried out. There are, however, numerous political and literary works portraying the struggle, social conflicts, and personal rage resulting from not attaining full nationhood among those members of ethnocultural groups who desire it (e.g., Vallières, 1968).

Among Spanish-speaking residents in the United States (who, like French speakers in Canada, are concentrated in a few defined geographic areas, and who have in some cases been established for centuries), a recent review by Rogler, Cortes, and Malgady (1991) reveals the existence of substantial research. To a large extent, acculturation research with this ethnocultural group has had difficulty distinguishing between phenomena resulting from continuing large-scale migration, and those that are characteristic of the longer-established part of the Hispanic population. The conventional indicator of the distinction between these two types of acculturating group is generational status, with higher generational status (e.g., second, third, or more) being used as an index of degree of acculturation experience. This index is based on assimilationist assumptions: the more generations a group has been interacting with a dominant society, the more it is assumed to change, and change in the direction of the dominant group. This assumption may be valid for this ethnocultural group in this particular context; however, for many others (e.g., French in Canada, Basques in Spain, Kurds in Turkey and Iraq) individual resistance and reactive social movements suggest the existence of a desire among some to avoid assimilation, and to pursue the separation mode of acculturation.

For Hispanic peoples in the United States this bipolar unidimentional assumption (contrasting Hispanicism and Americanism) has been the usual basis of research and has been identified by Rogler, Cortes, and Malgady (1991) as a serious impediment to interpreting most studies of Hispanic acculturation. Although some researchers developed bi-dimensional conceptualizations (similar to Figure 8–2; e.g., Szapoznik, Scopetta, & Kurtines, 1978; Padilla, 1980), most Hispanic acculturation research has been aligned with assimilationist assumptions. Despite these difficulties, Rogler, Cortes, and Malgady (1991) conclude that most studies show that the integration strategy promotes better mental health by allowing the retention of supportive traditional cultural elements while at the same time acquiring important features of the larger society.

A considerable amount of research has addressed the issue of ethnic or cultural identity of ethnocultural group members (e.g., Liebkind, 1984; Phinney, 1990; Camilleri & Malewska-Peyre, Volume 2). While identity is also of concern to other acculturating groups (especially Indigenous Peoples), ethnic identity appears to be a topic of foremost concern to ethnocultural groups. This is perhaps due to the greater need to make choices about ethnic identity in later generations: first generation immigrants and refugees (and sojourners) probably know who they are, while their offspring are in a situation where they have to decide.

There is a clear link (both theoretical and empirical) between identity choices and acculturation strategies. In their review of acculturation attitudes in Canada (Berry et al., 1989), there was considerable evidence for those with a heritage culture identity (e.g., Ukrainian) to prefer separation, for those with a national society identity (i.e., Canadian) to prefer assimilation, and for those with a bicultural identity (e.g., Ukrainian-Canadian) to prefer integration; those experiencing identity confusion were highest on marginalization. One recent empirical study (Phinney et al., 1994) with adolescents born and raised in the United States of varying cultural backgrounds (African, Hispanic, Asian, and "Whites") assessed participants' identity with "America" and "Ethnic" ideals and practices, and also measured their self-esteem. Results showed different identity patterns across groups: Whites were high on American, low on Ethnic (called "assimilated"); Africans were high on Ethnic, low on American (called "separated"); Hispanics were high on both (called "bicultural" or "integrated"); and Asians were divided (between "integrated" and "separated"). There is thus a strong empirical link shown between ethnic identity and the four modes of acculturation presented in Figure 8–2. With respect to self-esteem, all groups showed positive correlations with their level of "ethnic" identification, while only Whites showed a positive correlation with their "American" identity. Thus having a positive sense of oneself is linked to having an identity with a particular ethnic group, but not (except for whites) with an American identification.

This last finding leads directly to an issue that has been raised frequently in plural societies: Does having an "ethnic" identity in any way fragment an individual or create problems of national unity for a society? At the individual level, to the extent that a bicultural identity (combining a heritage and a national identity) is associated with the integration strategy, evidence generally suggests that this identity would be the most supportive of good adaptation (Berry et al., 1987). A study directly examining this issue with second and third generation Polish-Americans (Boski, 1994) shows that subjective well-being is indeed positively predicted by having an identification with both Polish and American cultures; there is no sign that such a dual identity diminishes a person's well-being. At the societal level, the evidence is similar: holding an ethnic (i.e., heritage culture) or dual identity does not diminish one's sense of attachment or commitment to Canada as a unified society (Kalin & Berry, 1996). Overall, then, having a "hyphenated-identity" undermines neither personal well-being nor attachment to a unified civic society. Whether this conclusion is valid for all culturally plural societies is not yet known.

Conclusions

Acculturation is one of the most complex areas of research in cross-cultural psychology, because the process involves more than one culture, in two distinct senses. First, acculturation phenomena result from contact between two or more cultures and second, research on acculturation has to be comparative (like all cross-cultural psychology) in order to understand variations in psychological outcomes that are the result of cultural variations in the two groups in contact. This complexity has made the reviewing of the field both difficult and selective. The initial framing of the field (in Figures 8–1, 8–2, and 8–3; and Tables 8–1 and 8–2) was an attempt to provide a structure that could identify the main features of acculturation phenomena (the "skeleton"), and into which illustrative studies could be inserted (bits of "flesh"). The questions naturally arise: to what extent has the review been able to establish some consistent findings? If it has, to what extent are these findings generalizable? And, what research still needs to be accomplished?

With respect to the first two questions, the empirical studies available seem to point to some consistent findings. First, psychological acculturation is influenced by numerous group-level factors in the society of origin and in the society of settlement, and by the interaction between them. What led the acculturating group to begin the process (whether voluntary, whether on their own lands, or elsewhere) appears to be an important source of variation in outcome. It is possible to discern a hierarchy of acculturating groups according to the probable degree of difficulty, risk, and eventual problems they face: risk appears to be greatest for refugees and asylum seekers, followed by indigenous peoples, sojourners, immigrants, and least for ethnocultural group members. However, other factors have also been identified as contributing; including national acculturation policies and attitudes in the dominant society, social support, residential concentration, and economic status. These population-level variables seem to be important in many studies, across many societies. However, their relative contributions will likely vary according to the specific acculturative context being considered. That is, they may be examples of a set of *universal* factors, ones that operate everywhere, but whose specific influence will vary in relation to the particular cultures in contact.

What is still needed are systematic comparative studies that will take these population-level factors into account in a research design (see Berry et al., 1987, for such a proposed design). For example, a single acculturating group (e.g., Chinese) who experience acculturation as members of refugee, immigrant, sojourner, and ethnocultural groups could be studied in societies with assimilationist, integrationist, and separationist policies; and within these settings, variations in ethnic attitudes, population concentration, and social support could be incorporated. Up until now, we have had to rely mostly upon sporadic ("one shot") studies of single acculturating groups, in single societies of settlement, with no control for other possibly important factors contributing to psychological acculturation.

Second, psychological acculturation is influenced by numerous individual-level factors. In particular, the integrationist or bicultural acculturation strategy appears to be a consistent predictor of more positive outcomes than the three alternatives of assimilation, separation, or marginalization. The availability and success of such a dual adaptation strategy, of course, depends on the willingness of the dominant society to allow (or even support) it. Thus, there is an apparent interaction between population-level and individual-level factors in contributing to psychological adaptations. But even in societies that tend toward assimilation policies, there was evidence that immigrants and ethnocultural group members generally prefer integration, and when they do, they tend to make more positive adaptations. Whether such a finding is valid for all groups acculturating to all dominant societies is an important question for researchers, policymakers, and those involved in counselling acculturating individuals. Once again, systematic comparative studies are essential to answer this question.

Third, how are the personal outcomes of the acculturation process to be interpreted? Are they a matter of acquiring essential social skills (making some rather easy behavioral shifts), of coping with stressors in order to avoid acculturative stress, or of succumbing to problems so serious that psychopathology will result? In this review, there is evidence that all three conceptualizations are valid, but that they may constitute a sequence or hierarchy of outcomes: If sufficient behavioral shifts (involving new culture learning and former culture shedding) do not occur, stressors may appear in the daily intercultural encounters that require appraisal and coping in order to prevent acculturative stress; and if these difficulties prove to be insurmountable, then psychopathologies may result. Because of the differing theoretical approaches taken by different researchers in their studies, such a conclusion has not been possible to draw from any one study. What is required are large-scale, longitudinal studies, carried out comparatively, in which all three approaches are combined. In the meantime, it is possible to say on the basis of this review that most acculturating individuals make rather positive adaptations (i.e., there is not widespread psychopathology in evidence), but that the acculturative transition is not always an easy one (i.e., changing one's culture presents challenges that are not easy to overcome). Acculturation is a risk, but risk is not destiny (Beiser et al., 1988). Because virtually all of the factors identified in this review are under human control, they should be amenable to change, guided by informed policy and program development. The contribution by cross-cultural psychologists to understanding these factors has been substantial, but much work remains to be done, both with respect to research, to communicating our findings and conclusions to acculturation policy and program developers, and to acculturating groups and individuals themselves.

Endnotes

1. Before leaving the concept of acculturation it is useful to note that contact and interaction among groups other than cultural groups have been described using the concept and the research literature on acculturation: in corporate mergers between two originally independent enterprises (Nahavandi & Malekzadeh, 1988), when female managers interact with male managers (Korabik, 1993), and between persons with a physical disability and the able bodied in society (Berry & Dalal, 1994). These other literatures suggest that the concept of acculturation may have a broader usefulness than the limited "cultural" focus in this chapter.

2. It should be noted here that the terms used in Figure 8–3 are those that are more appropriate to immigrants and refugees than to the other kinds of acculturating groups that were identified in Figure 8–1. For example, if Indigenous peoples are the acculturating group, their "pre-contact culture" would be examined rather than "Society of origin," and the "colonizing society" would be studied rather than the "Society of settlement."

References

Ager, A. (1993). *Mental health issues in refugee populations: A review.* Cambridge, MA: Harvard Center for the Study of Culture and Medicine.

Ahearn, F. & Athey, J. (Eds.). (1991). *Refugee children: Theory research and service.* Baltimore: Johns Hopkins University Press.

Aronowitz, M. (1992). Adjustment of immigrant children as a function of parental attitudes to change. *International Migration Review, 26,* 86–110.

Aslam, M., Davis, S., Farrar, N., & Rack, P. H. (1978). Health care needs of Asians in UK. Paper presented at *Third International Congress of Rehabilitation,* Orebro, Sweden, April, 1978.

Asoyek, A. (1991). Federal Republic of Germany: Thirty years of Turkish immigration. *Courier, 129,* 60–63.

Aycan, Z. & Berry, J. W. (1996). Impact of employment-related experiences on immigrants' adaptation to Canada. *Canadian Journal of Behavioral Science, 28,* 240–251.

Basu, A. K. & Ames, R. G. (1970). Cross-cultural contact and attitude formation. *Sociology and Social Research, 55,* 5–16.

Beiser, M., Barwick, C., & Berry, J. W. (1988). *Mental health issues affecting immigrants and refugees.* Ottawa: Health and Welfare Canada.

Beiser, M. (1994). *Longitudinal study of Vietnamese refugee adaptation.* Toronto: Clarke Institute of Psychiatry.

Beiser, M., Turner, R. J., & Ganesan, S. (1989). Catastrophic stress and factors affecting its consequences among Southeast Asian refugees. *Social Science and Medicine, 28,* 183–195.

Berry, J. W. (1970). Marginality, stress and ethnic identification in an acculturated Aboriginal community. *Journal of Cross-Cultural Psychology, 1,* 239–252.

Berry, J. W. (1976). *Human ecology and cognitive style: Comparative studies in cultural and psychological adaptation.* New York: Sage/Halsted.

Berry, J. W. (1980a). Social and cultural change. In H. C. Triandis & R. Brislin (Eds.), *Handbook of cross-cultural psychology* (Vol. 5, pp. 211–279). Boston: Allyn and Bacon.

Berry, J. W. (1980b). Acculturation as varieties of adaptation. In A. Padilla (Ed.), *Acculturation: Theory, models and findings* (pp. 9–25). Boulder, CO: Westview.

Berry, J. W. (1990a). Psychology of acculturation. In J. Berman (Ed.), *Cross-cultural perspectives: Nebraska symposium on motivation* (pp. 201–234). Lincoln: University of Nebraska Press.

Berry, J. W. (1990b). The role of psychology in ethnic studies. *Canadian Ethnic Studies, 22,* 8–21.

Berry, J. W. (1992). Acculturation and adaptation in a new society. *International Migration, 30,* 69–85.

Berry, J. W. (1994). *Aboriginal cultural identity: Its relation to social and psychological health.* Ottawa: Royal Commission on Aboriginal Peoples.

Berry, J. W. & Blondel, T. (1982). Psychological adaptation of Vietnamese refugees in Canada. *Canadian Journal of Community Mental Health, 1,* 81–88.

Berry, J. W. & Dalal, A. (1994). *Comparative studies of disability attitudes, beliefs and behaviors.* Paper presented at International Conference of International Association for Cross-Cultural Psychology, Pamplona, July, 1994.

Berry, J. W. & Hart Hansen, J. P. (1985). Problems of family health in circumpolar regions. *Arctic Medical Research, 40,* 7–16.

Berry, J. W. & Kalin, R. (1995). Multicultural and ethnic attitudes in Canada. *Canadian Journal of Behavioural Science, 27,* 301–320.

Berry, J. W. & Kim, U. (1988). Acculturation and mental health. In P. R. Dasen, J. W. Berry, & N. Sartorius (Eds.), *Health and cross-cultural psychology: Towards applications* (pp. 207–238). Newbury Park, CA: Sage.

Berry, J. W., Kim, U. Minde, T. & Mok. D. (1987). Comparative studies of acculturative stress. *International Migration Review, 21,* 491–511.

Berry, J. W., Kim, U., Power, S., Young, M., & Bujaki, M. (1989). Acculturation attitudes in plural societies. *Applied Psychology, 38,* 185–206.

Berry, J. W., Poortinga, Y. H., Segall, M. H., & Dasen, P. R. (1992). *Cross-cultural psychology: Research and applications.* New York: Cambridge University Press.

Berry, J. W., van de Koppel, J., Sénéchal, C., Annis, R., Bahuchet, S., Cavalli-Sforza, L., & Witkin, H. A. (1986). *On the edge of the forest.* Lisse, Netherlands: Swets and Zeitlinger.

Berry, J. W., Wintrob, R. Sindell, P., & Mawhinney T. (1982). Psychological effects of culture change among the James Bay Cree. In R. Rath et al. (Eds.). *Diversity and unity in cross-cultural psychology* (pp. 157–170). Amsterdam: Swets and Zeitlinger.

Bie, K. N. (1976). Norwegian students at a British

university: A case study of academic performance of foreign students. *Scandinavian Journal of Educational Research, 20,* 1–24.

Blue, A. & Blue, M. (1983). The trail of stress. In R. Samuda, J. W. Berry, & M. Laferriere (Eds.). *Multiculturalism in Canada* (pp. 301–308). Toronto: Allyn and Bacon.

Boski, P. (1994). Psychological acculturation via identity dynamics: Consequences for subjective well being. In A-M. Bouvy, F. van de Vijver, P. Boski, & P. Schmitz (Eds.), *Journeys into cross-cultural psychology* (pp. 197–215). Amsterdam: Swets and Zeitlinger.

Bourhis, R. (1994). Ethnic and language attitudes in Québec. In J. W. Berry & J. A. Laponce (Eds.), *Ethnicity and culture in Canada: The research landscape* (pp. 322–360). Toronto: University of Toronto Press.

Bouvy, A-M., van de Vijver, F., Boski, P., & Schmitz, P. (Eds.). (1994). *Journeys into cross-cultural psychology.* Amsterdam: Swets and Zeitlinger.

Breton, R. (1985). L'integration des francophones hors Québec. *Revue de l'Université d' Ottawa, 55,* 77–98.

Brislin, R., Landis, D., & Brandt, M. (1983). Conceptualizations of intercultural behaviour and training. In D. Landis & R. Brislin (Eds.), *Handbook of intercultural training* (Vol. 1, pp. 1–35). Elmsford, NY: Pergamon.

Britt, W. G. (1983). Pre-training variables in the prediction of missionary success overseas. *Journal of Psychology and Theology, 11,* 213–217.

Burnam, M. A., Telles, C. A., Karno, M., Hough, R. L., & Escobar, J. I. (1987). Measurement of acculturation in a community population of Mexican Americans. *Hispanic Journal of Behavioral Sciences, 9,* 105–130.

Burvill, P. W. (1984). Migration and mental disease. In J. E. Mezzich & C. E. Berganza (Eds.), *Culture and psychopathology* (pp. 243–256). New York: Columbia University Press.

Camilleri, C. (1990). Introduction. In C. Clanet, *L'interculturel: Introduction aux approches interculturelles en éducation et en sciences humaines* (pp. 2–4). Toulouse: Presses Univesitaires du Mirail.

Cawte, J., Bianchi, G., & Kiloch, L. (1968). Personal discomfort in Australian Aborigines. *Austra-

lian and New Zealand Journal of Psychiatry, 2,* 69–79,

Chance, N. A. (1965). Acculturation, self-identification and personality adjustment. *American Anthropologist, 67,* 372–393.

Chung, R. & Kagawa-Singer, M. (1993). Predictors of psychological distress among Southeast Asian refugees. *Social Science and Medicine, 36,* 631–639.

Church, A. (1982). Sojourner adjustment. *Psychological Bulletin, 91,* 540–572.

Clanet, C. (1990). *L'interculturel: Introduction aux approches interculturelles en éducation et en sciences humaines.* Toulouse: Presses Universitaires du Mirail.

Clément, R. & Noels, K. (1991). Langue, statut et acculturation. In M. Lavallée, F. Ouellet, & F. Larose (Eds.), *Identité, culture et changement social* (pp. 221–234). Paris: L'Harmattan.

Clément, R., Gauthier, R., & Noels, K. (1993). Choix langagiers en milieu minoritaire: attitudes et identité concomitantes. *Revue canadienne des sciences du comportement, 25,* 149–164.

Cochrane, R., Hashmi, F., & Stopes-Roe, M. (1977). Measuring psychological disturbances in Asian immigrants to Britain. *Social Science and Medicine, 11,* 157–164.

Cohon, J. D. (1981). Psychological adaptation and dysfunction among refugees. *International Migration Review, 15,* 255–275.

Dohrenwend, B. S. & Dohrenwend, B. P. (1978). Some issues in research in stressful life events. *Journal of Nervous and Mental Disease, 166,* 7–15.

Dona, G. (1993). *Acculturation, coping and mental health of Guatemalan refugees living in settlements in Mexico.* Unpublished doctoral dissertation, Psychology Department, Queen's University, Canada.

Dona, G. & Berry, J. W. (1994). Acculturation attitudes and acculturative stress of Central American refugees. *International Journal of Psychology, 29,* 57–70.

Eldering, L. & Kloprogge, J. (Eds.). (1989). *Different cultures, same school: Ethnic minority children in Europe.* Amsterdam: Swets and Zeitlinger.

Fong, S. & Peskin, H. (1969). Sex role strain and personality adjustment of Chinese-born students in America. *Journal of Abnormal Psychology, 74*, 563–568.

Freeman, M. (1988). Environment, society and health: An examination of quality of life issues in the contemporary North. In H. Linderholm (Ed.), *Circumpolar Health* (pp. 53–59). Oulu, Finland: Nordic Council.

Friedman, M. & Jaranson, J. (1994). The applicability of the post-traumatic stress disorder concept to refugees. In A. Marsella , T. Bornemann, S. Ekblad, & J. Orley (Eds.), *Amidst peril and pain: The mental well-being of the world's refugees* (pp. 207-227). Washington, DC: American Psychological Association.

Furnham, A. & Alibhai, N. (1985). The friendship networks of foreign students. *International Journal of Psychology, 9*, 365–375.

Furnham, A. & Bochner, S. (1982). Social difficulty in foreign culture: An empirical analysis of culture shock. In S. Bochner (Ed.), *Cultures in contact: Studies in cross-cultural interactions* (pp. 161–198). Oxford: Pergamon.

Furnham, A. & Bochner, S. (1986). *Culture shock: Psychological reactions to unfamilar environments*. London: Methuen.

Furnham, A. & Shiekh, S. (1993). Gender, generation, and social support correlates of mental health in Asian immigrants. *International Journal of Social Psychiatry, 39*, 22–33.

Garza-Guerrero, A. C. (1974). Culture shock: Its mourning and the vicissitudes of identity. *Journal of the American Psychoanalytic Association, 22*, 408–429.

Ghuman, P. A. S. (1991). Best or worst of two worlds? A study of Asian adolescents. *Educational Review, 33*, 121–132.

Gish, D. (1983). Sources of missionary stress. *Journal of Psychology and Theology, 11*, 243–250.

Glazer, N. & Moynihan, D. P. (1970). *Beyond the melting pot*. Cambridge, MA: MIT Press.

Golding, J. M. & Burnam, M. A. (1990). Immigration, stress and depressive symptoms in a Mexican-American community. *Journal of Nervous and Mental Disease, 178*, 161–171.

Gordon, M. M. (1964). *Assimilation in American life*. New York: Oxford University Press.

Graves, T. (1967). Psychological acculturation in a tri-ethnic community. *South-Western Journal of Anthropology, 23*, 337–350.

Grossarth-Maticek, R. & Eysenck, H. J. (1990). Personality, stress and disease: Description and validity of a new inventory. *Psychological Reports, 66*, 355–373.

Gulati, L. (1993). *In the absence of their men: The impact of male migration on women*. New Delhi: Sage.

Halpern, D. (1993). Minorities and mental health. *Social Science and Medicine, 36*, 597–607.

Hauff, E. & Vaglum, P. (1993). Integration of Vietnamese refugees into the Norwegian labour market: The impact of war trauma. *International Migration Review, 27*, 388–405.

Holtzman, W. & Bornemann, T. (Eds.). (1990). *Mental health of immigrants and refugees*. Austin: Hogg Foundation.

Honigmann, J. J. (1972). Social disintegration in five northern Canadian communities. *Canadian Review of Sociology and Anthropology, 2*, 199–214.

Honigmann, J. J. & Honigmann, I. (1965). *Eskimo townsmen*. Ottawa: Canadian Research Centre for Anthropology.

Hull, W. F. (1978). *Foreign students in the United States of America: Coping behavior within the educational environment*. New York: Praeger.

Ip, D. F. (1993). Reluctant entrepreneurs: Professionally qualified Asian migrants in small business. *Asian and Pacific Migration Journal, 2*, 57–74.

Jaenen, C. (1976). *Friend and foe*. Toronto: McClelland and Stewart.

Jayasuriya, L., Sang, D., & Fielding, A. (1992). *Ethnicity, immigration and mental illness: A critical review of Australian research*. Canberra, Australia: Bureau of Immigration Research.

Kagitçibasi, C. (1978). Cross-national encounters: Turkish students in the United States. *International Journal of Intercultural Relations, 2*, 141–160.

Kalin, R. & Berry, J. W. (1996). Ethnic and civic self-identity in Canada: Analyses of 1974 and 1991 National Surveys. *Canadian Ethnic Studies, 28*.

Kealey, D. J. (1989). A study of cross-cultural effectiveness: Theoretical issues, practical applications. *International Journal of Intercultural Relations, 13*, 387–428.

Kealey, D. J. & Ruben, B. D. (1983). Cross-cultural

personnel selection criteria, issues and methods. In D. Landis & R. W. Brislin (Eds.), *Handbook of Intercultural training* (Vol. 1, pp. 155–175). Elmsford, NY: Pergamon.

Klineberg, O. (1980). Stressful experiences of foreign students at various stages of sojourn: Counselling and policy implications. In G. V. Coelho & P. I. Amhed (Eds.), *Uprooting and development* (pp. 271–293). New York: Plenum.

Klineberg, O. & Hull, W. F. (1979). *At a foreign university: An international study of adaptation and coping*. New York: Praeger.

Knudsen, J. (1991). Therapeutic strategies, and strategies for refugee coping. *Journal of Refugee Studies, 4*, 21–38.

Korabik, K. (1993). Strangers in a strange land: Women managers and the legitimization of authority. *SWAP Newsletter, 17*, 26–34.

Krishnan, A. & Berry, J. W. (1992). Acculturative stress and acculturation attitudes among Indian immigrants to the United States. *Psychology and Developing Societies, 4*, 187–212.

Krupinski, J., Stoller, A., & Wallace, L. (1973). Psychiatric disorders in East European refugees in Australia. *Social Science and Medicine, 7*, 31–50.

LaFromboise, T., Coleman, H., & Gerton, J. (1993). Psychological impact of biculturalism: Evidence and theory. *Psychological Bulletin, 114*, 395–412.

Lane, B. (1992). Filipino domestic workers in Hong Kong. *Asian Migrant, 5*, 24–32.

Leopold, M. & Harrell-Bond, B. (1994). An overview of the world refugee crisis. In A. Marsella, T. Bornemann, S. Ekblad, & J. Orley (Eds.), *Amidst peril and pain: The mental well-being of the world's refugees* (pp. 17–31). Washington, DC: American Psychological Association.

Liebkind, K. (1984). *Minority identity and identification processes*. Helsinki: Societas Scientarum Fennica.

Liebkind, K. (1993). Self-reported ethnic identity, depression and anxiety among young Vietnamese refugees and their parents. *Journal of Refugee Studies, 6*, 25–39.

Linton, R. (1940). *Acculturation in seven American Indian tribes*. New York: Appleton-Century.

Littlewood, R. & Lipsedge, M. (1989). *Aliens and alienests: Ethnic minorities and psychiatry*. London: Unwin Hyman.

Lysgaard, S. (1955). Adjustment in a foreign society: Norwegian Fulbright grantees visiting the United States. *International Social Science Bulletin, 7*, 45–51.

Malzberg, B. (1940). *Social and biological aspects of mental disease*. Utica, NY: Utica State Hospital Press.

Malzberg, B. & Lee, E. (1956). *Migration and mental disease*. New York: Social Science Research Council.

Marville, A. (1981). The case of international students: A foreign student reports. *College Board Review, 120*, 23–26.

Matthiasson, J. & Waldram, J. (1983). The aftermath of a forced relocation: Anomie and its consequences for education. *Laurentian University Review, 15*, 97–97.

Mead, M. (1956). *New lives for old*. New York: Morrow.

Moghaddam, F. M. (1988). Individualistic and collective integration strategies among immigrants. In J. W. Berry & R. C. Annis (Eds.), *Ethnic psychology* (pp. 69–79). Amsterdam: Swets and Zeitlinger.

Murphy, H. B. M. (1965). Migration and the major mental disorders. In M. Kantor (Ed.), *Mobility and mental health* (pp. 221–249). Springfield, IL: Thomas.

Murphy, H. B. M. (1977). Migration, culture and mental health. *Psychological Medicine, 7*, 677–684.

Myambo, K. & O'Cuneen, P. (1988). Diplomatic wives: Acculturative stress in short-term multiple sojourners in Zimbabwe. In J. W. Berry & R. C. Annis (Eds.), *Ethnic psychology* (pp. 96–104). Amsterdam: Swets and Zeitlinger.

Nahavandi, A. & Malekzadeh, A. (1988). Acculturation in mergers and acquisitions. *Academy of Management Review, 13*, 79–90.

Naidoo, J. C. (1992). The mental health of visible ethnic minorities in Canada. *Psychology and Developing Societies, 4*, 165–186.

Neto, F. (1988). Migration plans and their determinants among Portuguese adolescents. In J. W. Berry. & R. C. Annis (Eds.), *Ethnic psychol-*

ogy (pp. 308–314). Amsterdam: Swets and Zeitlinger.

Neto, F. (1994). *Predictors of satisfaction with life among second generation migrants.* Paper presented at 23d International Congress of the International Association of Applied Psychology. Madrid, July 17–22, 1994.

Niezen, R. (1993). Power and dignity: The social consequences of hydro-electric development among the James Bay Cree. *Canadian Review of Sociology and Anthropology, 30,* 510–531.

Oberg, K. (1960). Culture shock: Adjustment to new cultural environments. *Practical Anthropology, 7,* 177–182.

Odegaard, O. (1932). Emigration and insanity: A study of mental disease among the Norwegian- born population of Minnesota. *Acta Psychiatrica Scandinavica,* Supplement 4.

Olmedo, E. L. (1979). Acculturation: A psychometric perspective. *American Psychologist, 34,* 1061–1070.

Olzak, S. (1983). Contemporary ethnic mobilization. *Annual Review of Sociology, 9,* 355–374.

O'Neil, J. (1986). Colonial stress in the Canadian arctic. In C. James et al. (Eds.), *Anthropology and Epidemiology* (pp. 249–274). Dordrecht, Netherlands: Reidel.

Padilla, A. (1980). The role of cultural awareness and ethnic loyalty in acculturation. In A. Padilla (Ed.), *Acculturation: Theory, models and some new findings* (pp. 47–84). Boulder, CO: Westview.

Padilla, A. (1994). Bicultural development: A theoretical and conceptual examination. In R. G. Malgady & H. Rodriguez (Eds.), *Theoretical and conceptual issues in Hispanic mental health* (pp. 16–31). Malabar, India: Krieger.

Partridge, K. (1988). Acculturation attitudes and stress of Westerners living in Japan. In J. W. Berry & R. C. Annis. (Eds.), *Ethnic psychology* (pp. 105–113). Amsterdam: Swets and Zeitlinger.

Phinney, J. (1990). Ethnic identity in adolescents and adults: A review of research. *Psychological Bulletin, 108,* 499–514.

Phinney, J., DuPont, E., Espinosa, C., Revill, J., & Sanders, K. (1994). Ethnic identity and American identification among ethnic minority youth. In A-M. Bouvy, F. van de Vijver, P. Boski, & P. Schmitz (Eds.), *Journeys into cross-cultural psychology* (pp. 167–183). Lisse, Netherlands: Swets and Zeitlinger.

Raaheim, A. (1987). Learning to learn at university. *Scandinavian Journal of Educational Research, 31,* 191–197.

Rack, P. (1982). *Race, culture and mental disorder.* London: Tavistock.

Rangaraj, A. (1988). The health status of refugees in Southeast Asia. In D. Miserez (Ed.), *Refugees: The trauma of exile* (pp. 39–44). Dordrecht, Netherlands: Nijhoff.

Redfield, R., Linton, R., & Herskovits, M. (1936). Memorandum on the study of acculturation. *American Anthropologist, 38,* 149–152.

Rogler, L. (1994). International migrations: A framework for directing research. *American Psychologist, 49,* 701–708.

Rogler, L., Cortes, D., & Malgady, R. (1991). Acculturation and mental health status among Hispanics. *American Psychologist, 46,* 585–597.

Rumbaut, R. (1991). The agony of exile: A study of the migration and adaptation of Indochinese refugee adults and children. In F. Ahearn & J. Athey (Eds.), *Refugee children: Theory, research and services* (pp. 53–91). Baltimore: Johns Hopkins University Press.

Sam, D. L. (1994). The psychological adjustment of young immigrants in Norway. *Scandinavian Journal of Psychology, 35,* 240–253.

Sam, D. L. (1995). Acculturation attitudes among young imigrants as a function of perceived parental attitudes to cultural change. *Journal of Early Adolescence, 15,* 238-258.

Sam, D. L. & Berry, J. W. (1995). Acculturative stress among young immigrants in Norway. *Scandinavian Journal of Psychology, 36,* 10–24.

Sam, D. L. & Eide, R. (1991). A survey of mental health of foreign students. *Scandinavian Journal of Psychology, 32,* 22–30.

Sayegh, L. & Lasry, J-C. (1993). Immigrants' adaptation in Canada: Assimilation, acculturation and orthogonal cultural identification. *Canadian Psychology, 34,* 98–109.

Schmitz, P. G. (1994). Acculturation and adaptation process among immigrants in Germany. In A-M. Bouvy, F. J. R. van de Vijver, & P. Schmitz (Eds.), *Journeys into cross-cultural psy-*

chology (pp. 142–157). Amsterdam: Swets and Zeitlinger.

Searle, W. & Ward, C. (1990). The prediction of psychological and sociocultural adjustment during cross-cultural transitions. *International Journal of Intercultural Relations, 14,* 449–464.

Segall, M. H., Dasen, P. R., Berry, J. W., & Poortinga, Y. H. (1990). *Human behavior in global perspective: An introduction to cross-cultural psychology.* New York: Pergamon.

Selby, H. M. & Wood, C. M. (1966). Foreign students at a high pressure university. *Sociology of Education, 39,* 139–154.

Seligman, M. (1975). *Helplessness: On depression, development and death.* San Francisco: Freeman.

Shisana, O. & Celentano, D. (1985). Depressive symptomatology among Namibian adolescent refugees. *Social Science and Medicine, 21,* 1251–1257.

Sinha, D., Mishra, R. C., & Berry, J. W. (1992). Acculturative stress in nomadic and sedentary tribes of Bihar, India. In S. Iwawaki, Y. Kashima, & K. Leung (Eds.), *Innovations in cross- cultural psychology* (pp. 396–407). Amsterdam: Swets and Zeitlinger.

Stewart, M. B. (1983). Racial discrimination and occupational attainment in Britain. *Economic Journal, 93,* 521–541.

Suarez-Orozco, M. M. (1991). Migration, minority status and education: European dilemmas and responses in the 1990s. *Anthropology and Educational Quarterly, 22,* 99–120.

Szapocznik, J. & Kurtines, W. (1993). Family psychology and cultural diversity. *American Psychologist, 48,* 400–407.

Szapocznik, J., Scopetta, M., & Kurtines, W. (1978). Theory and measurement of acculturation. *Interamerican Journal of Psychology, 12,* 113–130.

Tamura, T. & Furnham, A. (1993). Re-adjustment of Japanese returnee children from an overseas sojourn. *Social Science and Medicine, 36,* 1181–1186.

Thomas, T. & Balnaves, M. (1993). *New land, last home: The Vietnamese elderly and the family migration program.* Canberra, Australia: Bureau of Immigration and Population Research.

Trimble, J. (1980). Forced migration: Its impact on shaping coping strategies. In G. Coelho & P. Ahmed (Eds.), *Uprooting and development* (pp. 449–478). New York: Plenum.

UNESCO. (1985). *Cultural pluralism and cultural identity.* Paris: UNESCO.

U.S. Advisory Commission on International Educational and Cultural Affairs. (1966). *Foreign students in the United States: A national survey.* Washington, DC: U.S. Government Printing Office.

Vallières, P. (1968). *Nègres blancs d'Amerique.* Montreal: Edition Parti Pris. (English edition: *White niggers of America.* Published by McClelland and Stewart, Toronto, 1971.)

Vasquez, A. (1984). Les implications ideologiques du concept d'acculturation. *Cahiers de Sociologie Economique et Culturelle, 1,* 83–121.

Vega, W. & Rumbaut, R. (1991). Ethnic minorities and mental health. *Annual Review of Sociology, 17,* 18–39.

von Buchwald, U. (1994). Refugee dependency: Origins and consequences. In A. Marsella, T. Bornemann, S. Ekblad, & J. Orley (Eds.), *Amidst peril and pain: The mental well-being of the world's refugees* (pp. 17–31). Washington, DC: American Psychological Association.

Walton, B. J. (1971). Research on foreign graduate students. *International Educational and Cultural Exchange, 6* (3), 17–29.

Ward, C. & Kennedy, A. (1993a). Psychological and sociocultural adjustment during cross-cultural transitions: A comparison of secondary students overseas and at home. *International Journal of Psychology, 28,* 129–147.

Ward, C. & Kennedy, A. (1993b). Where's the "culture" in cross-cultural transition? Comparative studies of sojourner adjustment. *Journal of Cross-Cultural Psychology, 24,* 221–249.

Williams, C. & Westermeyer, J. (Eds.). (1986). *Refugee mental health in resettlement countries.* Washington, DC: Hemisphere.

Wintrob, R. & Sindell, P. (1972). Culture change and psychopathology: The case of Cree adolescents in Québec. In J. W. Berry & G. J. S. Wilde (Eds.), *Social psychology: The Canadian context* (pp. 259–271). Toronto: McClelland and Stewart.

Wolbert, B. (1991). More than a golden bangle . . . The significance of success in school and for returning Turkish migrant families. *Anthropology and Education Quarterly, 22*, 181–199.

Ying, Y-W. & Liese, L. H. (1991). Emotional well-being of Taiwan students in the U.S.: An examination of pre- to post-arrival differential.

International Journal of Intercultural Relations, 15, 345–366.

Zheng, X. & Berry, J. W. (1991). Psychological adaptation of Chinese sojourners in Canada. *International Journal of Psychology, 26*, 451–470.

9

CROSS-CULTURAL TRAINING AND MULTICULTURAL EDUCATION

RICHARD W. BRISLIN
University of Hawaii
United States

ANN-MARIE HORVATH
University of Hawaii
United States

Contents

Introduction

Contemporary difficulties in intercultural relations are both numerous and diverse. They include, for example:

- relations between Jews and Palestinian Arabs on the West Bank of the Jordan River; conflicts between Catholics and Protestants in Northern Ireland
- the separatist movement in Quebec, Canada
- demands by indigenous groups in the United States and Canada to have more political control over lands identified in various treaties
- conflicts brought on after the breakup of the Soviet Union into a large number of independent nations
- investments in East Germany, one of the causes of the most severe recession since World War II, in the aftermath of German reunification
- in France, government efforts to ban the introduction of words based on English transliterations
- in Fiji, conflicts between native Fijians and residents who trace their heritage to India
- and in Africa, conflicts between various factions within Burundi, Ethiopia, Nigeria, Rwanda, Somalia, South Africa, and Uganda

This list indicates that applied cross-cultural psychologists will have many opportunities in the coming years to work on intercultural relations. What is a common factor this list, which could be easily continued? All involve the frequent and often emotionally intense interactions among people from different cultural backgrounds. At times, cultural factors have been identified and policymakers have taken them into account in developing approaches to conflict reduction (e.g., in Israel: Erez, 1994; and in Ireland: Doob & Foltz, 1973).

One may distinguish between cross-cultural studies and intercultural studies; the latter are more often the focus of studies reviewed in this chapter. In cross-cultural studies, researchers often gather parallel sets of data from respondents in different cultures. For example, training programs for workers entering Japanese organizations might be compared with similar programs for workers entering American organizations; for example, Kashima and Callan (1994) found such programs more common in Japan. This finding could be related to certain "cultural" factors (e.g., individualism and collectivism: Triandis, 1989). In contrast, in intercultural studies, people from different cultural backgrounds are engaged in extensive fact-to-face interactions. Thus, an intercultural training study would examine the special issues facing American workers about to relocate to Japan, or Japanese workers assigned to organizations in the United States (Yoshida, 1994; Thomas & Ravlin, 1995).

The Integration of Culture into People's Thinking

That there are cultural factors involved in the above nine examples is far easier to say than to analyze in a sophisticated manner. Consider the following issues addressed over a period of years by prominent scholars. In analyzing the experiences of American Peace Corps Volunteers (PCVs) working in the Philippines during the early 1960s, Szanton (1966) noted a profound change in the thinking of many volunteers after they had experienced Filipino culture on a daily basis for many months:

> *After some while in the field, many PCVs did finally begin to accept emotionally the idea—and its extraordinary implications—that a people could be equally human, could be equally entitled to consideration, while at the same time they were significantly different in their values and behavior. Differences, in short, no longer implied inferiority. And to respect cultural differences meant first to understand them, which required one to take one's time, to empathize, to comprehend (Szanton, 1966, p. 51).*

This willingness to empathize and to comprehend is not universal, however. In introducing people to cultural differences as they affect workplace behavior, Hofstede (1980, p. 9) pointed to the amount of international exposure within [an audience] as one reason for the lack of willingness to consider these differences in a serious manner. "My general experience . . . is that the amount of international exposure within [an audience] strongly affects the way the subject is received. Internationally experienced audiences have little trouble seeing its importance and tolerating a certain amount of introspection into their own cultural constraints. Internationally naive audiences have difficulty seeing the points, and some members even feel insulted when their own culture is discussed."

Occasionally, even people who are sophisticated about their own culture take steps to learn even more. When Miriam Erez from Israel visited Japan to study management practices, Professor Tamao Matsui arranged a set of meetings with high-level Japanese executives. Professor Matsui attended these meetings, listening carefully to conversations between Dr. Erez and the Japanese business people. Dr. Erez wondered whether Professor Matsui attended these meetings out of politeness, or to reflect a cultural norm because he had arranged the meetings. Professor Matsui satisfied Dr. Erez's curiosity saying, "I am blind to the system since I am part of it. Please, open my eyes and let me know what you see in Japanese management." (Erez, 1994, p. 599). The ability to gather insights into one's own culture is one benefit of extensive intercultural interactions (Brislin, 1981). A forest/trees metaphor fits. As members of a culture, we grow up in a forest and learn how to satisfy various needs in an appropriate manner; "shared values and behaviors" is a phrase implied in most definitions of culture. Skilled in maneuvering within the forest, we still take individual trees and sometimes even clusters of trees for granted. The observations, questions, and puzzlement of people from other cultures can sensitize us to aspects of our own culture.

We have been puzzled, for example, at certain reactions of international students from Japan and South Korea studying in the United States. To meet Americans, these students often join campus clubs. They are sometimes dismayed when they observe Americans leaving the groups when they lose interest in their activities, get a part-time job, or are carrying a heavier-than-expected course load. The reactions of the Japanese and South Koreans encouraged us to examine our own culture. In our individualistic culture (e.g., Triandis, 1989; see also chapter by Kagitçibasi, this volume), a person is expected to develop a sense of the self that emphasizes separateness and uniqueness. One way to do this is to pursue interests through club memberships. But as interests change, so can one's club memberships. In the far more collectivist countries like Japan and South Korea, people are expected to develop loyalty to groups. In college, students often join one group and then spend a great deal of time with its members. Club membership is taken seriously, and, in effect, allows "practice" for the group loyalty they will later demonstrate to the organizations that employ them (Kashima & Callan, 1994). Students tempted to leave a club are typically dissuaded by other members.

These issues relate to the goals of cross-cultural training and education. While we distinguish training and education later, we note one commonality: Almost all participants in training and/or education programs will be neither psychologists nor psychology majors, but current and future business people, engineers, social service workers, health care specialists, counselors, elementary and secondary school teachers, military personnel, and so forth. So, the organizers of programs cannot assume that participants will have the necessary background to benefit from materials such as these *Handbook* chapters. Rather, organizers must study relevant materials and then find ways of presenting concepts, exercises, and recommendations in an attractive, engaging manner, while simultaneously addressing such sophisticated issues as:

1. Can people learn to look at cultural differences as just that, avoiding judgments that "those other ways are bad," which often stem from an ethnocentric starting point (Szanton, 1966)?
2. Can people be encouraged to talk about their own culture without becoming defensive (Hofstede, 1980)?
3. Can people learn to desire intercultural interactions, recognizing such potential benefits as insights into one's own culture, by observing contrasts in ways everyday needs are met in other cultures (Brislin, 1981; Erez, 1994)?
4. And, if these issues are sometimes not addressed in actual intercultural encounters (due to ethnocentrism or lack of interest in other cultures), can they be addressed in the sometimes artificial settings in which training and educational programs occur?

Cross-Cultural Training and Education: An Introduction

Cross-cultural training and education programs are relevant whenever people from different cultural backgrounds come into extensive contact, have misunderstandings, but must somehow deal with cultural differences. Examples are the conflicts among ethnic groups discussed previously; the movement of international students, business people, diplomats, and others across cultural boundaries; the adaptation of immigrants (Berry, 1990); interactions among people in newly integrated schools and neighborhoods; and the assignment of teachers from one cultural background to schools where many students are from other backgrounds (Cushner, 1994b).

A few distinctions between training and education programs should be noted here. Training refers to short-term programs of a few days duration, often with a very specific type of experience as their focus (e.g., training for a group of businesspeople about to be assigned to Japan). The general goal of training is to prepare people to live and work together effectively and to reduce conflicts based on cultural misunderstandings. Educational programs, on the other hand, are usually longer and are most often part of people's formal study for their high school diploma or for their college degree. They most often occur in the institutions that any given culture calls "our schools and colleges" and can extend over a semester or an entire academic year. While training programs can occur in a school or college (e.g., programs to help the adjustment of study abroad and international students: Pedersen, 1994), they can also occur in institutions such as businesses, hospitals, social service agencies, government offices, and counseling centers (Brislin & Yoshida, 1994a). Despite the difference in time frame, some of the content of programs and methods to communicate the nature of cultural differences can be very similar.

Cross-Cultural Training Programs: Methods and Content

Cross-cultural training programs (also called intercultural communication training programs) are short term efforts to prepare individuals to live and work effectively with people from other cultural backgrounds. Training can also prepare people for emotional experiences stemming from intercultural contact, such as culture shock, confrontations with their prejudices, and challenges to their existing stereotypes. Programs can be offered for people about to live in another country, or for individuals who interact with members of diverse cultural groups within any one country (e.g., Catholics and Protestants in Northern Ireland; Japanese and guest workers from the Philippines in Tokyo). Training programs often have a definite time frame, a paid staff, participants called "trainees," a site that is sometimes removed from the trainees' normal workplace, and an identifiable executive who recognizes the potential of training programs to improve intercultural communication. An executive is needed to plan training programs with their necessary pragmatic elements of a staff, budget, training site, and time off from trainees' normal work duties. Cross-cultural training has recently been the subject of specialized chapters and books (Bhawuk, 1990; Paige, 1993; Brislin & Yoshida, 1994a, 1994b; Triandis, Kurowski, & Gelfand, 1994).

There are three ways to organize the extensive literature on training programs: a framework based on the outcomes of research studies that have focused on the evaluation of training programs (Black & Mendenthall, 1990; Brislin & Yoshida, 1994b), a system based on the choice of methods that trainers use (Triandis,

Kurowski, & Hough, 1994); and a system based on the coverage of intercultural awareness, knowledge, emotions, and behaviors (Brislin & Yoshida, 1994b).

Training: Outcomes of Research on the Evaluation of Training Programs

Several reviews of training program evaluation studies have been published (Brislin, Landis, & Brandt, 1983; Black & Mendenthall, 1990; Brislin & Yoshida, 1994b); many studies have documented positive outcomes of well-designed programs. A broad framework for program outcomes focuses on changes in participants' thinking, affective reactions, and actual behaviors. This framework has long proven useful to social psychologists interested in attitude and attitude change, including changes in behaviors related to attitudes.

Changes in People's Thinking

Good training programs can increase people's knowledge of culture, cultural differences, and issues to be faced when interaction in other cultures occurs. For example, people can increase the complexity of their thinking, taking multiple points of view into account and multiple arguments related to the same issue (e.g., cultural, political and economic factors in addition to people's initial reaction of "good" vs. "bad" when faced with an unfamiliar concept). They can increase their understanding of people from other cultures and look at issues from the point of view of the others (Thomas & Ravlin, 1995). This goal is central to the development of culture assimilators (also called culture sensitizers), a set of training materials based on critical incidents and various interpretation of those incidents (Fiedler, Mitchell, & Triandis, 1971; Brislin, Cushner, Cherrie, & Yong, 1986; Triandis, 1994). Participants read about an incident involving people from two cultures. For example, a German businessperson might try to "get down to business" in negotiations with a Japanese counterpart. Various interpretations are offered from which trainees choose. Trainees then read expert commentary for each possible interpretation. In this case, they might identify the point that the German businessperson might be trying to use time efficiently.

The Japanese businessperson might prefer to engage in more general discussions with the German in the hopes of developing a trusting relationship that can be called upon if future business dealings ever run into stumbling blocks. The word "might" is carefully chosen because good training programs do not deal in stereotypes. Rather, they present information concerning possible cultural differences, but also cover the important point that there are wide individual differences within cultures. Indeed, the willingness to move beyond stereotypes is another documented outcome of training programs (Malpass & Salancik, 1977). Culture assimilators are especially useful for preparing people about the multiple viewpoints they will encounter during intercultural interactions. In many cases, people engage in very appropriate behaviors from the point of view of their own cultural background. Misunderstandings arise when they find that people in other cultures engage in other behaviors that are appropriate from their perspective.

Changes in People's Affective Reactions

Intercultural encounters produce affective reactions (Triandis, 1994). Affective reactions refer to people's feelings, emotions, and the intense sense of disruption in people's lives summarized by the terms "culture shock" (Furnham & Bochner, 1986) and "acculturative stress" (see chapter by Berry & Sam, this volume). People living in another culture may find cultural differences to be challenges to their culturally influenced view of equity, equality, fairness, loyalty, or some combination of these values. People can develop very negative views of the other culture and may look upon their cross-cultural experiences as highly unpleasant.

Training programs assist people to manage their affective reactions. For example, good programs can teach about challenges that, if overcome, can lead to active enjoyment of the intercultural interactions rather than mere tolerance of them (Landis, Brislin, & Hulgus, 1985). Active enjoyment helps to satisfy the four criteria of successful intercultural encounters: (1) active enjoyment itself, (2) reciprocity of these feelings by people from the other culture (Bhawuk, 1990), (3) task accomplishment, whether it be university degrees for international students, joint trade agreements for business people, or effective health care delivery for physicians and nurses, and (4) recovery from culture shock within a reasonable amount of time. It is assumed that people will experience the sense of helplessness, ineffectiveness, childishness, and stress (Johnson, 1989) that mark culture shock. In fact, if people do not experience some shock, they may be engaging in few intercultural interactions and, instead, may be communicating only with same-culture people who happen to be living and working in the same area. But what is a reasonable amount of time? This will differ for people with varying personalities, and it will differ according to the amount of cultural difference people expect, experience, and are prepared for (Adler, 1991; Brislin & Yoshida, 1994b). As a rough guide, six months is a reasonable amount of time for people to deal with culture shock. While still experiencing the normal stresses and strains of everyday life, people who successfully manage culture shock find no more stress in their lives than they would in their own culture.

Changes in People's Behaviors

Good training can also lead to changes in people's behavior in other cultures, and some of these behaviors can be considered as clearly leading to more productivity in the workplace (Black & Mendenthall, 1990). "Productivity" is of obvious interest to an organization's executives who would contract for training programs. A focus on observable behaviors moves evaluation studies beyond changes in cognitions and emotions toward the analysis of what people actually do.

Westwood and Barker (1990) developed a training program for international students, many from Asian nations, about to begin degree studies at Australian universities. Their program combined coverage of the steps needed for success in degree studies together with interactions with Australian peers who acted as "cultural informants" whenever the international students needed information. Compared to members of a control group who did not participate, participants received better academic grades and dropped out of their universities less frequently.

In a study aimed at assisting Mexican-American children succeed in the Houston, Texas school system, Johnson (1989) found that children who participated in a training program along with their parents were less disruptive during their actual classroom work. Such a program can address problems that lead to disruptive behavior, nondisruptive ways of dealing with problems, and differences in emic definitions of disruptive behavior in Anglo-American and Hispanic cultures.

This organization of program evaluation outcomes was influential in the development of Brislin and Yoshida's (1994b) recommendations for training program content. Whenever trainers make choices concerning content, they recommended that material and exercises be included that deal with (a) the awareness of what culture is and what cultural differences may exist, (b) new knowledge necessary for successful interactions in other cultures, (c) differences that often lead to emotional arousal as well as ways of dealing with these emotions, and (d) opportunities to practice unfamiliar behaviors that can increase the chances of success in other cultures.

Training: General Approaches in the Choice of Methods

A second framework for organizing the literature on cross-cultural training programs is to examine the general approach that trainers use (Triandis, Kurowski, & Hough, 1994) which then guides the selection of specific training techniques. While a combination of approaches may be used, looking at programs that predominantly use one approach is a useful heuristic. In the following descriptions, we focus on programs to help people about to live in another country.

Cognitive Training

Some training programs emphasize facts and information that trainees should find useful in other cultures. Such information can be either "culture specific" or "culture general." Specific information focuses on aspects of the culture in which trainees will be living, and it can include facts about climate, transportation, schooling, typical methods for reducing conflicts in interpersonal relations, male–female dating patterns, superior–subordinate relations in the workplace, and so forth. Culture general information includes treatments of issues of interest to people regardless of the specific culture in which they are about to live (Brislin et al., 1986), such as the nature of culture shock, other emotional reactions that people are likely to have when they find that their own cherished cultural assumptions are being violated, the challenges to people's typical methods of making attributions after observing the behavior of others, the need for working with the normal ingroup and outgroup formation activities of all people, and so forth. Culture general programs are especially useful when there is a large group of trainees but each of whom is about to live in another country. For example, a business contemplating overseas expansion might send representatives to Japan, South Korea, Germany, Singapore, and Mexico. Information useful to all trainees could be presented in a culture general program.

Specific techniques (Fowler & Mumford, 1995) for trainers using a cognitive approach can include short lectures from program staff members, presentations by "old hands" who have successfully made an adjustment to a specific culture, presentations by host nationals skilled at talking about their own culture, films and videotapes, assigned readings, and group discussions of critical incidents and case studies. Like all the approaches, the choice of cognitive methods and techniques has advantages and disadvantages. One advantage is that the cognitive approach is most often the easiest to plan and schedule because, with experience, trainers can judge the time necessary to cover various components. For example, trainers might know that people will be willing to listen to an "old hand" for 90 minutes, but then a change of pace represented by a 30-minute videotape is a wise programming decision. One disadvantage, however, is that programs based on the cognitive approach present so much information that the memories of trainees become severely taxed. In addition, trainees sometimes complain that while the facts presented are interesting, they remain a "laundry list" of unintegrated information.

Given the relatively low cost and administrative ease of cognitive methods, there will always be a place for them. Cognitive methods can often be used to convey basic information that trainees can later use, during the program, in the more active and experiential approaches to be reviewed. In addition, cognitive approaches (e.g., the formal lecture) are often expected by trainees in some cultures and trainers are culturally insensitive if they do not incorporate this fact into their programs. Goodman (1994a), for example, designed a critical incident concerning a trainer with a good reputation in his own country who did not meet trainee expectations of "high status lecturer" during a program in South Korea.

Attributional Training

To emphasize cultural relativity, attributional training is a good approach. Attributional training is based on differing interpretations of critical incidents involving interactions among people from different cultural backgrounds. In many incidents, the people involved do not disagree about the behaviors that occurred. Rather, they disagree about the causes of the behaviors. In an incident created to explain the applications of concepts developed by Hofstede (1980, 1991), for example, Brislin (1993) created an incident involving an American named Peter working on software development for a manufacturing firm in Japan. He was very productive and certainly not unpleasant with coworkers, but his work style involved going off alone to the company library and troubleshooting software problems on his own. Given his productivity, he downplayed the nonverbal messages from his supervisor that his total contributions to the organization were not at an acceptable level. Eventually, Peter was forced to consider leaving his job in order to find work elsewhere. What are the causes of the difficulties? A key aspect of the attributional approach is that there is not necessarily one correct interpretation of incidents involving interactions among people from different cultures. Rather, people often have different attributions based on what they have learned and experienced as members of their culture. Peter's attribution is that because he was productive and not unpleasant to others, he should be considered a successful employee. If his boss disapproves of something, then the boss should clearly communicate this to Peter. From the Japanese boss's viewpoint, however, Peter was not contributing to work group efforts. If Peter has special talents, he should not go off alone to solve problems. He should share his expertise with others and should also benefit from the contributions others can make. In addition, he should be more attentive to the reactions of his supervisor. Note that there is not a perfect explanation independent of people's culture. There is no right or wrong here; rather, people are making differing attributions based on their cultural backgrounds, and training can prepare people to understand the variety of reasons for the attributions people make.

Because culture assimilators contain 100 or more critical incidents, they can cover a wide variety of social situations that can lead to misunderstandings among people from different cultural backgrounds (Fiedler, Mitchell, & Triandis, 1971). They are effective in developing important cross-cultural skills, such as understanding the viewpoints of culturally different others, decreasing the use of stereotypes, problem solving when faced with difficulties, and the ability to identify culturally appropriate behaviors in which a person can engage (Albert, 1983; Cushner, 1989; Black & Mendenthall, 1990). An advantage is that the training materials can be used in a wide variety of ways. People can read and analyze critical incidents on their own time. They can discuss them in groups, thus obtaining practice in making contributions to a collective, an extremely important skill in many cultures (Kagitçibasi, this volume). The incidents can also provide the basic scripts for role plays in which trainees move from a passive to a more active role in training. Disadvantages include the time and expense necessary to develop materials and their relative unavailability to anyone without access to an excellent research librarian. Most assimilators are culture specific. They are designed for people from one cultural background about to live in another (e.g., Australian medical workers interacting with Aboriginal Australians). Further, given the small audience for any one set of materials, commercial publishers have not expressed enthusiasm about keeping culture assimilators in print. The one assimilator that is easily available is culture general, designed to help people adjust to cultural difference no matter where in the world they find themselves

(Cushner & Brislin, 1996). Given its general scope, however, the benefits stemming from presenting trainees specific helpful information about specific cultures has to be the task of trainers. Trainers can use the culture general themes (e.g., work, ingroups and outgroups, values, anxiety) as a guide for the selection of specific information and specific critical incidents in programs for people about to live in a particular culture.

Presenting critical incidents as a good training method may leave a false impression that all problematic incidents have clear solutions. We do not mean to give this impression, and indeed some advanced training workshops cover incidents in which there is no perfect solution. For example, Mullavey-O'Byrne (1994) developed an incident involving a health care worker in Australia who took a post at a large general hospital in Singapore. On her first day, she (Judy Evans) read a referral card and found that she was being asked to examine the painful right knee of a female traffic accident victim. Upon arriving at the examination room, she saw two women dressed in black with only eyes and hands visible. She could only hypothesize that they were Muslim women; that one was the patient and the other was a sister, aunt, or mother; and that they did not share a language in which they could readily communicate. So what was Judy to do? One purpose of this incident is to introduce the idea that people should not feel that their self-diagnosed "intercultural sensitivity" is enough to deal with every issue facing them. Rather, a well-honed sense of humility is often essential. In this case, Judy should be willing to call in her supervisor and to participate in the identification of a person who can act as an interpreter. Often, these interpreters will be bilingual staff members who take on the additional role of language interpreter without formal credentials, an issue for cross-cultural training discussed in detail by Freimanis (1994).

Experiential Approaches

When trainees move from passive roles as audience members for a lecture and assume more active roles in the training program, they are becoming involved in experiential approaches. Examples of this approach include:

1. A number of scenarios and guidelines for role plays in diverse programs for business people, health care professionals, teachers with students from diverse cultural backgrounds, volunteer information language interpreters, and others, have been published (Brislin & Yoshida, 1994a).
2. Field trips to places where cultural differences can be experienced, including visits to ethnic restaurants, the international arrivals area of large metropolitan airports, churches whose membership includes people socialized in a particular culture, activities sponsored by the international students' office at a university, and so forth. Brislin and Yoshida (1994b) have developed a list of such activities.
3. Case studies of issues certain to provoke intense discussion among trainees. For example, ethical issues that emerge when "business gifts" in one culture

are seen as "bribes" by members of another are certain to provoke discussion (Goodman, 1994a). Or, the transfer of funds to take honest advantage of tax laws in one country can be seen as illegal slush funds by officials in another country (Daniels & Radebaugh, 1995).

4. Structured simulations meant to capture and communicate key cultural differences (some available for purchase are described in Fowler & Mumford, 1995). A simulation called "Ecotonos," for example, engages participants in activities that introduce them to cultural differences in problem solving, decision making, and the exercise of power (Nipporica Associates & Hofner-Saphiere, 1993).

5. More open-ended simulations meant to capture as much as possible what life in other cultures will be like (three are described in Brislin & Yoshida, 1994b). For example, Everts (1988) described a program for "Pakeha" counselors in New Zealand who would be interacting with Maori clients and colleagues. A three-day training program took place in a village where Maori norms and customs were followed. The Pakehas learned to behave according to such norms as communal consensus in decision making, how to consult Maori elders for advice, and how to integrate the contributions of people knowledgeable about traditional views of mental, spiritual, and social welfare.

Experiential techniques can introduce trainees to aspects of other cultures that are as "real life" as possible, and they can introduce people to the emotional upheavals they may experience. A major disadvantage, however, is that when people do become emotionally involved, this may cause disruptions within the program. Unless the staff is prepared to deal with people's emotions during the training program, participants may become so aroused that the program will grind to a halt. The strong recommendation of experienced trainers (e.g., Paige, 1986) is that new trainers apprentice themselves to experts in the use of experiential techniques, who can deal with the wide range of trainee reactions.

Self-Awareness Training

A familiarity with experiential approaches is necessary to understand many of the techniques that come under the heading "self-awareness training." Especially useful when trainees are about to live in many different cultures, self-awareness deals with the trainees' own culture, and typical reactions people have when their sense of self-worth is challenged in other cultures. One of the best known methods is called "The Contrast-American Simulation" (Stewart, 1966), which we broaden here and call the "contrast culture" technique. Its basic feature is that the members of the training staff behave in ways that provide sharp contrasts with the preferred behavior of any trainee. Further, the trainers explain why their behavior makes sense according to their "cultural background." Given the sharp contrasts they experience and explanations that they hear, trainees should become aware that their own attitudes, values, and behaviors have been strongly influenced by their culture. Further, perhaps for the first time, they will be challenged to explain the cultural influences on their behavior. For example, a role play might involve two executives from different countries planning a joint business venture. They discuss policies for hiring mid-level managers. Trainers would be prepared to discuss their recommended policies based on the statements offered by a trainee, as in the following examples:

If the trainee recommends:	*Then the contrast offered is:*
Having no preference for married or unmarried managers	Preferring family men (who are thought to be more steady)
Looking for evidence of individual achievement	Looking for evidence of ability to contribute to group efforts
People who have initiative and who can make recommendations to company executives	People who will accept direction from company executives
Hiring on the basis of educational credentials and job experience	Hiring on the basis of family ties (Who would be more loyal than family?)

If the trainee makes a second-column suggestion, trainers would be just as prepared to draw their contrast from the first column. To add more structure to this exercise one can make a list of topics about which the training staff is comfortable discussing from various cultural viewpoints. Examples are arranged marriages versus people choosing their own mate; a vigorous free press contrasted with government-ordered limitations on press criticism; tolerance of extramarital affairs versus the expectation of marital fidelity; and differing examples of what people consider "human rights." Then, trainees are asked to present their cultural viewpoint on the topic, after which the staff presents the contrast. This approach loads the exercise in favor of what the staff is comfortable discussing, but this feature is central to the experience trainees are to have. Presented with views that contrast sharply, trainees should be encouraged to think about the cultural bases of their own behavior.

Behavioral Approaches

Cross-cultural training that focuses on people's overt behavior has had a checkered history. Used years ago in U.S. Peace Corps Training Programs (David, 1972; Brein & David, 1971), behavioral techniques derived from then "state of the art" reinforcement theory. One method was to ask program participants to list the activities they found to be reinforcing in their own culture. For example, people might list long periods of solitary reading, or working on a certain hobby, going to dances, or having opportunities to bring the latest technology to one's job. Then, trainers would engage participants in discussions concerning which of these reinforcing activities are possible in other cultures, which are impossible, and which might be modified. Further, they would be encouraged to find substitutes for some reinforcing activities that might also lead to the development of social networks, such as substituting learning about local dances for going out to nightclubs. Trainees might also be asked to list activities they actively dislike and find to be punishers. If they list an activity like gossiping (e.g., because of the trivial content and invasion of privacy), they might be told that gossip is a common activity in some cultures and that people who don't participate in gossip sessions are considered deviates.

During the 1970s and early 1980s, the behavioral approach to training fell into disfavor partly because the approach became associated with negative stereotypes of Skinnerian approaches to conditioning, including alleged denial of "free will" and control by outsiders manipulating rewards, among others. The pendulum swung from rejection to a more neutral point as different trainers found that focusing on behaviors led to successful training programs, and that the specialized Skinnerian terminology was not necessary. Moreover, trainers could focus on various complex reasons for people's behaviors. Diaz-Guerrero (1975) used the following example:

> *Tourists in Mexico City are walking around trying to find the museum. They ask a host national male, about 50 years old, who happens to be waiting for a bus. The host national chats with the tourists about their trip to Mexico, and then gives a set of very clear directions to help them get to the museum. After following the directions, however, the tourists find that they are nowhere near the museum. When they do find the museum the next day, they realize that the host national had no idea how to give directions. "Why didn't the person just say that he didn't know and then we would have asked someone else?"*

In analyzing this story, which clearly involves behaviors, Diaz-Guerrero points out that culture gives guidance on priorities when people interact (also analyzed with explicit implications for cross-cultural training by Yoshida, 1994). What is to be emphasized in the interaction, the facts (how to get to the museum) or the pleasantness of the interaction (a nice chat)? The tourists wanted the former, and the host national was interested in the latter. He may have thought that if he communicated ignorance concerning the directions, this behavior would interfere with the pleasant interaction they were having. So instead of potentially damaging the interaction, he tried to maintain the pleasantness by giving a set of directions. At that point, the tourists could leave the interaction in a happy mood. Yoshida (1994) argues that this emphasis on pleasant feelings is common in collective cultures and is one reason why people from a collective culture, like Japan, are sometimes stereotyped as "inscrutable." One reason for inscrutability is that outsiders to a culture can't figure out the true opinions held by hosts. But if hosts feel that giving their opinions might interfere with pleasant feelings, they may keep their true feelings to themselves. Maintaining positive relations (e.g., by not mentioning that a certain wedding gift would be inappropriate) is more important than putting one's opinions forward in a clear manner.

During training, people are given various recommendations for behaviors that are appropriate in other cultures (described more fully in Brislin & Yoshida, 1994b). Such recommendations can be culture specific (e.g., soften or even avoid public disagreements that would lead to loss of face, as in Japan or China) or culture general (e.g., identify host nationals who can serve as "cultural informants" when you have questions). Opportunities are then presented (e.g., role plays) so that trainees can practice the behaviors and receive feedback from the training staff. Concepts that allow trainees to put the various behaviors into a framework are offered (e.g., collectivism, goals people have during interpersonal interactions) so that the training does not become an oversimplified list of "do's and don'ts."

Training: Coverage of Awareness, Knowledge, Emotions, and Behaviors

Assuming that trainers would possess familiarity with frameworks based on research-based training outcomes and training methods, Brislin and Yoshida (1994b) recommended a four-part set of guidelines in the selection of content for training. They argued that the choice of content could be based on the sorts of communication difficulties (broadly defined) that people from one culture experience in another. Then, those difficulties could be analyzed in terms of four concepts: awareness of differences, knowledge, emotional confrontations, and behaviors. Because critical incidents are useful in capturing intercultural communication difficulties, they are often a good starting point. Here is a specific example (adapted from Singelis, 1994).

Critical Incident: "Japanese-Americans and Japanese"

Glenn Saito was a third-generation Japanese-American living in California. His parents, accepting American values and trying to prepare Glenn for success in America, did not speak Japanese at home and encouraged Glenn to do well in his English-speaking schooling. Still, interested in his ethnic heritage, Glenn took four years of college-level Japanese during his degree studies. After graduation, he took a job as a teacher of social studies in a private school.

To increase the cash flow into this school, administrators established some summer programs. One was designed for Japanese nationals, and it emphasized English language studies. Given his ethnicity, the administrators asked Glenn to be one of the teachers. He did so, and approached his job much like he did with his American students: He had a friendly style and an open-door policy when he was in his office at school, long, friendly discussions with students when they asked for his recommendations concerning what to do in America, and cooperative group learning activities during which the contributions of students were sought. Glenn found that his efforts seemed to increase the psychological distance between himself and his students. He became even more upset when he found that the Japanese organization that sponsored the students decided to send them to another school the next summer. What might have gone wrong?

Awareness of Cultural Differences

In analyzing any intercultural critical incident, first one must recognize that culture provides guidelines for behavior and that different cultures provide different guidelines. To communicate effectively in other cultures, people must be aware of what culture is and must recognize the possibility of cultural differences. This important step is often taken for granted: Doesn't everyone know that culture exists and that it leads to differences? In fact, no. In the incident, Glenn's administrators apparently presumed that a third-generation Japanese-American would be skillful at teaching Japanese nationals. Readers of this *Handbook* will undoubtedly be sensitive to the issue of awareness. Most readers will have college degrees in psychology or related disciplines and will surely know professors who study learning, personality development, interpersonal relations, and so forth, with absolutely no recognition that people's cultural background has an impact on their behavior.

Many critical incidents summarize "well-meaning clashes." People are engaging in appropriate behavior from the perspective of their own cultural background, but appropriateness clashes when people are from different backgrounds. Because the incidents are written so that no one is trying to be difficult, the reasons for misunderstandings are cultural. Working through a large number of critical incidents can move people from their initial position of "behavior is the same everywhere" to an awareness that "culture has an impact" (Albert, 1983). In the shared language of the field, people who make this move are said to have reached "the awareness stage."

Knowledge

When people focus on knowledge, they focus on what they think the facts are. If people have reached the awareness stage, they can entertain the possibility that in many cases, "facts" are in reality culturally based. There is no universal knowledge and no universally recognized set of facts that guide human behavior. Rather, cultures give emphasis to some types of knowledge rather than others, and the resulting "facts" reflect these differing emphases. In the critical incident, different people believe that various facts can be brought to bear on the issues involved. The school administrators are not making a distinction between Japanese and Japanese-Americans and apparently think that Glenn can be an effective teacher given his ethnicity. Glenn thinks that his informal teaching style will be as effective with Japanese students as with his American students. He is unaware that the "fact" for Japanese students is that teachers should be very knowledgeable people who present information directly and that to call a teacher by his first name is almost unthinkable.

Emotional Confrontations

People invest a great deal of time and energy learning the knowledge and behaviors necessary for success in their own culture. They spend many years on these tasks, either in a culture's formal schools, formal or informal apprenticeship programs (Rogoff, 1990), or specialized training programs sponsored by their organizations. When they find themselves working with individuals from other cultural backgrounds, the realization that familiar knowledge and behaviors are wrong or inappropriate causes emotional upheavals. In the incident, for instance, Glenn will not say to himself, "Isn't it interesting that Japanese respect for teachers leads students to expect direct instruction from an expert and does not prepare them to be at all comfortable with the type of cooperative group learning activities that I was using." Rather, he becomes emotionally upset when his efforts at decreasing power distance and increasing student participation are obvious failures. To deal with these emotional upheavals, trainers often borrow techniques developed by psychologists who have carried out research on stress and stress reduction (Walton, 1990).

Behaviors

In order to move their programs beyond coverage of knowledge, attitudes, and emotions, trainers may ask, "What behaviors (overt, observable) do people engage in frequently to satisfy their everyday needs? Are there other behaviors that hosts from the other culture employ frequently to meet their needs? Are some of those other behaviors going to be unfamiliar and perhaps uncomfortable when people are expected to employ them in cultures other than their own?" The answers may allow trainers to develop opportunities for trainees to practice unfamiliar behaviors.

In the incident, Glenn might practice giving very formal presentations to students on content related to the goals of his social studies class. He could also practice explaining to students why cooperative activities and other forms of classroom participation are valued in his culture. He might then begin with a very nonthreatening activity (Brislin & Yoshida, 1994b), such as small group discussions of a topic in social studies for which students prepare through a previously assigned reading requirement. Consequently, he would begin with activities familiar to his students (a formal lecture) but then move them slowly to more active participation. Students may become comfortable with active classroom participation because they are introduced to it gradually.

Other behaviors could be involved in follow-up training. If the program was for students (as is common: Cushner, 1989, 1994a), they could be gradually introduced to various behaviors that teachers look for in deciding "who the good students are." For example, in the United States, the behaviors include "speaking up in class" and even "disagreeing with positions taken by teachers." Administrators could be given exercises in which they have to make decisions that clearly go beyond facile generalizations about culture, such as their mistake that a Japanese-American will find it easy to work with Japanese nationals.

Moving from Training to Education

Issues in cross-cultural training and multicultural education have often been discussed in the same publications (e.g., Landis & Brislin, 1983; Cushner, 1994b) because there is some overlap in key concerns. Many of the goals of training and education are the same: increased awareness of cultural differences, increased knowledge, movement beyond stereotypes, introduction to emotional confrontations, coverage of different behaviors that meet similar everyday goals, and so forth. In addition, many of the cross-cultural training methods used to communicate information about culture can be integrated into a semester-long course, a contribution that often comes to mind when the term "multicultural education" is mentioned. Further, as another indicator of overlap, many colleges and universities have a course in cross-cultural training within their multicultural curricula. Additionally, much of the multicultural curricula and theoretical work has developed out of careful study of training studies on topics such as (1) identifying the challenges of diversity (e.g., intercultural miscommunication; Singelis, 1994), (2) supporting the need for changes in the educational system (e.g., additional services for international students; Pedersen, 1994), (3) implementing these changes in the school system (e.g., training teachers to recognize cultural variables within the student–teacher relationship; Goodman, 1994b), and (4) testing the effectiveness of changes to curriculum, in a feasible time period (e.g., presenting cultural specific material to teachers going abroad; Bird, Heinbuch, Dunbar, & McNulty, 1993). The most basic distinction is that cross-cultural training refers to short-term programs aimed at accomplishing specific goals set by trainers in collaboration with people who sponsor the training (e.g., businesses, health care agencies, counseling centers). Multicultural education takes place over a longer period of time in a culture's schools, especially the secondary and tertiary (college, university) levels. Another key difference is that the future cross-cultural interactions of students in a multicultural education course are less clear than for participants in a training program. While trainees most often have current or projected intercultural interactions, such certainty is not common for students in a college course. In a sense it could be argued that multicultural education is thus more pervasive and far-reaching than intercultural training. A more subtle difference pertains to the format of published work describing each approach; the intercultural training literature is rich with empirical studies while the current status of multicultural education draws heavily from descriptive or goal-oriented discussions. Other differences will become clear as we introduce the nature of multicultural education, with an emphasis on the wide range of meanings assigned to this term, the contributions of psychologists, and typical choices for course content.

Multicultural Education: Conceptualization, Key Issues, and Research Directions

Both intercultural training and multicultural education emphasize understanding of differences and acceptance of diversity. This is at times a psychologically challenging task (Paige, 1993a), requiring study of issues discussed in all fields of the social sciences. We have examined material from multiple academic disciplines, emphasizing current areas of study by psychologists, in order to examine ways psychologists can contribute to the research on and implementation of multicultural education.

Believing that multicultural education affects all students, we attempt here to explore issues potentially applicable to all students. We also examine some of the special factors that help to explain the experiences of ethnic minority students in many different countries. In our opinion, psychological research on multicultural education must not be limited by any one culture's or discipline's delineation of the concepts of culture, but must study the issues affecting majority and minority students as they interact in cultures around the world. This more expanded conceptualization of multicultural education allows for the recognition and acceptance of differences and similarities in the backgrounds, life experiences, and education of all students. Ethnic minorities and those in the majority culture need to learn about each other's lives (Feinberg, 1993) if true multicultural education is to occur.

Given the breadth of the concept, we have selected various issues that we believe are most relevant to psychological inquiry. We begin with an overview of major conceptualizations of multicultural education across disciplines, in various regions of the world, and as studied by various academics.

General Issues

In clinical psychology, a popular maxim is that clinicians should not ask "which treatment is best?", Rather, they should inquire about effectiveness, concerning which treatment, in what situations, for which problems when treated by whom, and for which patients? Likewise, in conceptualizing multicultural education, we must specify the issues and population under discussion. For instance, the creation of culturally compatible classrooms has been studied with ethnic minority students such as Native Hawaiians (see Tharp, 1989a), but this is of less practical significance to educators who work with culturally homogenous groups of students and are comfortable with their current teaching style. On the other hand, many instructors have had to deal with students of migrant workers or recent immigrants, and thus topics dealing with language study and curriculum for these students have received wider attention (see Batelaan & Gundara, 1991, for a broad review of studies).

The notion that multicultural issues are not relevant in some countries persists in part because the majority of widely available literature on the subject is produced in Western countries (primarily Australia, New Zealand, North America, and Western Europe). This imbalance in the source and dissemination of research has implications for the application of findings. This unequal distribution of literature, however, does not mean that the same issues are not relevant in many countries. Multicultural issues can be found beneath the surface of popular media, in nontranslated or nonpublicly distributed manuscripts, or in limited distribution government policies and practices. For example, the Chinese government has long been concerned about the "brain drain" of their students who study abroad and don't return to China upon completing their studies (Kao, 1971; Oh, 1977).

Though research is available on the educational systems and programs of non-Western nations (e.g., Asia: Yee, 1989), much of the work is anthropological in nature, often reported by Western observers (e.g., in China: English-Lueck, 1994). Other reasons for the Western dominance in this area include (1) a shorter history of widespread international migration to non-Western countries, implying less time to recognize cultural issues, (2) more attention in non-Western countries to basic properties of the educational system that apply to all students, such as the emphasis on rote memorization and entrance exams in many Asian schools, (3) the use of English as the primary publication language, often inhibiting contributions of fine scholars with limited command of English, as well as preventing widespread distribution of scholarly work in other languages, (4) differences in financial resources allocated for education in conjunction with other pressing areas of inquiry, and (5) societal or government pressure to avoid open discussion of controversial and delicate topics such as minority group concerns or the use of government moneys to finance study abroad while workers at home are unemployed.

Additionally, some cultures may not emphasize cultural issues in education. For instance, differences in thinking styles between Western and non-Western students may be less noticeable than differences between uneducated persons and those who have had formal education (Hansen, 1993); attempts at multicultural education may be a low priority for cultures with a high illiteracy rate. Yet cultural variables, to be discussed later in this chapter, do seem to play a role in the drop out rate and failure of minority students (e.g., McInerney, 1990) and may underlie higher illiteracy rates in pluralistic cultures (see Serpell & Hatano, volume 2 of this *Handbook*). Just as academics in certain countries have pursued distinct lines of research, differences in the handling of cultural factors involved in multicultural education are apparent.

Prevalent Terminology

Many of the definitions of multicultural education proposed by education specialists include a wide range of goals (see Baruth & Manning, 1992, for a review). According to Banks (e.g., 1989), multicultural education is multifaceted and may pertain to (a) the notion that all students should have an equal opportunity to learn, (b) a reform movement in the educational system to provide equal opportunity to all students, or (c) an ongoing process to improve students' academic achievement, rather than a one-shot effort.

While we agree with these conceptualizations of multicultural education, they are not helpful in clearly articulating the role psychology can play in this discussion. For work addressing equal learning opportunity, we refer readers to a review of educational policies of the OECD member countries or to an overview of the struggle in Canada to develop a multicultural policy in Quebec (Zinman, 1991) and concentrate here on other issues. Likewise, goals such as attempting to combat oppression or eradicate racism in the school system (e.g., Australia: Keeffe, 1992; Great Britain: Todd, 1991; New Zealand: Spoonley, 1993; U.S.: Sleeter, 1992) are laudable objectives, and we suggest several informative government documents such as the Swann Report (Great Britain, 1985) or the Hirsch Report (New Zealand, 1990) and prefer to concentrate here at a more psychological level of analysis.

Although we agree that multicultural education is an ongoing process, we believe this definition is more useful in separating the goals of training from those of education, rather than in defining the basis of the process or the method of achieving this goal. A more research-oriented conceptualization (with a focus on the people and processes involved) is needed to examine the contributions of psychologists.

Distinctive Terminology

Confusion as to the relevance of multicultural education may ensue when multicultural education is used to refer to specific purposes for improving intercultural interactions. Two generalized and divergent views of multicultural education, one highlighting material to integrate into the curriculum and the other emphasizing a "state of mind" have led to various approaches within the body of available research. Critical analysis of the terms involved is one approach to organizing this material. For an example of critical analysis applied to the education of a culturally diverse group, see Lane (1992) on multiculturalism and the Deaf culture. Likewise, confusion as to the relevance of multicultural education may ensue when the term "multicultural education" is used to refer to particular methods of implementing policies and procedures into educational settings. We have identified four specific uses of the term that have been studied across academic disciplines: global education, diversity (minority) education, intercultural education, and non-Western education. Psychologists have played a role to varying degrees in each of these areas and certainly have much more to offer within each perspective.

Diversity Education
Diversity education or ethnic education (e.g., Smolicz, 1979) addresses challenges facing ethnic minorities (whether in reference to migrants, immigrants, or native-born citizens). This view of multicultural education emphasizes the development of cultural pride and as well as "behaviors necessary for the economic and political success of minorities with market-driven identity formation as the educational norm" (Feinberg, 1993, p. 169). Much of this literature originates in countries with long histories of immigration, and the oppression of minorities in the school system is often a rationale for diversification (e.g., Modgill & Verma, 1985; Sleeter & Grant, 1994). Over the years predominant members of minority groups, such as in the West Indian community in Great Britain (Raynor, 1983), have fought against

diversity programs that they believe do not result in improved educational attainment for ethnic minority students. Major areas of research include decreasing minority failure and attrition rates, improving minority enrollment in tertiary education, creating culturally appropriate learning environments, boosting achievement levels, and fostering self-esteem and pride through organized cultural interventions. The identification of specific variables leading to successful outcomes for minority students is an area where psychologists potentially have much to offer.

Non-Western Education

A second view of multicultural education is that the issues involved are designed to educate Western countries (especially North American and European) about aspects of "non-Western" cultures (e.g., Asia, Africa, and the Middle East). Many college and university programs in the United States have begun to emphasize more coursework on non-Western cultures and much has been written about this movement under the heading of multicultural education. This view would be supported by a history department that decides to include material on early life in China or a religion course devoted to Buddhism. By offering "alternative" coursework to their students, school officials believe they are preparing students for future intercultural experiences. While little research on the benefits of providing such courses has been done by psychologists, we believe that multicultural education must move beyond the level of general curriculum reform.

Global Education

Global (e.g., Seelye, 1985), or international, education refers broadly to the education of students for the purpose of facilitating international relations, trade, and cooperative ventures throughout the world. This third view is concerned with the globalization of knowledge in a world in which it is becoming impossible to avoid intercultural interaction. This type of education is often designed to provide specific information to students on relevant aspects (often business related) of other cultures or nations. For instance, university courses in most Western countries include coursework designed to increase students' knowledge of Asian countries in which lucrative trade agreements are likely. Likewise, many Asian universities offer courses to instruct students in Western-based management and finance principles. Foreign language study, study abroad programs, and cross-cultural coursework are other methods used to expand students' knowledge of other "foreign" cultures.

Intercultural Education

A fourth view of multicultural education, that it is necessary in pluralistic environments, is more expansive than the other three. Often referred to as intercultural education (e.g., Paige, 1993b; Rey, 1986), its focus is on diversity in the classroom and the problems instructors may face in working with students from multiple cultural backgrounds. Much progress in this area has been made in European countries experiencing increasingly higher rates of migrant workers and movement across borders (see examples of research progress in Batelaan & Gundara, 1991; Reid & Reich, 1992). Several European Commonwealth working committees, led by Micheline Rey-von Allmen of Switzerland, have advocated a holistic approach to creating classrooms that allow all students to express their cultural identity while fostering respect for others.

Diversification of teaching methods and activities has been examined (such as lessons to teach the mother tongue and culture to migrant students, see Tocatlidou, 1992) as well as ways to improve interactions between students of various cultural backgrounds (e.g., Kehoe & Echols, 1984). The emphasis of this view is on bridging cultural differences. For instance, proponents of this type of multicultural education might seek new ways of incorporating recent immigrants from Greece into their classrooms, or examine the goals of various reception/welcome classes for migrants (e.g., Rey, 1986). While this view offers useful guidelines to educators in multiethnic/racial or multilingual environments, it suggests that students living in a seemingly monocultural environment do not need to be exposed to intercultural or cross-cultural material as their contact with other cultures may be limited. Though not the intent of its originators proponents of this view may overlook subtle cultural diversity (e.g., those related to gender, ethnicity, and religion) within races. Certain educators reflect this view of multicultural education when they claim that the movement toward a more diverse curriculum and more culturally sensitive teaching approach, is not relevant in their situation because their classrooms are not "diverse." This view, as originally conceptualized, addresses the need of all students to learn to engage in successful intercultural interactions whether inside or outside of the classroom.

The Contributions of Psychologists

Psychologists do not have any particularly extraordinary insights into the process of determining educational policies. Instead, psychologists attempt to offer educators an objective look at the issues and variables at play in the design and implementation of multicultural education (see Laosa, 1977). While the goals of psychology often differ from the more polemic or goal-directed stance of educators, psychologists' suggestions, whether on the design for educational programs for Africans dwelling in France or for Arabs residing in Mexico, aren't always as objective as is desirable. Distinguishing among polemic, goal-directed, and objective research remains a challenge.

At the same time, psychologists have an arsenal of techniques at their disposal for conducting solid empirical research. Psychologists conduct evaluation research (Campbell & Stanley, 1966) to illuminate the components of programs that seem to be related to positive outcomes, however they are defined. There is also a need for the sophisticated methods of data analysis used in psychological research, such as meta analysis, to organize findings across studies (see Lipsey & Wilson, 1993), which will guide program development. Psychologists can develop standards to increase the likelihood of success of future educational reforms.

As measures are designed and implemented, there is also a need for more assessment of the tools used to measure the constructs. Psychologists are trained in assessment techniques and can be involved in the testing and standardization of instruments to measure constructs such as communication proficiency in non-native speakers of a language (e.g., via The Assessment Instrument for Multicultural Clients: Adler, 1993). The assessment of minority students is one area in which much work is needed. In the application of the cultural practice perspective, it is acknowledged that sociocultural factors must be considered in the assessment of academic skills (Rogoff, 1982; Miller-Jones, 1989). While many studies of testing bias harmful to minority culture or language students have been done, (see chapter by Van de Vijver & Leung, Volume 1, this *Handbook*), psychologists must recognize and also assess cultural variables within a group that may affect educational attainment (Olmedo, Martinez, & Martinez, 1978).

The issues addressed by school psychologists have received less attention here as many of the themes in their work have been covered in various chapters of this *Handbook,* including learning and cognition differences among students (Mishra, Volume 2); counseling issues in working with students from diverse backgrounds (Beardsley & Pedersen, this volume); and testing, assessment and academic performance of minority students (Serpell & Hatano, Volume 2, this *Handbook*). Study habits (e.g., Gade, Huriburt, & Fuqua, 1986), personality and cultural related characteristics (e.g., Sue & Sue, 1972), and the psychological well-being of minority students as measured through constructs such as self-esteem (Verma & Bagley, 1982; Locke, 1989) are other widely discussed topics covered by school psychologists. Several chapters of this volume of the *Handbook* also review social--psychological constructs applicable to educating and training (for attitudes and values see Smith & Schwartz; for individualism/collectivism see Kagitçibasi; for acculturation see Berry & Sam; and for intergroup relations see Gudykunst & Bond).

Following the contributions of Vygotsky, the field of educational psychology in recent years has embraced the notion that all learning and cognitive processing occurs in a social context (e.g., Miller-Jones, 1989; Rogoff, 1981, 1990). From the work of the Laboratory of Comparative Human Cognition (e.g., 1982, 1983) and a review article by Miller-Jones (1989), recommendations for the inclusion of cultural considerations have been made for assessing the competence of children from culturally diverse backgrounds. Rogoff (1981, 1982, 1990) has included examples and concepts relevant to many cultures in her efforts to apply theory to practice. For instance, although she offers evidence that all cultures use guided participation (a teaching method involving observation and practice) to teach children, she discusses three features which differ among cultures. Accordingly, cultures differ in: (a) which skills the community considers important for children to learn and master (e.g., eating with the right hand in India), (b) approaches valued in the learning of the skill (e.g., speed in the performance of the task, accuracy, verbal vs. observation), and (c) opportunities and situations in which children may practice skills and learn values (e.g., formal school, home schooling, watching elders of the community; Rogoff, 1990). Additional progress in the field of educational psychology has been made in the work of Tharp and his colleagues in modifying the classroom to match the sociocultural context of the students' environment (Tharp, 1982; Tharp, 1989b; Tharp & Gallimore, 1988; Tharp & Yamauchi, 1994; Yamauchi, 1993) as we have discussed elsewhere in this chapter.

Multicultural Education and Psychology: Looking to the Future

Unlike the straightforward format of intercultural training (programs designed to impart certain skills or concepts), multicultural education extends beyond the boundaries of programs. Programs designed for implementing multicultural education do exist and consist of cross-cultural coursework or attempts at modifying the standard classroom environment. Yet multicultural education is often implemented or supplemented by training programs. These training programs are designed to facilitate aspects that fall under the rubric of multicultural education and are more difficult to clearly define than the goals of most intercultural training programs. The areas we have chosen to examine all could facilitate students' appreciation of diversity or could improve the level of achievement possible for previously disadvantaged students (disadvantaged because of the school culture rather than genetic flaws). These strategies for changing the school culture differ only in targeted action: (1) changes in the course content, especially in tertiary education coursework (e.g., area studies, broadening the curriculum, cross-cultural courses), (2) changes in the training of teachers (e.g., training issues, role of teachers, teaching assistants), and (3) changes in the movement of students, (e.g., studying abroad, migrating, returning home after a sojourn).

College and University Coursework

To re-emphasize an earlier comment, multicultural education is sometimes operationalized through the introduction of a certain course, or through a change in curriculum, although others view it in a much broader sense as "total school reform effort designed to increase educational equity for a range of cultural, ethnic, and economic groups" (Banks, 1989, p. 6). Currently, schools have a number of options for introducing culture into their coursework. The three most widely discussed methods—area/ethnic studies, broadening the general curriculum, and cross-cultural coursework—deserve further study by psychologists to ascertain the benefits and weaknesses of each approach. Some key issues of each approach are presented here.

Area Studies
Area studies (Tung, 1981), also referred to as ethnic studies (e.g., Bowser, Auletta, & Jones, 1993), is synonymous with informational training and is appropriate for ethnic minority and majority culture students. Area studies courses are often taught by minority faculty chosen for their expertise, usually on one topic with titles such as "The struggle of West Indians in Great Britain," or "The impact of Asian Immi-

grants in the Hawaiian Islands." Asian studies courses also fall into this category of coursework (see Kamada, 1994). Ethnic studies are considered by some educators to represent an earlier phase of multicultural education that has now been surpassed by a broadened range of goals for schools (Banks, 1988). Often these courses are viewed by administrators and taxpayers as less legitimate than mainstream "core" department offerings, and area studies faculty frequently fear being cut when (as is becoming more common) cultural topics are integrated into general coursework (Bowser, Auletta, & Jones, 1993).

In area studies, actual, conceptual, and sometimes attributional based (understanding of behaviors) knowledge is taught (Tung, 1981; Bird, Heinbuch, Dunbar, & McNulty, 1993) to increase students' empathy for members of other cultures. The acquisition of empathy should improve adjustment for those immersed into the unfamiliar culture. However, some research has shown that area studies may not be adequate to change empathy, or attitudes and emotions, and these concepts are both important in fostering improved intercultural interactions (Brislin & Yoshida, 1994b) and a goal of many ethnic studies programs. For instance (Bird et al., 1993), some American secondary school teachers in the United States received area studies training by experts on Japan during a workshop while others were taught material unrelated to Japanese culture and received another non-cultural workshop. All teachers were later tested on knowledge, attitude, and behavioral intentions pertaining to an upcoming visit to Japan. Results indicate that those receiving cultural training demonstrated increased knowledge of Japan, but not a more positive attitude, or behavioral intentions toward the Japanese. This study, (which highlighted the overlap between training and education) measured changes in participants after a brief time period; further study is needed before the impact of semester or year-long courses can be demonstrated. More psychological research assessing various domains of behavior, knowledge, and attitudes after participation in pre- and post- area studies courses would help to establish the utility of offering such coursework. It has yet to be determined whether area study courses are more effective than culturally focused specific topics dispersed into the general curriculum or even into traditional introductory psychology coursework.

Broadening the Curriculum

A major goal of multicultural educational is to implement the foundations of cultural awareness, knowledge, and skills into the general curriculum. Generally, the goals of globalizing the curriculum are not to design a more culturally compatible curriculum for one particular group of students, but to increase the amount of attention to diversity in existing materials, or to internationalize the range of topics covered. One way to expand the curriculum is by using examples that are relevant to the students using the materials. For instance, the experiences of migrant Turkish families could be included in texts used in European classrooms, or the life stories of Ethiopians could be incorporated into books used by African students. By incorporating ethnic minorities into texts that in the past have been overwhelmingly dependent on dominant culture males in stories, examples, and descriptions of history (e.g., Spoonley, 1993), it is hoped that minority students will better internalize and absorb the material (see Allen & Santrock, 1993). A second way to broaden the curriculum is through the inclusion of topics and viewpoints of scholars around the world. Rather than identifying a cultural group, as is often the case in area studies coursework, the instructor selects a general theme and seeks materials to support or refute the theme from various sources around the world. A major goal of the class is the examination of differing viewpoints in discussions of topics the students have primarily learned from an ethnocentric perspective while relating all arguments to the issues and concerns of the students (deBary & Bloom, 1990). As more and more cultural groups become vocal about their exclusion from curricula , there is an urgent need for assessment of the outcome of a more globalized curriculum, at the primary and secondary as well as the tertiary educational level.

Cross-Cultural Psychology: An Example of Cross-Cultural Instruction

The American Psychological Association (APA) has joined the ranks of cross-cultural psychologists advocating the integration of culture into the study of psychology and training of psychologists (McGovern, Furumoto, Halpern, Kimble, & McKeachie, 1991). According to this APA report, faculty have a responsibility to convey knowledge and understanding of cultural, ethnic, gender, class, and race issues to their students who will work with an increasingly diverse population and who themselves are now more likely to be from diverse origins. It has also been recognized that the profession of psychology must increase its recruitment of ethnic minorities and improve services to them (Bernal & Padilla, 1982; Peterson & Cox, 1988; Sue, Zane, & Young, 1994). Guidelines, however imperfect (see criticism by Yee, Fairchild, Weizmann, & Wyatt, 1993), have also been developed for persons delivering psychological services to minority populations (APA, 1993).

Yet, as is true for other disciplines, recognition of the value of culture has not yet radically changed the structure of psychology coursework. As more textbooks add cultural capsules (i.e., paragraphs on cultural differences, etc.) into the material (as separate boxes throughout the book, Zimbardo & Weber, 1994; or as a separate chapter, McConnell & Philipchalk, 1992; Santrock, 1994), additional effort is needed to assist students in applying their acceptance and understanding of cultural issues into their mainstream psychological studies and practice. To date, there has not been a widespread appreciation of the role of culture or ethnicity in basic psychological fundamental theories, and cultural studies remain a secondary line of research and study in mainstream psychology (Betancourt & Lopez, 1993). In many universities, these issues are primarily dealt with in specialized cross-cultural psychology courses, or courses geared toward specific minority populations (see Betancourt & Lopez, 1993; Jenkins, 1982). These courses, which are seldom required or even available to all students, even at the graduate level (Bernal, 1990), must cover an inordinate amount of complex material in a short time. While reputable resources are available to instructors (e.g., Berry, Poortinga, Segall, Dasen, 1992; Brislin, 1993; Brislin, Cushner, Cherrie, Young, 1986; Cushner & Brislin, 1996; Lonner & Malpass, 1994; Pedersen, 1988; Segall, Dasen, Berry, Poortinga, 1990; Triandis, 1994), it may be difficult to promote the material in a manner such that students may integrate cultural tenets into their repertoire of basic psychological knowledge. Students must employ contemporary cross-cultural perspectives to examine specific behaviors that once were thought to be universal. For instance, the application of cultural variables to a psychological phenomena such as motivation, whether one begins with a study of motivation and adds in cultural mediators (e.g., independent and interdependent self external locus of control), is preferable to mere replications of studies on various races or cultures (Betancourt & Lopez, 1993). Correlates of specific cultural variables originating in non-Western populations are being advanced in indigenous psychological studies (see Kim & Berry, 1993), and represent another much-needed direction for cross-cultural education programs.

Teaching and Teachers' Issues: Innovative Training

The implementation of equal educational opportunities for all must go beyond curriculum reform to include methods of instruction (Banks, 1989). Not all students learn in a similar manner, yet they tend to be taught in one standard classroom. For example, some African Americans and Mexican Americans were found to prefer a more "humanized" (story) style of learning than is generally used in mainstream classes (Ramirez & Castaneda, 1974). Differences in style of learning require teachers to adjust their lessons to better fit their students' needs. Teachers are not always prepared to teach in a diverse classroom in which the standard format does not "fit" some or most of the students (Brislin, 1993). Psychologists can help determine how best to prepare teachers to face the growing challenges of modern schools wherever they are located. Teacher training comprises multiple topics, including teacher self-growth and ethnocentrism, and actual teaching strategies and suggested materials.

Self-Growth and Ethnocentrism
It is difficult for teachers who themselves do not see the benefits of multicultural education to instill in students the desire for intercultural experiences. Teachers must first develop their own understanding of cultural diversity and its pervasive ramifications within the classroom. Psychologists have developed models (such as those discussed in the training portion of this chapter) for increasing intercultural learning. When implemented into teacher education programs, these models would offer teachers an opportunity for personal growth and cultural development. In addition to training teachers to work in a multicultural environment, psychologists can assist multicultural teachers in their adjustment to the classroom culture. Ross and Krider (1992) identified six themes or areas of challenge facing international student instructors: instructional preparation, class-

room procedures, English usage, cultural awareness, American students and intercultural communication. The two major components of these difficulties, technical teaching techniques and cultural differences, were described as attenuated with training.

Teachers must also be aware of their own ethnocentrism and cultural biases. Teachers and parents may differ in their perception of behaviors and criteria for achievement in the classroom. For instance, Lambert and colleagues (1993) found that when Jamaican children were rated by their teachers on the Jamaican youth checklist (modified from the Western version) there were low correlations between the parents' and the teachers' judgment of problematic behavior. In another study, Black and White adults were asked to judge recordings of children's narratives. The results indicated that the White adults found the narratives of the white children as more indicative of future academic ability while the Black adults came to the reversed conclusion (Rogoff, 1990). Studies such as these highlight the need for attention to the specific factors (age, gender, context) affecting teachers' judgment of both successful students and disruptive or disobedient students.

Teaching Strategies

Three components of the teaching process are advocated by Paige (1993a) in order to motivate students toward an appreciation of diversity, while avoiding the promotion of negative or limiting stereotypes and prejudices. He suggests that teachers first attempt to predict the level of psychological intensity of the lesson. Predicting whether a cultural topic will support or challenge students requires awareness of the students' own cultural identity (Bennett, 1993), as well as their intercultural sensitivity (see Bhawuk & Brislin, 1992). Yet clear and broadly usable standards for measuring either of these constructs do not exist and pose a challenge for interested psychologists. A second step of the teaching process involves the exploration and testing of hypotheses on intercultural learning. Psychologists should be involved in the design and testing of these hypotheses. Just as psychologists in the classroom have helped teachers deal with slow learners and behavior problems, they can assist teachers in identifying the culturally preferred learning styles and academic strengths of pupils and assess the overall classroom acceptance of diversity. The third recommendation from Paige is to prepare the students to learn. Again, an understanding of the students' cultural perception of the material to be learned would assist teachers in aligning their presentations with students' needs.

Moving across Cultures and Schools: Relevant Issues

Given the large numbers of persons moving across cultural and national borders, most countries have an investment in the education of students from a multitude of cultures and nations (see examples from European nations in Berg-Eldering, de Rijcke, & Zuck, 1983). Due in part to liberal family reunion policies, the number of immigrant students in classrooms worldwide has multiplied (see bibliography of European sources in Pornbacher, 1990, and international sources in Altbach & Wang, 1989; Altbach, Kelly, & Lulat, 1985; Batelaan & Gundara, 1991).

Migration in general has increased exponentially, with 70 percent of students moving from underdeveloped nations to Westernized, economically stable countries (Wagner & Schnitzer, 1991). This movement has been of several types and includes recent immigrants, linguistic minorities, refugees, and indigenous people such as Native Americans and Australian aboriginal students, thought to be at more risk for academic difficulties than others (Keeffe, 1992; Marsella, Bornemann, Ekblad, & Orley, 1994; Moyer & Motta, 1982; Steinberg, Blinde, & Chan, 1984; Tharp, 1989a; Tung, 1985). Migrant workers' or "guestworkers's" children, as they often travel back and forth between two or more countries, may also experience difficulties in school related to their transitory lifestyle and have been the focus of research (England: Gumbert, 1983; Germany: Rist, 1979; European Community: Rey, 1984; Rey-von Allman, 1993; Switzerland: Rey, 1979). We concentrate here on a few of the directions of psychological research.

As a result of migration, a need for improved educational opportunities for immigrant and migrant students has arisen (e.g., Bhatnager, 1981). Research has included topics such as reception classes for newcomers (e.g., in France: Demangeot, 1988), or efforts to improve schooling for migrant and Gypsy children in Europe (Council of Europe, 1988; Reid & Reich, 1992). Language issues seem to comprise the largest portion of the literature worldwide (e.g., Garcia & Otheguy, 1989), but have been especially salient in many countries of Europe. Both the teaching of language skills needed in the host culture (Porcher, 1981; Rey, 1981, 1986) as well as the desire to assist children in the maintenance of their home culture language (Kurmann, 1979) and cultural identity (Simila, 1988) have been addressed and offer rich areas of exploration.

Psychologists have devoted considerable attention to the adjustment of international students (see chapter by Berry & Sam, this volume). From Oberg's (1960) discussion of cultural shock to more recent works on various aspects of adjustment (e.g., Church, 1982; Kim, 1988; Searle & Ward, 1990), the well-being and satisfaction of international students in Western nations has most often been explored. One exception may be the literature on Japan's growing role as a host nation. Tanaka and colleagues examined the satisfaction of students studying in Japan (Tanaka, Takai, Kohyama, Fujihara, 1994). They showed that country of residence is one important variable affecting satisfaction with one's study experience in Japan, with unexpected results suggesting that non-Asian students tend to be more satisfied with their sojourn than Asian students. The traditional U-curve pattern of student adjustment (Lysgaard, 1955) was not found in this. Horowitz and Kraus (1984), comparing the adjustment of Soviet and American children in Israel, also found different patterns of adaptation for the two groups. Additional work, along the lines of work conducted with New Zealand students studying abroad in 23 countries (Ward & Kennedy, 1993), is needed to elucidate universal and culturally dependent factors that mediate adjustment.

The experiences of the spouses of international students is yet another area in need of research. Self-help groups for spouses have been designed (see Schwartz & Kahne, 1993) and follow-up studies on the effectiveness of such interventions would provide answers to questions about the long-term coping and adjustment of persons who often speak little of the host country's language and have access to few community services and resources.

The consequences of studying abroad on re-adjustment to the home culture have been documented in anecdotes, case studies, and research reports of returnees (see examples in Martin, 1984; Martin, Bradford, & Rohrlich, 1995). For example, the Japanese educational system is aware of the difficulties facing "returnees" who have spent time abroad. Upon return, children may enter special schools to catch up on the work they missed, do correspondence work while abroad, or even in some cases enter universities through affirmative action type programs when their return to Japan occurs just prior to university study (Feinberg, 1993).

By studying the experiences of high school exchange students from Australia, Ecuador, Norway, and Sweden, Wilson (1993) also highlights the positive side to re-entry, such as the opportunity to break down stereotypes and the seeking out of intercultural friendships and experiences within their home countries. Studies on the long-term outcome of study abroad would provide important information on effects on career paths, marriages, and interest in international affairs.

Goals and Outcomes of Multicultural Education

The outcomes of multicultural education are especially understudied. Culture learning as defined by Walsh (1979) is the understanding of the ways in which persons in other cultures perceive reality. This perception is subjective, influenced by feelings (toward one's own and other cultures), and dependent on skills for learning about cultures. One goal of multicultural education is to enhance the ability of students to predict the behaviors and opinions of persons of other cultures in a multitude of settings and occasions. The cultural learner goes beyond cognitions and is open to the possibility of his or her own feelings and thoughts being influenced by other cultures. In a sense it is "learning a culture" rather than "learning about a culture," and is meant to combat stereotypes and ethnocentrism.

According to Banks (1988), additional goals of multicultural education are to increase the potential academic-achievement potential of all students, to foster more positive attitudes and decrease stereotypes learned from society, to empower minority students, and to encourage all students to understand the perspectives of minorities and cultures throughout the world. Ramsey (1987) adds several other goals, namely those that would enable students to develop and accept their own membership in various groups, to relate to and cooperate with different others, to respect alternative lifestyles, and to bridge the cultures of family and school.

We wish to briefly address three possible outcomes of implementing multicultural curriculum and practices: student mastery, increasing the knowledge of students, and student empowerment.

Student Mastery

Argueta-Bernal (1990) defines mastery as "the degree to which an individual believes he or she can exercise control over events in the environment" (p. 211). Self-control, or internal locus of control as it is sometimes called, has been linked to lower stress and better mastery for ethnic minorities (Padilla, Wagatsuma, & Lindholm, 1985) and for immigrants (Seipel, 1988). However, it is not always possible for all students in the school system when the curriculum and teaching style does not "fit" all students. Recommendations for increasing students' feelings of mastery often focus on building language skills. Coates (1990) recommends cognitive procedures to help African-American adolescents replace external agents that impose standards of behavior with internalized feelings of self-control.

Increasing the Knowledge of Students

For immigrants, sojourners, and refugees, learning about the new environment improves the effectiveness of behaviors and decreases feelings of alienation by increasing one's ability to predict the outcome of events in that culture (Triandis, 1994; Triandis, Dunnette, & Hough, 1994). As stated earlier, in training with cultural assimilators or critical incidents, such students may learn to make the correct attributions of the behaviors of their classmates and teachers. Once they have the knowledge of the appropriate behaviors and reasons for them, they are free to choose to implement the behaviors or not. At the same time, the use of materials such as critical incidents may help students of the majority culture learn and accept different behaviors from their non-majority classmates, thus decreasing the imbalance of cultural change and fostering a more multicultural environment.

Student Empowerment

The alienation and feelings of powerlessness that can result from an inappropriate fit between students and the educational system may be reduced through a combination of empowerment strategies and the placing of a positive value on individual differences. Providing the members of subcultures with more control over the topics pursued, and the research process itself, also is empowering (Bishop, 1994). Personalization of material is facilitated when students are able to find contributions of their ethnic or cultural groups represented in the school curricula. Likewise, reference to minority students' culture further creates an invitation to learning, as students are better able to identify with the academic materials presented to them.

Conclusion

Students must be taught skills, attitudes, and knowledge which allow them to bridge between their own culture and that of the larger society and educational system (Banks, 1989). Culture has long played a role in psychological studies conducted in schools. While awareness of cultural differences and their implications is a necessary first step to implementing changes (Pedersen, 1988), awareness alone is not enough and can lead to superficial attempts at multicultural education. For example, some schools see a need for more diversity and implement ethnic food days into their cafeterias. Promoting ethnic holidays and customs can increase the acceptability of diversity (e.g., Semons, 1991), yet this form of intervention does not adequately attend to the students' diverse educational needs within a pluralistic school environment.

In the past, psychologists have made contributions to the field of education with research on topics such as ethnic/racial differences in intelligence testing, gender/ethnic differences in school performance, and attrition rates of minorities. Most of this past research was conducted in Western countries by Western researchers. International cross-cultural studies and collaborative works across borders and cultures are now more common and offer further insight into the psychological components of education. Much work needs to be done as culture becomes more and more a part of mainstream awareness and discussion. Just as basic courses in psychology have become a part of the standard education of many students, courses in multicultural education will also become necessary for students of the next decade to be effective members of the world community. It is time for psychological research on multicultural education to catch up to the needs and the interests of the educators and students who have the most to gain from psychologists' endeavors.

Recommendations for Psychologists' Contributions

1. While there is much discussion on the need to recognize diversity within the classroom, there is insufficient attention to diversity within cultural and ethnic groups (e.g., Ellemers, 1983) and students are divided into cultural groups in an inconsistent fashion. Some researchers group students according to their surname, others by obvious racial or physical characteristics. At the tertiary level, students may be asked to check off or write in their ethnic or racial background. Little attention has been paid to multiple group background or to students who identify with a cultural group other than that suggested by their family heritage or physical appearance. More attention to diversity related to ethnic identity, generational status, ethnic group pride, and participation in cultural activities and hobbies would ensure that researchers are sampling students who belong to the categories into which they are placed (see Banks, 1988; Bennett, 1993). Furthermore, the relationship between cultural identification and the learning process (as suggested by Branch, 1994) is an underexplored avenue and deserves attention.

2. Currently, the majority of educational interventions and intercultural training programs are designed as short term projects. Given financial and personnel constraints, short programs are likely to remain the norm in most countries. However, since short term training is usually beneficial (Triandis, 1994), we believe that even more positive outcomes are possible through more intensive and long-term programs. Ongoing training and maintenance of skills could be supported through peer education groups, mentor to mentee relationships, and regular refresher courses from community guest lecturers or academics from nearby universities or colleges.

3. It is unfortunate that many well-designed, meticulously implemented, and widely distributed studies are soon forgotten. Too often, researchers are rewarded for work designed to produce the ever bigger, better, or more explanatory variable behind cultural differences in the classroom. There is a dire need for researchers to return to the basics. Using contemporary methodological and statistical advances, replication studies would be of great value, as would more follow-up and long-term replication studies on the impact of intervention efforts. Follow-up studies of children have shown that early gains may be washed away once the active intervention is removed (Brislin, 1993). Do migrant children maintain language and cultural ties to their homeland or do they eventually absorb many of the cultural features of their host cultures until they represent a cosmopolitan world citizen? Will the bicultural-identifying Asian students in the United Kingdom and Canada (see Ghuman, 1993) demand major educational reforms as they progress through the system, or will they gradually integrate themselves into the current school milieu? Only through long-term follow up and longitudinal research will questions such as these be answered.

4. There is a need for more and better circulated indigenous research on emic cultural issues rather than etic Western comparisons across groups (see Hamaguchi, 1985, for a review of constructs addressed in Japanese studies). LaFromboise and Plake (1981) have long asserted the need to implement research methods relevant to various cultural groups. On a related note, Dasen (1992) has lamented the scarcity of published studies on topics relevant to non-Western countries. In fact, it seems that many researchers are unaware of the needs of the population they study. It is hoped that the involvement of members of the culture under study, in all stages of research, will lead to an increased emphasis on the educational issues deemed important by the studied community.

5. Collaborations allow researchers to examine issues facing educators and trainers across populations and in various formats. This integration and in-depth international review is necessary if widesweeping educational reforms are to become reality. There are numerous reasons why integrated studies should be encouraged. One advantage of multidisciplinary, multicultural reviews is that educators are able to look beyond their trees and see the entire forest in a more objective light. Once researchers understand the larger realm in which they operate, they will be more able to focus on their particular questions, building upon the established foundation of knowledge. Also, as in meta-analyses, subtle findings and interactions are more likely to be seen in large scale, international review studies. Trends across populations are also more easily seen, and may lead to a better understanding of the underlying constructs involved. Through collaboration, educators may also come to see that the issues raised within their school systems are neither esoteric nor unique. And finally, given the shortage of research funds, collaborations between leading scholars and educators are more likely to be approved and funded.

6. It is apparent that intercultural trainers, educators, and psychologists must work together for real progress to be made. Educators should receive training in cross-cultural psychology so that they are able to integrate sophisticated concepts with the pleasant but unexamined feelings that intercultural experiences engender (Dasen, 1992). On the other hand, there is a need for psychologists to design empirical and applied studies based on the theories and models generated from educators. Intercultural training programs have long been used to implement the goals of multicultural education and offer support for the value of professional collaboration.

References

Adler, N. (1991). *International dimensions of organizational behavior*, 2d ed. Boston: PWS- Kent.

Adler, S. (1993). *Multicultural communication skills in the classroom*. Boston: Allyn and Bacon.

Albert, R. (1983). The intercultural sensitizer or culture assimilator: A cognitive approach. In D. Landis & R. Brislin (Eds.), *Handbook of intercultural training* (Vol. 2, pp. 186–217). Elmsford, NY: Pergamon.

Allen, L. & Santrock, J. W. (1993). *Psychology: The contexts of behavior*. Dubuque: WCB Brown and Benchmark.

Altbach, P. G., Kelly, D. H., & Lulat, Y. G-M. (1985). *Research on foreign students and international study: An overview and bibliography*. New York: Praeger.

Altbach, P. G. & Wang, J. (Eds.). (1989). *Foreign students and international study: Bibliography and analysis, 1984–1988*. New York: University Press of America.

American Psychological Association (APA), Office of Ethnic Minority Affairs. (1993). Guidelines for providers of psychological services to ethnic, linguistic, and culturally diverse populations. *American Psychologist, 48*, 45–48.

Argueta-Bernal, G. A. (1990). Stress and stress-related disorders in Hispanics: Biobehavioral approaches to treatment. In T. C. Serafica, A. I. Schwebel, R. K. Russel, P. D. Isaac, & L. B. Myers (Eds.), *Mental health of ethnic minorities* (pp. 5–37). New York: Praeger.

Banks, J. A. (1988). *Multiethnic education: Theory and practice*, 2d ed. Boston: Allyn and Bacon.

Banks, J. A. (1989). Multicultural education: Characteristics and goals. In J. A. Banks & C. A. McGee Banks (Eds.), *Multicultural education: Issues and perspectives* (pp. 2–26). Boston: Allyn and Bacon.

Baruth, L. G. & Manning, M. L. (1992). *Multicultural education of children and adolescents*. Boston: Allyn and Bacon.

Batelaan, P. & Gundara, I. S. (1991). *Multicultural education: A bibliography*. Geneva: UNESCO/IBE (IBE Bulletin 65, no. 260).

Bennett, J. M. (1993). Cultural marginality: Identity issues in intercultural training. In R. M. Paige (Ed.), *Education for the intercultural experience* (pp. 109–136). Yarmouth, ME: Intercultural.

Berg-Eldering, L. v. d., de Rijcke, F. J. M., & Zuck, L. V. (Eds.). (1983). *Multicultural education: A challenge for teachers*. Dordrecht, Netherlands: Foris.

Bernal, M. E. (1990). Ethnic minority mental health training: Trends and issues. In F. C. Serafica, A. I. Schwebal, R. K. Russell, P. D. Isaac, & L. B. Myers (Eds.), *Mental health of ethnic minorities* (pp. 249–274). New York: Praeger.

Bernal, M. E. & Padilla, A. M. (1982). Status of minority curricula and training in clinical psychology. *American Psychologist, 37*, 780–787.

Berry, J. W. (1990). Psychology of acculturation:

Understanding individuals moving between cultures. In R. Brislin (Ed.), *Applied cross-cultural psychology* (pp. 232–253). Newbury Park, CA: Sage.

Berry, J. W., Poortinga, Y. H., Segall, M. H., & Dasen, P. R. (1992). *Cross-cultural psychology: Research and applications.* Cambridge: Cambridge University Press.

Betancourt, H. & Lopez, S. R. (1993). The study of culture, ethnicity, and race in American psychology. *American Psychologist, 48,* 629–637.

Bhatnager, J. (Ed.). (1981). *Educating immigrants.* London: Croom Helm.

Bhawuk, D. (1990). Cross-cultural orientation programs. In R. Brislin (Ed.), *Applied cross-cultural psychology* (pp. 325–346). Newbury Park, CA: Sage.

Bhawuk, D. P. S. & Brislin, R. W. (1992). The measurement of intercultural sensitivity using the concepts of individualism and collectivism. *International Journal of Intercultural Relations, 16,* 413–436.

Bird, A., Heinbuch, S., Dunbar, R., & McNulty, M. (1993). A conceptual model of the effects of Area Studies Programs and a preliminary investigation of the model's hypothesized relationships. *International Journal of Intercultural Relations, 17,* 415–436.

Bishop, R. (1994). Initiating empowering research? *New Zealand Journal of Educational Studies, 29,* 175–188.

Black, J. & Mendenthall, M. (1990). Cross-cultural training effectiveness: A review and a theoretical framework for future research. *Academy of Management Review, 15,* 113–136.

Bowser, M. P., Auletta, E. S., & Jones, T. (1993). *Confronting diversity issues on campus.* Newbury Park, CA: Sage.

Branch, C. W. (1994). Ethnic identity as a variable in the learning equation. In E. R. Hollins, J. E. King, & W. C. Hayman (Eds.), *Teaching diverse populations: Formulating a knowledge base* (pp. 207–223). Albany: State University of New York Press.

Brein, M. & David, K. (1971). Intercultural communication and the adjustment of the sojourner. *Psychological Bulletin, 76,* 215–230.

Brislin, R. (1981). *Cross-cultural encounters: Face-to-face interactions.* Elmsford, NY: Pergamon.

Brislin, R. (1993). *Understanding culture's influence on behavior.* Fort Worth: Harcourt.

Brislin, R., Cushner, K., Cherrie, C., & Yong, M. (1986). *Intercultural interactions: A practical guide.* Newbury Park, CA: Sage.

Brislin, R., Landis, D., & Brandt, M. (1983). Conceptualizations of intercultural behavior and training. In D. Landis & R. Brislin (Eds.), *Handbook of intercultural training* (Vol. 1, pp. 1– 35). Elmsford, NY: Pergamon.

Brislin, R. & Yoshida, T. (Eds.). (1994a). *Improving intercultural interactions: Modules for cross-cultural training programs.* Thousand Oaks, CA: Sage.

Brislin, R. & Yoshida, T. (Eds). (1994b). *Intercultural communication training: An introduction.* Thousand Oaks: SAGE.

Campbell, D. T., & Stanley, J. C. (1966). *Experimental and quasi-experimental designs for research.* Chicago: Rand McNally.

Church, A. (1982). Sojourner adjustment. *Psychological Bulletin, 91,* 540–572.

Coates, D. L. (1990). Social network analysis as mental health intervention with African American adolescents. In T. C. Serafica, A. I. Schwebel, R. K. Russel, P. D. Isaac, & L. B. Myers (Eds.), *Mental health of ethnic minorities* (pp. 5–37). New York: Praeger.

Council of Europe (Ed.). (1988). *Thirty-fifth council of Europe teachers' seminar "schooling for gypsies' and travellers' children": Evaluating innovation.* Strasbourg: Council for Cultural Co-operation.

Cushner, K. (1989). Assessing the impact of a culture-general assimilator. *International Journal of Intercultural Relations, 13,* 125–146.

Cushner, K. (1994a). Cross-cultural training for adolescents and professionals who work with youth exchange programs. In R. Brislin & T. Yoshida (Eds.), *Improving intercultural interactions: Modules for cross-cultural training programs* (pp. 91–108). Thousand Oaks, CA: Sage.

Cushner, K. (1994b). Preparing teachers for an intercultural context. In R. Brislin & T. Yoshida (Eds.), *Improving intercultural interactions: Modules for cross-cultural training programs* (pp. 109–128). Thousand Oaks, CA: Sage.

Cushner, K. & Brislin, R. (1996). *Intercultural inter-*

actions: A practical guide, 2d ed. Thousand Oaks, CA: Sage.

Daniels, D. & Radebaugh, L. (1995). *International business: Environments and operations.* Reading, MA: Addison-Wesley.

Dasen, P. R. (1992). Cross-cultural psychology and teacher training in cultural diversity and the schools. In J. Lynch, C. Modgil, & S. Modgil (Eds.), *Cultural diversity and the schools* (Vol. 2, pp. 191–204). London: The Falmer Press.

David, K. (1972). Intercultural adjustment and applications of reinforcement theory to problems of "culture shock." *Trends, 4,* 1–64.

deBary, W. T. & Bloom, I. (Eds.). (1990). *Approaches to the Asian classics.* New York: Columbia University Press.

Demangeot, P. (1988). Chronique d'une classe d'accueil. *Migrants-Formation, 73,* 78–81.

Diaz-Guerrero, R. (1975). *Psychology of the Mexican: Culture and personality.* Austin: University of Texas Press.

Doob, L. & Foltz, W. (1973). The Belfast Workshop: An application of group techniques to a destructive conflict. *Journal of Conflict Resolution, 17,* 489–512.

Ellemers, J. E. (1983). The study of ethnicity: The need for a differential approach. In L. v. d. Berg-Eldering, F. J. M. de Rijcke, & L. V. Zuck (Eds.), *Multicultural education: A challenge for teachers* (pp.19–26). Dordrecht, Netherlands: Foris.

English-Lueck, J. A. (1994). Neighbors and Neibu: An anthropological reflection of intergroup communication in a predeparture program in China. *International Journal of Intercultural Relations, 18,* 85–98.

Erez, M. (1994). Toward a model of cross-cultural industrial and organizational psychogy. In H. Triandis, M. Dunnette, & L. Hough (Eds.), *Handbook of industrial and organizational psychology,* 2d ed. (Vol. 4, pp. 559–607). Palo Alto: Consulting Psychologists Press.

Everts, J. (1988). The Marae-based Hui: Intensive induction to cross-cultural counselling: A New Zealand experiment. *International Journal for the Advancement of Counselling, 11,* 97–104.

Feinberg, W. (1993). *Japan and the pursuit of a new American identity: Work and education in a multicultural age.* New York: Routledge.

Fiedler, F., Mitchell, T., & Triandis, H. (1971). The culture assimilator: An approach to cross-cultural training. *Journal of Applied Psychology, 55,* 95–102.

Fowler, S. & Mumford, M. (Eds.). (1995). *Intercultural Sourcebook.* Yarmouth, ME: Intercultural.

Freimanis, C. (1994). Training bilinguals to interpret in the community. In R. Brislin & T. Yoshida (Eds.), *Improving intercultural interactions: Modules for cross-cultural training programs* (pp. 313–341). Thousand Oaks, CA: Sage.

Furnham, A. & Bochner, S. (1986). *Culture shock: Psychological reactions to unfamiliar environments.* London: Methuen.

Gade, E., Huriburt, C., & Fuqua, D. (1986). Study habits and attitudes of American Indian students: Implications for counselors. *The School Counselor, 34,* 135–139.

Garcia, O. & Otheguy, R. (Eds.). (1989). *English across cultures, cultures across English: A reader in cross-cultural communication.* Berlin: Mouton de Gruyter.

Ghuman, P. A. S. (1993). *Coping with two cultures: British Asian and Indo-Canadian adolescents.* Clevedon: Multilingual Matters.

Goodman, N. (1994a). Cross-cultural training for the global executive. In R. Brislin & T. Yoshida (Eds.), *Improving intercultural interactions: Modules for cross-cultural training programs* (pp. 34–54). Thousand Oaks, CA: Sage.

Goodman, N. R. (1994b). Intercultural education at the university level: Teacher-student interaction. In R. W. Brislin and T. Yoshida (Eds.), *Improving intercultural interactions: Modules for cross-cultural training programs* (pp. 129–147). Thousand Oaks, CA: Sage.

Gumbert, E. B. (Ed.). (1983). *Different people: Studies in ethnicity and education.* Atlanta: Center for Cross-Cultural Education, College of Education, George State University.

Hamaguchi, E. (1985). A contextual model of the Japanese: Toward a methodological innovation in Japanese studies. *Journal of Japanese Studies, 11,* 289–321.

Hansen, C. D. (1993). Culture, cognition, and literacy: Tales from Morocco. *International Journal of Intercultural Relations, 17,* 271–292.

Hirsch, W. (1990). *A report on issues and factors re-*

lating to Maori achievement in the education system. Auckland: Ministry of Education.

Hofstede, G. (1980). *Culture's consequences: International differences in work-related values*. Beverly Hills: Sage.

Hofstede, G. (1991). *Cultures and organizations: Software of the mind*. New York and London: McGraw-Hill.

Horowitz, R. T. & Kraus, V. (1984). Patterns of cultural transition: Soviet and American children in a new environment. *Journal of Cross-Cultural Psychology, 15*, 399–416.

Jenkins, A. H. (1982). *The psychology of the Afro-Americans: A humanistic approach*. Elmsford, NY: Pergamon.

Johnson, D. (1989). The Houston Parent–Child Development Center project: Disseminating a viable program for enhancing at-risk families. *Prevention in Human Services, 7*, 89–108.

Kamada, M. (1994). Asian studies in Australia: Approaches to Asia through education. *Australian Journal of International Affairs, 48*, 1–24.

Kao, C. H. G. (1971). *Brain drain: A case study of China*. Taipei: Mei Ya.

Kashima, Y. & Callan, V. (1994). The Japanese work group. In H. Triandis, M. Dunnette, & L. Hough (Eds.), *Handbook of Industrial and Organizational Psychology*, 2d ed. (Vol. 4, pp. 609–646). Palo Alto: Consulting Psychologists Press.

Keeffe, K. (1992). *From the centre to the city: Aboriginal education, culture and power*. Canberra, Australia: Aboriginal Studies Press.

Kehoe, J. & Echols, F. (1984). Educational approaches for combatting prejudice and racism. In S. Shapson & V. D'Oyley (Eds.), *Bilingual and multicultural education: Canadian perspectives* (pp.130–139). Clevedon, England: Multilingual Matters.

Kim, U. & Berry, J. W. (Eds.). (1993). *Indigenous psychologies: Research and experience in cultural context*. Newbury Park, CA: Sage.

Kim, Y. (1988). *Communication and cross-cultural adaptation*. Philadelphia: Multilingual Matters.

Kurmann, W. (1979). *Le retour au pays des travailleurs migrants italiens: Problemes lĩes a la scolarisation de leurs enfants*. Rapport de mission effectúee pour l'Unesco, cooperation internationale dans l'education, N. 36. Berne: Office federal de l'education et de la science.

Laboratory of Comparative Human Cognition. (1982). Culture and intelligence. In R. J. Sternberg (Ed.), *Handbook of human intelligence* (pp. 642–722). New York: Cambridge University Press.

Laboratory of Comparative Human Cognition. (1983). Culture and cognitive development. In W. Kessen (Ed.), *Mussen handbook of child development* (Vol. 1, pp. 295–356). New York: Wiley.

LaFromboise, T. D. & Plake, B. S. (1981). Cultural relevant training of American Indian researchers. Paper presented at the meeting of the American Educational Research Association, Los Angeles, April, 1981.

Lambert, M. C., Knight, F., Taylor, R., & Newell, A. L. (1993). Further comparisons of teacher and parent ratings of behavior and emotional problems in Jamaican children. *International Journal of Intercultural Relations, 17*, 1–18.

Landis, D. & Brislin, R. (Eds.). (1983). *Handbook of intercultural training* (3 vols.). Elmsford, NY: Pergamon.

Landis, D., Brislin, R., & Hulgus, J. (1985). Attributional training versus contact in acculturative learning: A laboratory study. *Journal of Applied Social Psychology, 15*, 466–482.

Lane, H. (1992). *The mask of benevolence: Disabling the deaf community*. New York: Knopf.

Laosa, L. M. (1977). Multicultural education: How psychology can contribute. *Journal of Teacher Education, 28*, 26–30.

Lipsey, M. W. & Wilson, D. B. (1993). The efficacy of psychological, educational, and behavioral treatment: Confirmation from meta-analysis. *American Psychologist, 48*, 1181–1209.

Locke, D. C. (1989). Fostering the self-esteem of African-American children. *Elementary School Guidance and Counseling, 23*, 254–259.

Lonner, W. J. & Malpass, R. (Eds.). (1994). *Psychology and culture*. Boston: Allyn and Bacon.

Lysgaard, S. (1955). Adjustment in a foreign society: Norwegian Fullbright grantees visiting the United States. *International Social Science Bulletin, 7*, 45–51.

Malpass, R. & Salancik, G. (1977). Linear and branching formats in culture assimilator training. *International Journal of Intercultural Relations,1*, 76–87.

Marsella, A. J., Bornemann, T., Ekblad, S., & Orley, J. (1994). *Amidst peril and pain: The mental health and well-being of the world's refugees.* Washington: American Psychological Association.

Martin, J. N. (1984). The intercultural reentry: Conceptualizations and suggestions for future research. *International Journal of Intercultural Relations, 8,* 115–134.

Martin, J. N., Bradford, L., & Rohrlich, B. (1995). Comparing predeparture expectations and post-sojourn reports: A longitudinal study of U.S. students abroad. *International Journal of Intercultural Relations, 19,* 87–110.

McConnell, J. V. & Philipchalk, R. P. (1992). *Understanding human behavior,* 7th ed. Fort Worth: Harcourt Brace Jovanovich.

McGovern, T. V., Furumoto, L., Halpern, D. F., Kimble, G. A., & McKeachie, W. J. (1991). Liberal education, study in depth, and the arts and sciences major: Psychology. *American Psychologist, 46,* 598–605.

McInerney, D. M. (1990). The determinants of motivation for urban aboriginal students: A cross-cultural analysis. *Journal of Cross-Cultural Psychology, 21,* 474–495.

Miller-Jones, D. (1989). Culture and testing. *American Psychologist, 44,* 360–366.

Modgill, S. & Verma, G. (Eds.). (1985). *Multiculturalism and education: The interminable debate.* London: The Falmer Press.

Moyer, T. R. & Motta, R. W. (1982). Alienation and school adjustment among black and white adolescents. *The Journal of Psychology, 112,* 21–28.

Mullavey-O'Byrne, C. (1994). Intercultural communication for health care professionals. In R. Brislin & T. Yoshida (Eds.), *Improving intercultural interactions: Modules for cross-cultural training programs* (pp. 171–196). Thousand Oaks, CA: Sage.

Nipporica Associates & Hofner-Saphiere, D. (1993). *Ecotonos.* Yarmouth, ME: Intercultural.

Oberg, K. (1960). Cultural shock: Adjustment to new cultural environments. *Practical Anthropology, 7,* 177–182.

Oh, T. K. (1977). *The Asian brain drain: A factual and causal analysis.* San Francisco: R and E Research Associates.

Olmedo, E. L., Martinez, J. L., Jr., & Martinez, S. R. (1978). Measure of acculturation for Chicano adolescents. *Psychological Reports, 42,* 159–170.

Padilla, A. M., Wagatsuma, Y., & Lindholm, K. (1985). Acculturation and personality as predictors of stress in Japanese and Japanese-Americans. *Journal of Social Psychology, 125,* 295–305.

Paige, R. M. (1986) Trainer competencies: The missing conceptual link in orientation. *International Journal of Intercultural Relations, 10,* 135–158.

Paige, R. M. (1993). On the nature of intercultural experiences and intercultural education. In R. M. Paige (Ed.), *Education for the intercultural experience* (pp. 1–20). Yarmouth: Intercultural Press.

Paige, R. M. (Ed.). (1993). *Education for the intercultural experience.* Yarmouth: Intercultural Press.

Pedersen, P. (1988). *A handbook for developing multicultural awareness.* Alexandria, VA: American Association for Counseling and Development.

Pedersen, P. (1994). International students and international student advisers. In R. Brislin & T. Yoshida (Eds.), *Improving intercultural interactions: Modules for cross-cultural training programs* (pp.148–167). Thousand Oaks: SAGE.

Peterson, P. D., & Cox, G. B. (1988). Community mental health staff utilization in Washington state: Characteristics and target groups. *Community Mental Health Journal, 24,* 65–82.

Porcher, L. (1981). *L'education des enfants de migrants en Europe, l'interculturalisme et la formation des enseignants.* Strasbourg: Conseil de l'Europe.

Pornbacher, U. (Ed.). (1990). *Migration und interkulturelle erziehung in Europa: Bibliography for 1988.* Clevedon: Multilingual Matters.

Ramirez, M., & Castaneda, A. (1974). *Cultural democracy, bicognitive development and education.* New York: Academic.

Ramsey, P. G. (1987). *Teaching and learning in a diverse world: Multicultural education for young children.* New York: Teachers College Press.

Raynor, J. M. (1983). Race and education: Interpreting British policies in the 1960s and 1970s. In E. B. Gumbert (Ed.), *Different people: Stud-*

ies in ethnicity and education (pp. 75–98). Atlanta: Center for Cross-Cultural Education, College of Education, George State University.

Reid, E. & Reich, H. H. (Eds.). (1992). *Breaking the boundaries: Migrant workers' children in the EC.* Clevedon, England: Multilingual Matters.

Rey, M. (1979). L'education des enfants (de) migrants dans le canton de Geneve: Vers une education interculturelle. *Etudes Pedagogiques*, 127–138.

Rey, M. (1981). Des classes d'accueil a une education interculturelle. In A. Gretler et al. (Eds.), *Etre migrant*, 2d ed. Berne: Lang.

Rey, M. (1984). *L'education des enfants des travailleurs migrants "La formation des enseignants".* Rapport final du groupe de travail. Strasbourg: Conseil de l'Europe.

Rey, M. (1986). *Former les enseignants a l'education interculturelle? (Training teachers in intercultural education).* Les travaux du Conseil de la Cooperation Culturelle 1977–1983. Strasbourg: Conseil de l'Europe.

Rey-von Allmen, M. (1993). Immigration, marginalisation et chances educatives. *Education et recherche, 15*, 99–118.

Rist, R. (1979). On the education of guestworker children in Germany: Public policy and equal opportunity. *Comparative Education Review, 23*, 355–369.

Rogoff, B. (1981). Schooling and the development of cognitive skills. In H. Triandis & A. Heron (Eds.), *Handbook of cross-cultural psychology* (Vol. 4, pp. 233–294). Boston: Allyn and Bacon.

Rogoff, B. (1982). Integrating context and cognitive development. In M. E. Lamb & A. L. Brown (Eds.), *Advances in developmental psychology* (Vol. 2, pp. 125–170). Hillsdale, NJ: Lawrence Erlbaum.

Rogoff, B. (1990). *Apprenticeship in thinking: Cognitive development in social context.* New York: Oxford University Press.

Ross, P. G. & Krider, D. S. (1992). Off the plane and into the classroom: A phenomenological explication of international teaching assistants' experiences in the American classroom. *International Journal of Intercultural Relations, 16*, 277–293.

Santrock, J. W. (1994). *Psychology*, 4th ed. Madison: WCB Brown and Benchmark.

Schwartz, C. G. & Kahne, M. J. (1993). Support for student and staff wives in social transition in a university setting. *International Journal of Intercultural Relations, 17*, 451–463.

Searle, W. & Ward, C. (1990). The prediction of psychological and sociological adjustment during cross-cultural transitions. *International Journal of Intercultural Relations, 14*, 449–464.

Seelye, H. N. (1993). *Teaching culture: Strategies for intercultural communication* 3rd ed. Lincolnwood, IL: National Textbook Company.

Segall, M. H., Dasen, P. R., Berry, J. W., Poortinga, Y. H. (1990). *Human behavior in global perspective: An introduction to cross-cultural psychology.* New York: Pergamon.

Seipel, M. M. (1988). Locus of control as related to life experiences of Korean immigrants. *International Journal of Intercultural Relations, 12*, 61–71.

Semons, M. (1991). Ethnicity in the urban high school: A naturalistic study of student experiences. *The Urban Review, 23*, 137–158.

Simila, M. (1988). The cultural identity of immigrant youth: A perspective from action theory. *Migration: A European Journal of International Migration and Ethnic Relations, 3*, 61–78.

Singelis, T. (1994). Non-verbal communication in intercultural interactions. In R. W. Brislin & T. Yoshida (Eds.), *Improving intercultural interactions: Modules for cross-cultural training programs* (pp. 268–294). Thousand Oaks, CA: Sage.

Sleeter, C. E. (1992). *Keepers of the American dream: A study of staff development and multicultural education.* London: The Falmer Press.

Sleeter, C. E. & Grant, C. A. (1994). *Making choices for multicultural education: Five approaches to race, class, and gender*, 2d ed. New York: Merrill.

Smolicz, J. J. (1979). *Culture and education in a plural society.* Canberra, Australia: The Curriculum Development Centre.

Spoonley, P. (1993). *Racism and ethnicity*, 2d ed. Auckland: Oxford University Press.

Steinberg, L., Blinde, P. L., & Chan, K. S. (1984). Dropping out among language minority youth. *Review of Educational Research, 54,* 113–132.

Stewart, E. (1966). The simulation of cultural differences. *Journal of Communication, 16,* 291–304.

Sue, D. W. & Sue, S. (1972). Psychological characteristics of Chinese-American college students. *Journal of Counseling Psychology, 6,* 471–478.

Sue, S., Zane, N., & Young, K. (1994). Research on psychotherapy with culturally diverse populations. In A. E. Bergin & S. L. Garfield (Eds.), *Handbook of psychotherapy and behavior change* (pp. 783–817). New York: Wiley.

Swann Report. (1985). *Education for all: Report of the Commission of Enquiry into the Education of Children from Ethnic Minority Groups.* London: Department of Education and Science (DES).

Szanton, D. (1966). Cultural confrontation in the Philippines. In R. Textor (Ed.), *Cultural frontiers of the Peace Corps* (pp. 35–61). Cambridge, MA: MIT Press.

Tanaka, T., Takai, J., Kohyama, T., & Fujihara, T. (1994). Adjustment patterns of international students in Japan. *International Journal of Intercultural Relations, 18,* 55–76.

Tharp, R. G. (1982). The effective instruction of comprehension: Results and description of the Kamehameha Early Education Program. *Reading Research Quarterly, 17,* 503–527.

Tharp, R. G. (1989a). Psychocultural variables and constants: Effects on teaching and learning in schools. *American Psychologist, 44,* 349–359.

Tharp, R. G. (1989b). Culturally compatible education: A formula for designing effective classrooms. In H. T. Trueba, G. Spindler, & L. Spindler (Eds.), *What do anthropologists have to say about dropouts?* (pp. 51–66). New York: The Falmer Press.

Tharp, R. G. & Gallimore, R. (1988). *Rousing minds to life: Teaching, learning and schooling in social context.* Cambridge: Cambridge University Press.

Tharp, R. G. & Yamauchi, L. (1994). *Instructional conversation in Native American classrooms.* Santa Cruz: National Center for Research on Cultural Diversity and Second Language Learning, University of California.

Thomas, D. & Ravlin, E. (1995). Responses of employees to cultural adaptation by a foreign manager. *Journal of Applied Psychology, 80,* 133–146.

Tocatlidou, V. (1992). Designing materials for mother tongue teaching. In E. Reid & H. H. Reich (Eds.), *Breaking the boundaries: Migrant workers' children in the EC* (pp. 179–212). Clevedon, England: Multilingual Matters.

Todd, R. (1991). *Education in a multicultural society.* London: Cassell Educational.

Triandis, H. (1989). The self and social behavior in differing cultural contexts. *Psychological Review, 96,* 506–520.

Triandis, H. C. (1994). *Culture and social behavior.* New York: McGraw-Hill.

Triandis, H. C. & Dunnette, M., & Hough, L. (Eds.). (1994). *Handbook of industrial psychology,* 2d ed. (Vol 4). Palo Alto, CA: Consulting Psychologists Press.

Triandis, H., Kurowski, L., & Gelfand, L. (1994). Workplace diversity. In H. Triandis, M. Dunnette, & L. Hough (Eds.), *Handbook of industrial and organizational psychology,* 2nd ed. (Vol. 4, pp. 769–827). Palo Alto: Consulting Psychologists Press.

Tung, R. (1981). Selecting and training of personnel for overseas assignments. *Columbia Journal of World Business, 6,* 68–78.

Tung, T. M. (1985). Psychiatric care for Southeast Asians: How different is different? In T. C. Owan (Ed.), *Southeast Asian mental health: Treatment, prevention, services, training, and research* (pp. 5–40). Washington, CD: National Institute of Mental Health.

Verma, G. & Bagley, C. (Eds.). (1982). *Self-concept, achievement and multicultural education.* London: MacMillan.

Walsh, J. E. (1979). *Humanistic cultural learning: An introduction.* Honolulu: The University Press of Hawaii.

Walton, S. (1990). Stress management training for overseas effectiveness. *International Journal of Intercultural Relations, 14,* 507–527.

Ward, C. & Kennedy, A. (1993). Psychological and socio-cultural adjustment during cross-cultural transitions: A comparison of secondary students overseas and at home. *International Journal of Psychology, 28,* 129–147.

Westwood, M. & Barker, M. (1990). Academic

achievement and social adaptation among international students: A comparison groups study of the peer-pairing program. *International Journal of Intercultural Relations, 14,* 251–263.

Wilson, A. H. (1993). A cross-national perspective on reentry of high school exchange students. *International Journal of Intercultural Relations, 17,* 465–492.

Yamauchi, L. A. (1993). *Visions of the ideal Zuni classroom: Multiple perspectives on Native American education.* Doctoral dissertation. Honolulu: University Press of Hawaii.

Yee, A. H. (1989). Cross-cultural perspectives on higher education in East Asia: Psychological effects upon Asian students. *Journal of Multilingual and Multicultural Development, 10,* 213–232.

Yee, A. H., Fairchild, H. H., Weizmann, F., & Wyatt, G. E. (1993). Addressing psychology's problems with race. *American Psychologist, 48,* 1132–1140.

Yoshida, T. (1994). Interpersonal versus non-interpersonal realities: An effective tool individualists can use to better understand collectivists. In R. Brislin and T. Yoshida (Eds.), *Improving intercultural interactions: Modules for cross-cultural training programs* (pp. 243–267). Thousand Oaks, CA: Sage.

Zimbardo, P. G. & Weber, A. L. (1994). *Psychology.* New York: Harper Collins College.

Zinman, R. (1991). Developments and directions in multicultural/intercultural education, 1980–1990, the Province of Quebec. *Canadian Ethnic Studies, 23,* 65–80.

10

INDUSTRIAL/ORGANIZATIONAL PSYCHOLOGY[1]

C. HARRY HUI
University of Hong Kong
Hong Kong

CHUNG LEUNG LUK[2]
University of Hong Kong
Hong Kong

Contents

Introduction

Global marketing is of growing importance as national economies are increasingly interdependent. The Asia-Pacific Economic Cooperation Summit in Jakarta in 1994, for example, issued a blueprint for the world's largest free trade area by 2020 (Spaeth, 1994), bringing together 2.2 billion culturally diverse consumers. The former Soviet Bloc countries now open their doors to the West. As companies enter this global market, we must ask whether psychological and management principles that originated in Europe and North America can effectively be applied elsewhere. Can we assume the same work values across culture? Does work mean the same thing to, and satisfy the same needs of, different peoples? What impacts does culture have on employees' attitudes and behaviors? What is it like to be in an ethnically heterogeneous workplace? Are there leadership theories and management techniques that apply universally? Do organization development approaches that help many companies in one country work in another country? Do cultures differ in the way business is done, and deals are negotiated?

To answer questions like these, this chapter reviews recent research in this field, focusing on studies published since the first edition of this *Handbook*.

Values and Motivation

Work-Related Values

While work ethics in most societies share the basic theme that work is good and honorable, they differ in the specifics.[3] For example, the Protestant work ethic (that people should work, individually, for personal salvation and to honor God; Weber, 1930) has been found to have different factor structures in different cultures (see Bluen & Barling, 1983, for a factor analytic study of white employees in South Africa). Similarly, the Meaning of Work (MOW) International Research Team (1987, chapter 6) found two distinguishable norms related to work: the entitlement norm (that individuals who work should gain outcomes in return) and the obligation norm (that everyone has a duty to work for society).[4] These contrasting ideas echo the individualism-collectivism dichotomy, which is discussed in greater detail by Kagitçibasi elsewhere in this volume.

In Asia, there are two work-related values, the Confucian work ethic and the Japanese style work ethic derived from it. Social scientists have attributed the strong economic growth of some Asian countries in the past two decades to Confucianism (e.g., Hicks & Redding, 1983a, b; Hofstede & Bond, 1988). Here, familial reputation and social stability rather than personal salvation are key values. Work becomes altruistic, a moral duty to the collectivity (Kao & Ng, 1988). Examining the Pacific Basin economic development, the Chinese Culture Connection (1987) identified the factor "Confucian work dynamism," which is positively loaded on such characteristics as persistence, thrift, sense of shame, ordering by status, and negatively on personal steadiness, protecting one's face, respect for tradition, and reciprocation of favors. Hong Kong, Taiwan, Japan, and South Korea ranked high on "Confucian work dynamism," while Pakistan, Nigeria, Philippines, and Canada ranked low. The research team also found the factor correlated with national economic growth between 1965 and 1987 (Hofstede, 1991; Hofstede & Bond, 1988; Franke, Hofstede, & Bond, 1991).

In Japan, work is central to a person's life (England & Misumi, 1986). Of the seven industrialized nations involved in the MOW project (Belgium, West Germany, Israel, Japan, Netherlands, United States, and Yugoslavia), Japan has the greatest number of workers willing to continue working even when wealthy enough to quit (Harpaz, 1989). Japanese workers associate physical exercise, spiritual training, and character building, with the workspace (Misumi, 1990). According to Cole (1979), work is seen as an end in itself in Japan.

Compared to their U.S. counterparts, Saudi managers are significantly more paternalistic in their value orientation toward their companies (At-Twaijri, 1989). In two Arab countries, Iraq and Saudi Arabia, managers believe that human growth and development on the job, together with serving the group's interests, are important work elements (Ali, 1989). Nevertheless, certain businesses essential to modern economies, such as banking or external financing involving interest, are considered sinful and prohibited (Kassem & Ariss, 1990).

There are some countries in Asia that devalue work; India is one (J. B. P. Sinha, 1994; see also Fyans, Maehr, Salili, & Desai, 1983). Given that the caste system allocates physical labor to slaves and "untouchables," exemption from physical labor becomes a sign of nobility. The way to spiritual maturity is meditation, not work. These values mesh with *chalega,* a fatalistic acceptance of the status quo (Kanungo, 1990; D. Sinha, 1991).

This is not to say, however, that Indians always hate work. Schuster, Forsterling, and Weiner (1989) compared causal attributions by taxi drivers and civil servants from Belgium, West Germany, South Korea, England, and India, and found Indians most distinct in making attributions that were external, variable, and uncontrollable by self. However, when work is construed as duty in service of in-group members, a positive ethic may be invoked (Kanungo, 1990; Rastogi, 1987; J. B. P. Sinha, 1990b). Indians will tend to emphasize the work-related values of embeddedness in family and caste, harmony and tolerance, duty over hedonism, preference for personalized relationships, and preference for hierarchy (J. B. P. Sinha, 1990a).

Needs and Work Goals

The work-related values previously discussed above can be readily translated into specific psychological needs and work goals. These needs energize a person toward specific acts (Ronen, 1986).

Structure of Needs
The five-tier hierarchy of needs described by Maslow (1954) and the three-factor structure of needs specified in Alderfer's (1972) ERG theory have not received much empirical support in cross-cultural studies (see, for example, Rauschenberger,

Schmitt, & Hunter, 1980). Ronen (1994) argued that the failure was due to methodological shortcomings and not theoretical deficiency. Using importance ratings on 14 specific work goals (collected from samples in Canada, France, the United Kingdom, Germany, Japan, China, and Israel), Ronen conducted multidimensional scaling and found very similar maps of work goals in all samples. Each of the maps from the seven countries can be partitioned into four quadrants by two general dimensions: individualism–collectivism and materialism–humanism. Each specific work goal can then be assigned a coordinate on each of these two general value dimensions. He further argued that this two-dimensional configuration of work goals was evidence for an underlying, universal structure of needs.

Ronen (1994) then conceptually reformulated the categorizations of needs by Maslow and Alderfer in terms of his configuration. Specifically, physiological, safety, and existence needs are equivalent to materialistic collectivism (collectivist in the sense that the goals are common to the group of paid employees), aiming at financially quantifiable work goals. Social needs and relatedness are equivalent to nonmaterialistic collectivism, which entails the pursuit of good interpersonal relations at work. Self-esteem needs and also relatedness are equivalent to materialistic individualism, involving recognition and advancement which are personal achievements with meanings endowed by others. Finally, self-actualization and growth are equivalent to nonmaterialistic individualism. This conceptualization is nonetheless arbitrary, and needs further validation.

Strength of Needs

While the structure of needs may be universal, their relative strengths are not. Nevis (1983a, b) revised Maslow's hierarchy of needs, and argued that the most basic needs in the People's Republic of China are belonging needs rather than physiological needs. Moreover, self-actualization is embodied in service to one's nation and community. Nevis explained these deviations in terms of adjustments of priority to environmental demands (1983b). A person who self-actualizes by means of contributing to the group is realizing the value of collectivist self-actualization.

Consistent with this line of thought, Shenkar and Ronen (1987b) found that Chinese government officials and enterprise managers ranked "making a contribution" and "co-workers who cooperate" as the most important work goals. ("Time for nonwork activities" and "promotion" were ranked the lowest.) The employer–employee relationship in collectivist cultures is colored with moral overtones and mutual obligations (Redding, Norman, & Schlander, 1994). Nonmaterial rewards are expected and valued. The pattern is partly reflective of the Confucian work ethic as well as socialist ideology that espouse harmony and cooperation.

Westernization nevertheless affects the workforce in many developing countries. "Autonomy," for instance, was ranked very important by Shenkar and Ronen's Chinese subjects. The percentage of Chinese workers who considered "contribution to nation and community" as the most important element in life, declined from 73 to 45 percent during the five years between 1986 and 1991 (for more details, see Hui & Tan, 1995), further evidence of the trend toward Westernization. A similar trend but at a slower rate can be detected in other countries. For example, Ali and Al-Shakhis (1991) found a decline, from 1982 to 1986, in "tribalistic" (being submissive to authority and tradition) and "conformist" values (being intolerant of ambiguity) among Saudi managers. "Manipulative" values (being materialistic, expressive, calculating) became more emphasized. "Egocentric" values (being aggressive, selfish, impulsive) remained the least endorsed, by a large margin, both in 1982 and 1986.

In the developed countries covered by the MOW project, "interesting work" was a dominant work goal. Harpaz (1990, p. 81) found that it was ranked the most important work goal in Belgium, Britain, Israel, and the United States. In the other three countries (Germany, Japan, and the Netherlands), it was ranked either the second or the third. We should note, however, that the definition ("work that you really like") provided in the questionnaire is confounded with other concepts such as fulfillment of needs (perhaps social for one person but security for another), and thus may have artificially led to higher rankings.

If we lay aside "interesting work" from Harpaz's mean intra-country ranks, national differences re-appear. Workers in the Netherlands ranked autonomy and interpersonal relations the highest and promotion the lowest. Ironically, emphasis on pay and job security was the highest in the United States, Belgium, Britain, and Germany. As the employer-employee relationship in individualist cultures is "a business relationship based on the calculation of mutual advantages" (Redding, Norman, & Schlander, 1994, p.653), employees only expect material rewards from their employers. Greater variation is found among the two more collectivist countries. Israelis ranked "interpersonal relations" the highest, and "job security and variety" the lowest, while Japanese chose "match between person and job" as the highest and "promotion" as lowest. In a separate study (Yamauchi, 1993), recognition and personal growth were found to be valued by Japanese employees.

Fulfillment of basic needs is still the concern of people living close to or below the poverty line. For example, for workers in Nigeria, economic return is the most important work goal (Ejiogu, 1983). In India, both workers and managers have a strong urge to hoard material resources (Sinha, 1994). Power is coveted as an essential means of acquiring resources. Female Indian workers, perhaps one of the most deprived groups in that country, are ready to forego short working hours, less strenuous work, and personal benefits for job status, prestige, income, and promotion opportunity (Ahmad, 1989). Maslow's prepotency principle seems to hold: Where basic needs have not been satisfied, other higher level motivators would not work.

Organizational Commitment and Communication

Organizational Commitment in Ethnically Homogeneous Organizations

In each country the culture and government policies can produce a dominant form for business organizations (Whitley, 1990). For example, companies in Argentina,

Brazil, and Uruguay were "flatter," or had fewer levels, than some Asian (Indian, Filipino, and Taiwanese) companies (Negandhi, 1984). Hofstede (1980) defined four organizational forms around the world according to their emphasis on power distance and uncertainty avoidance. An organization with high power distance and strong uncertainty avoidance is known as the *pyramid of people,* high power distance and weak uncertainty avoidance as the *family,* low power distance and strong uncertainty avoidance as the *well-oiled machine,* and low power distance and weak uncertainty avoidance as the *village market.*

In this section we shall examine the degree of organizational commitment in the organizational forms that are ethnically homogeneous. In these cases, the employees and employers share more or less the same set of cultural values.

The American

The American form of organizations, the *village market* (Hofstede, 1980), is characterized by low personal authority of the owner, low enterprise loyalty of the employees, and high role individuation according to Whitley's (1990) typology. This organizational form will be used as the anchoring point for comparisons that follow.

The Overseas Chinese

The small-scale Chinese family business, which takes the form of the *family* in Hofstede's (1980) terminology, is preserved in overseas Chinese societies. The values of paternalism and personalism, as well as a sense of insecurity, prevail in the organizational structure and mould the employer-employee relationship (Hui, 1990; Redding, Norman, & Schlander, 1994). Job satisfaction is higher among those who are collectivist (Hui, Eastman, & Yee, 1995). In this organizational form, personal authority of the owner is high, employee loyalty is medium, and role individuation is low (Whitley, 1990). Two distinct levels in the organizational structure can be identified: the core inside circle, and the peripheral, non-management employees (Kao, 1993). The core inside circle comprises the owner, his family members or close kin, and trusted non-kin who have been accepted as in-group members. Managerial and decision-making power is concentrated in this small circle and particularly on the owner. The peripheral non-management employees are considered as outsiders. They are not trusted or granted decision-making power on important issues. Empowerment does not go beyond the small circle. Loyalty to the organization is personalized and concentrated on the owner who is a father figure. Rewards and promotion are largely based on personalized loyalty in addition to performance. The employer–employee relationship is similar to a father–son relationship. Moral obligations are emphasized. The father figure is aloof, omnipotent, and autocratic.

Employees' commitment to the organization depends on whether they are in the core inside circle or in the peripheral level (Kao & Ng, 1992). Psychological commitment is high within because the father-son relationship and the moral overtones are salient in the circle. Moreover, employees who embrace Confucian values are more hard working and committed to the organization (Yang & Cheng, 1987).

The Mainland Chinese

The situation in the People's Republic of China is relatively unexplored. Under the rule of the Communist Party, the traditional organizational form had been demolished. Virtually all businesses had become state-owned. This situation has changed somewhat in the last decade of economic reform during which some non-state owned (i.e., private) companies emerged. Yu, Wang, and He (1992) compared employees' organizational commitment in state-owned and non-state owned enterprises. Organizational commitment is significantly lower in the former. Employees in state-owned enterprises feel that they are not receiving adequate managerial protection and that their jobs are less promising and satisfying. These state-owned enterprises may not be as capable of satisfying the employees' psychological needs as the more deep-rooted family businesses (see, for example, Kent, Lynn, & Mailer, 1991).

The Korean

The degree of collectivism of South Korea is somewhat similar to that of Chinese societies. Although the Korean organizational form is grouped with the Japanese form under the *pyramid of people* (Hofstede, 1980), it is more similar to the Chinese form in terms of the participants' mentality (Redding, Norman, & Schlander, 1994). The model South Korean organizational form is the *chaebol*, which is characterized by a "company familism" (Kim, 1988). As in the Chinese family business, personal authority of the owner is high, employee loyalty is medium, and role individuation is low (Whitley, 1990). Because of the support from government policies, South Korean firms can grow to a larger size than that of Chinese family businesses. Yet the typical *chaebol* is still controlled by the owner and/or his relatives, and authority is highly centralized. Managers play the paternal role in relation to their subordinates.

The Japanese[5]

Most Japanese organizations take the form of a *pyramid of people* (Hofstede, 1980), probably because that suits the culture best. Lincoln, Hanada, and Olson (1981) studied 28 Japanese-owned organizations in the United States. They found that employees with Japanese ancestry have higher work satisfaction and more personal ties with coworkers if the organizational structure is differentiated more vertically (i.e., "taller" structure). These employees also reacted negatively to horizontal role differentiation. Such relationships were absent among American employees in the same organizations.

In a Japanese enterprise, ownership and management are usually separated. Mutual trust can develop among non-kins, therefore rendering the organization far less personalized. The seniority-based promotion system suppresses employees' inter-organizational mobility. It also fosters loyalty, which is directed to a position in the hierarchy rather than to a particular person. According to Whitley's (1990) analysis, personal authority in the Japanese organization is low, enterprise loyalty is high, and role individuation is low. Smith (1984) reviewed studies contrasting Japanese firms with firms owned by people of other cultures. The general picture is that Japanese workers have lower absenteeism, and they work harder. Compared with their counterparts in other cultures, Japanese managers are more concerned with quality control, efficiency, and timekeeping. They also hold more meetings.

Contrary to the commonly held belief that Japanese employees are much more committed to their organizations than their American counterparts, empirical research is unequivocal that organizational commitment (as well as job satisfaction) among Japanese employees is actually lower than that among Americans (e.g., Kalleberg & Reve, 1992; Lincoln & Kalleberg, 1985; Luthans, McCaul, & Dodd, 1985; Near, 1986, 1989). Even Japanese chief executive officers were less content in their jobs than their American counterparts (DeFrank, Matteson, Schweiger, & Ivancevich, 1985). The MOW International Research Team (1987, chapter 6) further proffered indirect evidence of lower organizational commitment in Japan than in the United States. The Japanese, compared with Americans, reported higher preference for the entitlement norm and lower preference for the obligation norm. One explanation for this is that the reward systems in Japanese enterprises are more effective in enhancing behavioral commitment rather than attitudinal commitment (Redding, Norman, & Schlander, 1994).

Furthermore, Marsh and Mannari (1977) found that whether Japanese employees would stay in the same organization could not be predicted by their level of support for lifetime commitment norms and values. In other words, the employees stay with the same employer not because they are believers in lifetime commitment, but perhaps because they have no alternative. They comply, without private acceptance, with the group norms of working hard and staying with the same company (Near, 1986). On the contrary, organizational commitment is a function of employees' age and tenure regardless of the country, be it South Korea, Japan, or America (Luthans, McCaul, & Dodd, 1985). In addition to age and tenure, Kalleberg and Reve (1992) in their study of 4,567 U.S. and 3,735 Japanese employees further found that organizational commitment is related to perceived promotion opportunities. Moreover, organizational commitment is correlated with intrinsic rewards in the U.S. employees, but with earning in the Japanese employees.

A Synthesis

Generally speaking, organizations in more collectivist cultures base promotion and compensation decisions on employees' loyalty, seniority, and in-group membership. The in-group is narrowly defined. In special cases of collectivism, the in-group of an organization is defined solely in terms of familial ties to the owner. A characteristic of this familist organizational form is the personalized, paternal relationship between employer and employee, and discrimination between in-group members and non-trusted employees (see also Hofstede, 1987).

Similar familism can be found in organizations of other collectivist cultures such as India (Kanungo, 1990; J. B. P. Sinha, 1994) and Uruguay (Negandhi, 1984), with the in-group comprising of a few trusted employees. Because this in-group is more stable than those in individualist cultures, in-group members can adopt a longer time frame to conceptualize the employer–employee relationship and the leader–follower relationship (Chemers, 1994; Whitley, 1990). The consequence is that moral obligations and cooperation instead of calculative elements and individual achievement are emphasized among in-group members (Redding, Norman, & Schlander, 1994; Whitley, 1990). They do not have to settle their gain or loss hastily because they know they will get paid back in the future. Also, the group will encounter a variety of jobs and this will strengthen interdependence among group members as no single one of them can tackle all the jobs on his or her own. Hence, group achievement rather than individual expertise is valued (Rohlen, 1979). On the contrary, the ingress in other forms of organizations such as the *village market* are vaguely defined. Sometimes employees identify with their own professional group, and sometimes they identify with the organization as a whole. The employer–employee relationship is temporary and contractual. Therefore, they have to calculate accurately how much input each party has made so that they can allocate everybody's share on the group's dissolution. General levels of cultural collectivism do *not* necessarily lead to underlying attitudinal commitment. We speculate that cultural collectivism strengthens the ties between trusted employees and the management or the owner, thereby strengthening organizational commitment only in this particular group of employees. As for those employees not in the in-group, attitudinal commitment can be very low.

Interpersonal Dynamics in Ethnically Heterogeneous Organizations

The above organizational forms we have discussed are relatively simple because of internal value congruence. The situation becomes more complex when the cultural and ethnic origin of the employer is different from that of the employees, or when the staff force is made up of people from two or more cultural groups. In such multicultural organizations, issues of intergroup relations, intercultural communication, acculturation, and adaptation become salient (for more details, see chapters by Berry & Sam and Gudykunst & Bond, this volume).

Bochner and Hesketh's (1994) study of an Australian bank illustrated the complex issues facing this type of organization. The top management of the Australian bank is comprised of White native English-speakers, while the respondents sampled came from 28 different national/ethnic origins, broadly categorizable into two groups, one high on collectivism and power distance, and one low on both. Although there is a nondiscrimination policy, the two groups report very different relationships with the employer. The first group does not have much trust in their employer and members of other ethnic groups. Their contact with fellow workers is, however, more personal and informal. Teamwork is preferred. Quite the reverse is true for the second group.

According to Shaw's (1990) cognitive categorization model, the difficulties of intercultural management can be traced to the discrepancies between cultures in their employee/manager schemas, situational schemas, and behavioral scripts. People from different cultural backgrounds have different definitions of what comprises a good leader/manager and different understandings of situations and suitable behaviors. Therefore one's automatic responses may not be considered appropriate in the eyes of a party from another culture. These discrepancies can be reduced by more exposure to other cultures.

Cultural heterogeneity is not always a liability. For example, Anderson (1983) found that diversity within the work group in New Zealand manufacturing companies does not impede the effectiveness of certain managerial techniques nor affect the leader–follower relationship. In a mature leader–follower relationship (Graen & Wakabayashi, 1994), individuals have established a common ground of communication and a basis for mutual understanding. Cultural heterogeneity is less likely to be a hindrance to group functioning, and it can be a resource for the individuals' own learning and the organizations' development (see, e.g., Herriot & Pemberton, 1994). These observations can be explained in terms of Triandis, Kurowski, and Gelfand's (1994) theoretical model, which links interethnic attitudes and accommodation at the workplace with such variables as cultural distance, perceived similarity, and superordinate goals and sociotypes. According to this model, smaller cultural distance, greater perceived similarity, plus superordinate goals and sociotypes, can contribute to more positive interethnic attitudes and greater likelihood of accommodation. At the European Finance Centre of British Petroleum, a two-day training program for multicultural teamworking was implemented to facilitate communication and mutual understanding among its 40 members of 13 different nationalities (Neale & Mindel, 1992). Intervention techniques should be used to encourage and nurture innovative ideas generated as a result of perspective difference, so that large organizations can benefit more fully from their culturally diverse human resources (Rosenfeld & Servo, 1990).

Management of Ethnically Heterogeneous Organizations

Management of Overseas Subsidiaries

Multinational enterprises (MNEs) control and manage overseas subsidiaries in two ways—bureaucratic control and cultural control (Jaeger, 1983). The bureaucratic mode involves explicitly setting codified rules, regulations, and relatively well-defined job requirements, as well as controlling resources to fortify authority and power. The cultural mode involves exporting corporate culture from the headquarters. The local subsidiary is led by expatriate managers with long company service. It employs a large number of people who speak the language of the country of ownership. It encourages the use of that language, sends more local employees to headquarters for training, and arranges frequent staff visits to and from headquarters. Corporate values, customs and traditions are emphasized. Socialization is intense and holistic, although the rules transmitted are implicit, informal, and personal.

The cost of cultural control can be substantial as the firm has to invest more money to support the socialization processes and to arrange for relocating the expatriates (Jaeger, 1983). Moreover, the culture of the headquarters may be incompatible with the political and social environment of the host country. Hatch (1995) reported an extensive cross-cultural team building and training program conducted for a North American electronics company and its overseas subsidiaries in 41 countries. Some of the activities and the structure of the original program designed in the headquarters had to be modified to avoid conflicts with the local cultures. In the French subsidiary, for instance, use of English in instruction meant a threat to employees' Frenchness and was subsequently replaced by use of French. Ground rules were also strongly resisted because of the French style of not abiding by any authority. Bureaucratic control is more flexible and economical, but MNEs that practice cultural control justify their practice by insisting that the investment in socialization is worthwhile and will result in better human resources, which in turn will lead to higher profit. Jaeger (1983) studied two U.S.-owned MNEs that have subsidiaries in Brazil. The subsidiary that practices a cultural mode of control is more similar to the American headquarters in terms of physical structures and facilities than the subsidiary that practices bureaucratic control.

Compared to overseas subsidiaries owned by parent companies in countries such as the United States and Germany, overseas subsidiaries owned by Japanese are managed most autocratically (Negandhi, Eshghi, & Yuen, 1985). The Japanese top management exercises centralized decision making, does not trust local employees, has no confidence in local employees' ability, and is the most ethnocentric.

Management of Joint Ventures

International joint ventures are a new form of organization characterized by internationally shared ownership. By this very definition, the top management, not just the subordinates, is bound up with cultural heterogeneity. As a result, for example, in U.S.-Korea joint ventures, the Korean parent firms are more concerned with market share and growth than with profit, while the American counterparts hold a different view (Tung, 1991). Distrust and dispute at the top could easily lead to breakdown of the entire organization. Shenkar and Zeira (1987) further hypothesized that employees' loyalty, communication, and decision making would be impaired when the joint venture parents do not share similar objectives, and that loyalty would sway to the parent with a majority stake. Clearly more research is needed to evaluate the hypotheses.

Cultural Adaptation

Yavas, Luqmani, and Quraeshi (1990) compared local and expatriate managers working in Saudi Arabia, and found no difference in organizational commitment and work values, but a slightly higher job satisfaction among expatriate managers. However, there are also reports that Western managers assigned to non-Western or Third World settings find themselves less satisfied with their work, than those who are assigned to a Western, overseas country (see, for example, Dunbar, 1992).

Acculturation to the "mainstream" culture at the workplace has been found to be a significant determinant of intention to stay. For example, Hispanics not acculturated to the Anglo culture have a much higher turnover rate during the year after joining the U.S. navy than Hispanics who are high in acculturation and non-Hispanic whites (Booth-Kewley, Rosenfeld, & Edwards, 1993). A similar relationship was found for American expatriates assigned to countries in Europe and the Pacific Rim (Gregersen & Black, 1990).

Managerial Techniques

Managerial techniques fall into two general categories: the personal domain and the impersonal domain. The personal domain refers to managerial leadership. The impersonal domain includes situational variables such as participative management, team work arrangement, and reward schemes. This section will review application of these Western techniques in other cultures.

Managerial Leadership

All the usual management functions of planning, organizing, staffing, directing, and control can be subsumed under the broad category of leadership. As such, leadership theories have always occupied center stage in management research. This topic was covered extensively in A. S. Tannenbaum's (1980) chapter published in the first edition of this *Handbook.* Since then, research has added no theoretical upheaval, but only a fine-tuning of existing theories and adaptations for cross-cultural application. Researchers keep asking the same question: Is there a culture-free theory of leadership?

Two-Dimensional Approach
The Ohio State leadership theory postulates two basic behavioral dimensions of leadership: "initiating structure" and "consideration." Each serves a distinct set of functions to the subordinates, the first for structuring their task, and clarifying their roles and task requirements, the other for providing socioemotional support. Similar conceptualizations have been formulated in earlier works of Bales and Slater (1955) and Blake and Mouton (1964). Data from the West suggest that the more a person exhibits these two qualities, the more desirable the person is as a leader (e.g., Tjosvold, 1984). The transactional versus transformational leadership (Bass, 1985; Burns, 1978), a broader bi-dimensional paradigm of leadership theories, is functionally similar to initiating structure and consideration. Bass's (1985) factor analysis of data obtained from executives and army officers indicates that transactional leadership includes contingent reward and management-by-exception, whereas transformational leadership includes charisma, individualized consideration, and intellectual stimulation. A transformational leadership workshop to train Israeli infantry cadets was superior to traditional training programs based on a transactional model (Popper, Landau, & Gluskinos, 1992).

Using data collected in Japan, Misumi (1985) also depicts a leader's behavior on a two-dimensional plane. One dimension is an emphasis on subordinates' performance (P), which consists of "pressure (to work hard)" and "planning (the work, or expertise)." The other dimension is an emphasis on maintenance (M) of workgroup solidarity, harmony, and interpersonal relationships. His PM theory argues that the leadership style that emphasizes both P *and* M is always superior to other leadership styles. J. B. P. Sinha (1980) proposed a NT theory of Indian leadership, where N stands for nurturant style and T stands for task-oriented style (for more details, see J. B. P. Sinha, 1994). This view received empirical support by Ansari (1986) and Kool and Saksena (1989), who found that the majority of Indian managers preferred a "high task/high relationship" leadership style.

Data from the relatively unexplored areas in the Middle East also indicate a similar bi-dimensional structure of leadership behaviors. Using data collected from Iranian middle managers on Stogdill's (1963) Leader Behavior Description Questionnaire, Ayman and Chemers (1983) found two dimensions of leadership that are then labeled *benevolent paternalism* and *domineering*. Benevolent paternalism is associated with the Iranian father style which is a blend of warmth and sternness. Domineering is associated with exploitation and control. Conceptually, the factor of benevolent paternalism corresponds somewhat to the dimension of consideration or employee-centeredness, whereas domineering can be regarded as the Iranian version of the initiating structure or task-centered leadership. A leader's benevolent paternalism increases the Iranian foremen's work effectiveness and satisfaction with supervision, whereas domineering lowers subordinates' cohesiveness and satisfaction with supervision. Whether we can generalize these two factors of leadership to other Muslim cultures requires more research.

Despite the identification of two factors in the countries previously reviewed, we still have to understand whether (and how) task-orientation (or P, for that matter) would result in an overall positive or negative effect on the workgroup. The interaction effects between the two dimensions, a central theme in PM leadership, also needs to be explored in greater depth.

In addition, suggestions have been made that for adaptation of the PM theory to organizations in mainland China, a third dimensions, C (moral character), should be included (Ling, Chen, & Wang, 1987; Peterson, 1988). That is, to be a good leader in Chinese society, one has to display moral virtues in addition to enacting the performance and maintenance roles. Using a group of Chinese employees in Hong Kong, Tan (1995) recently found that this third dimension of Chinese leadership was more predictive than P and M of subordinates' job satisfaction, subjective feeling of leader's warmth, and satisfaction with the company. While the addition of a third set of qualities makes the theory more culturally appropriate, we must exercise caution so that this third set of qualities does not overlap with the existing P and M qualities and consequently render the theory less parsimonious.

Contingency Principles

Although research on PM leadership (e.g., Smith, Peterson, Misumi, & Tayeb, 1989) has demonstrated the general structure of P and M leadership and the superiority of the PM leadership style in all countries, the specific behaviors associated with each of the two factors vary substantially from country to country (Smith, Misumi, Tayeb, Peterson, & Bond, 1989). In a study by Smith, Peterson, Misumi, and Bond (1992) on British, American, Japanese, and Hong Kong Chinese workers, only partial support has been found for the cross-cultural generalizability of the PM theory. Of three criterion variables (i.e., subordinates' work quality, productiveness, and group cooperation), only the first one is affected by the bosses' maintenance and planning styles in all samples. Planning-P leadership can boost work effectiveness only in Japanese workers, but not in American or British workers. What is more, Pressure-P leadership has adverse effect on Western workers, whereas the opposite is true for Japanese workers.

The contextual dependency of managerial actions has recently been addressed in the framework of event-management (Peterson, Smith, Bond, & Misumi, 1990; Smith & Peterson, 1988; Smith, Peterson, & Misumi, 1994). These researchers define event-management processes as "information structures-in-use through which members interpret and respond to the work situations they encounter" (Peterson et al., 1990, p. 77). Smith, Peterson, and Misumi (1994) studied event management styles of workers and supervisors in Japan, the United Kingdom, and the United States. Japanese workers frequently refer to their supervisors and adhere to manuals and standard procedures to handle both familiar and unfamiliar events. On the other hand, British and American workers do not have consensus on the ways to handle any particular event. Some may refer to superiors, others may resort to personal knowledge. There is no clear norm governing event management. Such cultural differences can be interpreted in terms of power distance and individualism.

Podsakoff and his associates (Podsakoff, Todor, Grover, & Huber, 1984; Podsakoff, Todor, & Skov, 1982) advocated another notion of culture-free leadership effectiveness. They argued that a leader's task-structuring behaviors and socioemotional behaviors relate only "indirectly" to variables that can motivate subordinates. The most direct and fundamental factors driving subordinates' behaviors are the rewards and punishments delivered by the leader, which include acknowledgment, praise, and reproach. This view, with its roots in the behavioral school, suggests that a leader who administers contingent rewards and punishments is always more effective in enhancing subordinates' performance and job satisfaction than a leader who administers noncontingent rewards and punishments. Podsakoff et al. (1984) found that across six samples of American employees, the most effective leaders are always the ones who administer contingent rewards without administering noncontingent punishments. Noncontingent rewards and contingent punishments are not related to subordinates' work performance and satisfaction. Podsakoff, Dorfman, Howell, and Todor (1986) and Farh, Podsakoff, and Cheng (1987) replicated Podsakoff et al.'s (1984) findings in Mexico and Taiwan.

However, as was mentioned before, contingent rewards constitute just one facet of transactional leadership, which in turn is one dimension of the bi-dimensional paradigm. While the research of Podsakoff and his associates demonstrates that certain aspects of effective leadership are culture-free, what about the more personal aspects of leadership, the transformational leader?

Charismatic Leadership

Charisma is a central concept in transformational leadership (Bass, 1985). The charismatic leader is a role model with which the followers identify. Charisma is a personal quality that transforms the followers from valuing job security and pay toward pursuing, with enthusiasm, their highest level values, such as self-actualization. A charismatic leader is a leader who becomes personally attractive by taking heroic and unconventional actions (Conger & Kanungo, 1987). Waldman, Bass, and Yammarino (1990) found that charismatic leadership was more effective than leader contingent rewards among a group of American navy officers. This finding that the superman figure is attractive to individualists in the military has been replicated in managers and employees in private companies (Hater & Bass, 1988; Waldman, Bass, & Einstein, 1987).

Do charismatic leaders in collectivist cultures exhibit the same behavioral components as those in individualist cultures? While no study on charismatic leadership in work settings has been conducted in collectivist cultures, the research on PM, NT, and CPM leadership discussed earlier can provide a hint. We speculate that in collectivist cultures, charisma would be associated with behavioral components that increase group cohesiveness. Moreover, a charismatic leader in collectivist cultures transforms the followers toward pursuing collectivist self-actualization or contribution to the group. The model figure of a charismatic leader in a collectivist culture is not a superman, but, deducing from the findings of Ayman and Chemers (1983), J. B. P. Sinha (1980), and Tan (1995), is likely to be a benevolent father in Iran, a nurturant manager in India, and a moral person in China. The impression management view of leadership (Chemers, 1994) can help to define charisma in a cross-cultural context. From this perspective, a charismatic leader is someone who can project an impression of the appealing model leader figure specific to the culture onto the phenomenal world of the followers.

A Synthesis

To conclude this section on leadership, we propose a modified version of the PM leadership model, with all the above findings fitted tentatively into a universal bidimensional paradigm. The refinement is the addition of a new facet, Model-M, into the original theory. Model-M refers to a model leader figure in a certain culture, be it superman, moral person, or benevolent father. Consequently, PM leadership expands to have four facets under two factors:

Transactional leadership　　：Planning-P
　　　　　　　　　　　　　　　Pressure-P

Transformational leadership　：Maintenance-M
　　　　　　　　　　　　　　　Model-M

This model might guide future cross-cultural research on leadership.

Participative Management

One of the most popular topics in the management literature has been participative management (Tannenbaum, 1980; Whyte, 1983). This line of research can be dated back to Haire, Ghiselli, and Porter's (1966) 14-country study of managers' opinions of subordinates' participation. The general finding was that while these managers favored participative management, they did not really believe that their subordinates were capable of participating. This discrepancy in managerial beliefs has been subsequently replicated in countries of diverse cultural backgrounds including Cyprus (Banai & Katsounotos, 1993), Greece (Cummings & Schmidt, 1972), Malawi (Jones, 1988), and Turkey (Kozan, 1993).

It has been argued that the practice or eschewal of participative management depends not on cultural values but on managers' perception of the need to ensure quality and on team members' acceptance of and commitment to the decision. Bottger, Hallein, and Yetton (1985), who studied managers in Australia, Africa, Papua New Guinea and Pacific Islands, support this view. The researchers found that when problem structure and leader power are high, managers are less participative regardless of their own nationality. When problem structure and leader power are low, managers are generally more participative; Australian managers are so to a greater extent than their counterparts from the three developing countries. Bottger, Hallein, and Yetton (1985) attributed this contingency effect to the Australian managers' higher educational and industrializational levels, which made them more trusting in adverse situations where quality of the decision and degree of goal acceptance were questionable. Cultural explanations for participative management are de-emphasized.

On the other hand, an experiment conducted by Erez and Earley (1987) demonstrates that culture is not irrelevant to participative management. The researchers compared the effectiveness of three goal-setting strategies (assigned goals, representative goal-setting, and participative goal-setting) between American and Israeli students. Results suggest that, in both countries, participative goal-setting is superior to representative goal-setting, which in turn is superior to assigned goals in improving productivity. However, for the Israeli subjects, a work goal that is assigned is more damaging to their performance. This interaction between goal-setting strategies and culture can be explained in terms of the level of goal acceptance. Being more collectivist (and lower in power distance as well, see Hofstede, 1980) than the Americans, Israeli subjects find it difficult to accept a goal not generated by their collective but assigned to them by a superior.

The combination of high cultural collectivism with paternalism (i.e., high power distance), such as that found in Chinese societies, may result in a different reaction to an assigned goal (e.g., Nelson & Reeder, 1985). More specifically, the paternalistic emphasis and a feeling of belonging to the organization would make it totally legitimate to accept an assigned goal without resentment. Participative management may even have adverse effects on performance because the subordinates are not prepared to act without direction (Tannenbaum, 1980; Whyte, 1983). Chinese managers who took part in Graf,

Hemmasi, Lust, and Liang's (1990) study indicated that they did not want much change to the non-consultative approach of their superiors and the unquestioning attitudes of the subordinates.

Indeed, participative management can backfire in some developing countries. In India, a leader who invites subordinates to take part in business decisions is sometimes perceived by subordinates as weak (J. B. P. Sinha, 1973). For Nigerian workers and teachers, participative management can make the supervisors more likable, but it also reduces productivity markedly (Ejiogu, 1983). In the long run, it even induces resentment from the teachers who believe that it is a waste of their time to participate in setting school policy. Ali (1993) explains Arab managers' preference for consultative management over participative management in terms of the influence of Islamic and tribalistic values, which encourage consultation.

Participation has taken a distinctive form in Europe known as industrial democracy (Wilpert, 1990). Industrial democracy differs from the participative management discussed previously because it refers to "statutorily regulated forms of direct-personal or indirect-representative employee involvement in organizational decision making" (Wilpert, 1987, p. 232), instead of top-down endowments. The IDE-International Research Group (1981) conducted a survey of the formal rules for participation of each hierarchical level in an organization and the actual participative behavior in 12 European countries by collecting data from 1,000 managers or union leaders and 9,000 employees. Ten years later the Group collected data again in the same way as before from 10 of the original 12 European countries as well as Japan and Poland (Drenth & Wilpert, 1990). They observed different patterns of formal participation in these countries. For example, the 1978 data showed that British workers and first-line supervisors were expected to take part in as much (or even more) decision making as middle- and senior- management. This pattern persisted after ten years. A more hierarchical pattern, in which the more senior persons get to make more decisions, is observable in the Netherlands, Belgium, Denmark, Sweden, Japan, and Poland. In 1978 Yugoslavia, everyone from the manual worker to top management was expected to participate. The situation had only changed slightly by 1987. More work is needed to understand the cultural and sociopolitical roots of these patterns.

Team Work Arrangement

Working with the in-group is inherently motivating in some, usually collectivist cultures, whereas working alone is motivating to individualists. Earley (1993) conducted an experiment, using Chinese, Israeli, and American managers as subjects, to test the effects of psychological collectivism and work conditions (individual work, work with out-group, or work with in-group) on work performance. The interaction effect between the two independent variables is impressive. Performance was high either when individualists (mostly American subjects) worked individually or when collectivists (mostly Israeli and Chinese subjects) worked with the in-group. Working with an out-group had detrimental effects on the performance of all subjects. In a similar vein, another experiment of Earley (1989) demonstrated that social loafing could only be found in American managers, who are more individualist than PRC managers. Teamwork with in-group members is likely to have a social facilitating effect on collectivists. Jin (1993) conducted a field experiment using front-line workers in PRC organizations as subjects. Over a 3-month period, voluntarily formed work teams were superior to assigned work teams in enhancing work motivation, work performance, satisfaction with the team, and the job arrangement. A voluntarily formed work team is probably very similar to a naturally-occurring in-group, which can facilitate work performance. On the contrary, workers in the assigned work teams regard each other as outgroup members. The outcomes are inevitably disappointing.

In sum, autonomy as one of the five key motivating job characteristics in a Western theory of job design (Hackman & Oldham, 1980) may not be universal. Its motivating effects are restricted to individualist cultures. This explains why in Kalleberg and Reve's (1992) study autonomy is correlated with organizational commitment in the U.S. sample, but not in the Japanese sample, where only degree of close supervision from superiors and formalization can predict organizational commitment. In collectivist cultures, workers are more motivated when working within a group where responsibilities are shared. Work teams made up of in-group members are the key to work commitment and performance.

Reward Schemes

Certain rules of allocating rewards and penalties are not controlled by the leader and are relatively institutionalized. Three such resource and reward allocation rules recur in the literature: equity, equality, and need (Deutsch, 1983). Empirical research outside North America in the early eighties (for a review, see Cook & Hegtvedt, 1983) attempted to identify the allocation rule that is perceived to be fairest and most readily accepted by members of certain cultural groups.

According to such cross-cultural work, collectivism entails a sharp in-group—out-group distinction, which consequently leads to egalitarian assignment of rewards and cutbacks within the in-group to preserve in-group harmony. In contrast, proportional assignment of rewards and punishment to individual members according to merit or contribution is deeply embedded in individualist cultures in the form of performance-based appraisal practices. This basic contrast has generally been supported in a large body of research (e.g., Berman, Murphy-Berman, & Singh, 1985; Bond, Leung, & Wan, 1982; Hui, Triandis, & Yee, 1991; Krishnan, 1987; Leung & Bond, 1984; and Murphy-Berman, Berman, Singh, Pachauri, & Kumar, 1984).

Cultures have different conceptions about the functions of a work group (Sullivan, Suzuki, & Kondo, 1986). Japanese managers use the group as a means to enhance performance, while American managers use the group to reduce risk. They also differ in their willingness to reward team play. Along this line, Sullivan, Suzuki, and Kondo (1986) found that American managers allocate rewards according to an individual's performance, whereas Japanese managers reward the individual more if he works more closely with the group. A management-by-objective program reported by Gluskinos (1988) indicates that in another collectivist culture, Israel, workers prefer a bonus system that rewards team performance rather than individual performance.

In short, a characteristic of collectivist cultures is reward allocation on the basis of group performance rather than individual achievement. The rule of equality or need is implemented within the in-group, while the rule of equity is used in dealing with out-group members. In individualist cultures, the rule of equity is used both for in-group members and strangers. This cultural difference should be interpreted in light of the longer time frame adopted by members of an in-group in collectivist cultures. Equal sharing of a resource need not be regarded as an isolated event, but can be expected to balance out in the future. Even if nothing material is promised for the near future, the reputation for being the major contributor is itself very rewarding. This is perhaps the basis of Nevis's (1983a, b) observations and his reason for reconceptualizing self-actualization in terms of service to one's nation and community.

The undercurrent of conflict between organizational practices and cultural heritage can be demonstrated in a study by Meindl, Yu, and Lu (1990). This group of researchers found American managers flexibly apply either the proportionality rule or the equality rule in different contexts, depending on the level of workgroup interdependence. They use the equality rule when interdependence is high and the proportionality rule when interdependence is low. However, PRC managers are more rigid and use the proportionality rule regardless of the level of workgroup interdependency. This rigidity of the PRC managers is interpreted as an "attendant psychological reactance" (p. 7) against their cultural heritage in the face of the normative force of the national reform toward market economy, which includes the use of performance-based appraisal systems.

Organization Development and Change

Organization development (OD) emerged as a movement in the United States and the United Kingdom after the Second World War, as a result of work in training laboratories, survey feedback, and action research. Since then, it has flourished, even across national boundaries (see, for example, the review by Faucheux, Amado, & Laurent, 1982).

In its original form, OD was put forward to humanize the "machine bureaucracies found in many manufacturing organizations" (Leitko & Szczerbacki, 1987, p. 52). Along the lines of humanistic psychology and Theory Y in management, R. Tannenbaum and Davis (1969) saw the goals of OD as lying in expression of feelings, authenticity, risk, confrontation, and collaboration. OD aims to change the culture of an organization toward low power distance, low uncertainty avoidance, low masculinity, and medium individualism (Jaeger, 1986).

Specifically, OD is a set of planned interventions aimed at improving organizational performance and individual development (Alderfer, 1977; Faucheux,

Amado, & Laurent, 1982; Friedlander & Brown, 1974; Porras & Silvers, 1991). As this purpose suggests, OD is an all-encompassing term (Brown-Hinckley, 1989). Any behavioral technique or theory that is intentionally applied to induce certain organizational changes in a desired direction falls in the domain of OD. The managerial techniques mentioned in the last section have been part of many OD projects.

Cultural Relativity

The original OD programs have an "implicit belief in technical determinism" (Faucheux, Amado, & Laurent, 1982, p. 342), that is, that a certain managerial technique can determine productivity anywhere. However, these traditional OD programs have recurrently met with failure both within the United States and in other countries (Mirvis & Berg, 1977). Furthermore, many of the OD techniques widely used today have been developed recently in other cultures (Adler, 1983). People are becoming more aware that there are value conflicts both within the OD system (Alderfer, 1977) and between the OD system and the cultural environment (Faucheux, Amado, & Laurent, 1982; Preston, 1987). Even the goal of OD-induced cultural changes specified by Jaeger (1986) may not be universally desirable. Workers in an extremely individualist culture may abuse or react aversely to the implementation of a quality control circle, which might be suitable for cultures of medium individualism (or medium collectivism) only. On the other hand, employees in a culture of very high power distance may find it difficult to set work goals for themselves.

Therefore, OD programs should only be applied when there are "problem/process fit" and "process/culture fit" (Jaeger, 1986). First, techniques should be chosen on the basis of match between the values of a particular culture and the aforementioned OD values. Techniques that conflict with the most rigidly held values in the host culture should be avoided. For instance, a management training program in China does not use action learning, because its underlying values (e.g., openness, personal risk-taking, and individual initiative) are not part of the prevalent norm (Boisot, 1986). "Sensitivity training" is avoided in Iraq because the managers cannot tolerate open criticism (Atiyyah, 1993). Second, the goals of OD should be explicitly stated as they may be different in different cultures (Murrell & Wahba, 1987), otherwise the users will be disappointed and feel short-changed after the program.

OD in Various Countries

The principle of the "process/culture fit" can be demonstrated in several successful and unsuccessful OD programs.

Africa
Organizations in most developing countries in sub-Sahara Africa are characterized by autocratic and mechanistic practices. These prevalent organizational practices are in severe clash with the democratic and self-management values of the

sociotechnical system, a major OD concept. Kiggundu (1986) lamented the lack of success in the application of the sociotechnical system in some of these countries, which lacked "the necessary physical and institutional infrastructure" (Kiggundu, 1986, p. 350).

Arab Countries

Atiyyah (1992) reviewed a number of publications in Arabic and concluded that the rigid bureaucratic system, fatalistic attitudes, and overemphasis on control commonly found in some Arab organizations precludes successful introduction of modern managerial technology.

Japan

The PM theory of leadership, an indigenous theory, has been employed in OD programs in Japan with success (Misumi, 1990). Moreover, the quality control circle, a small group of employees committed to improving the quality of products or services, is probably the most well-known technology that has helped Japan achieve success in the production and manufacturing business. According to Heath (1990), its effectiveness depends on participants' positive quality attitudes, rich quality knowledge, sophisticated quality skills and high level of job involvement. Unfortunately, most of these qualities are absent in many developing countries.

Latin America

Bourgeois and Boltvinik (1981) commented on the applicability of North American OD practices to Latin America, suggesting that obstacles to the transfer of the technology included psychosocial, cultural, political, and economic ones.

Philippines

The assumption that goal-setting is a motivator may not apply well in the Philippines. Participants of a funding program to help them develop their own business set glamorous goals as a means to get more funds but did not care about how these goals could be accomplished (DiBella, 1993). Reyes-Sagun (1988) suggested that Filipino value orientations, such as unquestioning obedience to authority and resignation in the face of difficulty, are in sharp contrast with those of OD.

Scandinavia

The Results Management (ReMa) technique is a Finnish OD program which stresses results in a wide context ranging from mental welfare of the managers to the social responsibility of the firm. Tainio and Santalainen (1984) compared the effectiveness of the Blake-Mouton managerial grid with that of the ReMa in Finnish firms. The grid is more effective than the ReMa in bringing beneficial changes in individual managers. The ReMa, on the other hand, is more effective than the grid in bringing benefits for the organization as a whole. The researchers argued that ReMa matched the Finnish environment more than the Blake-Mouton grid did, given that this culture does not have high emphasis on individualism and benefits for individual managers.

Singapore

OD programs commonly found in Singapore emphasize behavioral changes more than structural and technical changes. However, the major barrier to importing North American OD programs into Singapore as well as other Asian countries lies in an organizational climate unfavorable to open discussion (Putti, 1989). OD in Singapore, therefore, should be regarded as special training sessions rather than a comprehensive change process. The most commonly used OD method in Singapore is survey feedback (Putti, 1989), a tool to help workers obtain a more accurate perception of how they do interpersonally so that they know what to improve on. As survey feedback is usually carried out in an anonymous manner, it is particularly popular in societies such as Singapore where open confrontation is not the fashion.

Turkey

The Village Institutes of Turkey in the 1940s have been the most significant attempt at cultural change toward modernizing rural areas in this country (Erdener, 1991). In fact, the Village Institutes should be regarded as a bold national development instead of mere organization development. The administration tried to cultivate in their adolescent participants a culture different from the traditional rural culture. In the ten years of operation, the Institutes successfully developed an elite group of workers with a strong belief in hard work, a need for (cooperative) achievement, and a distinctively different set of value orientations than that of the general public. Erdener (1991) called these cultural changes lower power distance, lower uncertainty avoidance, and higher individualism. Unfortunately, the original goal of the Village Institutes to modernize rural areas by these elites was not fulfilled, and widespread cultural change did not occur.

The Former U.S.S.R.

Simulations were used in firms and organizations of the former Soviet Union. The activity-inciting game (AIG), which lasts for several days, has been reported to be the most dominant OD practice (Tullar, 1992). Both the content and the backdrop of the game are specially tailor-made to be as real as possible. In addition to producing new ways of communication like other OD practices, AIG is claimed to be able to reframe the thoughts of managers and workers who have participated.

Estonia

Managers who were once alienated from and arrogant toward their subordinates, possibly as a result of being under Soviet ideological control for many years, are now different. They have learned to be more empathetic, and have become more socially competent (Krips, 1992).

Summary

Some OD programs have been implemented in developing countries, where productivity improvements are urgently needed (e.g., Murrell, 1988). Unfortunately, our review shows that such OD programs are not always successful, whereas in developed countries where productivity is already high, OD programs are more likely to bring observable results. Perhaps we have to seriously rethink the basic premises and utility of OD programs as they are applied in another culture.

It is possible that successful OD programs are the by-product of "something" that can raise productivity, not the cause of productivity. That "something" is probably a work-related value conducive to economic growth, plus a need for dominating achievement in individualist cultures or cooperative achievement in collectivist cultures. French and Bell (1990) have stated that an underlying assumption of OD about organization members is that they "desire to make, and are capable of making, a higher level of contribution to the attainment of organizational goals than most organizational environments will permit" (p. 44). Probably this assumption does not hold true in many developing countries. Thus applying OD programs there is fruitless. The implementation of an OD technique, for example, job enrichment, may only be welcomed by highly motivated workers, but rejected by workers who desire nothing more than a comfortable job.

The crux of the matter, therefore, becomes using OD to foster such a work-related value and to arouse the participants' need for achievement. For example, the economic motivation of Indian farmers is significantly related to their crop productivity (Sagar & Ray, 1985). In this case we cannot rely on prepackaged OD programs, for the failure of most existing OD programs in developing countries is due to the fact that they are not directly linked to the recipients' most salient needs. These OD programs as imported motivating techniques are not motivating at all. Indigenous OD programs have to be redesigned and customized to maximize the "process/culture fit." Whatever elements in the national culture that are conducive to organizational success should be distilled and used as a building block for the program. The Village Institutes project in Turkey seems to be promising in inculcating strong work-related values and achievement motivation.

Despite all that, the success of OD programs still cannot be guaranteed. One needs only to realize that if one objective of OD is to change organizational members' underlying values that are counterproductive, a clash with the existing values is inevitable. Moreover, when the (counterproductive) values that have to be changed are extensive, it is natural that the effect is less apparent than if the program is sharply focused to change a limited aspect of behaviors.

Business Activities

Doing business is more than handling internal affairs. It also involves forming innovative ideas, taking steps to implement them, and negotiating with external parties to see the ideas through. In the final major section of this chapter, we shall review literature in these areas.

Entrepreneurship

Entrepreneurship engenders innovativeness, calculated risk-taking, and proactiveness (e.g., Miller, 1983). The cultural repertoire of entrepreneurship would be high power distance, high individualism, low uncertainty avoidance, and high masculinity. As stated by Amit, Glosten, and Muller (1993), "Entrepreneurs have a tolerance for inequality; they will favor individual rather than collective action; they are prepared to take risks; and they tend to have a highly 'masculine' orientation" (p. 820). The cross-cultural validity of this set of entrepreneurial beliefs was verified by McGrath, MacMillan, and Scheinberg (1992), who compared 1,217 entrepreneurs with 1206 career professionals from Austria, Canada, Finland, Italy, Portugal, People's Republic of China, Sweden, the United States, and Puerto Rico on their responses to a questionnaire measuring various attitudes and beliefs regarding success, risk, changes, and management. With women subjects from the United States, Ireland, and Puerto Rico, Hisrich (1986) also found a difference between entrepreneurs and non-entrepreneurs that generalizes across culture: Entrepreneurs are more achievement oriented, better educated, and more energetic than non-entrepreneurs. However, American women embark on entrepreneurial activities because they want job satisfaction, sense of achievement, and independence. Puerto Rican women entrepreneurs are primarily motivated economically.

Zheng and Stimpson (1990) focused on national differences in four psychological characteristics of entrepreneurship, namely innovation, achievement orientation, self-esteem, and personal control. They found that while in the United States entrepreneurs and non-entrepreneurs are distinguishable on the four characteristics, such distinctions are not that clear in Korea, Thailand, and China. In terms of psychological needs as measured by Steers and Braunstein's (1976) Manifest Needs Questionnaire, Israeli entrepreneurs have higher needs for achievement, affiliation, and autonomy than non-entrepreneurs. In the American sample no such difference has been identified (Baum et al., 1993).

Confucianism, which has evolved into Confucian work dynamism (Chinese Culture Connection, 1987), is commonly regarded as the basis of successful entrepreneurial activities in East and South East Asia (e.g., Chinese Culture Connection, 1987; Cho & Kim, 1993; Kao, 1993; McGrath, MacMillan, Yang, & Tsai, 1992). This factor is important in consolidating effective, future-oriented hierarchical organizations, and cultivating harmonious interpersonal networks that are essential for business activities.

Some cultural values may be at odds with the entrepreneurial culture. Traditional Soviet culture favors egalitarianism and is negative toward risk-taking and profit-making motives (Herbig & McCarty, 1993; Hisrich & Grachev, 1993). There was also a lack of incentive for innovation and creativity. Adding to the problem were a restriction on initiatives, a pricing mechanism that did not reflect demand, an over-emphasis on full employment, and a blockage of horizontal communications. The environment was sterile for entrepreneurship. As a result, efficiency and productivity of organizations in the former Soviet Union were very low despite the abundance of natural resources. Vietnam, a close ally of the the former USSR, had many cultural and structural characteristics in common with the the former USSR, and thus faced similar economic difficulties (Dana, 1994; Herbig & McCarty, 1993). Fortunately, the adoption of a so-called *doi-moi* model of economic transformation since the mid-1980s, from a centrally planned command economy to a market economy, has sparkled numerous entrepreneurial activities. Many small businesses were set up and economic improvements have been remarkable (Dana, 1994).

Corporate entrepreneurship—entrepreneurial attitudes and behaviors displayed by employees and not owner of a company—has also been studied. Swierczek and Jatusripatak (1994) developed a questionnaire to measure entrepreneurial characteristics and administered it to senior managers of firms in Thailand, the Philippines, Singapore, and Malaysia. The latter two samples were mainly Chinese in ethnicity. Compared to the Filipinos, Malaysians, and Singaporeans, who are fairly alike among themselves, the Thai managers engage in more innovative activities, are less proactive, and are less ready to put their products or services in a market. Morris, Davis, and Allen (1994) conducted a questionnaire survey with senior executives in large manufacturing firms in the United States, South Africa, and Portugal. Among American and South African executives, there is a curvilinear relationship between the individualism–collectivism dimension and corporate entrepreneurship. In other words, a balance between individualism and collectivism is most conducive to corporate entrepreneurship. For the Portuguese no such pattern was found, possibly due to the small sample size.

Two issues have to be raised with regard to theorizing about entrepreneurship. First, the definition of the construct remains ambiguous (Amit, Glosten, & Muller, 1993). The second is that there are contradictory hypotheses about the relations between cultural factors and components of entrepreneurship. Specifically, one set of hypotheses postulates a positive relationship between high power distance and entrepreneurship (e.g., McGrath, MacMillan, & Scheinberg, 1992). According to another set of hypotheses (e.g., Shane, 1993; Takyi-Asiedu, 1993), free communication and decentralized authority can spur innovation, which is the core component of entrepreneurship. One possible reconciliation of this paradox is to argue that low power distance is conducive only to *corporate* entrepreneurship because in this environment the organizational structure would not suppress the entrepreneurs' desire for power. For entrepreneurs who resent being subordinate to authority of any form and want to be at the center of authority and power, a cultural milieu characterized by high power distance is more beneficial. This line of reasoning is consistent with Morris, Davis, and Allen's (1994) position that a medium level of individualism may be best for corporate entrepreneurship, but a high level of individualism is more prevalent among business-owners.

Probabilistic Thinking

One of the fundamental psychological processes underlying individual entrepreneurship is probabilistic thinking, which is subject to cultural influences (Wright et al., 1978). British students discriminated numerical uncertainty more finely and were more calibrated in their probability assessment than Indonesian, Malaysian, and Hong Kong students (Wright et al., 1978). These cultural differences were replicated among British civil servants, Hong Kong middle managers, and Indonesian businessmen working in Jakarta (Wright & Phillips, 1980). Whether probabilistic entrepreneurs make better decisions than non-probabilistic entrepreneurs do, however, is not clear. It is likely that greater calibration enables the owner of a firm to evaluate opportunities and threats more accurately, and exercise more precise budgetary control and long-term planning. However, Wright and Phillips (1980, p. 254) also noted that "the successful non-probabilistic thinker, realizing his inability to think probabilistically, may remain flexible in response to an uncertain future."

Risk-Taking Tendency
Research on the antecedents of risk-taking tendency at the individual level is sporadic. Roy and Chaudhary (1987) found that among Indian postgraduate students, psycho-emotional maturity is associated with moderate risk-taking tendency. A significant correlation is found between personal individualism and positive attitude toward risk-taking among Arab managers (Ali, 1993). In central Europe, Greece, and Scandinavia, executives are the most risk-averse. Spain is in the middle, while American executives are most positive toward risk-taking (Cummings, Harnett, & Stevens, 1971). Bass and Burger (1979) similarly found that American managers had highest tolerance for risk among ten other countries.

Tse, Lee, Vertinsky, and Wehrung (1988) compared international marketing decisions made by executives from Canada, Hong Kong, and People's Republic of China (PRC). They found that PRC executives are more likely than the Canadians to continue an unprofitable product line or a joint venture with a competitor who is in trouble, adopt a new design without subordinates' consensus, recall malfunctioning products, and go without adopting risk-adjustment strategies. These differences can be attributed to the specific values of the PRC executives, including face saving, long-term focus on exchange relationships, restriction on competition, unquestioned respect for leaders, and fatalistic views of the environment. Hong Kong executives are somewhere in between PRC and Canadian executives, possibly because their value orientation has shifted toward individualism as a result of greater exposure to the Western business world. An increase in international trade and cultural exchanges may reduce national differences.

There are, however, data suggesting that culture may not have much impact on one's risk taking tendency. Foxall and Payne (1989) found that the decision-making style of British and Australian mid-level managers is more strongly correlated with the nature of their task than their nationality. Internally-oriented occupational groups, such as the cost accountants, technical engineers, administrative managers, and operations/production managers, score significantly lower on the Kirton Adaption-Innovation Inventory (Kirton, 1987), indicating a more adaptive and conservative style. Externally-oriented groups, including financial accountants, management engineers, directive managers, and marketing managers, score higher on this inventory, indicating a more innovative and risk-taking tendency. However, the paucity of cross-cultural research on risk-taking tendency does not permit a very useful conclusion at this stage.

Conflict and Negotiation

Graham, Evenko, and Rajan (1992) linked culture to negotiation processes and outcomes, which included profits attained by the negotiator and partner's satisfaction. In their model, culture determines whether problem-solving strategies or distributive (competitive) bargaining strategies would be used. A negotiator who uses problem-solving strategies will attain *less* profit if the partner does not use problem-solving strategies. Nevertheless, by demonstrating use of problem-solving strategies, the negotiator may induce the partner to adopt problem-solving strategies, and thereby attain a higher profit. The relative strengths of the direct negative effect and the indirect positive effect of using problem-solving strategies varies in different cultures.

Intra-Cultural Conflict Management

Graham and his associates (Campbell, Graham, Jolibert, & Meissner, 1988; Graham, 1983; Graham, Evenko, & Rajan, 1992; Graham, Kim, Lin, & Robinson, 1988) studied intra-cultural dyadic buyer/seller negotiation to identify factors influencing negotiation outcomes in several cultures. In the United States, the successful negotiator is the person oriented toward problem-solving and exchanging information at the negotiation table. Japanese and Korean negotiators are similar in that both stress role status and the reciprocity norm. In these two groups, the effective negotiators, usually the buyers, are those who possess and maintain a higher status; use of problem-solving strategies by one side is likely to induce similar acts at the other side. For Taiwan Chinese and Soviet business people, distributive (competitive) bargaining strategies have been used to attain higher profits. To the French, buyer/seller similarity is most important. Germans demonstrate the harshest buyer/seller relationship, in which the benefits of one side are traded off for those of the other side. In Brazil, the most successful are those who exercise power and influence at the negotiation table, as well as those who are difficult to size up (i.e., using "deceptive bargaining strategies"). This is consistent with the observation that Brazilian managers, because of the emphasis on machismo, are more likely than their American counterparts to use power than communication to gain compliance (Rossi & Todd-Mancillas, 1987). The British results are unclear. The prior observations should be taken with caution, however, as laboratory simulation and use of business course participants appear to be Graham's dominant research strategy.

Cultures differ in the extent to which they tolerate or accept confrontations. Among British managers, the "collaborating" and "competing" styles (in Thomas's classification, 1976) are preferred ways of handling conflicts and asserting themselves (Westwood, Tang, & Kirkbride, 1992). Kozan (1989) found that Turkish managers avoid conflicts with peers, accommodate when conflict with superiors is imminent, and force their way when dealing with subordinates. Jordanian managers, on the other hand, collaborate and compromise with the other parties (Kozan, 1989). In general, both Turkish and Jordanian managers prefer the collaborating style. In other cultures that value harmony and reciprocity, the Chinese for example, the "compromising" and "avoiding" styles of conflict management come more naturally (e.g., Trubisky, Ting-Toomey, & Lin, 1991; Tse, Francis, & Walls, 1994). Nevertheless, the conflict-aversiveness of the Chinese ironically renders conflict resolution difficult (Kirkbride, Tang, & Westwood, 1991), probably because the conflicting parties cannot or would not discuss the issue, and they do not have much prior experience in handling conflicts.

Inter-Cultural Negotiation

Most reports on inter-cultural negotiation in natural settings are about bilateral talks between Americans and Japanese or between Americans and PRC representatives. This is partly due to the huge trade imbalance and subsequently the furious trade conflicts in the two dyads. Inter-cultural negotiation is full of uncertainties and risk because participating parties have no common ground of mutual understanding at the start. Misunderstanding of the other party's wishes and misinterpretation of the other party's overture may lead to very undesirable outcomes. Moreover, the two parties may be holding very different sets of assumptions about the negotiation. For instance, American trade representatives dealing with PRC negotiators may regard a trade deal as beneficial to both parties, while the PRC side have prepared to play a zero-sum game (Lavin, 1994). The situation can be further complicated when negotiators on the two sides has different concerns in handling the negotiation, for example, economic concerns for American negotiators but political concerns for PRC negotiators.

Chinese negotiators revolve around abstract principles before going into details and specifics (Pye, 1982). They like to reach agreement with their negotiating counterparts on issues of principles so that some sort of quasi-kinship allegiance can be built up. The PRC negotiators' emphasis on establishing mutual trust greatly increases the time for foreign negotiators to reach agreement with them (Pye, 1982; Shenkar & Ronen, 1987a; Tung, 1982).

Japanese negotiators are more oriented toward long-term interpersonal relationship than short-term profit, as compared to American negotiators (e.g., Graham, 1988; March, 1989). Understanding the Japanese insider's knowledge and communicating *ningensei,* (a concern of humanity) are necessary for foreigners to negotiate with Japanese successfully (Goldman, 1994). The Japanese tend to ask the foreign counterparts many questions to build up an understanding in them, avoid open confrontations by not giving feedback, and reach agreement rather "abruptly" on most problems once a mutual understanding has been established. Japanese executives involved in inter-cultural negotiations report higher interpersonal attraction in the counterpart but lower individual profits attained than in intra-cultural negotiations (Adler & Graham, 1989). March (1989) goes on to liken American-Japanese negotiation to a negotiation between an extrovert and an introvert.

Weiss (1994a, b) proposed a framework of inter-cultural negotiation, which stresses the fit between the negotiation strategy and the levels of familiarity of the negotiating parties with each other's culture. Simply doing what the counterpart would do as in an intra-cultural negotiation is naive and does not lead to success. Along the same line, Francis (1991) suggested that the relationship between inter-negotiator attraction and adjustment of communicative style is a curvilinear one.

In her study, American MBA students perceived Japanese business negotiators as more attractive if the Japanese exercised moderate adaptation of their communicative style than if they exercised no adaptation or over-adaptation. However, Americans have no intention to modify their intra-cultural negotiation strategies for use in an inter-cultural negotiation setting (Adler & Graham, 1989). They nevertheless report higher satisfaction from inter-cultural negotiation than in intra-cultural negotiation. Tse, Francis, and Walls (1994) also found that both Canadian and PRC executives had no intention to adjust their strategies when moving from an intra-cultural to an inter-cultural setting. (See Brislin & Horvath, this volume, for a discussion of intercultural training related to intercultural negotiation.)

Future Directions

A significant portion of the studies reviewed in this chapter were conducted by researchers who traveled and taught management courses outside of their own countries. The proliferation of international learning facilities as well as vendors of management development/consulting services has greatly expanded research opportunities in cross-cultural I/O psychology. Although the number of studies in cross-cultural I/O psychology has increased tremendously over the last decade or two, improvements are needed to keep pace with the market's demand.

Scope

We need to substantially expand the breadth and depth of research in the field. With regard to breadth, many important topics in I/O psychology, such as job design, work environment (including shiftwork, telecommuting, flexispace, etc.), and customer service, have not been covered in this review, because there have not been sufficient empirical studies on the topic. With regard to depth, we witness a bias in favor of theoretical issues rather than the more practical ones. For example, the research on work-related values is more mature than that on OD and entrepreneurship. Existing studies on practical issues are characterized by an impressionistic approach, relying mainly on unsystematic observations and anecdotal experiences. These constitute a good starting point, but rigorous research and perhaps controlled experiments are needed for the discipline to grow.

Theory

The construct of individualism–collectivism (and to a lesser extent, power distance) has been helpful in conceptualizing and explicating cultural variations, but also adds the danger of an oversimplified, dichotomistic view of world cultures.

We must not assume that cultural differences in organizational behaviors can be explained in terms of one or two constructs. By saying this, we are not arguing against the utility of these constructs in cross-cultural I/O research, but only that they must not be used mindlessly. A more comprehensive theory that takes into account other dimensions of cultural differences is needed.

One theoretical framework that has some potential to this end was put forward by Erez (1994). Her model of cultural self-representation takes culture as a contextual factor. The self processes this contextual factor and evaluates managerial and motivational techniques it encounters (e.g., participative goal-setting) in relation to their contribution to the fulfillment of self-derived needs. If there is a match, work behavior will improve; if not, work behavior will deteriorate. This model can be refined and expanded to incorporate cultural elements other than individualism-collectivism.

Methodology

Progress in empirical studies lags behind theoretical development. Two problems can be identified.

First, the majority of the studies reviewed did not directly measure subjects' level of individualism–collectivism, or power distance, or whatever cultural construct was presumed to be accounting for the cross-cultural differences observed. Without a direct measurement, interpretations resorting to this construct can at best be regarded as *post hoc* explanations (see Berry, 1996, for an elaboration of this problem).

Researchers can now measure their subjects' level of individualism or collectivism directly, and then incorporate this variable into statistical analyses to test whether it is able to explain the variance of the outcome variable. The INDCOL Scale (Hui, 1988; Hui & Yee, 1994) or Earley's (1989, 1993) collectivism measure can be used for this purpose. For example, Hui et al. (1991) formally incorporated the subjects' degree of psychological collectivism into an ANCOVA model to show that psychological collectivism can explain cultural variations in reward allocation.

A second, more serious limitation in research methodology lies in the distribution of the cultural groups selected or available for study. The most often studied national groups are the United States and Japan, as representatives of individualist cultures and high power distance cultures respectively. However, using only two or three cultures to make inferences is extremely risky. In such studies, the range of cultural differences on the cross-cultural constructs of interest is restricted. The explanatory power of these constructs is thereby compromised.

Now that economic development has made accessible many previously unexplored developing countries, I/O psychologists should position themselves to take advantage of opportunities to collect useful data from as many cultures as possible. As company headquarters and their subsidiaries are now linked together with sophisticated electronic communication systems, theories in I/O psychology can be conveniently tested with a large number of cultural groups.

Concluding Remarks

We began this chapter by stating that what was developed and found to work in one (often Western) culture may not be applicable in another. Most of the content of this chapter clearly demonstrates the validity of this statement. However, the utility of cross-cultural I/O psychology does not stop here. Its contribution lies not only in the unearthing of cultural specifics, but also in its sensitization of academics and practitioners to limitations of their theories and methods. With this comes an impetus to modify and even redevelop their tools, to answer the needs of the global marketplace. To this end the community of I/O psychologists has only made the first, albeit important, step.

Endnotes

1. The authors wish to thank Geert Hofstede for his critical comments on an earlier draft of this article, and Agnes Tse for her assistance in a later stage of writing it.

2. Author's names are arranged alphabetically.

3. A distinction between work and paid employment should be drawn (Cherns, 1984; Westwood, 1992). While in industrialized nations these two may be the same, in tribal societies a relatively large proportion of work done remains outside the realm of paid employment. In such societies, work is detached from economic activities and wage employment implies subordination. To a man approaching elderhood, being employed is a shame. On the other hand, work without pay is seen as the extension and continuation of education. This distinction between work and paid employment has to be borne in mind in our study of most underdeveloped and developing countries.

4. Because the MOW asked respondents "what should be," the findings may reveal merely the presumed ideal. Future research might have to ask which norms actually prevail in practice.

5. Paradoxically, the essence of "Japanese management" depicted here and other sources (such as Ouchi, 1981) is recently under challenge even in Japanese enterprises. Reports indicate that big Japanese enterprises are reviewing their traditional remuneration scheme. The traditional practice of seniority-based promotion and salary rise is now being replaced by more "equitable" performance-based appraisal systems ("Cost cutting actions," 1995). The practice that was once believed to be a critical factor leading to the superior performance of Japanese organizations is perhaps not that effective in reality. Alternatively, we can argue that cultural changes in Japan have led to the disposal of this traditional practice (e.g., Schwind & Peterson, 1985).

References

Adler, N. J. (1983). Organizational development in a multicultural environment. *The Journal of Applied Behavioral Science, 19,* 349–365.

Adler, N. J. & Graham, J. L. (1989). Cross-cultural interaction: The international comparison fallacy? *Journal of International Business Studies, 20,* 515–537.

Ahmad, S. (1989). Perceived importance of job factors by Indian women workers. *Journal of the Indian Academy of Applied Psychology, 15,* 93–99.

Alderfer, C. P. (1972). *Existence, relatedness, and growth.* New York: Free Press.

Alderfer, C. P. (1977). Organization development. *Annual Review of Psychology, 28,* 197–223.

Ali, A. (1989). A comparative study of managerial beliefs about work in the Arab states. *Advances* in *International Comparative Management, 4,* 95–112.

Ali, A. J. (1993). Decision-making style, individualism, and attitudes toward risk of Arab executives. *International Studies of Management and Organization, 23,* 53–73.

Ali, A. J. & Al-Shakhis, M. (1991). Changing managerial values in Saudi Arabia. *Advances in International Comparative Management, 6,* 81–102.

Amit, R., Glosten, L., & Muller, E. (1993). Challenges to theory development in entrepreneurship research. *Journal of Management Studies, 30,* 815–834.

Anderson, L. R. (1983). Management of the mixed-cultural work group. *Organizational Behavior and Human Performance, 31,* 303–330.

Ansari, M. A. (1986). Need for nurturant-task leaders in India: Some empirical evidence. *Management and Labour Studies, 11,* 26–36.

At-Twaijri, M. I. (1989). A cross-cultural comparison of American-Saudi managerial values in U.S.-related firms in Saudi Arabia: An empirical investigation. *International Studies of Management and Organization, 19,* 58–73.

Atiyyah, H. S. (1992). Research note: Research in Arab countries, published in Arabic. *Organization Studies, 13,* 105–112.

Atiyyah, H. S. (1993). Management development in Arab countries: The challenges of the 1990s. *Journal of Management Development, 12,* 3–12.

Ayman, R. & Chemers, M. M. (1983). Relationship of supervisory behavior ratings to work group effectiveness and subordinate satisfaction among Iranian managers. *Journal of Applied Psychology, 68,* 338–341.

Bales, R. F. & Slater, P. E. (1955). Role differentiation in small, decision-making groups. In T. Parsons, R. F. Bales, J. Olds, M. Zelditch, & P. E. Slater (Eds.), *Family, socialization, and interaction process* (pp. 259–306). New York: Free Press.

Banai, M. & Katsounotos, P. (1993). Participative management in Cyprus. *International Studies of Management and Organization, 23,* 19–34.

Bass, B. M. (1985). *Leadership and performance beyond expectations.* New York: Free Press.

Bass, B. M. & Burger, P. C. (1979). *Assessment of managers: An international comparison.* New York: Free Press.

Baum, J. R., Olian, J. D., Erez, M., Schnell, E. R., Smith, K. G., Sims, H. P., Scully, J. S., & Smith, K. A. (1993). Nationality and work role interactions: A cultural contrast of Israeli and U.S. entrepreneurs' versus managers' needs. *Journal of Business Venturing, 8,* 499–512.

Berman, J. J., Murphy-Berman, V., & Singh, P. (1985). Cross-cultural similarities and differences in perception of fairness. *Journal of Cross-Cultural Psychology, 16,* 55–67.

Berry, J. W. (1996). New approaches to the study of intercultural and international I/O psychology. In C. Earley & M. Erez (Eds.), *Frontiers of industrial and organizational psychology.* San Francisco: Jossey-Bass.

Blake, R. R. & Mouton, J. S. (1964). *The managerial grid.* Houston: Gulf.

Bluen, S. D. & Barling, J. (1983). Work values in white South African males. *Journal of Cross-Cultural Psychology, 14,* 329–335.

Bochner, S. & Hesketh, B. (1994). Power distance, individualism/collectivism, and job-related attitudes in a culturally diverse work group. *Journal of Cross-Cultural Psychology, 25,* 233–257.

Boisot, M. H. (1986). Action learning with Chinese characteristics: The China–EEC management programme. *Management Education and Development, 17,* 128–136.

Bond, M. H., Leung, K., & Wan, K. C. (1982). How does cultural collectivism operate? The impact of task and maintenance contributions on reward distribution. *Journal of Cross-Cultural Psychology, 13,* 186–200.

Booth-Kewley, S., Rosenfeld, P., & Edwards, J. E. (1993). Turnover among Hispanic and non-Hispanic blue-collar workers in the U.S. Navy's civilian work force. *Journal of Social Psychology, 133,* 761–768.

Bottger, P. C., Hallein, I. H., & Yetton, P. W. (1985). A cross-national study of leadership: Participation as a function of problem structure and leader power. *Journal of Management Studies, 22,* 358–368.

Bourgeois, L. J. & Boltvinik, M. (1981). OD in cross-cultural settings: Latin America. *California Management Review, 23,* 75–81.

Brown-Hinckley, B. P. (1989). Visions of current and future issues in organization development. *Group and Organization Studies, 14,* 271–279.

Burns, J. M. (1978). *Leadership.* New York: Harper & Row.

Campbell, N. C. G., Graham, J. L., Jolibert, A., & Meissner, H. G. (1988). Marketing negotiations in France, Germany, the United Kingdom, and the United States. *Journal of Marketing, 52,* 49–62.

Chemers, M. M. (1994). *A theoretical framework for examining the effects of cultural differences on leadership.* Paper presented at the International Congress of Applied Psychology, Madrid, Spain, July, 1994.

Cherns, A. (1984). Contribution of social psychology to the nature and function of work and its relevance to societies of the Third World. *International Journal of Psychology, 19,* 97–111.

Chinese Culture Connection. (1987). Chinese values and the search for culture-free dimensions of culture. *Journal of Cross-Cultural Psychology, 18,* 143–164.

Cho, Y. H., & Kim, Y. S. (1993). The cultural roots of entrepreneurial bureaucracy: The case of Korea. *Public Administrative Quarterly, 16,* 509–524.

Cole, R. E. (1979). *Work, mobility and participation.* Berkeley: University of California Press.

Conger, J. A. & Kanungo, R. N. (1987). Toward a behavioral theory of charismatic leadership in organizational settings. *Academy of Management Review, 12,* 637–647.

Cook, K. S. & Hegtvedt, K. A. (1983). Distributive justice, equity, and equality. *Annual Review of Sociology, 9,* 217–241.

Cost cutting actions of Japanese enterprises. (1995). *Sing Tao Daily* (January 14, 1995), B11. (In Chinese.)

Cummings, L. L., Harnett, D. L., & Stevens, O. J. (1971). Risk, fate conciliation and trust: An international study of attitudinal differences among executives. *Academy of Management Journal, 14,* 285–304.

Cummings, L. L., & Schmidt, S. M. (1972). Managerial attitudes of Greeks: The roles of culture and industrialization. *Administrative Science Quarterly, 17,* 265–272.

Dana, L. P. (1994). The *doi-moi* model: An ethno-graphic account of entrepreneurship, innovation, and change in former French Indo-China. *Entrepreneurship, Innovation, and Change, 3,* 61–83.

DeFrank, R. S., Matteson, M. T., Schweiger, D. M., & Ivancevich, J.M. (1985). The impact of culture on the management practices of American and Japanese CEOs. *Organizational Dynamics, 13,* 62–76.

Deutsch, M. (1983). Current social psychological perspectives on justice. *European Journal of Social Psychology, 13,* 305–319.

DiBella, A. J. (1993). The role of assumptions in implementing management practices across cultural boundaries. *The Journal of Applied Behavioral Science, 29,* 311–327.

Drenth, P. J. D. & Wilpert, B. (1990). Industrial democracy in Europe: Cross-national comparisons. In P. J. D. Drenth, J. A. Sergeant, & R. J. Takens (Eds.), *European perspectives in psychology* (Vol. 3, pp. 115–131). Chichester, England: Wiley.

Dunbar, E. (1992). Adjustment and satisfaction of expatriate U.S. personnel. *International Journal of Intercultural Relations, 16,* 1–16.

Earley, P. C. (1989). Social loafing and collectivism: A comparison of the United States and the People's Republic of China. *Administrative Science Quarterly, 34,* 565–581.

Earley, P. C. (1993). East meets West meets Mideast: Further explorations of collectivistic and individualistic work groups. *Academy of Management Journal, 36,* 319–348.

Ejiogu, A. M. (1983). Participative management in a developing economy: Poison or placebo? *The Journal of Applied Behavioral Science, 19,* 239–247.

England, G. W. & Misumi, J. (1986). Work centrality in Japan and the United States. *Journal of Cross-Cultural Psychology, 17,* 399–416.

Erdener, C. B. (1991). Reconfiguring work-related values in a modernizing country: The Village Institutes of Turkey. *Advances in International Comparative Management, 6,* 57–79.

Erez, M. (1994). Toward a model of cross-cultural industrial and organizational psychology. In H. C. Triandis, M. D. Dunnette, & L. M. Hough (Eds.), *Handbook of industrial and organizational psychology,* 2d ed. (Vol. 4, pp.

559–607). Palo Alto: Consulting Psychologists Press.

Erez, M. & Earley, P. C. (1987). Comparative analysis of goal-setting strategies across cultures. *Journal of Applied Psychology, 72,* 658–665.

Farh, J. L., Podsakoff, P. M., & Cheng, B. S. (1987). Culture-free leadership effectiveness versus moderators of leadership behavior: An extension and test of Kerr and Jermier's "substitutes for leadership" model in Taiwan. *Journal of International Business Studies, 18,* 43–60.

Faucheux, C., Amado, G., & Laurent, A. (1982). Organizational development and change. *Annual Review of Psychology, 33,* 343–370.

Foxall, G. R. & Payne, A. F. (1989). Adaptors and innovators in organizations: A cross-cultural study of the cognitive styles of managerial functions and subfunctions. *Human Relations, 42,* 639–649.

Francis, J. N. P. (1991). When in Rome? The effects of cultural adaptation on intercultural business negotiations. *Journal of International Business Studies, 22,* 403–428.

Franke, R. H., Hofstede, G., & Bond, M. H. (1991). Cultural roots of economic performance: A research note. *Strategic Management Journal, 12,* 165–173.

French, W. L. & Bell, C. H. (1990). *Organization development: Behavioral science interventions for organization improvement,* 4th ed. Englewood Cliffs, NJ: Prentice Hall.

Friedlander, F. & Brown, L. D. (1974). Organization development. *Annual Review of Psychology, 25,* 313–341.

Fyans, L. J., Maehr, M. L., Salili, F., & Desai, K. A. (1983). A cross-cultural exploration into the meaning of achievement. *Journal of Personality and Social Psychology, 44,* 1000–1013.

Gluskinos, U. M. (1988). Cultural and political considerations in the introduction of Western technologies: The Mekorot Project. *Journal of Management Development, 6,* 34–46.

Goldman, A. (1994). The centrality of "ningensei" to Japanese negotiating and interpersonal relationships: Implications for U.S.–Japanese communication. *International Journal of Intercultural Relations, 18,* 29–54.

Graen, G. B. & Wakabayashi, M. (1994). Cross-cultural leadership making: Bridging American and Japanese diversity for team advantage. In H. C. Triandis, M. D. Dunnette, & L. M. Hough (Eds.), *Handbook of industrial and organizational psychology,* 2d ed. (Vol. 4, pp. 415–446). Palo Alto: Consulting Psychologists Press.

Graf, L. A., Hemmasi, M., Lust, J. A., & Liang, Y. (1990). Perceptions of desirable organizational reforms in Chinese state enterprises. *International Studies of Management and Organization, 20,* 47–56.

Graham, J. L. (1983). Brazilian, Japanese, and American business negotiations. *Journal of International Business Studies, 14,* 47–61.

Graham, J. L. (1988). Negotiating with the Japanese: A guide to persuasive tactics. *East Asian Executive Reports, 10,* 19–21.

Graham, J. L., Evenko, L. I., & Rajan, M. N. (1992). An empirical comparison of Soviet and American business negotiations. *Journal of International Business Studies, 23,* 387–418.

Graham, J. L., Kim, D., Lin, C. Y., & Robinson, M. (1988). Buyer–seller negotiations around the Pacific Rim: Differences in fundamental exchange processes. *Journal of Consumer Research, 15,* 48–54.

Gregersen, H. B. & Black, J. S. (1990). A multifaceted approach to expatriate retention in international assignments. *Group and Organization Studies, 15,* 461–485.

Hackman, J. R. & Oldham, G. R. (1980). *Work redesign.* Reading, MA: Addison-Wesley.

Haire, M., Ghiselli, M. M., & Porter, L. W. (1966). *Managerial thinking: An international study.* New York: John Wiley.

Harpaz, I. (1989). Non-financial employment commitment: A cross-national comparison. *Journal of Occupational Psychology, 62,* 147–150.

Harpaz, I. (1990). The importance of work goals: An international perspective. *Journal of International Business Studies, 21,* 75–93.

Hatch, E. K. (1995). Cross-cultural team building and training. *Journal of Quality and Participation, 18,* 44–49.

Hater, J. J. & Bass, B. M. (1988). Superiors' evaluations and subordinates' perceptions of transformational and transactional leadership. *Journal of Applied Psychology, 73,* 695–702.

Heath, P. M. (1990). Quality — and how to achieve it. *Management Decision, 28,* 42–46.

Herbig, P. A. & McCarty, C. (1993). Structural and cultural influences on innovation: A case study of the former Soviet Union experience. *Entrepreneurship, Innovation, and Change, 2,* 345–357.

Herriot, P. & Pemberton, C. (1994). *Competitive advantage through diversity: Organizational learning from difference.* London: Sage.

Hicks, G. & Redding, S. G. (1983a). The story of the East Asian economic miracle: Part II. The culture connection. *Euro-Asian Business Review, 2,* 18–22.

Hicks, G. & Redding, S. G. (1983b). The story of the East Asian economic miracle: Part I. Economic theory be damned. *Euro-Asian Business Review, 2,* 24–32.

Hisrich, R. D. (1986). The woman entrepreneur: A comparative analysis. *Leadership and Organization Development Journal, 7,* 8–16.

Hisrich, R.D., & Grachev, M.V. (1993). The Russian entrepreneur. *Journal of Business Venturing, 8,* 487–497.

Hofstede, G. (1980). *Culture's consequences: International differences in work related values.* Beverly Hills: Sage.

Hofstede, G. (1987). The applicability of McGregor's theories in Southeast Asia. *Journal of Management Development, 6,* 9–18.

Hofstede, G. (1991). *Culture and organizations: Software of the mind.* London: McGraw-Hill.

Hofstede, G. & Bond, M. H. (1988). The Confucius connection: From cultural roots to economic growth. *Organizational Dynamics, 16,* 4–21.

Hui, C. H. (1988). Measurement of individualism–collectivism. *Journal of Research in Personality, 22,* 17–36.

Hui, C. H. (1990). Work attitudes, leadership styles, and managerial behaviours in different cultures. In R. W. Brislin (Ed.), *Applied cross-cultural psychology* (pp. 186–208). Newbury Park, CA: Sage.

Hui, C. H., Eastman, K. L., & Yee, C. (1995). The relationship between individualism-collectivism and satisfaction at the workplace. *Applied Psychology: An International Review, 44,* 276–282.

Hui, C. H. & Tan, C. K. (1995). Employee motivation and attitudes in the Chinese workforce. In M.H. Bond (Ed.), *Handbook of Chinese psychology* (pp. 364–378). Hong Kong: Oxford University Press.

Hui, C. H., Triandis, H. C., & Yee, C. (1991). Cultural differences in reward allocation: Is collectivism the explanation? *British Journal of Social Psychology, 30,* 145–157.

Hui, C. H. & Yee, C. (1994). The shortened individualism-collectivism scale: Its relationship to demographic and work-related variables. *Journal of Research in Personality, 28,* 409–424.

IDE-International Research Group. (1981). *Industrial democracy in Europe.* Oxford: Oxford University Press.

Jaeger, A. M. (1983). The transfer of organizational culture overseas: An approach to control in the multinational corporation. *Journal of International Business Studies, 14,* 91–114.

Jaeger, A. M. (1986). Organization development and national culture: Where's the fit? *Academy of Management Review, 11,* 178–190.

Jin, P. (1993). Work motivation and productivity in voluntarily formed work teams: A field study in China. *Organizational Behavior and Human Decision Processes, 54,* 133–155.

Jones, M. (1988). Managerial thinking: An African perspective. *Journal of Management Studies, 25,* 481–505.

Kalleberg, A. L. & Reve, T. (1992). Contracts and commitment: Economic and sociological perspectives on employment relations. *Human Relations, 45,* 1103–1132.

Kanungo, R. N. (1990). Culture and work alienation: Western models and Eastern realities. *International Journal of Psychology, 25,* 795–812.

Kao, H. S. R. & Ng, S. H. (1988). *Organizational behavior.* Taipei: Sanmin. (In Chinese.)

Kao, H. S. R. & Ng, S. H. (1992). Organizational commitment and culture. In R.I. Westwood (Ed.), *Organisational behaviour: Southeast Asian perspectives* (pp. 173–198). Hong Kong: Longman.

Kao, J. (1993). The worldwide web of Chinese business. *Harvard Business Review, 71,* 24–36.

Kassem, M. S. & Ariss, S. S. (1990). Strategy formulation in the Arab context. *Advances in International Comparative Management, 5,* 245–255.

Kent, D. H., Lynn, M., & Mailer, A. (1991). The nettlesome problem of post-socialist organizational control: Linking control and culture. *Advances in International Comparative Management, 6,* 143–158.

Kiggundu, M. N. (1986). Limitations to the application of sociotechnical systems in developing countries. *The Journal of Applied Behavioral Science, 22,* 341–353.

Kim, S. U. (1988). The role of social values and competitiveness in economic growth: With special reference to Korea. In D. Sinha & H. S. R. Kao (Eds.), *Social values and development: Asian perspectives* (pp. 76–92). New Delhi: Sage.

Kirkbride, P. S., Tang, S. F. Y., & Westwood, R. I. (1991). Chinese conflict preferences and negotiating behaviour: Cultural and psychological influences. *Organization Studies, 12,* 365–386.

Kirton, M. J. (1987). *KAI manual,* 2d ed. Hatfield, England: Occupational Research Center.

Kool, R. & Saksena, N. K. (1989). Leadership styles and its effectiveness among Indian executives. *Indian Journal of Applied Psychology, 26,* 9–15.

Kozan, M. K. (1989). Cultural influences on styles of handling interpersonal conflicts: Comparisons among Jordanian, Turkish, and U.S. managers. *Human Relations, 42,* 787–799.

Kozan, M. K. (1993). Cultural and industrialization level influences on leadership attitudes for Turkish managers. *International Studies of Management and Organization, 23,* 7–17.

Krips, H. (1992). Leadership and social competence in the declining years of communism. *Small Group Research, 23,* 130–145.

Krishnan, L. (1987). Equality and equity in reward distribution in an Indian setting. *Psychological Studies, 32,* 97–103.

Lavin, F. L. (1994). Negotiating with the Chinese. *Foreign Affairs, 73,* 16–22.

Leitko, T. A. & Szczerbacki, D. (1987). Why traditional OD strategies fail in professional bureaucracies. *Organizational Dynamics, 15,* 52–65.

Leung, K. & Bond, M. H. (1984). The impact of cultural collectivism on reward allocation. *Journal of Personality and Social Psychology, 47,* 793–804.

Lincoln, J. R., Hanada, M., & Olson, J. (1981). Cultural orientations and individual reactions to organizations: A study of employees of Japanese-owned firms. *Administrative Science Quarterly, 26,* 93–115.

Lincoln, J. R. & Kalleberg, A. L. (1985). Work organization and workforce commitment: A study of plants and employees in the U.S. and Japan. *American Sociological Review, 50,* 738–760.

Ling, W. Q., Chen, L., & Wang, D. (1987). Construction of CPM scale for leadership behavior assessment. *Acta Psychologica Sinica, 3,* 236–242.

Luthans, F., McCaul, H. S., & Dodd, N. G. (1985). Organizational commitment: A comparison of American, Japanese, and Korean employees. *Academy of Management Journal, 28,* 213–219.

March, R. M. (1989). No-nos in negotiating with the Japanese. *Across the Board, 26,* 44–51.

Marsh, R. M. & Mannari, H. (1977). Organizational commitment and turnover: A prediction study. *Administrative Science Quarterly, 22,* 57–75.

Maslow, A. H. (1954). *Motivation and personality.* New York: Harper.

McGrath, R. G., MacMillan, I. C., & Scheinberg, S. (1992). Elitists, risk-takers, and rugged individualists? An exploratory analysis of cultural differences between entrepreneurs and nonentrepreneurs. *Journal of Business Venturing, 7,* 115–135.

McGrath, R. G., MacMillan, I. C., Yang, E. A. Y., & Tsai, W. (1992). Does culture endure, or is it malleable? Issues for entrepreneurial economic development. *Journal of Business Venturing, 7,* 441–458.

Meindl, J. R., Yu, K. C., & Lu, J. (1990). Distributive justice in the workplace: Preliminary data on managerial preferences in the PRC. In B. B. Shaw & J. E. Beck (Eds.), *Research in personnel and human resource management* (Supplement 2, pp. 221–236). Greenwich, CT: JAI Press.

Miller, D. (1983). The correlates of entrepreneurship in three types of firms. *Management Science, 29,* 770–791.

Mirvis, P. H. & Berg, D. N. (1977). *Failures in organization development and changes: Cases and essays for learning.* New York: Wiley.

Misumi, J. (1985). *The behavioral science of leadership:*

An interdisciplinary Japanese research program. Ann Arbor: University of Michigan Press.

Misumi, J. (1990). The Japanese meaning of work and small group activities in Japanese industrial organizations. *International Journal of Psychology, 25,* 819–832.

MOW International Research Team. (1987). *The meaning of work.* New York: Academic.

Morris, M. H., Davis, D. L., & Allen, J. W. (1994). Fostering corporate entrepreneurship: Cross-cultural comparisons of the importance of individualism versus collectivism. *Journal of International Business Studies, 24,* 65–89.

Murphy-Berman, V., Berman, J., Singh, P., Pachauri, A., & Kumar, P. (1984). Factors affecting allocation to needy and meritorious recipients: A cross-cultural comparison. *Journal of Personality and Social Psychology, 46,* 1267–1272.

Murrell, K. L. (1988). Organization development in post-war Afghanistan. *Organization Development Journal, 6,* 13–17.

Murrell, K. L. & Wahba, M. R. (1987). Organization development and action research in Egypt: A consulting case study. *Organization Development Journal, 5,* 57–63.

Neale, R. & Mindel, R. (1992). Rigging up multicultural teamworking. *Personnel Management, 24,* 36–39.

Near, J. P. (1986). Work and nonwork attitudes among Japanese and American workers. *Advances in International Comparative Management, 2,* 57–67.

Near, J. P. (1989). Organizational commitment among Japanese and U.S. workers. *Organization Studies, 10,* 281–300.

Negandhi, A. R. (1984). Management in the third world. *Advances in International Comparative Management, 1,* 123–154.

Negandhi, A. R., Eshghi, G. S., & Yuen, E. C. (1985). The management practices of Japanese subsidiaries overseas. *California Management Review, 27,* 93–105.

Nelson, J. A. & Reeder, J. A. (1985). Labor relations in China. *California Management Review, 27,* 13–32.

Nevis, E. C. (1983a). Cultural assumptions and productivity: The United States and China. *Sloan Management Review, 24,* 17–29.

Nevis, E. C. (1983b). Using an American perspective in understanding another culture: Toward a hierarchy of needs for the People's Republic of China. *The Journal of Applied Behavioral Science, 19,* 249–264.

Ouchi, W. (1981). *Theory Z: How American business can meet the Japanese challenge.* Reading, MA: Addison-Wesley.

Peterson, M. F. (1988). PM Theory in Japan and China: What's in it for the United States? *Organizational Dynamics, 16,* 22–38.

Peterson, M. F., Smith, P. B., Bond, M. H., & Misumi, J. (1990). Personal reliance on alternative event-management processes in four countries. *Group and Organization Studies, 15,* 75–91.

Podsakoff, P. M., Dorfman, P. W., Howell, J. P., & Todor, W. D. (1986). Leader reward and punishment behaviors: A preliminary test of a culture-free style of leadership effectiveness. *Advances in International Comparative Management, 2,* 95–138.

Podsakoff, P. M., Todor, W. D., Grover, R. A., & Huber, V. L. (1984). Situational moderators of leader reward and punishment behaviors: Fact or fiction? *Organizational Behavior and Human Performance, 34,* 21–63.

Podsakoff, P. M., Todor, W. D., & Skov, R. (1982). Effects of leader contingent and noncontingent reward and punishment behaviors on subordinate performance and satisfaction. *Academy of Management Journal, 25,* 810–821.

Popper, M., Landau, O., & Gluskinos, U. M. (1992). The Israeli defence forces: An example of transformational leadership. *Leadership and Organization Development Journal, 13,* 3–8.

Porras, J. I. & Silvers, R. C. (1991). Organization development and transformation. *Annual Review of Psychology, 42,* 51–78.

Preston, J. C. (1987). Cultural blinders: Take them off before attempting international organization development. 16th Annual Information Exchange of the Organization Development Institute, Williams Bay, Wisconsin, 1986. *Organization Development Journal, 5,* 50–56.

Putti, J. M. (1989). Organization development scene in Asia: The case of Singapore. *Group and Organization Studies, 14,* 262–270.

Pye, L. W. (1982). *Chinese commercial negotiating style.* Cambridge, MA: Oelgeschlager, Gunn & Hain.

Rastogi, P. N. (1987). Improving productivity: Do human relations theories provide the answers? *Vikalpa, 12,* 3–12.

Rauschenberger, J., Schmitt, N., & Hunter, J. E. (1980). A test of the need hierarchy concept by a Markov model of change in need strength. *Administrative Science Quarterly, 25,* 654–670.

Redding, S. G., Norman, A., & Schlander, A. (1994). The nature of individual attachment to the organization: A review of East Asian variations. In H. C. Triandis, M. D. Dunnette, & L. M. Hough (Eds.), *Handbook of industrial and organizational psychology,* 2d ed. (Vol. 4, pp. 647–688. Palo Alto: Consulting Psychologists Press.

Reyes-Sagun, L. (1988). Philippine value system: Its implications to a successful organization development effort. *Organization Development Journal, 6,* 73–75.

Rohlen, T. P. (1979). The company work group. In E. F. Vogel (Ed.), *Modern Japanese organisation in anthropological perspective* (pp. 185–209). Tokyo: Tuttle.

Ronen, S. (1986). *Comparative and multinational management.* New York: Wiley.

Ronen, S. (1994). An underlying structure of motivational need taxonomies: A cross-cultural confirmation. In H. C. Triandis, M. D. Dunnette, & L. M. Hough (Eds.), *Handbook of industrial and organizational psychology,* 2d ed. (Vol. 4, pp. 241–269. Palo Alto: Consulting Psychologists Press.

Rosenfeld, R. & Servo, J. C. (1990). Facilitating innovation in large organizations. In M. A. West & J. L. Farr (Eds.), *Innovation and creativity at work* (pp. 251–263). West Sussex, England: Wiley.

Rossi, A. M., & Todd-Mancillas, W. R. (1987). Machismo as a factor affecting the use of power and communication in the managing of personnel disputes: Brazilian versus American male managers. *Journal of Social Behavior and Personality, 2,* 93–104.

Roy, G. S., & Chaudhary, P. (1987). Personality maturity and risk-taking behaviour. *Asian Journal of Psychology and Education, 19,* 38–41.

Sagar, R. L. & Ray, G. L. (1985). Economic motivation and farmers' productivity. *Psychological Research Journal, 9,* 33–34.

Schuster, B., Forsterling, F., & Weiner, B. (1989). Perceiving the causes of success and failure: A cross-cultural examination of attributional concepts. *Journal of Cross-Cultural Psychology, 20,* 191–213.

Schwind, H. F. & Peterson, R. B. (1985). Shifting personal values in the Japanese management system. *International Studies of Management and Organisation, 15,* 60–74.

Shane, S. (1993). Cultural influences on national rates of innovation. *Journal of Business Venturing, 8,* 59–73.

Shaw, J. B. (1990). A cognitive categorization model for the study of intercultural management. *Academy of Management Review, 15,* 626–645.

Shenkar, O. & Ronen, S. (1987a). The cultural context of negotiations: The implications of Chinese interpersonal norms. *The Journal of Applied Behavioral Science, 23,* 263–275.

Shenkar, O. & Ronen, S. (1987b). Structure and importance of work goals among managers in the People's Republic of China. *Academy of Management Journal, 30,* 564–576.

Shenkar, O. & Zeira, Y. (1987). Human resources management in international joint ventures: Directions for research. *Academy of Management Review, 12,* 546–557.

Sinha, D. (1991). Values and work behaviour. *Abhigyan,* 1–14.

Sinha, J. B. P. (1973). *Some problems of public sector organizations.* Delhi: National.

Sinha, J. B. P. (1980). *The nurturant task leader.* New Delhi: Concept.

Sinha, J. B. P. (1990a). The salient Indian values and their socio-economic roots. *Indian Journal of Social Science, 3,* 477–488.

Sinha, J. B. P. (1990b). *Work culture in the Indian context.* New Delhi: Sage.

Sinha, J. B. P. (1994). Cultural embeddedness and the developmental role of industrial organizations in India. In H. C. Triandis, M. D. Dunnette, & L. M. Hough (Eds.), *Handbook of industrial and organizational psychology,* 2d ed. (Vol. 4, pp. 727–764). Palo Alto: Consulting Psychologists Press.

Smith, P. B. (1984). The effectiveness of Japanese styles of management: A review and critique. *Journal of Occupational Psychology, 57*, 121–136.

Smith, P. B., Misumi, J., Tayeb, M., Peterson, M. F., & Bond, M. H. (1989). On the generality of leadership style measures across cultures. *Journal of Occupational Psychology, 62*, 97–109.

Smith, P. B. & Peterson, M. F. (1988). *Leadership, organizations and culture: An event management model.* London: Sage.

Smith, P. B., Peterson, M. F., & Misumi, J. (1994). Event management and work team effectiveness in Japan, Britain and the USA. *Journal of Occupational and Organizational Psychology, 67*, 33–43.

Smith, P. B., Peterson, M. F., Misumi, J., & Bond, M. H. (1992). A cross-cultural test of the Japanese PM leadership theory. *Applied Psychology: An International Review, 41*, 5–19.

Smith, P. B., Peterson, M. F., Misumi, J., & Tayeb, M. (1989). Testing leadership theory cross culturally. In J. P. Forgas & J. M. Innes (Eds.), *Recent advances in social psychology: An international perspective* (pp. 383–391). North Holland: Elsevier Science Publishers B.V.

Spaeth, A. (1994). Dressed for success. *Time*, (November 28, 1994), pp. 24–25.

Steers, R. M. & Braunstein, D. N. (1976). A behaviorally based measure of manifest needs in work settings. *Journal of Vocational Behavior, 9*, 251–266.

Stogdill, R. M. (1963). *Manual for the Leader Behavior Description Questionnaire* (Form XII). Columbus: Ohio State University Bureau of Business Research.

Sullivan, J. J., Suzuki, T., & Kondo, Y. (1986). Managerial perceptions of performance: A comparison of Japanese and American work groups. *Journal of Cross-Cultural Psychology, 17*, 379–398.

Swierczek, F. W. & Jatusripatak, S. (1994). Exploring entrepreneurship cultures in Southeast Asia. *Journal of Enterprising Culture, 2*, 687–708.

Tainio, R. & Santalainen, T. (1984). Some evidence for the cultural relativity of organizational development programs. *The Journal of Applied Behavioral Science, 20*, 93–111.

Takyi-Asiedu, S. (1993). Some socio-cultural factors retarding entrepreneurial activity in sub-Saharan African. *Journal of Business Venturing, 8*, 91–98.

Tan, C. K. (1995). *The Chinese employees' view of effective leadership: A test of the CPM model.* Unpublished master's thesis. Department of Psychology, University of Hong Kong.

Tannenbaum, A. S. (1980). Organizational psychology. In H. C. Triandis & R. W. Brislin (Eds.), *Handbook of Cross-Cultural Psychology* (Vol. 5, pp. 281–334). Boston: Allyn and Bacon.

Tannenbaum, R. & Davis, S. A. (1969). Values, man and organizations. *Industrial Management Review, 10*, 67–83.

Thomas, K. W. (1976). Conflict and conflict management. In M. D. Dunnette (Ed.), *Handbook of industrial and organizational psychology* (pp. 889–935). Chicago: Rand McNally.

Tjosvold, D. (1984). Effects of leader warmth and directiveness on subordinate performance on a subsequent task. *Journal of Applied Psychology, 69*, 422–427.

Triandis, H. C., Kurowski, L. L., & Gelfand, M. J. (1994). Workplace diversity. In H. C. Triandis, M. D. Dunnette, & L. M. Hough (Eds.), *Handbook of industrial & organizational psychology*, 2d ed. (Vol. 4, pp. 769–827). Palo Alto: Consulting Psychologists Press.

Trubisky, P., Ting-Toomey, S., & Lin, S. L. (1991). The influence of individualism-collectivism and self-monitoring on conflict styles. *International Journal of Intercultural Relations, 15*, 65–84.

Tse, D. K., Francis, J., & Walls, J. (1994). Cultural differences in conducting intra- and inter-cultural negotiations: A Sino–Canadian comparison. *Journal of International Business Studies, 25*, 537–555.

Tse, D. K., Lee, K. H., Vertinsky, I., & Wehrung, D. A. (1988). Does culture matter? A cross-cultural study of executives' choice, decisiveness, and risk adjustment in international marketing. *Journal of Marketing, 52*, 81–95.

Tullar, W. L. (1992). Organizational change in the USSR: The activity-inciting game. *Leadership and Organization Development Journal, 13*, 17–20.

Tung, R. L. (1982). U.S.–China trade negotiations: Practices, procedures and outcomes. *Journal of International Business Studies, 13*, 25–38.

Tung, R. L. (1991). Handshakes across the sea: Cross-cultural negotiating for business success. *Organizational Dynamics, 19*, 30–40.

Waldman, D. A., Bass, B. M., & Einstein, W. O. (1987). Leadership and outcomes of performance appraisal processes. *Journal of Occupational Psychology, 60*, 177–186.

Waldman, D. A., Bass, B. M., & Yammarino, F. J. (1990). Adding to contingent-reward behavior: The augmenting effect of charismatic leadership. *Group and Organization Studies, 15*, 381–394.

Weber, M. (1930). *The Protestant ethic and the spirit of capitalism* (Talcott Parsons, transl.). London: Unwin University Books.

Weiss, S. E. (1994a). Negotiating with "Romans," Part 1. *Sloan Management Review, 35*, 51–61.

Weiss, S. E. (1994b). Negotiating with "Romans," Part 2. *Sloan Management Review, 35*, 85–99.

Westwood, R. I. (1992). The meaning and experience of work. In R. I. Westwook (Ed.), *Organizational behaviour: Southeast Asian perspectives* (pp. 201–242). Hong Kong: Longman.

Westwood, R. I., Tang, S. F., & Kirkbride, P. S. (1992). Chinese conflict behavior: Cultural antecedents and behavioral consequences. *Organization Development Journal, 10*, 13–19.

Whitley, R. D. (1990). Eastern Asian enterprise structures and the comparative analysis of forms of business organization. *Organization Studies, 11*, 47–74.

Whyte, W. F. (1983). Worker participation: International and historical perspectives. *The Journal of Applied Behavioral Science, 19*, 395–407.

Wilpert, B. (1987). Participation and industrial democracy. In B. M. Bass, & P. J. D. Drenth (Eds.), *Advances in organizational psychology: An international review* (pp. 232–241). Newbury Park, CA: Sage.

Wilpert, B. (1990). How European is work and organizational psychology? In P. J. D. Drenth, J. A. Sergeant, & R. J. Takens (Eds.), *European perspectives in psychology* (Vol. 3, pp. 3–20). Chichester, England:Wiley.

Wright, G. N. & Phillips, L. D. (1980). Cultural variation in probabilistic thinking: Alternative ways of dealing with uncertainty. *International Journal of Psychology, 15*, 239–257.

Wright, G. N., Phillips, L. D., Whalley, P. C., Choo, G. T., Ng, K. O., Tan, I., & Wisudha, A. (1978). Cultural differences in probabilistic thinking. *Journal of Cross-Cultural Psychology, 9*, 285–299.

Yamauchi, H. (1993). Work values of Japanese, Korean, and Chinese business workers. *Psychologia, 36*, 250–258.

Yang, K. S. & Cheng, P. S. (1987). Confucianized values, individual modernity, and organizational behavior: An empirical test of the post-Confucian hypothesis. *Bulletin of the Institute of Ethnology Academia Sinica, 64*, 1–49 (in Chinese).

Yavas, U., Luqmani, M., & Quraeshi, Z. (1990). Organisational commitment, job satisfaction, work values: Saudi and expatriate managers. *Leadership and Organization Development Journal, 11*, 3–10.

Yu, K. C., Wang, D. C., & He, W. (1992). A study of the organizational commitment of Chinese employees. *Advances in Chinese Industrial Studies, 3*, 181–195.

Zheng, R. & Stimpson, D. V. (1990). A cross-cultural study of entrepreneurial attitude orientation. *Information on Psychological Sciences, 6*, 23–25. (In Chinese.)

11

HEALTH AND
CULTURE-CENTERED INTERVENTION

LISA MARIE BEARDSLEY
University of Illinois
United States

PAUL PEDERSEN
University of Alabama
United States

Contents

Introduction

The purpose of this chapter is to integrate biological factors with social, cultural, and psychological factors relevant to health, illness, and disease and to draw conclusions from them that inform cross-cultural psychologists, as well as health care providers, counselors, and public health policymakers. Culture is the matrix within which all human behavior operates and is that which distinguishes human from animal behavior. In this chapter, it will be shown that when culture is made central to health interventions, behavior can be measured more accurately, personal identity becomes clearer, the consequences of problems are better understood, and situations become more meaningful. Not only are cultural variables filters through which health and the treatment of illness are perceived but they also enter into the biological processes of health and disease.

Cross-cultural research can help to clarify the nature of interactions among biological, psychological and cultural factors (Ilola, 1990). In this chapter we will (1) define health, illness, and disease, (2) examine reasons for differences in health morbidity and mortality, (3) review cross-cultural diagnosis and treatment issues, and (4) provide recommendations for training culture-centered counselors and health care workers. Stolley and Lasky (1995) have written a highly readable account of epidemiology and interested readers are directed there for a review of landmark studies in and methods employed by this exciting discipline. The purpose of this chapter is not to reiterate what they have already written, but to focus on those examples that illuminate cultural correlates of disease and health.[1]

Broad-Based Definition of Health

Sheikh and Sheikh (1989) describe the breakdown of the Westernized "dualistic-materialistic-paradigm" accompanied by a conceptual revolution in which an Easternized holistic perspective is gaining importance. "Western medicine has tended to look upon the body as a sort of machine that can be treated in total isolation from the mind, but even before the major paradigm shifts, it was becoming clear that this mechanical approach was simply not working. This was especially apparent in areas where psychosomatic linkages were showing that the mind does have a major impact upon bodily functions (Sheikh & Sheikh, 1989, p. v)." A biological model of health is obsolete. When the World Health Organization (WHO) launched its Health for All by the Year 2000 (HFA 2000) primary health care campaign in 1977, health was broadly defined to be a "state of complete physical, mental, and social well-being, and not merely the absence of disease or infirmity." In 1981, the WHO further operationalized this definition with 12 indicators of health that were grouped into four areas: health policy indicators, social and economic indicators, primary healthcare service indicators, and indicators of health status (morbidity, mortality, literacy). To illustrate the far-reaching implications of a broad definition of health, specific HFA 2000 indicators are summarized below (WHO, 1993, pp. A-3, A-4).

A. Health policy indicators are:
   1. The number of countries in which health for all is continuing to receive endorsement at the highest official level
   2. The number of countries in which mechanisms for involving people in implementing health for all are fully functioning or are being further developed
   3. The percentage of gross national product spent on health

B. Social and economic indicators are:
   4. The percentage of the national health expenditure devoted to local health services
   5. Resources for primary health care that are becoming more equitably distributed
   6. The amount of international aid received or given for health

C. Indicators of primary healthcare services are:
   7. The percentage of population covered by primary healthcare, with at least the following: safe water in the home or with reasonable access, and adequate excreta-disposal facilities available; immunizations against diphtheria, tetanus, whooping cough, measles, poliomyelitis, and tuberculosis; local health services, including access to essential drugs within one hour's walk or travel; attendance by trained personnel for pregnancy and childbirth, and, caring for children up to at least one year of age; the percentage of women of childbearing age using family planning

D. Indicators of health status are:
   8. The percentage of newborns weighing at least 2,500 grams, and the percentage of children whose weight-for-age and/or weight-for-height are acceptable
   9. The infant mortality rate, maternal mortality rate and probability of dying before the age five
   10. Life expectancy at birth, by sex
   11. The adult literacy rate, by sex
   12. The per capita GNP

Progress toward achieving these measurable health indicators is monitored and reported at regional and global levels. Reports of 151 member states, representing 96 percent of the world population in 1990, were included in the World Health Statistics Annual (WHO, 1993). The United Nations Development Program uses similar macro indicators to operationalize and monitor human development globally. The point in outlining these indicators is to promote a definition of health that is more comprehensive than "a state in which disease is absent." The social and behavioral sciences potentially have much to contribute to achieving these health goals but are stymied by transcultural portability of intervention approaches (Berry et al., 1992, pp. 376–377). In discussing the Turkish Early Enrichment Program in particular, Kagitçibasi (1995) demonstrated that its remarkable long-term success was precisely because it was a culturally-adapted, theory-based intervention program. Without a strong partnership with psychology, wide-scale interventions that perhaps meet with initial success are destined to fail because fundamental psychological and social support systems are missing. As both the Turkish program and other interventions, which we describe later, amply support, psychology is a relevant, indeed, an essential discipline to successful and sustainable health interventions both at macro (programmatic/policy) and micro (individual) levels.

Most health research is based on measures of poor health (morbidity and mortality data). This poses a significant problem in that "reverse logic" is then used to draw inferences from them about what contributes to good health. It is the righting of disease, the promotion of health, and the identification of positive predictors of good health rather than disease that is of ultimate interest. Too few studies identify factors that correlate with and predict health rather than disease. Recognizing and developing criteria that define disease does not thereby establish the gold standard for good health. What are the "risk factors" (if they can be called that) for good health? Research on the beneficial effects of social support, for instance, has identified it as a "risk factor" promoting health (House, Landis, & Umberson, 1988; Fraser, Haller-Wade, & Morrow, 1995). A few such studies are available (Benfante, Reed, & Brody, 1985) and more are needed but much of what we currently know about health is inferred from studies of morbidity and mortality.

Nevertheless, the collection of accurate vital statistics is essential to monitor and evaluate progress toward national and international HFA 2000 objectives. Even though data collection is more reliable in some countries than in others, chronic disease (e.g., cardiovascular disease, cancer) and accidents cause more morbidity and mortality in industrialized countries than in developing countries. And, although the incidence of infectious and parasitic disease is worldwide, they are most prevalent in Africa, Asia, and Latin America. Respiratory infections (pneumonia, influenza) and Acquired Immunodeficiency Syndrome (AIDS) are exceptions, and in 1993, AIDS surpassed accidents to become the leading cause of mortality in the 25–44 year-old age group in the United States (NCHS, 1994; CDC, 1995).

What accounts for international health differences? Some variations in disease can be traced to geographic features such as waterways, country boundaries, rainfall, latitude, and average temperature (as is the case with malaria). Patterns such as malnutrition are directly linked to socioeconomic factors. Much of what we now understand about these differences comes from data collected through ethnographic field methods, household surveys, and clinic records. Through the application of statistics and cartography, epidemiologists and medical geographers can then analyze morbidity and mortality over time and space. These macro-level analyses describe disease and health in specific populations and regions, but experimental research is still needed to confirm inferences drawn about culture-related etiology. The problem is that it is very difficult, if not impossible to manipulate cultural variables. Migrant groups constitute a "natural experiment," however, allowing cultural factors that affect health to be examined without raising the ethical concerns of experimentation with human subjects.

Variability in Disease Patterns: Communicable and Parasitic Diseases

River Blindness

The etiologic cycle of many communicable and parasitic diseases involves a single pathogen or microorganism and a simple route of infection. By breaking the etiologic cycle of disease, a number of public health projects have achieved remarkable success. The case of *onchocerciasis* (river blindness) is a good example. With high infection rates in endemic pockets in savanna and river basin areas, such as the Volta River basin, this major public health problem has significantly obstructed development in fertile river valleys throughout Western Africa for at least the past 100 years. On the basis of entomological and ophthalmic disease surveys and aerial photographs of abandoned settlements, Hunter (1966; 1980) mapped geographic "frontiers of blindness." These areas demarcated a frontier along which a historical, cyclical pattern of advancement and retreat occurred: advancement due to hunger, followed by retreat due to disease. As a result, some of the most fertile soils in the Upper Volta and northeast Ghana areas were abandoned and not farmed.

A thorough understanding of the epidemiology of this skin and eye disease was key to successful intervention efforts. The route of infection starts when infected female blackflies inject the parasitic worm into animal and human hosts. The worms live and breed in their human host from eleven to sixteen years, causing humans to become a long-term parasitic reservoir. These worm bundles breed thousands of microfilariae which in turn cause skin lesions, subcutaneous nodules, cysts, and eye lesions that may be severe enough to cause blindness. In 1974 about 1.5 million people were infested and 35,000 of them were blinded by eye lesions. At least as many had their vision severely impaired.

Because there is no viable treatment or medication for onchocerciasis, the WHO-coordinated Onchocerciasis Control Program focused its efforts on prevention. After 12 years of larviciding the river rapids (where the blackfly breeds) and enforcing other vector-controlled activities, the program dramatically changed incidence with a greater than 95 percent drop in the intensity and severity of disease (WHO, 1987). The prevalence of eye lesions and blindness had already fallen by 50 percent after ten years of control. Present projections indicate that 15 years of control will eliminate the human reservoir of infection.

Guinea Worm Disease

A similar dramatic drop was achieved with dracunculiasis (Guinea worm disease) in the high- incidence countries of Ghana and Nigeria. Active surveillance and eradication efforts were coordinated by the WHO and the CDC starting in the period 1987–1988. These efforts included health education, distribution of nylon filters, provision of safe water sources, and medical treatment of those affected. By the end of 1993, a 90 percent reduction in incidence was reported (CDC, 1994).

Many other infectious and communicable diseases have likewise been controlled through medical and environmental interventions that include immunizations, vaccines, larvicides, pesticides, sanitation, and the proper disposal of waste materials.

Although there is no cure for onchocerciasis, many such diseases can be treated and cured. The American Public Health Association (APHA) has identified four basic approaches to the control of communicable disease: prevention and treatment, sanitation, proper nutrition, and research (see APHA, 1985, for disease-specific detection, treatment, and control measures).

Malaria: Biological and Behavioral Interactions

Malaria control in Sri Lanka and UNICEF's child survival efforts in Bangladesh are other intervention programs that succeeded at first. But both failed to achieve long-term success because human factors involved in the transmission and maintenance of these problems were inadequately taken into account (Harkness, Wyon, & Super, 1988). Both projects demonstrated that if long-term solutions to malnutrition and child welfare are to be achieved, intervention must involve adequate understanding of the human behaviors that are part of the morbidity cycle. Health education is most successful when key behavioral changes are culturally-supported and sustained.

Malaria continues to be the major public health problem in most countries in the African region (WHO, 1993). West Africa was once referred to as the "White man's grave," but availability of antimalarial drugs has reduced barriers to economic development. Although antimalarials such as chloroquine have effectively opened malaria-endemic areas to economic development, chloroquine therapy is associated with significant noncompliance among Black Africans who are less likely to use malaria prophylaxis or to obtain early treatment until after the symptoms of malaria cause them considerable distress. When they do come for treatment, compliance has been poor.

The temptation to "blame the victim" for failed projects should be resisted, however. Behavioral noncompliance with treatment may be rooted in biological factors over which those affected have little control. Chloroquine is a popular antimalarial medication because it is less toxic and more effective than is quinine. However, research by Osifo (1989) suggests that because of its affinity for melanin, it disproportionately causes adverse side effects in Black patients. Although chloroquine-induced itching has been found in various ethnic groups and races, skin pigmentation is involved in the metabolism of this drug. Skin melanocytes are distributed more diffusely in black than in white skin. As the drug is metabolized, black skin, in effect, "traps" the chloroquine. Fever causes constriction of peripheral vascular tissue (the skin) which is why those with malarial fever (or fever of any kind for that matter) experience skin discomfort and sensitivity. When a Black patient who is being treated with chloroquine develops malarial fever, the chloroquine that accumulates in the melanin of the skin further amplifies itch receptors and creates a hypersensitivity to the itch sensation. Following up on these findings, Asawalam, Osifo, and Haller (1993) used questionnaires to assess the subjective experience of "feeling itchy." They also used a fascinating device to corroborate the subjective data with an objective measure of scratching. They modified self-winding watches to record the movement of subjects' arms and legs while they slept. In addition to finding that less total scratch time was employed by the dominant versus non-dominant hand (probably because it was more efficient in locating and administering a palliative scratch), the researchers also found a drug that reduced the need to scratch. An understanding of these pharmacodynamics sheds light on the "compliance problem" in antimalarial therapy with Black patients and led to the recommendation to co-administer chloroquine with a drug (Dapsone) used to effectively treat the dermatological itching of leprosy (Asawalam, Osifo, & Haller, 1993). At least this particular "compliance problem" appears to be rooted in biological rather than psychosocial factors that result in differential benefits of medications for members of one group over another. Unfortunately, the noncompliance is also a likely contributor to the emergence of chloroquine-resistant strains of malaria. Greater understanding of the molecular basis of human disease has opened new therapeutic and diagnostic modalities. The field of genetics is expanding at a rapid pace and Tay-Sachs disease, sickle-cell anemia, emphysema and liver disease, once only associated with demographic markers, can now be traced to specific molecular lesions. Gene therapy holds promise for these and other diseases, such as AIDS.

Acquired Immunodeficiency Syndrome (AIDS)

A June 1981 report of five homosexual males in Los Angeles with pneumonia, and a month later another report of a rare malignant tumor (Kaposi's sarcoma) in 26 homosexual males, marked the beginning of the AIDS epidemic in the United States (CDC, 1981a). Since then it has been reported in more than 163 countries, becoming a modern global epidemic (Cotran, Kumar, & Robbins, 1994). It is of great research interest to social, behavioral and basic scientists alike because of its epidemiology (and also probably because of the availability of funds for AIDS research). It has been closely studied in the United States where the five major risk groups clearly point to behavioral risk factors. The case distribution among these groups currently is as follows: homosexual/bisexual males (60%), intravenous (IV) drug users (23%), hemophiliacs (1%), recipients of blood and blood components (2%), and heterosexual contacts of high-risk groups, mostly intravenous drug users (6%). The pool of infected people in Africa, Asia, and Europe is large and expanding to include women and children, and in the United States, also ethnic minorities. As the epidemic evolves, bidirectional venereal transmission is outpacing all other modes of transmission. Outside Europe and the United States, heterosexual venereal transmission continues to be the major route of infection.

The immune and central nervous system are the major targets of infection by the human immunodeficiency virus (HIV). The hallmark of the disease is profound immunosuppression that culminates in a final crisis phase within seven to ten years of infection. HIV is a classic Trojan horse, destroying from within by sabotaging the immune system and then using the immune system to disseminate the virus throughout body tissue. As a result of severe immunosupression, those with HIV infection are susceptible to recurrent and severe infections by a wide range of opportunistic pathogens (fungal, bacterial, and viral) and of certain tumors.

The immune system is the first line of defense against disease. A healthy immune system is also critical to the healing process once disease develops. Research on AIDS has heightened awareness of behavioral, psychological, and social factors that compromise the immune system. Psychoimmunological studies in the United States have found associations between feelings of distress or depression and an increased risk of clinical and subclinical infection. Levy (1988) reviewed ten psychobiological studies that linked affect and behavior to cancer mortality. Studies suggest that feelings of depression suppress the immune system and thereby increase vulnerability to disease. In one study, more persons with AIDS were found to have had a prior history of depression than did matched homosexual males without AIDS (Rubinow et al., 1988).

Conversely, lowered risk is associated with social support and "hardiness," a sense of control, commitment, and challenge (Temoshok, 1988). A sense of well-being and happiness predicted reduced cancer incidence and mortality from hormonally-dependent tumors for women (Reynolds & Kaplan, 1990). The perception of inadequate social support, helplessness, and inadequate expression of negative emotions were associated with progression of cancer and with cancer mortality.

Other studies indicate that severe and chronic stressors such as depression, marital discord, or caring for a family member with Alzheimer's disease can decrease cellular immunity and thereby increase vulnerability to disease (Glaser & Glaser-Kiecolt, 1988; Glaser-Kiecolt & Glaser, 1988). The researchers conclude that humans do not appear to adapt to chronic stress and that over time, it compromises immunity.

Cohen (1988) also identified social support as important to undergirding a healthy immune system. He drew a parallel between the social withdrawal that is part of a voodoo curse or Hmong Sudden Death Syndrome with what is experienced by persons with cancer and AIDS. In all of these, the withdrawal of social support magnifies the individual's feelings of separation, loss, depression, and hopelessness, thereby hastening the progression of disease. Citing studies that support the healing power of hope, humor, community support, meditation, prayer, relaxation, and positive mental imagery, Cohen advocates a "biology of hope." Social support, he argues, is essential to self-esteem and a sense of mastery over illness.

Research with animals has identified exogenous substances such as cocaine and THC (marijuana) that can suppress the immune system. The researchers theorize that the recreational use of these drugs by humans increases vulnerability to AIDS, cancer, and other diseases in which a compromised immune system is part of disease etiology (Friedman et al., 1988; Klein, Newton, & Friedman, 1988). If drugs like this suppress the immune system, then sharing "dirty needles" is not the only reason why intravenous drug users are at high risk for contracting AIDS. The effects of social support, attitude toward life, and illicit drug use on the immune system are not yet well understood, but it seems clear that AIDS is of multifactorial etiology. The most prominent risk factor worldwide is sexual behavior (in the United States and Europe), and behaviors associated with intravenous drug use. Consequently, current health education and prevention efforts center around "safe sex" practices (e.g., use of latex condoms, a monogamous relationship with an AIDS-free partner) and safer intravenous drug-use behaviors (e.g., use of clean needles). At the health policy level, blood and blood products are now routinely screened in many countries to minimize transmission through this route (FDA, 1994). There is still much that needs to be understood about the epidemiology of the disease. For example, why do drug users share needles even though it is a well-established high-risk behavior? This is an area for research and future application to health education efforts.

Even though the etiology, epidemiology, and pathogenesis of AIDS is fairly well understood, and some prevention efforts are in place, effective treatment is not yet available. Gene therapy holds promise for treating AIDS, cancer, diabetes, and heart disease, but is not yet a reality. Because psychological and behavioral factors are key epidemiological features of these diseases, it is of paramount importance that health education efforts include behavioral interventions.

Behavioral and Psychological Components of Chronic Disease

Framingham Heart Study

The effects of diet and other lifestyle factors have been demonstrated in the health status of different ethnic groups and in different countries. In the period 1948–1949, the Framingham Heart Study enrolled a cohort of 5,209 middle-aged men who were free of coronary heart disease (CHD), in Framingham, Massachusetts (U.S.), Honolulu (a sample of Japanese-Americans), and Puerto Rico (Gordon, Garcia-Palmieri, Kagan, Kannel, & Schiffman, 1974). The prospective study found that the U.S. White population had twice the CHD death rate of Puerto Ricans and four times that of Honolulu Japanese. In all three populations, elevated serum cholesterol and hypertension were related to CHD incidence.

Cigarette smoking was related to CHD in the first two sites but not in Puerto Rico. Another difference was that relative weight (obesity) was less of a risk factor for the U.S. White population than it was for the other two groups. This landmark study established CHD to be complex in etiology, with multiple risk factors, distinguishing it from most infectious diseases that can usually be traced to a single pathogen, or lung cancer for which smoking is a primary, significant risk factor. There is little that can be done to control etiologic and environmental factors such as radiation exposure or genetic factors, except perhaps through genetic counseling. There is nothing that can be done about significant risk factors such as one's age, race, or gender. Much can be done, however, to modify behavior, and for this reason it is particularly important to understand the behavioral components of not just CHD, but also other diseases that cause premature death and preventable suffering. For CHD, the Framingham Study found age, sex, and race to be unmodifiable risk factors that predicted risk (with older White males at highest risk). Modifiable risk factors included smoking, alcohol consumption, diet, psychosocial factors, and exercise.

Ni-Hon-San Study and the Honolulu Heart Study

Research studies of migrant ethnic groups are a natural experiment in which the genetic pool (ethnicity) is held constant while external factors change. The Ni-Hon-San Study, part of the on-going, prospective Honolulu Heart Study, provides a good model of health status changes associated with migration. In this study, data were collected from about 12,000 Japanese men in Hiroshima and Nagasaki in Japan, Honolulu, and San Francisco. Data points included anthropometric measures, body fluid and tissue samples (blood, urine, tissue), and morbidity and mortality indices. When the study began in 1964, Japan had one of the lowest rates of CHD worldwide and the United States had one of the highest. Conversely, Japan had one of the highest rates of cerebrovascular disease (CBVD) worldwide. Stroke remained the leading cause of death in Japan for years until it was surpassed by cancer mortality in 1981.

The concept of acculturation (see chapter by Berry & Sam, this volume) can explain why the Japanese in Japan had the lowest rates of CHD with intermediate rates in Hawaii and highest rates among those who migrated to California. The process of acculturation involves changes in the physical environment, biological factors (e.g., dietary patterns), cultural factors (e.g., language, religion), and psychological factors, such as values. As the Japanese migrated and underwent a process of acculturation, their serum cholesterol, glucose levels, uric acid levels, relative weight, and blood pressures all increased. Japanese in California weighed approximately 8 kilos more than did those in Japan. Their dietary patterns also changed. Total calories were slightly lower in Japan, but average dietary fat intake was only 40 percent that of the Hawaii and California cohort. Consumption of fish, complex carbohydrates, vegetables, fruits, unrefined grain, and soybean curd (tofu) decreased during migration. There was an increase in consumption of bread, pork items (ham, bacon, and sausage), and high fat foods (butter, margarine, and cheese). In Hawaii and California, more traditional foods were replaced by consumption of sandwiches and hamburgers, and for breakfast, processed meat and eggs. A consistent and positive correlation was found between elevated serum cholesterol levels and greater dietary intake of saturated fat, animal protein, and dietary cholesterol.

Indices of psychological acculturation paralleled indicators of biological acculturation. The number of years lived in Japan, frequency of speaking the Japanese language, ability to read a Japanese newspaper, and ethnicity of coworkers all correlated with CHD and CHD risk factors, especially if subjects were classified as Type A according to the Jenkins Activity Survey (Cohen, Syme, Jenkins, Kagan, & Zyzanski, 1979). Those men who were more traditionally Japanese had lower serum cholesterol and lower uric acid levels. They smoked fewer cigarettes, were less obese, and were more physically active than those who were more Westernized, that is, those who infrequently spoke or read Japanese or associated with Japanese coworkers (Kato, Tillotson, Nickaman, Rhoads, & Hamilton, 1973; Tillotson et al., 1973; Kagan, Marmot, & Kato, 1980; Lichton, Bullard, & Sherrell, 1983; Reed et al., 1982).

Although the association of risk factors with CHD was stronger in the cohort in Hawaii than in Japan, these differences were not statistically significant. Systolic blood pressure was the greatest and most consistent CHD risk factor. Other factors were age, elevated serum cholesterol, cigarette smoking, and elevated serum glucose. Alcohol consumption and physical activity were negatively correlated with CHD, suggesting that they protected the individual from developing CHD (Yano et al., 1988; Donahue, Abbott, Reed, & Yano, 1988).

Brislin (1980) notes that cross-cultural studies are essential to understanding the interplay between environmental factors and the core aspects of a phenomenon. In the case of CHD, cross-cultural studies have helped outline a more complete understanding of disease etiology. Deviant cases and research findings that at first seem puzzling have provided insights into the epidemiology of disease that could not have been gained from monocultural research. For example, Levine and Bartlett (1984) examined the role of stress in CHD etiology by correlating CHD with pace of life and punctuality in Japan, Taiwan, Indonesia, Italy, England and the United States. The greatest number of deaths from CHD per 100,000 was in England (317), followed by the United States (295), and Italy (152). Japan had the lowest mortality (40); however, mortality data were unavailable for Taiwan and Indonesia. The researchers used three measures of pace of life (pace of walking, accuracy of clocks, and pace of working) and found that these measures were highly correlated with each other and with the degree of economic development and city size. But they did not find these variables to be correlated with CHD. Japan had the fastest pace of life using these measures. In Japan, people walked quickly, clocks were more accurate, and postal service more prompt. But Japan had the lowest incidence of death from CHD. These findings contradicted the hypothesis that a faster pace of life would be positively correlated with CHD.

Further consideration of reasons why a correlation between stress and CHD was not found yields interesting hypotheses. There are undoubtedly cultural variations in the construct of psychological stress. Beyond this, there is reason to hypothesize that greater availability of social support in collectivistic cultures mediates stress. Chronic disease epidemiology has cultural variations, as already noted with smoking not being the risk factor for heart disease in Puerto Rico that it was in the other two populations in the Framingham Heart Study. Furthermore, the Levine and Bartlett pace of life study emphasizes the overriding importance of hypertension, smoking, diet, obesity, and a sedentary lifestyle in CHD etiology.

However, the most important aspect of the study that the researchers did not discuss is that Japan at that time had the highest worldwide mortality for stroke.

Clinical records and autopsy findings have shown that stroke shares the very same risk factors as does CHD, namely hypertension, high serum cholesterol, severe atherosclerosis of the coronary arteries and aorta, diabetes, and smoking. A notable difference between CHD and stroke risk profiles is that while alcohol consumption is negatively correlated with CHD (or has a protective effect), it is positively related to hemorrhagic stroke. More than twice the risk of stroke was found for light drinkers and a three-to-fourfold increased risk for moderate to heavy drinkers compared with nondrinkers (Donahue, Abbott, Reed, & Yano, 1986). As with CHD, the presence of multiple risk factors magnified the risk of stroke. Another indication of the similarity of the etiology and pathophysiology of CHD and stroke is that autopsies of Japanese men in Hawaii revealed evidence of prior strokes in 58 percent of CHD cases (Abbott, Donahue, MacMahon, Reed, & Yano, 1987; Abbott, Yin, Reed, & Yano, 1986; Stemmermann et al., 1984; Kagan, Popper, Rhoads, & Yano, 1985).

The Ni-Hon-San data show two synchronous but asymmetrical processes unfolding as Japanese males migrated from Japan to Hawaii and California. In the first pattern, incidence of CHD gradually increased. In the second, stroke incidence markedly dropped to a level less than one-third that of the cohort in Japan. By 1960, the stroke death rate for Japanese-American men dropped to figures equivalent to that of U.S. White men of the same age. In the older age groups it was significantly lower in the United States compared to the Japanese cohort. This indicates that in a Western environment, risk factors for stroke can be reversed more quickly than can risk factors for CHD. It has been proposed that the critically low protein and/or fat-poor diet of postwar Japan and a relatively greater amount of alcohol intake are involved in the epidemiology of stroke in Japan. Among all cohorts however, hypertension was the single most important risk factor. Alcohol consumption, smoking, and diabetes were also important independent risk factors (Worth, Kato, Rhoads, Kagan, & Syme, 1975; Kagan, et al., 1985).

Twenty years of data from the Honolulu Heart Study have helped to develop a clearer picture of interactions among cultural, behavioral, and environmental factors in CHD epidemiology. This understanding provides an evidence-based foundation for intervention and prevention efforts (Benfante, 1992). Both a strength and a drawback in the data is that genetic background is held constant; all members of the study sample are Japanese. While this is an experimental advantage, it could be argued that CHD epidemiology is fundamentally different for Japanese than it is for Finns, so data from other groups are needed to confirm generalizability of CHD etiology. Comparisons of members of different ethnic groups and cross-national studies address such concerns and illuminate their associations with cultural factors. We turn next to such studies.

The Adventist Health Study

In a review of over 70 national and international studies of gastrointestinal cancer, Miller (1982) found that total fat and animal protein intake, especially of beef, and deficiency of dietary fiber were correlated with colon cancer incidence and mortality. But a limitation of correlational studies is that long periods of time often lapse between exposure to risk factors and the eventual development of disease. As Miller acknowledges, although current dietary habits and other factors are correlated with current indices of disease, to truly understand the epidemiology and etiology of gastric cancer, it would be more appropriate to correlate dietary habits of 20 to 30 years earlier. Unfortunately, such data are often unavailable and unreliable. Other methods are needed to supplement our understanding when the etiologic latency period is long as it is with colon cancer.

Prospective and cross-cultural studies of ethnically diverse groups with a history of fixed health behaviors are helpful in overcoming the confounding due to interactions among risk factors, ethnicity, and time. This is the opposite research model of the Ni-Hon-San Study. There have been several studies of religious groups that would meet these criteria. The Adventist Health Study (239 studies, 1954–1995) has been helpful in identifying cancer and CHD risk factors and has shown that diet plays an important role in disease etiology over and above that of genetics or geographic variables. Numerous studies in different countries have shown that Seventh-day Adventists (SDAs) live longer and are healthier than are their countrymen. SDAs in the United States also have less cancer of the breast, pancreas, and colorectal canal but have a higher risk for prostate and endometrial cancer (Mills, Beeson, Phillips & Fraser, 1994). The incidence of circulatory system diseases (CHD, stroke) is also significantly lower than in comparable cohorts.

These biological indices are directly related to their religious value that health maintenance is important. In a survey of 40,000 SDAs in the United States, one-half were non-vegetarian (with restricted meat consumption, e.g., no pork), one-fourth were lacto-ovo vegetarians, and one-fourth had adopted the vegetarian diet sometime in their life. About 84 percent drank less than one cup of coffee per day, 99 percent were nonsmokers, and 90 percent were nondrinkers (Phillips, Kuzma, Beeson, & Lotz, 1980). A trend toward delayed onset of dementia in vegetarians was found, with matched subjects who ate meat more than twice as likely to become demented as their vegetarian counterparts (Giem, Beeson, & Fraser, 1993). Because smoking is the primary etiology of most lung cancer, low incidence of lung cancer among SDAs is obviously attributable to the virtual absence of smoking in this population. Surprisingly, Phillips and colleagues (1980) found a lower incidence of lung cancer in non-smoking SDAs compared to non-smoking non-SDAs. Following up on this interesting finding, a later study found that fruit consumption has a strong and statistically significant protective association with lung cancer that is independent of smoking (Fraser, Beeson, & Phillips, 1991). As with CHD and stroke, lung cancer is not as simple in etiology as once thought and diet here, too, is of significance.

Cross-national studies of SDAs have shown similar patterns. SDAs in Australia have a lower prevalence of the risk factors that are associated with CHD and respiratory diseases. They had higher lung ventilator capacity and lower levels of systolic and diastolic blood pressure, plasma cholesterol, plasma urate concentrations, and obesity (Webster & Rawson, 1979; Simons, Gibson, Jones, & Bain, 1979).

In a ten-year study of mortality patterns in the Netherlands, SDAs were found to have significantly lower standardized mortality ratios for total mortality, cancer, and cerebrovascular disease compared to the total Dutch population (Berkel & deWaard, 1983). The Tromsö Heart Study found the same favorable coronary risk factor profiles for Norwegian SDAs. They had lower serum cholesterol (men and women) and blood pressure levels (women only) compared to other Norwegians (Fønnebø, 1985).

The SDA lifestyle does not seem to uniformly benefit all subgroups equally. Analysis of data from a high-risk subset in the United States, African Americans, showed that while of some benefit, these lifestyle factors were not equivalent for Black Adventists. Conceding that "Black Americans are not as biologically homogeneous as they are socially portrayed, [that] their gene pool compared to the original African stock, has undergone extensive selection," Sumbureru (1990, p. 35) found that longevity was lower for Black Adventists compared to Whites. He observed that, "variables such as beer and wine consumption which showed a positive relationship with mortality among Blacks failed to show the same among Whites" and suggested, "that lifestyle risk factors for mortality are not necessarily equivalent cross-culturally" (p. 173). Along the same lines, Melby, Goldflies, and Toohey (1993) found that a vegetarian diet did afford some protection for older Blacks compared to nonvegetarian Blacks in the United States. In their study, Black vegetarians had lower average systolic blood pressure, less hypertension, and they were significantly leaner than were Black nonvegetarians. But compared to older White adults, hypertension continued to pose a health concern for them.

The initial Framingham Heart Study and the Ni-Hon-San Study only included men, so generalizations from them to women's health are not warranted. Do the same "healthy behaviors" benefit women? A subset of the Adventist Health Study suggests that they do. Vegetarian compared to nonvegetarian women had significantly fewer overnight hospitalizations and surgeries during the previous year. They reported fewer chemical and drug allergies, were less likely to use medications and health services, and had a lower incidence of chronic disease (Knutsen, 1994). Moreover, lower incidence rates were accompanied by higher survival rates for cancer and for breast cancer in particular.

A value system in which health is a priority also affects behavior after disease develops. Lower breast cancer death rate among SDA women as compared to the general population is attributed in part to better survival patterns due to a shorter interval between onset of symptoms and subsequent diagnosis and treatment. These women were more likely to quickly obtain health care and comply with treatment once their health was endangered (Zollinger, Phillips, & Kuzma, 1984).

What explains these better health measures? Better health is in part a function of those behaviors that replace risk-related ones. For example, in the Ni-Hon-San study, lower levels of animal protein consumption in Japan were accompanied by higher levels of vegetable protein consumption (beans, lentils, peas). In the case of fatal pancreatic cancer, the Adventist Health Study also found that a lower level of animal protein consumption correlated with increased consumption of vegetable protein and dried fruits, the latter of which was associated with a significant protective relationships to risk (Mills, Beeson, Abbey, Fraser, & Phillips, 1988). A diet rich in unprocessed foods and low in animal protein and fat contribute to the health of SDAs but so did exercise, indirectly. In industrialized countries where so many have sedentary occupations, engaging in exercise is promoted as a healthful activity because of its strong negative association with CHD mortality. Fraser and colleagues (1992) found that regular exercise by itself did not prevent the development of heart disease (morbidity). Instead, they found a significant negative association with fatal CHD events (mortality). Regular exercise sufficiently strengthened the heart muscle, lessening the likelihood that the "heart attack" was a fatal one.

What about psychological measures of risk? In the Ni-Hon-San Study, Westernized subjects had a higher CHD risk gradient than did those men who were more traditionally Japanese. A similar gradient of risk was found upon examination of psychological and values-related variables in Norwegian SDAs. Fønnebø (1992b, 1994) showed that degree of adherence to the SDA lifestyle was related to health status, that entering the church at an early age had a large effect on later mortality, and that later lifestyle changes had a smaller effect on death risk. An increasing gradient of risk was found with decreasing adherence to the SDA lifestyle. Those who were religiously inactive were found to have risk factor profiles similar to that of non-SDAs. Their risk profiles were significantly higher than were the profiles of those who complied with the SDA lifestyle (Fønnebø, 1992a). The same pattern was found for SDAs in the United States. Those with poor adherence to the SDA lifestyle had a risk of disease that was only slightly less than or statistically equal to the risk of nonsmoking, non-SDAs (Phillips et al., 1980). Simple identification with the SDA church then, offered little protection from disease. Adherence to its values and lifestyle did.

Processes of acculturation provide a useful model to explain why SDAs who are more secular have risk profiles comparable to that of non-SDAs. Those who were more "acculturated" in their religious values, health behaviors, and lifestyle were also the ones whose health indicators were more positive. As in the Ni-Hon-San Study, acculturation is seen to be a mix of values, behaviors, and biological indices of morbidity and mortality. Changes in the physical environment (housing, geographic location), although part of the acculturation model, do not appear to be prominent in CHD epidemiology.

Dayan (1994) found similar gradients of risk-related values and behaviors in a study of the health beliefs, behaviors, and health status of Orthodox, Conservative, and Reform Jews in Canada. Orthodox Jews had the most conservative health values and tended to view maintaining health as an obligation to God. But should illness develop, they demonstrated greater belief in divine intervention in recovery from illness. Their faith in God's power to heal them was coupled with greater motivation to behave in ways that would maintain or reinstate health, making such individuals more likely to be compliant with treatment protocols.

In line with their more conservative health values, Orthodox Jews also engaged in healthier behaviors than did Conservative or Reform Jews. This was particularly true in regard to a lesser use of drugs, tobacco, and alcohol. Not surprisingly, Orthodox Jews were found to have better physical health status. They did not, however, have better mental health status. They used fewer coping strategies than did the other two groups, which Dayan interpreted to be due to a greater tendency of religious individuals to rely on God in times of trouble. The belief that one can simply "trust in God" decreases a need for that individual to have a large repertoire of other coping strategies. Such individuals were also hypothesized to espouse a more simplistic explanation for why they have become ill, for example, that "illness is a punishment from God." The better indicators of health among SDAs and the Orthodox Jewish population in Canada show the profound impact that a values-driven lifestyle can have on a variety of physiological measures. The confirming cross-national SDA data suggest that these values appear to be independent of other cultural variables, such as the physical environment, language, national history and identity, politics, and national origin. Clearly, values can affect behavior with measurable health outcomes.

The North Karelia Project

An understanding of how values relate to health behaviors, coping strategies, and disease risk factors is the basis of effective health education efforts. It is well established that the presence of multiple risk factors magnifies the risk of developing disease. Consequently, programs that succeed in reducing the presence of risk factors in a population also succeed in changing morbidity and mortality patterns. The Karelia area in eastern Finland has had among the highest cardiovascular mortality rates in the world for years. In 1972 the North Karelia Project began systematically to treat hypertension and, through community-based prevention programs, to reduce the risk factors already discussed: serum cholesterol, blood pressure, and consumption of animal (saturated) fat. These efforts yielded excellent dividends. From 1972 to 1984, mortality from stroke, ischaemic heart disease, and from all cardiovascular disease declined more steeply in Karelia than in the rest of Finland, even though it remains higher than in the United States or other Western European countries (Tuomilehto, et al., 1986; Nissinen, Tuomilehto, & Puska, 1989; Tuomilehto, Piha, Nissinen, Geboers, & Puska, 1989).

The application of the behavioral sciences to the solution of health problems is promising but requires both effort and knowledge so that macro-level interventions are culturally appropriate and medically sound. We can expect to see improvements in public health programs as bridges are made by contributions from indigenous psychologies to epidemiology and the biomedical sciences. The remainder of the chapter will focus on intervention at the micro level. Specifically, assessment, clinical decision-making, counseling, and treatment issues will be discussed next.

Assessment, Clinical Decision Making, and Practice

Diagnostic Reliability and Validity

A number of factors contribute to disagreement in clinical assessment and practice when cultural boundaries are crossed. Differences exist among the many manuals used internationally to describe signs, symptoms, and other criteria used to classify disease. The WHO has developed and published guidelines and manuals to standardize the worldwide collection, coding, monitoring, and reporting of disease. Some of these manuals include *The International Classification of Disease* (WHO, 1992) and the *International Nomenclature of Diseases: Infectious Diseases* (WHO, 1985). Classification manuals like these contribute to the increasing degree of cross-national agreement on the diagnosis of biopathological indices such as infant mortality and coronary heart disease. The degree of agreement declines, however, when diagnosing psychopathology. Highest interrater reliability is generally found for organic syndromes (e.g., senile dementia), with intermediate levels of agreement for schizophrenia, and the lowest agreement for depressive and affective disorders. For example, substantial agreement was found when using the ICD-10 with an Arab population in Egypt with organic mental disorders, substance use disorders, schizophrenic, schizotypal, delusional, affective, neurotic, and stress-related disorders (Okasha & Seif el Dawla, 1992). The *Diagnostic and Statistical Manual of Mental Disorders (DSM)* of the American Psychiatric Association has been translated into Danish, Dutch, Finnish, Japanese, Spanish, and other languages and is another standard reference. However, even though the Chinese Classification of Mental Disorders is based on the DSM, one study found only 75 percent agreement when Chinese and American psychiatrists evaluated the same Chinese patients (Altshuler et al., 1988). Diagnoses of schizophrenia were identical. But the American psychiatrist was more likely to use a diagnosis of major depression, whereas the Chinese psychiatrist was more likely to diagnose those patients with anxiety disorder or neurasthenia, a type of neurosis not commonly reported in the United States. (See chapter by Tanaka-Matsumi & Draguns, this volume, for a further discussion of these issues.)

Diagnostic accuracy is also compromised with the use of culturally-biased tests (intelligence tests, questionnaires, etc.). Lonner (1990) demonstrates (1) that testing and assessment are not familiar procedures in much of the non-Western world, (2) psychological constructs and concepts are not universally valid, (3) the basis of comparison across cultures is often not equivalent, (4) test stimuli are more frequently in a verbal rather than visual form and language conveys strong bias, and (5) test score differences frequently imply a "deficit" in one or another culture by the language used to describe those differences. In another area of study, Kohlberg's measures of moral development, for example, are biased toward an individualistic norm reflecting the values of an urban middle-class group (Segall, Dasen, Berry, & Poortinga, 1990; Eckensberger & Zimba, volume 2, this *Handbook*) and with a bias favoring the male perspective (Gilligan, 1982, 1987).

Cultural bias in the use of tests and measurements is likely to result in over-diagnosis, under-diagnosis, or misdiagnosis. While it is generally accepted that biases exist in the use of counseling tests and measures (Paniagua, 1994; Dana, 1993), this does not necessarily mean that those tests and measures cannot or should not be used. The search first for "culture free" tests and later for "culture fair" tests has not been successful (Lonner & Ibrahim, 1989; Irvine & Berry, 1983). Flaherty and colleagues (1988) suggest that any culture-fair test would need to fulfill five validity criteria of (1) content equivalence, (2) semantic equivalence across cultures, (3) technical equivalence, (4) criterion equivalence, and (5) conceptual equivalence across cultures. Escobar (1993) contends that no test or assessment can fulfill these five criteria.

Nor would it be desirable to screen out culture altogether. All illness has a psychological component that is influenced by culture and that interacts with biological processes of disease. Just how does the personal experience of pain and the social expression of illness relate to pathophysiology, and to what degree is it important that the uniqueness of a condition be eliminated for the sake of being able to make cross-cultural comparisons? How important is it to determine whether psychosomatic symptoms, such as upset stomach or insomnia, are "imagined" or "real"? Kleinman (1986) concluded that the more than 150 cases of diagnosed neurasthenia that he saw in the outpatient psychiatry clinic of Hunan Medical College were related to China's cultural revolution. He proposed that by telling their sickness stories these patients could safely tell others about their grief without censorship. They could also use their illness to negotiate improvements in their work conditions or to return home from distant locations to which they had been involuntarily sent. For them, their pain was a symbol of resistance to the values, priorities, and practices of post-revolution China.[2] Illness communicated emotional and psychological needs in a socially recognized, acceptable, and safe manner.

In this way, illness identifies cultural values and has psychological significance in and of itself. A study of immigrants to Israel of Western and Oriental origin found that culture of origin did not affect the subjective experience of physical distress (Silver, 1987). However, when comparing depressed versus nondepressed individuals, there was a difference in the quantity of physical ailments each group experienced. Patients who were depressed had more physical complaints than did controls. Not only did the depressed individuals feel worse affectively, they also had more physical complaints about which to feel bad than did those who were not depressed. While not affecting the prevalence of complaints, Silver did find that culture affected the voicing of complaints, the weight attached to them, and the significance the examining physicians attached to them.

Certainly, there are complaints and behavioral patterns that are more prevalent in specific populations, or are unique to certain cultures or locales. Eating disorders, for example, are considered to be culture-specific to industrialized countries, where about 90 percent of cases are women, with greatest incidence for Euroamerican females (Banks, 1992). First-degree biological relatives are at increased risk and twin studies further suggest a genetic factor in anorexia nervosa and bulimia nervosa (Woodside, 1993). Eating disorders are rarely seen in impoverished countries where there is competition for economic and food resources. Primary etiology is thought to be related to Westernized values that are popularized for women in the media and fashions. Some of the best studied culture-bound syndromes, identified by their local names, have been included in an appendix to the DSM-IV (APA, 1994). Examples include to run *amok* (impulse-control disorder traditionally seen in males in Southeastern Asia and originally in Malaysia), *susto* in Latin America ("fright" or "soul loss" characterized by severe anxiety, restlessness, fear of black magic, and of evil eye), and *taijin-kyofusho* (anthropophobia) in Japan and Korea.

The emic–etic distinction is useful to describe the plasticity that comes from the interaction of a biological process (disease) and illness behavior (the psychological experience and social response to disease). In a discussion of culture-bound syndromes, Berry et al. (1992) indicate the likelihood of a universalistic position, that is, that for many conditions there exists underlying symptoms that are universal (insomnia, upset stomach, anxiety) that are further expressed in a culturally-stereotyped manner. For example, in the United States, Hispanics and Asians are more likely than Caucasians to express their illness as physical illness. A distinct repertoire of somatic manifestations has been reported even among highly-acculturated Hispanics in the United States and research is underway to better define the somatization construct for inclusion as a diagnostic criterion (Escobar, 1987). Another example is taijin-kyofusho (anthropophobia syndrome) already mentioned. It affects mostly males and, at core, is a type of social phobia characterized by the etic components of anxiety and fear of evaluation and rejection. The culturally-stereotyped emic components include fear of eye contact, concern about body odor, and easy blushing.[3] Figure 11–1 (Beardsley, 1994) shows how the emic components of a culture-bound syndrome relate to the etic aspects of the more

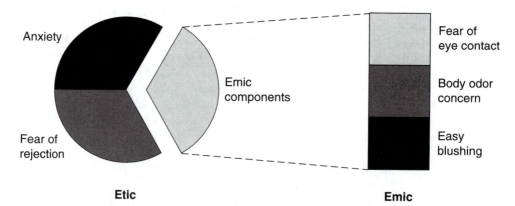

FIGURE 11–1   Etic and emic aspects of social phobias (as illustrated by Taijin-Kyofusho)

general condition of, in this case, social phobias. The percentages are meant to illustrate the relationship between emic and etic components of the condition and not to indicate the exact proportions of one component to another.

Cross-cultural validity is as important as that of diagnostic reliability. Even though clinicians from different cultures may agree about a diagnosis, it can still be wrong. The diagnosis must really be what it is judged to be; it must have construct validity. This is determined by observing the natural course of the condition and the effects of treatment over time. For example, it has been argued that episodic heavy alcohol consumption by American Indians is not alcoholism. However, Westermeyer and Peake (1983) found higher mortality from alcohol-related causes and deteriorated health and social status in those who continued to drink heavily in a ten-year follow-up study of 45 American Indians. Those who had abstained for three to ten years improved in health and/or social status. This is the same pattern as for alcoholics in the general U.S. population, supporting the cross-cultural validity of an initial diagnosis of alcoholism in this sample.

What about the construct validity of psychological correlates of alcoholism in a wine-drinking culture? In France, Weill and Le Bourhis (1994) identified psychological and behavioral predictors of future drinking behavior in a five-year prospective study of French teenage males. They found that the males who in 1985 were more dissatisfied with life and were unconstrained and pessimistic were the heaviest drinkers in 1990. Those who were "docile, contented, religious" and well aware of the dangers of alcohol consumption in 1985 drank the least in 1990. They also went out less, smoked less, and drank less coffee than did the heaviest drinkers.

Both reliability and validity are needed for an accurate, culture-centered diagnosis. To increase reliability, Lonner and Ibrahim (1989) conclude that an accurate assessment should (1) take into consideration the client's world view, beliefs, values, and culturally unique assumptions, (2) incorporate culture-specific, norm grouping criteria, and (3) be related to a combination of approaches and standardized or objective measures appropriate to the client. It is also important to validate that the construct really is what it is thought to be. The natural course of the disease or the result of treatment is usually the final judge in cross-cultural construct validity of physical and mental health diagnoses.

Consequences of Misdiagnosis

The consequences of a misdiagnosis can be serious and costly. The patient may receive painful, useless, or expensive tests and treatments without any relief from what is really causing the illness. In summarizing the controversy that surrounds educational placement in U.S. public schools, Trent and Artiles (1995) note that historically "minority and poor children were disproportionately placed into special education programs—particularly programs for children with mental retardation" (p. 215). In other cases, social controls, such as psychiatric institutionalization, were imposed because it was deemed that the person was of danger to self or others. Altshuler and colleagues (1988) found that Chinese psychiatrists were more likely to hospitalize manic but not depressed patients, concluding that this was probably because a nonsuicidal, withdrawn person is well-tolerated by the family and society in Chinese culture but not in American culture. In one study of the reliability of diagnoses, 109 Cuban refugees to the United States appealed the psychiatric diagnoses of an initial review in the United States that barred them from entry and led to institutionalization or incarceration while awaiting being sent back to Cuba (Boxer & Garvey, 1985). The second medical board that reviewed the cases overturned 43 percent of the exclusionary certifications. The most common diagnosis that was overturned was that of antisocial personality disorder. The majority (72%) of the 54 diagnoses of schizophrenic disorders, organic mental disorders, mental retardation, and psychoses were upheld.

Why were the diagnoses of antisocial personality disorder overturned so frequently? One reason is that the diagnosis was made on what the person chose to tell the physician about past behavior. Information from medical or prison records, family members, friends, or employers still in Cuba was unavailable. Another cause of variability is that a technicality in the immigration law allowed someone with adult antisocial behavior to immigrate but excluded someone who had evidenced antisocial behavior before the age of 15. Such information is difficult to obtain for refugees. Another problem is that "antisocial behavior" is also in part culturally defined and environmentally determined. Such behavior may be the "street smarts" necessary for survival by someone growing up in a rough and deprived social context. "Even our definitions of health and pathology can be culture-bound, especially in the area of mental health. Thus what constitutes healthy human development may also vary according to the sociocultural context" (Kagitçibasi, 1988, p. 25). A rater bias toward greater leniency on the part of the second medical board that reviewed the Cuban refugees reflects sensitivity to the cultural issues in psychopathology.

Group differences have been found in the diagnosis of and clinical treatment of patients. For example, Saikh (1985) found that the behavior of Asian patients was interpreted as more bizarre than that of indigenous (English) psychiatric patients in England. Consequently, more Asian than English patients were diagnosed with schizophrenia. Along with the diagnostic label of schizophrenia, this sample of Asian patients also received more electro-convulsive or "shock" therapy.

Being a member of the majority group does not prevent one from becoming a victim of misdiagnoses. The table is turned when the physician is culturally different and is an international medical graduate. Even though medical training may have been completed in the host country, these physicians still bring with them some of their own cultural assumptions. Language difficulties increase the potential for misunderstanding and a feeling by the patient that the physician is too different to be trusted. This can have negative effects on patient compliance with treatment and satisfaction with the care provided by the physician.

Implications of Culture for Counseling

The psychological study of cultures often assumed that there was a fixed state of mind whose observation was obscured by cultural distortions. The underlying assumption is that there exists a single universal definition of normal behavior. A contrasting anthropological position assumed that cultural differences were clues to divergent attitudes, values, or perspectives that differentiated one culture from another, based on a culture-specific viewpoint. The anthropological perspective assumed that different groups or individuals had somewhat different definitions of normal behavior as a result of their own unique cultural contexts. Anthropologists have tended to take a relativist position when classifying and interpreting behavior across cultures. Psychologists, by contrast, have linked social characteristics and psychological phenomena with minimum attention to the different cultural viewpoints. When counseling psychologists have applied the same interpretation to the same behavior regardless of the cultural context, cultural bias has resulted (Pedersen, Draguns, Lonner, & Trimble, 1996).

"Person-centered" approaches wrongly assume that individuals decide and function independently from their culturally defined perception of reality. "Problem-centered" approaches sometimes presume that if external problems can be solved the intervention is successful, without regard for the necessity that "apparent problems" may fulfill in a culturally-defined context. For example, in a six-country study of chronic low back pain, Sanders et al. (1992) found that patients in the United States reported the most dysfunction (psychosocial, behavioral, vocational, and avocational). Patients in Mexico and New Zealand reported the least amount of functional impairment. Back pain patients in all six countries (Japan, Mexico, Columbia, Italy, New Zealand, and the United States), however, had more functional impairment than did controls, verifying reliability of the diagnoses. The researchers interpreted the greater amount of dysfunction reported by patients in the U.S. as a function of financial gains, (disability insurance payments), availability of health care, and greater lenience in social expectations, attitudes toward, and political protection for those who are disabled in general.

As counseling interventions have become more implemented around the world, each cultural context has also become more broadly defined. "Situation-centered" approaches sometimes explain the world through transactions or interactions of collectivities without regard for an individual's cultural identity aside from any "particular" cultural context. The culture-centered approach to interventions, however, is directly focused on the culturally learned assumptions that control behavior in each cultural context (Pedersen & Ivey, 1993). In it, the centrality of culture is unambiguously highlighted. The consequences of this broad and inclusive definition of terms is to fundamentally change the function of cultural and cross-cultural perspectives of traditional counseling interventions. A broad and inclusive definition of interventions includes both the educational and the medical model to accommodate the diversity of culturally different consumer populations. The task is to match aspects of each cultural context with significant and salient antecedents to achieve appropriate outcomes in a purposive way. This is a complicated process. According to the "educational model" the consumer is typically regarded as an essentially healthy, normal person with a serious problem. The provider's task is to "teach" the client ways of dealing with the problem and the consumer's task is to "learn" new strategies. Just as all counseling interventions are to some extent educative, so educational change also has a therapeutic dimension to it. In many non-Western cultures the "teacher" is expected to guide persons toward appropriate personal growth goals. Seeking help from a mental health specialist for a "mental" problem in these cultures almost certainly reduces that person's status in the community. However, a teacher can provide almost the same functions of guidance and learning in ways that will enhance one's status.

In many cultures the client may seek help from "intra-psychic resources" within the person, using "self-righting mechanisms" such as natural support systems. These endogenous resources are frequently overlooked as one of the treatment modes available. In many cultures conditions of stress lead to a mobilization of these self-healing modes that might result in altered states of consciousness as in dreams, dissociated states, religious experiences, or even what appears to be psychotic reactions. Torrey (1986) cites numerous examples where self-righting approaches have been mobilized by healers and through spirits. Prince (1976, 1980; Valla & Prince, 1989) describes the role of endorphins as a physiologically endogenous resource that can be mobilized without bringing in outside mental health experts.

The psychological study of altered states of consciousness has been suppressed by a behavioral bias against internal, intangible, inaccessible mental states that do not lend themselves to experimental research (Ward, 1989). In recent years the medical model is being challenged by psychosocial approaches, and Valla and Prince (1989) demonstrate, for example, how religious experiences can provide self-healing mechanisms that change the physiological as well as the psychological states. Katz (1993) describes the Fijian "straight path" as a healing tradition emphasizing the spiritual dimensions of health and their relevance to the community through healing through a way of "honorable living."

Counseling and therapy have a history of protecting the status quo against change, as perceived by minority cultures (i.e., racial minorities, women, and those without power). These attitudes are documented in "scientific racism" and "Euro-American ethnocentrism" (Pedersen, Fukuyama, & Heath, 1989). Cultural differences were explained by some via a "genetic deficiency" model that promoted the superiority of dominant cultures. This was matched to a "cultural deficit" model that described minorities as deprived or disadvantaged by their culture. Minorities in the United States were under-represented among professional counselors and therapists, the topic of culture was trivialized at professional meetings, minority views were underrepresented in the research literature, and, consequently, the counseling profession was discredited among minority populations because they viewed it as a tool to maintain differences between those who have power and access to resources and those who do not.

With this historical backdrop, the culture-centered counselor too often has to choose between following professional ethical guidelines or acting in an ethical manner (Casas & Thompson, 1991; Pedersen, in press). All professional counselor associations with ethical guidelines emphasize the ethical responsibility of counselors to know their client's cultural values before delivering a mental health service to those clients, but professional guidelines continue to support the perspective of a dominant culture (Pedersen, 1994), sometimes requiring the counselor to demonstrate "responsible disobedience" (Pedersen & Marsella, 1982) to the formal ethical guidelines.

The American Psychological Association (APA, 1992) *Ethical Guidelines* provide numerous examples of how cultural biases are implicit within the principles themselves (Pedersen, 1994; Pedersen, in press). The APA (1992) *Ethical Standards* are even more blatant in their cultural bias beginning with Standard 1.08. It presumes that differences of age, gender, race, ethnicity, national origin, religion, sexual orientation, disability, language and socioeconomic status are not usually significant in all psychological interventions! The presumption of generalized and abstract standards or guidelines for ethical behavior is that all counselors of goodwill share the same cultural assumptions. Seeking safety in abstractions has allowed the individual provider to project her or his own self-referenced cultural assumptions into the professional guidelines at the expense of culturally-different clients.

Pathologizing mystical experiences would be an example of Western models going beyond their boundaries in some cultures. Can optional outcomes of counseling be identified that would be more inclusive and culturally sensitive? Walsh (1989) describes the relationship between Asian and Western psychologies as complementary to one another. Asian and Western psychologies both focus on development with the Asian systems focused on advanced stages of development in a more "transpersonal" focus and well-being while Western systems focus on psychopathology and physical/mental development. Accurate and appropriate cultural awareness is the foundation for culture-centered intervention. Those who have developed an appropriate awareness will know what facts they need and will be motivated to gather that information before proceeding with their intervention. This second step of gathering knowledge and developing an informed comprehension is the homework a culture-centered counselor must complete before an intervention. Without an appropriate foundation of awareness, the facts and information gathered will have no meaning (Sue, Arredondo, & McDavis, 1992). Having mastered these competencies of knowledge can help the counselor be more accurate and competent with each client regardless of that client's cultural background. Through training the culture-centered counselor is able to manage more complexity, send and receive verbal and nonverbal messages more accurately, and perceive each client from the viewpoint of the client's cultural context.

Psychological factors that are the products of socialization within any given culture and that affect the diagnoses a clinician makes are of particular interest because culturally-based psychological factors affect perceptions and the attributions used to explain those observations. The culture-centered health professional is aware of personal assumptions and can use a knowledge of the culturally-related expectations of the client for therapeutic benefit. For example, one of the four value dimensions along which Hofstede (1980) found countries to differ is power distance. In Japan where there is high power distance, patients are more likely to be compliant with physician directives than in a country with low power distance. Although the health professional from an individualistic culture may feel uncomfortable with a non-egalitarian hierarchy, the potential benefits of assuming the culturally-ascribed role should outweigh personal discomfort. In this volume, Tanaka-Matsumi and Draguns discuss in more detail relationships involving culture and psychopathology and related diagnostic problems. Elsewhere, Draguns (1990) identifies specific techniques for the psychotherapist who crosses cultures. Critical incidents that illustrate differences in role expectations, social hierarchies, and other common culture-general areas of conflict and how they can affect day-to-day interactions are available for training purposes (Cushner & Brislin, 1995). By defining interventions broadly according to their helping functions, a more inclusive framework is developed that reflects the cultural diversity and complexity of each client's context in a global context. By enlarging our repertoire of culture-centered intervention resources we become better able to match the right method and context.

Toward Theory Building

Culture is complex, but it is not chaotic. There are patterns that make it possible to manage the complexity. This inclusive definition of culture has been addressed by a "theory of complexity." Complexity theory in the social sciences (Waldrop, 1992) grew out of chaos theory in the physical sciences. Seeking to redefine conventional categories, proponents in this movement "believe that they are forging the first rigorous alternative to the kind of linear, reductionistic thinking that has dominated science since the time of Newton—and that has now gone about as far as it can go in addressing the problems of our modern world." (p. 13). The concepts of chaos, nonlinear dynamics, and self-organization (Barton, 1994) have been gaining the attention of psychologists from a wide variety of areas (Abraham & Gilgen, 1995) and comprise a promising movement in counseling and cross-cultural psychology. When chaos theory was originally conceived to describe weather forecasting (Geleick, 1987), it described chaotic systems as unpredictable locally. But when viewed globally or over long periods of time they were essentially stable. Butz (1992a, 1993) applies this metaphor to the experience of anxiety in psychotherapy and systems theories of family therapy. The new paradigm emphasizes convergence of hard and soft sciences toward complexity rather than simplicity, subjectivity rather than objectivity, constructivist rather than "discovered" reality, and a contextual rather than abstract description of human behavior.

Ideas from nonlinear dynamics have been applied to Jungian therapy (Abraham, Abraham, & Shaw, 1990; Butz, 1992a; Eenwyk, 1991), psychoanalysis

(Langs, 1992), posttraumatic stress (Glover, 1992), psychic development and individual psychopathology (Guidano, 1991), family systems (Elkaim, 1981), multiple personality disorders (Putnam, 1988, 1989), schizophrenia (Schmid, 1991), and psychiatric disorders (Sabelli, Carlson-Sabelli, & Javaid, 1990). Chaos is the starting point for most psychotherapies where the therapist becomes the companion to guide clients through their apparent chaos. Western cultures have tended to disregard or resolve chaos and thus lack conceptual tools for dealing with this level of complexity.

The functional precursors of mental health services have been documented in a wide variety of cultures, although usually not differentiated as a separate specialty. The labels of counseling, therapy, and human services are relatively new, but the functions described by those labels have a long history going back to the beginning of recorded social relationships. We know (1) that formal counseling and therapy has spread with the worldwide rise of urbanization and industrialization, (2) that "talk therapy" is only one alternative counseling intervention, (3) that counseling is the treatment of choice for a relatively small number of people worldwide, and (4) that counseling and therapy are becoming more responsive to people worldwide (Lefley & Pedersen, 1986).

How to reconceptualize counseling in light of distinguishing features of cultures such as individualism or collectivism is another area for theory building. A "Westernized" description of the self presumes a separate independent and autonomous individual guided by traits, abilities, values, and motives that distinguish that individual from others. (See chapter by Kagitçibasi, this volume). Western cultures are described by Triandis (1988) as more "individualistic," emphasizing competition, self-confidence, and freedom whereas "collectivistic" emphasize communal responsibility, social usefulness, and acceptance of authority. The Westernized perspective has traditionally defined the optional outcomes of counseling and problems stemming from Westernized versus non-Westernized thinking are most vivid in majority/minority culture relationships. The two large-scale multicenter, longitudinal studies sponsored by the WHO found significantly better outcomes for schizophrenia in non-Western countries compared to Europe and North America (Linn & Kleinman, 1988; see also chapter by Tanaka-Matsumi & Draguns, this volume). More work opportunities, and a greater tolerance of (and more social support for) the mentally ill by family members and the community in non-Western countries are mediating factors that have been thought to contribute to these better outcomes. In this case, collectivism emphasizes other goals for therapy, the perception of illness, its social meaning, and rehabilitation outcomes.

What other progress can we anticipate in theory building? Berry (1995) recently developed a model for cross-cultural health psychology, in which categories of health phenomena are analyzed by levels, macro (community/cultural) or micro (individual/psychological). Such theory development is a promising indicator of progress and is anticipated to provide direction for future cross-cultural health research. The publication of several new volumes (Kavanagh & Kennedy, 1992; Paniagua, 1994; Ridley, 1995; Padilla, 1995) indicates that theory is being informed more by an understanding of culturally-different clients and that theoretical structures are being extrapolated from examples of success with culturally-different populations. It will be important to remember that the counseling audience of the future is a global population and that solutions to problems of culture-centered counseling will need to draw from all cultures. By moving from practice to theory in the field of counseling we can become responsive to cultural similarities and differences in each cultural context. By making culture central to the intervention, we have attempted to demonstrate the ways that culture can improve the quality of counseling and the effectiveness of counselors. Attempts to disregard the cultural context, on the other hand, will lead health professionals toward abstract projections of their own self-referenced criteria and the fatal illusion of a monocultural future.

Conclusions

What have we learned from cross-cultural studies of health that we would not have otherwise known? They have helped unravel the threads that weave patterns we recognize as disease. They have helped identify significant risk factors of disease and explain why some benefit from treatment more than do others. Monocultural studies of disease are, by their very nature, limited in their generalizability to other settings and groups of people. Cross-cultural studies have helped to identify disease risk factors so significant that they could be considered to be culture-general. They have also identified significant risk factors that are amplified or, in some cases, mitigated through culture. In the Framingham Heart Study, cigarette smoking was a risk factor for heart disease in Massachusetts and Honolulu but not in Puerto Rico. In the Adventist Health Study, two nonsmoking groups were compared and the Adventist group had lower lung cancer rates. The benefits of not smoking were magnified by consumption of fruit in the diet—a strong and significant protective factor that was independent of smoking. Just as the presence of multiple risk factors increases the risk of developing disease, likewise the presence of multiple health behaviors increases the likelihood of good health and helps explain why some cigarette smokers live long, healthy lives and why others who never smoke develop heart disease. In this case, eating a healthy diet increased the protection afforded by not smoking.

Mixed reports on which behaviors are healthy and which are unhealthy are perplexing. What can be made of popular reports that drinking red wine helps prevent heart disease? The Honolulu Heart Study and the Adventist Health Study are explanatory here. Researchers in both studies found moderate alcohol consumption to be protective against developing heart disease. But the Honolulu Heart Study also found alcohol consumption to be positively correlated with hemorrhagic stroke. The primary risk factors are the same for both of these vascular diseases: hypertension, high serum cholesterol, diabetes, and smoking. The tentative answer to this puzzle is that even moderate alcohol consumption is not without some risk.

It makes sense to target those behaviors that pose greatest risk so consensus about which risk factors are the most serious is important to achieve. The North Karelia Project is a good model of this. By targeting and reducing primary risk factors (uncontrolled hypertension, smoking, high dietary intake of saturated fat), marked success was achieved in a short time period. The WHO-coordinated Onchocerciasis Control Program provides another dramatic example of the success that can be achieved through a rational, systematic, and focused approach to health promotion.

Cross-cultural studies also clarify the interaction among genetics, the environment, and lifestyle behaviors. Beyond that, they help us understand those risk factors that are most likely to predispose one to developing disease. It was noted that some significant risk factors are unmodifiable, such as age, race, and gender. Others, such as diet and hypertension, however, have been modified with demonstrated success (e.g., in the North Karelia Project) and for this reason it is particularly important to understand the behavioral components of CHD, cancer, AIDS, and other diseases that cause premature death and preventable suffering. Cross-cultural studies illuminate factors that increase vulnerability to disease—psychological and social factors that lower the immune response. Findings from AIDS-related research and the Adventist Health Study show that social support boosts immunity and is associated with health. Feelings of isolation and depression, on the other hand, suppress the immune system. Intravenous drug users are at risk for contracting the HIV-virus through cross-contamination when sharing needles. But at least in animal models (yet to be cross-culturally demonstrated!), cocaine and THC also increase susceptibility to disease by suppressing the immune system. Cross-cultural studies help physicians, counselors, and other health care providers to better understand patients' compliance with treatment and how values may reduce or enhance compliance with treatment plans. The Adventist Health Study indicates that when health is highly valued, individuals are more likely to seek treatment early and to comply with treatment when disease is diagnosed. Research also demonstrates that physiological differences in the way medication is metabolized by Blacks versus Whites makes it more difficult for Black patients to tolerate the standard treatment for malaria. In this light, compliance is seen to be part motivation, and part physiological tolerance for treatment.

Findings from cross-cultural research are an important part of the medical and epidemiological literature because they confirm and, in some cases, clarify confusing observations limited to specific populations. Together with the main body of medical literature, cross-cultural studies of health provide direction for macro level disease prevention and health promotion efforts. At the micro-level, the findings enable health practitioners to better serve their patients and clients. They distill the experiences of others so that those who are studying to be health practitioners are more informed and better skilled than if they relied on personal experience alone. Valuable lessons are also to be learned from projects that faltered after initial success were achieved. For long-term health promotion to succeed, educational efforts must continue. Health maintenance systems must be established, accessible, and culturally appropriate.

There is also an important effect of culture in making a medical diagnosis. Misdiagnosis may be the result of using different systems that classify diseases or simply from cross-cultural differences in the perception, attribution, and expression of signs and symptoms of disease. The confounding effects of emic and etic aspects of illness and the existence of culture-specific syndromes add more complexity to the clinical picture. For these reasons, in this chapter we have emphasized the importance of training culture-centered health professionals. By defining interventions broadly according to their helping functions, a more inclusive framework is promoted, one that reflects the cultural diversity and complexity of each client. By enlarging our repertoire of culture-centered intervention resources we become better able to match the right method and context to client needs. The more skilled the physician, nurse practitioner, psychologist, counselor, or other health professional is at gathering and applying this information, the more likely it is that they will provide medically sound, culturally appropriate, timely, and efficacious care.

Endnotes

1. Neither are factors associated with environmental-occupational diseases or the delivery and use of health services discussed. These are important related areas but are beyond the scope of this chapter.

2. See the *DSM-IV Case Book* for a description of a typical case of neurasthenia (Spitzer, Gibbon, Skodol, Williams, & First, 1994).

3. The *DSM-IV Case Book* (Spitzer et al., 1994) and Takano (1977) provide case studies of anthropophobia.

References

Abbott, R. D., Donahue, R. P., MacMahon, S. W., Reed, D. M., & Yano, K. (1987). Diabetes and the risk of stroke: The Honolulu Heart Program. *Journal of the American Heart Association, 257,* 949–952.

Abbott, R. D., Yin, Y., Reed, D. M., & Yano, K. (1986). Risk of stroke in male cigarette smokers. *New England Journal of Medicine, 315,* 717–720.

Abraham, F. D., Abraham, R. H., & Shaw, C. D. (1990). *A visual introduction to dynamical systems theory for psychology.* Santa Cruz: Aerial.

Abraham, F. D. & Gilgen, A. R. (Eds.). (1995). *Chaos theory in psychology.* Westport, CT: Praeger.

Altshuler, L. L., Wang, X., Qi, H., Hua, Q., Wang, W. & Xia, M. (1988). Who seeks mental health care in China? Diagnoses of Chinese outpatients according to DSM-III-R criteria and the Chinese Classification System. *American Journal of Psychiatry, 145,* 872– 875.

American Psychological Association. (1992). Ethical principles of psychologists and code of conduct. *American Psychologist, 47,* 1597–1611.

American Psychiatric Association. (1994). *Diagnostic and statistical manual of mental disorders,* 4th ed. Washington, DC: American Psychiatric Association.

American Public Health Association. (1985). *Control of communicable disease in man,* 14th ed. Washington, DC: American Public Health Association.

Asawalam, B., Osifo, G., & Haller, L. (1993). Drugs

against chloroquine antimalarial itch. *Journal of the European Academy of Dermatology and Venereology, 2,* 193–99.

Banks, C. G. (1992). "Culture" in culture-bound syndromes: The case of anorexia nervosa. *Social Science and Medicine, 34,* 867–884.

Barton, S. (1994). Chaos, self-organization and psychology. *American Psychologist, 49,* 5–14.

Beardsley, L. M. (1994). Medical diagnosis and treatment across cultures. In W. J. Lonner & R. S. Malpass (Eds.), *Psychology and culture* (pp. 279–284). Boston: Allyn and Bacon.

Benfante, R. (1992). Studies of cardiovascular disease and cause-specific mortality trends in Japanese-American men living in Hawaii and risk factor comparisons with other Japanese populations in the Pacific region: A review. *Human Biology, 64,* 791–805.

Benfante, R., Reed, D., & Brody, J. (1985). Biological and social predictors of health in an aging cohort. *Journal of Chronic Disease, 38,* 385–395.

Berkel, J, & deWaard, F. (1983). Mortality pattern and life expectancy of Seventh-day Adventists in the Netherlands. *International Journal of Epidemiology, 12,* 455–459.

Berry, J. W. (1995). Culture and ethnic factors in health. In R. West (Ed), *Cambridge handbook of psychology, health and medicine* (pp. 84–96). New York: Cambridge University Press.

Berry, J. W., Poortinga, Y. H., Segall, M. H., & Dasen, P. J. (1992). Cross-cultural psychology: *Research and applications.* Cambridge: Cambridge University Press.

Boxer, P. A. & Garvey, J. T. (1985). Psychiatric diagnoses of Cuban refugees in the United States: Findings of medical review boards. *American Journal of Psychiatry, 1421,* 86–89.

Brislin, R. W. (1980). Cross-cultural research methods: Strategies, problems, applications. In I. Altman, A. Rapoport, & J. W. Wohlwill (Eds.), *Human behavior and environment* (Vol. 4) (pp. 47–82). New York: Plenum.

Butz, M. R. (1992a). Chaos: An omen of transcendence in the psychotherapeutic process. *Psychological Reports, 71,* 827–843.

Butz, M. R. (1992b). The factual nature of the development of the self. *Psychological Reports, 71,* 1043–1063.

Butz, M. R. (1993). Systemic family therapy and

symbolic chaos. *Humanity and Society, 17,* 200–223.

Casas, J. M. & Thompson, C. E. (1991). Ethical principles and standards: The racial ethnic minority perspective. *Counseling and Values, 35,* 186–195.

Centers for Disease Control. (1981a). Kaposi's sarcoma and pneumocystis pneumonia among homosexual men—New York and California. *MMWR, 30,* 305.

Centers for Disease Control. (1981b). Pneumocystis pneumonia—Los Angeles. *MMWR, 30,* 250.

Centers for Disease Control. (1994). Update: Dracunculiasis, Eradication—Ghana and Nigeria, 1993. *MMWR, 43,* 293–294.

Centers for Disease Control. (1995). Update: Acquired immunodeficiency syndrome—United States, 1994. *MMWR, 44,* 64–67.

Cohen, J. B., Syme, S. L., Jenkins, C. D., Kagan, A., & Zyzanski, S. J. (1979). Cultural context of Type A behavior and risk for CHD: A study of Japanese American males. *Journal of Behavioral Medicine, 2,* 375–384.

Cohen, S. I. (1988). Voodoo death, the stress response, and AIDS. In T. P. Bridge & A. F. Mirsky (Eds.), *Psychological, neuropsychiatric, and substance abuse aspects of AIDS: Advances in biochemical psychopharmacology* (Vol. 44, pp. 95–110). New York: Raven.

Cotran, R. S., Kumar, V., & Robbins, S. L. (1994). *Robbins pathologic basis of disease,* 5th ed. Philadelphia: W.B. Saunders.

Cushner, K. & Brislin, R. W. (1995). *Intercultural interactions: A practical guide,* 2d ed. Thousand Oaks, CA: Sage.

Dana, R. H. (1993). *Multicultural assessment perspectives for professional psychology.* Boston: Allyn and Bacon.

Dayan, J. (1994). *Health beliefs, health behaviors, health status, and coping among Orthodox, Conservative, and Reform Jews.* Unpublished Masters Thesis, Psychology Department, Queen's University.

Donahue, R. P., Abbott, R. D., Reed, D. M., & Yano, K. (1986). Alcohol and hemorrhagic stroke: The Honolulu Heart Program. *Journal of the American Medical Association, 255,* 2311–2314.

Donahue, R. P., Abbott, R. D., Reed, D. M., & Yano,

K. (1988). Physical activity and coronary heart disease in middle-aged and elderly men: The Honolulu Heart Program. *American Journal of Public Health, 78,* 683–685.

Draguns, J. (1990). Applications of cross-cultural psychology in the field of mental health. In R. W. Brislin (Ed.), *Applied cross-cultural psychology* (pp. 302–324). Newbury Park, CA: Sage.

Eenwyk, J. R. (1991). Archetypes: The strange attractors of the psyche. *Journal of Analytical Psychology, 36* 1–25.

Elkaim, M. (1981). Non-equilibrium, chance and change in family therapy. *Journal of Marital and Family Therapy, 7,* 291–297.

Escobar, J. I. (1987). Cross-cultural aspects of the somatization trait. *Hospital Community Psychiatry, 38,* 174–180.

Escobar, J. I. (1993). Psychiatric epidemiology. In A. C. Gaw (Ed.), *Culture, ethnicity and mental illness* (pp. 43–73). Washington, DC: American Psychiatric Press.

Flaherty, J. H., Gaviria, F. M., Pathak, D., Mitchell, T. M., Wintrob, R., Richman, J. A., & Birz, S. (1988). Developing instruments for cross-cultural psychiatric research. *Journal of Nervous and Mental Disease, 176,* 257–263.

Fønnebø, V. (1992a). Coronary risk factors in Norwegian Seventh-day Adventists: A study of 247 Seventh-day Adventists and matched controls. *American Journal of Epidemiology, 135,* 504–508.

Fønnebø, V. (1992b). Mortality in Norwegian Seventh-day Adventists 1962–1986. *Journal of Clinical Epidemiology, 45*(2), 157–167.

Fønnebø, V. (1994). The healthy Seventh-day Adventist lifestyle: What is the Norwegian experience? *American Journal of Clinical Nutrition, 59* (suppl.), 1124S–1129S.

Fønnebø, V. (1985). The Tromsö heart study: Coronary risk factors of Seventh-day Adventists. *American Journal of Epidemiology, 122,* 789–793.

Food and Drug Administration. (1994). *Code of federal regulations* (Vol. 21, Section 610.45). Washington, DC: U.S. Government Printing Office.

Fraser, G. E., Beeson, W. L., & Phillips, R. L. (1991). Diet and lung cancer in California Seventh-day Adventists. *American Journal of Epidemiology, 133,* 683–693.

Fraser, G. E., Haller-Wade, T. M., & Morrow, S. (1995). *Social support and traditional risk factors for coronary heart disease in middle-aged Seventh-day Adventist men and their neighbors.* Manuscript submitted for publication, Loma Linda University, Loma Linda, California.

Fraser, G. E., Strahan, T. M., Sabate, J., Beeson, W. L., & Kissinger, D. (1992). Effects of traditional coronary risk factors on rates of incident coronary events in a low-risk population: The Adventist Health Study. *Circulation, 86,* 406–413.

Friedman, H., Klein, T., Specter, S., Pross, S., Newton, C., Blanchard, D. K., & Wilden, R. (1988). Drugs of abuse and virus susceptibility. In T. P. Bridge & A. F. Mirsky (Eds.), *Psychological, neuropsychiatric, and substance abuse aspects of AIDS: Advances in biochemical psychopharmacology* (Vol. 44, pp. 125–137). New York: Raven.

Geleick, J. (1987). *Chaos making a new science.* New York: Viking-Penguin.

Giem, P., Beeson, W. L., & Fraser, G. E. (1993). The incidence of dementia and intake of animal products: Preliminary findings from the Adventist Health Study. *Neuroepidemiology, 12,* 28–36.

Gilligan, C. (1982). *In a different voice.* Cambridge, MA: Harvard University Press.

Gilligan, C. (1987). Moral orientation and moral development. In E. F. Kittay & D. T. Meyers (Eds.), *Women and moral theory* (pp. 19–33). Totowa, N J: Rowman & Littlefield.

Glaser, R. & Glaser-Kiecolt, J. (1988). Stress-associated immune suppression and acquired immune deficiency syndrome (AIDS). In T. P. Bridge & A. F. Mirsky (Eds.), *Psychological, neuropsychiatric, and substance abuse aspects of AIDS: Advances in biochemical psychopharmacology* (Vol. 44, pp. 203–215). New York: Raven.

Glover, H. (1992). Emotional numbing: A possible endorphin-mediated phenomenon associated with post-traumatic stress disorders and other allied psychopathological states. *Journal of Traumatic Stress, 5,* 643–675.

Gordon, T., Garcia-Palmieri, M. R., Kagan, A., Kannel, W. B., & Schiffman, J. (1974). Differences in coronary heart disease in Framingham, Honolulu, and Puerto Rico. *Journal of Chronic Disease, 27,* 329–344.

Guidano, V. R. (1991). *The self in process.* New York: Guilford.

Harkness, S., Wyon, J. B., & Super, C. M. (1988). The relevance of behavioral sciences to disease prevention and control in developing countries. In P. R. Dasen, J. W. Berry, & N. Sartorius (Eds.), *Health in cross-cultural psychology: Toward applications* (pp. 241–255). Newbury Park, CA: Sage

Hofstede, G. (1980). *Culture's consequences: International differences in work-related values.* London: Sage.

House, J. S., Landis, K. R., & Umberson, D. (1988). Social relationships and health. *Science, 241,* 540–45.

Hunter, J. M. (1966). River blindness in Nangodi, Northern Ghana: A hypothesis of cyclical advance and retreat. *The Geographical Review, 56,* 398–416.

Hunter, J. M. (1980). Strategies for the control of river blindness. In M. Meade (Ed.), *Conceptual and methodological issues in medical geography* (pp. 38–76). Chapel Hill: University of North Carolina.

Ilola, L. M. (1990). Culture and health. In R. W. Brislin (Ed.), *Applied cross-cultural psychology* (pp. 278-301). Newbury Park, CA: Sage.

Irvine, S. H. & Berry, J. W. (1983). *Human assessment and cultural factors.* New York: Plenum Press.

Kagan, A., Marmot, M. B., & Kato, H. (1980). The Ni-Hon-San Study of cardiovascular disease epidemiology. In N. H. Kesteloot & J. V.Joossens (Eds.), *Epidemiology of arterial blood pressure* (pp. 423–426). The Hague: Nijhoff.

Kagan, A., Popper, J. S., Rhoads, G. G., & Yano, K. (1985). Dietary and other risk factors for stroke in Hawaii–Japanese men. *Stroke, 16,* 390–396.

Kagitçibasi, C. (1995). Is psychology relevant to global human development issues? Experience from Turkey. *American Psychologist, 50,* 293–300.

Kagitçibasi, C. (1988). Diversity of socialization and social change. In P. Dasen, J. Berry, & N. Sartorius (Eds.), *Health and cross-cultural psychology: Towards applications* (pp. 25–47). Newbury Park, CA: Sage.

Kato, H. Tillotson, J., Nickaman, M. Z., Rhoads, G. G., & Hamilton, H. D. (1973). Epidemiological studies of coronary heart disease and stroke in Japanese men living in Japan, Hawaii, and California. *American Journal of Epidemiology, 97,* 376–384.

Katz, R. (1993). *The straight path: A story of healing and transformation in Fiji.* Reading, MA: Addison- Wesley.

Kavanagh, K. H. & Kennedy, P. H. (1992). *Promoting cultural diversity.* Newbury Park, CA: Sage.

Klein, T. W., Newton, C. A., & Friedman, H. (1988). Suppression of human and mouse lymphocyte proliferation by cocaine. In T. P. Bridge & A. F. Mirsky (Eds.), *Psychological, neuropsychiatric, and substance abuse aspects of AIDS: Advances in biochemical psychopharmacology* (Vol. 44, pp. 139–143). New York: Raven.

Kleinman, A. M. (1986). *Social origins of distress and disease: Depression, neurasthenia, and pain in modern China.* New Haven: Yale University Press.

Knutsen, S. F. (1994). Lifestyle and the use of health services. *American Journal of Clinical Nutrition, 59* (suppl.), 1171S–1175S.

Langs, R. (1992). Towards building psychoanalytically based mathematical models of psychotherapeutic paradigms. In R. L. Levine & H. E. Fitzgerald (Eds.), *Analysis of dynamic psychological systems* (Vol. 2, pp. 371–393). New York: Plenum.

Lefley, H. & Pedersen, P. (Eds.). (1986). *Cross-cultural training for mental health professionals.* Springfield, IL: Thomas.

Levine, R. V. & Bartlett, K. (1984). Pace of life, punctuality, and coronary heart disease in six countries. *Journal of Cross-Cultural Psychology, 15,* 233–255.

Levy, S. M. (1988). Behavioral risk factors and host vulnerability. In T. P. Bridge & A. F. Mirsky (Eds.), *Psychological, neuropsychiatric, and substance abuse aspects of AIDS: Advances in biochemical psychopharmacology* (Vol. 44, pp. 225–239). New York: Raven.

Lichton, I. J., Bullard, L. R., & Sherrell, B. U. (1983). A conspectus of research on nutritional status in Hawaii and Western Samoa 1960–1980 with references to diseases in which diet has been implicated. *World Review of Nutrition and Dietetics, 41,* 40–75.

Linn, K. & Kleinman, A. M. (1988). Psychopathology and clinical course of schizophrenia: A cross-cultural perspective. *Schizophrenia Bulletin, 144,* 550–557.

Lonner, W. (1990). An overview of cross-cultural testing and assessment. In R. W. Brislin (Ed.), *Applied cross-cultural psychology* (pp. 56–76). Newbury Park, CA: Sage.

Lonner, W. J. & Ibrahim, F. A. (1989). Assessment in cross-cultural counseling. In P. Pedersen, J. Draguns, W. Lonner, & J. Trimble (Eds.), *Counseling across cultures,* 3d ed. (pp. 229–334). Honolulu: University of Hawaii Press.

Melby, C. L., Goldflies, D. G., & Toohey, M. L. (1993). Blood pressure differences in older Black and White long-term vegetarians and nonvegetarians. *Journal of the American College of Nutrition, 2,* 262–269.

Miller, A. B. (1982). Risk factors from geographic epidemiology for gastrointestinal cancer. *Cancer, 50,* 2533–2540.

Mills, P. K., Beeson, W. L, Abbey, D. E., Fraser, G. E., & Phillips, R. L. (1988). Dietary habits in past medical history as related to fatal pancreas cancer risk among Adventists. *Cancer, 61,* 2578–2585.

Mills, P. K., Beeson, W. L., Phillips, R. L., & Fraser, G. E. (1994). Cancer incidence among California Seventh-day Adventists, 1976–1982. *American Journal of Clinical Nutrition, 59* (suppl.), 1136S–1142S.

National Center for Health Statistics. (1994). *Annual summary of births, marriages, divorces, and deaths: United States, 1993* (Monthly vital statistics report, Vol. 42(13), pp. 18–20). Hyattsville, MD: U.S. Dept. of Health and Human Services, Public Health Service.

Nissinen, A., Tuomilehto, J., & Puska, P. (1989). From pilot project to national implementation: Experiences from the North Karelia Project. *Scandinavian Journal of Primary Health Care 1,* 49–56.

Okasha, A. & Seif el Dawla, A. (1992). Reliability of ICD-10 research criteria: An Arab perspective. *Acta Psychiatrica Scandinavica, 86,* 484–8.

Osifo, N. G. (1989). Mechanisms of enhanced pruritogenicity of chloroquine among patients with malaria: A review. *African Journal of Medical Science, 18,* 121–129.

Padilla, A. M. (Ed.). (1995). *Hispanic psychology: Critical issues in theory and research.* Thousand Oaks, CA: Sage.

Paniagua, F. A. (1994). *Assessing and treating culturally diverse clients: A practical guide.* Thousand Oaks, CA: Sage.

Pedersen, P. (1994). *A handbook for developing multicultural awareness.* Alexandria, VA: American Counseling Association.

Pedersen, P. (In press). *The ethical dilemma of a multicultural counselor.* New York: Directions in Mental Health Counseling, National Program of Continuing Education and Certification Maintenance.

Pedersen, P., Draguns, J., Lonner, W. J., & Trimble, J. (1996). *Counseling across cultures,* 4th ed. Thousand Oaks, CA: Sage.

Pedersen, P., Fukuyama, M. A., & Heath, A. (1989). Client, counselor and contextual variables in multicultural counseling. In P. Pedersen, J. Draguns, W. Lonner, & J. Trimble (Eds.), *Counseling across cultures,* 3d ed. (23–53). Honolulu: University of Hawaii Press.

Pedersen, P. & Ivey, A. E. (1993). *Culture-centered counseling and interviewing skills.* Westport, CT: Greenwood/Praeger.

Pedersen, P. & Marsella, A. C. (1982). The ethical crisis for cross-cultural counseling and therapy. *Professional Psychology, 13,* 492–500.

Phillips, R. L., Kuzma, J. W., Beeson, W. L., & Lotz, T. (1980). Influence of selection versus lifestyle on risk of fatal cancer and cardiovascular disease among Seventh-day Adventists. *American Journal Epidemiology, 112,* 296–314.

Prince, R. H. (1976). Psychotherapy as the manipulation of endogenous healing mechanism: A transcultural survey. *Transcultural Psychiatric Research Review, 13,* 155–233.

Prince, R. H. (1980). Variations in psychotherapeutic experience. In H. C. Triandis & J. G. Draguns (Eds.), *Handbook of cross-cultural psychology* (Vol. 6, pp. 291–349). Boston: Allyn and Bacon.

Putnam, F. (1988). The switch process in multiple personality disorder and other state-change disorders. *Dissociation, I,* 24–32.

Putnam, F. (1989). *Diagnosis and treatment of multiple personality disorder.* New York: Guilford.

Reed, D., McGee, D. Cohen, J., Yano, K., Syme, S.

L., & Feinleib, M. (1982). Acculturation and coronary heart disease among Japanese men in Hawaii. *American Journal of Epidemiology, 115,* 894–905.

Reynolds, P. & Kaplan, G. A. (1990). Social connections and risk for cancer: Prospective evidence from the Alameda County Study. *Behavioral Medicine, 16,* 101–110.

Ridley, C. R. (1995). *Overcoming unintentional racism in counseling and therapy: A practitioner's guide to intentional intervention.* Thousand Oaks, CA: Sage.

Rubinow, D. R., Joffe, R. T., Brouwers, P., Squillace, K., Lane, H. C., & Mirsky, A. F. (1988). Neuropsychiatric impairment in patients with AIDS. In T. P. Bridge & A. F. Mirsky (Eds.), *Psychological, neuropsychiatric, and substance abuse aspects of AIDS: Advances in biochemical psychopharmacology* (Vol. 44, pp. 111–116). New York: Raven.

Sabelli, H. C., Carlson-Sabelli, L., & Javaid, J. I. (1990). The thermodynamics of bipolarity: A bifurcation model of bipolar illness and bipolar character and its psychotherapeutic publications. *Psychiatry, 53,* 346–368.

Saikh, A. (1985). Cross-cultural comparison: Psychiatric admission of Asian and indigenous patients in Leicestershire. *International Journal of Social Psychiatry, 31,* 3–11.

Sanders, S. H., Brena, S. F., Spier, C. J., Beltrutti, D., McConnell, H., & Quintero, O. (1992). Chronic low-back pain patients around the world: Cross-cultural similarities and differences. *Clinical Journal of Pain, 8,* 317–323.

Schmid, G. B. (1991). Chaos theory and schizophrenia: Elementary aspects. *Psychopathology, 24,* 185–198.

Segall, M. H., Dasen, P. R., Berry, J. W., & Poortinga, Y. H. (1990). *Human behavior in global perspective: An introduction to cross-cultural psychology.* New York: Pergamon.

Sheikh, A. & Sheikh, K. S. (1989). *Eastern and Western approaches to healing: Ancient wisdom and modern knowledge.* New York: Wiley.

Silver, H. (1987). Physical complaints are part of the core depressive syndrome: Evidence from a cross-cultural study in Israel. *Journal of Clinical Psychiatry, 48,* 140–142.

Simons, L., Gibson, J., Jones, A., & Bain, D. (1979).

Health status of Seventh-day Adventists. *Medical Journal of Australia, 2,* 148.

Spitzer, R. L., Gibbon, M., Skodol, A. E., Williams, J. B., First, M. B. (Eds.). (1994). *DSM-IV casebook.* Washington, DC: American Psychiatric Press.

Stemmermann, G. N., Hayashi, T., Resch, J. A., Chung, C. S., Reed, D. M., & Rhoads, G. G. (1984). Risk factors related to ischemic and hemorrhagic cerebrovascular disease at autopsy: The Honolulu Heart Study. *Stroke, 15,* 23–28.

Stolley, P. D., & Lasky, T. (1995). *Investigating disease patterns: The science of epidemiology.* New York: Freeman.

Sue, D. W., Arredondo, P., & McDavis, R. J. (1992). Multicultural counseling competencies and standards: A call to the profession. *Journal of Counseling and Development, 70,* 477–486.

Sumbureru, D. (1990). The influence of lifestyle on longevity among Black Seventh-day Adventists in California: An epidemiologic approach. (Doctoral dissertation, Department of Epidemiology, Loma Linda University, 1988). *Dissertation Abstracts International, 51*(1-B), 165–166.

Takano, R. (1977). Anthropophobia and Japanese performance. *Psychiatry, 40,* 259–269.

Temoshok, L. (1988). Psychoimmunology and AIDS. In T. P. Bridge & A. F. Mirsky (Eds.), *Psychological, neuropsychiatric, and substance abuse aspects of AIDS: Advances in biochemical psychopharmacology* (Vol. 44, pp. 241–247). New York: Raven.

Tillotson, J. L., Kato, H., Nickaman, M. Z., Miller, D. C., Gay, M. L., Johnson, K. G., & Rhoads, G. G. (1973). Epidemiology of coronary heart disease and stroke in Japanese men living in Japan, Hawaii, and California: Methodology for comparison of diet. *American Journal of Clinical Nutrition, 26,* 177–184.

Torrey, E. F. (1986). *Witchdoctors and psychiatrists: The common roots of psychotherapy and its future.* New York: Harper & Row.

Trent, S. C. & Artiles, A. J. (1995). Serving culturally diverse students with emotional or behavioral disorders: Broadening current perspectives. In J. M. Kauffman, J. W. Lloyd, D. P. Hallahan, & T. A. Astuto (Eds.), *Issues in edu-*

cational placement: Students with emotional and behavioral disorders* (pp. 215–249). Hillsdale, NJ: Lawrence Erlbaum.

Triandis, H. C. (1988). Collectivism vs individualism: A reconceptualization of a basic concept in cross-cultural social psychology. In C. Bagley & G. K. Verma (Eds.), *Personality, cognition and values* (pp. 60–95). London: Macmillan.

Tuomilehto, J., Geboers, J., Salonen, J. T., Nissinen, A., Kuulasmaa, K., & Puska, P. (1986). Decline in cardiovascular mortality in North Karelia and other parts of Finland. *British Medical Journal, 293,* 1068–1071.

Tuomilehto, J., Piha, T., Nissinen, A., Geboers, J., & Puska, P. (1989). Trends in stroke mortality and in antihypertensive treatment in Finland from 1972 to 1984 with special reference to North Karelia. *Journal of Human Hypertension, 1,* 201–208.

Valla, J. P. & Prince, R. H. (1989). Religious experiences as self-healing mechanisms. In C. Ward (Ed.), *Altered states of consciousness and mental health* (pp. 149-166). Newbury Park, CA: Sage.

Ward, C. (Ed.). (1989). *Altered stages of consciousness and mental health.* Newbury Park, CA: Sage.

Waldrop, M. M. (1992). *Complexity: The emerging science at the edge of order and chaos.* New York: Touchstone.

Walsh, R. (1989). Toward a synthesis of Eastern and Western psychologies. In A. A. Sheikh & K. S. Sheikh (Eds.), *Eastern and Western approaches to healing* (pp. 542–555). New York: Wiley.

Webster, I. W. & Rawson, G. K. (1979). Health status of Seventh-day Adventists. *Medical Journal of Australia, 1,* 417–420.

Westermeyer, J. & Peake, E. (1983). A ten-year follow up of alcoholic Native Americans in Min-

nesota. *American Journal of Psychiatry, 140,* 189–194.

Weill, J. & Le Bourhis, B. (1994). Factors predictive of alcohol consumption in a representative sample of French male teenagers: A five-year prospective study. *Drug and Alcohol Dependence, 35,* 45–50.

Woodside, D. B. (1993). Genetic contributions to eating disorders. In A. S. Kaplan & P. E. Garfinkel (Eds.), *Medical issues and the eating disorders: The interface* (pp. 193–212). New York: Brunner/Mazel.

World Health Organization. (1985). *International nomenclature of diseases: Infectious diseases,* Vol. 2. Geneva: WHO.

World Health Organization. (1987). *World health statistics manual, 19.* Geneva: WHO.

World Health Organization. (1992). *The international classification of disease and related health problems,* 10th rev. Geneva: WHO.

World Health Organization. (1993). *World health statistics annual: 1992.* Geneva: WHO.

Worth, R. M., Kato, H., Rhoads, G. G., Kagan, A., & Syme, S. L. (1975). Epidemiological studies of coronary heart disease and stroke in Japanese men living in Japan, Hawaii and California: Mortality. *American Journal of Epidemiology, 102,* 481–490.

Yano, K., McLean, C. J., Reed, D. M., Shimizu, Y., Sasaki, H., Kodama, K., Kato, H., & Kagan, A. (1988). A comparison of the twelve year mortality and predictive factors of coronary heart disease among Japanese men in Japan and Hawaii. *American Journal of Epidemiology, 127,* 476–487.

Zollinger, T. W., Phillips, R. L., & Kuzma, J. W. (1984). Breast cancer survival rates among Seventh-day Adventist and non–Seventh-day Adventist. *American Journal of Epidemiology, 119,* 503–509.

12

CULTURE AND PSYCHOPATHOLOGY

JUNKO-TANAKA-MATSUMI
Hofstra University
United States

JURIS G. DRAGUNS
Pennsylvania State University
United States

Contents

Introduction

This chapter appraises the current state of knowledge on the relationship between culture and psychopathology, following earlier reviews in the first edition of the *Handbook* by Draguns (1980), Guthrie and Tanco (1980), Marsella (1980), Sanua (1980), and Tseng and Hsu (1980). This chapter emphasizes recent developments and findings from a variety of perspectives.

Formulations on the interplay of abnormal behavior and culture are rooted in one of the three general orientations that have been described as absolutist, universalist, and relativist, (Berry, Poortinga, Segall, & Dasen, 1992). Of these three positions, the absolutist, which posits invariance of psychopathological phenomena across cultures, remains only a "logical possibility" (Berry et al., 1992, p. 358). Virtually all writers on the subject are in agreement that culture exerts some degree of influence upon psychopathological processes and manifestations. As to the extent of this influence, estimates vary from trivial and superficial (e.g., Berne, 1959; Vyncke, 1958) to pervasive and fundamental (e.g., Marsella, 1980, 1994). Evidence produced shows that even organically based mental disorders exhibit the effect of their place and time (Pfeiffer, 1994). Draguns (1980) concluded that "no disorder has been found to be immune to cultural shaping" (p.155). Therefore, this chapter includes information based on the remaining two conceptual options, the universalist and the relativist. As Berry et al. (1992) noted, these two viewpoints overlap greatly with the etic and emic positions (Berry, 1969). In relation to psychopathology, the etic or universalist view emphasizes comparability of cross-culturally or even globally applicable dimensions or categories. Frequently, but not always, these categories are equated with the major entries of the Western Kraepelinian diagnostic system. Emic or culturally relativist investigators eschew comparison and categorization and caution against the dangers of the "category fallacy" (Kleinman, 1977). Instead, they focus on the context of a phenomenon within a culture and prize the ability to investigate and comprehend such a phenomenon within the culture's frame of reference (Draguns, 1996a).

In addition to these two "pure" and opposite orientations, there is a hybrid position rooted not in conceptual distinction, but in practical and clinical realities. In pluralistic nations, such as Australia, Canada, Singapore, the United States, and many others, members of diverse ethnic groups live side by side, but develop adaptive and maladaptive reactions based on their cultural and social experience (see chapter by Berry & Sam, this volume). Increasingly, a similar situation is observed in many formerly homogeneous cultures in Europe and elsewhere, as exemplified by France, Germany, and Great Britain. Many of these countries have experienced a major influx of migrants and sojourners. Faced with the imperative of developing effective interventions, researchers and clinicians have typically opted for an amalgam of etic and emic, culturally universal, and relative features. It is therefore more expedient to group these reports from multicultural milieus separately on the basis of the setting and topic rather than their abstract conceptual orientation. Therefore, the balance of the chapter will consist of universalist, relativist, and multicultural sections. We will also examine the relation of the "individualism–collectivism" dimensions to culture and psychopathology. Finally, therapeutic systems will be briefly reviewed and cultural accommodation in the development of services will be introduced. Readers of this chapter will find related matters in this *Handbook* volume by Kagitçibasi on individualism–collectivism, Berry and Sam on acculturation; Best and Williams on sex differences, and Beardsley and Pedersen on culturally sensitive counseling techniques.

The Universalist Approach: Substantive Findings

Biomedical Models and Standardization of Diagnosis across Cultures

Current editions of the International Classification of Disorders (ICD-10; World Health Organization [WHO], 1992) and DSM-IV (American Psychiatric Association [APA], 1994) have promoted the use of standardized diagnostic systems around the world (Mezzich, Fabrega, Mezzich, & Goffman, 1985). The neo-Kraepelinian approach that has guided the development of these manuals emphasizes diagnosis based upon explicit criteria in order to establish reliability and consensual validity. The principal criteria for inclusion of a behavior pattern in DSM-IV are *distress* and *disability*. In addition to these two hallmarks, the current definition of mental disorder also posits "increased risk of suffering death, pain, disability, or an important loss of freedom" (APA, 1994, p. xxi). By restricting mental disorder to those dysfunctions that primarily occur within the individual, these inclusion criteria attempt to differentiate mental disorder from social deviance.

To increase the cross-cultural applicability of DSM-IV, its authors have taken three new steps: (1) presentation of information in the text regarding cultural variations in the clinical manifestations of the disorders, (2) a description of 25 culture-bound syndromes in an appendix, and (3) an outline of cultural formulation for the evaluation of the individual's cultural context. This latter was designed to provide a review of the individual's cultural background, cultural explanations of the individual's illness (e.g., cultural idioms of distress), cultural factors related to the psychosocial environment and levels of functioning, cultural elements of the relationship between the individual and the clinician, and the overall cultural assessment necessary for diagnosis and care.

These modifications hold the promise of contributing toward a culturally more sensitive, reliable, and informative diagnosis of the individual. However, the cross-cultural applicability of DSM-IV remains to be tested. As yet, DSM-IV does not allow for the recognition of indigenous, within-culture distinctions that traditional healers take into account when they choose among alternative intervention strategies (Eisenbruch, 1992).

Beyond the culture-specific critiques of DSM-IV, some generic diagnostic problems remain to be addressed: What are the defining criteria of normal and abnormal functioning of the individual in different cultural contexts, and how does the diagnostician recognize whether a behavior disorder is clinically significant within the unique cultural context of the individual? DSM-IV does not provide a generic set of decision rules to be applied across all of the diagnostic categories. Thus, the authors of DSM-IV explicitly recognize that cross-cultural diagnostic decisions will continue to be based on clinical judgment.

DSM-IV may not, in fact, provide a universal diagnostic framework that may be used across diverse cultures. Everything known about the cross-cultural manifestation of most psychological disturbances strongly suggests not (Draguns, 1986, 1996a). The publication of standardized diagnostic instruments has, however, dramatically altered the nature of cross-cultural research by attempting to use the same criteria for abnormality and collecting comparable data in different cultures.

International and Cross-Cultural Studies

Affective Disorders
In his review of depression and culture, Marsella (1980) concluded that "depression does not assume a universal form" (p. 260) and stated that "the psychological representation of depression occurring in the Western world is often absent in non-Western societies" (p. 261). WHO (1983) conducted an international project on the diagnosis and classification of depression in Switzerland, Canada, Japan, and Iran. WHO's goal was to test the feasibility of using standardized instruments. Patients ($N = 573$) were diagnosed using the Schedule for Standardized Assessment of Depressive Disorders (WHO/SADD) by project psychiatrists. The WHO/SADD examines 39 symptoms of depression. Its overall reliability was .96, with no specific item reliability falling below .90.

WHO (1983) found that more than 76 percent of the depressed patients reported core depressive symptoms that included "sadness, joylessness, anxiety, tension, lack of energy, loss of interest, loss of ability to concentrate, and ideas of insufficiency" (p. 61). Suicidal ideation was present in 59 percent of patients. The WHO project also discovered cross-cultural variation in the expression of depression. Specifically, 40 percent of patients displayed "other symptoms," such as somatic complaints and obsessions, that were not part of the original 39 symptoms of depression measured by the WHO/SADD. Variations existed both within and across cultures. For example, in Japan, more depressed patients in Nagasaki displayed core symptoms than patients in Tokyo. Marsella, Sartorius, Jablensky, and Fenton (1985) interpreted these findings as a strong demonstration of cultural factors.

Guilt was defined in the SADD as "painful awareness of having committed offenses against one's moral code, or having failed to perform a duty or a task" (WHO, 1983, p. 137). In the WHO project, guilt feelings were elicited according to semi-structured interviews and not necessarily expressed spontaneously by patients. Interviewers used specific probe questions concerning religious, social, and familial duties. The WHO results attenuate the implications of previous studies that found an absence of guilt in many non-Western depressed patients (e.g., Singer, 1975). Murphy (1982a) and Jackson (1986) both observe that personal guilt is historically associated with the development of individualism in the Judeo-Christian tradition in the West. In fact, in the WHO study, guilt was expressed less frequently by depressed patients in Iran (32 percent) and Japan (48 percent in Tokyo; 41 percent in Nagasaki) than those in Canada (58 percent) and Switzerland (68 percent). That in itself may be a substantive finding rather than a methodological artifact. Reports from several East Asian and South Asian cultures converge in suggesting that guilt is differently experienced, conceptualized, and communicated in these settings than in the West (Kimura, 1967; Pfeiffer, 1994; Sethi, Prakash, & Aurora, 1980; Rao, 1973, 1984; Yap, 1971). The WHO results suggest that, rather than being absent in depression, guilt may be overshadowed by more obtrusive, often psychophysiological features, and thus less prominent.

It should be kept in mind that the WHO research included no samples from Africa. However, Orley and Wing (1979) developed the Luganda version of the Present State Examination (PSE) and conducted an epidemiological survey in two villages in the East Mengo District in Uganda. One striking and unexpected finding of this study was the high frequency of depressive disorders for both Ugandan men (14.3 percent) and women (22.6 percent). Moreover, "pathological guilt" was reported by 71 percent of male and 83 percent of female Ugandan subjects with depressive disorders. German (1987) stated that "current workers are unanimous in agreeing that depressive illness, psychotic or otherwise, is common in Africa" (p. 441).

Orley and Wing's (1979) findings of the high prevalence of guilt stand in contrast to the virtual consensus of the earlier investigators of depression in Francophone Africa who found an underemphasis on guilt in the symptomatology of their clients (e.g., Collignon, 1978; Collignon & Gueye, 1995; Diop, 1967; Zeldine et al., 1975). Is the Luganda culture, which is located in an Anglophone country, atypical in this respect, have Orley and Wing's procedures been more effective in eliciting guilt, or is the picture of depression changing in Africa (Prince, 1968)? Draguns (1995, 1996a) and Tanaka-Matsumi (1992, 1995) have proposed that expression and communication of depressive experiences and other related negative affective states is a subtle and complex process. These formulations posit the interviewer's empathy, the social distance between the client and the interviewer, and the existence and nature of stereotypes as important determinants of the degree and nature of self-reported information obtained in depression. Future studies should incorporate these variables into formal research designs and also note their observable effect in clinical interview settings.

Ulusahin, Basoglu, and Paykel (1994) conducted a cross-cultural study of depressive symptoms in British and Turkish outpatients. Patients were selected according to the Research Diagnostic Criteria and interviewed using the Clinical Interview for Depression (CID; Paykel, 1985) and the Hamilton Depression Rating Scale (Hamilton, 1967). The results showed that depressed British and Turkish patients shared core depressive symptoms. However, the Turkish patients had higher scores for somatic complaints (e.g., somatic anxiety, hypochondriasis, insomnia), while the British patients had higher scores for core psychological complaints (e.g., guilt, pessimism, depressed mood). Guilt feelings were frequent among both British and Turkish patients.

In recent Chinese epidemiological studies, the prevalence of depressive disorders was consistently lower in Hong Kong and Taiwan than in Western nations. In a comparative epidemiologic study, Compton et al. (1991) conducted a *post-hoc* analysis of the data from the Taiwan Psychiatric Epidemiological Project and found that the prevalence of depression, as measured by the DSM-III Diagnostic Interview Schedule (DIS: Robins, Helzer, Croughan, & Ratcliff, 1981), was lower in Taiwan than in the United States. Perceptive and sophisticated discussions of the reasons for the low incidence of depression in Chinese culture have been presented by Lin (1985) and Tseng, Lin, and Yee (1995); these authors emphasize how the traditional communal orientation of the Chinese both alleviates the impact of object loss and provides strong social support in the wake of losses and disappointments.

Nakane et al. (1991) reported that 20 to 30 percent of first-contact psychiatric patients were diagnosed with depression in Shanghai, Seoul, and Nagasaki. Woo et al. (1994) found that 41 percent of elderly men and 29 percent of women living in Hong Kong met the depression criteria on the Chinese version of the Geriatric Depression Scale (GDS). Subjects with high GDS scores had more somatic symptoms, such as headaches, dizziness, stomach pain, and joint pains, and their high depression scores were associated with poor social networks.

Nakane et al. (1988) examined diagnostic practices for depressive disorders in Asia. Using ICD-9 and DSM-III, psychiatrists in Shanghai, Seoul, and Nagasaki evaluated videotaped patients from three centers with "typical depression, atypical depression, or depression as a comorbid condition." The raters tended to diagnose the Japanese cases as affective psychosis, while they diagnosed the Chinese cases as neurotic disorder. The Korean cases were evenly distributed between diagnoses of an affective psychosis and neurotic disorder. These results show that, across the three centers in Asia, clinicians differ significantly in the pattern of symptoms to which they assign the diagnostic category "depression."

International and cross-cultural studies of depression that employed standardized instruments suggest that: (1) universal core symptoms of depression include dysphoria, anxiety, tension, lack of energy, and ideas of insufficiency, (2) more patients from Western countries express guilt feelings spontaneously than do non-Western patients, (3) beyond core symptoms, there are cultural variations in the expression of depression, and (4) diagnostic practices may in part explain the low reported prevalence of depression, particularly in Asian countries.

Suicide

Suicide is a leading cause of death in young people. As such, it has been a prominent topic of cross-cultural investigations (Jilek-Aal, 1988). Based on the 10 volumes of the WHO Annual (WHO, 1973–1985), Barraclough (1988) analyzed international variation in the suicide rate of 15 to 24 year olds. Great cross-national variation was observed in youth suicide, with regard to rate, sex ratio, and trend over time. Arabic states (Egypt, Jordan, Kuwait, and Syria) have low rates, as do many of the Latin states, excepting El Salvador, Surinam, and Cuba. Scandinavian, Central and Eastern European states, and some Asian states (Japan, Singapore, Sri Lanka) have higher suicide rates. Except in Cuba, Paraguay, Thailand, and Martinique, there is a higher suicide rate for males. For both males and females, Sri Lanka has the highest youth suicide rate.

Despite the cross-national variability in youth suicide, its causes remain elusive. Jilek-Aal (1988) suggests that weakening of family structure, religious values, child rearing practice, increased drinking, and cultural value judgments about suicidal behavior are contributing factors in youth suicide. In the United States, interpersonal problems are prominent among young suicidal individuals. They report feeling depressed, hopeless, socially isolated, and view death as escape (Lester, 1988). Paris (1991) also notes an increase in youth parasuicidal behavior. Parasuicidal behavior is associated with the spread of drug abuse, a breakdown of societal norms, and severe family pathology. Paris argues that many parasuicidal individuals meet current Western criteria (DSM) for borderline personality.

In addition to the youth suicide, international and cross-cultural suicidology has addressed several important issues. The world's highest reported suicide rates, in Sri Lanka (47 per 100,000) and Hungary (38.6 per 100,000) (Desjarlais, Eisenberg, Good, & Kleinman, 1995), have attracted a lot of attention. In the case of Sri Lanka, high suicide rates have been explained *post hoc* on the basis of endemic group violence (Silva, in press). In reference to Hungary, retrospective explanations have capitalized on intrafamily and socialization processes that exercise a push toward achievement and easily induce a sense of failure and guilt (Buda & Föredi, 1995). The relevance of political and macrosocial factors has also been explored. In Hungary, the population had to contend with an unpopular, externally imposed totalitarian regime that stifled hope and inhibited initiative (Varga & Katona, 1991). The influence of these factors upon the Hungarian suicide rate has not as yet been definitively established.

Suicide investigators have studied the gender ratio of suicide victims. In most countries, the adult suicide rate for men is at least as high as that of women. In Hong Kong, Taiwan, and China, this ratio approaches equality (Desjarlais et al., 1995; Draguns, 1996b; Peng & Tseng, 1992). In light of one recent statistical indicator (WHO, 1991), in China, women's suicide rates have been reported to be higher than men's. Moreover, gender ratios have also been found to be low in Japan, Singapore, India, and Thailand, though not in South Korea and Sri Lanka. Is this regional trend stable and significant? If so, what are its underpinnings? The problem obviously calls for concerted future investigation.

The relationship of diagnostic categories (e.g., depression) to suicide appears also to be cross-culturally variable. Pfeiffer (1994) reported a lesser relationship between suicidal ideation and depression in Indonesia than in Germany, although the likelihood of actual suicide attempts was equal in both countries. However, all of these impressions remain tentative.

Paris (1991) has suggested that attempted suicide rates fluctuate much more across space and time than do the rates for completed suicide. Therefore, variations in attempted suicide are potentially a more sensitive and relevant cultural indicator than the nationally and internationally reported statistics on completed suicides.

The relationship of suicide to social change and its pace and nature, to the experience of hope and hopelessness, and to the vicissitudes of destructiveness and aggression continue to be active subjects of cultural investigation (Desjarlais et al., 1995; Pfeiffer, 1994; Draguns, 1994). There is little support for the theory of an inverse compensatory relationship between suicide and homicide (Palmer, 1965; Pfeiffer, 1994). The connection between social change and suicide is complex; rapid social transformation has only sometimes produced increases in suicide rates (Desjarlais et al., 1995). Rapid social change does not inevitably breed alienation (Guthrie & Tanco, 1980), nor does migration predictably increase the incidence of mental disorder (Bemak, Chung, & Bornemann, 1996). The impact and meaning of social change remains to be studied, and hope and hopelessness need to be operationalized and incorporated into hypotheses and research designs.

Schizophrenia

In the last 25 years WHO has conducted three major studies on the course and outcome of schizophrenia at 20 research centers in 17 countries. Prominent features of the WHO schizophrenia program include: (1) simultaneous case finding and data collection, (2) standardized instruments, (3) trained project psychiatrists, (4) the combined clinical and computer-based reference categorization of the case, and (5) multiple follow-up assessments (Jablensky, 1989).

In the International Pilot Study of Schizophrenia (WHO, 1973) 1,202 patients were evaluated at nine centers in Africa (Nigeria), Asia (India, Taiwan), Europe (Czech Republic, Denmark, Russia, the United Kingdom), Latin America (Colombia), and North America (the United States). The purpose of the IPSS was to develop and test a standardized method of diagnosis using the Present State Examination (Wing, Cooper, & Sartorius, 1974). WHO (1973) reported universality in the core symptoms of schizophrenia. These symptoms included lack of insight, predelusional signs (such as delusional mood, ideas of reference, perplexity), flatness of affect, auditory hallucinations, and experiences of control.

In a two-year follow-up study (WHO, 1979) that investigated the course and outcome of schizophrenia, project psychiatrists interviewed 75.6 percent of the patients. Across most centers, the subjects lacked positive psychotic symptoms, such as delusions and hallucinations. However, they exhibited negative psychotic symptoms, such as flatness of affect, lack of insight, and difficulties in cooperation. The percentages of patients who showed negative psychotic symptoms varied across cultures (Katz et al., 1988). In Ibadan (Nigeria) 17.5 percent of patients showed lack of insight, with higher percentages of patients presenting this symptom in Aarhus (Denmark) (69.4%), Taipei (Taiwan) (59.0%), and Prague (Czech Republic) (50.9%). Acute undifferentiated and catatonic cases of schizophrenia were more prevalent in developing countries (Sartorius, Jablensky, Korten, & Ernberg, 1986).

The prognosis for schizophrenia was operationalized as the percentage of the follow-up period characterized by psychosis. Prognosis was better for patients in developing countries (Colombia, Nigeria, and India) than for those in developed countries (the United States, Great Britain, and Denmark). During the follow-up period, 48 percent of the subjects in Aarhus, 47 percent in Washington, and 36 percent in Prague were still psychotic more than 75 percent of the time. During this same period 7 and 19 percent of the subjects in Cali and Agra were judged to be psychotic.

In the developed countries the predictive power of the five best variables explained 24 to 30 percent of the variance on course and outcome measures. In the developing countries the best five predictors captured 13 to 21 percent of the variance. Social isolation and unmarried status were associated with a poor outcome in both developed and developing countries (WHO, 1979). High educational status was predictive of chronicity in non-Western and developing countries, but not in the West. Warner (1994) observes that in rural Agra, India, outcome for schizophrenia is worse among the better educated and attributes this to the greater labor market stresses affecting the educated in the Third World. Observing that schizophrenic disorders vary greatly in their course, Jablensky (1989) concluded on the basis of cross-cultural data that "schizophrenia is highly malleable by internalized or extrinsic environmental influences (or both)" (p. 521).

WHO has also conducted a *prospective* epidemiological study to compare the true prevalence of schizophrenia across cultures (Jablensky et al., 1992; Sartorius, Jablensky, Korten, & Ernberg, 1986). In this case-finding project, 1,379 subjects were evaluated at 12 centers in 10 countries: Aarhus (Denmark), Agra and Chandigarh (India), Cali (Colombia), Dublin (Ireland), Ibadan (Nigeria), Moscow (Russia), Nagasaki (Japan), Nottingham (UK), Prague (Czech Republic), and Honolulu and Rochester (U.S.). The project identified all individuals who contacted "helping agencies" for the first time over two consecutive years in specified geographical catchment areas. Identified subjects were then screened for symptoms of a functional psychosis. The helping agencies included indigenous healers and religious institutions. The incidence rates were found to be comparable in developed and developing countries. However, more patients in the developing countries had an acute onset of schizophrenia.

The second purpose of the WHO case-finding study was to investigate the role of stressful life events occurring two to three weeks preceding the development of schizophrenic episodes (Day et al., 1987). Six of the nine centers were similar in the mean number of stressful life events, which were coded into five categories (personal, livelihood, family/household, social network, and additional). The subjects in the three remaining centers (Agra, Chandigarrh, and Ibadan) reported lower rates of stressful events within these categories. These results suggest that specific events described by the subjects from developing countries may not be easily classified into predetermined categories. Cultural knowledge is necessary to identify unique stressors.

A considerable amount of literature exists on the association between stressful events and the onset of schizophrenic episodes. Murphy (1982b) focused on faulty information processing as a risk factor for developing schizophrenia. Faulty information processing develops through (1) mistraining in information processing, (2) the complexity of the information to which one is exposed, (3) the degree to which decisions are expected on the basis of complex or unclear information, and (4) the degree to which schizophrenia-bearing families are discouraged or encouraged to have children (Murphy, 1982b, p. 223). Murphy proposed that the noted high prevalence rate of schizophrenia among Irish Catholics and Irish immigrants in Canada was due to the complicated communication style of Irish people.

Although Sanua's review (1980) suggested that conflicts in the family could hasten a breakdown in vulnerable individuals, family research in schizophrenia has declined in prominence during the last two decades, both within and across cultures. The shift from a psychodynamic to a biological paradigm is probably responsible for this trend. Nonetheless, the recent model that capitalizes on the "embeddedness" of cultural influences within the family (Szapocznik & Kurtines, 1993) provides a wedge for a possible revival of family-oriented research on the prehistory of schizophrenia and other disorders. On the basis of their experience as family therapists with a multiethnic clientele, Tseng and Hsu (1991) assert that the major developmental transitions, for example, from infancy to childhood and from adolescence to adulthood, occur in all cultures. They differ across cultures, however, in their meaning, nature, impact, and other variables (Greenfield, 1994). Thus, culture would be expected to shape the adaptive and maladaptive consequences of these developmental marker experiences. Methodological critiques of the WHO schizophrenia project concern differences in access to hospitals across countries. Cohen (1992) attributes the differences in prognosis to differing rates of hospital contact rather than to illness. In Cohen's view, the greater proportion of acute cases in developing countries merely reflects differing access to modern psychiatric centers. Waxler-Morrison (1992), however, found that differential access could not account for prognostic findings in her five-year follow-up study of hospitalized schizophrenics in Sri Lanka (Waxler, 1979). Other researchers (Hopper, 1992; Sartorius, 1992; Warner, 1992) have pointed to the standardized procedures and exhaustive follow-up evaluation of the patients in the WHO study as safeguards against contamination by artifacts. Jablensky and Sartorius (1988) concluded that "the position of cultural relativism vis-a-vis the *identification* of schizophrenia in different populations finds little support" (p. 68).

Alcoholism
Although excessive alcohol use is observed across cultures, the differentiation of normal and abnormal drinking is extremely difficult especially when it is attempted on a cross-cultural basis. Across cultures the consequences of excessive alcohol use are highly variable (Murphy, 1992). They may or may not lead to serious social, legal, or medical problems. Developing universal criteria for alcoholism poses a challenge to cross-cultural researchers.

As a first step toward that goal, WHO began studying the concept of normal drinking through detailed interviews with local informants in the Cross-Cultural Applicability Research project (CAR) (Bennett, Janca, Grant, & Sartorius, 1993). CAR has gathered interview data from participants in nine cultures reflecting linguistic, religious, and geographic diversity. The results confirmed that the concept of "normal" drinking was subject to major cultural variation. For example, Navajos in Arizona (U.S.) and Indians in Bangalore (India) denied the very possibility of normal drinking. Spanish respondents in Santander and Greek respondents in Athens considered drinking as an essential part of their culture. No single, universal criterion consistently distinguished normal from abnormal drinking. The amount of alcohol consumed and the context in which consumption took place emerged as two reliable indicators across cultures.

Helzer and Canino (1992) conducted the largest international epidemiological study of alcoholism; it was based on 48,000 respondents in North America, Europe, and Asia. Researchers in different countries used the Diagnostic Interview Schedule (DIS), which was based on DSM-III, to diagnose alcoholism. They found that, in every culture investigated, men had higher rates of alcohol abuse/dependence than women. The prevalence of alcoholism was dramatically greater for men than women, particularly in Taiwan, China, and Korea.

In comparison with the United States (17.4%), lifetime prevalence of alcoholism was lower for Chinese in Taiwan (7.4%) and Hong Kong (3.3%), and lowest in Shanghai (0.45%) (Wang et al., 1992; Yeh & Hwu, 1992). Lin and Lin (1982) described the Chinese as a "low-risk population" for alcoholism because of the interdependent social and familial networks that regulate their behavior. Korea (22%), on the other hand, has one of the highest rates of alcohol consumption in the world (Lee, 1992; Lee et al., 1990). Although Korean culture also emphasizes interdependent and familial networks, Korean men have frequent opportunities to drink socially. The Korean public tolerates drunken behavior (Lee, 1992).

Canino, Burnam, and Caetano (1992) reported that alcohol abuse is related to the acculturation status of immigrants. Mexican Americans born in the United States (23%) are almost twice as likely to develop alcohol abuse/dependence problems than Mexican American (13%) and Puerto Rican (13%) immigrants. The drinking patterns of American-born Mexican Americans resemble those of non-Hispanic whites.

Anxiety Disorders

Draguns (1980), Marsella (1980), and Tseng and Hsu (1980) are in agreement that there is great cross-cultural variability for ambulatory anxiety disorders. However, there is ambiguity as to which disorders within this category deviate from normative behavior of the general population.

Tseng et al. (1990) investigated the symptomatology of patients with "neuroses, situational adjustment reaction or acute emotional reaction" (p. 252) at five research centers in Asia. The sites included Ching-Mai (Thailand), Bali (Indonesia), Kao-Hsiung (Taiwan), Shanghai (China), and Tokyo (Japan). The study assessed the similarities and differences between normal and clinical populations within the same culture and then compared their data across cultures. Symptom profiles of the patients in each city deviated from the profiles of the normal subjects toward exaggeration. In addition, there was cross-cultural variability across the five centers, together with a greater similarity between the groups in Taiwan and China than between any other centers.

Differences in diagnostic practices account in part for cross-cultural differences in reported symptoms of "neurosis." Tseng, Xu, Ebata, Hsu, and Cui (1986) had psychiatrists in Beijing, Tokyo, and Honolulu diagnose six videotaped Chinese patients undergoing a mental status examination. Psychiatrists from Beijing diagnosed them with neurasthenia when their colleagues in Tokyo and Honolulu diagnosed them with adjustment reactions. Tseng, Asai, Kitanishi, McLaughlin, and Kyomen (1992) also compared diagnostic judgments of Japanese psychiatrists in Tokyo and American psychiatrists in Honolulu. Patients with the project diagnosis of social phobia were presented on videotape. The diagnostic agreement of the Japanese psychiatrists was greater than that of the American psychiatrists for the Japanese cases of social phobia *(taijin kyofusho)*. The agreement rate of the Japanese psychiatrists for the two American cases was only 6.5 percent. Tseng's two international studies demonstrate that diagnostic practices contribute to cross-cultural variability in observed symptoms. For this reason, researchers endorse the use of a standardized diagnostic system to control for differences in diagnostic practice. To the extent that ambulatory psychiatric disorders reflect an exaggeration of a culture's baseline, however, standardization of diagnostic criteria may miss culturally unique deviations.

Weissman et al. (1994) compared the common data on obsessive-compulsive disorder (OCD) from common epidemiological studies published in the United States, Canada, Puerto Rico, Germany, Taiwan, Korea, and New Zealand. Each project had used identical OCD criteria based on the DIS. Except for Taiwan (0.7%), the rates of OCD in other nations fell between 1.9 and 2.5 percent. Across cultures, a large proportion of persons with the diagnosis of OCD also met the criteria for major depression and for other anxiety disorders.

Personality Disorders

The establishment of Axis II for personality disorders in DSM-III stimulated the development of a standardized procedure to diagnose personality disorders. A total of 716 patients from India, Switzerland, the Netherlands, England (two sites), Luxembourg, Germany, Kenya, the United States, Norway, Japan, and Austria were involved in the development of the International Personality Disorder Examination, which is a semi-structured interview designed to be compatible with ICD-10 and DSM-III-R (Loranger et al., 1994). The IPDE contains 157 items and uses a semi-structured interview format. The inter-rater reliabilities of the IPDE were .64 for current diagnosis and .68 for lifetime diagnosis. Loranget et al. (1994) concluded that cross-cultural application of the IPDE is feasible. Lewis-Fernandez and Kleinman (1994), however, point out that the very definition of personality disorder is culture-bound. They argue that conceptualizing personality without considering context disregards both the social origins of disorders and the norms for expected behaviors. Thus, personality disorders are construed as culture-bound disorders that can be diagnosed only against their culture's norms and limits of tolerance.

Childhood Disorders

There has been a steady increase in publications on the use of empirically based assessment systems. One controversy concerns the cross-cultural diagnosis of childhood hyperactivity as specified by different diagnostic manuals (Werry, 1985). Prendergast et al. (1988) examined variability in the diagnostic rate of hyperactivity in the United States and the United Kingdom. Case histories of 21 American and 20 British boys were evaluated by American and British research teams as well as American and British clinician panels using both ICD-9 and DSM-III. The results revealed (1) a higher rate of diagnosed hyperactivity in American than British children across rater nationalities and instruments, (2) strikingly higher diagnostic reliability of the research teams as compared with that of each clinical panel, and (3) an interactive influence of the diagnostic system used and clinician nationality on the rate of diagnosed hyperactivity. Clinicians of both nationalities generated more diagnoses of hyperactivity when using the DSM-III than when using the ICD-9, but the effect was larger for U.K. clinicians.

Mann et al. (1992) used a behavior checklist to examine cross-cultural differences in the disruptive behavior ratings of two Japanese and two American boys by mental health professionals ($N = 37$) from China, Indonesia, Japan, and the United States. Each child was videotaped alone and in a group. Overall, the country of residence of both the rater and child were associated with significant differences in ratings of disruptive behavior without any interaction effect of the two factors. Raters from China and Indonesia consistently rated the boys as more disruptive than did raters from Japan and the United States. In a study of videotaped parent–child interaction (Tseng, McDermott, Ogino, & Ebata, 1982), cross-cultural differences were observed between American and Japanese mental health professionals who viewed and rated six American children of different ethnic backgrounds and two Japanese children. The cultural background of the diagnosticians influenced their ratings of the presence or absence of target child behaviors as well as their intensities.

In sum, diagnosis of hyperactive and disruptive behaviors of children appears to be culturally variable as a function of the nationality of both the child and the diagnostician. Diagnostic reliability for childhood disorders using standardized instruments needs to be established across cultures.

The Childhood Behavior Checklist (CBCL) (Achenbach & Edelbrock, 1983) is an empirically-derived measure of childhood psychopathology that may be viewed as an alternative to syndromal diagnosis. The CBCL is designed to obtain standardized parent reports of children's competencies and behavioral and emotional problems. The CBCL also has the Teacher's Report Form (TRF) and Youth Self-Report (YSR). The CBCL is potentially useful in cross-cultural assessment for two reasons. First, the CBCL accommodates the possibility that informants' evaluations may differ depending on the context of the child's activities. Second, the CBCL defines childhood problem severity in terms of deviation from the normative performance of the population.

Achenbach and his colleagues demonstrated the feasibility of using the CBCL in a series of cross-cultural epidemiologic studies of childhood disorders. They have compared the CBCL profiles of American children with children in the Netherlands (Achenbach, Verhulst, Baron, & Akkerhuis, 1987; Achenbach, Verhulst, Edelbrock, Baron, & Akkerhuis, 1987), Puerto Rico (Achenbach, Bird, Canino,

Phares, Gould, & Rubio-Stipec, 1990), and Australia (Achenbach, Hensley, Phares, & Grayson, 1990), among others. The findings indicate that (1) parents and teachers of low SES children report more behavior problems and less competencies than those of upper SES children, (2) while total CBCL scores were cross-culturally comparable, differences in specific items were observed in every study, and (3) boys were reported to have more problems of undercontrol than girls.

Weisz (1989) developed a "problem suppression–facilitation" model of child psychopathology and culture. He hypothesized that cultural differences in values and socialization practices affect the incidence of certain child problems. Cultures have different thresholds for problem behaviors of children. In both Jamaica (Lambert et al., 1992) and Thailand (Weisz et al., 1987; Weisz, 1989) parents discourage "undercontrolled, acting out behavior" and encourage "politeness and respectfulness" in comparison with American parents. Overall, undercontrolled problems outnumbered overcontrolled problems among all three groups of children. Consistent with the conception of disorder as an exaggeration of normative behavior (Draguns, 1988, 1990a), both Jamaican and Thai children were predicted to score higher on items coded as "overcontrolled" (e.g., shyness, anxiety, depression) than American children. As hypothesized, Thai children scored higher on the overcontrolled dimension than American children on the CBCL as rated by parents. Similarly, Jamaican children were referred more frequently for problems of overcontrol than American children, and American children presented more frequently problems of undercontrol than Jamaican children.

The Cultural Relativist Approach: Substantive Findings

Emic Orientations

The development of "indigenous psychologies" has contributed to a diversity of views, particularly from Third World countries and has infused the emic approach with new vitality (Sinha, 1989; Kim & Berry, 1993). Emically-oriented investigators have studied psychopathology in relation to the sociocultural context (Fabrega, 1989a; Good, 1992; Kleinman, 1986, 1991; Littlewood, 1990; Marsella & White, 1982).

Kleinman's (1977) paper on the "category fallacy" marked the beginning of the "new cross-cultural psychiatry." Kleinman (1977, p. 4) stated that "psychiatric categories are bound to the context of professional psychiatric theory and practice in the West." Cross-cultural researchers commit "the most crucial error" when they impose illness categories of their own culture on deviant behavior patterns in other cultures. Emic researchers seek to investigate (1) the meanings of indigenous idioms of distress, (2) culture-specific classifications of disorders, (3) the role of culture in identifying and shaping the form and meaning of antecedent risk factors, and (4) attributions for consequences of illness (Marsella & Dash-Scheur, 1988; Weiss & Kleinman, 1988). In the last two decades, culture-oriented investigators have contributed numerous analyses of the cultural context of psychopathology. Such studies have addressed folk idioms of distress (Nichter, 1981), cultural conceptions of depression (Kleinman & Good, 1985; Marsella, 1980), anxiety (Good & Kleinman, 1985), ethnographic descriptions and folk models of "madness" in Black Africa (Patel, 1995; Sow, 1980), and many other issues. Some of these studies are reviewed in the ensuing sections.

Cultural Idioms of Distress

Cultural relativists are highly skeptical about the applicability of Western diagnostic criteria in other cultures (Hinton & Kleinman, 1993). Indigenous views and concepts of distress are considered fundamental to understanding the cultural context of illness behaviors (Angel & Thoits, 1987; Kirmayer, 1984). Culture-oriented researchers have intensively studied the question of how members of a culture express distress and understand meanings of idioms of distress (Nichter, 1981).

The Explanatory Model Interview Catalogue (EMIC) has been developed to identify culture-specific idioms of distress, perceived causes of illness, and help-seeking behavior (Weiss et al., 1992). The authors used the EMIC in a cultural study of leprosy and mental health in India. Reported interrater agreement of the EMIC items using kappa ranged from .62 to .90. Beliefs in magico-religious causation were as frequent as beliefs in infection/germs among leprosy patients. The EMIC responses were examined along with responses to the Structured Clinical Interview for DSM-III-R and the combined Hamilton Depression and Anxiety Rating Scale. Consistent with the hypothesized relationship between social stigma and distress, half of the leprosy patients met the criteria for depression, anxiety, or somatoform disorder, as compared with only 8 percent of patients with a similar but non-stigmatizing fungal infection. Investigating the EMIC's relationship to standardized diagnostic methods such as DSM-III-R promises to be an important area of cross-cultural validation.

Somatization, Neurasthenia, and Depression

The mind–body distinction and its relationship to the expression of distress have been investigated, with particular attention to Asian patients (Lin, 1989). The question concerns the cultural meaning of somatic complaints. As White (1982), Kirmayer (1984), and Kleinman (1986) point out, it may be ethnocentric to view bodily complaints as the simple result of a lack of "psychological mindedness" (Draguns, 1996a). Different cultures may selectively encourage or discourage the reporting of psychological or physiological components of the stress response.

Neurasthenia is a very common diagnosis in China. In China neurasthenia is called *shenjing shuairuo*, literally meaning neurological weakness. Symptoms of neurasthenia include bodily weakness, fatigue, tiredness, headaches, dizziness, and a range of gastrointestinal and other complaints (Kleinman & Kleinman, 1985). Kleinman (1980, 1982, 1986), with the assistance of a Chinese psychiatrist, interviewed 100 Chinese patients with the diagnosis of *shenjing shuairuo*. He used the

Chinese language version of the Schedule of Affective Disorders and Schizophrenia (SADS; Endicott & Spitzer, 1978) modified to yield DSM-III diagnoses. Kleinman reported that 93 neurasthenic patients met the criteria for depressive disorder, of whom 87 patients met the criteria for major depressive disorder. "Depressed" patients spontaneously complained of headaches (90%), insomnia (78%), dizziness (73%), pain (48%), and loss of or poor memory (43%), among others. However, when Kleinman specifically asked the patients about psychological and affective symptoms, they acknowledged dysphoric mood (100%), trouble concentrating (84%), anhedonia (61%), hopelessness (50%), and low self-esteem (60%).

Zhang (1989) investigated the "Western" diagnostic status of 40 Chinese patients diagnosed as neurasthenic by Chinese psychiatrists in Shanghai. Only 22.5 percent of the 40 cases met the ICD-9 definition of neurasthenia. Lacking the category of neurasthenia, the PSE/CATEGO program classified 55 percent of the cases as depressive neurosis. When the DSM-III was used, a total of 80 percent of the 40 cases of neurasthenia were diagnosed as anxiety (60%) or depressive (20%) disorders. Using the DIS, a structured interview format of the DSM-III, a total of 70 percent of the 40 cases were classified as major depression episodes or bipolar affective disorder, but only 5 percent were diagnosed as anxiety disorder. Thus, the "Western" diagnostic status of Chinese-diagnosed neurasthenia varies with the particular Western-derived standardized instruments are employed.

From an emic standpoint, the discrepancy between *spontaneous* expression of somatic complaints and *elicited* symptoms (e.g., dysphoria) suggests that cultural meanings of symptoms are altered by interpretations based upon Western-derived standardized instruments and imposed criteria. Elicited symptoms may not conform to culturally accepted ways of expressing distress. Somatic complaints are less stigmatized among Chinese and somatization justifies an acceptable medical intervention. Chinese in Hong Kong, Taiwan, and China do not readily recognize psychological symptoms as problems that justify seeking help in a medical setting (Cheung, 1989). The setting (e.g., general medical versus psychiatric clinic) and problem conceptualization influence reasons given for help-seeking and reported symptoms (Cheung, 1986; Cheung, Lee, & Chan, 1983).

Critics (e.g., Young, 1989) of Kleinman's biopsychosocial model of neurasthenia as depression contend that neurasthenia is a distinctive disorder that should not be confused with the imposed diagnosis of depression. In other words, somatic complaints are not the equivalent of "somatization." In fact, Kawanishi (1992) argues that the so-called somatization of Asians is an artifact of ethnocentric bias due to Western medicalization of distress. Tung (1994) studied subjective meanings of body-related verbal expressions in Chinese by asking Chinese informants to interpret the meanings of 182 body-related verbal expressions selected from Chinese literary works. Tung found that the meaning of the body *(shen ti)* is equivalent to that of the self or the person. Heart *(xin)* shares meaning with affective states and emotions. Tung (1994) concluded that Chinese body-related words are "idioms of human conditions," so that "to treat these expressions as merely 'somatizing' what should be 'psychological' is both misleading and too limited in scope" (p. 489). Ots (1990) was able to link liver with anger, heart with anxiety, and spleen with depression in a large scale study of hospitalized patients in Nanjing. Somatization no more signifies a lack of "psychological mindedness" in Chinese, than does psychologization represent a lack of somatic awareness in Western cultures.

Somatization is prevalent in Saudi Arabia, Iraq, African nations, India, Japan, the Philippines, Taiwan, Hong Kong, Iran, and Turkey (German, 1987; Odejide, Oyewunmi, & Ohaeri, 1989; Kleinman & Kleinman, 1985; Ulusahin, Basoglu, & Paykel, 1994) and among Hispanics in the United States and elsewhere (Koss, 1990). Leff (1988) stated that "only in the contemporary West is depression articulated principally as an intrapsychic experience (e.g., 'I feel blue')" (p. 74). Starcevic (1991) suggested that as a society undergoes a period of difficult and chaotic transition, as exemplified by the fall of communism and the breakup of Yugoslavia, people experience neurasthenic symptoms as an expression of loss of control. Case studies of chronic neurasthenia among the victimized survivors of the Cultural Revolution in China (Kleinman & Kleinman, 1995) provide extensive information on the somatic effects of alienation and extreme stress. Compatible with these observations, Skultans (1995) in Latvia ventured the hypothesis that neurasthenia constitutes a mode of passive resistance against political oppression and other intolerable circumstances when more direct and active, avenues of self-assertion are blocked.

Nervios

Mexican-Americans and Puerto Ricans use *nervios* (nervousness) as an illness category (Guarnaccia, Good, & Kleinman, 1990). Symptoms of nervios include trembling, headaches, sleeping disorder, dizziness, stomach ailments, and dysphoric emotions (fear, worry, anxiety, and rage). *Ataque de nervios* is experienced in response to a stressful event, such as the death of a loved one or a conflict within a family. Patients report that they have a "sense of heat in the chest rising into the head" (Guarnaccia, Good, & Kleinman, 1990, p. 1450). Ataque de nervios occurs in culturally stressful and familiar settings, such as during a funeral or at the scene of an accident. Jenkins (1988) interviewed relatives of Anglo-American and Mexican-American patients who had a diagnosis of schizophrenia according to the PSE and DSM-III. The majority (67%) of the relatives of Mexican-American patients said that the problem was one of *nervios*, but for Anglo-Americans (68%) the problem was due to *mental illness*.

Culture-Bound Syndromes

The diagnostic status of culture-bound syndromes continues to be controversial particularly in the context of increased diagnostic system standardization. Culture-bound syndromes are considered to occur in specific cultures, where their expressions are determined by cultural factors (Simons & Hughes, 1985). They are "exotic" because they do not fit into the existing Western nosology (Prince & Tcheng-Laroche, 1987). More important, "cultural beliefs or rules and patterns of interaction are constitutive of the disorder . . . there is no way to intelligibly describe the problem without invoking cultural particulars" (Kirmayer, 1991, p. 26) from a Western standpoint.

Simons and Hughes (1985) proposed to integrate various culture-bound disorders into a set of *taxons,* or general patterns of behavior, based on similarities in phenomenology. Culture-bound syndromes are considered to be a subset of folk psychiatric disorders with culturally meaningful names. Simons and Hughes present a glossary of culture-bound or folk psychiatric syndromes, describing alternative names, geographic locale, and symptoms. Furthermore, Hughes (1985) states that culture-bound disorders can be classified according to DSM-III by providing culture-relevant information on Axis IV, an axis used to describe psychosocial stressors. This universal classification scheme is consistent with Yap's (1974) point that culture-bound disorders should be integrated into a universal classification system.

DSM-IV provides an outline for cultural formulation and an appendix of 25 culture-bound syndromes without providing explicit diagnostic criteria for them. This new attempt at integration has several implications. First, there is the presumption that over 350 mental disorders listed in the DSM-IV text are cross-culturally applicable, demonstrating a universalist position. Second, because all of the presently identified culture-bound disorders are known to occur in non-Western regions, DSM-IV advocates a distinctly Western epistemology. Third, such classification attempts are likely to miss the cultural context within which these disorders occur and which is necessary for their diagnosis (Hinton & Kleinman, 1993; Tanaka-Matsumi & Higginbotham, 1996).

Koro has been reported most frequently among men, in Southern China and Southeast Asia, who become convinced that their genitals are withdrawing into their abdomen. Koro victims fear eventual death due to a female ghost. Tseng et al. (1992) conducted an empirical assessment of 214 of the 2,000 victims of the koro epidemic that occurred during the period 1984–85 and in 1987 on Hainan Island, Guangdong, China. The koro patients were compared with a group of clinic patients with "phobic and other anxiety disorders," and with a group of normal individuals. The koro group showed elevations on anxiety and phobia scales of the modified Symptom Checklist (SCL-90), but scored lower than the clinical anxiety group on all SCL-90 scales. The koro subjects expressed a strong belief in koro and the existence of a supernatural power. They had also completed fewer years of schooling than the other two groups.

Taijin Kyofusho is a Japanese culture-bound syndrome. It is a form of social phobia frequently seen in the Japanese cultural context. Patients with Taijin Kyofusho are fearful of offending others by blushing, emitting offensive odors, staring inappropriately, or presenting an improper facial expression, a blemish, or physical defect (Tanaka-Matsumi, 1979). Taijin Kyofusho patients are obsessed with shame. Taijin Kyofusho has been attributed to the Japanese value of extreme interpersonal sensitivity and to the culturally fostered inhibition of expressing negative emotions, even in a nonverbal manner (Russell, 1989). In Japan, the development of an "interdependent self" (Markus & Kitayama, 1991) is reinforced through specific interpersonal codes. Hypersensitivity to one's bodily conditions in social situations may explain the cultural prominence of Taijin Kyofusho in Japan (Takahashi, 1989; Kirmayer, 1991).

Anthropophobia has been reported in China. This syndrome appears to be the Chinese counterpart of Taijin Kyofusho, with some distinctive features. Zhong (1993) and Zhang and Zhong (1993) presented clinical information on 113 anthropophobic patients in Beijing. Their symptoms focused on the fear of being looked at. These patients were described as socially conforming, rigid, and introverted. Zhang and Zhong (1993) pointed to a probable etiology involving sexual curiosity and self-exploration. A systematic comparison of anthropophobic clients in Beijing with their neurasthenic counterparts and normal controls amplified these observations (Zhang, 1995). Anthropophobics were found to share a great many similarities with neurasthenics, but exhibited numerous differences from normals. Loss of a family member, however, was more frequently reported by neurasthenics than anthropophobics. Anthropophobics also emerged as more shy, lonely, and collectivistic in their social orientation than neurasthenics. The former tended to express their anxiety in psychological rather than somatic terms. In their school years, anthropophobics obtained higher grades than neurasthenics, but reported fewer friendships with classmates or peers. Their reports of childhood were less happy than those of neurasthenics. Anthropophobics also acknowledged a conjunction of early sexual activity and interest with a greater shyness with members of the opposite sex. This finding is consonant with the hypothesized sexual embarrassment or guilt as an etiological factor in anthropophobia.

Anorexia nervosa is self-starvation marked by fear of gaining weight and distorted perception of one's bodily image. Although it is not classified as a culture-bound disorder, anorexia is particularly common among young women from predominantly Western countries. Self-starvation syndrome is culturally reactive and is considered a historical product of affluence, modernization, and distress over personhood (Di Nicola, 1988). Lee (1995), however, challenges the assumption that anorexia nervosa is a Western culture-bound disorder in light of recent reports from Asian countries including Hong Kong, Taiwan, China, Malaysia, India, Singapore, and Japan.

In conclusion, recent studies of culture-bound disorders demonstrate that (1) cultures have specific meaningful labels for behavior disorders, (2) these disorders are culturally acquired ways of expressing one's inability to control oneself in culturally delimited stressful situations, (3) cultures have their own folk models for disorders, and (4) culture-bound syndromes challenge any universal nosology because of their geographically circumscribed occurrence and culturally specific content.

Multiculturalism and Ethnic-Minority Research

Three related worldwide phenomena have increased the relevance of cross-national and cross-ethnic investigation and the search for culturally sensitive assessment, diagnostic, and treatment models for psychopathology. They are: (1) intra-national multiculturalism, (2) worldwide migration, and (3) acculturation and adaptation problems (see also Berry and Sam, this volume). Both emic and etic positions are competing for primacy in prediction, assessment, and intervention throughout the range of psychopathology.

The Epidemiological Catchment Area (ECA) Survey

The ECA survey, which is the largest epidemiological survey ever conducted in the United States, involved five centers located in St. Louis, Baltimore, New Haven, Durham, and Los Angeles (Eaton et al., 1984; Regier, Myers, Kramer, Robins, & Blazer, 1984; Robins & Regier, 1991). The ECA survey has generated epidemiological research data according to ethnicity, age, gender, and socioeconomic status. Over 20,000 randomly selected community residents were interviewed using the NIMH-DIS for case identification. The DIS assesses major psychiatric disorders described in the DSM-III to determine lifetime and current diagnoses based on a set of explicit criteria (Robins et al., 1981). The DIS was translated into Spanish (Karno, Burman, Escobar, Hough, & Eaton, 1983). In the validation study (Burman, Karno, Hough, Escobar, & Forsythe, 1983), the Spanish DIS tended to underdiagnose depression and affective disorders and overdiagnose alcohol abuse, when compared with trained clinicians' diagnosis using the DSM-III.

The ECA data suggest the interplay of ethnicity and acculturation status on the prevalence of affective disorders. The lifetime prevalence of affective disorders was 11 percent for Non-Hispanic Whites and 7.8 percent for Mexican Americans. The same trend was observed for the specific categories of manic episode, major depressive episode, and dysthymia (Karno et al., 1987). In comparison with Mexican-American women, the rate of major depressive episode was 2.5 times higher for non-Hispanic white women under 40 years of age. However, Mexican Americans born in the United States resembled the non-Hispanic whites in exhibiting increased rates for specific symptoms of major depression (e.g., dysphoria, appetite disturbances, sleep disturbances, etc.) (Golding, Karno, & Rutter, 1990). The rates for Mexican Americans born in Mexico were lower in eight of the nine symptom categories examined.

Some of the ECA findings may be the result of confounding ethnicity with acculturation and acculturative stress (López, 1994). In the ECA study, birthplace and language served as the index of acculturation status. With acculturation, Mexican Americans may learn to experience and/or express depression through more cognitive and affective symptoms rather than through the somatic channel.

Worldwide Migration, Acculturation and Adjustment Problems

Acculturation Models

With an upsurge in migration around the world, there has been an increased interest in the mental health status of migrants. Migrants have been grouped into "immigrant," "refugee," and "guest worker" categories (Rack, 1988). Adaptation problems develop through the interactive effects of many factors, including the conditions in the host culture, upbringing in the country of origin, and the experience of voluntary versus forced migration (Arpin, Comba, & Fleury, 1988; Berry & Kim, 1988). Berry (1980) and Berry and Sam (this volume) present frameworks for acculturation and mental health according to integration, assimilation, separation, and marginalization modes applied to the predicament of the acculturating individual. There are differences in the preferred mode of acculturation and in associated mental health problems. In the United States, Asian Indian immigrants who had an attitude of separation and marginalization reported more stress than those who endorsed integration (Krishnan & Berry, 1992). Berry, Kim, Minde, and Mok (1987) studied a total of 1,197 acculturating individuals in Canada (native peoples, refugees, sojourners, immigrants, and ethnic groups) during the 1969–1979 period. Native peoples of Canada and refugees scored the highest on the acculturative stress measure, while the immigrants reported the least amount of stress. Education was a consistent predictor of low stress. Moyerman and Forman's (1992) meta-analytic study of acculturation and adjustment based on 49 reports found that lower socioeconomic status was associated with acculturative stress. Among immigrant Mexican-American women in California, their scores on the Center for Epidemiological Studies-Depression Scale (CES-D; Radloff, 1977) significantly correlated with the variables of education, income, perceived economic opportunity, perceived distance between the home country and the host country, and the loss of interpersonal ties in the home country (Vega, Kalody, & Valle, 1987).

Refugees

It is estimated that the number of international and internal refugees exceeds 40 million people worldwide (Leopold & Harrell-Bond, 1994). The growing literature on refugees emphasizes their losses, adjustment difficulties, and stressors. Evidence of the high incidence of psychiatric problems among refugees makes urgent the need for a valid assessment of their problems, effective interventions, and social policies addressing their difficulties (Kroll et al., 1989; Marsella, Bornemann, Ekblad, & Orley, 1994; Westermeyer, 1989). In Sweden, Latin-American refugees report more psychological distress than South European and Finnish labor migrants or Swedish matched community controls (Sundquist, 1994).

Depression is prevalent among Southeast Asian refugees (Beiser, Cargo, & Woodbury, 1994; Westermeyer, Vang, & Neider, 1983) and their mode of expressing depression requires cultural accommodation strategies on the part of helping agencies (Fraser & Pecora, 1986). Post-traumatic stress disorder and culture shock are very common among Indo-Chinese refugees in the United States (Draguns, 1996c).

Voluntary Migrants

Most studies of voluntary migrants rely for their data on psychiatric hospital admission rates (Leff, 1988; Rack, 1988). In Great Britain, Cochrane and Bal (1989) conducted a study of psychiatric hospital admissions based on the largest data set to date, collected in the census years 1971 and 1981 and encompassing all of England and Wales. Cochrane and Bal found that both Irish-born and Caribbean-born migrants to Britain had higher admissions rates than the native-born British, while Asian-born migrants had lower admission rates. The Irish-born migrant men and women had the highest rates of admissions for alcohol abuse and depression, respectively. The Caribbean-born migrants to Britain had the second highest psychiatric hospital admission rate, and both Caribbean men (359 per 100,000) and women (235 per 100,000) had exceedingly high rates of admission for schizophrenia, when compared with those of native-born British men (61 per 100,000) and women (58 per 100,000). Cochrane and Bal (1987, 1989) have examined various possible explanations for the alarmingly high rates of the hospital diagnosis of schizophrenia among Afro-Caribbeans. No single explanation, including possible misdiagnosis, migration-induced stress, or predisposition, is consistently supported by data.

In India, psychiatric morbidity rates were highest among urban slum dwellers who migrated from Pakistan and lowest among families who moved from nearby villages (Sharma, Michael, Venkataswamy-Reddy, & Gehlot, 1985). In Japan, mental health professionals have recently established the Society of Transcultural Psychiatry (Nishizono, 1994) in response to the increase in Japanese returnees from overseas (Minoura, 1988), international students (Tanaka, Takai, Kohyama, & Fujihara, 1994), and labor migrants from Southeast Asia and South America (Abe, 1994).

Epidemiological and clinical research has also been vigorously pursued with guest workers in Germany (Pfeiffer, 1994). The symptoms presented, the course of the disorder, and its outcome represent a complex amalgam of the characteristics of the original and host culture, the stresses encountered, and personal resources. Still, a number of characteristic reaction patterns have emerged. Among them, the acute paranoid reaction with dramatic emotional display is prominent. It has often been traced to the partial understanding of the host culture and its customs and language. This state is said to bring about misunderstandings and personalized interpretations (Böker & Schwarz, 1977), and has been interpreted as an aggravation of normal nostalgia that may lead to a reactive depressive condition with culturally distinctive modes of manifestation (Larbig, Xenakis, & Onishi, 1979). At other times, anxiety tends to be expressed in its raw, pure, and intense form resulting in dramatic, but relatively benign, states of acute distress. The common denominator of these syndromes is their relatively favorable prognosis, provided that the therapists take into account the cultural context of symptom presentation. Prognosis is worse if the symptoms are mistaken for more serious pathology.

Clinician's Bias in Diagnosis

Findings of cross-cultural differences in diagnostic practices suggest the need for incorporating characteristics of the professional observer as research variables.

Typically, cross-cultural differences that have been systematically identified in the judgment of professional observers across cultures have been treated as "error" to be reduced and eventually eliminated (Draguns, 1982). However, these discrepancies constitute genuine cross-cultural phenomena worthy of investigation.

Patient variables, such as race, gender, and social class produce "bias" in clinical judgment (Adebimpe, 1981, 1984; Adebimpe, Chu, Klein, & Lange, 1982; Cheetham & Griffiths, 1981; López, 1989; Neighbors, Jackson, Campbell, & Williams, 1989; Paradis, Friedman, Lazar, Gruber, & Kesselman, 1992; Westermeter, 1987). This bias can promote either overdiagnosis or underdiagnosis. López (1989) hypothesized that (1) clinicians have differential subjective base rates of disorders for different groups (e.g., Anglo-Americans versus Mexican-Americans), (2) they differ in information processing activity as a function of their cultural background, and (3) they engage in their own hypothesis testing in diagnosis. These predictions are yet to be fully tested empirically.

The epidemiologic study of affective disorders among the Amish in Pennsylvania (Egeland, Hostetter, & Eshleman, 1983) showed the impact of cultural factors on the diagnosis of bipolar disorders. In this study, which employed the Research Diagnostic Criteria, 71 percent of the cases were diagnosed with affective disorders, of which bipolar disorders accounted for 34 percent. However, according to medical records, 79 percent of these bipolar cases had previously been misdiagnosed as schizophrenia. This was interpreted by the authors as due to clinicians' lack of cultural knowledge regarding the strict religious codes regulating Amish behaviors resulting in clinicians' misinterpretation of culturally normative behaviors.

Fabrega et al. (1994) found that older African-American inpatients were initially more likely to be diagnosed as psychotic and less likely to receive a diagnosis of a mood disorder than their Anglo-European counterparts. At discharge, however, African-American patients received higher ratings of improvement. The question remains as to whether the initial diagnostic differences were due to clinicians' misjudgments of similar symptoms, or whether they misinterpreted real differences in symptom expression by African-Americans and Anglo-Europeans (Neighbors, Jackson, Campbell, & Williams, 1989).

Cross-cultural diagnostic differences are also documented in communication with patients. McDonald-Scott, Machizawa and Satoh (1992) found that over 80 percent of American and Canadian psychiatrists ($n = 112$) and Japanese psychiatrists ($n = 166$) would inform patients of the diagnosis of affective and anxiety disorders. However, only 30 percent of Japanese psychiatrists said they would inform patients of the diagnosis of schizophrenia, while 70 percent of American and Canadian psychiatrists would convey this diagnosis. Japanese psychiatrists preferred to use alternative diagnosis, such as neurasthenia, while American and Canadian psychiatrists preferred to discuss differential diagnosis with the patient. Munakata (1989) states that Japanese psychiatrists use neurasthenia as a "disguised diagnosis" for schizophrenia, because it is more easily accepted by patients and their families due to its absence of social stigma.

In conclusion, value judgments and perceptions of professionals, even when they use standardized instruments, can influence diagnosis, the selection of treatment, and communication with patients (Westermeyer, 1987). Clinician behavior in the cross-cultural diagnostic context should be investigated as a significant source of cultural variability in diagnosis.

Cultural Adaptation and Validation of Assessment Instruments

Irvine and Caroll (1980) proposed stringent psychometric criteria for establishing the cross-cultural reliability and validity of assessment instruments (see also chapter by van de Vijver & Leung, Volume 1, this *Handbook*). Moreover, the cultural relevance of adapted measures must be established (Geisinger, 1994). Weiss and Kleinman (1988) pointed to the divergent pull of the etic and emic orientations: "Cosmopolitan frames are essential for comparative analysis within and across cultures, but are incomplete without the local conceptual frames derived from the indigenous experience that renders comparison valid and meaningful" (p. 193). Several measurement studies have sought to attain an integration of the etic and emic approaches in the cultural adaptation of their measures.

The CES-D (Radloff, 1977) has been validated for Korean immigrants in Canada (Noh, Avison, & Kaspar, 1992) and Hispanic populations in California (Aneshensel, Clark, & Freichs, 1983). These studies used back translations, studied item equivalence, and compared factor structures of the scale. One major concern in adapting a standardized instrument is that the content may systematically omit culture-specific expressions. Kinzie et al. (1982) examined specific items of the Beck Depression Inventory (BDI) to assess depression among Vietnamese refugees in the United States; their analyses led them eventually to construct the Vietnamese Depression Scale (VDS), replacing in the process most of the original BDI items.

Manson, Shore, and Bloom's (1985) research on the development of the American Indian Depression Scale (AIDS) used both emic and etic criteria and resulted in a culturally sensitive and clinically useful instrument. Through interviews with informants, the authors came up with five Hopi illness categories that are relevant to depression. The categories were translated as (1) worry sickness, (2) unhappiness, (3) heartbroken, (4) drunken-like craziness, and (5) disappointment.

The AIDS included questions on the five indigenous categories of illness and the NIMH-DIS items representing depression, alcohol abuse, and somatization. The AIDS was administered to the clinical index group (*n* =22) and a matched community group of Hopis (*n* =32). Fifty subjects said that they could not find a single Hopi word equivalent to the term "depression," even though all of them were familiar with the five Hopi illness categories. The various Hopi categories of illness were differently related to the major DSM-III criteria of depression. "Unhappiness" was most strongly associated with the DSM-III criterion of dysphoric mood. The indigenous category of "heartbroken" was more broadly marked by "weight loss, disrupted sleep, fatigue, psychomotor retardation and agitation, loss of libido, a sense of sinfulness, shame, not being likable, and trouble thinking clearly" (Manson, Shore, & Bloom, 1985, p. 350).

Cultural adaptation of diagnostic instruments has been demonstrated to be critical in preventing misdiagnosis. The development of culture-relevant, emic assessments, such as the AIDS, also contributes to the cross-validation of standardized instruments, such as the DIS, in establishing the relationship between emic and etic concepts.

Individualism–Collectivism Dimensions and Psychopathology: Conceptual Advances

Draguns (1980) and Marsella (1979) hypothesized that the expression of psychopathology represents elements of the person's culture, be it in the form of an exaggeration (Draguns, 1988, 1990a) or as culture-relevant coping responses to stress (Coyne & Downey, 1991; Marsella, 1979; Marsella & Dash-Scheur, 1988). Betancourt & López (1993) called for hypothesis-driven research identifying cultural variables (e.g., religiosity) that could predict specific symptom expressions (e.g., content of delusions).

One major question concerns the contribution of cultural values and self-orientation to the expression of and social responses to abnormal behavior. Hofstede (1980) has identified four dimensions that distinguish employees within a multinational corporation in different nations: individualism–collectivism, uncertainty avoidance, power distance, and masculinity–femininity. Of these dimensions, individualism–collectivism has been most intensively studied (Kim, Triandis, Kagitçibasi, Choi, & Yoon, 1994). It has been applied to social and work behaviors across cultures (see chapter by Kagitçibasi, this volume, for details). To a much lesser extent, the individualism–collectivism dimension has also been linked to clinical findings from Japan, China, and in North and South America (Draguns, 1990a).

Radford, Nakane, Ohta, Mann, and Kalucy (1991) conducted a comparative study of the decision making of depressed patients in Australia and Japan. This study illustrates the importance of assessing cultural orientation in order to understand differences in stress reactions. A total of 104 Japanese and Australian clinically depressed patients were screened according to the WHO/SADD criteria. Normal Japanese and Australian students were included as control groups. Radford hypothesized that a depressed person's location along the individualism–collectivism dimension influences their decision making. On a Decision Behavior Questionnaire the Japanese normal subjects' predominant complacency and collateral decision-making styles reflected a collectivist orientation. The normal Australian subjects stressed the more individualistic orientation of ability, responsibility, and individual decision making. The results indicated an interaction of culture and group. In Japan, depressed patients and normals did not differ in their decision-making style. However, Australian patients experienced individual decision making as more stressful than normal controls. These results were explained in terms of the extent to which depression interferes with culturally determined responsibilities of the individual. In the collectivist Japanese culture, decision making is not the sole responsibility of the individual and the Japanese depressed patients could rely on others to make decisions for or with them. In the individualistic Australian culture, however, depressed patients' difficulty in individual decision making was role-dystonic and thus was associated with lowered self-esteem, hypervigilance, and avoidance.

In the WHO study (1979) reviewed earlier, prognosis for schizophrenia was better for patients from collectivist cultures (e.g., Colombia, India, and Nigeria) that reinforce an interdependent or allocentric self. In contrast, patients from individualistic cultures (e.g., Denmark, United Kingdom, United States) that endorse an independent self did more poorly at follow-ups. These differences in the course of schizophrenia have been linked to family factors. Strong family ties can buffer the stresses of social isolation, and the support of the family system may reduce the individual consequences of a mental disorder (Lin & Kleinman, 1988; Sanua, 1980; Warner, 1994). When the "illness" experience is shared by the family as in India (Sinha, 1988), the subjective experience of an individual's distress is apparently minimized.

The individualism–collectivism dimension has been measured empirically and it has been used to classify the countries of the world. Investigating the relationship between variations in abnormal behavior and cultural dimensions and values should be the goal of future cross-cultural research in the area of psychopathology. The design of such an investigation should include normal control groups to establish each culture's normative behavior and shared values. Summarizing their major review of psychopathology in China, a traditionally collectivist society, Tseng, Lin, and Yee (1995) described the family as both the resource of social support the originator of personal problems. Its dual role in cultures around the world remains to be systematically investigated.

Culture's Responses to Abnormal Behavior: Models for Therapy

Cultural Accommodation and Psychotherapy

Western psychiatry continues to spread throughout the Third World and this movement has caused cultural and institutional conflicts between the Western biomedical orientation and indigenous practices (Higginbotham & Marsella, 1988; Littlewood, 1990). Higginbotham (1984) surveyed and interviewed the staffs of 22 mental health systems in Taiwan, the Philippines, and Thailand to illustrate the impact of Western biomedical psychiatry. He also documented the barriers preventing modern Western Psychiatry from achieving its goal of establishing "community acceptability, integration, and continuity with prevailing health beliefs" (Higginbotham, 1984, p. xv).

The goal of cultural accommodation is the integration of the cultural context with the design of services. Cross-cultural therapists practice cultural accommodation by analyzing the indigenous meanings of deviant behaviors, their perceived causes and the social reactions they provoke (Kleinman, 1978; Marsella & White, 1982; Higginbotham, 1984). In Africa, strong beliefs in supernatural causation of disorders have imposed social and cultural limitations on psychotherapy (Sow, 1980). Analyzing the devastating problems of hunger, infectious disease, education, and basic living conditions, African specialists today voice an urgent need to integrate mental health services with the primary health care program (Odejide, Oyewunmi, & Ohaeri, 1989).

Kleinman (1978) advocates "therapy as negotiation." He suggests four procedures for negotiating both the meaning of the client–therapist interaction and the cultural meaning of the client's presenting problem. First, the therapist encourages clients to give their own explanation of the presenting problem. Second, the therapist discloses the explanation, or "explanatory model," that he or she uses to interpret the problem. Third, the two frameworks are compared for similarities and discrepancies. Finally, the client and clinician translate each explanatory model into mutually acceptable language, so that they may jointly set the content of therapy, target behaviors, and outcome criteria.

This model is consistent with that of Higginbotham, West, and Forsyth (1988) which emphasizes the importance of assessing the client's views in developing effective interventions in different cultures. To achieve community legitimacy and acceptance, a therapeutic system should accommodate (1) a culture-specific definition of deviancy, (2) accepted norms for role behavior, (3) expectations of intervention, and (4) culturally sanctioned change agents (Higginbotham, 1984).

Indigenous Therapies and Western Therapies in Cultural Context

Prince (1980) concluded that Western conceptions of psychotherapy must be drastically expanded if one is to understand the therapeutic procedures of other cultures. His view is still supported (Prince, 1992; Ward, 1989). A shared worldview and shared beliefs concerning the presenting problem are considered universal features of effective therapy in its cultural forms (Torrey, 1986).

Kakar (1982), an Indian psychoanalyst, states that indigenous therapies have both etic and emic aspects. As a participant observer, Kakar studied ancient healing practices in India as practiced by shamans and mystics. The success of traditional healing practices in India is attributed to sharing of the Indian worldview by the healer, the patient, and his or her extended family. The goal of therapy is to restore the "relational self." Healing practices often involve the patient's family members, who participate in rituals to expel the bad spirits believed to be the cause of the disorder. Roland (1988, 1991), who has practiced psychoanalysis in Japan and India, proposes that the various concepts of psychoanalysis are universal, but that the content is highly culture specific as is the training of therapists. He uses the individualism and collectivism dimensions to describe cultural differences in the types of therapist–patient relationships, communication style, and the extent to which individual-oriented confrontation can be used in therapy.

In Japan, within the framework of psychoanalytic psychotherapy, interdependence has been analyzed by using the concept of *amae* (Doi, 1973; Johnson, 1992). Doi defines amae, or "indulgent dependency" (Johnson, 1992, p. 201), as a basic desire. In Japan, there are implicit cultural rules of communication governing the expression of amae by one person to another. Taketomo (1986), therefore, conceptualizes amae as a metalanguage within the Japanese cultural context, and maintains that successful psychoanalytic therapy with Japanese clients must attend to the metacommunicational function of amae.

Outside of the psychoanalytic tradition, Reynolds (1980) describes the "silent therapies" developed in Japan. Both Morita therapy and Naikan therapy are influenced by Buddhism and minimize the verbal interaction between the therapist and the client. Instead, the therapist provides a structured setting for self-reflection; the client is encouraged to focus on his or her relationships with specific others in order to reduce self-centeredness in the interpersonally-oriented Japanese cultural context.

Mullings (1984) gives ethnographical accounts of traditional and spiritualist healing practices in urban Ghana. She reports cases of indigenous African healers who provide patients with culturally acceptable explanations of their diagnoses and interventions. Indigenous therapies, such as possession rituals and fights against sorcery, should be effective from a cultural standpoint. On the basis of providing therapy to Arab and African clients in Paris, Nathan (1994) proposed that psychotherapists should adopt a cultural frame of reference when explaining a client's etiology and should take seriously their indigenous explanations of disorder and distress.

Snacken (1991) distinguished three models of intervention with non-Western clients: intercultural, bicultural, and polycultural. "Intercultural therapy," pioneered in Belgium and France, involves either a single anthropologist–psychologist familiar with the client's language and culture (and sometimes belonging to the client's culture) or two anthropologist–psychologists working in collaboration. Although indigenous terminology may be employed (e.g., "sorcery"), intercultural intervention draws upon Western theory (systems, behavioral, or analytic). What Snacken calls "bicultural therapy," as developed by Collomb in Dakar, includes a native healer as member of the treatment team. According to Snacken, one weakness of the bicultural model is that the client is often caught between two different approaches. Although the Western practitioner and traditional healer try to work together, the client consults with each separately and receives both Western and traditional forms of intervention. Snacken's third category, "polycultural therapy," best represented by the work of Nathan in France, is an ambitious undertaking in which the client meets at the same time with approximately 15 therapists of diverse national or ethnic backgrounds. In addition, the client is invited to attend with his or her own doctor, psychologist, psychiatrist, or social worker. In polycultural therapy, a multicultural environment is created which transcends the Western–non-Western dichotomy between therapist and client, and in which client's fears of traditional charlatanism or Western "black magic" are allayed (Snacken, 1991).

Focusing on the cross-cultural applicability of behavior therapy, Tanaka-Matsumi and Higginbotham (1996) stressed the importance of identifying the client's explanatory model in order to facilitate communication during the functional analysis of the presenting problem. The functional analysis identifies antecedent events and consequences of problem behaviors within the client's social network. In this approach, cultural factors are embedded in the client's larger social environment and reinforcement history (Higginbotham & Tanaka-Matsumi, 1991; Tanaka-Matsumi, Seiden, & Lam, in press).

In the United States, there has been a rapid increase in publications on therapies with ethnic minority adults, adolescents, and children (e.g., chapter by Beardsley & Pedersen, this volume; Boyd-Franklin, 1989; Comas-Diaz & Griffith, 1988; Paniagua, 1994; Pedersen, 1994; Pedersen, Draguns, Lonner, & Trimble, 1996; Tharp, 1991). Accommodating cultural and ethnic diversity has become a goal of psychotherapy. Sue and Zane (1987) assert that therapists must both possess cultural knowledge and be competent in the use of culture-consistent strategies; each may enhance therapist credibility and thereby avoid premature termination of therapy. However, very limited research on psychotherapy with ethnic minority groups has been conducted so far, and there has been an even greater paucity of studies on specific conditions that are supposedly crucial for therapeutic effectiveness (Neal & Turner, 1991; Sue, Zane, & Young, 1994).

In sum, therapy often is construed as a social influence process; both client and therapist variables play an important role in treatment selection and outcome (Draguns, 1990b; Leff, 1988, pp. 69–85). The context of therapy should be consistent with the client's culture to achieve the goal of cultural accommodation (Tanaka-Matsumi, 1989).

Summary and Conclusions

A vast amount of literature has developed since the publication of the first edition of this *Handbook*. Both emic and etic perspectives are strongly reflected in the aggregate of studies reviewed in this chapter. The field of culture and psychopathology is now characterized by methodologically solid sophisticated research, which increasingly incorporates culture-oriented anthropological and ethnographic information. The following conclusions are offered:

1. The universalist position has registered advances in developing standardized diagnostic methods based on the biomedical model of psychopathology. Comparisons of epidemiological data in two cultures across the entire range of disturbances have been implemented and multi-national studies of specific disorders have been conducted. The inclusion of normal and clinical samples within the same investigation has permitted a bridging of the gulf between the cross-cultural study of normal and abnormal behavior.

2. In the process, the culturally invariant and variable components of psychopathology have been identified, especially in relation to the major disorders of depression and schizophrenia. At the same time, research has been extended to an ever widening spectrum of disorders, from anorexia nervosa to borderline personality.

3. The context of symptom manifestation has been elucidated and the transactional and interpersonal character of mental disorder has come to be better understood. The interplay of somatic and experiential factors in psychopathology around the world has been explored. The "New Cross-Cultural Psychiatry" movement and indigenous psychologies have made major contributions to contextual analyses of psychopathology.

4. The multicultural perspective has stimulated research on specific ethnic groups within pluralistic societies. Worldwide migrations have prompted researchers to investigate the nature of adjustment problems and to develop culturally sensitive measures.

5. Links are beginning to be discerned between major dimensions of culturally differentiating behavior and modes of expression of psychopathology. The dimension of individualism–collectivism, and the self-orientation dimension of interdependent–independent self, are promising parameters for the integration of the diverse and polarized approaches in this field.

6. Theorists of culture-oriented therapeutic systems have proposed that cultural accommodation is associated with intervention effectiveness. The field of cross-cultural psychopathology is in need of empirical programmatic studies evaluating the clinical utility of culture-accommodating assessment and treatment practices.

7. One major line of division of the world, namely into the communist versus capitalist, predominantly democratic, camps, has been virtually ignored by cross-cultural investigators of psychopathology. Pflanz (1970) asserted that the psychiatric disorders in the Federal Republic of Germany and in the German Democratic Republic were virtually identical. Tseng et al. (1990) found that similarity of culture among the Chinese overrode the contrast in political systems as far as psychiatric symptoms were concerned. But the surface has been barely scratched on the possible psychiatric ramifications of the great ideological clash of the 20th century. Its investigation should be vigorously pursued (see Draguns, 1995).

8. The question "Does culture make a difference in psychopathology?" (Al-Issa, 1982, p. 3) has been answered in the affirmative. At the same time, it is conceded that the scope of the universal, invariant factors in psychopathology is vast (Al-Issa, 1995). Between these two reference points lie the established facts and unmet challenges of research on culture and psychopathology.

References

Abe, Y. (1994). Nikkei Latin Amerikajin no seishinshogai: Chiryo to sono bunkateki haikei (Mental disorders of Latin Americans of Japanese descent: Intervention and its cultural background). In *Proceedings of the Japanese Society of Transcultural Psychiatry* (pp. 5–7). Yamagata, Japan: Yamagata University.

Achenbach, T. & Edelbrock, C. S. (1983). *Manual for the Child Behavior Checklist and Revised Child Profile*. Burlington: Department of Psychiatry, University of Vermont.

Achenbach, T. M., Bird, H. R., Canino, G., Phares, V., Gould, M. S., & Rubio-Stipec, M. (1990). Epidemiological comparisons of Puerto Rico and U.S. mainland children: Parent, teacher, and self-reports. *Journal of the American Academy of Child and Adolescent Psychiatry, 29*, 84–93.

Achenbach, T. M., Hensley, V. R., Phares, V., & Grayson, D. (1990). Problems and competencies reported by parents of Australian and American children. *Journal of Child Psychology and Psychiatry, 31*, 265–286.

Achenbach, T. M., Verhulst, F. C., Baron, G. D., & Akkerhuis, G. W. (1987). Epidemiological comparisons of American and Dutch children: I. Behavioral/emotional problems and competencies reported by parents for ages 4–16. *Journal of the American Academy of Child and Adolescent Psychiatry, 26*, 317–325.

Achenbach, T. M., Verhulst, F. C., Edelbrock, C., Baron, G. D., & Akkerhuis, G. W. (1987). Epidemiological comparisons of American and Dutch children: II. Behavioral/emotional problems reported by teachers for ages 6–11. *Journal of the American Academy of Child and Adolescent Psychiatry, 26*, 326–332.

Adebimpe, V. R. (1981). Overview: White norms and psychiatric diagnosis of black patients. *American Journal of Psychiatry, 138*, 279–285.

Adebimpe, V. R. (1984). American Blacks and psychiatry. *Transcultural Psychiatric Research Review, 21*, 81–111.

Adebimpe, V., Chu, C. C., Klein, H. E., & Lange, M. H. (1982). Racial and geographic differences in the psychopathology schizophrenia. *American Journal of Psychiatry, 139*, 888–891.

Al-Issa, I. (1982). Does culture make a difference in psychopathology? In I. Al-Issa (Ed.), *Culture and psychopathology* (pp. 3–32). Baltimore: University Park Press.

Al-Issa, I. (1995). Culture and mental illness in international perspective. In I. Al-Issa (Ed.), *Handbook of culture and mental illness: An international perspective* (pp. 3–49). Madison, CT: International Universities Press.

American Psychiatric Association. (1994). *Diagnostic and statistical manual of mental disorders*, 4th ed. Washington, DC: American Psychiatric Association.

Aneshensel, C. S., Clark, V. A., & Freichs, R. R. (1983). Race, ethnicity, and depression: A confirmatory factor analysis. *Journal of Personality and Social Psychology, 44*, 385–394.

Angel, R. & Thoits, P. (1987). The impact of culture on the cognitive structure of illness. *Culture, Medicine and Psychiatry, 11*, 465–494.

Arpin, J., Comba, L., & Fleury, F. (Eds.). (1988). Migrazione e salute mentale in Europa. *Antoropologia Medica, 4*.

Barraclough, B. (1988). International variation in the suicide rate of 15–24 year olds. *Social Psychiatry and Psychiatric Epidemiology, 23*, 75–84.

Beiser, M., Cargo, M., & Woodbury, M. A. (1994). A comparison of psychiatric disorders in different cultures: Depressive typologies in Southeast Asian refugees and resident Canadians. *International Journal of Methods in Psychiatric Research, 4*, 157–172.

Bemak, F., Chung, R. C., & Bornemann, T. H. (1996). Counseling and psychotherapy with refugees. In P. B. Pedersen, J. G. Draguns, W. J. Lonner, & J. Trimble (Eds.), *Counseling across cultures*, 4th ed. (pp. 243–265). Thousand Oaks, CA: Sage.

Bennett, L. A., Janca, A., Grant, B. F., & Sartorius, N. (1993). Boundaries between normal and pathological drinking. *Alcohol, Health and Research World, 17*, 190–195.

Berne, E. (1959). Difficulties of comparative psychiatry. *American Journal of Psychiatry, 113*, 193–200.

Berry, J. W. (1969). On cross-cultural comparability. *International Journal of Psychology, 4*, 119–128.

Berry, J. W. (1980). Acculturation as varieties of adaptation. In A. Padilla (Ed.), *Acculturation: Theory, models and some new findings* (pp. 9–25). Boulder, CO: Westview.

Berry, J. W., Kim, U., Minde, T., & Mok, D. (1987). Comparative studies of acculturative stress. *International Migration Review, 11*, 491–510.

Berry, J. W. & Kim, U. (1988). Acculturation and mental health. In P. Dasen, J. W. Berry, & N. Sartorius (Eds.), *Health and cross-cultural psychology: Towards applications* (pp. 207–236). Newbury Park, CA: Sage.

Berry, J. W., Poortinga, Y. H., Segall, M. H., & Dasen, P. J. (1992). *Cross-cultural psychology: Research and applications.* Cambridge: Cambridge University Press.

Betancourt, H. & López, S. R. (1993). The study of culture, ethnicity and race in American psychology. *American Psychologist, 48,* 629–637.

Böker, W. & Schwarz, P. (1977). Die akute paranoide Reaktion-ein charakteristisches Phänomenon der transkulturellen und Migrationspsychiatrie. In A. Boroffka & W. M. Pfeiffer (Eds.), *Fragen der transkulturell-vergleichenden Psychiatrie in Europa* (pp. 96–102). Münster, Germany: Westfälische Wilhelms Universität.

Boyd-Franklin, N. (1989). *Black families in therapy: A multisystem approach.* New York: Guilford.

Buda, B. & Föredi, J. (1995). Hungarian culture and mental illness. In I. Al-Issa (Ed.), *Handbook of culture and mental illness: An international perspective* (pp. 303–313). Madison, CT: International Universities Press.

Burman, M. A., Karno, R. L., Hough, J. I., Escobar, J. I., & Forsythe, A. B. (1983). The Spanish Diagnostic Interview Schedule. *Archives of General Psychiatry, 40,* 1189–1196.

Canino, G. L., Burman, A., & Caetano, R. (1992). The prevalence of alcohol abuse and/or dependence in two Hispanic communities. In J. E. Helzer & G. J. Canino (Eds.), *Alcoholism in North America, Europe, and Asia* (pp. 131–158). New York: Oxford University Press.

Cheetham, R. S. W. & Griffiths, J. A. (1981). Errors in the diagnosis of schizophrenia in Black and Indian patients. *African Medical Journal, 59,* 71–75.

Cheung, F. M. C. (1986). Psychopathology among Chinese people. In M. H. Bond (Ed.), *The psychology of the Chinese people* (pp. 171–212). Hong Kong: Oxford University Press.

Cheung, F. M. C. (1989). The indigenization of neurasthenia in Hong Kong. *Culture, Medicine and Psychiatry, 13,* 227–241.

Cheung, F. M. C., Lee, S-Y., & Chan, Y. Y. (1983). Variations in problem conceptualization and intended solutions among Hong Kong students. *Culture, Medicine and Psychiatry, 7,* 263–278.

Cochrane, R. & Bal, S. S. (1987). Migration and schizophrenia: An examination of five hypotheses. *Social Psychiatry, 22,* 181–191.

Cochrane, R. & Bal, S. S. (1989). Mental hospital admission rates of immigrants to England: A comparison of 1971 and 1981. *Social Psychiatry and Psychiatric Epidemiology, 24,* 2–12.

Cohen, A. (1992). Prognosis for schizophrenia in the Third World: A reevaluation of cross-cultural research. *Culture, Medicine and Psychiatry, 16,* 53–75.

Collignon, R. (1978). Vingt ans de travaux à la clinique psychiatrique de Fann Dakar. *Psychopathologie Africaine, 19,* 326–328.

Collignon, R. & Gueye, M. (1995). The interface between culture and mental illness in French speaking West Africa. In I. Al-Issa (Ed.), *Handbook of culture and mental illness: An international perspective* (pp. 93–112). Madison, CT: International Universities Press.

Comas-Diaz, L. & Griffith, E. E. H. (1988). *Clinical guidelines in cross-cultural mental health.* New York: Wiley.

Compton, W. M., Helzer, J. E., Hwu, H. G., Yeh, E. K., McEnvoy, L., Topp, J. E., & Spitznagel, E. L. (1991). New methods in cross-cultural psychiatry in Taiwan and the United States. *American Journal of Psychiatry, 148,* 1697–1704.

Coyne, J. C. & Downey, G. (1991). Social factors and psychopathology. *Annual Review of Psychology, 42,* 401–425.

Day, R., Nielsen, J. A., Korten, A., Ernberg, G., Dube, K. C., Gebhart, J., Jablensky, A., Leon, C., Marsella, A. J., Olatawura, M., Sartorius, N., Stromgren, E., Takahashi, R., Wig, N., & Wynne, L. C. (1987). Stressful life events preceding the acute onset of schizophrenia: A cross-national study from the World Health Organization. *Culture, Medicine and Psychiatry, 11,* 123–205.

Desjarlais, R., Eisenberg, L., Good, B., & Kleinman, A. (1995). *World mental health: Problems and priorities in low-income countries.* New York: Oxford University Press.

Diop, M. (1967). La dépression chez le noir Africain. *Psychopathologie Africaine, 3,* 183–195.

Di Nicola, V. F. (1990). Anorexia multiforms: Self-starvation in historical and cultural context. *Transcultural Psychiatric Research Review, 27,* 165–196, 245–287.

Doi, T. (1973). *The anatomy of dependence.* Tokyo: Kodansha International.

Draguns, J. G. (1980). Psychological disorders of clinical severity. In H. C. Triandis & J. G. Draguns (Eds.), *Handbook of cross-cultural psychology* (Vol. 6, pp. 99–174). Boston: Allyn and Bacon.

Draguns, J. G. (1982). Methodology in cross-cultural psychopathology. In I. Al-Issa (Ed.), *Culture and psychopathology* (pp. 33–70). Baltimore: University Park Press.

Draguns, J. G. (1986). Culture and psychopathology: What is known about their relationship? *Australian Journal of Psychology, 38,* 329–338.

Draguns, J. G. (1988). Personality and culture: Are they relevant for the enhancement of quality of mental life? In P. R. Dasen, J. W. Berry, & N. Sartorius (Eds.), *Health and cross-cultural psychology: Toward applications* (pp. 141–161). Newbury Park, CA: Sage.

Draguns, J. G. (1990a). Normal and abnormal behavior in cross-cultural perspective: Specifying the nature of their relationship. In J. J. Berman (Ed.), *Cross-cultural perspectives: Nebraska Symposium on Motivation, 1989* (Vol. 37, pp. 235–278). Lincoln and London: University of Nebraska Press.

Draguns, J. G. (1990b). Applications of cross-cultural psychology in the field of mental health. In R. W. Brislin (Ed.), *Applied cross-cultural psychology* (pp. 302–324). Newbury Park, CA: Sage.

Draguns, J. G. (1994). Pathological and clinical aspects. In L. L. Adler & U. P. Gielen (Eds.), *Cross-cultural topics in psychology* (pp. 165–178). Westport, CT: Greenwood.

Draguns, J. G. (1995). Cultural influences upon psychopathology: Clinical and practical implications. In A. Bergman & J. Fish (Eds.), *Special issue: Multicultural perspectives on mental illness, Journal of Social Distress and the Homeless,4,* 89–114.

Draguns, J. G. (1996b). Abnormal behavior in Chi-nese societies: Clinical, epidemiological, and comparative studies. In M. Bond (Ed.), *Handbook of psychology of the Chinese people* (pp. 395–411). Hong Kong: Oxford University Press.

Draguns, J. G. (1996a). Multicultural and cross-cultural assessment of psychological disorder: Dilemmas and decisions. In J. Impara & G. R. Sodowsky (Eds.), *Buros–Nebraska Symposium on Motivation and Testing* (Vol. 9, pp. 37–84). Lincoln, NE: Buros Institute of Mental Measurements.

Draguns, J. G. (1996c). Ethnocultural considerations in the treatment of post-traumatic stress disorder: Theory and service delivery. In A. J. Marsella (Ed.), *Ethnocultural aspects of post-traumatic disorder* (pp. 459–481). Washington, DC: American Psychological Association.

Eaton, W. W., Holzer, C. E., II, Von Korff, M., Anthony, J. C., Helzer, L. E., George, L., Burman, M. A., Boyd, J. H., Kessler, L. G., & Locke, B. Z. (1984). The design of the Epidemiological Catchment Area surveys. *Archives of General Psychiatry, 41,* 942–948.

Egeland, J. A., Hostetter, A. M., & Eshleman, S. K. (1983). Amish Study: III. The impact of cultural factors on diagnosis of bipolar illness. *American Journal of Psychiatry, 140,* 67–71.

Eisenbruch, M. (1992). Toward a culturally sensitive DSM: Cultural bereavement in Cambodian refugees and the traditional healer as a taxonomist. *Journal of Nervous and Mental Disease, 180,* 8–10.

Endicott, J. & Spitzer, R. L. (1978). A diagnostic interview: The Schedule for Affective Disorders and Schizophrenia. *Archives of General Psychiatry, 35,* 837–844.

Fabrega, H. (1989a). On the significance of an anthropological approach to schizophrenia. *Psychiatry, 52,* 45–65.

Fabrega, H. (1989b). Cultural relativism and psychiatric illness. *Journal of Nervous and Mental Disease, 177,* 415–425.

Fabrega, H., Mulsant, B. M., Rifai, H., Sweet, R. A., Pasternak, R., Ulrich, R., & Zubenko, G. S. (1994). Ethnicity and psychopathology in an aging hospital-based population: A comparison of African-American and Anglo-American patients. *Journal of Nervous and Mental Disease, 182,* 136–144.

Fraser, M. W. & Pecora, P. J. (1986). Psychological adaptation among Indochinese refugees. *Journal of Applied Social Sciences, 10,* 20–39.

Geisinger, K. F. (1994). Cross-cultural normative assessment: Translation and adaptation issues influencing the normative interpretation of assessment instruments. *Psychological Assessment, 6,* 304–312.

German, G. S. (1987). Mental health in Africa: II. The nature of mental disorders in Africa today. Some clinical observations. *British Journal of Psychiatry, 151,* 440–446.

Golding, J. M., Karno, M., & Rutter, C. M. (1990). Symptoms of major depression among Mexican-American and non-Hispanic whites. *American Journal of Psychiatry, 147,* 861–866.

Good, B. J. (1992). Culture and psychopathology: Directions for psychiatric anthropology. In T. Schwartz, G. M. White, & C. A. Lutz (Eds.), *New directions in psychological anthropology* (pp. 181–205). Cambridge: Cambridge University Press.

Good, B. & Kleinman, A. (1985). Culture and anxiety: Cross-cultural evidence for the patterning of anxiety disorders. In A. H. Tuma & J. D. Maser (Eds.), *Anxiety and anxiety disorders* (pp. 297-324). Hillsdale, NJ: Lawrence Erlbaum.

Greenfield, P. M. (1994). Independence and interdependence as developmental scripts: Implications for theory, research, and practice. In P. M. Greenfield & R. R. Cocking (Eds.), *Cross-cultural roots of minority child development* (pp. 1–40). Hillsdale, NJ: Lawrence Erlbaum.

Guarnaccia, P. J., Good, B. J., & Kleinman, A. (1990). A critical review of epidemiological studies of Puerto Rican mental health. *American Journal of Psychiatry, 147,* 1449–1456.

Guthrie, G. & Tanco, P. P. (1980). Alienation. In H. C. Triandis & J. G. Draguns (Eds.), *Handbook of cross-cultural psychology* (Vol. 6, pp. 9–59). Boston: Allyn and Bacon.

Hamilton, M. (1967). Development of a rating scale for primary depressive illness. *British Journal of Social and Clinical Psychology, 6,* 278–296.

Helzer, J. E. & Canino, G. J. (1992). Comparative analysis of alcoholism in ten cultural regions. In J. E. Helzer & G. J. Canino (Eds.), *Alcoholism in North America, Europe, and Asia* (pp. 289–308). New York: Oxford University Press.

Higginbotham, H. N. (1984). *Third world challenge to psychiatry.* Honolulu: University Press of Hawaii.

Higginbotham, H. N. & Marsella, A. J. (1988). International consultation and the homogenization of psychiatry in Southeast Asia. *Social Science and Medicine, 27,* 553–561.

Higginbotham, H. N. & Tanaka-Matsumi, J. (1991). Cross-cultural application of behavior therapy. *Behaviour Change, 8,* 35–42.

Higginbotham, H. N., West, S., & Forsyth, D. (1988). *Psychotherapy and behavior change: Social, cultural and methodological perspectives.* New York: Pergamon.

Hinton, L. & Kleinman, A. (1993). Cultural issues and international psychiatric diagnosis. *International Review of Psychiatry, 1,* 111–134.

Hofstede, G. (1980). *Culture's consequences.* Beverly Hills: Sage.

Hopper, K. (1992). Cervantes' puzzle: A commentary on Alex Cohen's "Prognosis for schizophrenia in the Third World: A reevaluation of cross-cultural research." *Culture, Medicine and Psychiatry, 16,* 89–100.

Hughes, C. C. (1985). Culture-bound or construct-bound? In R. C. Simons & C. C. Hughes (Eds.), *The culture-bound syndromes* (pp. 3–24). Boston: D. Reidel.

Irvine, S. H. & Carroll, W. K. (1980). Testing and assessment across cultures: Issues in methodology and theory. In J. W. Berry (Ed.), *Handbook of cross-cultural psychology* (Vol. 2, pp. 181–244). Boston: Allyn and Bacon.

Jablensky, A. (1989). Epidemiology and cross-cultural aspects of schizophrenia. *Psychiatric Annals, 19,* 516–524.

Jablensky, A. & Sartorius, N. (1988). Is schizophrenia universal? *Acta Psychiatrica Scandinavica, 78,* 65–70.

Jablensky, A., Sartorius, N., Ernberg, G., Anker, M., Korten, A., Cooper, J. E., Day, R., & Bertelsen, A. (1992). *Schizophrenia: Manifestations, incidence, and course in different cultures: A World Health Organization ten country study.* Psychological Medicine Monograph Supplement 20. Cambridge: Cambridge University Press.

Jackson, S. W. (1986). *Melancholia and depression.* New Haven: Yale University Press.

Jenkins, J. H. (1988). Conceptions of schizophrenia as a problem of nerves: A cross-cultural comparison of Mexican-Americans and Anglo-Americans. *Social Science and Medicine, 26,* 1233–1243.

Jilek-Aal, L. (1988). Suicidal behavior among youth: A cross-cultural comparison. *Transcultural Psychiatric Research Review, 25,* 87–106.

Johnson, F. A. (1992). *Dependency, independency and amae: Psychoanalytic anthropological observations.* New York: New York University Press.

Kakar, S. (1982). *Shamans, mystics and doctors.* New York: Knopf.

Karno, M., Burman, M. A., Escobar, J. I., Hough, R. L., & Eaton, W. W. (1983). Development of the Spanish-language version of the National Institute of Mental Health Diagnostic Interview Schedule. *Archives of General Psychiatry, 40,* 1183–1188.

Karno, M., Hough, R. L., Burman, A., Escobar, J. I., Timbers, D. M., Santana, F., & Boyd, J. H. (1987). Lifetime prevalence of specific psychiatric disorders among Mexican Americans and non-Hispanic whites in Los Angeles. *Archives of General Psychiatry, 44,* 695–701.

Katz, M. M., Marsella, A. J., Dube, K. C., Olatawura, M., Takahashi, R., Nakane, Y., Wynne, L. C., Gift, T., Brennan, J., Sartorius, N., & Jablensky, A. (1988). On the expression of psychosis in different cultures: Schizophrenia in an Indian and in a Nigerian community: A report from the World Health Organization project on determinants of outcome of severe mental disorders. *Culture, Medicine, and Psychiatry, 12,* 331–355.

Kawanishi, Y. (1992). Somatization of Asians: An artifact of Western modernization? *Transcultural Psychiatric Research Review, 29,* 5–36.

Kim, U. & Berry, J. W. (Eds.). (1993). *Indigenous psychologies: Research and experience in cultural context.* Newbury Park, CA: Sage.

Kim, U., Triandis, H. C., Kagitçibasi, C., Choi, S-C., & Yoon, G. (Eds.), (1994). *Individualism and collectivism: Theory, method and applications.* Thousand Oaks, CA: Sage.

Kimura, B. (1967). Phänomenologie des Schulderlebnisses in einer vergleichenden psychiatrischen Sicht. In N. Petriolowitsch (Ed.), *Beiträge zue vergleichenden Psychiatrie* (Vol. 11, pp. 54–83). Basel, Switzerland: Karger.

Kinzie, J. D., Manson, S. M., Vinh, D. T., Tolan, N. T., Anh, B., & Pho, T. N. (1982). Development and validation of a Vietnamese-language Depression Scale. *American Journal of Psychiatry, 139,* 1276–1281.

Kirmayer, L. J. (1984). Culture, affect, and somatization: Parts 1 and 2. *Transcultural Psychiatric Research Review, 21,* 159–262, 237–262.

Kirmayer, L. J. (1991). The place of culture in psychiatric nosology: Taijin Kyofusho and DSM-III-R. *Journal of Nervous and Mental Disorder, 179,* 19–28.

Kleinman, A. (1977). Depression, somatization, and the "new cross-cultural psychiatry." *Social Science and Medicine, 11,* 3–9.

Kleinman, A. (1978). Clinical relevance of anthropological and cross-cultural research: Concepts and strategies. *American Journal of Psychiatry, 135,* 427–431.

Kleinman, A. (1980). *Patients and healers in the context of culture.* Berkeley: University of California Press.

Kleinman, A. (1982). Neurasthenia and depression: A study of somatization and culture in China. *Culture, Medicine, and Psychiatry, 6,* 117–189.

Kleinman, A. (1986). *Social origins of distress and disease: Depression, neurasthenia, and pain in modern China.* New Haven: Yale University Press.

Kleinman, A. (1991). *Rethinking psychiatry: From cultural category to personal experience.* New York: Free Press.

Kleinman, A. & Good, B. (Eds.). (1985). *Culture and depression: Studies in the anthropology and cross-cultural psychiatry of affect and disorder.* Berkeley: University of California Press.

Kleinman, A. & Kleinman, J. (1985). Somatization: The interconnections in Chinese society among culture, depressive experiences, and the meaning of pain. In A. Kleinman & B. Good (Eds.), *Culture and depression* (pp. 429–490). Berkeley: University of California Press.

Kleinman, A. & Kleinman, J. (1995). Remembering the cultural revolution: Alienating pains and the pain of alienation/transformation. In T. Y. Lin, W-S Tseng, & E. Yeh (Eds.), *Mental health in Chinese societies* (pp. 141–155). Hong Kong: Oxford University Press.

Koss, J. D. (1990). Somatization and somatic complaint syndromes among Hispanics: Overview and ethnopsychological perspectives. *Transcultural Psychiatric Research Review, 27*, 5–29.

Krishnan, A. & Berry, J. W. (1992). Acculturative stress and acculturation attitudes among Indian immigrants to the United States. *Psychology and Developing Societies, 4*, 187–212.

Kroll, J., Habenicht, M., Mackenzie, T., Yang, M., Chan, S., Vang, T., Nguyen, T., Ly, M., Phommasouvanh, B., Nguyen, H., Vang, Y., Souvannasoth, L., & Cabugao, R. (1989). Depression and post-traumatic stress disorder in Southeast Asian refugees. *American Journal of Psychiatry, 146*, 1592–1597.

Lambert, M. C., Weisz, J. R., Knight, F., Desrosiers, M. F., Overly, K., & Thesiger, C. (1992). Jamaican and American adult perspectives on child psychopathology: Further exploration of the threshold model. *Journal of Consulting and Clinical Psychology, 60*, 146–149.

Larbig, W., Xenakis, C., & Onishi, M. S. (1979). Psychosomatische Symptome und funktionelle Beschwerden bei Arbeitnehmern in Ausland. *Zeitschrift für Psychosomatische Medizin und Psychoanalyse, 25*, 49–63.

Lee, C. K. (1992). Alcoholism in Korea. In J. E. Helzer & G. J. Canino (Eds.), *Alcoholism in North America, Europe, and Asia* (pp. 247–263). New York: Oxford University Press.

Lee, C. K., Kwak, Y. S., Yamamoto, J., Rhee, H., Kim, Y. S., Han, J. H., Choi, J. K., & Lee, Y. H. (1990). Psychiatric epidemiology in Korea: Part I. Gender and age differences in Seoul. *Journal of Nervous and Mental Disease, 178*, 242–246.

Lee, S. (1995). Self-starvation in context: Towards a culturally sensitive understanding of anorexia nervosa. *Social Science and Medicine, 41*, 25–36.

Leff, J. (1988). *Psychiatry around the globe: A transcultural view.* London: Gaskell.

Leopold, M. & Harrell-Bond, B. (1994). An overview of the world refugee crisis. In A. J. Marsella, T. Bornemann, S. Ekblad, & J. Orley (Eds.), *Amidst peril and pain: The mental health and well-being of the world's refugees* (pp. 17–33). Washington, DC: American Psychological Association.

Lester, D. (1988). Youth suicide: A cross-cultural perspective. *Adolescence, 23*, 955–958.

Lewis-Fernandez, R. & Kleinman, A. (1994). Culture, personality, and psychopathology. *Journal of Abnormal Psychology, 103*, 67–71.

Lin, K. & Kleinman, A. (1988). Psychopathology and clinical course of schizophrenia: A cross-cultural perspective. *Schizophrenia Bulletin, 14*, 555–567.

Lin, T. Y. (1985). Mental disorders and psychiatry in Chinese cultures: Characteristic features and major issues. In W-S. Tseng & D. Y. H. Wu (Eds.), *Chinese culture and mental health* (pp. 369–393). Orlando, FL: Academic.

Lin, T. Y. (1989). Neurasthenia revisited: Its place in modern psychiatry. *Culture, Medicine and Psychiatry, 13*, 105–129.

Lin, T. Y. & Lin, D. T. C. (1982). Alcoholism among the Chinese: Further observations of a low-risk population. *Culture, Medicine and Psychiatry, 6*, 109–116.

Littlewood, R. (1990). From categories to contexts: A decade of the new cross-cultural psychiatry. *British Journal of Psychiatry, 156*, 308–327.

López, S. R. (1989). Patient variable biases in clinical judgment: Conceptual overview and methodological considerations. *Psychological Bulletin, 106*, 184–204.

López, S. R. (1994). Latinos and the expression of psychopathology: A call for the direct assessment of cultural influences. In C. A. Telles & M. Karno (Eds.), *Mental disorders in Hispanic populations* (pp. 109–127). Los Angeles: UCLA.

Loranger, A. W., Sartorius, N., Androls, A., Berger, P., Buchheim, P., Channabasavanna, S. M., Coid, B., Dahl, A., Dickstra, R. F. W., Ferguson, B., Jacobsberg, L. B., Mombauer, W., Pull, C., Ono, Y., & Regier, D. A. (1994). The International Personality Disorder Examination. *Archives of General Psychiatry, 51*, 215–224.

Mann, E. M., Ikeda, Y., Mueller, C. W., Takahashi, A., Tao, K. T., Humris, E., Li, B. L., & Chin, D. (1992). Cross-cultural differences in rating hyperactive-disruptive behavior in children. *American Journal of Psychiatry, 149,* 1539–1992.

Manson, S. M., Shore, J. H., & Bloom, J. D. (1985). The depressive experience in American Indian communities: A challenge for psychiatric theory and diagnosis. In A. Kleinman & B. Good (Eds.), *Culture and depression* (pp. 331–368). Berkeley: University of California Press.

Markus, H. R. & Kitayama, S. (1991). Culture and the self: Implications for cognition, emotion and motivation. *Psychological Review, 98,* 224–253.

Marsella, A. J. (1979). Cross-cultural study of mental disorders. In A. J. Marsella, R. G. Tharp, & T. J. Ciborowski (Eds.), *Perspectives on cross-cultural psychology* (pp. 233–262). New York: Academic.

Marsella, A. J. (1980). Depressive experience and disorder across cultures. In H. C. Triandis & J. G. Draguns (Eds.), *Handbook of cross-cultural psychology* (Vol. 6, pp. 233–262). Boston: Allyn and Bacon.

Marsella, A. J. (1994). *Cross-cultural psychopathology: Foundations, issues, and directions.* Master lecture presented at the Annual Meeting of the American Psychological Association, Los Angeles, August, 1994.

Marsella, A. J., Bornemann, T., Ekblad, S., & Orley, J. (Eds.). (1994). *Amidst peril and pain: The mental health and well-being of the world's refugees.* Washington, DC: American Psychological Association.

Marsella, A. J. & Dash-Scheur, A. (1988). Coping, culture, and healthy human development: A research and conceptual overview. In P. Dasen, J. W. Berry, & N. Sartorius (Eds.), *Cross-cultural psychology and health: Toward applications* (pp. 162–178). Newbury Park, CA: Sage.

Marsella, A. J., Sartorius, N., Jablensky, A., & Fenton, F. (1985). Cross-cultural studies of depressive disorders: An overview. In A. Kleinman & B. Good (Eds.), *Culture and depression: Studies in the anthropology and cross-cultural psychiatry of affect and disorders* (pp. 299–324). Berkeley: University of California Press.

Marsella, A. J. & White, G. (Eds.). (1982). *Cultural*

conceptions of mental health and therapy. Boston, MA: D. Reidel /Kluwer.

McDonald-Scott, P., Machizawa, S., & Satoh, H. (1992). Diagnostic disclosure: A tale of two cultures. *Psychological Medicine, 22,* 147–157.

Mezzich, J. E., Fabrega, H., Mezzich, A. C., & Goffman, G. A. (1985). International experience with DSM-III. *Journal of Nervous and Mental Disease, 173,* 738–741.

Minoura, Y. (1988). The psychological reorganization process of overseas experience after returning to Japan: A symbolic interactionist approach to returnees. *Shakai Shinrigaku Kenkyu (Research in Social Psychology), 3,* 3–11. (In Japanese.)

Moyerman, D. R. & Forman, B. D. (1992). Acculturation and adjustment: A meta-analytic study. *Hispanic Journal of Behavioral Sciences, 14,* 163–200.

Mullings, L. (1984). *Therapy, ideology and social change.* Berkeley: University of California Press.

Munakata, T. (1989). The socio-cultural significance of the diagnostic label "neurasthenia" in Japan's mental health care system. *Culture, Medicine and Psychiatry, 13,* 203–213.

Murphy, H. B. M. (1982a). *Comparative psychiatry: The international and intercultural distribution of mental illness.* Berlin: Springer-Verlag.

Murphy, H. B. M. (1982b). Culture and schizophrenia. In I. Al-Issa (Ed.), *Culture and psychopathology* (pp. 221–250). Baltimore: University Park Press.

Murphy, J. M. (1992). Contributions of anthropology and sociology to alcohol epidemiology. In J. E. Helzer & G. J. Canino (Eds.), *Alcoholism in North America, Europe, and Asia* (pp. 21–32). New York: Oxford University Press.

Nakane, Y., Ohta, Y., Radford, M., Yan, H., Wang, X., Lee, H. Y., Min, S. K., Michitsuji, S., & Ohtsuka, T. (1991). Comparative study of affective disorders in three Asian countries: II. Differences in prevalence rates and symptom presentation. *Acta Psychiatrica Scandinavica, 84,* 313–319.

Nakane, Y., Ohta, Y., Uchino, J., Takada, K., Yan, H. Q., Wang, X. D., Min, S. K., & Lee, H. Y. (1988). Comparative study of affective disorders in three Asian countries: I. Differences in diagnostic classification. *Acta Psychiatrica Scandinavica, 78,* 698–705.

Nathan, T. (1994). *L'influence qui guerit.* Paris: Editions Odile Jacob.

Neal, A. M. & Turner, S. M. (1991). Anxiety disorders research with African Americans: Current status. *Psychological Bulletin, 109,* 400–410.

Neighbors, H. W., Jackson, J. S., Campbell, L., & Williams, D. (1989). The influence of racial factors on psychiatric diagnosis. *Community Mental Health Journal, 25,* 301–311.

Nichter, M. (1981). Idioms of distress. *Culture, Medicine, and Psychiatry, 5,* 379–408.

Nishizono, A. (1994). Tabunka kan seishin igakukai no hassoku. (Founding of Japanese Society of Transcultural Psychiatry.) *Kokoro no Rinsho a la Carte,* (February, special issue), 2–3.

Noh, S., Avison, W. R., & Kaspar, V. (1992). Depressive symptoms among Korean immigrants: Assessment of a translation of the Center for Epidemiologic Studies—Depression Scale. *Psychological Assessment, 4,* 84–91.

Odejide, A. O., Oyewunmi, L. K., & Ohaeri, J. U. (1989). Psychiatry in Africa: An overview. *American Journal of Psychiatry, 146,* 708–716.

Orley, J. & Wing, J. K. (1979). Psychiatric disorders in two African villages. *Archives of General Psychiatry, 36,* 513–520.

Ots, T. (1990). The angry liver, the anxious heart and the melancholy spleen: The phenomenology of perceptions in Chinese culture. *Culture, Medicine and Psychiatry, 14,* 21–58.

Palmer, S. (1965). Murder and suicide in forty nonliterate societies. *Journal of Criminal Law, Criminology, and Political Science, 56,* 320–324.

Paniagua, F. A. (1994). *Assessing and treating culturally diverse clients.* Thousand Oaks, CA: Sage.

Paradis, C. M., Friedman, S., Lazar, R. M., Gruber, J., & Kesselman, M. (1992). Use of a structured interview to diagnose anxiety disorders in a minority population. *Hospital and Community Psychiatry, 43,* 61–64.

Paris, J. (1991). Personality disorders, parasuicide, and culture. *Transcultural Psychiatric Research Review, 28,* 25–39.

Patel, V. (1995). Explanatory models of mental illness in sub-Saharan Africa. *Social Science and Medicine, 40,* 1291–1298.

Paykel, E. S. (1985). The Clinical Interview for Depression: Development, reliability and validity. *Journal of Affective Disorders, 9,* 85–96.

Pedersen, P. B. (1994). *Psychological interventions in a cross-cultural context.* Master lecture presented at the Annual Meeting of the American Psychological Association, Los Angeles, CA, August, 1994.

Pedersen, P. B., Draguns, J. G., Lonner, W. J., & Trimble, J. E. (Eds.). (1996). *Counseling across cultures* 4th ed. Thousand Oaks, CA: Sage.

Peng, K. L. & Tseng, W-S. (Eds.). (1992). *Suicidal behaviour in the Asia–Pacific region.* Singapore: University of Singapore Press.

Pfeiffer, W. (1994). *Transkulturelle psychiatrie,* 2nd ed. Stuttgart, Germany: Thieme.

Pflanz, M. (1970). Soziale Krankheitsfaktoren. In W. J. Schraml (Ed.), Klinische Psychologie: Ein Lehrbuch fur *Psychologen Ärzte, Heilpädagogen und Studierende* (pp. 27–45). Berne: Huber

Prendergast, M., Taylor, E., Rapoport, J. L., Bartko, J., Donnelly, M., Zametkin, A., Ahearn, M. B., Dunn, G., Wieselberg, H. M. (1988). The diagnosis of childhood hyperactivity: A U.S.–U.K. cross-national study of DSM-III and ICD-9. *Journal of Child Psychology and Psychiatry, 29,* 289–300.

Prince, R. H. (1968). The changing picture of depressive syndromes in Africa: Is it fact or diagnostic fashion? *Canadian Journal of African Studies, 1,* 177–192.

Prince, R. H. (1980). Variations in psychotherapeutic procedures. In H. C. Triandis & J. G. Draguns (Eds.), *Handbook of cross-cultural psychology* (Vol. 6, pp. 291–350). Boston: Allyn and Bacon.

Prince, R. (1992). Religious experience and psychopathology: Cross-cultural perspectives. In J. F. Schumaker (Ed.), *Religion and mental health* (pp. 281–290). New York: Oxford University Press.

Prince, R. & Tcheng-Laroche, F. (1987). Culture-bound syndromes and international disease classifications. *Culture, Medicine and Psychiatry, 11,* 3–20.

Rack, P. (1988). Psychiatric and social problems among immigrants. *Acta Psychiatrica Scandinavica, 78,* 167–174.

Radford, M. H. B., Nakane, Y., Ohta, Y., Mann, L.,

& Kalucy, R. S. (1991). Decision making in clinically depressed patients: A transcultural social psychological study. *Journal of Nervous and Mental Disease, 179,* 711–719.

Radloff, L. S. (1977). The CES-D Scale: A self-report depression scale for research in the general population. *Applied Psychological Measurement, 1,* 385–401.

Rao, A. V. (1973). Depressive illness and guilt in Indian cultures. *Indian Journal of Psychiatry, 23,* 213–221.

Rao, A. V. (1984). Unipolar and bipolar depression: A review. *Indian Journal of Psychiatry, 26,* 99–105.

Regier, D. A., Myers, J. K., Kramer, M., Robins, L. N., & Blazer, H. (1984). The NIMH Epidemiological Catchment Area program. *Archives of General Psychiatry, 41,* 934–941.

Reynolds, D. K. (1980). *The quiet therapies: Japanese pathways to personal growth.* Honolulu: University Press of Hawaii.

Robins, L. N., Helzer, J. E., Croughan, J. L., & Ratcliff, K. (1981). The NIMH Diagnostic Interview Schedule: Its history, characteristics and validity. *Archives of General Psychiatry, 38,* 381–389.

Robins, L. N. & Regier, D. A. (Eds.). (1991). *Psychiatric disorders in America: The Epidemiologic Catchment Area Study.* New York: Free Press.

Roland, A. (1988). *In search of self in India and Japan: Toward a cross-cultural psychology.* Princeton: Princeton University Press.

Roland, A. (1991). Psychoanalysis in India and Japan: Toward a comparative psychoanalysis. *American Journal of Psychoanalysis, 51,* 1–10.

Russell, J. G. (1989). Anxiety disorders in Japan: A review of the Japanese literature on Shinkeishitsu and Taijin Kyofusho. *Culture, Medicine, and Psychiatry, 13,* 391–403.

Sanua, V. (1980). Familial and sociocultural antecedents of psychopathology. In H. C. Triandis & J. G. Draguns (Eds.), *Handbook of cross-cultural psychology* (Vol. 6, pp. 175–236). Boston: Allyn and Bacon.

Sartorius, N. (1992). "Prognosis for schizophrenia in the Third World: A reevaluation of cross-cultural research.": Commentary. *Culture, Medicine, and Psychiatry, 16,* 81–84.

Sartorius, N., Jablensky, A., Korten, A., & Ernberg, G. (1986). Early manifestation and first contact incidence of schizophrenia. *Psychological Medicine, 16,* 909–928.

Sethi, B. B., Prakash, R., & Aurora, U. (1980). Guilt and hostility in depression. *Indian Journal of Psychiatry, 22,* 156–160.

Sharma, P., Michael, A., Venkataswamy-Reddy, M., & Gehlot, P. S. (1985). Migration and mental illness. *Indian Journal of Psychological Medicine, 8,* 47–52.

Silva, K. T. (In press). Suicide, self-destructive violence, and armed conflict in Sri Lanka. *Studies in Conflict and Terrorism.*

Simons, R. & Hughes, C. (1985). *The culture-bound syndromes: Folk illnesses of psychiatric and anthropological interest.* Boston: D. Reidel/Kluwer.

Singer, K. (1975). Depressive disorders from a transcultural perspective. *Social Science and Medicine, 9,* 289–301.

Sinha, D. (1988). The family scenario in a developing country and its implications for mental health: The case of India. In P. R. Dasen, J. W. Berry, & N. Sartorius (Eds.), *Health and cross-cultural psychology: Toward applications* (pp. 48–70). Newbury Park, CA: Sage.

Sinha, D. (1989). Cross-cultural psychology and the process of indigenisation: A second view from the Third World. In D. M. Keats, D. Munro, & L. Mann (Eds.), *Heterogeneity in cross-cultural psychology* (pp. 24–40). Amsterdam and Lisse: Swets and Zeitlinger.

Skultans, V. (1995). Neurasthenia and political resistance in Latvia. *Anthropology Today, 11,* 14–17.

Snacken, J. (1991). Guide pour le pratique dans un contexte multiculturel et interdisciplinaire. In J. Leman & A. Gailly (Eds.), *Therapies Interculturelles* (pp. 135–140). Bruxelles, Belgium: Editions Universitaires, De Boeck Universite.

Sow, I. (1980). *Anthropological structures of madness in Black Africa.* New York: International Universities Press.

Starcevic, V. (1991). Neurasthenia: A paradigm of social psychopathology in transitional society. *American Journal of Psychotherapy, 45,* 544–553.

Sue, S. & Zane, N. (1987). The role of culture and

cultural techniques in psychotherapy: A critique and reformulation. *American Psychologist, 42,* 37–45.

Sue, S., Zane, N., & Young, K. (1994). Research on psychotherapy with culturally diverse populations. In A. E. Bergin & S. L. Garfield (Eds.), *Handbook of psychotherapy and behavior change,* 4th ed. (pp. 783–817). New York: Wiley.

Sundquist, J. (1994). Refugees, labor migrants and psychological distress: A population-based study of 338 Latin-American refugees, 161 South European and 396 Finnish labour migrants, and 996 Swedish age-, sex-, and education-matched controls. *Social Psychiatry and Psychiatric Epidemiology, 29,* 20–24.

Szapocznik, J. & Kurtines, W. M. (1993). Family psychology and cultural diversity: Opportunities for therapy, research and application. *American Psychologist, 48,* 400–407.

Takahashi, T. (1989). Social phobia syndrome in Japan. *Comparative Psychiatry, 30,* 45–52.

Taketomo, Y. (1986). Amae as metalanguage: A critique of Doi's theory of amae. *Journal of the American Academy of Psychoanalysis, 14,* 525–544.

Tanaka, T., Takai, J., Kohyama, T., & Fujihara, T. (1994). Adjustment patterns of international students in Japan. *International Journal of Intercultural Relations, 18,* 55–75.

Tanaka-Matsumi, J. (1979). Taijin Kyofusho: Diagnostic and cultural issues in Japanese psychiatry. *Culture, Medicine and Psychiatry, 3,* 231–245.

Tanaka-Matsumi, J. (1989). The cultural difference model and applied behavior analysis in the design of early childhood intervention. In L. L. Adler (Ed.), *Cross-cultural research in human development: Lifespan perspectives* (pp. 37–46). New York: Praeger.

Tanaka-Matsumi, J. (1992). *Culture and communication of depression.* Unpublished manuscript. Department of Psychology, Hofstra University.

Tanaka-Matsumi, J. (1995). Cross-cultural perspectives on anger. In H. Kassinove (Ed.), *Anger disorders: Definition, diagnosis and treatment* (pp. 80–89). Washington, DC: Francis & Taylor.

Tanaka-Matsumi, J. & Higginbotham, N. H. (1996).

Behavioral approaches to cross-cultural counseling. In P. B. Pedersen, J. G. Draguns, W. J. Lonner, & J. E. Trimble (Eds.), *Counseling across cultures,* 4th ed. (pp. 266–292). Newbury Park, CA: Sage.

Tanaka-Matsumi, J., Seiden, D. Y., & Lam, K. (In press). Cross-cultural functional analysis: A strategy for culturally-informed clinical assessment. *Cognitive and Behavioral Practice.*

Tharp, R. G. (1991). Cultural diversity and treatment of children. *Journal of Consulting and Clinical Psychology, 59,* 799–812.

Torrey, F. (1986). *Witchdoctors and psychiatrists: The common roots of psychotherapy and its future.* New York: Harper & Row.

Tseng, W-S., Asai, M., Jieqiu, L., Wibulswasd, P., Suryani, L. K., Wen, L-K., Brennan, J., & Heiby, E. (1990). Multicultural study of minor psychiatric disorders in Asia: Symptom manifestations. *The International Journal of Social Psychiatry, 36,* 252–264.

Tseng, W-S., Asai, M., Kitanishi, K., McLaughlin, D., & Kyomen, H. (1992). Diagnostic patterns of social phobia: Comparison in Tokyo and Hawaii. *Journal of Nervous and Mental Disease, 180,* 380–385.

Tseng, W-S., & Hsu, J. (1980). Minor psychological disturbances of everyday life. In H. C. Triandis & J. G. Draguns (Eds.), *Handbook of cross-cultural psychology* (Vol. 6, pp. 61–98). Boston: Allyn and Bacon.

Tseng, W-S. & Hsu, J. (1991). *Culture and family.* New York: Haworth.

Tseng, W-S., Lin, T. Y., & Yee, E. (1995). Concluding comments. In T. Y. Lin, W-S. Tseng, & E. Yee (Eds.), *Mental health in Chinese societies* (pp. 346–357). Hong Kong: Oxford University Press.

Tseng, W-S., McDermott, J., Ogino, K., & Ebata, K. (1982). Cross-cultural differences in parent-child assessment: U.S.A. and Japan. *International Journal of Social Psychiatry, 28,* 305–317.

Tseng, W-S., Mo, K-M., Li, L-S., Chen, G-Q., Ou, L-W., & Zheng, H-B. (1992). Koro epidemics in Guangdong, China: A questionnaire survey. *Journal of Nervous and Mental Disease, 180,* 117–123.

Tseng, W-S., Xu, N., Ebata, K., Hsu, J., & Cui, Y. (1986). Diagnostic pattern of neurosis among

China, Japan and America. *American Journal of Psychiatry, 143,* 1010–1014.

Tung, M. P. M. (1994). Symbolic meanings of the body in Chinese culture and "somatization." *Culture, Medicine and Psychiatry, 18,* 483–492.

Ulusahin, A., Basoglu, M., & Paykel, E. S. (1994). A cross-cultural comparative study of depressive symptoms in British and Turkish clinical samples. *Social Psychiatry and Psychiatric Epidemiology, 29,* 31–39.

Varga, G. & Katona, E. (1991). *The political change in Uruguay: Its effect on suicide and substances abuse.* Paper presented at the Second European Congress of Psychology, Budapest, Hungary, July, 1991.

Vega, W. A., Kolody, B., & Valle, J. R. (1987). Migration and mental health: An empirical test of depression risk factors among immigrant Mexican women. *International Migration Review, 21,* 512–532.

Vyncke, J. (1958). L'Assistence Psychiatrique au Ruanda-Urûndi. CCTA/CSA-WFMH-WHO. Meeting of Specialists on Mental Health. Bukavu, The Congo.

Wang, C-H., Liu, W., Zhang, M-Y., Yu, E. S. H., Xia, Z-Y., Fernandez, M., Lung, C-T., Xu, C-L., & Qu, G-Y. (1992). Alcohol use, abuse, and dependency in Shanghai. In J. E. Helzer & G. J. Canino (Eds.), *Alcoholism in North America, Europe, and Asia* (pp. 264–288). New York: Oxford University Press.

Ward, C. (Ed.). (1989). *Culture and altered state of consciousness.* Beverly Hills: Sage.

Warner, R. (1992). "Prognosis for schizophrenia in the Third World: A reevaluation of cross-cultural research": Commentary. *Culture, Medicine, and Psychiatry, 16,* 85–88.

Warner, R. (1994). *Recovery from schizophrenia: Psychiatry and political economy,* 2d ed. New York: Routledge.

Waxler, N. E. (1979). Is outcome for schizophrenia better in nonindustrial societies? The case of Sri Lanka. *Journal of Nervous and Mental Disease, 167,* 144–158.

Waxler-Morrison, N. E. (1992). "Prognosis for schizophrenia in the Third World: A reevaluation of cross-cultural research": Commentary. *Culture, Medicine and Psychiatry, 16,* 77–80.

Weiss, M. G. & Kleinman, A. (1988). Depression in cross-cultural perspective: Developing a culturally informed model. In P. Dasen, J. W. Berry, & N. Sartorius (Eds.), *Cross-cultural psychology and health: Toward applications* (pp. 179–206). Newbury Park, CA: Sage.

Weiss, M. G., Doongaji, D. R., Siddhartha, S., Wypij, D., Pathare, S., Bhatawdekar, M., Bhave, A., Sheth, A., & Fernandes, R. (1992). The Explanatory Model Interview Catalogue (EMIC) contribution to cross-cultural research methods from a study of leprosy and mental health. *British Journal of Psychiatry, 160,* 819–830.

Weissman, M. M., Bland, R. C., Canino, G., Greenwald, S., Hwu, H., Lee, C. K., Newman, S. C., Oakley-Browne, M., Rubio-Stipec, M., Wickramaratne, P. J., Wittchen, H., & Yeh, E. (1994). The cross-national epidemiology of obsessive–compulsive disorder. *Journal of Clinical Psychiatry, 55,* 5–10.

Weisz, J. R. (1989). Culture and the development of psychopathology: Lessons from Thailand. In D. Cicchetti (Ed.), *The emergence of a discipline: Rochester Symposium on Developmental Psychopathology* (pp. 89–117). Hillsdale, NJ: Lawrence Earlbaum.

Weisz, J. R., Suwanlert, S., Chaiyasit, W., Weiss, B., Achenbach, T., & Walter, B. R. (1987). Epidemiology of behavioral and emotional problems among Thai and American children: Parent reports from 6–11. *Journal of the American Academy of Child and Adolescent Psychiatry, 26,* 890–897.

Werry, J. S. (1985). ICD-9 and DSM-III classification for the clinician. *Journal of Child Psychology and Psychiatry, 26,* 1–6.

Westermeyer, J. (1987). Cultural factors in clinical assessment. *Journal of Consulting and Clinical Psychology, 55,* 471–478.

Westermeyer, J. (1989). *Mental health for refugees and other immigrants: Social and preventive approaches.* Springfield, IL: Thomas.

Westermeyer, J., Vang, T. F., & Neider, J. (1983). Migration and mental health among Hmong refugees. *Journal of Nervous and Mental Disease, 171,* 92–96.

White, G. (1982). The role of cultural explanations

in "somatization." *Social Science and Medicine, 16,* 1519–1530.

Wing, J. K., Cooper, J. E., & Sartorius, N. (1974). *Measurement and classification of psychiatric symptoms: An instruction manual for the PSE and CATEGO program.* Cambridge: Cambridge University Press.

Woo, J., Hoo, S. C., Lau, J., Yuen, Y. K., Chiu, H., Lee, H. C., & Chi, I. (1994). The prevalence of depressive symptoms and predisposing factors in an elderly Chinese population. *Acta Psychiatrica Scandinavica, 89,* 8–13.

World Health Organization. (1973). *Report of the international pilot study of schizophrenia.* Geneva: WHO.

World Health Organization. (1973–1985). *World health statistics Aanuals 1973–85.* Geneva: WHO.

World Health Organization. (1979). *Schizophrenia: An international follow-up study.* Geneva: WHO.

World Health Organization. (1983). *Depressive disorders in different cultures: Report of the WHO collaborative study of standardized assessment of depressive disorders.* Geneva: WHO.

World Health Organization. (1991). *Statistics annual for 1989.* Geneva: WHO.

World Health Organization. (1992). *The ICD-10 classification of mental and behavioural disorders: Clinical descriptions and diagnostic guidelines.* Geneva: WHO.

Yap, P. M. (1971). Guilt and shame, depression and culture: A psychiatric cliché reexamined. *Community Contemporary Psychology, 1,* 35–53.

Yap, P. M. (1974). *Comparative psychiatry: A theoretical framework.* Toronto: University of Toronto Press.

Yeh, E-K. & Hwu, H-G. (1992). Alcoholism in Taiwan Chinese communities. In J. E. Helzer & G. J. Canino (Eds.), *Alcoholism in North America, Europe, and Asia* (pp. 214–246). New York: Oxford University Press.

Young, D. (1989). Neurasthenia and related problems. *Culture, Medicine and Psychiatry, 13,* 131–138.

Zeldine, G., Ahvi, R., Leuckx, R., Boussat, M., Saibou, A., Haanck, C., Collignon, R., Tourame, G., & Collomb, H. (1975). A propos de l'utilisation d'une échelle d'évaluation en psychiatrie transculturelle. *Encéphale, 1* (NS), 133–145.

Zhang, A. Y. (1995). *Anthropophobia in Chinese young adults.* Unpublished doctoral dissertation, Interdisciplinary Studies Department, Pennsylvania State University, University Park, Pennsylvania.

Zhang, J. & Zhong, Y. (1993). Discussion on psychopathological nature and pathogenesis of anthropophobia. *Chinese Journal of Neurology and Psychiatry, 19,* 269–271. (In Chinese.)

Zhang, M-Y. (1989). The diagnosis and phenomenology of neurasthenia: A Shanghai study. *Culture, Medicine and Psychiatry, 13,* 147–161.

Zhong, Y. (1993). *Treatment of anthropophobia.* Guiyang City, China: Gizhou Press of Science and Technology. (In Chinese.)

Author Note

The authors would like to thank Douglas Seiden for his valuable editorial assistance.

NAME INDEX

SUBJECT INDEX